Spatialities of Byzantine Culture from the Human Body to the Universe

The Medieval Mediterranean

PEOPLES, ECONOMIES AND CULTURES, 400–1500

Managing Editor

Frances Andrews (*University of St Andrews*)

Editors

Corisande Fenwick (*University College London*)
Paul Magdalino (*University of St Andrews*)
Maria G. Parani (*University of Cyprus*)
Larry J. Simon (*Western Michigan University*)
Daniel Lord Smail (*Harvard University*)
Jo Van Steenbergen (*Ghent University*)

Advisory Board

David Abulafia (*Cambridge*)
Benjamin Arbel (*Tel Aviv*)
Hugh Kennedy (*SOAS, London*)

VOLUME 133

The titles published in this series are listed at *brill.com/mmed*

Spatialities of Byzantine Culture from the Human Body to the Universe

Edited by

Myrto Veikou and Ingela Nilsson

BRILL

LEIDEN | BOSTON

Cover illustration: *Modern landscape seen through the ruins of a Byzantine niche* (*Mystras, Greece*). Photograph by Lisa Jeppesen. © Myrto Veikou.

Library of Congress Cataloging-in-Publication Data

Names: Veikou, Myrto, editor. | Nilsson, Ingela, editor.
Title: Spatialities of Byzantine culture from the human body to the
   universe / edited by Myrto Veikou and Ingela Nilsson.
Description: Leiden ; Boston : Brill, [2022] | Series: Medieval
   Mediterranean, 0928-5520 ; volume 133 | Includes index.
Identifiers: LCCN 2022030195 (print) | LCCN 2022030196 (ebook) |
   ISBN 9789004518742 (hardback) | ISBN 9789004523005 (ebook)
Subjects: LCSH: Byzantine Empire–Civilization. | Spatial
   history–Byzantine Empire.
Classification: LCC DF521 .S65 2022 (print) | LCC DF521 (ebook) |
   DDC 949.5/02–dc23/eng/20220707
LC record available at https://lccn.loc.gov/2022030195
LC ebook record available at https://lccn.loc.gov/2022030196

Typeface for the Latin, Greek, and Cyrillic scripts: "Brill". See and download: brill.com/brill-typeface.

ISSN 0928-5520
ISBN 978-90-04-51874-2 (hardback)
ISBN 978-90-04-52300-5 (e-book)

Copyright 2022 by Koninklijke Brill NV, Leiden, The Netherlands.
Koninklijke Brill NV incorporates the imprints Brill, Brill Nijhoff, Brill Hotei, Brill Schöningh, Brill Fink, Brill mentis, Vandenhoeck & Ruprecht, Böhlau, V&R unipress and Wageningen Academic.
All rights reserved. No part of this publication may be reproduced, translated, stored in a retrieval system, or transmitted in any form or by any means, electronic, mechanical, photocopying, recording or otherwise, without prior written permission from the publisher. Requests for re-use and/or translations must be addressed to Koninklijke Brill NV via brill.com or copyright.com.

This book is printed on acid-free paper and produced in a sustainable manner.

Contents

Acknowledgements XI
List of Figures XII
Abbreviations XX
Notes on Contributors XXI

(Byzantine) Space Matters! An Introduction 1
   Myrto Veikou and Ingela Nilsson with Liz James

PART 1
The (Most) Private Space: The Human Body

Editorial Note on Part 1   19

1   The Human Belly as a 'Natural Symbol'
    The Greek and Byzantine Anthropology of γαστήρ   20
      Tomek Labuk

2   *Crime et châtiment* à Byzance
    Le corps humain comme espace public   44
      Charis Messis

3   The World from Above
    Divine Amphitheatres, Spiritual Watchtowers, and the Moral Spatialities of κατασκοπή   72
      Veronica della Dora

4   Space and Identity, a Located Negotiation
    A Case Study on Mobile Bodies in Byzantine Hagiography   98
      Myrto Veikou

PART 2
Experienced Spaces: Human Bodies within Their Natural Environments

Editorial Note on Part 2   113

5   Space-environment as Historical Actor in Byzantium   114
      Adam Izdebski

6   In the Shadow of Virgil
      The Significance of Butrint's Liminality in Deep Mediterranean History   128
      Richard Hodges

7   At Home in Cappadocia
      The Spatialities of a Byzantine Domestic Landscape   152
      Robert Ousterhout

8   A Byzantine Space Oddity
      The Cultural Geography of Foodways and Cuisine in the Eastern Mediterranean (700–1500)   171
      Joanita Vroom

9   Space and Identity
      Byzantine Conceptions of Geographic Belonging   212
      Johannes Koder

PART 3
Anthropogenic Spaces: Byzantine Landscapes

   Editorial Note on Part 3   241

10   What Is a Byzantine Landscape?   243
      Michael J. Decker

11   Adapting to the Cypriot Landscape
      A Study of Medieval to Modern Occupation of the Malloura Valley   262
      P. Nick Kardulias

12   Constructing New Cities, Creating New Spatialities
      An Ethnoarchaeological Experiment   288
      Enrico Zanini

13   'The Humility of the Desert'
      The Symbolic and Cultural Landscapes of Egyptian Monasticism   313
      Darlene L. Brooks Hedstrom

14 From the Ancient Demes to the Byzantine Villages
Transformations of the Landscape in the Countryside of Athens 339
   Georgios Pallis

PART 4
Empowered Spaces: Byzantine Territories

Editorial Note on Part 4   357

15 L'inscription du pouvoir impérial dans l'espace urbain constantinopolitain à l'époque des Paléologues   358
   Tonia Kiousopoulou

16 Byzantine Notions of the Balkans
Symbolic, Territorial and Ethnic Conceptions of Space, Sixth to Ninth Centuries   369
   Konstantinos Moustakas

17 The Partitioned Space of the Byzantine Peloponnese
From History to Political and Mythical Exploitation   384
   Ilias Anagnostakis and Maria Leontsini

18 Spatial Concepts and Administrative Structures in the Byzantine-Turkish Frontier of Twelfth-Century Asia Minor   400
   Alexander Beihammer

19 The Other Than Self
Byzantium and the Venetian Identity   425
   Sauro Gelichi

PART 5
Performed Spaces: Spatialities of Cultural Practices

Editorial Note on Part 5   459

20 Tents in Space, Space in Tents   460
   Margaret Mullett

21 Variations on the Definition of Sacred Space from Eusebius of Caesarea to Balsamon 482
    Béatrice Caseau

22 "Dwelling Place and Palace"
    The Theotokos as a "Living City" in Byzantine Hymns, Icons and Liturgical Practice 503
    Helena Bodin

23 The Development of Religious Topography at Constantinople in the Fourth to Seventh Centuries 522
    Isabel Kimmelfield

24 Mind the Gap
    Mosaics on the Wall and the Space between Viewer and Viewed 537
    Liz James

PART 6
Imaginary Spaces: Byzantine Storyworlds

Editorial Note on Part 6 557

25 The Phenomenology of Landscape in the *Menologion* of Basil II 558
    Rico Franses

26 Pachon's Progressive Return
    Figurativity, Framing and Movement in Historica Lausiaca 23 577
    David Westberg

27 Spaces Within, Spaces Beyond
    Reassessing the Lives of the Holy Fools Symeon and Andrew (BHG 1677, 115z) 595
    Paolo Cesaretti and Basema Hamarneh

28 Textualization of Space and Travel in Middle Byzantine Hagiography 613
    Yulia Mantova

29 The Visual Structure of Epigrams and the Experience of Byzantine Space
    A Case Study on Reliquary Enkolpia of St Demetrios   631
        Brad Hostetler

Afterword
Byzantine Spacetime: A Rough Guide For Future Tourists to the Past   656
    Adam J. Goldwyn and Derek Krueger

Index   667

Acknowledgements

We would like to express our heartfelt thanks to Riksbankens Jubileumsfond for their generous support of the conference "From the Human Body to the Universe: Spatialities of Byzantine Culture", held at Uppsala University on May 18–21, 2017. This volume is the outcome of that conference, but it cannot be considered as the conference proceedings: some participants in the conference are not included here, while other contributions have been added. We remain grateful to all participants in the conference for their papers and their willingness to engage in discussion.

This book has been finalized within the frame of the research programme 'Retracing Connections' (https://retracingconnections.org/), financed by Riksbankens Jubileumsfond (M19-0430:1). Its production was supported by an additional grant from The Royal Swedish Academy of Letters, History and Antiquities, for which we would like to express our sincere thanks. We are most thankful to Uppsala University Museum (Cecilia Ödman and Ragnar Hedlund) for their kind contribution of photographic material. Last but not least, we would like to thank Marcella Mulder for her constant kindness, efficiency and patience.

Figures

0.1 The Anatomical Theatre of Uppsala University, internal view. Photograph: Gustavianum, Uppsala universitetsmuseum. © Uppsala University Museum.   5
1.1 Visualization of the webs of meaning associated with the space of γαστήρ in the Greek tradition.   26
6.1 Map showing the location of Butrint and the Butrint National Park. © Butrint Foundation Archives.   129
6.2 Aerial view of Butrint and the Straits of Corfu, in the distance. Photograph by Alket Islami. © Butrint Foundation Archives.   130
6.3 Portrait of S.S. Clarke (1897–1924). Courtesy of the British School at Athens. Photograph © Butrint Foundation Archives.   132
6.4 Portrait of Luigi Maria Ugolini (1896–1936). Photograph © Butrint Foundation Archives.   133
6.5 Nikita Khruschchev and Enver Hoxha at Butrint, May 1959. Photograph © Butrint Foundation Archives.   135
6.6 Ugolini's excavations of the Butrint theatre, spring 1928. Photograph © Butrint Foundation Archives.   136
6.7 Butrint's Sceaen Gate during clearance by Ugolini's team in ca. 1930. Photograph © Butrint Foundation Archives.   137
6.8 Beyond Butrint: field surveys by the Butrint Foundation. © Butrint Foundation Archives.   139
6.9 Reconstruction of the Roman bridge across the Vivari channel at Butrint. © Butrint Foundation Archives.   139
6.10 Map showing the location of the (archaic Greek) Dema Wall (refurbished in the 11th century and Venetian times). © Butrint Foundation Archives.   144
6.11 View of the late antique settlement at Diaporit, showing the small chapel, residence, bath-house and, in the distance, the 6th-century basilica. Photograph © Butrint Foundation Archives.   147
7.1 Ortahisar (near), Hallaç Manastırı, view into courtyard, looking northeast. Author's copyright.   155
7.2 Ortahisar (near), Hallaç Manastırı, plan. Author's copyright, redrawn after L. Rodley.   156
7.3 Ortahisar (near), Hallaç Manastırı, interior of the hall, looking north. Author's copyright.   157
7.4 Selime-Yaprakhisar, Area 11, façade. Author's copyright.   158
7.5 Selime, Kale complex, kitchen. Author's copyright.   160
7.6 Akhisar (near), Çanlı Kilise settlement, courtyard Area 13, view of dovecotes behind partially fallen façade. Author's copyright.   161

FIGURES XIII

7.7   Açık Saray, Area 1 stable, interior. Author's copyright.   161
7.8   Erdemli, wine press. Author's copyright.   162
7.9   Erdemli, mill. Author's copyright.   163
7.10 Keşlikköy, rock-cut beehive, interior. Author's copyright.   164
7.11 Akhisar (near), Çanlı Kilise settlement, plan of Areas 1–4. Author's copyright.   165
7.12 Akhisar (near), Çanlı Kilise settlement, Area 4, rolling stone door to refuge. Author's copyright.   168
8.1   Left above: Scene from the story 'La Giara' in the Italian movie *Kaos* (1984) (Wikimedia italia); Left below: Fresco of St George in a cauldron, Agios Nikolaos church, Mouri, ca. 1300; Right below: Fresco of St George in a cauldron, Agios Georgios church, Mourni, beginning of 14th century. Author's copyright.   172
8.2   Athenian Agora, section MM, Distribution map of two types of pithoi (blue = masonry built and green = terracotta/ceramic), plus photograph of Byzantine terracotta/ceramic pithoi buried in the ground of the eastern building in this complex (after Vroom and Boswinkel 2016, Figures 6 and 7; photo number 2012.50-098 (X-72), ASCSA); cross-section drawing of a terracotta/ceramic pithos by A. Hoton, ASCSA)   175
8.3   Athenian Agora, Dimensions of masonry built and terracotta/ceramic pithoi in section MM (after Vroom and Boswinkel 2016, tables 2–3; based on the excavation diaries of the ASCSA; cross-section drawing of a terracotta/ceramic pithos by A. Hoton, ASCSA   177
8.4   Istanbul, Chora Monastery, vault mosaic depicting the scene 'Wedding at Cana', 14th century. Author's copyright.   180
8.5   Butrint, Western Defences, Reconstructed drawing of Tower 1 with a selection of pottery finds from this tower. Author's copyright. Drawing by W.R. Euverman. Photographs © Butrint Foundation.   182
8.6   Butrint, Western Defences, Photographs and drawings of a cooking pot (left) and a chafing dish (right) from Tower 1. Drawings: Author's copyright. Photographs © Butrint Foundation.   183
8.7   Drawing and photographs of culinary techniques of cooking vessels in a 'designated space' above a fire or in a tripod (after Dark 2001, colour plate 13; Papanikola-Bakirtzi 2002, no. 402; Pellegrino 2007, Fig. 3a). Left below: miniature of an angel with a cooking vessel on a tripod, Octateuch Manuscript, Vatopedi Monastery, Vatopedi cod. 802 (fol. 417a), Mount Athos, 13th century (after Bakirtzis 1989, Fig. 34a).   184
8.8   Cappadocia, Peristrema Valley, Drawings and photographs of the kitchen of Selime Kalesi with the remains of a *tandir* or *tabun* in the floor (left below) and a pyramidal chimney (right below). After Kalas 2009, Figures 2, 4–6.   186
8.9   Drawing of four types of permanent fire-place installations. Left above: cylindrical, hollow clay installation (*tannur, tandoor*). Right

above: smaller 'iglo-shaped' clay installation (*tabun*). Left below: domed metal pan (*saj*). Right below: domed cylindrical-shaped clay installation (*waqdiah*). © J. Vroom and S. van der Vlugt. 187

8.10 Drawings and photographs of cooking installations/techniques for food preparation with heat in a 'special space' (after Yehuda 2011, Fig. 6). Left below: miniature of the sorceress Medea, Venice Codex of Pseudo-Oppian's *Cynegetica*, Biblioteca Nazionale Marciana, cod. Gr. Z 479 (fol. 47r), ca. 1060 (after Spatharakis 2004, Fig. 99). Right below: detail from a miniature of the Alexander Romance made in Trebizond, Hellenic Institute of Byzantine and Post-Byzantine Studies, Cod. Gr. 5, Venice, 14th century (after Bakirtzis 1989, 35b). 189

8.11 Drawings and photographs of hearths as a 'specialised space' for food preparation with heat in Crusader houses and towers in Greece and Israel (after Williams II and Zervos 1993, pl. 3; Yehuda 2011, Fig. 3). Photograph: Author's copyright. 191

8.12 An overview of Late Byzantine/Crusader ceramic cooking vessels from Greece, Cyprus and Israel (after Yehuda 2011, Fig. 4; Gabrieli 2005, rig. 4; Gabrieli et al. 2017, Fig. 7; photograph left above: Author's copyright). 192

8.13 Three phases of food preparation with heat: left: a 'designated space', centre: a 'special space', and right: a 'specialized space' (Drawings centre below and right after Yehuda 2011). 193

8.14 Architectural reconstruction of three phases of food preparation with heat. Left: a 'designated space'. Centre: a 'special space'. Right: a 'specialized space'. © J. Vroom & S. van der Vlugt. 193

8.15 Rim average and base average diameters of Middle Byzantine (left), of Late Byzantine (centre), and of Post-Medieval tableware (right) (Drawings after Vroom 2003, table 7.3). 195

8.16 Average vessel height and volume of Byzantine tablewares. (Drawing after Vroom 2016, Fig. 13.5 and table 13.C). 196

8.17 Dining scene and schematic table setting in Early Byzantine times. Miniature of Story of Joseph, Ahburnham or Tours Pentateuch, Bibliothèque Nationale de France lat. 2334, Paris, ca. late 6th-early 7th century (after Vroom 2016, Fig. 13.6). 198

8.18 Dining scene and schematic table setting in Middle Byzantine times. Miniature of Job's Children, St Catherine's Monastery gr. 3 (fol. 17v), Sinai, 11th century (after Vroom 2016, Fig. 13.7). 199

8.19 Composition image of Late Byzantine glazed and unglazed tablewares from the Athenian Agora (above; after Vroom and Tzavella 2017, Fig. 7, ASCSA) in relation to Late Byzantine dining scenes (below). Left below: Miniature of Job's Children, Ms. Grec. 135, fol. 18v, Bibliothèque Nationale de France Grec.

FIGURES   XV

       135 (fol. 18v), Paris, ca. 1361–1362 (after Vroom and Tzavella 2017, Fig. 9). Right
       below: Icon of the Hospitality of Abraham, Benaki Museum, Athens, 14th
       century (after Vroom 2003, Fig. 11.32). 200
8.20   Dining scene and schematic table setting in Late Byzantine/Late Medieval
       times. Miniature in a *croce dipinta*, Museo Nazionale di San Matteo, Pisa, ca.
       12th–13th century (after Vroom 2016, Fig. 13.8). 203
11.1   Map of the Eastern Mediterranean. © David Massey; AAP Archives. 268
11.2   Map of Cyprus showing location of Athienou Archaeological Project survey
       area in red rectangle. © David Massey; AAP Archives. 274
11.3   Late medieval Frankish sugar mill at Kolossi Castle, Cyprus. Author's
       copyright. 277
11.4   Map of AAP survey area showing locations of sites and distribution of pottery
       by period. © AAP Archives. 279
11.5   Millstone at Athienou-*Malloura*. © AAP Archives. 280
11.6   Venetian period burials at Athienou-*Malloura*. © AAP Archives. 283
11.7   Cattle in pen in AAP project area. Author's copyright. 283
12.1   The plain of Dara in 1980. Author's copyright. 293
12.2   Sketch-plan of the archaeological site of Dara. Author's copyright, redrawn
       based on different sources. 295
12.3   First zoning plan of Littoria by architect O. Frezzotti (after Mariani
       1976). 296
12.4   Arrival of the settlers at Littoria (after Mariani 1976). 298
12.5   Aerial view of Littoria's first monumental setting, a few years after the
       foundation (after Mariani 1976). 300
12.6   Mussolini depicted as an urban planner in a lost wall mosaic, originally in
       Pomezia (after Mariani 1976). 301
12.7   The main cistern of Dara. Author's copyright. 303
12.8   Littoria shaped as a full-size city in 1940. © Aerofototeca del Ministero della
       Cultura. 306
13.1   Private kitchen from a monastic residential building in Wādī al-Naṭrūn, Egypt.
       Author's copyright. 317
13.2   Leather sandal (#870-1903) from Byzantine Egypt showing punchwork,
       incising, and foot straps. Courtesy of the Victorian and Albert Museum. 318
13.3   Fishing net (14.1.560) found at the Topos of Apa Epiphanius in Western Thebes.
       Courtesy of the Metropolitan Museum of Art. 318
13.4   The proximity of the Nile, cultivated fields and desert cliffs. Author's
       copyright. 319
13.5   Thin border walls provided visual markers of settlements for travellers and
       residents of the desert in Middle Egypt near Dayr al-Bala'yzah. Author's
       copyright. 321

13.6	Accumulation of natron salt deposits at one of the four lakes in Wādī al-Naṭrūn. Author's copyright. 324
13.7	One of over eighty monastic dwellings in the hills around Gebel Naqlun in the Fayyum Oasis. Author's copyright. 326
13.8	The Monastery of Apa Thomas at Wadi Sarga. The North Building was built into and against the bed rock of the wadi with a combination of small boulders, mud brick, and plaster. Courtesy of the Trustees of the British Museum. 329
13.9	Documentary source from the Topos of Apa Epiphanius, Western Thebes (*P.Mon.Epi.* 198). Photograph © Metropolitan Museum of Art. 331
14.1	The Athenian plain and the sites under examination (Map: Eleutherios Tsouris). 340
14.2	The inscription of 850/1 from Maroussi, squeeze of the now lost stone (after Orlandos 1933, 202, Fig. 272). 343
14.3	The surviving part of Hagios Ioannis church at modern Vouliagmenis avenue. Author's copyright. 346
14.4	The fortified monastery of Daphni, inner view of the north wall. © S. Topouzi. 347
14.5	The central part Athenian olive grove as it was preserved in 1908 (after D. Aiginites, *Το κλίμα της Αττικής*, Athens 1908, 88–89). 348
14.6	The church complex at Penteli cave. Author's copyright. 350
17.1	The longitudinal division of Peloponnese (after Jones 1968, Book VIII, vol. 4, map n. 8). 387
17.2	Metropolitan sees of Middle Byzantine Peloponnese (after Yannopoulos 1993, 390). 388
19.1	Venice, Museo Archeologico Nazionale, medieval wellhead. © Martina Secci. 429
19.2	Forks (after Rabano Mauro, *De Rerum Naturis*: XVI.4 *De civibus*; XXII, 1 *De mensis et escis*). 430
19.3	Venice, presbytery in St Mark's Basilica, Pala d'Oro: the Last Supper (after Lorenzoni 1965, p. 6, n. 31). 431
19.4	Athens, Stoà of Attalus, Museum, photograph of a "Glazed White Ware" chafing dish. © Giovanni Dall'Orto. 434
19.5	The distribution of Byzantine chafing-dishes in the Mediterranean and Black Sea (after Arthur 2007, p. 15, Fig. 1). 435
19.6	"Forum Ware" from Rome (after Whitehouse 1965, p. 57, Fig. 16). 438
19.7	Comparing "Glazed White Ware" (on the left) and "Forum Ware" (on the right). Re-elaborations of drawings after Hayes 1992, p. 22, Fig. 7.8 and Whitehouse 1965, p.57, Fig.16.2a. © Laboratory of Medieval Archaeology, University of Ca' Foscari Venice. 438

FIGURES   XVII

19.8   Map indicating the line of Venice's hypothetical city walls. © Laboratory of
       Medieval Archaeology, University of Ca' Foscari Venice.   441
19.9   Roman inscription reused in a Venetian palace. © Laboratory of Medieval
       Archaeology, University of Ca' Foscari Venice.   442
19.10 Monastery of St Hilary and Benedict in Gambarare, early medieval grave.
       © Laboratory of Medieval Archaeology, University of Ca' Foscari Venice.   444
19.11 Venice, Museo Archeologico Nazionale, sarcophagus from monastery of St
       Hilary and Benedict in Gambarare (after Polacco, *Marmi*, p. 27, n. 12).   445
19.12 Venice, Museo Archeologico Nazionale, sarcophagus from monastery of St
       Hilary and Benedict in Gambarare (after Polacco, *Marmi*, p. 25, n. 10).   445
19.13 Sant'Apollinare in Classe (RA), sarcophagus of Archbishop *Iohannis* (after
       Valenti Zucchini and Bucci, *"Corpus"*, p. 58, Fig. 60).   447
19.14 Sant'Apollinare in Classe (RA), sarcophagus of Archbishop *Gratiosu*s (after
       Valenti Zucchini and Bucci, *"Corpus"*, pp. 58–59, Fig. 61).   447
19.15 Ravenna, Museo Arcivescovile, sarcophagus of *Gregorius* and *Maria* (after
       Valenti Zucchini and Bucci, *"Corpus"*, p. 59, Fig. 62).   448
19.16 Ravenna, Museo Nazionale, sarcophagus (after Valenti Zucchini and Bucci,
       "Corpus", p. 60, Fig. 65).   448
21.1   Istanbul, Byzantine Cathedral of Hagia Sophia, photograph of the
       catechoumena. Author's copyright.   488
22.1   "Encompass us beneath the precious veil of your protection". *Pokrov*
       (Protection of the Theotokos). Russian icon, 15th c., Vladimir-Suzdal Museum.
       Photograph from Wikimedia Commons. Public domain. (https://commons.
       wikimedia.org/wiki/File:Pokrov_(15th_c.,_Vladimiro-Suzdal_museum)
       .jpg)   514
22.2   "In Thee, O Full of grace, doth all creation rejoice". *O Tebe raduetsia*. Russian
       icon, last quarter of 16th c., Novgorod (?). NMI 297. Photograph
       @Nationalmuseum, Stockholm.   516
24.1   Church of Hosios Loukas, Phokis, Greece, general view of the south-east
       pendentif. Photograph © Rebecca Raynor.   547
25.1   Empress Theodora II, *Menologion* of Basil II, Biblioteca Apostolica Vaticana,
       Vatican, Vat. gr. 1613, p. 392. Reproduced by permission of Biblioteca
       Apostolica Vaticana, with all rights reserved.   560
25.2   The Execution of Autonomous, *Menologion* of Basil II, Biblioteca Apostolica
       Vaticana, Vatican, Vat. gr. 1613, p. 30. Reproduced by permission of Biblioteca
       Apostolica Vaticana, with all rights reserved.   561
25.3   Isidore of Pelusium, *Menologion* of Basil II, Biblioteca Apostolica Vaticana,
       Vatican, Vat. gr. 1613, p. 371. Reproduced by permission of Biblioteca
       Apostolica Vaticana, with all rights reserved.   562

25.4   Paul Cezanne, La Montagne Sainte-Victoire, 1902–1906. Oil on canvas, 63 x 83 cm. Kunsthaus Zurich. Purchased with a contribution of Emil Bührle, 1946.   566

25.5   Discovery of the Head of John the Baptist, *Menologion* of Basil II, Biblioteca Apostolica Vaticana, Vatican, Vat. gr. 1613, p. 420. Reproduced by permission of Biblioteca Apostolica Vaticana, with all rights reserved.   573

29.1   Reliquary Casket of the Four Martyrs of Trebizond, 11th/12th or 14th/15th centuries. Tesoro di San Marco, Venice (inv. no. 33). Photo: Archivio Fotografico della Procuratoria di San Marco Procuratoria di San Marco. Courtesy of the Procuratoria di San Marco.   634

29.2   Reliquary Casket of the Four Martyrs of Trebizond, diagram indicating the placement of verses. Tesoro di San Marco, Venice (inv. no. 33). Photo: Archivio Fotografico della Procuratoria di San Marco Procuratoria di San Marco, with drawing by Brad Hostetler. Courtesy of the Procuratoria di San Marco.   635

29.3   Reliquary Enkolpion of St Demetrios, view of the front showing the image of St. Demetrios and verses 1 & 2, 12th–13th cent. Photo: © Dumbarton Oaks, Byzantine Collection, Washington, DC (BZ.1953.20).   637

29.4   Reliquary Enkolpion of St Demetrios, view of the back showing the image of Ss. Sergios & Bakchos, 12th–13th cent. Photo: © Dumbarton Oaks, Byzantine Collection, Washington, DC (BZ.1953.20).   638

29.5   Reliquary Enkolpion of St Demetrios, interior view showing inner doors closed, 12th–13th cent. Dumbarton Oaks, Byzantine Collection, Washington, DC (BZ.1953.20). Photo: Brad Hostetler. Courtesy of Dumbarton Oaks, Byzantine Collection, Washington, DC.   638

29.6   Reliquary Enkolpion of St Demetrios, interior view showing inner doors open, 12th–13th cent. Dumbarton Oaks, Byzantine Collection, Washington, DC (BZ.1953.20). Photo: Brad Hostetler. Courtesy of Dumbarton Oaks, Byzantine Collection, Washington, DC.   639

29.7   Reliquary Enkolpion of St Demetrios, multiple views of the side showing verses 3 & 4, 12th–13th cent. Dumbarton Oaks, Byzantine Collection, Washington, DC (BZ.1953.20). Photo: after Grabar 1954, Figs. 31–34. Courtesy of Dumbarton Oaks, Byzantine Collection, Washington, DC.   640

29.8   Reliquary Enkolpion of St Demetrios, oblique view showing the lid with the image of St. Demetrios, 11th cent. Kulturstiftung Sachsen-Anhalt, Domschatz Halberstadt, Inv.-Nr. DS024. Photo: after Janke 2006, 162. Courtesy of Kulturstiftung Sachsen-Anhalt.   643

29.9   Reliquary Enkolpion of St Demetrios, oblique view showing the lid removed, inner doors closed, and the epigram on the side, 11th cent. Kulturstiftung Sachsen-Anhalt, Domschatz Halberstadt, Inv.-Nr. DS024. Photo: Bertram Kober/punctum. Courtesy of Kulturstiftung Sachsen-Anhalt.   644

FIGURES

29.10   Reliquary Enkolpion of St Demetrios, interior view showing the inner doors open, 11th cent. Kulturstiftung Sachsen-Anhalt, Domschatz Halberstadt, Inv.-Nr. DS024. Photo: Bertram Kober/punctum. Courtesy of Kulturstiftung Sachsen-Anhalt.   645

29.11   Reliquary Enkolpion of St Demetrios, composite image showing the arrangement of the epigram on three sides, splayed out, 11th cent. Kulturstiftung Sachsen-Anhalt, Domschatz Halberstadt, Inv.-Nr. DS024. Photo: Bertram Kober/punctum, compositing by Brad Hostetler. Courtesy of Kulturstiftung Sachsen-Anhalt.   649

29.12   Reliquary Enkolpion of St Demetrios, 12th cent. Photo: Courtesy of the Holy and Great Monastery of Vatopedi, Mount Athos.   651

29.13   Reliquary Enkolpion of St Demetrios, composite image showing all four sides, splayed out, 11th cent. Photo: Athanasios Lavriotis, compositing by Brad Hostetler. Courtesy of Franz Alto Bauer and the Holy Monastery of the Great Lavra, Mount Athos.   652

Abbreviations

AASS	*Acta sanctorum* (Paris, 1863–1940)
BMGS	*Byzantine and Modern Greek Studies*
BZ	*Byzantinische Zeitschrift*
CFHB	Corpus Fontium Historiae Byzantinae
CSHB	Corpus Scriptorum Historiae Byzantinae
DChAE	*Deltion Christianikis ke Archaeologikis Etaireias* (Δελτίον της Χριστιανικής και Αρχαιολογικής Εταιρείας)
DOP	*Dumbarton Oaks Papers*
JÖB	*Jahrbuch der Österreichischen Byzantinistik*
ODB	A. P. Kahzdan (ed.), *The Oxford Dictionary of Byzantium,* Oxford: OUP 1991.
PG	J. P. Migne, *Patrologiae Cursus Completus, Series Graeca,* 161 vols. Paris 1857–1866.
RéB	*Revue des études byzantines*
TLG	Thesaurus Linguae Graecae (https://stephanus.tlg.uci.edu)

Notes on Contributors

Ilias Anagnostakis
is Research Director at the Institute of Historical Research/Section of Byzantine Research/National Hellenic Research Foundation Athens, IHR/NHRF. He holds a Ph.D. from the University of Paris I Panthéon-Sorbonne (1983). He is supervisor of the research program "Everyday and Social Life in Byzantium" and a member of the team of "Historical Geography of Byzantine Peloponnese, 395–1204". His research interests include everyday and social life in Byzantium; Byzantine Greece and Peloponnese; production, consumption and use of nutrition products in Byzantium (esp. wine, olive oil and cooking); Byzantine gastronomy. He is a member of the editorial board of *Oinon Istoro* and a founding member of the research team "The history of Greek wine: technology and economy."

Alexander Beihammer
is the Heiden Family Professor of Byzantine history at the University of Notre Dame. His research interests include Byzantine diplomatics, political and cultural relations between Byzantium and Islam, and Asia Minor from the Seljuk conquests to the Early Ottoman period. His most recent monograph is *Byzantium and the Emergence of Muslim Turkish Anatolia, ca. 1030–1120* (London–New York: Routledge, 2017). He currently works on a project on the transformation of the Smyrna region and western Asia Minor from Byzantine to Early Ottoman times.

Helena Bodin
is Professor of Literature at the Department of Culture and Aesthetics, Stockholm University, Sweden. Her research concerns the functions of literature at the boundaries between languages, nations, arts, and media. In particular, she has studied modern literature's engagement with the Byzantine Orthodox Christian tradition from the various perspectives of intermedial studies, cultural semiotics, and translation studies, including aspects of multilingualism.

Darlene L. Brooks Hedstrom
is the Myra and Robert Kraft and Jacob Hiatt Chair in Christian Studies at Brandeis University in Classical Studies and Near Eastern and Judaic Studies. She is Senior Archaeological Consultant for the Yale Monastic Archaeology Project-North. As an archaeologist and historian, Brooks Hedstrom specializes

in the material culture and archaeological history of Eastern and Byzantine Christianity. She is the award winning author of *The Monastic Landscape of Late Antique Egypt: An Archaeological Reconstruction* (Cambridge 2017) and editor of the forthcoming *Late Antique Monasticism: An Archaeological and Historical Guide* (Cambridge).

Béatrice Caseau Chevallier
is Professor of Byzantine history at Sorbonne University, in Paris. She is a senior member of the Institut universitaire de France, and a member of the research lab Orient & Méditerranée. Her research interests are varied and include canon law.

Paolo Cesaretti
is Professor of Byzantine Civilization at the University of Bergamo where he also teaches Greek Literature and Roman History. His research and publications (including critical editions) mainly focus on the continuity of scholarly literature in Byzantium, on Byzantine hagiography, on the Late Antique world, and on the relationships between Byzantium and the Medieval West. Three Byzantine "narrative non-fiction" books of his have been translated into various languages.

Michael J. Decker
specializes in the economic and social history and archaeology of the eastern Mediterranean of the fifth-twelfth centuries. He has been an Andrew Mellon Postdoctoral Fellow (Rice University) and the recipient of a Fulbright Research Fellowship. His publications include *The Byzantine Dark Ages*, *The Byzantine Art of War*, and *Life and Society in Byzantine Cappadocia* (w/J. Eric Cooper). Decker is currently Maroulis Professor of Byzantine History and Orthodox Religion at the University of South Florida, where he has taught and researched since 2004.

Veronica della Dora
is Professor of Human Geography at Royal Holloway, University of London and a Fellow of the British Academy. Her research interests and publications span historical and cultural geography, the history of cartography and Byzantine studies with a specific focus on landscape, sacred space and the geographical imagination. She is the author of *Imagining Mount Athos: Visions of a Holy Place from Homer to World War II* (University of Virginia Press, 2011), *Landscape, Nature and the Sacred in Byzantium* (Cambridge University Press, 2016), *Mountain: Nature and Culture* (Reaktion, 2016), and *The Mantle*

of the Earth: Genealogies of a Geographical Metaphor (University of Chicago Press, 2021).

Rico Franses
has held teaching positions at Pratt Institute, the Australian National University and the American University of Beirut, where he was also Founding Director of the University Art Galleries and Collections. His publications include *Donor Portraits in Byzantine Art. On the Vicissitudes of Contact between Human and Divine* (Cambridge University Press, 2018); "Lacan and Byzantium. In the Beginning was the Image", in R Betancourt and M. Taroutina (eds), *Byzantium/ Modernism: Art, Cultural Heritage, and the Avant-Gardes* (Brill, 2015), 311–329; and "To Not Know God. Geometrical Abstraction and Visual Theology in Islamic Art," in E. Baboula and L. Jessop (eds), *Art and Material Culture in the Byzantine and Islamic Worlds. Essays in Honour of Erica Cruikshank Dodd* (Brill, 2021), 265–85.

Sauro Gelichi
is Professor of Medieval Archaeology at the University of Ca' Foscari of Venice. He has been director of many archaeological research projects in Italy and beyond, including Tunisia, Syria, Turkey and Montenegro, and has published monographs and articles on archaeological and historical subjects. He is also principal editor of the journal *Archeologia Medievale*.

Adam J. Goldwyn
is Associate Professor of English at North Dakota State University. He is the author of *Byzantine Ecocriticism: Women, Nature, and Power in the Medieval Greek Romance* (Palgrave MacMillan: 2018), co-translator with Dimitra Kokkini of John Tztezes' *Allegories of the Iliad* (Harvard University Press: 2015) and *Allegories of the Odyssey* (Harvard University Press: 2019) and, with Ingela Nilsson, co-editor of *Reading the Late Byzantine Romance: A Handbook* (Cambridge University Press: 2018).

Basema Hamarneh
is Professor of Late Antique and Early Christian Archaeology, at the Department of Classical Archaeology, University of Vienna. Her research and publications focus on urban and rural settlements in the Late Antique and Early Christian periods; Christianisation of Roman Castra; archaeology and artistic expression of Late Antique, Early Christian/Byzantine and Early Islamic Near East; monastic and religious identities and hagiography applied to topographic

studies. She is co-editor of the Mitteilungen zur Christlichen Archäologie, and directs an archaeological excavation in central Jordan.

Richard Hodges
is the President Emeritus of the American University of Rome. He was Professor at the Universities of East Anglia and Sheffield; Director of the British School at Rome (1988–95); Director of the Prince of Wales's Institute of Architecture (1996–98); Director of the Institute of World Archaeology at the University of East Anglia (1996–2007); Williams Director of the University of Pennsylvania Museum of Anthropology and Archaeology (2007–12). He joined the Butrint Foundation as its scientific director (1993–2012) to initiate new excavations and site management strategies at the UNESCO World Heritage Site of Butrint (Albania). He is currently Principal Investigator of a major EU-funded project in Tuscany (2015–20).

Brad Hostetler
is Assistant Professor of Art History at Kenyon College in Gambier, Ohio. His research focuses on epigraphy and the relationship between text and image in Byzantine material culture. He has held fellowships at Dumbarton Oaks Research Library and Collection and the Metropolitan Museum of Art.

Adam Izdebski
is an environmental historian. He is Associate Professor at the Jagiellonian University in Krakow and the leader of the Independent Research Group "Palaeo-Science and History" at the Max Planck Institute for the Science of Human History in Jena.

Liz James
is Professor of Art History at the University of Sussex. She is interested in all things to do with Byzantine art but perhaps especially with mosaics. Her most recent publication is the very large and ridiculously expensive *Mosaics in the Medieval World* (Cambridge 2017).

P. Nick Kardulias
is the Marian Senter Nixon Professor of Classical Civilization and Professor of Anthropology and Archaeology, Emeritus, at the College of Wooster (USA). His research interests include the analysis of stone tools as they relate to the study of agriculture and craft specialization in ancient cultures, and the use of world-systems analysis and evolutionary theory in archaeological contexts. He

has directed projects in Greece, Cyprus, and the United States. Recent publications include *The Ecology of Pastoralism* (editor; 2015) and *Lithics Past and Present: Perspectives on Chipped Stone Studies in Greece* (co-editor; 2016).

Isabel Kimmelfield
is an independent researcher based in Bristol. Her research focuses on the suburbs of Constantinople and their relationship with the city centre over the early and middle Byzantine periods. She received an MA in History from Radboud University, an MLitt in Art History from the University of Glasgow, and a BA in History and English Literature from the University of Durham. Recent publications include 'Argyropolis: A diachronic approach to the study of Constantinople's suburbs' in *Constantinople as Centre and Crossroad*, Olof Heilo and Ingela Nilsson eds. (Stockholm, 2019) and 'Defining Constantinople's suburb through travel and geography', *Scandinavian Journal of Byzantine and Modern Greek Studies* (Uppsala, 2016).

Tonia Kiousopoulou
is Professor of Byzantine History in the History and Archaeology Department, National and Kapodistrian University of Athens. Her research focuses on the social history during the late byzantine period. She has published the following books: *Ο θεσμός της οικογένειας στην Ήπειρο κατά τον 13ο αιώνα* (Athens 1990); *Χρόνος και ηλικίες στη βυζαντινή κοινωνία. Η κλίμακα των ηλικιών από τα αγιολογικά κείμενα της μέσης εποχής (7ος-11ος αι.)* (Athens 1997); *Βασιλεύς ή Οικονόμος: Πολιτική εξουσία και ιδεολογία πριν την Άλωση* (Athens 2007, translated into English as *Emperor or Manager: Power and Political Ideology in Byzantium before the Fall*, Geneva 2011, and into Serbian in 2014); *Οι "αόρατες" βυζαντινές πόλεις στον ελλαδικό χώρο (13ος-15ος αιώνας)* (Athens 2013).

Johannes Koder
is Professor emeritus of Byzantine Studies at the University of Vienna. He was Professor at the University of Mainz (1978–1985) before taking up the chair in Vienna (1985–2010). He has served as interim director of the Austrian Archaeological Institute and of the excavations in Ephesos 2007–2009. He was also the president of the Association Internationale des Études Byzantines (AIEB) in 2012–2016. He is a member of the Austrian Academy of Sciences since 1989 and editor of *Tabula Imperii Byzantini*, foreign member of the Academy of Athens since 2007, and member of Academia Europaea since 2012. He is also Dr. (h.c.) at the Universities of Athens (2006), Ioannina (2011) and Thrake (2016).

Derek Krueger
is Joe Rosenthal Excellence Professor of Religious Studies at the University of North Carolina at Greensboro. He is the author of numerous studies of late antique and Byzantine cultural and religious history, including *Liturgical Subjects: Christian Ritual, Biblical Narrative, and the Formation of the Self in Byzantium* (2014) and *Writing and Holiness: The Practice of Authorship in the Early Christian East* (2004). He is chair of the United States National Committee for Byzantine Studies and a Senior Fellow in Byzantine Studies at Dumbarton Oaks.

Tomasz Labuk
is keenly interested in the appropriation of ancient Greek iambic and comic tradition in Byzantine literature. In his PhD thesis, "Gluttons, Drunkards, and Lechers. The Discourses of Food in 12th-Century Byzantine Literature: ancient themes and Byzantine innovations", he analysed the re-use and appropriation of ancient Greek iambic tradition by 11th and 12th century Byzantine authors, from Michael Psellos, through Nikolaos Mesarites, to Niketas Choniates.

Maria Leontsini
is Senior researcher at the Institute of Historical Research/Section of Byzantine Research/National Hellenic Research Foundation Athens, IHR/NHRF. She holds a PhD in Byzantine History from the University of Athens (2001). She is a member of the research programs "Everyday and Social Life" and "Historical Geography of Byzantine Peloponnese, 395–1204". She is supervisor of the project "Byzantine literary sources for the history and civilization of Arabs and Arabia". Her research interests include historical, behavioural and geographical perspectives on diet; urban/rural contexts and the environment; Byzantium and the East: Interaction, exchanges and cross-cultural communication.

Yulia Mantova
graduated from the Moscow State University's department of Byzantine and Modern Greek philology in 2002. Her dissertation was devoted to the origin and dating of the *Life of David, Symeon and George*. The paper included commentary and translation into Russian which was later published. In 2016 she defended her doctoral thesis on the literary motif of travel in Mid-Byzantine hagiography and the same year joined the Department of Byzantine and Modern Greek philology at Moscow University as a lecturer. Her research interests focus on the literary aspects of hagiography, and she has recently begun work on the socio-cultural use of invective in Byzantium.

Charis Messis

holds a PhD in Byzantine Studies from Écoles des Hautes Études en Sciences Sociales in Paris and an habilitation from the Sorbonne University. He now teaches Byzantine literature at the National and Kapodistrian University of Athens, where his research interests concern Byzantine history and literature, especially the history of gender, along with other social and anthropological aspects of the Byzantine world. He is author and co-editor of several books and articles on such topics.

Konstantinos Moustakas

received his PhD in Byzantine and Ottoman studies at the University of Birmingham in 2001. Since then, he teaches Byzantine history at the University of Crete. He has published extensively on economic and demographic matters concerning the transition from late Byzantium to early Ottoman times at a localized level; on ideological and historiographical matters related with the fall of Byzantium and the advent of the Ottoman Empire; as well as on medieval Balkan history.

Margaret Mullett

is Professor emerita of Byzantine Studies at Queen's University Belfast and Director of Byzantine Studies emerita at Dumbarton Oaks. She is now honorary Professor at the University of Edinburgh. Recent edited volumes are (with S. Harvey) *Knowing Bodies, Passionate Souls: Sense Perceptions in Byzantium* (2017), (with I. Nilsson and C. Messis) *Storytelling in Byzantium: Narratological Approaches to Byzantine Texts and Images* (2018), and (with R. Ousterhout) *The Church of the Holy Apostles: a Lost Monument, a Forgotten Project, and the Presentness of the Past* (2020). She is currently working on tents, on Byzantine emotion, and on the *Christos Paschon*. At the time of the Spatialities conference she was Visiting Professor of Byzantine Greek at Uppsala working with the narratology research group.

Ingela Nilsson

is Professor of Greek and Byzantine Studies at Uppsala University. She is a specialist in Byzantine literature with a particular focus on issues of literary adaptation, often from a narratological perspective. Her most recent publications include the co-edited volumes *Storytelling in Byzantium: Narratological Approaches to Byzantine Texts and Images* (2018), *Reading the Late Byzantine Romance: A Handbook* (2019) and the monograph *Writer and Occasion in Twelfth-Century Byzantium: The Authorial Voice of Constantine Manasses* (2021).

Nilsson is editor of the series Studia Byzantina Upsaliensia, associate editor of Brill's Narratological Commentaries to Ancient Texts, and editor (with David Ricks) of *Byzantine and Modern Greek Studies*.

Robert G. Ousterhout
is Professor emeritus in the History of Art at the University of Pennsylvania. He is the author of *Visualizing Community: Art, Material Culture, and Settlement in Byzantine Cappadocia*, Dumbarton Oaks Studies 46 (Washington, DC, 2017); and *Eastern Medieval Architecture*, (Oxford University Press, 2019), as well as co-editor of *Piroska and the Pantokrator*, with M. Sághy (Budapest: Central European University Press, 2019); and *The Holy Apostles: A Lost Monument, a Forgotten Project, and the Presentness of the Past*, with M. Mullett (Dumbarton Oaks Symposia and Colloquia) (Washington, DC, 2020).

Georgios Pallis
is Assistant Professor of Byzantine and Post-Byzantine Archaeology and Art at the Faculty of History and Archaeology of the National and Kapodistrian University of Athens. His research focuses on Byzantine sculpture and epigraphy and issues of topography. His field experience includes excavations in sites in Attica, Central Greece, and the Cyclades, where he is currently participating in the excavation of the ancient and early Christian capital of Andros. He is also member of the board of the Christian Archaeological Society at Athens and an active member of the Greek Epigraphic Society and the Greek Committee of Byzantine Studies.

Myrto Veikou
is researcher at Uppsala University within the international research project *Retracing Connections – Byzantine Storyworlds in Greek, Arabic, Georgian, and Old Slavonic, c. 950 – c. 1100* led by I. Nilsson (UU / Riksbankens Jubileumsfond). She specializes in Byzantine Studies through philology, archaeology and geography, taking particular interest in the investigation of the concepts of space and spatiality in Byzantine cultures. She has published on theory of settlement and a wide range of spatial studies, based on Byzantine material culture and literary texts. Her first doctoral thesis, published as 'Byzantine Epirus, a Topography of Transformation. Settlements of the 7th–12th Centuries in Southern Epirus and Aetoloacarnania, Greece' (Leiden 2012), addressed the history of medieval settlement as a result of interaction between physical/social space and human agency, setting forth new theory on the historicity of space. Her second doctoral thesis (forthcoming in *Studia Byzantina Upsaliensia*) proposes a narratological inquiry of the broader meaning of 'spatialities' in Byzantine

texts, which focuses on the employment of a 'spatial' language or 'spatial' narrative techniques and strategies. She is also cooperation partner at the project *Medieval Smyrna/İzmir: The Transformation of a City and its Hinterland from Byzantine to Ottoman Times* led by A. Külzer (Austrian Academy of Sciences / Austrian Science Fund).

Joanita Vroom
is Professor of the Archaeology of Medieval and Early Modern Eurasia at the Faculty of Archaeology, Leiden University (NL), specializing in Medieval and Post-Medieval archaeology in the eastern Mediterranean and the Near East (including the Byzantine, Islamic, Crusader and Ottoman periods). She takes a particular interest in the social-economic (production and distribution) and cultural aspects (cuisine and eating habits) of ceramics in these societies, and is series editor of the 'Medieval and Post-Medieval Mediterranean Archaeology Series' (MPMAS) at Brepols Publishers (Turnhout).

David Westberg
is senior lecturer in Greek at Uppsala University. His previous work is mainly concerned with the rhetorical school of Gaza and the Christian reception of classical traditions.

Enrico Zanini
is Full Professor in Methodologies of Archaeological Research at the University of Siena, where he also teaches Late Antique and Byzantine Archaeology. At present he manages two archaeological fieldwork projects: the excavations in the Early Byzantine District of Gortys (Crete) (www.gortinabizantina.it), and the excavation on the Roman and Late Antique settlement of Vignale (Tuscany) (www.uominiecoseavignale.it). Recent books: D. Michaelides, Ph. Pergola, E. Zanini (eds), *The Insular System of the Early Byzantine Mediterranean: Archaeology and history*, Oxford 2013; P. Basso, E. Zanini (eds), *Statio amoena: Sostare e vivere lungo le strade romane*, Oxford 2016.

(Byzantine) Space Matters! An Introduction

Myrto Veikou and Ingela Nilsson with Liz James

The injunction to historicize space is a recent development in Byzantine studies; traditionally, philologists, archaeologists, historians, and art-historians have been tempted to take space for granted. However, within the so-called Spatial Turn, evolving in the Humanities and the Social Sciences from the 1970s onwards, research on spatial paradigms and practices has been expanding, gaining attention across disciplines and vastly different periods.[1] Doreen Massey and John Allen's highly influential co-edited volume 'Geography Matters!' constitutes a landmark in cultural geography, because it clearly articulates the new conceptualizations of space within the context of this turn.[2] We paraphrase Massey's and Allen's title for introducing the present volume in Byzantine studies for a number of reasons. First of all, their title performs a word-play in which 'matters' – used as either noun or verb – calls readers to perceive the book's twofold meaning: in the first case (noun), as a volume that offers an outline of current issues in geography; in the second case (verb), as a volume underpinning the Spatial Turn's main principle and central statement – geography's critical importance for society. The present volume has been conceived as a work with a similar twofold meaning. On one hand, it aims to epitomize the current main issues around, discussions about, and approaches to space within Byzantine studies. On the other hand, it seeks to stimulate the 'critical reassertion of space' within Byzantine studies with the help of postmodern geography.[3]

In the context of postmodern geography and the Spatial Turn, space has been attributed a complex involvement in historical developments, as a comprehensive concept constituted by the integration of absolute and relative, relational and materially-sensed, physical and social, conceptualized and lived space. The investigation of historical developments with focus on spatial aspects of historical cultures initially developed to counterpoise the overemphasis on temporality, which was prevailing in historical studies until the 1970s.[4] It gradually gained even greater importance and came under the spotlight for two reasons: first, because the spatial approaches proved to be a great

---

1 Warf & Arias 2009.
2 Massey & Allen (eds) 1984.
3 Soja 1989.
4 Withers 2009.

means for alternative interpretations of human agencies and, second, because it offers many good opportunities for discussing crucial issues of contemporary social life, such as ecologic life-styles, natural-resources management, private- and public-space planning etc. The Spatial Turn turned out to be a paradigm shift in outlook and perspective, spanning far beyond the academic discipline of geography: it has, for example, deeply affected and largely shaped the way in which people think about contemporary politics.[5]

Byzantium itself provides an excellent opportunity for discussions about space. It offers an example of a medieval culture which was deeply aware of nature and very closely related to it. Its populations had a strong sense of belonging to their land, which in turn determined their personal and collective identities. These residents were very sensitive in producing their own appropriated space specifically designed to be of human-friendly scale; the translation of space to place. Accordingly, Byzantine spaces, whose abundant traces have come down to us either as material, artistic, or literary remains, constitute a remarkable kaleidoscope of late antique and medieval cultures of the Eastern Mediterranean. Moreover, this raw data of Byzantine space constantly increases, through surveys, excavations, and archival research. The analysis and interpretation of these manifold spatial vestiges open a large window towards our understanding of medieval people.

And yet, the Spatial Turn, which has been developing in many other areas of research and remains most relevant to the present day, has been somewhat overlooked in the study of Byzantine cultures. While the last decade has witnessed a decisive change in the overall attitude to theory in Byzantine studies, there is still a certain reluctance to understand, absorb, or even discuss and reject new theoretical developments.[6] In the case of Spatial studies, Byzantinists have been rather slow in producing a theoretically contemporary dialogue with other scholarly fields, a situation that has produced an unbalanced development of the concept of space in Byzantine studies. On the one hand, certain of its aspects (its materiality and physical transformation) have been largely investigated within the fields of historical topography and landscape archaeology, an accomplishment which deserves ample credit per se.[7]

---

5 Bourdieu 1989; Pugh 2009.
6 Cf. Messis and Nilsson 2018, 1–2.
7 Alongside the very first historiographical works in the field, by Johannes Koder (see his ergography in Külzer & Popović 2017, 407–35), this treatment can be seen in numerous archaeological projects in the Balkans, Asia Minor, and Near East, as well as in compendia such as the *Tabula Imperii Byzantini* Series of the Austrian Academy of Sciences, and the *Late Antique Archaeology* Series by Brill NV (see Külzer et al. 2020; Lavan 2003–2018).

On the other, its multiple involvement in social developments and cultural expressions have hardly been interpreted with using the wide range of tools provided by cultural geography. This has been more intense during the last couple of decades, as technology allows intensive documentation and thorough analyses of the physical space once belonging to the Byzantine Empire,[8] but all this work does not develop hand-in-hand with an equal amount of theoretical interpretations of that space as a socio-cultural component of the empire. Hence, Byzantine studies do not always display a clear focus on research 'of space' (Spatial studies), but rather historical research 'with space', having missed, partly due to conservatism, a paradigm shift in historical theory (from the Annales School to the Spatial Turn).

That said, there is a mindful and determined chain of efforts to bridge the gap between spatial analysis and spatial interpretation.[9] It is significant that such efforts often occurred under the direct influence from other fields of studies which are more open to theoretical reconsiderations and shifts of attention.[10] The present volume aspires to be one link in this chain by offering a theoretical update of the Byzantine paradigm within the particular area of Medieval Spatial studies. An engagement of Byzantinists with a geographic mentality and approach, who are involved in the Spatial Turn, opens up entirely new ranges of possibilities for understanding the Byzantine world. Many cultural aspects speak for the crucial importance of spatialities for the Byzantines: their bodies and minds have been performed as their most personal spaces – their places – of social identity and control. Byzantine people interacted with their natural

---

[8] Spatial documentation and analysis can be seen in an exemplary form in the results of the Avkat Survey (Haldon, Elton & Newhard 2018), published as a combination of a printed overview and an extensive digital repository of visual information (some 51,000 photographs associated with GIS maps).

[9] Art history has been a main field of such research; see e.g. Safran 1988; Lidov 2006, 2009, 2016; Kordi 2014, 2016. In Byzantine archaeology there is a range of publications such as Hodges 2016; Zavagno 2009; Zanini 2017, 2019; Veikou 2009, 2012a–b, 2015, 2019; Bogdanović 2011, 2014, 2017, 2018. In history, see works by Tonia Kioussopoulou (2011, 2013) and in historical geography, see those by Andreas Külzer (2016, 2018, 2019). The editors have offered previous publications in literary studies in the same direction (Messis, Nilsson & Mullett 2018; Veikou & Nilsson 2018; Veikou 2016, 2018, 2020). See also the forthcoming monographs by Christodoulos Papavarnavas and Milan Vukašinović.

[10] In field archaeology see e.g. Bevan, Conolly & Tsaravopoulos 2007; Bevan & Conolly 2013; Caraher, Scott Moore & Pettegrew 2014. In history of settlement and networks see e.g. Çaykent & Zavagno 2014; Çaykent & Zavagno 2016. Anne-Marie Yasin has developed this area of studies in reference to Byzantine cultures (indicatively, Yasin 2009, 2016, 2017). Veronica Della Dora has extended the same scope to Byzantine historical and literary studies (2013, 2016, 2018).

environments in their struggle to survive and create, thus producing their spatial experiences. In that way they have constructed their own culturally appropriated spaces, producing Byzantine landscapes. These landscapes have been dominated by power relations, which divided them into territories, and they have been performed by cultural practices. Passing from the body to the mind, imaginary spaces have hosted moments of a universe of heaven and human passions. These are the spatial aspects of Byzantine cultures dealt with by each of the six sections in this volume: the space of the body; the body in its natural environment; the dialectic natural and human landscape; the territories of Byzantium; the spatial practices; the spatial imaginaries.

As a whole, the volume aspires to provide various answers to the question: How are all these Byzantine spaces relevant to us, today, and in what ways can we grasp them? To ensure diversity and pluralism, this question has been addressed by numerous scholars working in most fields of Byzantine studies: philology and literary studies, history, art history, archaeology, historical geography, historical topography, epigraphy. There has also been a conscious effort to embrace interdisciplinarity and intradisciplinarity in a more specific manner. The concept of space has been established as a platform on which many different conceptualizations and developments offer a fruitful intradisciplinary dialogue on theory and method in contemporary Byzantine studies. A wide range of different conceptualizations of space is articulated through a variety of topics and approaches in the twenty-nine chapters of this book. An afterword then offers a critical consideration of the multiple answers given to the central question by the authors of the volume, as well as to the dialogue on theory and method developed through them.

This volume is the outcome of an international conference held at Uppsala University in May 2017, but it cannot be considered as the conference proceedings. While the conference aimed to present all possible theoretical stances and bring them into dialogue, the volume has been designed as a much more focused project. The aim has been to bring forth spatiality as a crucial dimension of Byzantine culture, interrogate the various understandings of space in Byzantine culture, introduce new methodological approaches to the topic, and present case studies placed within a wider theoretical context, from all fields of Byzantine studies. Spatial experience was not merely focused upon as a scholarly tool; it was considered determinative as a connecting web of social relations.

Based on the principle that space is not simply a symbolic container of social relations but a composer of the contents happening in it, the conference in Uppsala opened in an amazing room at the Museum Gustavianum: the Anatomical Theatre of Uppsala University, built by the medical professor and

(BYZANTINE) SPACE MATTERS! AN INTRODUCTION

FIGURE 0.1　The Anatomical Theatre of Uppsala University, internal view
PHOTOGRAPH: GUSTAVIANUM, UPPSALA UNIVERSITETSMUSEUM. © UPPSALA UNIVERSITY MUSEUM

amateur architect Olof Rudbeck the Elder in 1663.[11] Rudbeck had received the idea of a cone-formed theatre inside a cupola from similar theatres in Leiden and Italy, where anatomy lessons with the help of dissections had already been established during the fifteenth and sixteenth centuries.[12] The hall's peculiar form is based on the principle of a funnel-shaped space, a cone with the cone pointing downwards (Figure 0.1). The main focus area, the dissecting table, is found at the tip of the cone; the funnel is fitted with tiers where people stood during the dissecting lecture. The tiers are very narrow (at a 40cm distance from the parapets), so people had to stand (which had a kind of practical meaning, as they were prone to faint during dissections). The outcome of this shape is astonishing. It allows the person at the tip of the cone to look at all people at the tiers at any time, and those never know when they will be looked at. At the same time, it allows all people at the tiers to look at the person in the centre and at each other at all times – and no one ever knows when one is looked at.

11　Eriksson 2004. See different approaches on space as container and as content, in Mondragon & Lopez 2012; Ryan 2014, §2.3.
12　Ferrari 1987; Klestinec 2004.

A development of this architectural form was a type of institutional building, the Panopticon, designed by the English philosopher and social theorist, Jeremy Bentham, in the eighteenth century.[13] The design consists of a circular structure with an 'inspection house' at its centre, from which the manager or staff of an Institution was able to watch the inmates stationed around the perimeter. Bentham devoted most of his efforts to developing a plan for a Panopticon prison in which all inmates might be observed by a single watchman without the inmates being able to tell whether or not they were being watched. The fact that the inmates cannot know when they are being watched means that all inmates must act as though they are watched at all times, effectively controlling their own behaviour constantly.[14] There is accordingly much more to this architectural plan than mere architecture. As Michel Foucault realised, "the Panopticon is a machine for dissociating the see/being seen dyad: in the peripheric ring one is totally seen, without ever seeing; in the central tower, one sees everything without ever being seen. It is an important mechanism for it automatizes and disindividualizes power."[15] The Panopticon, according to Foucault, must not be understood as a dream building, but as

> a generalizable model of functioning; a way of defining power relations in terms of the everyday life of men. [...] It is polyvalent in its applications; it serves to reform prisoners, but also to treat patients, to instruct schoolchildren, to confine the insane, to supervise workers. [...] It is a type of location of bodies in space, of distribution of individuals in relation to one another, of hierarchical organization, of disposition of centres and channels of power, of definition of the instruments and modes of intervention of power, which can be implemented in hospitals, workshops, schools, prisons. [...] The panoptic mechanism is not simply a hinge, a point of exchange between a mechanism of power and a function; it is a way of making power relations function in a function, and of making a function function through these power relations.[16]

Foucault invoked the idea of the panopticon as a metaphor for modern "disciplinary" societies and their pervasive inclination to observe and normalize. He obviously wrote inspired by his actuality but one, in fact, wonders about his knowledge of medieval texts. In Byzantine hagiography one encounters

---

13   Bentham 1843.
14   Foucault 1995, 195–228.
15   Foucault 1995, 201–2.
16   Foucault 1995, 205–6.

Byzantine perceptions of disciplinary spaces similar to his, as early as the 11th century. As narrated in version B of the *Life of St Athanasios the Athonite*, the holy man constructs a monastery by intentionally giving it the shape of a 'panopticon':

> Καὶ μετὰ τοῦτο τῆς τῶν κελλίων ἀπαρξάμενος οἰκοδομῆς, κύκλῳ ταῦτα τῆς ἐκκλησίας κατεσκεύασεν ἐν τετραγώνῳ τῷ σχήματι, κελλίον τῷ κελλίῳ συνάψας, ὧντινων μέσον ἵσταται ἡ ἐκκλησία ὥσπέρ τις ὀφθαλμὸς βλεπόμενος πάντοθεν.[17]

> And after this he began the construction of cells round about those parts of the church in the form of a square, and having connected cell to cell in the middle of these stood the church like an eye observing from every angle.[18]

The visit to the Anatomical Theatre in Uppsala was intended, firstly, so as to make the participants realise, by personal experience, that spaces make people feel, think, perceive and act in specific ways, and, secondly, that this is not a modern concept. Just as the conception of such a space can be traced back to around the last century of the Byzantine Empire (with dissections in Italy beginning around 1405), the great importance of space in Byzantine culture is also very clear and deserves investigation by means of appropriate interdisciplinary methodology.

A prerequisite for a productive interdisciplinary approach is the disambiguation of terminology. This rule is often not followed. It is common for various items of vocabulary (such as space, place, landscape, environment) to be used in the study of Byzantine spaces undefined and without regard to an interdisciplinary dialogue. Sometimes they are used simply as common words without any specification; at other times they are employed as terms, yet they refer to many different theoretical traditions and disciplinary fields. 'Landscape' is a good example of ambiguity: it is most often used undefined in Byzantine Archaeology, yet a close reading reveals that it may refer to contradictory theoretical frameworks deriving from different academic traditions in Art History, Geography, and History-Archaeology.[19] Such neglect may create a remarkable confusion; this issue is exemplified by three case studies in this

---

17   *Life of Athanasios of Athos B*, 25.2.1–5.
18   Stephenson 2003.
19   See Mina & Veikou 2020.

volume, by Darlene Brooks Hedstrom, Nick Kardulias, and Georgios Pallis, and it is discussed by Adam Izdebski and Michael Decker.

Because of the integral spatiality of social life (it all happens somewhere), all archaeologists – whether specializing more with landscape and architecture or with material culture – deal with space even when they do not openly acknowledge it. It is of great importance to comprehend the spatial parameter of the human past and its heritage for the present and the future, at a local level;[20] this principle is here defended by Richard Hodges, Enrico Zanini, and Nick Kardulias. But how can we, as Byzantinists, approach this parameter in regard to a society and culture of the past, which is essentially remote and unknown to us? A potential measure for Byzantine spaces is the Byzantine human bodies, as archaeologically attested: by material remains of garments, accessories, pieces of furniture etc. Aspects to consider, regarding this material culture, are the size and capacity of vessels and furniture, immobility or portability of objects, their position within buildings and rooms, as well as their role in place-making and identity, for instance in the case of garments and jewellery. Such issues are discussed by Joanita Vroom in this volume.

Architecture, too, is important evidence of Byzantine spatialities. On the one hand, domestic and public spaces have been constructed as to accommodate medieval human bodies in dependence on materials from the natural environments; on the other, they constitute responses to Byzantine spatial perceptions, conceptions and imaginaries at a local and a global level. These two parameters of architecture, the physical and the conceptual, are entangled and they have developed interconnected in the course of the empire. Archaeologists have been considering a variety of aspects around the practical expressions of this development, such as location, size, scale, dimensions and analogies, building materials, accessibility and movement, light and visibility, colours, and decoration by paintings, sculptures and objects or fabrics. All these were involved in the particular spatial experiences of Byzantine people, as exemplified by the studies of Joanita Vroom and Robert Ousterhout in this volume.

Also, the body is a measure for the experience of natural space, such as the sea, the rivers, the mountains, the deserts, the islands etc. Critical issues for Byzantine culture and religion are the perception of the earth as cosmos as well as the experience of the sky as an immense, unreachable, and unpredictable, overlying space. These issues are dealt with by Veronica della Dora's discussion of *kataskope* in this volume. Location is connected to spatial practices and

---

20 See e.g. Hodges 2016; Maddrell et al. 2015.

processes of place-making as well as to collective memory and identities; these issues are discussed by Johannes Koder, Sauro Gelichi, and Liz James. Last but not least, human bodies together with the natural environment of which they are part, are the substance of the empire as a political body: humans and the land to which they belong constitute the empire's territory – political space par excellence.[21] This mechanism is exemplified by four Byzantine examples in the chapters by Tonia Kioussopoulou, Konstantinos Moustakas, Ilias Anagnostakis and Maria Leontsini, and Alexander Beihammer.

But space is a crucial aspect not only of human experience and physical circumstances; it is also essential to any linguistic and artistic representation. In order for you to make sense of the text you are now reading, the space between words, lines, and sections is significant; so is the spatial setting of this piece, which without the volume it introduces would make little sense. Yet 'natural' or indispensable as they may be, spaces of representations are not neutral or free from ideological implications. Inspired by Yuri Lotman, perhaps the first cultural historian to approach literary space from a semiotic perspective, one could say that any artist or writer creates their own vision of the world only as a model of 'real space', relying on description of spatial relationships that are both factual (up vs. down) and metaphorical (up is better than down, as in social hierarchies or Heaven vs. Hell).[22] Spatial representations of any kind accordingly convey much more than geographical or locational information – a setting can be symbolic rather than 'real',[23] literary spatiality can subvert the basically temporal structure of a story,[24] and imaginaries can transfer the reader or beholder to basically any space or storyworld.[25]

In this context, spaces and spatialities of representations may be seen as reflections of experienced spaces, in the sense that it is difficult to imagine

---

21   Foucault 1995, 206, cited above.
22   Lotman 1990. See also Lotman (1977), 218: "Literary space represents an author's model of the world, expressed in the language of spatial representation. In a literary work, space models different relations of the world-picture: temporary, social, ethical and others." Space, according to Lotman, "sometimes metaphorically adopts meanings of relations in the modelled world-structure, that are themselves not spatial at all." On Lotman's theory of literary space and spatial language, see e.g. Hansen Löve 1994, 33–37.
23   On the different functions of space in narrative, see e.g. de Jong 2014, 122–29; in a Byzantine context, see Nilsson 2021a and 2021b, 25–57.
24   For an analysis of such 'spatializing' strategies in Byzantine literature, influenced by the approach of Frank 1991, see Nilsson 2000 and 2001, esp. 139–45. On the workings of ekphrasis from this perspective, see also Nilsson 2005.
25   See e.g. the contributions by Myrto Veikou, Ellen Söderblom Saarela, Milan Vukašinović, and AnnaLinden Weller in Messis, Mullett & Nilsson 2018.

anything that cannot be grasped by human cognition – even descriptions of outer space tend to refer to spatial conceptions known to us, otherwise they would make little sense. They thus range from the innermost parts of our bodies to the universe, including its spiritual and phenomenological aspects. The contributions in this volume cover a considerable part of such considerations and thus offer a substantial advancement of a field still under development. The chapters exploring various aspect of the human body, mentioned above, are complemented by literary studies of corporeal representations by Tomek Labuk, Charis Messis, and Myrto Veikou. It may seem evident, but still worth noting, that genres under investigation here range from legal texts to poetry; there is no text type for which space is irrelevant, although the chapters of this volume express a certain leaning towards hagiography (see the chapters by Myrto Veikou, David Westberg, Paolo Cesaretti & Basema Hamarneh, and Yulia Mantova). Such a tendency is probably indicative of the increasing literary interest in hagiography rather than a lack of interest in the spatialities of other genres; while early studies of literary spatiality in Byzantium focused on novelistic and ekphrastic texts,[26] time has now come to a genre that brims with spatial notions on linguistic, factual, and literary levels.

Space in art and literature is sometimes seen as an indispensable but not necessarily important setting: merely the backdrop against which images or stories are placed. The aesthetic, symbolic or emotional implications of such spatial settings are then left out of the discussion, as if they had no significance for the overall interpretation of the work. To an even greater extent, the impact of the space in which works of art were placed, texts were performed or stories told is often overlooked, with the result that their spatial context is underestimated or neglected. Nonetheless, whenever Byzantinists engage with ideas around landscapes or places or architecture, be they in texts, in images or in the material world, they are engaging with spaces. Byzantine objects exist in space and spaces; are displayed in spaces; have homes in different places. How those spaces acted, with or without reference to the objects within them, is proving a fruitful source of inquiry: light and sound in Hagia Sophia; acoustics in churches in Thessaloniki.[27]

Indeed, throughout Byzantine art, there are images of spaces and places, from depictions of the Cosmos or the end of time (in the form of the Last Judgement) to idyllic pastoral landscapes and gardens, spaces both real and imaginary (and sometimes both at the same time). Often these space/place

---

26   As indicated above, n. 21.
27   Pentcheva 2017; Peers 2013; Gerstel et al. 2021.

aspects of the image are overlooked – little has been said about 'landscape' as a Byzantine pictorial concept, for example, other than to dismiss it.[28] Veronica Della Dora and Helen Saradi have, in different ways, looked to explore the Byzantines' own conceptualisations of space made visible in their images.[29] Della Dora has considered sacred topographies, both real (Mount Sinai) and depicted (images of Mount Sinai). Saradi has engaged with architecture and images of architecture – how were cities represented, for example, and why, and what changed – the differences apparent in floor mosaics such as that from the eighth-century church of St Stephen at Umm al-Rasas in Jordan to the city held by Constantine in the tenth-century mosaic of the south-west vestibule in Hagia Sophia.

So Byzantine images – pictorial as well as literary – exist in space and as spaces. They can depict spaces and places. They can turn spaces into places. Spaces in an image, on an image and around an image can all affect its reception, its effect. Images both define and help us see how the Byzantines perceived, conceived, and defined space, the world around them. Even taking space as a backdrop is to define it or to banish it. This becomes clear in the contributions of Margaret Mullett, Béatrice Caseau, Liz James, and Rico Franses, forcing us to reconsider some preconceived notions of what represented spaces actually are and what they mean. The implications and meaning of spiritual representations of spaces and places are investigated by Helena Bodin and Isabel Kimmelfield, both with a certain focus on one of the central spaces of Byzantium: Constantinople. The question about the workings of language in actual, physical space, both in the presence of made words (carved on a building, written on or into an image) within images and as words as images themselves, is addressed by Brad Hostetler. The very ordering of words was a spatial statement in itself – an ordering and management of space prevalent in Byzantine society through its visibility on buildings, objects, and in manuscripts.

We are matter, and material space includes us and surrounds us. We seek to conceive and manage it by translating it into different idioms: physical space, conceptual spaces, social space, and place. Space is a natural feature and concurrently a human construction; it lies on us to perceive, label, experience, share and divide.

---

28   Clark 1984.
29   Della Dora 2016; Saradi 2010.

Bibliography

Primary Sources

Life of Athanasios of Athos B, ed. R. P. Greenfield & A.-M. Talbot, *Holy Men of Mount Athos*, Dumbarton Oaks Medieval Library, London 2016, 127–367. English translation by Paul Stephenson 2003, online publication at https://web.archive.org/web/20050528000730/ http://homepage.mac.com/paulstephenson/trans/athanasios1.html (last accessed on 11-03-2022).

Secondary Sources

Bentham, J. 1843. *The Works of Jeremy Bentham*, vol. 4 (Panopticon, Constitution, Colonies, Codification). Edinburgh.

Bevan, A., J. Conolly, & A. Tsaravopoulos 2007. "The fragile communities of Antikythera", *Archaeology International* 10, 32–36.

Bevan, A. & J. Conolly 2013. *Mediterranean Islands, fragile communities and persistent landscapes: Antikythera in long-term perspective*, Cambridge.

Bogdanović, J. 2011. "The Performativity of Shrines in a Byzantine Church: The Shrines of St Demetrios", in A. Lidov (ed.), *Spatial Icons. Performativity in Byzantium and Medieval Russia*, Moscow, 275–316.

Bogdanović, J. 2014. "The Rhetoric and Performativity of Light in the Sacred Space: A Case Study of The Vision of St Peter of Alexandria", in A. Lidov (ed.), *Hierotopy of Light and Fire in the Culture of the Byzantine World*, Moscow, 282–304.

Bogdanović, J. 2017. *The Framing of Sacred Space: The Canopy and the Byzantine Church*, Oxford.

Bogdanović, J. 2018. *Perceptions of the Body and Sacred Space in Late Antiquity and Byzantium*, New York.

Bourdieu, P. 1989. "Social Space and Symbolic Power", *Sociological Theory* 7/1, 14–25.

Caraher, W. R., R. Scott Moore & D. K. Pettegrew 2014. *Pyla-Koutsopetria I: archaeological survey of an ancient coastal town*, Boston, MA.

Çaykent, Ö. & L. Zavagno (eds) 2014. *Islands of the Eastern Mediterranean: a history of cross-cultural encounters*, London – New York.

Çaykent, Ö. & L. Zavagno (eds) 2016. *People and Goods on the Move. Merchants, Networks and Communication Routes in the Medieval and early Modern Mediterranean*, Fisciano.

Clark, K., ²1984 (¹1976). *Landscape into art*. New York.

de Jong, I. 2014. *Narratology and Classics*. Oxford.

Della Dora, V. 2013. "Gardens of Eden and Ladders to Heaven: Holy Mountain Geographies in Byzantium", in K. D. Lilley (ed.), *Mapping Medieval Geographies: Geographical Encounters in the Latin West and Beyond, 300–1600*, Cambridge, 271–98.

Della Dora, V. 2016. *Landscape, Nature, and the Sacred in Byzantium*, Cambridge.

Della Dora, V. 2018. "Mountains as a Way of Seeing: From Mount of Temptation to Mont Blanc", in Ch. Kakalis & E. Goetsch (eds), *Mountains, Mobilities and Movement*, London, 189–211.

Eriksson, G. 2004. "Olof Rudbeck som vetenskapsman och läkare: Lars Thorén föreläsning 2003. Sammandrag", *Svensk Medecinhistorisk Tidskrift* 8/1, 39–44.

Ferrari, G. 1987. "Public Anatomy Lessons and the Carnival: The Anatomy Theatre of Bologna," *Past & Present* 117, 50–106.

Foucault, M., 1995. "Panopticism", in *Discipline & Punish: The Birth of the Prison*, translated by A. Sheridan, New York, 195–228.

Frank, J. 1991. *The Idea of Spatial Form*, New Brunswick.

Gerstel, S. E. J., C. Kyriakakis, S. Antonopoulos, K. T. Raptis, J. Donahue, 2021. "Holy, Holy, Holy: Hearing the Voices of Angels", *Gesta* 60/1, 31–49.

Haldon, J., H. Elton & J. Newhard (eds.) 2018. *Archaeology and urban settlement in Late Roman and Byzantine Anatolia: Euchaïta- Avkat-Beyözü and its environment*, Cambridge (https://opencontext.org/search/?q=Avkat#11/40.5681/35.3156/15/any/ Google-Satellite, last accessed on 09-06-2021).

Hansen Löve, K. 1994. *The Evolution of Space in Russian Literature: A Spatial Reading of 19th and 20th century narrative literature*, Amsterdam – Atlanta, GA.

Hodges, R. 2016. *The Archaeology of Mediterranean Placemaking. Butrint and the Global Heritage Industry*, London.

Kioussopoulou, T. 2011. *Emperor or Manager: Power and political ideology in Byzantium before 1453*, transl. Paul Magdalino, Geneva.

Kioussopoulou, T. 2013. *Οι «αόρατες» βυζαντινές πόλεις στον ελλαδικό χώρο (13ος-15ος αιώνας)*, Athens.

Klestinec, C. J. 2004. "A History of Anatomy Theatres in Sixteenth-Century Padua", *Journal of the History of Medicine and Allied Sciences* 59/3, 375–412.

Kordi, S. 2014. *The Chora parekklesion as a space of becoming*, Diss. Leeds.

Kordi, S. 2016. "Corporeal Perceptions of the Immaterial: Agency and Rhythm in Palaeologan Monumental Painting", *IKON* 9, 153–62.

Külzer, A. 2016. "Byzantine Lydia: Some Remarks on Communication Routes and Settlement Places", in P. Magdalino & N. Necipoğlu (eds.), *Trade in Byzantium: Papers from the Third International Sevgi Gönül Byzantine Studies Symposium.* Istanbul, 279–95.

Külzer, A. 2018. "Reconstructing the Past in a changing Landscape: Reflections on the Area of Ephesus and other Sites in Western Asia Minor", *Gephyra* 16, 75–90.

Külzer, A. 2019. "Roads and Routes: Communication Networks in the Hinterland of Ephesos", in Sabine Ladstätter & Paul Magdalino (eds.), *Ephesos from Late Antiquity until the Late Middle Ages*. Vienna, 149–60.

Külzer, A. & M. Popović (eds.) 2017. *Space, Landscapes and Settlements in Byzantium: Studies in Historical Geography of the Eastern Mediterranean*. Studies in Historical Geography and Cultural Heritage 1. Novi Sad – Vienna.

Külzer, A., V. Polloczek, M. Popović & J. Koder 2020. *Raum und Geschichte: der Historische Atlas 'Tabula Imperii Byzantini' an der Österreichischen Akademie der Wissenschaften*, Studies in Historical Geography and Cultural Heritage 3, Novi Sad.

Lavan, L. (ed.) 2003–2018. Late Antique Archaeology Series vols. 1–12, Leiden (https://brill.com/view/serial/LAA.).

Lidov, A. M. (ed.) 2006. *Hierotopy: The Creation of Sacred Spaces in Byzantium and Medieval Russia*, Moscow.

Lidov, A. M. 2009. *Hierotopy: Spatial Icons and Image-Paradigms in Byzantine Culture*, Moscow.

Lidov, A. M. 2016. "Iconicity as Spatial Notion. A New Vision of Icons in Contemporary Art Theory", *IKON* 9, 17–28.

Lotman, J. 1977. *The Structure of the Artistic Text*, translated by Ronald Vroon, Ann Arbor.

Lotman, J. 1990. *Universe of the Mind: A Semiotic Theory of Culture*, translated by Ann Shukman; introduction by Umberto Eco, London.

Maddrell, A., V. Della Dora, A. Scafi and H. Walton 2015. *Christian Pilgrimage, Landscape and Heritage*, New York.

Massey, D. & J. Allen, (eds), 1984. *Geography matters!* Cambridge.

Messis, Ch., M. Mullett & I. Nilsson (eds), 2018. *Storytelling in Byzantium: Narratological Approaches to Byzantine Texts and Images*, Uppsala.

Mina, M. & M. Veikou, 2020. "Art Studies, Post-Processual Perspectives on Gender, Landscape", in *Encyclopedia of Global Archaeology*, ed. C. Smith, New York.

Mondragon, M. & Lopez, L. 2012. "Space and Time as Containers of the 'Physical Material World' with some Conceptual and Epistemological Consequences in Modern Physics", Cornell University (https://arxiv.org/abs/1205.1715, last accessed on 09-06-2021).

Nilsson, I. 2000. "Spatial time and temporal space: Aspects of narrativity in Makrembolites", in P. A. Agapitos and D. R. Reinsch (eds), *Der Roman im Byzanz der Komnenenzeit*, Frankfurt am Main, 94–108.

Nilsson, I. 2001. *Erotic Pathos, Rhetorical Pleasure: Narrative Technique and Mimesis in Eumathios Makrembolites' Hysmine & Hysminias*, Uppsala.

Nilsson, I. 2005. "Narrating Images in Byzantine Literature: The Ekphraseis of Konstantinos Manasses", *Jahrbuch der Österreichischen Byzantinistik* 55, 121–46.

Nilsson, I. 2021a. "Byzantine Narrative: Theory and Practice", in S. Papaioannou (ed.), *Oxford Handbook of Byzantine Literature*, Oxford, 273–93.

Nilsson, I. 2021b. *Writer and Occasion in Twelfth-Century Byzantium: The Authorial Voice of Constantine Manasses*, Cambridge.

Papavarnavas, Ch. forthcoming. *Gefängnis als Schwellenraum in der byzantinischen Hagiographie. Eine Untersuchung früh- und mittelbyzantinischer Märtyrerakten*, Berlin – Boston.

Peers, G. (ed.) 2013. *Byzantine Things in the World.* Yale.

Pentcheva, B. (ed.) 2017. *Aural Architecture in Byzantium: music, acoustics and ritual.* London.

Pugh, J. 2009. "What are the consequences of the 'spatial turn' for how we understand politics today? A proposed research agenda", *Progress in Human Geography* 33/5, 579–86.

Ryan, M.-L., 2014. "Space", in: P. Hühn et al. (eds.), *The living handbook of narratology*, Hamburg: Hamburg University (http://www.lhn.uni-hamburg.de/article/space, last accessed on 09-06-2021).

Safran, L. (ed.) 1988. *Heaven on Earth: Art and the Church in Byzantium.* University Park, Penn.

Saradi, H. D., 2010. 'Space in Byzantine thought' in S. Curcic & E. Hadjitryphonos (eds), *Architecture as Icon: Perception and reception of architecture in Byzantine art*, Yale, 73–113.

Soja, E. W., 1989. *Postmodern Geographies: The Reassertion of Space in Critical Social Theory.* London and New York.

Veikou, M. 2009. "'Rural Towns' and 'In-between Spaces'. Settlement Patterns in Byzantine Epirus (7th–11th centuries) in an Interdisciplinary Approach", *Archeologia Medievale* 36, 43–54.

Veikou, M. 2012(a). *Byzantine Epirus: A Topography of Transformation: Settlements of the seventh-twelfth centuries in southern Epirus and Aetoloacarnania, Greece*, Leiden – Boston.

Veikou, M. 2012(b). "Byzantine Histories, Settlement Stories: Kastra, "Isles of Refuge", and "Unspecified Settlements" as In-between or Third Spaces", in T. Kioussopoulou (ed.), *Οι Βυζαντινές πόλεις, 8ος–15ος αιώνας. Προοπτικές της έρευνες και νέες ερμηνευτικές προσεγγίσεις*, Rethymno, 159–206.

Veikou, M. 2015. "One island, three capitals. Insularity and the successive relocations of the capital of Cyprus from late antiquity to the middle ages", in S. Rogge & M. Grünbart (eds), *Medieval Cyprus – a Place of Cultural Encounter*, Münster – New York, 357–387.

Veikou, M. 2016. "Space in Texts and Space as Text – A new approach to Byzantine spatial notions", *Scandinavian Journal of Byzantine and Modern Greek Studies* 2, 143–75.

Veikou, M. 2018. "'Telling Spaces' in Byzantium: Ekphraseis, place-making and 'thick' description", in Messis, Mullett & Nilsson (eds) 2018, 15–32.

Veikou, M. 2019. "The Reconstruction of Byzantine Lived Spaces: A Challenge for Survey Archaeology", in Vassileiou, A., Diamandi, Ch. (eds), *'Εν Σοφία μαθητεύσαντες,*

Essays in Byzantine Material Culture and Society in Honour of Sophia Kalopissi-Verti, Oxford, 17–24.

Veikou, M. 2020. *Spatial Paths to Holiness: Literary 'Lived Spaces' in eleventh-century Byzantine saints' Lives*, Diss. Uppsala.

Veikou, M. & I. Nilsson 2018. "Ports and harbours as heterotopic entities in Byzantine literary texts", in C. von Carnap-Bornheim, F. Daim, P. Ettel, U. Warnke (eds), *Harbours as objects of interdisciplinary research – Archaeology + History + Geoscience, Interdisziplinäre Forschungen zu Häfen von der Römischen Kaiserzeit bis zum Mittelalter Series*, Mainz, 265–77.

Vukašinović, M. forthcoming. *Ideology as Narrative Worldmaking: Subjects and Space in Roman and Serbian Lands after 1204*.

Warf, B. & S. Arias (eds) 2009. *The Spatial Turn: Interdisciplinary Perspectives*. Abingdon – New York.

Withers, C. W. J. 2009. "Place and the 'Spatial Turn' in Geography and in History", *Journal of the History of Ideas* 70/4, 637–58.

Yasin, A.-M. 2009. *Saints and Church Spaces in the Late Antique Mediterranean: Architecture, Cult, and Community*, Cambridge.

Yasin, A.-M. 2016. "Beyond Spolia: Architectural Memory and Adaptation in the Churches of Late Antique North Africa", in S. T. Stevens & J. P. Conant (eds), *North Africa under Byzantium and early Islam*, Washington, D.C., 215–36.

Yasin, A.-M. 2017. "The Pilgrim and the Arch: Channelling Movement and Transforming Experience at Late Antique Holy Sites", in T. M. Kristensen & W. Friese (eds), *Excavating Pilgrimage: Archaeological Approaches to Sacred Travel and Movement in the Ancient Mediterranean and Near East*, London, 166–86.

Zanini, E. 2017. "La 'mansio' di Vignale (Piombino): l'archeologia di un 'sito minore' in una lettura antropologica 'surmoderna'", in S. Santoro Bianchi (ed.), *Emptor e mercator: spazi e rappresentazioni del commercio romano*, Bari, 513–32.

Zanini, E. 2019. "Macro-economy, Micro-ecology, and the Fate of Urbanized Landscape in Late Antique and Early Byzantine Crete", in M.A. Cau Ontiveros & C. Mas Florit (eds), *Change and Resilience: The Occupation of Mediterranean Islands in Late Antiquity*, Oxbow – Philadelphia, 139–62.

Zavagno, L. 2009. *Cities in Transition: Urbanism in Byzantium Between Late Antiquity and the Early Middle Ages (500-900 A.D.)*, Oxford.

PART 1

The (Most) Private Space: The Human Body

∴

Editorial Note on Part 1

The first section of this collection considers attitudes towards the very first space that one perceives, the most personal and private yet also exposed hence interactional: the corporeal space. The section explores notions of the body as a space within spaces and ways in which it shaped and constrained thought in Byzantine cultural expressions. It also investigates the concept of embodied space, as the location where human experience and consciousness takes on material and spatial form. The four chapters present embodied space as a model for understanding the creation of place through spatial orientation, movement, use of space, and language. Tomek Labuk scrutinizes the belly (γαστήρ) as a critical part of corporeal space, which allows the human body to exert social control by means of hosting and regulating nourishment. This chapter exemplifies the control of bodies and bodily behaviours—or a Byzantine 'government of the bodies'. Charis Messis offers a discussion on the relation between the socialization and spatialization of the body. Through his study on Byzantine legal and literary texts, Messis argues for political dimensions of the physical human body. Veronica della Dora focuses upon symbolic aspects of embodied space. Della Dora presents a Byzantine symbolic visual experience (κατασκοπή, i.e. a 'synoptic experience of space produced through elevation') as active engagement and not passive observation. Last but not least, Myrto Veikou discusses the moving and relocating human body as a literary performed space, which is used as a narrative device in Byzantine hagiography. Veikou also offers an introduction to the geographical concept of spatial mobility—a recurrent theme in the following chapters.

1
The Human Belly as a 'Natural Symbol'
The Greek and Byzantine Anthropology of γαστήρ

Tomek Labuk

It seems difficult to conceive of any specific space which is more private and intimate to us than our bodies. They are crucial to our sustenance and well-being; their diagrams are deeply inscribed within our brain structures, and they facilitate our sensory perception of both the world and any imaginable space.[1] This intimacy of our own bodily 'universe' is strengthened by the fact that no one could have any direct access and understanding of how we perceive our own body or how we feel within it. That said, the body seems to pose a curious paradox: being the most private space, it is simultaneously the most public one. It is through our body that we interact with other bodies and spaces; living within in it, we live in the society of other individuals, and how we comport ourselves in our bodies is a marker of our social and political identity.

The inevitable consequence of our embodiment reveals itself in the simple fact that to live and thrive we need to nourish ourselves. And because the individual body is simultaneously a public or social entity, one of the most effective ways of exerting control upon it is to discipline its dietary habits. Discussing this intimate interconnection between nutritional and social control, Brian Turner noticed that the Latin noun *regimen* conveys a closely connected double meaning both: "dietary regimen", thus a set of rules which control the intake of food, and "political regime", which can be broadly understood as the "government of the bodies".[2] They both strive to control individual and social bodies by producing and exercising sets of rules which rationalize bodily behaviours. From this perspective, the control of the belly and its needs ensures the orderly composition of any given social group.

---

1 As neuro-biological research shows, we possess a virtual map of our body which is imprinted in our brain since the time of its formation in the pre-natal phase (the so-called 'homunculus'). What is astonishing is that those born without a limb (or limbs) might suffer from 'phantom limb pain' (PLP) and feel members of their bodies which they have never possessed; for this, see Kean 2014, 129–214 with an extensive scientific bibliography on the subject, and Subedi & Grossberg 2011.
2 Turner 1982, 3.

Thus, there is an apparent analogy between what is organic and social: the body is easily translated into social and political spheres. For this reason, we are accustomed to conceiving of society as an organism: a living entity whose parts (organs and limbs) need to function properly, and such a relation between what is bodily and social is universal to all human cultures.[3] Yet, it is one thing to acknowledge such interconnection, but something else to understand the semiotics of the human body within a specific culture. Mary Douglas has shown that each 'natural symbol', including the body itself, is a construct of both bodily experience and the socio-cultural setting within which it exists.[4] Thus, despite the fact that the concept of the body and its parts is always "a model of any bounded system",[5] it is a product of social convention, an artifice that needs to be interpreted within its specific context and in relation to other sets of symbols.[6]

While some common patterns and structures of conceiving of the body and its parts exist which are universal, the symbolic significance attached to bodily members and physiological processes may differ.[7] While in the polytheistic structures of Hinduism, the anthropomorphized representations of gods are possible, in the Judeo-Christian framework, the intermingling of the divine and the worldly is strictly prohibited. Douglas has illustrated this point with an excerpt taken from Maimonides' reflections on the anthropomorphic representations of God in the Old Testament. According to him, while it is possible to assign the external organs (shoulders, hands, feet, etc.) figuratively to God, one should never associate God with the internal organs of digestion. It is simply inconceivable to present God as truly possessing bowels, as "they are at once recognized as the signs of imperfection".[8]

In the present discussion, I would like to focus on one of the most vital parts of the human body, namely the belly, and its symbolic significance in Byzantine culture. Following the insights and methodological framework put forward by Douglas, I disclose the prevailing patterns of social and religious

---

3   Temkin 1942.
4   Douglas 1996.
5   Douglas 1984.
6   Douglas 1984, 116: "The body is a complex structure. The functions of its different parts and their relation afford a source of symbols for other complex structures. We cannot possibly interpret rituals [...] unless we are prepared to see in the body a symbol of society, and to see the powers and dangers credited to social structure reproduced in small on the human body".
7   Douglas 1996, xxxv: "A basic question for understanding natural symbolic systems will be to know what social conditions are the prototype for the one or the other set of attitudes to the human body and its fitness or unfitness for figuring godhead".
8   Maimonides 1956, 61. See the discussion in Douglas 1996, xxxiv.

conceptualization of the space of γαστήρ (belly), στόμαχος (stomach) and κοιλία (gut) in Byzantium. Surely, if our bodies are crucial to both our individual and social lives, and if our bellies are vital to the sustenance of our bodies, then particular symbolic significance must have been attached to it. Hence, in what follows, I address the following questions: what patterns of meaning were concealed behind the social concept of the belly as a 'natural symbol'? What are the ultimate sources of Byzantine conceptualization of γαστήρ? What are the implications of characterizing someone through their belly? Last, but not least, if the belly can be universally understood as a "sign of imperfection", to what extent should its urges be controlled to ensure social well-being? I will proceed with the search for the answers to these in two steps. First, I engage in an 'archaeology of an idea', to seek the sources of the Byzantine conceptualization of the belly. Secondly, I put forward several case studies based primarily but not exclusively on written Byzantine sources to uncover the patterns of conceptualizing the space of the belly in the Medieval Greek tradition.

1   Peeping into Darkness: γαστήρ in the Greek-Byzantine Tradition

The moral problematization of the space of the human belly seems to date back to the earliest period of Greek literature.[9] Already in the archaic iambic poetry, γαστήρ was conceptualized as a threatening space: the greediness of public officials and kings, who were the main targets of iambic insult, was explicitly associated with their insatiable bellies. One of the most conspicuous examples of such a connection is a famous mock-epic purportedly composed by the iambic poet, Hipponax. In the poem, he emphasizes the monstrous voraciousness of the politician Eurymedontiades: he is like the all-devouring Charybdis and "a stomach with a knife inside it" (ἐγγαστριμάχαιρα), hence he swallows the foodstuffs whole:

> Μοῦσά μοι Εὐρυμεδοντιάδεα, τὴν παντοχάρυβδιν,
> τὴν ἐγγαστριμάχαιραν, ὃς ἐσθίει οὐ κατὰ κόσμον, ἔννεφ',
> ὅπως ψηφῖδι <κακὸς> κακὸν οἶτον ὀλεῖται
> βουλῇ δημοσίῃ παρὰ θῖν' ἁλὸς ἀτρυγέτοιο […]

> Tell me, Muse, of the sea swallowing, the stomach carving of
> Eurymedontiades who eats in no orderly manner, so that through a

---

9   For the "moral problematization" of consumption see Foucault 1990, 14–32.

baneful vote determined by the people he may die a wretched death along the shore of the undraining sea [...]¹⁰

The passage reveals vividly the close linkage between the insatiable γαστήρ, the unruly eating habits (ἐσθίει οὐ κατὰ κόσμον), and the social threat. This interconnection of the uncontrolled belly and danger is visible in the fact that the ones like Eurymedontiades, who were decreed to be stoned to death in archaic Athens, were those public officials who abused the people for their use: the tyrants, the fraudulent generals, and the traitors of the πόλις, hence all those who threatened the social order and stability of the city.¹¹ Similarly, in Athenian Old Comedy, the inability to curb the urges of the belly was emblematic of the manipulative and parsimonious demagogues who were living at the expense of the people. For this reason, the costumes worn by the comic actors included a padded protruding belly which pointed to its uncivil character, since it indicated slackness, effeminacy, and unrestrained appetites, and hence pointed to the lack of civic control over their bodies.¹²

The belly and its beastly needs stand at the core of the *Iliad* and the *Odyssey*. Pucci and Egbert showed that γαστήρ and concerns over orderly consumption form the leitmotifs of the *Odyssey* and are one of the drivers of its plot.¹³ Thus, both Odysseus' companions, who consumed the forbidden meat of the Cattle of Helios, and Penelope's suitors, who broke the divine law of ξενία and were unlawfully filling their bellies with Odysseus' substance, had to be punished and killed; indeed, γαστήρ is characterized in the *Odyssey* as a wretched thing which causes much evil to men.¹⁴ Correspondingly, the entire plot of the *Iliad* is triggered by the belly-driven δημοβορία of Agamemnon, who unjustly takes Briseis for himself and thereby prompts Achilles' anger (μῆνις).¹⁵ Agamemnon's uncontrollable private urges are mapped directly onto his public rapaciousness.

These ideas were further elaborated on and organized by Plato and Aristotle. In the *Timaeus*, Plato argues that gods placed the lowest part of the mortal

---

10 Hipponax, *Fragments* 128. Cf. Hesychius, *Lexikon* ε 155: ἐγγαστριμάχαιραν· τὴν ἐν τῇ γαστρὶ κατατέμνουσαν. The fragment from Hipponax has been discussed by Brown 1988. English translation by Gerber 1999, 459.
11 Worman 2008.
12 Foley 2000, 275.
13 Pucci 1995, 157–208; Bakker 2013, 135–56.
14 Homer, *Odyssey* 17.473–74: γαστέρος εἵνεκα λυγρῆς, οὐλομένης, ἣ πολλὰ κάκ' ἀνθρώποισι δίδωσιν.
15 Worman (2008, 29) points out that the δημοβορία, literally 'people-eating,' of Agamemnon is driven directly by the urges of his own γαστήρ.

soul in the belly (γαστήρ).[16] As a result, it became the seat of beastly/feminine urges, which included the worst drive for bodily satisfaction. Since this nethermost part of the soul is responsible for the most basic, irrational, animal-like appetites (which include craving for food, drink, and sex) Plato likens it to a savage beast (θρέμμα ἀγρίον).[17] Aristotle argues along similar lines. In the *Nicomachean Ethics*, he identifies taste and touch as brutish sensations which humans share with other animals.[18] The latter is even more pernicious than the sensation of taste: it is the act of touching food which gratifies a licentious person, being seemingly close to sexual pleasure.[19] A man who takes enjoyment in these sensations can be compared to a wild animal and is characterized by savagery (θηριῶδες). Therefore, gluttons, who are maddened by their bellies (γαστριμάργοι), prove themselves to be extremely crude types of people (ἀνδραποδώδεις). Indeed, such wariness towards γαστήρ is particular to every philosophical system of Greek antiquity. The Pythagoreans, with their elaborate rules which prohibited the intake of certain kinds of food, are a particularly good case in point:[20] Pythagoras' idea of strict ἐγκράτεια entailed holding the belly in constant check against its propensity towards luxury.[21] In the same vein, Philo Judaeus perceived control over the belly, the genitals, and the tongue (an organ which consumes and produces speech) to be the primary concern of philosophy.[22]

Such a conceptualization of the belly as a natural symbol, associated with a threat both to the individual and to society as a whole, became even stronger with the advent of Christianity. It seemed only natural that γαστήρ began to be associated with the deadly sins of gluttony, lust and greed and, by extension, with Original Sin. This can be gleaned from the writings of the Greek Church

---

16 Plato, *Timaeus* 69c–70e. Certainly, Plato was profoundly inspired by Socrates, who was purportedly the most self-controlled man towards the urges for sex, food, and wine. For this see Xenophon, *Memorabilia* 1.2.1.
17 As Plato argues further, it is for this reason that the gods decided to place it near the genitals, so that the belly as the seat of the most irrational passions is maximally distanced from the rational soul and does not interfere with it: Plato, *Timaeus* 69e. Plato perceives the belly as the ultimate source of immorality, irrationality, infirmity, and hence links it to effeminacy. See the discussion of these in Hill 2011, 45–55.
18 Aristotle, *Nicomachean Ethics* 1118a–b.
19 In order to illustrate his point, Aristotle quotes story of a glutton who wished his neck was as long as a crane's so that he might enjoy the sensation for a longer time, Ibid. 1118a.30–32.
20 Garnsey 1999, 87–89; Simoons 1998, 192–210.
21 Porphyry, *Life of Pythagoras* 22.18–22.
22 Philo Judaeus, *De Congressu* 80.1–2. For the discussion of this see Hultin 2008, 78–81. The triad of talking, eating, and lust is discussed by Worman (2008, 275–318) in relation to Aristoteles and Theophrastus.

fathers, which advocate for a rigorous ἐγκράτεια towards one's body and one's belly. It was through the maintenance of absolute control over one's σῶμα that one could live up to the ideal of a Christian. Indeed, living by one's γαστήρ was believed to be the polar opposite of godly existence. Clement of Alexandria's famous discussion on gluttony in the *Paedagogus* is a conspicuous case in point here. His ideas related to γαστήρ blend concepts associated with it in antiquity (hence foolishness, bestiality/animality, effeminacy, social danger) with the main tenets of Christianity.[23] In Clement's eyes, those who live only by their bellies resemble savage beasts, for they live only to eat. Clement links them to Satan, who himself was fashioned in Christian thought in the mould of a gluttonous beast. Hence belly, with its uncontrolled and unquenchable desires, leads inevitably to sin and perdition of an individual.

Therefore, for the sake of recapitulation, the webs of meaning associated with the space of γαστήρ in the Greek tradition might be illustrated in the form of the diagram below (Figure 1.1). Against this background, let us turn to the Byzantine period to examine the continuities and developments of such a conceptualization.

2 Case Study No. 1: Γαστὴρ in the Byzantine Ascetic Tradition

Perhaps one of the best places to move the investigation into the Byzantine period is the famous *Ladder of Divine Ascent* written by John Klimax somewhere around the beginning of the seventh century. It should not come as a surprise that the treatise, which was written primarily for the use of ascetic monks, includes an entire chapter entitled "On the beloved and knavish mistress, the belly" (Περὶ τῆς παμφίλου καὶ δεσποίνης πονηρᾶς γαστρός).[24] The title itself is rich with references to ancient and early Christian ideas. John Klimax plays here with the grammatical gender of the Greek noun γαστήρ, which is feminine: we have already seen that in the ancient tradition the belly is a gendered space associated with what was believed to be 'feminine', and thus irrational, urges.[25] The link between the pleasure derived from the consumption of food and sexual fulfilment is present here as well: after all, the Greek noun

---

23 For this, see an in-depth analysis in Hill 2011, 110–20.
24 John Klimax, *Ladder* 14. English translation by Moore 1959 misses this wordplay and renders the title "On the clamorous, yet wicked master—the stomach".
25 Worman 2008, 8–19 points out that such a conceptualization was a product of a male-dominated society, in which every behavioral pattern that endangered the prevailing norms of 'masculinity' was thought to be 'feminine'.

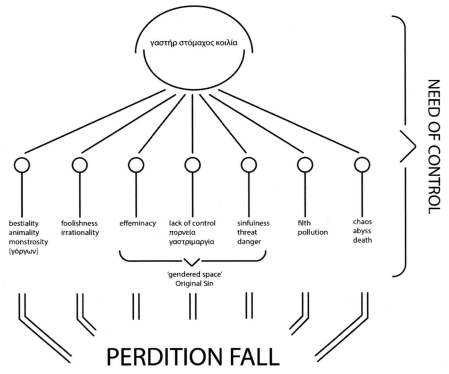

FIGURE 1.1 Visualization of the webs of meaning associated with the space of γαστήρ in the Greek tradition

γαστήρ stood not only for the belly as a digestive organ, but as an organ for sexual procreation. Further in the chapter John Klimax shows how belly-driven gluttony and fornication go hand in hand: the ever-insatiable demon within the belly can never be satisfied, even if it ate all of Egypt and drank up the river Nile, it would still fail to deafen its drive for fornication (πορνεία).[26]

Identification of the belly as a 'mistress' clearly alludes to the original sin, instigated by Eve and the insatiable belly of Adam. This interconnection can be seen in one of the illuminations included in the mss Vat. Gr. 394, which is an important witness to the text. On folio 74 r., gluttony is depicted as a classicizing figure of a richly clad woman, who wears a golden crown on her head and wields an apple in her left hand. She is portrayed while staring lasciviously at

---

26 John Klimax, *Ladder* 14 κζ''. The image emphasizes the insatiability of the belly: the Nile was the biggest river which was known back that, while Egypt, due to its fertile delta, was associated with abundance of food.

the figures of the monks, who are being instructed by John Klimax about her dangers.[27] The apple, which she holds in her left hand, points to the sinister character of the belly/gluttony, while the crown underscores the fact that the urges of the belly are the 'ruling passions' and the springboard of every sin. Finally, the extravagant attire of the personification of γαστριμαργία casts it into the role of a biblical whore (πορνή), hence a seditious, precarious, sinful, and lascivious woman.[28] The link between γαστριμαργία, threat, and the original sin is rounded up by next illumination in the manuscript (fol. 78 r.). It portrays two scenes: in the first one we can see Adam and Eve in the Garden of Eden, who are standing near the apple tree, whereas in the second one they are being expelled from the Garden by an angel.

The entire chapter of the Ladder emphasizes the dire threats which are posed to humans by the belly. Human life seems to be infinite wavering between hunger and satiety, and John Klimax doubts that anyone could set themselves free of this cruel mistress.[29] He does not merely limit the urges of γαστήρ to the lowest and beastly appetites, but identifies the belly as the seat of purely demonic forces that bewitch the individual: indeed, it is Lucifer himself who settles in the stomach.[30] For this reason, it can never be tamed or coddled: it must be overwhelmed, pruned, and treated with the utmost violence and only thereby tamed.[31] At times, John Klimax pictures this struggle in openly military terms—those who struggle against their all-devouring bellies are like combatants (ἀγωνιστής).[32] The threat posed by the passions of one's belly never ceases, and the fight is constant: "Master your gut before it masters you", threatens John Klimax.[33] Within the framework of the Ladder, the belly is the ultimate source and the pinnacle of every conceivable sin.[34] The one who lives by it will never have a share in the divine kingdom,[35] the vices which stem

---

27 Martin 1954, 68–68; Maguire 2012, 112. In the second (left-hand side) section of the scene, she lays conquered by Klimax who is scaling up the divine ladder.
28 For the discussion of the social dangers of πορναί in the biblical tradition see Gaca 1999. Cf. John Klimax, Ladder 14 γ': Κόρος βρωμάτων, πορνείας πατήρ.
29 John Klimax, Ladder 14.α': Θαυμάζω γὰρ εἰ μήτις τάφον οἰκήσας, ἐγένετο ταύτης [scil. γαστρός] ἐλεύθερος.
30 Ibid. 14 λ': Ἄρχων δαιμόνων, ὁ πεσὼν ἑωσφόρος· καὶ ἄρχων παθῶν ὁ λαιμὸς τῆς κοιλίας.
31 Ibid. 14 ιζ'; 14 ιη'; 14 κδ'; 14 κς''.
32 Ibid. 14 ι''.
33 Ibid. 14 ιζ': Κράτει κοιλίας, πρὶν αὐτὴ σοῦ κρατήσει.
34 Ibid. 14 λδ': "Let us ask this foe, or rather this supreme chief of our misfortunes, this door of passions, this fall of Adam, this ruin of Esau, this destruction of the Israelites, this laying naked of Noah's shame, this betrayer of Gomorrah, this reproach of Lot, this death of the sons of Eli [...]" For Noah, drunkenness and shame see the section 3 of this article.
35 14 κθ'; 14 λβ''.

from it defile one's soul and body with "impurities, dreams, and emissions",[36] and when it is not mastered, it leads to the unavoidable fall and perdition.

3   Case Study No. 2: The Gnawing Teeth of γαστήρ/ὕστερα and the Gorgon's Head

That γαστήρ, κοιλία, and στόμαχος are associated with a grave threat to the integrity of an individual in a treatise, which was primarily addressed to ascetic monks, should come as no surprise. Nevertheless, γαστήρ was perceived as a natural symbol associated with the sphere of danger, even in the non-literary folkloric tradition. This point might be well illustrated by the extremely popular Byzantine *hystera* amulets. These were thought to be magical pendants, which endowed its owners with protection against illnesses, especially uterine conditions. On their obverse side, they include various images of the *gorgoneion*, hence a female head with the heads of snakes encircling it.[37] The use of gorgon-related imagery becomes clearer if we take a look at the Byzantine redaction of *Physiologus*. A gorgon was believed to be a creature that resembled a beautiful harlot whose hair was composed of snakes, while her face looked like death itself.[38] Whenever the time of coitus came, the gorgon supposedly emitted frightful sounds and seduced whoever heard her. When anyone glimpsed her, they died immediately.[39]

The deceptive attractiveness and the deadly threat posed by gorgons makes it clear why their resemblance was carved in the prophylactic amulets. The amulets were supposed to ward off the dangers linked with the belly or the womb from its possessors.[40] Foskolou points out that the magical inscriptions which were carved on their reverse side mention, alongside ὕστερα, the belly (<γ>αστέρα) and the stomach (<σ>τόμαχος). Some of the inscriptions refer to the beastly gnawing of teeth and voraciousness of the belly.[41] These were 'performative' engravings: they were supposed to be read aloud and thereby repel the imminent threat related to the belly/womb.

---

36   14 κζ′: τὴν ψυχὴν καὶ τὸ σῶμα ἐν μολυσμοῖς, καὶ φαντασίαις, καὶ ἐκκρίσεσι καταμιάνας.
37   For the discussion of the amulets see Spier 1993, Barb 1953, Foskolou 2014.
38   *Physiologus* 23.1–3: Ἔστι γὰρ ἡ γοργόνη μορφὴν ἔχουσα γυναικὸς [εὐμόρφου] πόρνης· αἱ δὲ τρίχες τῆς κεφαλῆς αὐτῆς ὡσεὶ ὄφεις, τὸ δὲ εἶδος [τοῦ προσώπου] αὐτῆς θάνατος.
39   Ibid. 23.9–10.
40   Cf. the comely figure of the deadly gorgon with the personification of γαστριμαργία in Vat. gr. 394 discussed above.
41   Spier 1993, 46.

The identification of γαστήρ with the gorgon dates back to extremely early periods.[42] Barb noticed that, in the ancient Greek tradition, στόμαχος was thought to be the entering-mouth which led to the womb, while the Greek terms denoting the 'womb,' the 'heart' and the 'belly/stomach' were frequently confused.[43] In the *Lexicon* by Hesychius, such a linkage is overt: he glosses the term ὄδερος (Lat. *uterus*) with the noun γαστήρ.[44] Certainly, the amulets were connected to a widespread belief that the womb was an independent animal-like being which could travel throughout the body, wreak havoc on it, and cause serious illnesses.[45] For this reason, they include the above-mentioned inscriptions, which were supposed to tame the maddened γαστήρ. Furthermore, the conceptualization of γαστήρ as the beastly space of danger is underscored by the fact that, since time immemorial, the womb has been connected in the Greek tradition to the ultimate place of rebirth and death. It stood as a symbol of both the primeval chaos, from which everything sprang, and the hellish abyss. Interestingly enough, in Christian iconography its gulf was represented as the jaws of Leviathan, whose prototype was a dolphin, the womb-fish.[46]

4 Case Study no. 3: Die Like Arius!

It comes as no surprise that within the Greek tradition, the sphere of the belly (γαστήρ) and the bowels (κοιλία, ἔντερα) were associated with pollution and socially/religiously unwanted elements. This can be gleaned from the story of Judas' disembowelment preserved in the Acts of Apostles: the body of the traitor supposedly burst open and his intestines spilled out in an act of divine retribution for his hateful deed.[47] According to Josephus Flavius, a similarly horrid fate was shared by another enemy of Christianity, Herod. In his *Jewish War*, Flavius reports how Herod died from intestinal inflammation. Josephus

---

42   Barb 1953 notes that in almost every iconography the womb is associated with round objects: vessels, jars, or even the navel, hence the connection of the womb with a round face surrounded by the snakes. The connection of the gorgon and gluttony can be gleaned from Aristophanes *Peace* 810 and is preserved in *Suda* γ 392.
43   Griffiths & Barb 1959, 368 n.14.
44   Hesychius, *Lexicon* o 74; Barb 1953, 222 n.106.
45   Foskolou 2014, 344.
46   Cf. the Greek term δελφύς, the close connection of δελφύς and δελφίς have been discussed by Barb 1953, 200.
47   Acts of the Apostles 1:18: "With the payment he received for his wickedness, Judas bought a field; there he fell headlong, his body burst open and all his intestines spilled out". I am following the English version from *NIV*.

describes this horrid disease in minute detail: Herod's body started to decompose, he suffered from chronic pain in his colon, his abdomen was inflamed, his penis putrefied and produced worms.[48] He recovered for a short while only to devise a massacre of those Jews from the illustrious families who plotted against him and died shortly thereafter.[49]

The trope of the 'intestinal death' of heretics and tyrants continued into Byzantine times. A widely-known story recounted in Socrates of Constantinople's *Historia Ecclesiastica* is an excellent case in point here. Arius supposedly dissimulated during his confession of the Orthodox faith: he signed the declaration of 'true' faith whilst holding a small scroll with his own heretical opinions hidden under his armpit, then he took communion from Alexander, the Patriarch of Constantinople. Convinced that he had successfully fooled everyone, he paraded through the streets of the city, but once he reached the Forum of Constantine, he was caught by a strange sensation in his bowels and rushed to a place at the back of the forum, where his bowels burst open, spilling fountains of blood.[50]

I have argued above that the space of the belly enclosed everything that was thought to be socially and religiously threatening: uncontrolled appetites, ungodliness, defilement, and sinfulness. Hence, linking γαστήρ with heretics should come as no surprise at all: what has spilled out of Arius' body symbolized not only the social danger which his heterodox opinions posed but also epitomized what he was: socially rejected filth. Moreover, the meaning of the entire story, which later became an established motif in anti-heretical Byzantine literature (and beyond it), might be elucidated by what Douglas has labelled as a "rule of distance from the physiological origin". According to this rule, the more important a social occasion is, the more the organic processes have to be set outside it, since they defile it and divest it of any dignity.[51] Muehlberger has noticed that Arius' 'intestinal' death gained immense popularity and quickly became a trope of heresy, and many other heretics were reported to have died

---

48   Joseph Flavius, *Jewish War* 1.656–58.
49   For a discussion of other literary tropes of good and bad death, see Agapitos 1998 and 2004.
50   Socrates Scholasticus *Historia Ecclesiastica*, 1.38. The story and its immediate reception has been extensively analyzed by Muehlberger 2015. Idem 2015, 7 notes that Judas' disembowelment in the Acts was the prototype for the story of Arius "intestinal death".
51   Douglas 1996, XXXIII: "According to the rule of distance from physiological origin (or the purity rule) the more the social situation exerts pressure on persons involved in it, the more the social demand for conformity tends to be expressed by a demand for physical control. Bodily processes are more ignored and more firmly set outside the social discourse, the more the latter is important. A natural way of investing a social occasion with dignity is to hide organic processes".

like Arius.[52] In later centuries, the trope was used not only for the deaths of the apostates but also for tyrants, usurpers, and ungodly emperors. This point can be elucidated by an example of the ungodly jester Lampoudios from the tenth-century *Vita Euthymii*. He was hired to heap violent insults during the official banquet against the guileless patriarch Euthymios. His malicious words make everyone blush and the emperor himself throws him out of the court. Soon he pays for the irreverent tone towards the patriarch: he was striding through the city with his associates when they passed through the gate on which there was a chapel of St Athenogenes. At that moment, Lampoudios suddenly fell ill, and his intestines, dung, and blood gushed out of his body.[53] It is by no means an accident that Lampoudios is compared to Judas:[54] both of them received bribes for their hateful deeds and both died instantaneously when their innards burst out.[55]

A similar fate is shared by several literary characters in the later periods of Byzantine literature. In Michael Psellos' *Chronographia*, Emperor Romanos III Argyros is pictured vomiting out some thick dark-coloured liquid; Theodora dies after severe diarrhoea, which resulted in a complete evacuation of her intestines.[56] In a similar vein, in Niketas Choniates' *History*, the tyrant Andronikos dies after a long execution when some Latin soldiers burst his entrails (ἔγκατα) with their swords.[57] Likewise, in Nicholas Mesarites' narrative of the failed palace coup led by John Komnenos 'the Fat' (Παχύς), the would-be usurper gives life, once he is decapitated and his bowels gush forth, which were loosened by the imperial soldiers with a two-edged sword.[58]

---

52 Muehlberger 2015, 7–8 with reference to the relevant sources.
53 *Life of Euthymius*, 7.45.7–10.
54 Ibid. 7.45.4: ὁ δὲ παρέχει τούτῳ ὡς ἄλλῳ τινὶ Ἰούδᾳ τριάκοντα ἀργύρια.
55 Ibid. 7.45.10–13. The author of the *vita* identifies Lampoudios' unjustified abuse as the direct cause of his bloody death.
56 On Romanos III Argyros' death: Michael Psellos, *Chronographia* III.26.35–38. On Theodora's death, Ibid. VI.222.4–7.
57 Niketas Choniates, *History* 350.47–351.51. As I argue elsewhere, Andronikos' tyrannical δημοβορία (people-eating) stems from the uncontrollable urges of his γαστήρ; Cf. Worman 2008, 29.
58 Mesarites Nicholas, *Narrative of the Coup* §28 46.21–24: εἰς οὖν τῶν στρατιωτῶν ἀμφικώπῳ σπάθῃ τὰς λαγόνας αὐτοῦ ἐξεκέντησε, καὶ βαρέως ὁ Ἰωάννης ἀνῴμωξε χαμάζε πεσών, τῶν κρυφίων ἐκχυθέντων ἐγκάτων.

5 Case Study no. 4: The 'Non-Ascetic' Asceticism of the Drunken Monk Jacob

Let us return for a moment to the ascetic tradition, or rather to its subversion, namely the famous invective against the drunken monk Jacob composed by Michael Psellos.[59] It is an extremely interesting piece of literature which reveals several insights into the Byzantine conceptualization of the belly. Indeed, γαστήρ, στόμαχος and κοιλία stand as the leitmotifs of the entire piece: within the 160 verses of the canon, Psellos wittily shows that the only ἄσκησις which is practiced by Jacob comes down to constant emptying of the ἀσκοί of wine, which flows directly into the chasm of his insatiable gut. Douglas' rule of the distance from physiological origin can be thus applied to it as well: γαστήρ not only subverts the social role which was supposed to be played by the monk, it also shatters the traditional context of singing a religious canon.[60]

Throughout the canon-invective, Michael Psellos reveals how Jacob rejected the virtuous life of a monk and spends entire nights and days hard-drinking and glutting himself: he reduced himself to his insatiable gut and is consistently presented as such. Due to his incessant drinking, he is nothing more than an insatiable animal (ζῷον ἀκόρεστον, ἀκόρεστε). Instead of praying to God and exercising ascetic practices, which he openly despises,[61] he fills his insatiable gut to the very brim,[62] presses wine directly from the grapes into the *pithos* in his belly;[63] he even baptizes himself with litres of consumed wine.[64] Jacob seems to be nothing more than an enormous belly-wineskin which leaks with fountains of foul-tasting wine through its pores.[65] Indeed, nothing can satiate

---

59 Michael Psellos, *Poem* 21.
60 For an extended analysis of the subverted form of the poem, see my discussion in Labuk (forthcoming).
61 Michael Psellos, *Against Jacob* 5–8.
62 Ibid. 4: κοιλίαι πίθων πληρούμεναι.
63 Ibid. 11: καὶ σφίγγων [βότρυας] ἐν τῷ λάρυγγι ἀποθλίβει τὸν οἶνον.
64 Ibid. 110–18; 131–36. Of course, the very idea of baptism was to cleanse oneself from sin and sickness and to incorporate the baptized into the community of the Christians. The only thing that Jacob can do is to "baptize" himself in the bodily waste produced by his belly: he can never be cleansed and incorporated into the "divine" community. Jensen 2012, esp. 7–90.
65 Ibid. 45–50: "Ὤφθης ἐν γῇ ἄμπελος, πάτερ, πολύκαρπος,|οἶνον στάζων πάντοθεν παχύτατον, | ἐκ τοῦ λαιμοῦ, ἐκ τῶν ὀφθαλμῶν, | ἐκ τῆς κάτω θύρας, ἀπὸ παντός σου τοῦ σώματος | ἱδρῶτας γὰρ ἐκχέεις, ἀλλὰ μέθην βαρεῖαν | ὡς ἀσκὸς διαρρεύσας, Ἰάκωβε; also see 149–54. Again, it is a pun on a phonetic similarity between the nouns ἀσκός and ἄσκησις: the only ascetic practice known to Jacob is related to emptying up wineskins. More than that, Psellos alludes to

Jacob's raging gut;[66] neither the constantly emptied *pithoi* brimming with wine, nor the proverbial river of the Nile, nor even if he drank up the entire ocean of wine.[67] As Michael Psellos jokingly remarks, even God himself, who had filled the void, would not be able to fill the huge belly of Jacob: his gut accepts everything like a sewer (ὡς σωλήν).[68]

Almost every verse and strophe of the canon emphasizes the unbridled drunkenness driven by an enormous and insatiable γαστήρ of Jacob. Under the humorous surface of the invective, Michael Psellos hides much deeper sense and explores the web of meanings hidden behind the natural symbol of the belly. The striking and, at times, repulsive physicality of the poem works to distance Jacob maximally from the godly life of ascetic monks: having gulped down enormous volumes of wine, he lies naked on his bed, still drinking unceasingly, farting, and "baptizing" himself in his bodily discharges, which he subsequently "vomits" (ἀποβλύζει) through all the orifices of his body: through his throat, eyes, even his "back door" (ἐκ τῆς κάτω θύρας).[69] Moreover, he belches, burps, and "sends out howling winds".[70] Of course, such repulsive physiology is well-grounded within the aesthetics of the Greek/Byzantine tradition of invective. At the same time, it conveys a deeper symbolic meaning: in her study of pollution and taboo, Douglas noticed that the leaking body is always regarded as socially unclean, unwanted, or threatening.[71]

The unsocial and anti-religious character of Jacob, who lives only to satiate his raging gut, is moreover emphasized in the canon by moulding him as the opposite of several biblical figures. Unlike his biblical counterpart, Noah, the first man to get drunk, Jacob did not even bother to plant a vine-tree: he

---

a widely-used biblical motif which likened the stomach to wineskin. For this see *Suda* α 4177, Psalm 118:83, 1 Corinthians 9:27; Eustathius, *Opera* 176.11–15 (discussed by Stone 2005, 39).

66 Michael Psellos, *Against Jacob* 87–88: στόμαχον οἱ πίθοι ἐκκενούμενοι οὐκ ἤμβλυναν.
67 Ibid. 55–56.
68 Ibid. 21–24: Ὁ πληρώσας ἀβύσσους δημιουργὸς κύριος | καὶ τὴν τῆς θαλάσσης κοιλίαν μεστώσας ὕδατος | σὴν οὐκ ἐπλήρωσε, πάτερ, πλατεῖαν γαστέρα· | ὡς σωλὴν γὰρ ἅπαντα κενοῖς δεχόμενος.
69 Ibid. 45–50. Also Ibid. 109–12: Δάκρυσι πλύνεις σου τὴν κλίνην | καὶ βαπτίσματι βαπτίζῃ καθ' ἡμέραν· | ἡ γαστήρ σου καὶ γὰρ τὸν οἶνον μὴ χωροῦσα | δι' ὀχετῶν τοῦ σώματος ἀποβλύζει τοῦτον, πάτερ. Similarly Ibid. 33–36: Ἀναπεσὼν ὕπτιος ἐπὶ τῆς κλίνης σου | καὶ γυμνώσας στῆθος καὶ τὸν τράχηλον | καὶ τὸν μηρὸν ἄχρι τῆς αἰδοῦς | πίνεις ἀνενδότως, ἴσως καὶ πέρδεις, Ἰάκωβε. In medieval art nakedness was associated with both drunk Noah and Dionysios: Anagnostakis and Papamastorakis 2004.
70 Ibid. 73–74: πληρωθεὶς γὰρ μέθης βορβορυγμούς, ὀξυρεγμίας ὠρυγάς τε ἐκπέμπεις καὶ πνεύματα.
71 Douglas 1984.

limits himself to feeding on the work of others and drinks all day and night.[72] Similarly, Michael Psellos subversively introduces the Old Testament story of Jonah's swallowing by the sea monster and spending three days in its κοιλία (*Jon.* 2:2–9). Through his incessant filling of his voracious γαστήρ/κοιλία, Jacob proved himself to be a greater Jonah (μείζων Ἰωνᾶς): he spends his entire life in the belly of his *pithos* and, unlike Jonah, Jacob does not even want to be rescued by God from it.[73] Moreover, the roar (κραυγή) of Jonah's ardent prayers to God, which went up from the belly of the monster in the biblical story, is only a rumble which is emitted by the sickly γαστήρ of Jacob, destroyed by the seas of consumed wine. It thus stands as yet another sign of Jacob's ungodliness.[74]

Moreover, Jacob is cast as the direct opposite of a protagonist of yet another biblical tale associated with baptism and resurrection, namely the story of the three brothers who were cast into the fiery furnace in *Dan.* 3. Jacob seems to be another Azarias (ὡς ἄλλος Ἀζαρίας), but the likeness is merely superficial. While the biblical Azarias was delivered from the ungodly fire because of his unwavering belief in God, Jacob is burnt by the fiery furnace of his drunkenness, which he quenches by pouring more and more wine into his stomach.[75]

In the end, the real identity of the drunken Jacob is fully revealed: he seems better suited to being a bacchant who drinks and sings hymns to the pagan god Dionysos than to being a Christian monk.[76] Even more, the way he drinks

---

[72] Ibid. 57–62. The first verse οὐ φυτεύσας ἀμπέλους is an overt allusion to the opening line of the famous scene of drunkenness of Noah in Genesis 9:20–23 (Καὶ ἤρξατο Νωε ἄνθρωπος γεωργὸς γῆς καὶ ἐφύτευσεν ἀμπελῶνα). Anagnostakis & Papamastorakis 2004, 233 remark that the verbs related to reclining (ἀναπεσών, ἀνάπαυσις) present in the poem have been traditionally associated with Noah: Michael Psellos, *Against Jacob* 33: Ἀναπεσὼν ὕπτιος ἐπὶ τῆς κλίνης σου and Ibid. 64 οὐδὲ τῇ γαστρί σου ἀνάπαυσιν δέδωκας. At the same time, Psellos indicates that the gut-loving Jacob breaks the social rules according to which the monks were supposed work and cultivate the land to secure the provisions of comestibles for their monasteries.

[73] Michael Psellos, *Against Jacob* 29–32.

[74] Ibid. 69–72: Ἐκ κοιλίας κραυγή σου | ἤκουσται, Ἰάκωβε, ἐν τῇ τοῦ πίθου γαστρί, | καὶ ὑπήκουσέ σου | ὁ τὸν οἶνον ἐκχέων σοι, πάντιμε· | πληρωθεὶς γὰρ μέθης / βορβορυγμούς, ὀξυρεγμίας | ὠρυγάς τε ἐκπέμπεις καὶ πνεύματα. On top of that, the story of Jonah's swallowing and his subsequent rescue was liked in Greek tradition with baptism and already in the *New Testament* (Matt. 12.39–40) it was believed to be a prefiguration of Christ's resurrection (Jensen 2012, 154).

[75] Michael Psellos, *Against Jacob* 105–8. Just like the story of Jonah, the tale of the three brothers was believed to be a prefiguration of Christ's resurrection. Here again, Jacob, because of his ungodly, belly-driven life, is set as in opposition to his biblical counterpart. For other anti-religious and anti-monastic guises of Jacob, see also my discussion in Labuk (forthcoming).

[76] Michael Psellos, *Against Jacob* 101–4.

unceasingly and the sheer volume of consumed wine evoke the feeling of ἔκπληξις in those who witness it. Already in the ancient tradition, ἔκπληξις signified a sensation of terror or awe which was believed to be created by the deadly gaze of a gorgon, a monster that epitomized all the deadly threats posed by the γαστήρ/στόμαχος/κοιλία.[77]

6 A Final Case Study: The Monstrous Body and the Disembowelment of a Usurper

Finally, I would like to discuss some of the aspects of a bulky body of texts related to the infamous failed coup led by John Komnenos, nicknamed the 'Fat' (Παχύς). They are of special relevance to the present discussion since all of them make use of the vast array of negative symbols and conceptualizations related to the space of the belly in the Byzantine tradition. Surely, the two speeches by Nikephoros Chrysoberges and Euthymios Tornikes, a narrative account by Nicholas Mesarites, along with a short excerpt from Niketas Choniates' *History* are the only texts from within the Byzantine tradition which use obesity and insatiable belly at such length.[78]

Interestingly enough, the belly is mentioned directly only in the speech by Tornikes: using a biblical quotation from *Phil.* 3:19, he identifies John with the enemies of Christianity, "whose god is their belly" (οὗ θεὸς κοιλία).[79] At the same time, however, all the sources related to the coup revolve around the threatening insatiability of the belly, its dire consequences, and the threats posed by those who live by it. John's morbid fatness is certainly the focal point of all the accounts. Hence Tornikes, for instance, constantly underscores the bulkiness, meatiness, and fleshiness of John's monstrous body (κρεωβαρής, πλατύσαρκός, βαρύκρεως, βαρύσαρκος, κοῦφος). Niketas Choniates emphasizes John's bulging gut (προκοίλιος, πιθώδης τὴν πλάσιν τοῦ σώματος) as well as his enormous body, which was stuffed with meat (κρεωβριθής). Similarly, Mesarites speaks of John as the one who was verily fat (τὸν ὄντως παχύν), he is described as a useless burden (ἀχθός τι ἐτώσιον), who was so heavy that he could not even walk by himself and had to be carried on a bed.[80] His body was so huge that

---

77 Ibid. 143–44. For ἔκπληξις and gorgon see van Eck 2016.
78 The only literary analysis of them was put forward by Kazhdan & Franklin (1984, 224–55). Also see Angold 2017, 31–42.
79 "Their destiny is destruction, their god is their stomach, and their glory is in their shame. Their mind is set on earthly things".
80 Nicholas Mesarites, *Narrative of the Coup* §8 25.10–18.

even the proverbially insatiable Hades would not be able to consume it in one go.[81]

Undoubtedly, there is a deeper logic in this obsessive focus on John's fat body. After all, John led the coup (or rather was a straw man behind it) against the ruling emperor, Alexios III Angelos.[82] In all the sources, the monstrously bulky body, which resulted from John's gluttony,[83] is used as an emblem of his sinfulness, anti-civic character, and utter uselessness. Of course, the connection between the fat John and Original Sin and evil is easily established by the authors through evoking the notion of sinful flesh (σάρξ): his body presented as a huge sack filled with flesh, even his mind seems to be fleshy (νοῦς σάρκινος).[84] Moreover, in Tornikes' speech and Mesarites' narrative, the sheer weight of John's fat body epitomizes his ungodly and un-kingly character. Tornikes humorously describes how the 'useless burden' of the usurper's body was pushed onto the imperial throne, which then crumbled to pieces,[85] while Mesarites, in a similarly joking tone, tells how a bunch of prostitutes and catamites that followed John wanted to see him "borne aloft despite being grossly fat", and to put the imperial crown on his foolish head.[86] Later in the text, Nicholas Mesarites shows how John drinks himself into a stupor while he is seated on the ground, which "symbolizes the unbearable weight of disaster".[87] Again, Euthymios Tornikes, referring to Aristotelian physics, perorates that such a heavy 'object' like John was bound to fall by its very nature.[88]

Furthermore, John's heaviness is not merely limited to his weight: in all accounts, he is presented as a dim-witted blockhead followed by a foolish rabble and not suited to wear the imperial crown.[89] His irrationality and insatiable appetites reveal themselves in numerous comparisons of John to wild

---

81 Ibid. §28 46.26–32.
82 For a discussion of the coup, see Angold 2015.
83 Alluded to by Tornikes, *Speech 1* §12 67.7–8 by a biblical quotation: φάγων γὰρ ἐνεπλήσθη καὶ ἀπελάκτισεν, ἐπαχύνθη, ἐπλατύνθη καὶ τοῦ τρέφοντος αὐτὸν ἐπελάθετο καὶ ἀπέστη ἀπ' αὐτοῦ.
84 Euthymios Tornikes, *Speech 1* §14 68.3. Cf. Michael Psellos, *Against Jacob* 25–28, 75–80. The notion of the 'fleshy' mind simply underscores John's sinful nature.
85 Euthymios Tornikes, *Speech 1* §13:14–30.
86 Nicholas Mesarites, *Narrative of the coup* §5 22.12–16.
87 Ibid. §28 45.10–18.
88 Euthymios Tornikes, *Speech 1* §17 70.3–6. The inevitable fall of those who live by their insatiable bellies was a standard motif since the times of the Church Fathers. See for instance Nikolaos Kataskepenos, *Life of St Cyril Phileotes* 40.6.21–31; Eustathios, *Speech IX* 165.62–73.
89 Nicholas Mesarites, §2 20.1; §2 20.16–20; §11 28.33–37; § 28 21–22; Euthymios Tornikes, *Speech 1* §14 68.2–4; §17 70.3–6; Niketas Choniates, *History* 526.46–47.

animals: Euthymios Tornikes sees in him a proverbial ape,[90] Nikephoros Chrysoberges perceives him, not coincidentally, as a savage beast (θήρ). Both Niketas Choniates and Euthymios Tornikes compare the monstrous corpse of the dead John to an enormous ox (βοῦς), an animal which was used in Byzantine literature as an emblem of foolishness, lack of education, and rusticity.[91] Tornikes adds that the corpse (πτῶμα) appeared as if it was pricked with a mattock and de-aired (οἷον οἱ ἐκ μακέλλης φύσωσιν), an image which not only emphasizes John's foolishness and boorishness, but also his ungodly character: in Ancient Greek literature μακέλλα was a weapon used by Zeus to kill the blasphemers.[92]

Surely, John's morbid fatness and his bulging gut made it easy to present him as an apostate and an enemy of Christianity.[93] It should not come as a surprise that the belly-living usurper is linked with the concept of social filth. Nicholas Mesarites openly connects John to social scum: in his narrative, he identifies John's followers as drunkards, catamites, male and female prostitutes, panderers, adulterers, pimps and gluttons, and all sorts of shady types.[94] Even more than that, Tornikes, Mesarites, and Choniates, just as was the case in Psellos' invective against Jacob, focus on the sickly bodily constitution of the belly-living John. While Euthymios Tornikes' limits himself to a short mention of John's heavy panting (τὰ πολλὰ ἀσθμαίνοντα),[95] Mesarites describes that the usurper looked as if he had already been half dead, breathed heavily and was perspiring so profusely that he constantly wiped the excess of sweat with a towel.[96] Niketas Choniates pushes the sickly imagery one step further: because of his morbid fatness John sweated so heavily that he had to continuously drink up the entire vessels of water, which he leaked through all the pores in his body and sprouted fountains of it "like a dolphin".[97] The function of the sickly body evokes once again the social conceptualization of the leaking σῶμα as something to be shunned and cast out of the borders of social order.

---

90   Euthymios Tornikes, *Speech 1* §12 67.5–6.
91   Bernard 2014, 266–80.
92   Euthymios Tornikes, *Speech 1* §15 68.23–24. *Suda* μ 67.
93   For instance, Euthymios Tornikes, *Oration 1* §12 66.19–20; §12 67.9–10; §13.25–30; Nicholas Mesarites, *Narrative of the Coup* §6 23.
94   Nicholas Mesarites, *Narrative of the Coup* §4 22.5–8; §7 23.33–24.6. Interestingly enough, already in the archaic iambic tradition fatness (παχεῖα) was associated with the lowest strata of society, especially the cheapest prostitutes, for which see *Suda* μ 1470.
95   Euthymios Tornikes, *Oration 1* §13 67.16.
96   Nicholas Mesarites, *Narrative of the Coup* §28 45.15–18; §11 28.10–13.
97   Niketas Choniates, *History* 527.50–53. For the symbolism of dolphin see n.46.

Finally, the monster was killed by the imperial troops who easily disposed of the rebels: John is decapitated and, if we are to believe Mesarites, gutted and decapitated by one of the soldiers, while his enormous body is chopped up into pieces.[98] The decapitation itself is interesting for several reasons. Mesarites conveys an image of John's head having been loosely attached to his bulky body, even while he was still alive. This was yet another sign of his foolishness and total lack of capacity to rule anyone.[99] Tornikes (and Chrysoberges) explores this imagery further and casts John's body in the form of the proverbial Empedoclean monster,[100] which had deformed half-human half-animal limbs and roamed the world in its primeval state:

> Οὕτω γοῦν παντοίοις ξίφεσι μελιζόμενος, αὐτοῦ πού κατέπεσεν ἐπὶ τοῦ δώματος τοῦ βασιλικοῦ, "τοῦ καὶ φθεγγομένοιο κάρη κονίησιν ἐμίχθη·" ἐν ἐκστάσει γὰρ ἡ τούτου κεφαλὴ διεκόπτετο καὶ πρὸς γῆν ἐφίπτετο καὶ πρὸς ᾅδου βάραθρον ἐσφαιρίζετο [...]· καὶ ἦν ἰδεῖν κόρσην μὲν ἀναύχενα, αὐχένα δ' ἀκόρσωτον, ταῦτα δὴ τὰ ἐμπεδόκλεια τέρατα, κεφαλὴν οὐ μόνον εἰδεχθῆ τε καὶ μυσαρὰν ἀποστρέφειν τε τὸ πρόσωπον καὶ ταχὺ τὰ βλέφαρα μύειν τοὺς εἰς αὐτὴν ἀτενίζοντας ἀναπείθουσαν, ἀλλὰ καὶ φοβερὰν τοῖς ὑπαντιάζουσι καὶ οἵαν ἄντικρυς τὴν τῆς Γοργόνης μυθεύουσι, τὸν δέ γε λοιπὸν ὁλκὸν τοῦ σώματος, ἠΰν τε μέγαν τε κείμενον, κατερραγμένον ἐπ' ἐδάφους ὡσεὶ πάχος, κατὰ τὸν ψαλμογράφον, τῆς γῆς, καὶ περὶ τὰς τῆς πόλεως διεξόδους προκείμενον "τοῖς πετεινοῖς εἰς κατάβρωμα".

Dismembered in this way by all sorts and kinds of swords, and [in the place] where he fell in the chamber of the imperial palace "his head was mingled with the dust;" *with his own spear you pierced his head (Hab. 3:14)*, and it flew to the ground, and it rolled towards the pit of Hades [...]. One could see a neckless head, and a headless neck, those Empedoclean monsters, a head which was not only hateful to look at, but also [so] ugly so that it made the ones looking at it earnestly turn their look away and close their eyelids quickly. But those who chanced upon it, they straight away spoke of it as if it had been a gorgon's head, and the remaining "tail" of his body[101] was lying there, enormous and

---

98 Nicholas Mesarites, *Narrative of the Coup* § 28 46.20–32.
99 Ibid. §11 28.10–17.
100 Empedocles, *Fragments* B 57; B 61.
101 The Greek term ὁλκός literally signifies "that which is dragged" and it signified the body of a serpent.

huge, torn in pieces *like the broken earth which has been ploughed* (Ps 140:7).[102]

The imagery of the passage is extremely dense, and the act of beheading is coloured with a quotation from Homer's *Iliad* and the Old Testament. All of them serve a similar purpose. John's monstrosity is further accentuated by the reference to the frightful sight of his severed head, which resembled not only the grotesque Empedoclean monster but also the dreadful gorgon. Indeed, Euthymios Tornikes, just like Michael Psellos, seems to be revolving around the notion of ἔκπληξις, which was traditionally linked to the feeling of awe incited by the appearance of gorgon's head. The remnant of John's body seems to have stirred the very same reaction: it was so sickening and fascinating at the very same time that no one could restrain themselves from viewing it. More than that, given the sheer popularity of the *hystera* amulets with the image of the *gorgoneion* inscribed on them, it is plausible that Tornikes alludes to this widely popular belief when describing the final fate of the fat John.

⋯

One could easily conclude that the moral landscape, to use Sam Harris' words, of γαστήρ, bristles with traps, obstacles, and bottomless pits. It is extremely easy to fall into them and to fall prey to the insatiable and dangerously alluring savage beasts which are indigenous to this 'territory'. Of course, one cannot escape the needs of one's belly: while we cannot sustain our bodies without 'feeding' it, there exists an extremely thin line between necessity and luxury.

Here I have shown that the space of γαστήρ was morally problematized in the Greek tradition, both ancient and medieval. Γαστήρ seems to have been the focus of special concern since ancient times and the significance which was attached to it within the broad circle of Greek culture was not merely limited to a person. Quite the contrary: the individual γαστήρ, στόμαχος, or κοιλία and the pressing need to exert unceasing control over it were, in essence, social concerns. For this very reason, γαστήρ was relegated to the sphere of negativity and became used as a symbol associated with a threat. Since the time of archaic Greek poetry, the insatiable belly was linked with dangerous types who posed a threat to the social *status quo*. Within the masculinised setting of the Greek πόλις, γαστήρ was perceived as the seat of effeminizing and beastly urges

---

102   Euthymios Tornikes, *Oration 1* §15. 9–24, my translation. Cf. Niketas Choniates, *History* 527.68–71.

which had to be held in constant check. The Christian setting of Byzantine culture further developed these ideas: the belly started to be associated with Original Sin, ungodly living, and even Satan himself, as we have seen in John Klimax's *Ladder*. Some of the *hystera* amulets include the image of a saint who conquers the raging stomach.[103] In these ways, the web of symbolic meanings associated with the space of the belly was expanded, and γαστήρ began to be associated with heretics, tyrants, and other unwanted social types.

Bibliography

Primary Sources

Aristophanes, *Peace*. Ed. N. G. Wilson, *Aristophanis fabulae, tomus 1: Acharnenses, Equites, Nubes, Vespae, Pax, Ave*s. Oxford 2007.

Archilochus, Semonides, Hipponax. *Greek Iambic Poetry: From the Seventh to the Fifth Centuries BC*. [*LCL* 259]. Tr. & ed. D. E. Gerber. Cambridge, MA 1999.

Aristotle, *Nicomachean Ethics*. Ed. I. Bywater, *Aristotelis ethica Nicomachea*. Oxford 1962.

Empedocles, *Fragments*. Ed. H. Diels and W. Kranz, *Die Fragmente der Vorsokratiker*, vol. 1. Berlin 1951, 308–74.

Eustathios of Thessaloniki, *Commentary in Iliad*. Ed. M. van der Valk. *Eustathii archiepiscopi Thessalonicensis commentarii ad Homeri Iliadem pertinentes*, vols. 1–4. Leiden 1971–1987.

Eustathios of Thessaloniki, *Speech IX*. Ed. P. Wirth, *Eustathii Thessalonicensis opera minora (magnam partem inedita)*. Berlin 1999, 152–69.

Euthymios Tornikes, *Speech 1*. Ed. J. Darrouzès, "Les discours d'Euthyme Tornikès (1200–1205)" *Revue des études byzantines* 26 (1968), 49–121.

Gen.; Phil.; Jon.; Dan.; Hab.; Ps.; Ed. A. Rahlfs, *Septuaginta, id est Vetus Testamentum Graece iuxta LXX interpretes*. Stuttgart 2006.

Hesychius, *Lexicon*. Ed. K. Latte, *Hesychii Alexandrini lexicon*, vols. 1–2. Copenhagen 1952–1966.

Hipponax, *Fragments*. Ed. D. E. Gerber, *Archilochus, Semonides, Hipponax. Greek Iambic Poetry: From the Seventh to the Fifth Centuries BC*. [*LCL* 259]. Cambridge, MA 1999.

Homer, *Odyssey*. Ed. P. von der Mühll, *Homeri Odyssea*. Basel 1962.

John Klimax, *The Ladder of Divine Ascent*. Ed. S. Eremitos, *Klimax tou osiou patros emon Ioannou kathegoumenou tou sinaiou oros*. Konstantinoupolis 1883.

John Klimax, *The Ladder of Divine Ascent*. Tr. A. L. Moore. London 1959.

Life of Euthymius. Ed. P. Karlin-Hayter, *Vita Euthymii patriarchae Constantinopolitani*. Brussels 1970.

---

103   Foskolou 2014, 342.

Michael Psellos, *Against Jacob*. Ed. L. G. Westerink, *Michael Psellus, Poemata*. Stutgart & Leipzig 1992.

Michael Psellos, *Chronographia*. Ed. D.-R. Reinsch, *Michaelis Pselli Chronographia*. Berlin & Boston 2014, 270–76.

Nicholas Kataskepenos, *Life of St Cyril Phileotes*. Ed. É. Sargologos, *La Vie de Saint Cyrille le Philéote moine byzantin (†1110)*. Brussels 1964.

Nicholas Mesarites, *Narrative of the Coup*. Ed. A. Heisenberg, *Nikolaos Mesarites, Die Palastrevolution des Johannes Komnenos*. Würzburg 1907.

Nicholas Mesarites, *Nicholas Mesarites. His life and works (in translation)*. Trans. M. Angold. Edinburgh 2017.

Niketas Choniates, *History*. Ed. J.-L. van Dieten, *Nicetae Choniatae Historia*. Berlin & New York 1975.

Nikephoros Chrysoberges, *Speech 1*. Ed. M. Treu, *Nicephori Chrysobergae ad Angeloi orationes tres*. Breslau 1892, 1–12.

Photius, *Lexicon*. Ed. C. Theodoridis, *Photii patriarchae lexicon*, vol. 1–4. Berlin 1982.

Physiologus. Ed. F. Sbordone, *Physiologus*. Hildesheim 1976.

Plato, *Timaeus*. Ed. J. Burnet, *Platonis opera*, vol. 4. Oxford 1968.

Porphyrius, *Life of Pythagoras*. Ed. A. Nauck, *Porphyrii philosophi Platonici opuscula selecta*. Hidelsheim 1963, 17–52.

Socrates Scholasticus, *Historia Ecclesiastica*. Ed. P. Maraval and P. Périchon, *Socrate de Constantinople, Histoire ecclésiastique*. Paris 2004–2007.

Suda. Ed. A. Adler, *Suidae lexicon* vol. 1–v. München & Leipzig 2001.

Xenophon, *Memorabilia*. Ed. E. C. Marchant, *Xenophontis opera omnia*, vol. 2. Oxford 1949.

Secondary Sources

Agapitos, P. A. 1998. Ὁ λογοτεχνικός θάνατος τῶν ἐχθρῶν στην αὐτοβιογραφία τοῦ ... "Αὐτοβιογραφία" τοῦ Νικηφόρου Βλεμμύδη, *Hellenica* 48, 29–46.

Agapitos, P. A. 2004. "Mortuary typology in the lives of saints: Michael the Synkellos and Stephen the Younger", in Odorico (ed.) 1999, 103–35.

Anagnostakis I. & T. Papamastorakis 2004. "Ekmanes neos Bakchos: Drunkenness of Noah in Medieval Art", in Angelidi (ed.) 2004, 209–56.

Angelidi, C. (ed.) 2004. *Byzantium matures. Choices, Sensitivities and Modes*. Athens.

Angold, M. 2015. "The Anatomy of a Failed Coup: The Abortive Uprising of John the Fat (31 July 1200)", in Simpson (ed.) 2015, 113–34.

Bakker, E. J. 2013. *The Meaning of Meat and the Structure of the Odyssey*. Cambridge.

Barb, A. A. 1953. "Diva Matrix: A Faked Gnostic Intaglio in the Possession of P. P. Rubens and the Iconology of a Symbol", *Journal of the Warburg and Courtauld Institutes* 16.3/4, 193–238.

Bernard, F. 2014. *Reading and Writing Byzantine Secular Poetry 1025–1081*. Oxford.

Brown, Ch. G. 1988. "Hipponax and Iambe", *Hermes* 116.4, 478–81.
Cohen, B. (ed.) 2000. *Not the Classical Ideal. The Construction of the Other in Greek Art.* Leiden & Boston.
Douglas, M. 1984. *Purity and Danger. An Analysis of the Concepts of Pollution and Taboo.* London & New York.
Douglas, M. 1996. *Natural Symbols. Explorations in Cosmology.* London & New York.
van Eck, C. 2016. "Petrifying Gaze of Medusa: Ambivalence, Ekplexis, and the Sublime", *Journal of Historians of Netherlandish Art* 8.2, 1–22.
Foley, H. 2000. "The Comic Body in Greek Art and Drama", in Cohen (ed.) 2000, 275–311.
Foskolou, V. A. 2014. "The Magic of the Written Word: The Evidence of Inscriptions on Byzantine Magical Amulets", *DChAE* 35, 329–48.
Foucault, M. 1990. *The History of Sexuality*, vol. 2: *The Use of Pleasure.* New York.
Gaca, K. L. 1999. "The sexual and social dangers of Pornai in the Septuagint Greek stratum of patristic Christian Greek thought", in James (ed.) 1999, 35–40.
Garnsey, P. 1999. *Food and Society in Classical Antiquity.* Cambridge.
Griffiths, J. G & A. A. Barb 1959. "Seth or Anubis?", *Journal of the Wartburg and Courtauld Institutes* 22.3/4, 367–71.
Hill, S. E. 2011. *Eating to Excess: The Meaning of Gluttony and the Fat Body in the Ancient World.* Santa Barbara.
Hultin, J. F. 2008. *The Ethics of Obscene Speech in Early Christianity and its Environment.* Leiden & Boston.
James, L. (ed.) 1999. *Desire and Denial in Byzantium.* Aldershot.
Jensen, R. M. 2012. *Baptismal Imagery in Early Christianity. Ritual, Visual, and Theological Dimensions.* Grand Rapids.
Kazdan, A. & S. Franklin 1984. *Studies on Byzantine Literature of the Eleventh and Twelfth Centuries.* Cambridge.
Kean, S. 2014. *The Tale of the Dueling Neurosurgeons: The History of the Human Brain as Revealed by True Stories of Trauma, Madness, and Recovery.* New York.
Labuk, T. (forthcoming). "The 'Drunken' Canon by Michael Psellos: *In Iacobum* Reconsidered".
Maimonides 1956. *The Guide for the Perplexed.* Tr. M. Friedlander. London.
Maguire, H. 2012. *Nectar and Illusion: Nature in Byzantine Art and Literature.* Oxford.
Meyer, W. & S. Trzcionka (eds) 2005. *Feast, Fast or Famine. Food and Drink in Byzantium.* Brisbane.
Muehlberger, E. 2015. "The Legend of Arius' Death: Imagination, Space and Filth in Late Ancient Historiography", *Past and Present* 227.1, 3–29.
Martin, J. R. 1954. *The Illustration of The Heavenly Ladder of John Climacus.* Princeton.
Odorico, P. (ed.) 1999. *Les Vies des saints a Byzance: genre litteraire ou biographie historique?: actes du IIe colloque international "Ερμηνεία".* Paris.

Pucci, P. 1995. *Odysseus Polutropos: Intertextual Readings in the Odyssey and the Iliad*. Ithaca & London.

Simoons, F. 1998. *Plants of Life, Plants of Death*. Madison.

Simpson, A. (ed.) 2015. *Byzantium 1180–1204. The Sad Quarter of the Century?* Athens.

Spier, J. 1993. "Medieval Byzantine Magical Amulets and Their Tradition", *Journal of the Warburg and Courtauld Institutes* 56, 25–62.

Stauffer, R. (ed.) 1949. *Science and Civilization*. Madison, WI.

Stone, A. F. 2005. "Eustathios and the Wedding Banquet", in Meyer & Trzcionka (eds) 2005, 33–42.

Subedi, B. & G. T. Grossberg 2011. "Phantom Limb Pain: Mechanisms and Treatment Approaches", *Pain Research and Treatment* 10, 1–8.

Tomekin, O. 1949. "Metaphors of Human Biology", in Stauffer (ed.) 1949, 169–94.

Turner, B. 1982. "The Discourse of Diet", *Theory, Culture and Society* 1, 23–32.

Worman, N. 2008. *Abusive Mouths in Classical Athens*. Cambridge.

2

Crime et châtiment à Byzance

Le corps humain comme espace public

Charis Messis

Resumé

Through the study of a series of legislative and literary texts (historiography, hagiography, poetry, etc.), as well as texts from the 'minor sciences', such as *oneirocritica*, this contribution examines the way in which the body of the culprit turns into a surface where crime and punishment are inscribed at the same time. This process of "monumentalization" of the body has a rather complex ritual, the διαπόμπευσις (the infamous procession). A series of literary testimonies, ranging from Late Antiquity to 12th-century Byzantium and concerning the infamous procession, has been examined in detail in order to identify its constants and propose a typology. The διαπόμπευσις announces and prepares the punishment and it is deployed in a fairly precise geographical (the hippodrome or the main street of towns or villages) and social space (the populace). The culprit is exposed to public ridicule and ritually and gradually loses all professional and gender attributes, even his social identity, and from a respectable and untouchable individual it is transformed into a simple guilty body, expropriated and 'spatialized' by the intervention of the whole community. The offending body, dissocialised and transformed into raw material, receives the inscription of the fault and of the punishment (or of the only punishment which also indicates the fault committed) and displays it in view of all in a temporal (cross-dressing, hair burning) or permanent way (bodily mutilation). The body thus manipulated replaces the person. This contribution thus tries to trace the evolution of certain manifestations of social violence, while examining the notions of space that the Byzantines handle and the complex relationships they have with corporeality.

Au VIIe siècle, à une époque où est mise en route la codification des connaissances anciennes et leurs remaniements chrétiens, Anastase le Sinaïte propose dans son *Guide* (Ὁδηγός) une définition du corps qui synthétise des élaborations diverses, philosophiques, médicales et théologiques. Selon cette définition :

Σῶμά ἐστι κατὰ μὲν τοὺς ἔξω πᾶν τὸ τριχῇ διαστατὸν ἤγουν τὸ ἔχον μῆκος καὶ πλάτος καὶ πάχος· κατὰ δὲ τὴν ἐκκλησίαν σῶμά ἐστι πᾶν τὸ ἐκ τοῦ μὴ ὄντος εἰς τὸ εἶναι γενόμενον […] Εἰδέναι μέντοιγε προσήκει, ὅτι πᾶσα σὰρξ πρόδηλον ὅτι καὶ σῶμα εἴρηται, οὐ πᾶν δὲ σῶμα σὰρξ ὀνομάζεται […] Τὸ σῶμα μὲν οὖν εἴρηται διττῶς· ποτὲ μὲν ὑλικόν, ποτὲ δὲ λεπτόν. Σῶμα ὑλικόν ἐστι τὸ δι' ἁφῆς κρατούμενον καὶ φθορᾷ ὑποκείμενον· σῶμα δὲ λεπτόν ἐστι τὸ ἀνέπαφον καὶ ἀψηλάφητον. Σάρξ ἐστι στοιχείων συνδρομή. Σάρξ ἐστιν οὐσία ῥευστὴ ἐξ αἵματος καὶ φλέγματος καὶ χολῆς καὶ χυμοῦ συνισταμένη […] τουτέστιν ἐκ θερμοῦ καὶ ψυχροῦ καὶ ὑγροῦ καὶ ξηροῦ.

Le mot *corps* signifie pour les savants de la culture païenne tout ce qui a trois dimensions, c'est-à-dire tout ce qui a une longueur, une largeur et une épaisseur. Pour l'Église, le corps est tout ce qui va de la non-existence à l'existence […] Il faut aussi savoir que toute chair est appelée évidemment corps, mais que tout corps ne peut pas être appelé chair […] Le mot *corps* a une double signification ; on parle de corps matériel et de corps subtil. Le corps matériel est appréhendé par le sens du toucher et est soumis à la corruption ; le corps éthéré est intouchable et intact. La chair est une confluence d'éléments. C'est une substance liquide, constituée de sang, de flegme, de bile noire et de bile jaune […], à savoir les qualités du chaud, du froid, du sec et de l'humide.[1]

Durant la période byzantine, il n'existe pas une notion unique du corps mais plusieurs perceptions, complémentaires ou antagonistes, qui posent la question de la corporéité et de la spatialité en des termes divers.[2] Entre les deux perceptions extrêmes proposées par la définition d'Anastase, à savoir le corps médicalisé qui n'est qu'un mécanisme objectivé (confluence d'éléments et de qualités—trois dimensions, longueur, largeur et épaisseur, qui définissent l'espace corporel) et le corps subtil et éthéré qui transforme la matérialité en essence, en *pneuma*, plusieurs degrés existent de ce que nous pourrions définir comme un corps social ou socialisé, un corps qui obéit à des codes établis par la communauté et qui est conditionné par différents critères sociaux dont les plus importants sont le sexe (corps masculin et féminin) et le statut (corps honorable/du riche ou du *honestior*, selon la terminologie légiste, et corps sans honneur/du pauvre ou du *humilior*, corps du laïc, du clerc ou du moine,

---

1 Anastase le Sinaïte, *Guide*, 5, 74–80 et 5, 83–91. Sur Anastase et son époque, voir Haldon 1990.
2 Il manque une monographie sur la perception du corps à Byzance. Sur les perceptions du corps au Moyen-Age occidental, voir en général Le Goff & Truong 2003 ; sur les perceptions chrétiennes du corps, Larchet 1996.

corps sain et corps malade etc.). Ce corps socialisé combine les deux dimensions exposées par Anastase le Sinaïte : il dispose d'abord d'une matérialité ; on lui reconnaît par la suite une sorte de subtilité que nous appellerons, par convention, intimité ou intériorité, ainsi qu'un espace minimal autour du corps matériel qui doit rester inviolable en étant l'espace vital dont le corps a besoin pour exister. Matérialité et intimité définissent la corporéité de la personne sociale.

Ce corps socialisé n'est pas un lieu social neutre, mais un espace où se jouent les enjeux sociaux concernant la construction de l'individu et de ses rapports avec les autres. C'est aussi un texte où se lisent les rapports de pouvoir, la place sociale, les manières civilisatrices, les attentes et les frustrations de son possesseur. Comme le souligne Maurice Godelier, "dans toute société existe un *corpus* de représentations plus ou moins fantasmatiques du corps, qui sont des ensembles d'idées, d'images, de valeurs et de symboles partagés par les deux sexes, et qui encodent l'ordre social en inscrivant les normes dans le corps de chacun".[3] Perçu comme un espace social, le corps physique devient ainsi un "objet concret d'investissement collectif, support de mises en scène et de mises en signes, motif de ralliement ou de distinction à travers les pratiques et les discours qu'il suscite".[4]

Tous les corps se réalisent différemment dans l'espace et entretiennent des rapports différents avec lui. Dans le processus de spatialisation du corps, tous les sens jouent un rôle central, et particulièrement la vue et le toucher. Nous ne prenons conscience de notre corps que dans le miroir, autrement dit toute surface qui reflète notre corps et lui attribue des dimensions ; les autres ont un rapport direct avec notre corps à travers le regard qu'ils nous adressent et qui nous circonscrit dans l'espace et comme espace. Ce regard doit être bien contrôlé ; il doit s'exercer sans porter visiblement atteinte à l'intimité de la personne regardée ; il ne doit pas être indiscret, scrutateur, pénétrant, provoquant ; il peut en revanche être admiratif, bienveillant, approbateur et, dans certains cas, même réprobateur. Ce type de regard a été analysé et codifié par une science de l'Antiquité tardive et de Byzance, la physiognomonie, qui vise à juger l'intimité par la matérialité du corps et par les rapports que celui-ci entretient avec l'espace (manière de marcher, de se placer, de bouger, etc.)[5]

---

3 Godelier 2001, 102. Voir aussi Le Breton 1997, 18, 28, etc.
4 Le Breton 1997, 96.
5 Sur la tradition physiognomonique de l'Antiquité et de Byzance, voir Evans 1969 ; Gleason 1990 et 1995, 55–81 ; Wilgaux 2008. Sur la tradition physiognomonique à Byzance, Dagron 1987.

L'autre moyen de spatialiser le corps est de le toucher ; toucher un corps signifie le dépersonnaliser, faire irruption dans son intimité, le transformer en *hétérotopie*.[6] D'abord, on touche les corps morts et les corps malades, qui sont des corps privés d'intimité, qui ne sont que des corps matérialisés ; le corps mort pour l'éternité, le corps malade pour une période indéterminée. Ensuite, il y a le toucher affectif, les gestes qui font communiquer les corps apparentés (parents/enfants, frères/sœurs au sens propre et figuré, famille élargie et amis). Deux procédés plus au moins ritualisés, destinés à toucher un corps qui n'appartient pas aux catégories précédentes (les morts, les malades, les "parents") et à le définir comme un espace "autre" sont l'acte sexuel[7] et le châtiment.[8] C'est pourquoi dans plusieurs logiques historiques et sociales les deux actes ne sont perçus que comme complémentaires : actes sexuels et châtiment sont des rapports qui dépersonnalisent le corps d'autrui, voire le singularisent et le spatialisent.

Dans le cadre de cette contribution nous allons examiner les objectifs et les conséquences de la spatialisation punitive des corps à Byzance, en laissant toutefois en suspens certaines questions concomitantes, comme celle de la distinction entre agent et victime de sévices. L'un et l'autre subissent-ils la même dépersonnalisation à cause du contact, ou est-ce seulement le statut du corps de la victime qui est *touché*, c'est-à-dire spatialisé ? Le bourreau est-il une personne qui subit des conséquences en touchant les autres corps ou est-il simplement un corps qui agit sur ordre, à savoir un corps déjà complètement dépossédé ? La réponse à ces questions est complexe et demande une autre investigation.

Nous essaierons ensuite de tracer les étapes de cette désocialisation/spatialisation punitive du corps humain mis au service de l'ordre public, à travers l'examen de la manière avec laquelle le corps des coupables à Byzance se transforme en surface où s'inscrivent en même temps le crime et le châtiment, afin qu'ils deviennent "un triste récit pour la postérité et un modèle d'amélioration (διήγημα σκυθρωπὸν τοῖς μετέπειτα καὶ πρὸς τὸ κρεῖττον ἐπανόρθωσις)".[9]

---

6 Foucault 1994.
7 Sur le toucher érotique à Byzance, voir Nilsson 2017. L'acte sexuel en tant que rapport hégémonique au corps et créateur d'hétérotopie est analysé par Foucault en plusieurs occasions, en particulier dans la première partie de son *Histoire de la sexualité*, intitulée *La volonté du savoir*. Sur le toucher punitif dans les miniatures à Byzance, voir Tirnanic 2017. Sur ces deux sens à Byzance dans un contexte plus général, voir Betancourt 2018.
8 Le châtiment est un symptôme des "états de crise" qui génèrent des hétérotopies, selon Foucault 1994, 756–57. Le même auteur examine la question du châtiment au Moyen Age et dans la modernité dans *Surveiller et punir*. Plusieurs de ses conclusions ont imprégné notre travail.
9 Attaleiatès, *Histoire*, 14, 13–14.

Ce processus de 'monumentalisation' déshonorante du corps dispose d'un rituel assez complexe dont nous nous occuperons maintenant.

1 La διαπόμπευσις comme procédé exemplaire de spatialisation du corps

L'atteinte au corps d'une personne en tant que moyen d'y exercer un contrôle prend à Byzance plusieurs formes, officielles et officieuses. Dans ces procédés de spatialisation, les mécanismes étatiques et les mécanismes sociaux agissent en convergence ou de manière complémentaire.

De tous les procédés punitifs, la procession infamante (διαπόμπευσις) est l'acte le plus important et le plus significatif.[10] Dans les textes, le mot διαπόμπευσις, ses synonymes (θεατρισμός, δήμευσις, θρίαμβος, etc.) et ses multiples dérivés ont deux significations principales, l'une, littérale, dans laquelle διαπόμπευσις a le sens de *pompe de dérision publique* organisée soit par les représentants du pouvoir politique soit de façon 'spontanée' par la population face à des actes délictueux et scandaleux, et une autre, métaphorique, exprimée principalement par des verbes (διαπομπεύω, θεατρίζω, περιβομβίζω, δημεύω, θριαμβεύω, etc.) qui signifient dévoiler un secret honteux et devenir spectacle ou être la risée de tous, sans toutefois que l'humiliation imposée prenne les formes officielles de la pompe de dérision. La διαπόμπευσις est la réponse efficace et théâtrale (ou efficace, parce que théâtrale) d'une société qui se veut unie et solidaire envers tous ceux qui transgressent les normes, les habitudes et les prescriptions morales communément partagées. Ce moyen de théâtralisation de la faute fonctionne d'une manière exemplaire pour la population, tandis que pour le coupable il constitue une sorte de dépossession momentanée ou permanente de son corps, en rapport avec la gravité de la faute commise. Ce procédé ancien, qui convenait aux mécanismes de contrôle d'une société close, de droit élémentaire et à la justice immédiate, et qui était pratiqué dans toutes les sociétés historiques du pourtour méditerranéen sous des formes différentes,[11] retrouve une nouvelle vigueur à partir du VIIe siècle quand la société

---

10 Magdalino 2007, 64–70. Sur les parades infamantes à Byzance, voir encore Koukoulès 1948–1956, III, 284–311 ; Politis 1975 ; Patlagean 1984.

11 Sur les supplices corporels en Grèce ancienne, voir Halm-Tisserant 1998 ; plus particulièrement sur les processions infamantes, 97–106. Sur les tortures mortelles dans le droit romain et dans le Code Théodosien, voir Grodzynski 1984. Sur les procédés infamants et les mises à mort en Occident, voir Gauvard 2005. Plus généralement, sur l'humiliation et sa signification dans la culture occidentale, voir Zink 2017.

byzantine, pour assurer sa survie, tourne en partie le dos aux réalisations du droit romain classique, monumentalisé par la codification de Justinien.

A partir de la promulgation de l'*Ecloga* par Léon III en 741, qui est présentée comme un choix des dispositions du droit de Justinien et une amélioration de celui-ci vers plus d'humanisation (Ἐκλογὴ τῶν νόμων […] ἀπὸ τῶν ἰνστιτούτων, τῶν διγέστων, τοῦ κώδικος, τῶν νεαρῶν τοῦ μεγάλου Ἰουστινιανοῦ διατάξεων καὶ ἐπιδιόρθωσις εἰς τὸ φιλανθρωπότερον),[12] on assiste à un tournant important dans le droit byzantin, qui affiche un changement considérable d'attitudes concernant la faute, le corps et la subjectivité de la personne fautive. L'un des changements les plus caractéristiques de l'*humanisation* pénale proclamée est l'abandon de la peine capitale au profit de peines qui prévoient des mutilations corporelles et la diffamation sociale.[13]

Comme clairement indiqué par les textes, le corps du coupable est le principal visé dans la διαπόμπευσις.[14] Les lois prévoient les mauvais traitements et les mutilations, mais elles ne parlent pas explicitement du procédé de la διαπόμπευσις.[15] Les rares textes qui la prévoient comme une peine en soi sont le *Livre du préfet*, daté de l'époque de Léon VI[16] et les *Lois des Homérites*, texte datable du VIIIe siècle.[17] Ce silence des lois sur une pratique largement attestée dans la littérature byzantine s'explique par le fait que la διαπόμπευσις n'était pas une peine mais un rituel qui conduisait à l'application d'une peine.[18] Nous

---

12   *Ecloga*, tit.
13   L'évocation de l'humanisation, à chaque fois qu'une telle peine est appliquée, est un lieu commun dans les textes. Cf. par exemple, lorsque Basile Ier punit les participants à la révolte de Kourkouas et qu'il applique, selon son biographe (*Vie de Basile Ier*, ch. 45), une peine clémente : des coups et l'élimination du poil, au lieu de la mort.
14   Patlagean 1984, 421, qui souligne que dans le droit romain antérieur le corps était placé entre l'intégrité et la mort.
15   Dans l'*Ecloga*, 2.8.1, par exemple, la femme qui se remarie dans les douze mois suivant la mort de son premier mari se diffame (ἄτιμος ἔσται), sans précision sur la manière avec laquelle l'infamie est atteinte. Pour Armenopoulos, *Procheiron* 6.15.1–6, il y a une liste assez longue de personnes à diffamer (περὶ τοῦ τίνες ἀτιμοῦνται) : celui qui insulte un juge, celui qui fait un procès pour gagner de l'argent, les comédiens, les proxénètes, les calomniateurs, les usuriers, etc.
16   Léon VI, *Le livre du préfet*, 8.5, qui prévoit pour les boulangers fautifs "la flagellation, la tonsure et la procession infamante (τὴν διὰ δαρμοῦ καὶ κουρᾶς καὶ θριάμβου)". La flagellation et la tonsure sont prévues aussi pour les notaires (1.12), les joailliers (2.8), les marchands de soie (6.14 et 7.1) et les entrepreneurs (22.2).
17   Les termes δήμευσιν, δημευθείς (*Lois des Homérites*, lig. 77 ; 151 ; 239 ; 262 ; 279–80 ; 295), δημευθεῖσα (*Lois*, lig. 351) δημευόμενοι (*Lois*, lig. 147 ; 235) posent un problème d'interprétation. Dans ce contexte, les termes renvoient plutôt au procédé de la diffamation publique ; voir Messis 2012.
18   Troianos 2002, 281.

examinerons ensuite certaines formes de la diffamation publique sans toujours faire une distinction claire entre application des lois et actes spontanés de violence sociale visant à la dépréciation publique d'autrui.

Les voleurs, les joueurs de jeux de hasard,[19] les prostituées et les adultères,[20] les sodomites,[21] les archontes injustes,[22] les accusés d'escroquerie,[23] parmi beaucoup d'autres, sont les victimes ordinaires de la διαπόμπευσις.[24] Les historiens insistent cependant sur des cas 'politiquement' significatifs, à savoir la punition d'ennemis intérieurs de l'État (révoltés malchanceux contre la personne sacrée de l'empereur ou empereurs déchus) ou de la foi (moines iconodoules pendant l'iconoclasme).[25] Dans ces cas, la διαπόμπευσις constitue l'autre face, la face obscure du triomphe du vainqueur,[26] à savoir un "triomphe

---

19   Malalas, *Histoire*, 379, 70–72.
20   Selon une tradition courante, ce sont les anciens Pisidiens qui ont commencé ce traitement envers les adultères (Nicolas de Damas, *Recueil de coutumes*, 2011, F 103 l, 186–87). Malalas, *Histoire*, 17, 15–16, transpose cette peine dans la mythologie, en parlant de la réaction d'Héphaistos lorsqu'il surprend Aphrodite dans les bras d'Arès ; une allusion à la ridiculisation des prostituées est contenue dans un texte du IXe siècle, la *Vie d'Antoine le Jeune*, où le saint, devenant le représentant de l'empereur Michel II dans la province de Cibyrrhéotes, ordonne que tout fornicateur et toute prostituée soient appréhendés, tonsurés et congédiés, ridiculisés. Voir aussi une épigramme adressée à un responsable pour la parade infamante des femmes, in Lambros 1911, no 7 : εἰς τὸν Βουμῆν δαίροντα τὰς γυναῖκας γυμνὰς καὶ πληροῦντα τὸ πρόσωπον αὐτῶν αἰθάλης καὶ οὕτω δημεύοντα.
21   Procope, *Anecdota*, ch. 11, 36 ; Malalas, *Histoire*, 364–65.
22   Voir par ex., la punition que Justin II impose à un magistros injuste chez Manassès, *Histoire*, v. 3364–73.
23   Dans la *Vie de saint Antoine le Jeune*, 210, 4–11, le saint, accusé de malversations alors qu'il gouvernait la ville d'Attaleia, est conduit devant l'empereur Théophile qui transmet l'affaire à Stéphane, responsable du palais. Stéphane fait subir au saint une procession infamante, afin que le saint se décide à rendre l'argent censé avoir été volé. Toute la procession est arrosée de coups de fouets. Théophile se décide finalement à relâcher le saint et punit de la même façon l'injuste Stéphane (211, 26–28).
24   Georges de Chypre, au début du XIIIe siècle, présente comme un fait courant l'élimination du poil facial pour la transgression des lois, dans *Éloge de la chevelure*, ch. 12 : "Synèse ignore, comme il semble, tous ceux qui sont conduits par la loi chez les coiffeurs pour couper la chevelure ou la barbe, s'ils s'avèrent avoir commis une faute de décence ou s'ils n'agissent pas selon les prescriptions des lois".
25   Nicéphore, *Histoire*, ch. 83, 1–8 ; *Vie de Stéphane le Jeune*, 158, 2–4 : traitement des moines amis des images par Constantin V, et aussi 161, 18–20.
26   Constantin Porphyrogénète, *Strategicon*, C 808–79, 146–51 ; Léon Diacre, *Histoire*, 23, 17–20 ; 24, 2–5 et 163, 3–9. Voir aussi Théophane, *Histoire*, 433, 10–14 ; Caminiatès, *Prise de Thessalonique*, ch. 77, 50–56. La pression pour un triomphe après une bataille conduit souvent à des triomphes extravagants, tel que celui organisé à Thessalonique en 1185 par David Comnène, in Eustathe, *Prise de Thessalonique*, 68, 25–31. Sur les triomphes impériaux, McCormick 1986.

honteux" (ἄτιμος θρίαμβος),[27] "un théâtre ridicule et très dégradant (καταγέλαστον καὶ πανευτελέστατον θέατρον)".[28]

Comme toute pièce théâtrale répétée, comme tout spectacle public institutionnalisé, la διαπόμπευσις avait une cérémonie riche qui s'appliquait suivant les cas et avec des variations. Pour en dégager ses éléments standardisés, nous examinerons de près quatre exemples de διαπόμπευσις, les plus complets : les deux premiers tirés de l'historiographie, le troisième de l'épistolographie et le quatrième de la poésie profane.

Le premier texte historiographique, extrait de la synthèse de Théophane, évoque les événements de l'année 767 et décrit la procession infamante subie par Constantin, le patriarche de Constantinople, victime de l'empereur Constantin v. Le prétexte de cette punition était sa participation supposée à une conspiration ratée contre l'empereur. Dans le texte, la διαπόμπευσις est le chemin qui conduit à la mise à mort du patriarche et à l'exposition publique de sa tête coupée :

τῇ δὲ ἑξῆς ἡμέρᾳ ἱπποδρομίας οὔσης, ἐψίλωσαν αὐτοῦ τὴν ὄψιν καὶ ἐγύμνωσαν αὐτοῦ τὴν γενειάδα καὶ τὰς τῆς κεφαλῆς τρίχας καὶ τῶν ὀφρύων, καὶ ἐνδύσαντες αὐτὸν σηρικὸν καὶ ἀμανίκωτον κοντὸν ἐκάθισαν αὐτὸν ἐπὶ ὄνου σαγματωμένου ἐξανάστροφα κρατοῦντα τὴν οὐρὰν αὐτοῦ, καὶ ἐξήνεγκαν διὰ τοῦ διϊππίου εἰς τὸ ἱπποδρόμιον, τοῦ λαοῦ παντὸς καὶ τοῦ δήμου ἀνασκάπτοντος καὶ ἐμπτύοντος αὐτόν. ἔσυρε δὲ τὸν ὄνον Κωνσταντῖνος ὁ ἀνεψιὸς αὐτοῦ ῥινοκοπημένος. ἐλθόντος δὲ αὐτοῦ ἐν τοῖς δήμοις, κατῆλθον καὶ ἐνέπτυσαν καὶ κόνιν ἐπέρριπτον ἐπ' αὐτόν. ἐνέγκαντες δὲ αὐτὸν εἰς τὸ στάμα ἔρριψαν αὐτὸν ἐκ τοῦ ὄνου καὶ ἐπάτησαν τὸν τράχηλον αὐτοῦ· καὶ καθίσαντες αὐτὸν ἀπέναντι τῶν δήμων, ἤκουε παρ' αὐτῶν σκωπτικοὺς λόγους ἕως τῆς ἀπολύσεως τοῦ ἱππικοῦ. καὶ οὕτω λαβὼν τὴν ἀπόφασιν ἀπεκεφαλίσθη εἰς τὸ Κυνήγιον. καὶ τὴν μὲν κεφαλὴν αὐτοῦ ἐκ τῶν ὤτων δήσαντες ἐπὶ τρισὶν ἡμέραις ἐν τῷ Μιλίῳ ἐκρέμασαν εἰς ἔνδειξιν τοῦ λαοῦ. τὸ δὲ σῶμα αὐτοῦ δήσαντες καλωδίῳ τὸν πόδα, διὰ τῆς Μέσης σύραντες εἰς τὰ Πελαγίου μετὰ τῶν βιοθανάτων ἔρριψαν· ὁμοίως καὶ τὴν κεφαλὴν αὐτοῦ μετὰ τὰς τρεῖς ἡμέρας ἐκεῖσε ἀπαγαγόντες ἔρριψαν.

Le jour suivant, en pleine activité de l'Hippodrome, on lui rasa le visage, élimina la barbe ainsi que la chevelure et le poil des sourcils. Ensuite on l'habilla d'un vêtement court de soie sans manches et on l'assit à

---

27 Zonaras, *Histoire*, III, 346, 9.
28 Attaleiatès, *Histoire*, 149, 24–25.

l'envers sur le dos d'un âne bâté en l'obligeant à tenir la queue de l'animal. On le fit sortir par le *diippion* dans l'Hippodrome, et tout le peuple le maudissait et crachait sur lui. Constantin, son neveu, le nez coupé, tirait les brides de l'âne. Quand il arriva devant les dèmes, leurs représentants descendirent, crachèrent sur lui et lui jetèrent de la poussière. Ils le transférèrent ensuite sur le lieu où se déroulaient les compétitions et là ils le jetèrent à terre et posèrent leurs pieds sur son cou. Ensuite, ils le firent asseoir en face des dèmes où on lui adressa des paroles railleuses jusqu'à la fin des courses. Recevant ainsi le jugement, il fut décapité sur la place appelée *La chasse* ; on suspendit sa tête par les oreilles pendant trois jours à l'emplacement appelé Milion, pour que le peuple le voie. On lia son corps et on le tira par une corde attachée à son pied, et on le jeta là où on jette ceux qui ont subi une mort violente. On jeta là aussi sa tête après trois jours.[29]

D'après le texte, les mutilations précèdent parfois la διαπόμπευσις (comme c'est le cas de Constantin, le neveu, qui parade le nez coupé), alors que d'autres fois elles la suivent (le patriarche a été décapité après la parade).

Le deuxième texte historiographique concerne la διαπόμπευσις de Michel Anemas, qui s'était soulevé contre l'autorité d'Alexis Ier au début du XIe siècle. La peine prévue pour consacrer la procession était l'aveuglement mais, grâce à l'intervention d'Anne Comnène et de sa mère, la reine Irène Doukaina, la punition d'Anemas se limita à la seule διαπόμπευσις :

τὸν δὲ Ἀνεμᾶν καὶ τοὺς σὺν αὐτῷ ὡς προταιτίους καὶ τὴν ἐν χρῷ κουρὰν τῆς κεφαλῆς καὶ τοῦ πώγονος ψιλώσας διὰ μέσης πομπεῦσαι τῆς ἀγορᾶς παρεκελεύσατο, εἶτα ἐξορυχθῆναι τοὺς ὀφθαλμούς. παραλαβόντες οὖν τούτους οἱ σκηνικοὶ καὶ σάκκους περιβαλόντες, τὰς δὲ κεφαλὰς ἐντοσθίοις βοῶν καὶ προβάτων ταινίας δίκην κοσμήσαντες, ἐν βουσὶν ἀναγαγόντες καὶ ἐγκαθίσαντες οὐ περιβάδην, ἀλλὰ κατὰ θατέραν πλευρὰν τούτους διὰ τῆς βασιλικῆς ἦγον αὐλίδος. ῥαβδοῦχοι ἔμπροσθεν τούτων ἀφαλλόμενοι καὶ ἀσμάτιόν τι γελοῖον καὶ κατάλληλον τῇ πομπῇ προσᾴδοντες ἀνεβόων, λέξει μὲν ἰδιώτιδι διηρμοσμένον, νοῦν δὲ ἔχον τοιοῦτον. Ἐβούλετο γὰρ τὸ ᾆσμα πάνδημον πᾶσι παρακελεύεσθαι <ἐξελθεῖν> τε καὶ ἰδεῖν τοὺς τετυραννευκότας τούτους κερασφόρους ἄνδρας, οἵτινες τὰ ξίφη κατὰ τοῦ αὐτοκράτορος ἔθηξαν.

---

29   Théophane, *Histoire*, 441, 19–30 et 442, 8–13. Voir aussi Nicéphore, *Histoire*, ch. 84 ; Georges le Moine, *Histoire*, 756–57.

> Anémas et ceux qui étaient avec lui les instigateurs du complot, après avoir eu la tête complètement rasée et la barbe coupée, furent condamnés au milieu de l'agora, puis à avoir les yeux crevés. Les organisateurs du spectacle s'en saisirent donc, les revêtirent de sacs, et ceignirent leurs têtes avec des viscères de bœufs et de moutons en guise de diadème ; on les plaça sur des bœufs, assis non pas à califourchon, mais de côté, et on les promena ainsi dans la cour du palais. Des apparitueurs dansaient devant eux, chantant alternativement à pleine voix un refrain bouffon, digne de cet appareil : il était en langue vulgaire et son sens était celui-ci. Cette chanson populaire invitait le public à venir voir ces séditieux porter des cornes, eux qui avaient aiguisé leurs armes contre l'autocrator.[30]

De ce texte, nous retenons que l'organisation de la διαπόμπευσις était confiée à des professionnels, les σκηνικοί, qui préparaient la mise en scène de la victime pour un spectacle grandiose qui ne se limitait pas seulement au rasage du poil, à la flagellation et aux insultes.

Le troisième texte, tiré de l'épistolographie, nous conduit à Rome en 998 et montre que les mêmes procédés de châtiment étaient appliqués en Occident, ou du moins l'auteur byzantin ne signale aucun écart entre l'usage byzantin et l'usage italo-germanique. La victime est ici l'antipape Jean XVI Philagathos, l'empereur justicier est Otton III et l'auteur qui décrit l'incident est Léon, évêque de Synada :

> Πρὸ παντὸς ἀνάθεμα γέγονε τῆς δυτικῆς ἐκκλησίας, εἶτα τοὺς ὀφθαλμοὺς ἐξωρύχθη, τὴν ῥῖνα τρίτον ἐξετμήθη καὶ τὸ χεῖλος τέταρτον, πέμπτον τὴν γλῶτταν τὴν πολλὰ καὶ ἄρρητα λαλοῦσαν καὶ ἄμαχον· ἐπόμπευσεν ἐπὶ τούτοις ἕκτον ὀνίσκῳ πτωχῷ σεμνυνόμενος οὐροκρατῶν καὶ τοῦτον, τὴν δὲ κεφαλὴν ἔσκεπε ἀσκοῦ παλαιοῦ τεμάχιον τὰς προτομὰς ἔχον ὀρθίους· τὸ δὲ ἕβδομον εἰς κρίσιν ἦλθε, κατεψηφίσθη, τὴν ἱερατικὴν ἐνεδύθη καὶ ἐξεδύθη στολήν, ὀπισθοφανῶς ἐσύρη <κατὰ> τὸν ναὸν αὐτόν, τὸν πρόναον, τὴν φιάλης αὐλὴν καὶ ὡς εἰς ἀναψυχὴν εἰς τὸν κάρκαρον ἐνεβήθη.

> (Le pape Philagathos) subit d'abord l'anathème de l'Église d'Occident, puis ses yeux furent crevés, son nez et ses lèvres coupés, de même que sa langue implacable qui proférait beaucoup de choses indicibles. Ensuite, il parada en chevauchant un âne misérable qu'il tenait par la queue. Sa tête était

---

30 Anne Comnène, *Alexiade*, 12.6.5 (tr. fr., Leib 1946, III, 72–73). Sur cet épisode, voir aussi Heher 2015, 18.

couverte d'un morceau de peau de chèvre dont le museau se tenait droit. Il fut ensuite conduit devant le tribunal, fut condamné, vêtu et dévêtu de son habit ecclésiastique et traîné par arrière à travers l'église, le narthex, la cour avec la fontaine et jeté dans la prison pour trouver le repos.[31]

Dans le texte cité, les mutilations et la parade de la διαπόμπευσις suivent l'anathème mais précèdent la décision du tribunal. La décision de la justice consiste à la destitution officielle de l'antipape par le rituel de son déshabillage des attributs de son office.

Dans le dernier cas, Jean Géomètre s'adresse à une victime de la parade infamante en décrivant les étapes du châtiment :

> Ὁ δραματουργός, τοῦ τράγου τὸ παιδίον,
> κήρυξον, εἰπὲ τὴν νέαν τραγῳδίαν·
> πῶς ἐξυβρίσθης, πῶς ἐτύφθης, πῶς μέσον
> πάντων ἐσύρθης, πῶς ἐχρίσθης τὴν θέαν,
> πῶς ἐρραπίσθης, πῶς ἐτίλθης τὰς τρίχας.
> ταῦτα, τραγῳδέ, νῦν τραγῴδει, καὶ τράγον
> εἴπερ θέλοις, καὶ τοῦτον εὕροις ἐγγύθεν,
> σὲ τὸν φύσαντα φημὶ τὸν κερασφόρον,
> τὸν ἐκφύσαντα τεσσάρων πλέθρων κέρας [...]

> Toi, le dramaturge, le fils de bouc, prêche à haute voix la nouvelle chanson de bouc : comment tu as été insulté, battu, traîné au milieu de tous avec le visage barbouillé, giflé, tonsuré. Toi, fils de bouc, chante maintenant ces chansons de bouc et, si tu cherches un vrai bouc, tu le trouveras à côté de toi, à savoir ce cocu qui t'as engendré et qui dispose d'une corne longue de quatre plèthres [...][32]

Dans ces quatre cas, comme dans la plupart des autres, le rituel essentiel se réduit à certains points qui se succèdent dans le temps et qui se déroulent dans un espace bien délimité, celui de l'Hippodrome[33] et de l'agora pour Constantinople, l'équivalent de l'agora dans les autres villes et villages ou, pour ce qui concerne les délits militaires, les campements militaires qui constituent une agora en mouvement :

---

31 Léon de Synada, *Lettres*, no 1, 10–19. Au même épisode se réfère la *Vie de Nil de Rossano*, ch. 89.
32 Géomètre, *Poèmes*, no 4. Cf. aussi Lauxterman 2019, 128–30.
33 Sur l'Hippodrome de Constantinople et les spectacles qui s'y déroulaient, Dagron 2011.

a) les mutilations symboliques ou effectives. Dans les mutilations effectives sont rangées l'ablation du nez ou du pénis, de la langue, de la main ou du pied, des seins pour les femmes ; certaines de ces mutilations s'inscrivent dans le cadre des peines-miroir (*Spiegelstrafe*), assez communes dans le droit de l'époque (mains, langue, pénis, seins),[34] tandis que d'autres constituent des métaphores : l'ablation du nez pour les crimes sexuels[35] ne s'explique que par un jeu d'analogies où le nez "signifie l'honneur" de la personne qui le porte, selon un *oneirocriticon* byzantin[36] ou, selon une conviction de l'anthropologie moderne, il constitue l'équivalent du pénis dans le visage humain, le pénis visible de chacun. Dans cette logique agit, par exemple, Syméon de Bulgarie qui, pour provoquer la honte des Byzantins (εἰς αἰσχύνην Ῥωμαίων), coupe le nez de leurs alliés chazares et envoie à Constantinople ce don insultant.[37] Dans les mutilations symboliques se classent la tonte des cheveux et le rasage de la barbe.[38] On élimine les signes de la masculinité (barbe, poil facial, chevelure), étant donné que l'écrasante majorité des victimes citées dans les textes historiographiques sont des hommes. Cela pourrait signifier un rituel symbolique de castration, car la barbe et le poil facial renvoient à la puissance du pénis et les cheveux renvoient à l'activité sexuelle.[39]

b) le changement de vêtement et les autres indices de dégradation sociale : ôter le vêtement auquel quelqu'un prétend signifie sa "nudité", tant sociale que sexuelle, et la nudité "signifie toujours un dommage".[40] Le vêtement symbolise le sexe et le statut de celui qui le porte et son changement génère plusieurs significations, sociales ou sexuées : en changeant des habits luxueux ou indicatifs d'une profession ou d'un office pour des

---

34 Sur la notion de *peine-miroir* dans le cadre byzantin, Pitsakis 2002. Sur les peines, en général, dans le système juridique byzantin, Troianos 1997.

35 Patlagean 1984, 406 et 422–23. L'ablation du nez que les lois prévoient pour les délits sexuels semble être pratiquée pour d'autres comportements socialement non acceptables, comme la démonstration de lâcheté pendant la bataille. Sur un tel épisode, voir Léon Diacre, *Histoire*, 57, 20–21. Malgré le fait que la punition reste une menace, la décision impériale rend claire la liaison entre le nez et l'honneur masculin.

36 *Onirocriticon de Manuel Paléologue*, 516, 24. Pour *Achmed Oneirocriticon*, 35, 21–22 : "Le front et le nez sont pour les humains ornement et abondance (τὸ μέτωπον καὶ ἡ ῥὶς κόσμος εἰσὶ καὶ πλοῦτος ἐνώπιον τῶν ἀνθρώπων)".

37 Georges le Moine, *Continué*, 853, 19.

38 Sur la signification du poil à Byzance, Auzépy 2002 ; Sideris 2011.

39 Leach 1980, 335–37, où il est question des cheveux utilisés comme symboles publics avec une signification explicitement sexuelle ; 352, où il est question de la barbe et du poil comme symbole du phallus.

40 *Oneirocriticon Atheniensis BN 1275*, 169, 20.

vêtements de peu de valeur ou des habits de moines, la victime subit une transformation/dégradation sociale ; en portant des vêtements féminins, la victime se voit nier publiquement son identité d'homme. Dans ce second cas, le changement du vêtement masculin en vêtement féminin est un acte qui réaffirme et réconforte les valeurs sociales bafouées par le comportement lâche ou délictueux de la personne concernée. L'incapacité, par exemple, des saints Serge et Bacchus de remplir leur devoir de soldats romains, à savoir d'offrir un sacrifice aux dieux de l'État, conduit Maximien à leur imposer le changement de vêtement, de militaire en féminin, ainsi qu'une procession infamante. Si Serge et Bacchus n'avaient pas été des vrais saints, ils auraient très mal vécu ce changement vestimentaire humiliant. Mais les deux héros de la foi réagissent contrairement à ce qui était attendu, ils acceptent pleinement ce changement en le réinterprétant théologiquement : "Seigneur, tu nous as parés d'un habit féminin comme des jeunes mariées, dans un mariage préparé pour nous unir à toi".[41] La plupart des Byzantins, et particulièrement les soldats, bien qu'ils aient peut-être admiré l'exemple des saints, n'auraient pas eu la même attitude. Bien au contraire, "pour des hommes pratiquant le métier des armes, ce châtiment était pire que la mort".[42] Cette pratique, ordinaire chez les voisins orientaux et chez les ennemis de l'empire,[43] se rencontre à Byzance de façon sporadique avant le XIe siècle. Pendant la période médiobyzantine, ce traitement était plutôt réservé aux prétendants vaincus du trône. Après sa révolte malheureuse contre Constantin IX Monomaque, Théophile Erotikos subit cette peine (ἀχθέντα δὲ θῆλυν ὁ βασιλεὺς ἐνδύσας στολὴν καὶ ἐν τῷ ἱππικῷ ἱπποδρομίας ἀγομένης θριαμβεύσας καὶ τῶν ὑπαρχόντων ψιλώσας ἀπέλυσε).[44] Ici, l'empereur vainqueur, prototype de la masculinité, féminise symboliquement son adversaire vaincu après l'avoir 'féminisé' réellement sur le champ de

---

41 *Passion de Serge et Bacchus*, ch. 7 ; sur le sujet, voir aussi Halsall 1999, 165.

42 Zosime, *Histoire*, III, 3, 5.

43 Zonaras, *Histoire*, III, 185, 10–13, où Hormisdas, le roi des Perses, apprenant que son stratège Varam a perdu une bataille contre les Romains, lui envoie un costume féminin et lui retire la stratégie ; voir aussi, Bryenne, *Histoire*, 93, 29–34, à propos du sultan Mouhemed (998–1030) qui, "fort mécontent de la tournure des événements, fit aveugler à leur retour ses dix généraux et menaça les soldats qui avaient fui le danger de les exposer à la risée publique vêtus en femmes".

44 Skylitzès, *Histoire*, 429. Un tel sort attend Critoplos qui n'a pas pu éviter la défection des Serbes, "ce qui amena le basileus (Jean II) à châtier Critoplos qui en avait la garde : il le fit revêtir de vêtements de femme et promener sur la place publique, monté sur un âne", selon Kinnamos, *Histoire*, 12.9–13 (tr. fr., Rosenblum 1972, 22). Michel VIII punit ainsi ses familiers qui n'ont pas obéi à ses ordres, selon Pachymère, *Histoire*, III, 25.

bataille. Parfois, la lâcheté est punie par le seul fait d'ôter un vêtement masculin déshonoré sans que celui-ci soit remplacé par un vêtement féminin.[45] Le changement de vêtement dans le processus d'humiliation n'est pas imposé aux femmes, car pour elles ce changement pourrait au contraire être perçu comme un grand honneur. Les *onirocritica* byzantins nous disent que si une femme rêve d'un tel travestissement, elle gagnera de l'honneur ou donnera naissance à un enfant mâle : "Si une femme voit en rêve qu'elle porte un habit d'homme, cela lui apporte de la gloire et le signe est considéré comme bon [...] si une femme voit qu'elle porte des armes de guerre masculins, elle gagnera du pouvoir sur son mari et n'aura pas peur d'ennemis".[46] Au-delà du monde permissif des rêves, seules deux catégories de femmes portent l'habit masculin mais elles vivent dans les marges de la société, en peuplant l'imaginaire des hommes : les saintes femmes travesties en hommes et les femmes guerrières, telles les Amazones. La dégradation sociale est aussi soulignée par l'emploi, lors de la procession du coupable, d'un animal peu ou pas noble (âne, bœuf, mule, chameau)[47] ; la victime est le plus souvent assise en sens inverse ou sur le côté (posture féminine), et tient, comme bride, la queue de l'animal.

c) violences physiques venant du peuple, comme le crachement et le lancement de poussière, de cendres ou d'entrailles d'animaux au visage du malheureux condamné, et violences verbales, telles que les chansonnettes infamantes, improvisées ou composées à l'avance, insultes le concernant personnellement ou concernant sa famille.[48] Le peuple qui participe au spectacle devient souvent le crieur de la faute commise, comme dans le cas de l'higoumène du monastère de saint Philippe à Constantinople, sous l'empereur Anastase I (491–518).[49] Quelquefois un crieur public précède et porte à la connaissance de tous le crime

---

45 Psellos, *Histoire*, VIII, 161, tr. fr. Renauld 1967, II, 170 : "un des guerriers qui poursuivaient Hataouris l'Arménien, l'apercevant, s'élança pour le tuer ; mais, le voyant pleurer, il le dépouilla de son vêtement, le laissa tout nu sous le fourré, et partit" ; Bryenne, *Histoire*, 135.31–33.
46 Achmed, *Oneirocriticon*, 218, 11–12 et 18–20. Cf. aussi *ibid.* 81–82 et 115, 22–25.
47 A propos plus particulièrement du chameau, voir *Chronicon Paschale,* 546, 4–11 ; Théophane, *Histoire*, 47, 18 ; Choniatès, *Histoire*, 349–50.
48 Sur les insultes byzantines, voir en général Koukoulès 1948–1956, III, 284–311; Politis 1975 ; Morris 2002, 313–26.
49 Georges le Moine, *Histoire*, 621.3–4 : (le peuple crie) : "celui-ci est l'ami de l'ennemi de la sainte Trinité".

commis.⁵⁰ Justinien II, par exemple, durant son deuxième règne "captura avec des chaînes Apsimaros et Leontios et les transféra à l'Hippodrome. Là, il foula leurs cous jusqu'à la fin de la première course et le peuple criait : 'tu foules des serpents, aspic et basiliskos, et tu écrases un lion et un dragon'".⁵¹ Thomas le Slave, à son tour, capturé et ridiculisé est obligé de chanter lui-même : "ô vrai roi, aie pitié de moi".⁵²

d) capitulation totale et/ou mise à mort du coupable. La capitulation est exemplifiée par le foulage de son cou, surtout pour le cas des ennemis extérieurs.⁵³ Quelquefois, offrir volontairement son cou aux pieds d'un empereur signifie accepter son plein pouvoir,⁵⁴ c'est un acte éloquent de soumission. Enfin, la mise à mort de la victime arrive à la suite des violences ou selon un verdict préexistant ; si a lieu une mise à mort, il y a souvent une exposition publique de la tête⁵⁵ ou de l'un des membres coupés, voire du corps entier des morts.⁵⁶ Parmi les membres coupés et exposés, les parties génitales tiennent une place particulière. En 610, les révoltés laissent leur rage se déchaîner contre l'empereur déchu Phokas ; après l'avoir appréhendé, "ils lui coupent la main droite et les parties génitales qu'ils fixent sur une lance ; le reste du corps, après l'avoir entraîné dans les rues, ils le brûlent dans le marché du Boos", selon la version des faits par le patriarche Nicéphore.⁵⁷ Georges le Moine, dans sa version des faits, attribue le traitement réservé aux parties honteuses de Phokas à ses mœurs dissolues (ἀσέλγεια) et au fait que ce dernier avait

---

50 Dans une des traductions grecques du conte arabe intitulé *Syntipas* (*Retractatio*, 146), une femme qui agit contre le roi est punie par une parade infamante. Sa punition consiste à ce "que sa tête soit rasée, que son visage soit enduit de cendres, qu'elle soit assise sur un âne par derrière et qu'elle soit conduite à travers toute la ville ; deux hérauts appelés *plantzarioi* (δύο δὲ κήρυκες ἤτοι πλατζάριοι) marchent devant et derrière elle et crient sa faute à haute voix pour qu'ils soient écoutés de tous". Dans la version longue (164) est décrit le même épisode, sans la glose *plantzarioi*.

51 Choniatès, *Histoire*, 131–32.

52 Théophane, *Continué*, 69.16. Sur la diapompeusis de Thomas le Slave, Georges le Moine, *Histoire*, 797.10–16 ; Zonaras, *Histoire*, III, 346.8–9.

53 Voir par ex., Théophane, *Histoire*, 375.11–12, où Justinien II pose son pied sur le cou d'Apsimaros et de Léonce sous les acclamations du dème.

54 Eustathe, *La prise de Thessalonique*, 36, 17–19 : "Andronic se jeta aux pieds de l'empereur, et de ses mains posa le frêle pied du souverain sur son large cou, pour manifester que l'empereur pouvait toujours le piétiner" (tr. fr. Odorico 2005, 168).

55 Choniatès, *Histoire*, 284, 42–44, pour la tête de Cantacuzène.

56 *Chronicon Pascale*, 546, 4–11, époque de Julien à Alexandrie ; le même épisode chez Théophane, *Histoire*, 47, 16–20.

57 Nicéphore, *Histoire*, ch.1, 44–48.

abusé de plusieurs femmes mariées.⁵⁸ Mais cette interprétation semble être une rationalisation postérieure. Comme pour Bardas, qui subit le même traitement avec, en outre, une procession infamante de ses parties génitales coupées,⁵⁹ ce traitement vise à l'anéantissement de l'identité sexuée de la victime. La profanation du cadavre prenait souvent les dimensions d'un spectacle d'horreur grandiose où participait le menu peuple, spontanément ou en suivant les directives royales, comme dans le cas de Stéphane le Jeune.⁶⁰

Ce rituel de base comprend des variations, des omissions et des additions considérables. On brûle au lieu de couper ou de raser le poil de la victime,⁶¹ on bat jusqu'à la mort le malheureux.⁶² Parfois on ridiculise en permanence une personne à travers sa statue érigée dans ce seul but. Selon les *Patria de Constantinople*, l'empereur Théodose fit ériger des statues d'Arius et d'autres hérétiques pour que les passants crachent dessus, y jettent de la crotte, de l'urine, etc.⁶³ D'autres fois, c'est la dépouille d'un empereur ou d'un patriarche de jadis, comme celle de Constantin V ou celle de Jean le Grammairien, présentée par Michel III devant le peuple de Constantinople, à laquelle on fait subir une διαπόμπευσις posthume et le feu purificateur de la condamnation.⁶⁴ La διαπόμπευσις ne prend pas toujours les formes extrêmes qui conduisent à la mort de la personne concernée. Souvent elle constitue une première étape qui conduit à l'exil ou à l'enfermement. Dans ce cas, la διαπόμπευσις ne comporte que l'élimination du poil et une correction⁶⁵ et très rarement des mutilations.⁶⁶ Une autre forme d'inscription permanente de la faute commise est d'écrire un texte entier sur le visage de la personne coupable. L'empereur iconoclaste Théophile inscrit sur le visage des frères Graptoi un poème entier,⁶⁷

---

58   Georges le Moine, *Histoire*, 665–66 ; Zonaras, *Histoire*, III, 203.7–10.
59   Génesios, *Histoire*, livre IV, 23.49–51 ; Selon Théophane, *Continué*, 292.43–46, les assassins de Bardas, oncle de Michel III, le découpèrent en morceaux, puis ses parties génitales furent accrochées sur une hampe et on en fit une procession (εἶτα κοντῷ τὰ παιδογόνα τούτου ἀπαιωρήσαντες μόρια παραδειγματίζουσί τε καὶ θριαμβεύουσι) ; Skylitzès, *Histoire*, 111.7–18.
60   *Vie de Stéphane le Jeune*, 170, 10–171, 4 (tr. Auzépy 1997, 270).
61   Pseudo-Syméon, *Histoire*, 699, 13–15 ; Georges le Moine *Continué I*, 24.1–10 et 30.17–20, où Léon VI brûle aussi le poil d'un parent de Zaoutzas.
62   *Vie de Stéphane le Jeune*, 161, 19–20 ; Choniatès, *Histoire*, 131–32 ; Pachymérès, *Histoire*, 503.25–30, etc.
63   *Patria de Constantinople*, I, 39 ; II, 43.
64   Georges le Moine, *Continué*, 834–35 ; Georges le Moine, *Continué I*, 15, 9–17.
65   Georges le Moine, 40–41 ; 47, 29–33 ; 65, 25–26 ; *Vie de Théophylacte de Nicomédie*, ch. 15 ; Kinnamos, *Histoire*, 64, 7–9.
66   Georges le Moine, *Continué I*, 65, 27–32.
67   Théophane, *Continué*, 150–52.

tandis que Constantin VI punit mille insurgés en inscrivant sur leur visage la phrase : "comploteur du thème d'Arméniakos" et les envoie en exil en Sicile.[68]

Dans les textes sont attestés aussi des cas de διαπόμπευσις 'simulée', comme celle organisée à Constantinople au tournant du VIIe siècle, lorsque "les dèmes trouvèrent un homme qui ressemblait à l'empereur Maurice, le vêtirent d'un habit noir, une couronne d'ail sur la tête et, assis sur un âne, ils lui firent faire le tour de la ville accompagné d'une chanson improvisée sur son comportement sexuel : 'il a trouvé une biche douce, et comme un coq commun l'a sautée, et il a acquis plusieurs enfants'".[69] Le peuple canalise sa violence contre le pouvoir en simulant une διαπόμπευσις et le spectacle fictif préconise ainsi une réalité désirée. D'autres exemples, organisés cette fois par le pouvoir, visent à afficher la clémence et la magnanimité de l'empereur envers son peuple, comme la mascarade organisée sous l'ordre de Basile Ier qui, en guise d'avertissement aux marins stationnés dans le Péloponnèse et pour leur inspirer de la peur, transfère là-bas des prisonniers arabes, le visage barbouillé de cendre, et donc méconnaissables, afin qu'ils soient empalés à la place des déserteurs byzantins.[70] Une clémence analogue envers les soldats byzantins est manifestée par Alexis I Comnène, qui préfère utiliser les procédés diffamatoires plutôt que d'imposer la peine de mort à des déserteurs, comme le relate son chantre Théophylacte d'Achrida dans un texte qui dévoile en même temps le vrai but de l'élimination du poil facial et de la chevelure :

> Πῶς τοὺς ἄχειρας ξιφηφόρους ἠμείψατο; ἐψίλωσε μὲν αὐτοῖς τὰς κεφαλάς, τοῦ φυσικοῦ κόσμου στερήσας, ὡς περὶ τὴν κεφαλὴν ἀσχημονήσαντάς τε καὶ ἐξυβρίσαντας· ἐψίλωσε δὲ καὶ τὸ γένειον, τὸ οἶμαι ἄνανδρον αὐτῶν καὶ ἀγενὲς ἐκπομπεύων διὰ συμβολικοῦ τοῦ προσχήματος. Σκόλοπα δὲ ἀνέστησε μὲν καὶ τὸν πλάνον ἐκεῖνον ἐπέδησεν· ἐπεγέλα δὲ ἄρα τῷ σκόλοπι ὁ φιλάνθρωπος, φόβητρον αὐτὸν μόνον ὀξύνας καὶ οἷον μορμολύκειον τεκτηνάμενος· οὐδὲ γὰρ εἶναι τῆς Ἀλεξίου βασιλείας ἀνδρὸς Ῥωμαίου φόνον θεάσασθαι.

> Comment a-t-il puni les piètres spadassins? Il leur fit raser le chef, leur ôtant cet ornement naturel, parce qu'ils avaient offensé et outragé leur chef. Il leur fit même couper la barbe pour se moquer, j'imagine par ce traitement symbolique de leur veulerie et de leur vilenie. Il fit dresser un pal et y fit attacher ce séducteur, mais il se gaussait bien du pal, notre bon

---

68 Zonaras, *Histoire*, III, 295, 6–10.
69 Théophane, *Histoire*, 283, 16–20. Cf. aussi Magdalino 2007, 63 ; Lauxtermann 2019, 130–31.
70 *Vie de Basile Ier*, ch. 62, 25–46 ; Zonaras, *Histoire*, III, 431, 5–11. Sur cet épisode, voir Anagnostakis—Lambropoulou 2002, 52–53.

basileus, puisqu'il ne l'avait épointé qu'en guise d'épouvantail et fabriqué qu'en guise de croque-mitaine. Car il ne convenait pas au règne d'Alexis de donner en spectacle l'exécution d'un Romain.[71]

Souvent, la διαπόμπευσις s'en tient au niveau de la menace. Ainsi le silentiaire Anastase, qui deviendra par la suite empereur, lorsqu'il apprend les agissements d'Eutychès, grand hérésiarque, lui lance que "s'il ne reste pas tranquille, on lui éliminera le poil du visage et on lui préparera une procession infamante"[72] ; de même Jean Tzetzès, au XIIe siècle, invite le sébaste Isaac Comnène à punir par une procession infamante l'un de ses ennemis, une personne détestable et efféminée.[73] L'efficacité de la menace dépend de la personne à qui elle s'adresse et de son univers de valeurs. Il y a des personnes qui, non seulement ne sentent rien devant la menace d'un tel traitement, mais quand elles le subissent n'ont aucune honte à se montrer devant le monde. Il s'agit de personnes abjectes, comme Stéphane Hagiochristophoritès : "il en eut le nez coupé, puisqu'il s'ébrouait sans honte comme un bouc en rut là où il ne fallait pas, et, en outre, les lanières qui savent corriger avaient bien dansé sur son dos. Toutefois, cet effronté ayant chassé toute honte de sa face, il n'hésita pas à se montrer en public sans craindre qu'on se moque de lui, et fréquenta les mêmes endroits qu'il pratiquait naguère, comme s'il n'avait rien fait de mal. Il se délectait à exhiber son indécence et montrait qu'il n'avait pas honte, en s'efforçant de prouver qu'il n'avait ni fait ni subi rien de mal".[74] Le comportement d'Hagiochristophoritès était socialement inattendu.

Du procédé de la διαπόμπευσις, il est clair alors que ce que le vainqueur nie c'est la valeur sexuelle et sociale du vaincu. Tout ce que nous venons de voir ne constitue qu'une mosaïque d'une violence polymorphe qui fait du corps sa cible principale. L'élimination du poil, les mutilations corporelles, le changement vestimentaire, le foulage du cou, les insultes qui sont adressées et qui souvent sont liées à l'honneur sexuel de la victime et de sa famille, le déshonneur du visage par les excréments jetés, la flagellation et les coups, la profanation du cadavre, sont autant de flèches portées à l'honneur de la personne ciblée. Les victimes perdent ainsi possession de leur corps, cet espace privilégié où le naturel et le social s'unissent pour attribuer une identité à l'individu qui le porte.

---

71   Théophylacte d'Achrida, *Discours*, 231, 7–15.
72   Georges le Moine, *Histoire*, 624, 1–2.
73   Tzetzès, *Lettres*, no 6, 12, 9–11.
74   Eustathe de Thessalonique, *La prise de Thessalonique*, 44–46 (tr. fr. Odorico 2005, 174).

La logique de la διαπόμπευσις dévoile, mieux que tout autre logique, la manière avec laquelle les Byzantins conçoivent les rapports entre personnes sur une base antagoniste, ainsi que plusieurs de leurs notions de la corporéité. Celui qui subit la διαπόμπευσις devient une sorte d'étranger pour la société à laquelle il appartient. Dans les cas rapportés par l'historiographie byzantine, qui traitent le plus souvent des luttes pour le pouvoir, le peuple s'amuse de ces spectacles qui le tirent de son quotidien. Ces peines théâtrales confortent son sentiment d'assurance sociale et valident ses valeurs morales. Il se réjouit finalement de l'esprit 'démocratique' d'une punition qui concerne principalement les personnes dont le corps est protégé par la loi civile et qui obéit à un strict code d'honneur.

Les formes officielles et institutionnalisées des violences exercées sur une personne sont la partie visible de l'iceberg, qui dissimule mal une violence sociale endémique[75] ayant recours aux mêmes moyens pour régler les affaires entre particuliers. Ces actes de violence quotidienne n'ont pas la valeur du grand spectacle de la διαπόμπευσις, mais elles gardent pour autant leur efficacité sociale à l'échelle de la microsociété où ils se réalisent. Ainsi Basile II, se sentant insulté par le comportement insolent de Kontostephanos, sous un coup de colère l'attrape par la barbe et le jette face contre terre[76] ; de même un certain Alexios, qui prétendait être le fils de Manuel Comnène, attaque à la cour du sultan d'Ikonion un ambassadeur byzantin en essayant vainement de l'attraper par la barbe.[77] Au Xe siècle dans le Péloponnèse, Nikon le Métanoeite expérimente dans son corps toute cette violence ambiante quand des agriculteurs de la région veulent le tuer après l'avoir impitoyablement battu et lui avoir tiré les cheveux.[78] A Thessalonique en 1185, "un de ces importuns—et il ne s'agissait pas pourtant d'un homme du peuple—se fit casser la figure, blesser au visage à coup de bâton, parce qu'il avait osé critiquer cette façon maladroite de conduire les opérations" du stratège David Comnène.[79] Les exemples peuvent se multiplier à loisir.

---

75   Sur certains aspects de cette violence endémique, voit Guillou 1993 ; Magdalino 2007, 57–58.
76   Skylitzès, *Histoire*, 331, 47–51. Sur le comportement d'Alexandre envers le patriarche Euthyme, voir Georges le Moine, *Continué 1*, 37, 26–29.
77   Choniatès, *Histoire*, 421, 40–41. Sur Euthyme le patriarche, qui a été déchu par Alexandre et dont il reçoit des insultes et qui lui arrache les poils de sa barbe (ἀτίμως), voir Pseudo-Syméon, *Histoire*, 716, 3–6.
78   *Vie de Nikon*, ch. 57, 29–32.
79   Eustathe de Thessalonique, *La prise de Thessalonique*, 76, 9–11 (tr. fr. Odorico 2005, 196). L'expression 'tenir par la barbe', dans le vocabulaire byzantin du XIIe siècle prend le sens métaphorique de 'humilier' chez Eustathe de Thessalonique, *La prise de Thessalonique*, 106, 22 : "A la fin, j'ai été traîné par la barbe—*comme on dit*".

Les fous, les personnes impotentes, les malades chroniques ou les personnes mentalement dérangées deviennent souvent les cibles d'une violence gratuite et sans conséquences légales. Dans l'Alexandrie du VIIe siècle, par exemple, un nommé Pierre devient de son plein gré serviteur et, perçu comme un fou, affronte le dédain, les coups et le rire moqueur de ses compatriotes.[80] A la fin du XIIe siècle à Constantinople, les eunuques, exclus progressivement du pouvoir, deviennent souvent les cibles d'une violence machiste, signe de "la folie du temps", selon le jugement de Nicétas Choniatès : Jean Cantacuzène, un jeune noble, "administra à l'eunuque Tzitas des coups meurtriers [...] de sorte qu'il perdit ses dents et que ses lèvres se tuméfièrent et saignèrent, cela parce qu'il avait été surpris en train de parler à l'empereur Alexis II Comnène des désastres de l'État".[81]

En ce qui concerne les formes officieuses de contrôle social et la violence des particuliers, pour la première période byzantine, Evelyne Patlagean a collecté les signes de la présence dans les villes d'une 'milice' de jeunes gens qui exercent "une gamme codifiée de violences [...] pour manifester deux tensions subtilement articulées entre elles, l'une politique, l'autre sociale".[82] Patlagean examine le côté sociopolitique de ces groupes, et cet examen révèle la formation, parmi les jeunes, de solidarités affirmatives d'une identité masculine en construction dans le cadre de la ville byzantine. Il est raisonnable alors de situer ces jeunes gens dans la foule qui ridiculise et brutalise les victimes de la διαπόμπευσις et génère et propage la violence quotidienne.

Si pour la plupart des hommes la menace qui pèse sur l'intégrité et l'intégralité de leur corps constitue une source d'angoisse permanente, une catégorie de personnes est exempte de telles peurs : les moines et les saints qui, pour atteindre la spiritualité, doivent aliéner leur corps, autrement dit le spatialiser. Au lieu d'éviter les défis adressés à leur honneur, ces derniers se préparent à les affronter avec une patience exemplaire. Les martyrs de jadis montraient leur dévouement à Dieu en subissant des traitements humiliants, comme par exemple Théodoret d'Antioche à qui "les uns frappaient les joues, d'autres lui crachaient sur le visage ou lui arrachaient la barbe ; certains se moquaient de lui en lui adressant des propos indécents ; d'autres, faisant un creux avec leurs mains et lui giflant le cou produisaient du vacarme et riaient aux éclats".[83] Le saint patriarche d'Alexandrie Jean l'Aumônier conseille à son neveu de se préparer à affronter non seulement le déshonneur public, mais

---

80   *Vie de Jean l'Aumônier*, 49, 14–18.
81   Choniatès, *Histoire*, 258.17–20.
82   Patlagean 1981, 123.
83   *Passion de Théodoret d'Antioche*, 126 (tr. 141).

aussi les coups et le mépris de tous, s'il veut "se manifester en vrai neveu de mon humilité",[84] et Euthyme le Jeune "montrait de la patience quand il était insulté, donnait sa bénédiction à ceux qui lui faisaient des reproches, priait pour ceux qui lui lançaient des blasphèmes, n'adressait pas des menaces contre ceux qui lui administraient des coups".[85] Niant leur personne sociale, les moines dépassent les conventions et les frontières entre la honte et l'honneur et préfigurent une nouvelle échelle de valeurs dans le voisinage de Dieu. La forme la plus extrême de cette négation des valeurs sociales est représentée par les saints fous en Christ, tel Syméon qui reçoit plusieurs coups des habitants d'Emèse, ou André le Salos qui subit les mêmes traitements de la part des habitants de Constantinople, des saints qui provoquent la violence sociale par leur comportement.[86]

...

L'une des hantises les plus puissantes de l'imaginaire collectif pendant l'Antiquité tardive et à Byzance est le corps maltraité, nié, stigmatisé et exposé, en un mot, le corps spatialisé. Les péripéties des héros du roman ancien, qui subissent d'innombrables sévices (mais préservent cependant l'intégrité de leur corps), de même que les histoires sanglantes des martyrs (qui préservent leur liberté d'esprit malgré la mutilation de leurs corps), nourrissent une conception du corps en tant que surface où un pouvoir, qu'il soit abusif ou légitime, marque ses prérogatives de contrôle partiel ou absolu.[87] Mauvais traitements et mutilations ne sont que des formes de la réappropriation du corps individuel du citoyen par les mécanismes du contrôle politique et social.

La διαπόμπευσις, et le système pénal qu'elle préfigure, en accord ou dans les marges du droit civil, constitue la manière 'signifiante' et extrême de spatialiser un corps. A Byzance, le corps du coupable se transforme en surface où s'inscrivent en même temps le crime et le châtiment : il est sous haute surveillance sociale et finit par devenir une voix qui narre des histoires d'inconduite

---

84   *Vie de Jean l'Aumônier*, 42, 5–10.
85   *Vie d'Euthyme le Jeune*, 23, 22–25.
86   Sur le comportement scandaleux de saints *saloi*, voir Browning 1981 ; Rydén 1981 ; Dagron 1990 ; Angelidi 1993 ; Déroche 2000.
87   Sur les différents modes de torture appliqués aux chrétiens, voir l'œuvre classique de Antonio Gallonio, *Trattato degli instrumenti di martirio e delle varie maniere di martirizare*, paru à Rome en 1591 (tr. fr., A. Gallonio, *Traité des instruments de martyre*, Grenoble 2002). Sur le martyre et l'arène pendant l'Antiquité tardive, voir Castelli 2005.

politique et de chute morale.[88] Le coupable est exposé à la risée publique lors des processions infamantes qui annoncent et préparent la punition et qui se déploient dans un espace géographique (l'hippodrome ou la rue principale des villes et des villages) et social (la populace) précis. Le coupable perd rituellement et graduellement tout attribut professionnel et sexué, voire son identité sociale, et d'individu respectable et intouchable se transforme en simple corps fautif, exproprié et 'spatialisé' par la volonté du pouvoir politique et la complicité de toute la communauté. Transformé en matière brute, le corps fautif reçoit l'inscription de la faute et du châtiment (ou du seul châtiment qui indique aussi la faute commise) et l'affiche au vu de tous de manière temporelle (travestissement, élimination du poil) ou permanente (mutilations). Le corps, et son traitement, préfigure ainsi une évolution de taille : on passe d'une conception où le corps est défini par des critères sexués et statutaires très rigides et par son caractère inviolable dans le cadre de la cité gréco-romaine ancienne, à une conception du corps au statut fragile et continuellement négociable dans le cadre d'un empire autoritaire.

Tandis que dans la législation cette transformation est lente et timide, puisque les lois, suivant la tradition romaine, distinguent fondamentalement les riches, punis le plus souvent par une amende, des pauvres, qui paient de leur corps, les textes historiographiques, en revanche, qui traitent des crimes contre l'État, présentent les riches et les aristocrates comme les premiers à subir des peines corporelles. Le pouvoir autoritaire vise à éliminer la stratification sociale au profit d'une société de sujets au statut indifférencié face au monarque. Selon Foucault, le supplice de ce type n'avait pas comme objectif de rétablir la justice ou de servir d'exemple, mais seulement de réactiver le pouvoir, de le réifier et le concrétiser, en soulignant jalousement à qui appartient le monopole de son exercice ou, comme il écrit de manière provocatrice, "la souveraineté faisait mourir et laissait vivre".[89] La place de la réification et de la sublimation du pouvoir était l'Hippodrome, "a public space in which the religious and political imagination of the society was repeatedly constituted and acted on the bodies".[90]

Si on compare l'expérience de la *diapompeusis* à une autre forme d'humiliation/ dépossession/ dépersonnalisation du corps, celle des saints et à un plus grand degré des saints *saloi* qui s'humilient eux-mêmes et subissent mille violences dans l'espace public, on constate que la spatialisation du corps est un

---

88   Patlagean 1984, 422.
89   Foucault 1997, 220.
90   Castelli 2005, 108. Cf. aussi Magdalino 2007, 70–1.

chemin à double tranchant : si les saints humilient leur corps, c'est pour en faire une essence divine, pour abolir la matérialité et la spatialité ; ils mettent en avant leur *personne*, leur corps subtil. Le châtiment en revanche, en suivant un procédé parallèle, abolit la personne, il se substitue à elle, pour rendre au corps sa pure matérialité : dans les deux cas, ce sont les situations liminales qui attribuent une autonomie spatiale au corps ; le corps ainsi manipulé remplace la personne, il se substitue à elle, il devient le corps d'un aliéné, un espace exproprié par la vertu extrême ou par le crime abominable.

Bibliographie

Sources primaires

Achmed, *Oneirocriticon*. Ed. F. Drexl, *Achmes Oneirocriticon*. Leipzig, 1925.

Anastase le Sinaite, *Guide*. Ed. K.-H. Uthemann, *Anastasii Sinaitae, Viae Dux*. Turnhout, 1981.

Anne Comnène, *Alexiade*. Ed. D. Reinsch and A. Kambylis, *Annae Comnenae Alexias*. Berlin & Boston, 2001 (tr. fr. B. Leib, Anne Comnène, Alexiade, 3 vols. Paris, 1937–1946).

Armenopoulos, *Procheiron*. Ed. C. Pitsakis, Κωνσταντίνου Ἀρμενοπούλου Πρόχειρον Νόμων ἢ Ἑξάβιβλος. Athènes, 1971.

Attaleiatès, *Histoire*. Ed. E. Tsolakis, *Michaelis Attaliatae Historia*. Athènes, 2011.

Bryenne, *Histoire*. Ed. P. Gautier, *Nicéphore Bryennios, Histoire*. Bruxelles, 1975.

Caminiatès, *La prise de Thessalonique*, Ed. G. Böhlig, *Ioannis Caminiatae De expugnatione Thessalonicae*. Berlin & New York, 1973.

Choniatès, *Histoire*. Ed. I. A. Van Dieten, *Nicetae Choniatae Historia*. Berlin—New York, 1972.

Chronicon Paschale. Ed. L. Dindorf. Bonn, 1832.

Constantin Porphyrogénète, *Strategicon*. Ed. J. Haldon, *Constantine Porphyrogenitus Three Treatises on Imperial Military Expeditions*. Wien, 1990.

Ecloga. Ed. L. Burgmann, *Ecloga, das Gesetzbuch Leons III und Konstantinos V*. Frankfurt, 1983.

Eustathe de Thessalonique, *La prise de Thessalonique*. Ed. S. Kyriakidis, *Eustazio di Tessalonica, La espugnazione di Tessalonica*. Palermo, 1961.

Genesios, *Histoire*. Ed. A. Lesmueller-Werner et I. Thurn, *Iosephi Genesii Regum libri quattuor*. Berlin & New York, 1978.

Géomètre, *Poèmes*. Ed. M. Tomadaki, Ἰωάννης Γεωμέτρης. Ἰαμβικὰ ποιήματα. Κριτικὴ ἔκδοση, μετάφραση καὶ σχόλια, Diss. Thessalonique, 2014.

Georges de Chypre, *Éloge de la chevelure*. Ed. I. Perez-Martin, *El patriarca Gregorio de Chipre (ca. 1240–1290) y la transmisión de los textos clásicos en Bizancio*, Madrid, 1996, 362–396.

Georges le Moine, *Histoire*. Ed. C. De Boor et P. Wirth, *Georgii Monachi Chronicon*. Stuttgard, 1978.

Georges le Moine, *Continué*. Ed. I. Bekker, *Georgii Monachi Vitae imperatorum recentiorum*. Bonn, 1838.

Georges le Moine, *Continué 1*. ed. B. Istrin, *Chronika Georgij Amartola*, v. II. Petropoli, 1922.

Kinnamos, *Histoire*. Ed. A. Meineke, *Ioannis Cinnami Epitome*. Bonn. 1836 (tr. fr., J. Rosenblum, *Jean Kinnamos, Chronique*. Paris, 1972).

Léon VI, *Le livre du préfet*. Ed. J. Koder, *Das Eparchenbuch Leons des Weisen*. Wien, 1991.

Léon Diacre, *Histoire*. Ed. C. Hasius, *Leonis Diaconi Caloensis Historiae Libri decem*. Bonn, 1828.

Léon de Synada, *Lettres*. Ed. M. Pollard Vinson, *The Correspondence of Leo, Metropolitan of Synada and Syncellus*. Washington, 1985.

Lois des Homérites. Ed. A. Berger, *Life and works of Saint Gregentios, archbishop of Taphar*. Berlin, 2006, 411–49.

Malalas, Histoire. Ed. I. Thurn, *Ioannis Malalae Chronographia*. Berlin-New York, 2000.

Manassès, Histoire. Ed. O. Lampsidis, *Constantini Manassis Breviarium Chronicum*. Athènes, 1996.

Nicéphore, *Histoire*. Ed. C. Mango, *Nikephoros Patriarch of Constantinople, Short History*. Washington, 1990.

Nicolas de Damas. Ed.-trad. E. Parmentier et F. P. Barone, *Histoires, Recueil de coutumes, Vie d'Auguste, Autobiographie*. Paris, 2011.

Onirocriticon Atheniensis BN 1275. Ed. A. Delatte, *Anecdota Athenensia*. Liège-Paris, 1927, 165–81.

Onirocriticon de Manuel Paléologue. Ed. A. Delatte, *Anecdota Athenensia*, Liège-Paris, 1927, 511–24.

Pachymère, *Histoire*. Ed. A. Failler, *Georges Pachymérès, Relations historiques*. I. livres 1–3. Paris, 1984.

Passion de Serge et Bacchus. Ed. Van den Gheyn, "Passio Antiquior ss. Sergii et Bacchi," *An. Boll.* 14 (1895), 373–95.

Passion de Théodoret d'Antioche. Ed. F. Halkin, *Hagiologie byzantine*, SH 71. Bruxelles, 1986, 123–51.

Patria de Constantinople. Ed. T. Preget, *Scriptores originum Constantinopolitanarum*. Leipzig, 1901.

Procope, *Anecdota*. Ed. J. Haury et G. Wirth, *Procopii Caesariensis opera omnia. III. Historia Arcana*. Leipzig, 1963.

Psellos, *Histoire*. Ed. D. Reinsch, *Michaelis Pselli Chronographia*. Berlin & Boston, 2014 (tr.fr. F. Renauld, *Michel Psellos Chronographie*, vol. 2. Paris, 1967).

Pseudo-Syméon, *Histoire*. Ed. I. Bekker, *Theophanis Continuatus, Ioannes Cameniata, Symeon Magister, Georgius Monachus*. Bonn, 1838.
Skylitzès, *Histoire*. Ed. I. Thurn, *Histoire, Ioannis Scylitzae Synopsis Historiarum*. Berlin—New York, 1973.
Syntipas, *Retractatio*. Ed. F. Boissonnade, *De Syntipa et Cyri filio Andeopuli narratio*, Paris, 1828; version longue, ed. F. Conca, *Novelle Bizantine. Il libro di Syntipas*. Milan, 2004.
Théophane, *Histoire*. Ed. C. de Boor, *Theophanis Chronographia*. Leipzig 1883.
Théophane, *Continué*. Ed. M. Featherstone et J. Signes Codoner, *Theophanis Continuati libri I–IV*, Boston & Berlin, 2015.
Théophylacte d'Achrida, *Discours*. Ed. P. Gautier, *Theophylacti Achridensis, Opera*. Thessalonique, 1980.
Tzetzès, *Lettres*. Ed. P.A. Leone, *Ioannis Tzetzae Epistulae*. Leipzig, 1972.
Vie d'Antoine le Jeune. Ed. A. Papadopoulos-Kerameus, Συλλογὴ παλαιστινῆς καὶ συριακῆς ἁγιολογίας. Saint Petersburg, 1907, 186–216.
Vie de Basile Ier. Ed. I. Ševčenko, *Chronographiae quae Theophanis Continuati nomine fertur liber quo Vita Basilii imperatoris amplectitur*. Berlin—New York, 2011.
Vie d'Euthyme le Jeune. Ed. L. Petit, *Vie et Office de saint Euthyme le Jeune*, Paris, 1904.
Vie de Jean l'Aumônier. Ed. H. Delehaye, "Une Vie inédite de saint Jean l'Aumonier," *An. Boll.* 45 (1927), 5–74.
Vie de Nikon. Ed. D. Sullivan, *The Life of Saint Nikon*, Brookline Massachusetts, 1987.
Vie de Stéphane le Jeune. Ed. M.-F. Auzépy, *La Vie d'Étienne le Jeune par Étienne le Diacre*, Aldershot, 1997.
Vie de Syméon Salos. Ed. L. Ryden (tr.fr. A.J. Festugière), *Léontios de Néapolis, Vie de Syméon le fou et Vie de Jean de Chypre*. Paris, 1974.
Vie de Théodora de Thessalonique. Ed. S. Paschalidis, Ὁ Βίος τῆς ὁσιομυροβλύτιδος Θεοδώρας τῆς ἐν Θεσσαλονίκῃ. Thessalonique, 1991.
Vie de saint Théophylacte de Nicomédie. Ed. A. Vogt, "S. Théophylacte de Nicomédie,"*An. Boll.* 50 (1932), 67–82.
Zonaras, *Histoire*. Ed. M. Pinder et T. Büttner-Wobst, *Ioannis Zonarae Annales*, 3 vol. Bonn, 1841–1897.
Zosime, *Histoire*. Ed. F. Paschoud, *Zosime Histoire Nouvelle*, vol. 3. Paris, 1971–1989.

Sources secondaires

Anagnostakis, I. & A. Lambropoulou, 2002. "Καταστολή : μια μορφή ανοχής στην Πελοπόννησο του 9ου και 10ου αιώνα," in *Ανοχή και καταστολή στους μέσους χρόνους*, ed. K. Nikolaou. Athènes, 47–61.
Angelidi, C. 1993. "Η παρουσία των σαλών στη βυζαντινή κοινωνία," in *Πρακτικά Ημερίδας : Οι περιθωριακοί στο Βυζάντιο*, ed. C. Maltezou. Athènes, 85–102.

Auzépy, M.-F. 2002. "Prolégomènes à une histoire du poil," *TM* 14 (= *Mélanges Gilbert Dagron*), 1–12.

Betancourt, R. 2018. *Sight, Touch, and Imagination in Byzantium*. Cambridge.

Castelli, E. 2005. "Persecution and Spectacle. Cultural Appropriation in the Christian Commemoration of Martyrdom," *Archiv für Religionsgeschichte* 7, 102–36.

Dagron, G. 1987. "Image de bête ou image de Dieu. La physiognomonie animale dans la tradition grecque et ses avatars byzantins," in *Poikilia. Etudes offertes à Jean-Pierre Vernant*. Paris, 69–80.

Dagron, G. 1990. "L'homme sans honneur ou le saint scandaleux," *Annales ESC* 4, juillet-août, 929–39.

Dagron, G. 2011. *L'Hippodrome de Constantinople. Jeux, peuple et politique*. Paris.

Déroche, V. 2000. *Syméon Salos. Le fou en Christ*. Paris.

Evans, E. 1969. *Physiognomics in the Ancient World*. Philadelphia.

Foucault, M. 1975. *Surveiller et punir*. Paris.

Foucault, M. 1976. *La volonté du savoir*. Paris.

Foucault, M. 1994. "Des espaces autres," in Id. *Dits et écrits 1954–1988, t. IV(1980–1988)*. Paris, 752–62.

Foucault, M. 1997. *"Il faut défendre la société". Cours au Collège de France 1976*. Paris.

Gauvard, C. 2005. *Violence et ordre public au Moyen Age*. Paris.

Gleason, M. 1990. "The Semiotics of Gender: Physiognomy and Self-Fashioning in the Second Century c.e.," in *Before Sexuality: the Construction of Erotic Experience in the Ancient Greek World*, eds. D. Halperin, J. Winkler and F. Zeitlin. Princeton, 389–415.

Gleason, M. 1995. *Making Men. Sophists and Self-Representation in Ancient Rome*. Princeton.

Godelier, M. 2001. "La sexualité est toujours autre chose qu'elle-même." *Esprit, mars-avril 2001 : L'un et l'autre sexe*. Paris, 96–104.

Grodzynski, D. 1984. "Tortures mortelles et catégories sociales," in *Du châtiment dans la cité*. Rome, 361–403.

Guillou, A. 1993. "Ceux que conscience populaire condamne," Βυζαντιακά 13, 11–23.

Haldon, J. 1990. *Byzantium in the Seventh Century: The Transformation of a Culture*. Cambridge.

Halm-Tisserant, M. 1998. *Réalités et imaginaire des supplices en Grèce ancienne*. Paris.

Halsall, P. 1999. *Women's Bodies, Men's souls: Sanctity and Gender in Byzantium*. Diss. th. New York.

Heher, D. 2015. "Heads on Stakes and Rebels on Donkeys. The Use of Public Parades for the Punishment of Usurpers in Byzantium (c. 900–1200)," *Porphyra*, dicembre, 12–20.

Koukoulès, F. 1948–1956. Βυζαντινῶν βίος καὶ πολιτισμός. Athènes.

Lambros, S. 1911. "Ὁ Μαρκιανὸς κῶδιξ 524," Νέος Ἑλληνομνήμων 8, 3–59.

Larchet, J.-C. 1996. *Ceci est mon corps. Le sens chrétien du corps selon les Pères de l'Église*. Genève.

Lauxtermann, M. 2019. *Byzantine Poetry from Pisides to Geometres. Texts and Contexts*, v. II. Wien.

Leach, E. 1980. *L'unité de l'homme et autres essais*. Paris.

Le Breton, D. 1997. *La sociologie du corps*. Paris.

Le Goff, J. & N. Truong, 2003. *Une histoire du corps au Moyen Age*. Paris.

MacCormick, M. 1986. *Eternal Victory. Triumphal Rulership in Late Antiquity, Byzantium and Early Medieval West*. Cambridge.

Magdalino, P. 2007. "Tourner en dérision à Byzance," in *La dérision au Moyen-Age. De la pratique sociale au rituel politique*, eds. E. Crouzet-Pavan et J. Verger. Paris, 55–72.

Messis, Ch. 2012. "La famille et ses enjeux dans l'organisation de la cité idéale chrétienne. Le cas des *Lois* des 'Homérites,'" in *Les réseaux familiaux : Antiquité tardive et Moyen Age*, ed. B. Caseau. Paris, 87–120.

Morris, R. 2002. "Curses and Clauses: The Language of exclusion in Byzantium," in *Ανοχή και καταστολή στcυς Μέσους Χρόνους*, ed. K. Nikolaou. Athènes, 313–26.

Nilsson, I. 2017. "To Touch or not to Touch. Erotic Tactility in Byzantine Literature," in *Knowing Bodies, Passionate Souls. Sense Perceptions in Byzantium*, eds. S. Ashbrook Harvey and M. Mullett. Washington, 239–57.

Odorico, P. 2005. *Jean Caminiatès, Eustathe de Thessalonique, Jean Anagnostès, Thessalonique. Chroniques d'une ville prise*. Toulouse.

Patlagean, E. 1981. "Les 'jeunes' dans les villes byzantines : émeutiers et miliciens", in *Le charivari*, eds. J. Le Goff et J.-C. Schmitt. Paris—La Haye—New York, 123–29.

Patlagean, E. 1984. "Byzance et le blason pénal du corps," in *Du châtiment dans la cité*. Rome, 405–26.

Rydén, L. 1981. "The Holy Fool," in *The Byzantine Saint*, ed. S. Hackel. Birmingham, 106–13.

Pitsakis, K. 2002. "Μερικές σκέψεις για τις 'ποινές-κάτοπτρο' στον ελληνικό μεσαιωνικό χώρο," in *Ανοχή και καταστολή στους Μέσους Χρόνους*, ed. K. Nikolaou. Athènes, 285–312.

Politis, N. 1975. "Υβριστικά σχήματα", in Id., *Λαογραφικά Σύμμεικτα Β*. Athènes, 384–442.

Sideris, G. 2011. "Jouer du poil à Byzance : anges, eunuques et femmes déguisées en moines, "in *Histoire du poil*, eds. M.-F. Auzépy et J. Cornette. Paris, 93–114.

Tirnanic, G. 2017. "A Touch of Violence. Feeling Pain, Perceiving Pain in Byzantium," in *Knowing Bodies, Passionate Souls. Sense Perceptions in Byzantium*, eds. S. Ashbrook Harvey and M. Mullett. Washington, 223–37.

Troianos, S. 1997. "Οι ποινές στο βυζαντινό δίκαιο," in *Έγκλημα και τιμωρία στό Βυζάντιο*, eds. S. Troianos. Athènes, 13–65.

Troianos, S. 2002. "Το ποινικό σύστημα του 'Επαρχικού Βιβλίου'", in *Ανοχή και καταστολή στους μέσους χρόνους*, ed. K. Nikolaou. Athènes, 277–83.

Wilgaux, J. 2008. "La physiognomonie antique : bref état de lieux," in *Langages et métaphores du corps dans le monde antique*, eds. V. Dasen & J. Wilgaux. Rennes, 185–95.

Zink, M. 2017. *L'humiliation, le Moyen Age et nous*. Paris.

3
The World from Above
Divine Amphitheatres, Spiritual Watchtowers, and the Moral Spatialities of κατασκοπή

Veronica della Dora

> Again, the devil taketh him up into an exceeding high mountain, and sheweth him all the kingdoms of the world, and the glory of them. (Mt. 4:8)

∵

In Matthew's Gospel, the beginnings of Christ's terrestrial ministry are marked by drama. Fresh off his baptism, Jesus is led into the wilderness to be tempted by the devil three times. Firstly, having fasted for forty days, he is asked to turn stones into bread to satisfy his hunger. He is then taken to the top of the highest pinnacle of the temple of Jerusalem and told by the devil to cast himself down to give proof of his divinity. Having refused for the second time, he is eventually taken to an even higher and more vertiginous spot, the top of a lofty mountain. Here the drama reaches its climax: through a spectacular zooming out movement, Christ—and the reader—are offered a sweeping view of all the earthly kingdoms in the twinkle of an eye.

According to John Chrysostom, the passage offers a lesson in endurance to the chief human temptations: slavery to the belly, vainglory, and subjection to the madness of riches. The three temptations are presented in order of strength. Chrysostom regards the boundless want for more as the most powerful of all temptations, for it lies at the root of Adam's fall, that is, of his desire to "make himself out to be God, the artificer of the universe".[1] In its sweeping grasp, the view from the Mount of Temptation pushes the gaze beyond the constraints of the human field of vision. This is why, Chrysostom explains, the devil kept this as the last of the three temptations, "as being of more force than

---

[1] John Chrysostom, *Homily on the Gospel of Matthew*, 13.5 Prevost.

the rest".² Why is the totalizing view from above so alluring and dangerous? From where does it draw its strength and appeal? Which kind of spatiality does it generate?

The synoptic experience of space produced through elevation is a quintessentially visual experience. It demands physical distancing. It requires a real or imaginary elevated spot from which to survey the lie of the land. Gazing down into the world—what the ancient Greeks called κατασκοπή—has been traditionally regarded as an empowering act, the epitome of territorial control and cartographic knowledge. Ironically, however, the view from above can also prove an exhilarating as much as disorientating experience: seen from an elevated spot, familiar landscapes and surfaces can become utterly, and wonderfully, unfamiliar. As a metaphor of omniscience and a source of aesthetic pleasure, the view from above is at once divine and diabolic; hence, as John Chrysostom acknowledged, it can cause dangerous vertigo.

The view from above nonetheless enshrines moral connotations that transcend sheer aesthetic pleasure and mundane desires. The Greek word κατασκοπή holds the strong sense of reconnaissance, spying, looking out, and keeping watch in order to observe and consider things from on high, and thus to 'contemplate'.³ In a broad sense, it relates to the ancient θέατρον, a 'place for seeing'. By setting the spectator at a distance from the stage, the θέατρον provides the rational detachment necessary to attain wisdom. It turns the viewer (θεατής) into a sort of θεός, or divinity—a prime example of the agency of space in shaping specific human experiences, as discussed in the introduction to this volume. Scaled up from urban theatres and from landscapes to the entire planet, the view from above was promptly appropriated in Roman *somnia* narratives and absorbed in the philosophical trope of the heavenly journey. Confronted with the vastness of the earth, in these narratives the κατάσκοπος suddenly realized the insignificance of his place on it and the futility of human affairs.

Whereas the *somnia* tradition had a lasting impact in the West and much has been written about it, the spatial and moral registers of κατασκοπή have not received equal attention by scholars of Byzantium.⁴ Elevated views have

---

2   Ibid. The temptations of Christ are also described in Luke's Gospel (4:1–13). Luke, however, reverses the order of the second and third temptations. The temple is kept at the end perhaps to stress the role of Jerusalem in the broader narrative, his Gospel ending in Jerusalem (the centre of the world).
3   Constas 2018, 187 n.26. *Κατάσκοπος* was the surveyor, but he was also the spy, the inspector, the examiner (Liddell & Scott 1977). See Clement of Alexandria, *Paedagogus* 1.5.21.
4   On the reception of the *somnia* tradition in Renaissance cartography, see for example, Cosgrove 2001 and 2003. Earlier examples include canto XXII in Dante Alighieri's *Paradise*.

usually been referred to in studies of gardens and architecture, from late antique descriptions of villas set on scenic spots to medieval urban ἐκφράσεις.⁵ In all these cases, the elevated prospect is generally approached as a literary topos, or as an object for aesthetic consumption adding beauty to a specific building or garden.⁶ Wider views and their moral implications, however, have not yet been the object of specific enquiry. This chapter explores metaphorical uses of κατασκοπή in Patristic and Byzantine hagiographic literature. While scant when compared to Classical literature, imaginary views from above were nonetheless occasionally employed by the Greek Church Fathers as devices for imparting spiritual teachings, and in the Middle Ages, as part of journeys to the afterlife. Mediated through the symbolic language of Scripture, such κατασκοπαί conjured up a distinctive type of spiritual spatiality.

The first section of this chapter introduces kataskopic spatialities in Classical and Late Antiquity, including views produced by the imaginary flights of rulers and philosophers and their resulting *theatra mundi*. The following sections turn to Byzantine 'spiritual θέατρα': Basil of Caesarea's 'amphitheatre of creation' as a metaphor for the contemplation of nature; John Chrysostom's world and celestial theatres as metaphors for the contemplation of Christian life and afterlife; and finally, the watchtower as a metaphor for ascetic watchfulness and a privileged observation point from which to witness the drama of Christ's Second Coming and the creation of a new earth and heaven. Altogether, these images and metaphors give expression to a symbolic approach to space that was at the heart of Byzantine spiritual culture.

As Dante is about to enter the eighth heaven, Beatrice invites him to gaze down. A view of the firmament and the seven heavens he has ascended opens up to him. Evoking Cicero's *Somnium Scipionis*, he thus reflects on the misery of human affairs as witnessed from above: 'L'aiuola che ci fa tanto feroci,/ volgendom'io con li etterni Gemelli/ tutta m'apparve dai colli alle foci' (*Paradise* 12.151–53). I am grateful to Mario Ricca for bringing this passage to my attention.

5   See, for example, Maguire 2000; Littlewood 1992; Nicholas Mesarites, *Description of the Church of the Holy Apostles*, Downey, 864.

6   The most famous description scenic view from a Roman villa is found in Pliny the Younger's letter to Gallus. Here Pliny takes his friend on a virtual tour through landscape views framed through folding-doors, windows and porticoes (Pliny, *Ep.* 23 Melmoth). Such views were painted on the walls of Roman villas in the so-called *topia*, a genre which, according to some, was linked to the invention of the stage screen in Hellenistic theatres in Alexandria (see, for example, Pearsall & Salter 1973).

1   From *Skopiai* to *Theatra Mundi*

According to the Classical scholar Alex Purves, two modes of experiencing and narrating space characterize ancient Greek literature, from Homeric epic all the way through Classical texts. The first approach, argues Purves, is closely aligned with prose and the practice of investigating through walking. "It takes the road as its dominant metaphor and sets forth a view of the plot that is sequential, rather than simultaneous, requiring time to reach the end".[7] The second, which Purves terms 'protocartographic', aspires to an impossible holistic view of space and time—the view of the Muses and of the Olympian gods surveying human destinies from the height of their abodes.[8] This view is achieved through what Irene de Jong calls 'panoramic standpoint', whereby the narrator is set at a considerable distance from a scene and oversees a large stretch of space. The protocartographic view, however, transcends the panoramic view in that it is not mono-focal; by contrast, it encompasses multiple angles and temporalities.[9]

In his study of space in Apollonius of Rhodes' *Argonautica*, William Thalmann operates a similar, yet more subtle distinction. He identifies three modes of experiencing space: from ground level, as a horizontal succession of places (which is the experience of the Argonauts); synoptically, through a God's-eye view (a privilege reserved to the immortals); and through panoramas that mortals can attain under special conditions (for example, from a mountain top). In the last two cases, argues Thalmann, space is perceived as a totality, but it is not abstract in the modern sense.[10] How was this experience of space achieved?

Geography partly accounts for the answer. The Mediterranean, it has been argued, "is not so much the sea between the lands, as the name asserts, but the sea among the mountains".[11] Sailing around the basin, except for part of the North African coast, one is virtually almost never out of sight of a range or peak. Isolated summits, abrupt promontories and lonely watchtowers provided ancient navigators with a system of landmarks essential to coastwise navigation.[12] At the same time, these features afforded commanding views and were often part of complex visual networks that extended inland and were

---

7   Purves 2010, 2.
8   Ibid.
9   de Jong 2012, 11.
10 Thalmann 2011, 6–8.
11 McNeill 1992, 12.
12 Semple 1932.

used for both military and religious purposes.[13] Ancient Greeks and Byzantines both referred to mountain heights as σκοπιαί and Romans as *speculae*, or "lookout places".[14] The Greek poet Simonides (556–468 BCE), for instance, spoke of the summits of Cithaeron as "lonely watchtowers", whereas Strabo (64 BCE–24 CE) provided descriptions of an actual belvedere built on one of the summits of Mount Tmolus in Lydia (western Anatolia). Similarly, *speculae* signposted Egeria's pilgrimage to the lands of the Bible (384 CE). Elevated churches and chapels equipped with (or functioning as) panoramic platforms enabled the pilgrim to identify in the landscape the places associated with the lives of Moses and Christ, as if on a giant map unfolding under her feet.[15]

In Classical and Hellenistic literature, the view from the mountaintop featured as an approximation of divine knowledge, a sort of compromise between the totalizing 'god's eye' view and the view from the ground of mortals. The Argonauts climbed Mount Dindymon to gain a prospective understanding of the region through which they were about to travel.[16] Philip of Macedon ascended the highest peak of the Haemus range in order to see the lie of the land as he planned his war against Rome—it was widely believed that this summit commanded a view over the Danube and the Alps, and both the Adriatic and the Black seas.[17] Likewise, Hadrian ascended Aetna in Sicily and Mount Casius in Syria to observe the sunrise and obtain a view over a wide swath of country, whereas Atlas, the legendary ruler of Mauretania, who was

---

13   Lofty peaks were used as beacons to convey long-distance messages by the Assyrians. In 480 BCE the Persians too had deployed an efficient system stretching out from the coast of Asia Minor across the Aegean by way of the islands to Attica during their invasion of Greece. The employment of fire signals by the Greeks became common by the time of the Peloponnesian War and was maintained by the Byzantines (see Pattenden 1983). The Minoans set their sanctuaries on Cretan peaks in sight of each other, on the top of which large sacrificial bonfires were lit as part of ceremonies, providing spiritual comfort to those villagers in the valley. During festival nights a network of sacred beacons would unite various regions and allow faithful to perform a 'visual' pilgrimage through the peaks (see Peatfield 1983). In Classical Greece, coastal promontories were often topped by temples signalling places of severe storms, as the high relief on which the sanctuaries were located often converted the straits and bays below into sea canyons through which winds seasonally blew with restless violence. These landmarks were also the first familiar features the returning seaman would have glanced on return to his homeland (see Semple 1932, 616; Mavian 1992).

14   Tozer 1897, 327.

15   Egeria, *Travels* Wilkinson, 121.

16   Apollonius of Rhodes, *Argonautics* 2.311–407. The passage is discussed in Thalmann 2011, 6–7.

17   Tozer 1897, 313–14.

also a philosopher, astronomer and mathematician, was said to have climbed up to the highest summit in his kingdom to gain a view of the entire inhabited world.[18]

Empowering and exhilarating as it might have appeared to individuals unacquainted with aerial photography and satellite imagery, the view from the mountain top was nonetheless but a humble surrogate of what the Latins called *somnium*, "the imaginative dreaming associated with the rising over the earth".[19] Unlike the military survey or the traveller's landscape reconnaissance, the long tradition of the *somnium* demanded an imaginary viewpoint external to the earth. Appropriate elevation was usually achieved through interstellar flight and spiritual ascent, and it provided the human mind with a perspective over the world denied to the physical eye. The resulting synoptic view implied raising over the mundane and was therefore "a mark of the exceptional being, the call to heroic destiny of the paradigmatic human".[20] For Plato, this paradigmatic human was the philosopher. In his account of the death of Socrates, the philosopher is portrayed as he comforts his mourning disciples with a description of the polychrome terrestrial globe silently floating in the darkness of the *kosmos*:

> Well then, my friend, first of all the true earth, if one views it from above, is said to look like those twelve-piece leather balls, variegated, a patchwork of colours, of which our colours here are, as it were, samples that painters use. There the whole earth is of such colours, indeed colours far brighter still and purer than these: one portion is purple, marvellous for its beauty, another is golden, and all that is white is whiter than chalk or snow; and the earth is composed of the other colours likewise, indeed of colours more numerous and beautiful than any we have seen.[21]

The most famous protagonists of *somnia* were nonetheless military heroes— in other words, the same individuals who in real life would have surveyed the land from the height of garrisons, watchtowers and mountain tops. In Cicero's *Somnium Scipionis*, for example, the conqueror of Carthage and hero of Rome's imperial expansion into Africa dreams of looking down upon Carthage "from a high place full of stars, shining and splendid", only to find out the limits of even "so great an empire as his own":

---

18   Tolias 2011, 147.
19   Cosgrove 2001, 3.
20   Ibid. 27.
21   Plato, *Phaedo* 110–15 Gallop.

And as I surveyed them from this point, all the other heavenly bodies appeared to be glorious and wonderful,—now the stars were such as we have never seen from this earth; and such was the magnitude of them all as we have never dreamed; and the least of them all was that planet, which farthest from the heavenly sphere and nearest to our earth, was shining with borrowed light, but the spheres of the stars easily surpassed the earth in magnitude—already the earth itself appeared to me so small, that it grieved me to think of our empire, with which we cover but a point, as it were, of its surface.[22]

Likewise, in a famous romance attributed to Pseudo-Callisthenes (third century CE), Alexander the Great questions whether he has reached the end of the world in his march of conquest. To find out, he devises an ingenious 'flying machine' powered by two griffins. As in Scipio's dream, the Macedonian king's ascent to heaven culminates in a humbling aerial view. Seen in the wider terrestrial context, the vast extents of land he struggled to conquer turn out to be nothing but part of "a tiny circle like a threshing floor".[23]

The *somnium*, and the figure of the κατάσκοπος more generally, were closely connected with the *theatrum mundi*, the idea of the world stage on which humans enact their lives under the eyes of the gods—and of the philosopher who has successfully separated himself from mundane affairs. Controversially traced back to Democritus, Pythagoras and Heraclitus, the metaphor was embraced and popularized by writers influenced by Stoicism, including Cicero himself.[24] Stoic philosophy bore witness to the diffusion of the exercise of κατασκοπή, both in the sense of a detached gaze relativizing human values and achievements and of "a spiritual gaze that discloses the beauty and order of the world beyond the shimmering appearances and the limitations of human knowledge".[25] For Seneca, the good actor, the wise man, was "a sight worthy of divine spectators".[26] Similarly, Marcus Aurelius, the emperor-philosopher, invited his audience to

---

22 Cicero, *Somnium Scipionis* 3–14 Pearman.
23 Pseudo-Callisthenes, *Alexander Romance* Stoneman, 123. Representations of the scene recur in Byzantine art as reminders of the futility of mundane affairs and anticipations of Christ's Ascension to heaven to show human weakness: Alexander ascended to the heavens transitorily and artificially; by contrast, Christ ascended without external aids and for eternity. A bas-relief, for example, is found on the exterior of the *katholikon* of Docheiariou monastery, Mount Athos. See Theoktistos 2006 and Schmidt 1995.
24 Christian 1987.
25 Jacob, cited in Cosgrove 2001, 49.
26 Seneca, *De Providentia* 12.7–12. See Hijmans 1966.

Survey, as from a high watchtower, the things of the earth; its assemblies for peace or war, its husbandry, matings and partings, births and deaths, noisy law courts, lonely wastes, alien peoples of every kind, feasting, mourning, bargaining—observing all the motley mixture and harmonious order that is wrought out of contrariety.[27]

According to Marcus Aurelius, one should not separate oneself from the organic whole, but seek to play one's part in it, and do so with appropriate seriousness. "For we are part of the skein and web of the one whole; our lot in society is assigned, woven into our particular web".[28]

By the same token, the spatial detachment of the κατάσκοπος enabled satirists to describe and laugh at the folly of humans. The wise man watched the action from the height of the world theatre, while his laughter mingled with that of the Olympians.[29] Lucian of Samosata (125–180 CE), for example, adopted the view Charon and Hermes obtained by piling up the highest mountains of Greece to survey human lives and fortunes, but only to find out the tiny space Charon—that is, Death—seems to occupy in the thoughts of those acting on the world stage.[30]

2 The Theatre of Creation

While the view enjoyed from a lofty mountain top or from the imaginative heights of *somnia* was an extraordinary experience reserved to divinities and few exceptional individuals, less dramatic views were ordinarily consumed by (usually wealthy) citizens of the Roman Empire and, later, of Byzantium. Spaces specifically architected 'for seeing' ranged from amphitheatres, hippodromes, circuses and watchtowers to villas overlooking the countryside and evocative marine scenes or elevated gardens commanding urban and suburban views. As Henry Maguire notes, from Cicero to Basil the Great, a standard element in the praise of a villa or estate was indeed "the pleasure to be obtained from gazing at its surrounding scenery".[31] From Lazio to Cappadocia, commanding prospects delighted happy estate owners and their visitors, and occasionally served as backdrops for late antique romances.[32] So essential were such views

---

27 Marcus Aurelius, *Meditations* 7.48, 9.30 Staniford.
28 Ibid. 4.26–40.
29 Christian 1987, 12.
30 Lucian, *Dialogues of the Dead* 6.1–14.
31 Maguire 2000, 262. See also Rossiter 1989.
32 For example, see Longos, *Daphnis and Chloe* 4.1–3.

to the ideal country retreat that when, in the early fifth century, Melania the Younger sold her estates to devote herself to Christ, we are told by her biographer, the devil tried to divert the saint from the chosen path by reminding her of the splendid views she used to enjoy from her elevated pool—a micro-scale re-enactment of the Mount Temptation drama.[33]

The most evocative Patristic description of such a scene comes from Basil of Caesarea. In a letter to his friend Gregory of Nazianzus, Basil fondly praises the charms of his alpine retreat near the banks of the river Iris in northern Cappadocia:

> My hut is so situated on the summit of the mountain that I can overlook the whole plain, and follow throughout its course the Iris, which is more beautiful, and has a more abundant body of water, than the Strymon near Amphipolis. The river of my wilderness, which is more impetuous than any other that I know of, breaks against the jutting rock, and throws itself foaming into the abyss below: an object of admiration to the mountain wanderer, and a source of profit to the natives, from the numerous fishes that are found in its waters. Shall I describe to thee the fructifying vapours that rise from the moist earth, or the cool breezes wafted over the rippled face of the waters? Shall I speak of the sweet song of the birds, or of the rich luxuriance of the flowering plants? What charms me beyond all else is the calm repose of this spot.[34]

The landscape surveyed by Basil of Caesarea from the height of his abode was an idealized microcosm which encompassed all the *topoi* of the *locus amoenus* (and terrestrial paradise): trees, streams, animals (wild but not dangerous to man).[35] Elevation enabled the saint to visually embrace this microcosm in its fullness. At the same time, it also set him closer to the vault of heaven and its stars, what Basil elsewhere called "everlasting blossoms"—a reminder, according to Alexander von Humboldt, of "the mildness of the constantly clear nights of Asia Minor".[36]

For Basil, however, the view from above did more than satisfying the senses or aesthetic taste. It facilitated meditation, or θεωρία φυσική, the contemplation of nature which the Greek Fathers considered the first stage by which the

---

33   *Vitae Sanctae Melaniae Junioris*, 18.33. The passage is discussed by Maguire (2002), 32.
34   Basil of Caesarea, *Epistle* 24 von Humboldt 40–41.
35   Earlier in the text Basil describes it as a 'fortress', or a sort of island on the land bounded by two ravines and the river.
36   von Humboldt 1997 (1858), 41.

soul attains knowledge of God.[37] Located near the top of the mountain, Basil's hut functioned as an observatory of what he called "the vast and varied workshop of divine creation".[38] From this lonely retreat, the hierarch's eye wandered over the humid leafy roof of the forest below; it followed the silvery ribbon of the Iris through the valley; it paused on the fine detail, be it a plant or an animal; finally, turning upwards, it zoomed out again to encompass the celestial vault of heaven and chase some distant constellation or lonely flickering star. Elevation granted the holy man visual mastery over that self-contained microcosm, while at the same time connecting him to the wider cosmos and its Creator. Basil's mountain was thus a sort of 'anti-Mount of Temptation'. Unlike the tempted Christ, the holy man found in the wilderness an edifying view as he contemplated the works of the Creator from within, and not those of men from an external viewpoint.

Views like this are likely to have inspired, or at least informed, the poetic lines of Basil's *Hexaemeron*, a series of influential sermons on the six days of creation in Genesis written around 370 CE and delivered to his congregation during Lent.[39] Here, emblematically, the hierarch invites the faithful to enter what he calls "the amphitheatre of creation" and to explore with him the mysterious depths of nature:

> If sometimes, on a bright night, whilst gazing with watchful eyes on the inexpressible beauty of the stars, you have thought of the Creator of all things; if you have asked yourself who it is that has dotted heaven with such flowers, and why visible things are even more useful than beautiful; if sometimes, in the day, you have studied the marvels of light, if you have raised yourself by visible things to the invisible Being, then you are a well prepared auditor, and you can take your place in this august and blessed amphitheatre (τοῦ σεμνοῦ τούτου καὶ μακαρίου θεάτρου).[40]

As with most metaphors, the 'amphitheatre of creation' draws its strength from the juxtaposition of such an ungraspable reality as the cosmos and the

---

37 According to Clement of Alexandria, θεωρία φυσική was conducive to piety, being a kind of preparatory training (Wallace-Hadrill 1968, 7). "Through the sight of visible things", argued Basil, "the mind is led to the invisible" (Basil of Caesarea, *Hexaemeron* 1.6 Jackson).
38 Basil of Caesarea, *Hexaemeron* 4.1 Jackson.
39 Basil's was the first *hexaemeron*, preceded by the mediating work of Philo of Alexandria with his synthesis of Judaic theology and Hellenistic philosophy. Among the Latin Fathers, Ambrose and Augustine wrote some of the earliest extant hexaemeral literature. On differences between different *hexaemera* see de Beer 2015.
40 Basil of Caesarea, *Hexaemeron* 6.1 Jackson.

familiarity of the theatre to its audience. Theatres, circuses and spectacles were popular attractions as well as common targets of criticism and hostility among early Christian preachers. They were also the subject of repeated condemnation by ecclesiastical synods.[41] Novatian, for example, urged Christians to turn away from dissolute theatres to the much more magnificent theatre of creation and Salvation history.[42] Basil of Caesarea himself likewise deemed theatres "full of impure sights" and therefore "common schools of vice". Instead, he summoned his flock, "shall we not rather stand round the vast and varied workshop of divine creation and, carried back in mind to the times of old, shall we not view all the order of creation?"[43]

More characteristically, the amphitheatre metaphor conjured up the global, synoptic vision that Basil aimed at conveying to his audience—"we propose to study the world as a whole".[44] Setting his audience in the midst and yet at the same time above the earthly stage, the Cappadocian presented the six days of creation as a continuously unfolding revelation, from the lifting of the veil of waters and darkness enveloping the earth at the beginning of Genesis to its clothing in a "brilliant garment" of vegetation.[45]

In his Second Theological Oration, Gregory of Nazianzus likewise presented his audience with a sweeping overview of the terrestrial surface and invited them to:

> Traverse the length and breadth of earth, the common mother of all, and the gulfs of the sea bound together with one another and with the land, and the beautiful forests, and the rivers and springs abundant and perennial, not only of waters cold and fit for drinking, and on the surface of the earth [...] Tell me how and whence are these things? What is this great web unwrought by art?[46]

Only from an imaginary elevated spot could the web come into view as a whole and patterns of connection start to emerge (like the threads of human lives surveyed from Marcus Aurelius' imaginary watchtower). For the Cappadocians, beauty lay in these very interconnections, or rather, in the realization that all things, from the most majestic natural feature to the tiniest grain of sand, were

---

41 On the Church's attitude towards theatre, see von Balthasar 1988, 89–105.
42 Ibid. 95.
43 Basil of Caesarea, *Hexaemeron* 4.1 Jackson.
44 Ibid. 6.1.
45 Ibid. 5.2.
46 Gregory of Nazianzus, *Second Oration* 26 Schaff & Wace.

there for a purpose and as part of the same God-created whole—like inextricable threads of a giant tapestry imprinted with the face of its Creator:

> He welded all the diverse parts of the universe by links of indissoluble attachment and established between them so perfect a fellowship and harmony that the most distant, in spite of their distance, appeared united in one universal sympathy.[47]

While encouraging the close observation of natural phenomena, Basil of Caesarea was nonetheless conscious of the limits of human vision. Ironically, in order to demonstrate such limits, he, once again, turned to high places—this time to reverse the ancient myth of the κατάσκοπος. From the top of a high mountain, the hierarch noted, the ploughmen in the valley appear as tiny as ants and the sails of a large ship "smaller than a dove". This, he argued, has to do with the weakness of vision, for "sight [...] loses itself in the air, becomes weak and cannot seize with exactness the object which it sees". Likewise, high mountains intersected by valleys appear rounded and smooth, because sight "reaches only to the salient parts, and is not able, on account of its weakness, to penetrate into the valleys which separate them. It does not even preserve the form of objects, and thinks that all square towers are round". Thus, Basil concluded, "all proves that at a great distance sight only presents to us obscure and confused objects".[48]

Rather than an object of aesthetic contemplation bound to human vision and the other human senses, Basil of Caesarea challenged his audience to see creation through the eyes of God, to see it, that is, holistically and for the end for which it was created—for the union of all things in the person of his incarnate Son.[49] As opposed to the fallible eyes and limited field of vision of humans, Basil explained, "God's eye never sleeps", but "watches over all".[50] In

---

47　Basil of Caesarea, *Hexaemeron* 2.2 cf. 1.7.
48　Basil of Caesarea, *Hexaemeron* 6.9. Basil recognized "the limitations of the human condition when he asserted that the most difficult of sciences is to know oneself, since our eye cannot see itself and our mind is slow to recognize its own faults" (de Beer 2015, 20).
49　As he explained, God does not form the same idea of beauty that we do: "It is not with eyes that the Creator views the beauty of His works. He contemplates them in His ineffable wisdom. A fair sight is the sea all bright in a settled calm; fair too, when, ruffled by a light breeze of wind, its surface shows tints of purple and azure,—when, instead of lashing with violence the neighbouring shores, it seems to kiss them with peaceful caresses. However, it is not in this that Scripture makes God find the goodness and charm of the sea. Here it is the purpose of the work which makes the goodness" (Basil of Caesarea, *Hexaemeron* 4.6 cf. 3.10 Jackson).
50　Ibid. 7.5. Cf. Athanasios of Alexandria, *Contra Gentes*, 3.3.

the 'amphitheatre of creation', Basil's addressees were to be no mere spectators, but active participants. It was not enough for Christians to remain detached κατάσκοποι, or onlookers, Basil argued. Rather, embracing their limits, they had to become fellow combatants (συναγωνισταί) committed to the investigation (ἐξέτασις) and contemplation (θεωρία) of the mysteries of the cosmos and the discovery of truth:

> To investigate the great and prodigious show of creation, to understand supreme and ineffable wisdom, you must bring personal light for the contemplation of the wonders which I spread before your eyes, and help me, according to your power, in this struggle.[51]

Like the interpretation of Scripture (θεωρία γραφική), the contemplation of nature (θεωρία φυσική) required more than sight. It demanded existential and ascetical discipline.

> Christians are to engross themselves in creation as though they were in the middle of a grand contest or drama still unfolding in time and space. Wonder and admiration do not suffice. They must be players, engaged participants, in solidarity not only with Basil himself, their guide, but with the Creator who intends every intricate detail of the world—like every detail in the scriptural text—to reveal his gracious and providential purposes.[52]

3   The Theatre of Salvation

For the Greek Church Fathers θεωρία φυσική and θεωρία γραφική were deeply interwoven. According to Maximos the Confessor, creation was a Bible whose letters and syllables were the particular aspects of creatures and whose words were the more universal aspects of creation. After Gregory of Nazianzus, Maximos emphasized how the visible physical phenomena were "naturally interconnected so that the harmonious web of the universe is contained within it like the various elements in a book".[53] Conversely, Scripture was like a cosmos constituted of heaven and earth "and what comes between them, by

---

51 Basil of Caesarea, *Hexaemeron* 6.1 Jackson.
52 Blowers 2009, 147.
53 Maximos the Confessor, *Ambiguum* 10.18 Constas. On the book of nature metaphor in Maximos and previous writers, see Constas 2018, 30–32.

which I mean ethical, natural, and the theological philosophy, proclaiming the ineffable power of the One who has spoken through it".[54]

God, argued Maximos, "educates us first of all using the picture book of nature; then, when we are older, he uses the play of Holy Scripture to lead us to true insight into the Divine".[55] In both cases, θεωρία was essentially visionary; it presupposed that "the Bible in its totality points towards an overarching objective or σκοπός, the fullness of the revelation of God in Jesus Christ".[56] Composed of the words θέα ('view') and ὁρᾶν ('to see'), θεωρία implied a broad, unified vision of things; a comprehensive view from above that enabled the detection of the deep structures of cosmos and Scripture as "economies of revelation".[57] It is therefore not surprising that theatrical metaphors, including Maximos' "God's play", were often used with reference to Salvation history—and to human life itself.

In spite of the Church's adversity to theatre, the Stoic motif of the 'world theatre' repeatedly appears in Patristic writing, whether to illustrate the world's futility[58] or to justify the sufferings the wise man has to endure to "faultlessly play the role God has given him in the drama of life".[59] However, unlike pagan world stages watched upon by amused goddesses and detached philosophers untroubled by the actions of their fellow men, the Christian world theatre implied, and emphasized, an inversion between the place occupied by the actors and that of the impassible κατάσκοπος watching from above. For Clement of Alexandria, for example, "the celestial Word, the true athlete", had stepped onto the stage to be "crowned in the theatre of the whole universe".[60]

Others stressed the inversion of human roles after death: while on the earthly stage the righteous were exposed to the gaze of fellow-men spectators who enjoyed the tragedy of their martyrdom as if it were a comedy, in heaven they would watch down on the eternal torments of their former godless spectators. "If a man has insulted you unjustly", John Chrysostom wrote, "you ought not to grieve at all but to pity him: [you will be derided by spectators on earth, but praised by spectators in heaven] [...] delight yourself in the theatre of heaven. For there all will praise and applaud and welcome you".[61] Here

---

54 Maximos the Confessor, *Ambiguum* 10.18 Constas; see also 10.30–31.
55 Balthasar 1988, 156 (see *Ambiguum* 71.7).
56 Blowers 2009, 150.
57 Ibid.
58 See, for example, John Chrysostom, *Second Homily on Lazarus*.
59 Clement of Alexandria, *Stromata* 7.11.65, cited in von Balthasar 1988, 156.
60 Clement of Alexandria, *Exhortation to the Heaten* 1 Roberts et al.
61 John Chrysostom, *Homily on the Gospel of John* 17.36. Cited in Christian 1987, 36. Other examples are discussed in Balthasar 1988, 151–55.

one is reminded of Paul's words to the Corinthians, whereby the apostles are said to be "made a spectacle unto the world, and to angels, and to men" (1 Cor. 4:9). Elsewhere in Paul's letters, the whole community is brought on stage and made "a gazingstock (θεατριζόμενοι) both by reproaches and afflictions" and yet reminded that "ye have in heaven a better and an enduring substance" (Heb. 10:32–34). Faithful are therefore invited to "enter the holy places by the blood of Jesus, by the new and living way that he opened for us through the curtain [of the Temple], that is, through his flesh" (Heb. 10:19–20).

John Chrysostom nonetheless pushed the theatrical metaphor further. He appropriated the language and imagery of the popular theatre in order to draw people to the heavenly theatre.[62] In the introduction to his homilies on the Gospel of Saint John, for example, he juxtaposes eager spectators rushing to the theatre to watch a distinguished athlete, musician or rhetorician to the audience of the evangelist, "whose stage is heaven and whose theatre is the inhabitable earth". Interestingly, here sight turns into sound, and the view from above into a reverberation filling the entire universe:

> If in the case of rhetoricians, musicians, and athletes, people sit in the one case to look on, in the other to see at once and to listen with such earnest attention; what zeal, what earnestness ought ye in reason to display, when it is no musician or debater who now comes forward to a trial of skill, but when a man is speaking from heaven, and utters a voice plainer than thunder? For he has pervaded the whole earth with the sound; and occupied and filled it, not by the loudness of the cry, but by moving his tongue with the grace of God.[63]

Were the faithful ready to receive and keep the evangelist's words, argues John Chrysostom, "they could no longer be mere men nor remain upon the earth, but would take their stand above all the things of this life, and having adapted themselves to the condition of angels, would dwell on earth just as if it were heaven".[64] But the world's reality is different. In order to convey its misery, in another homily Chrysostom turns to the Stoic κατάσκοπος:

> For if anyone could, as though seated on the highest bench of a theatre, look down upon all the world—or rather, if you will, let us for the present

---

62 Rylaarsdam 2014, 229–30.
63 John Chrysostom, *Homilies on the Gospel of John* 1.1–2 Schaff & Wace.
64 Ibid.

THE WORLD FROM ABOVE 87

take in hand a single city—if then a man seated on an elevated spot could take in at a glance all the doings of the men there, consider what folly he would condemn, what tears he would weep, what laughter he would laugh, with what hatred he would hate; for we commit such actions as deserve both laughter, and the charge of folly, and tears, and hatred.[65]

Unlike Stoic and other pagan world stages, the Christian theatre of life, however, was not a space the actor simply exited, having finished to play his or her role. It was rather the preamble to another theatre—the heavenly theatre of eternal life. "Now if you look to that theatre, learn what crowns are there, transport yourself into the applause which comes hence", argues John Chrysostom, "never will earthly things be able to hold you; neither when they come will you deem them great, nor when they are away seek after them".[66] Unlike the Stoic κατάσκοπος, the true Christian was not simply meant to gaze at the foolishness and misery of humans from high, but to re-direct the gaze upwards, to that other theatre, and inwards, that is, to his or her own soul and conscience. According to Chrysostom, poverty and wealth were but the masks of present life.[67] It was only at the moment of death, having "quit the theatre of life", that all masks would be stripped away and each man would be judged by his works alone. "Pull off [the] mask, explore [the] conscience, enter into [the] mind".[68]

4   Spiritual Watchtowers

Applied to spiritual life, κατασκοπή conjured up further spatial metaphors and symbolic geographies. Unlike θέατρον and θεωρία, which suggest a broad, general view and therefore the contemplation of universals, κατασκοπή enshrines a sense of closer inspection, as well as of 'keeping watch'.[69] In this latter sense, it was used by Maximos the Confessor in connection with ascetic practice. Maximos related the word to the etymology of Joppa, the city where Peter had his vision (Acts 11:1–18). In his words,

---

65   Ibid. 82.4.
66   Ibid. 17.36.
67   Cf. also e.g. Lucian, *Timon the Misanthrope*.
68   John Chrysostom, *Homily on Lazarus* 2.3 Allen. The passage is discussed in Christian 1987, 35.
69   From the verb σκοπεύω, which indicates the contemplation of particulars (Liddell & Scott 1977).

'Joppa' means 'observation' (κατασκοπή) and signifies the guarding of the mind appropriate to those engaged in the practice of asceticism. Located near the shore of the sea, such a city, were it not located on a height, would be struck by many waves. From this it seems to me that it points to the one who builds virtue, as if it were a city, upon the height of knowledge. Such a person is not far from involuntary trials, and—having nearby and next to him, just like the sea, an attachment to sense perception that he has not yet completely beaten back,—he is in need of observation. Otherwise, the unclean demons, slipping in undetected through involuntary trials, will launch a sudden attack of voluntary passions against him.[70]

Maximos then contrasts the topography of Joppa with that of Zion, "the watchtower oriented with a view toward peace". While the former city overlooks the troubled sea from the height of its coastal location, the latter is far removed from it. Hence, unlike the ascetic battered by the waves of temptation, the one living on Zion, "while on the height of knowledge, observes solely the intelligible visions of beings" and "receives the impressions of divine realities". Anyone dwelling in Joppa, Maximos the Confessor therefore concludes, "is devoted to the practical life of asceticism, carefully observing the traps of the opposing powers, while the one who makes his home in Zion is a man of knowledge, contemplating in his intellect solely the beauty of divine visions".[71]

The watchtower metaphor was part of the complex spiritual topography of Salvation history, with its economy of revelation through prophecy and symbols. Watchtowers feature in the Old Testament as sites revealing devastating views, as well as prophetic visions.[72] Here the gaze of the beholder is not passively fixed on the spectacle underneath, as in a theatre, but actively scans the horizon; it is pushed to a distance, like the gaze of Moses standing on Mount Nebo as he contemplates a view of the Promised Land unfolding in different directions (Deut. 34:1–4). Most notably, the prophet Habakkuk is said to have stood on his watchtower and "watched to see" what God would say to him (Hab. 2:1). He thus foresaw the freeing of Israel and the return from Babylon. In a homily that became closely associated with Easter symbolism in Byzantium, Gregory of Nazianzus interpreted the prophecy as foretelling the Resurrection of Christ and the victory over death:

---

70 Maximos the Confessor, *Reponses to Thalassios* 27.7, Constas.
71 Ibid. 27.8.
72 See, for example, Habakkuk 2:1; Isaiah 21:8, 32:14; 2 Chronicles 20:24.

> Well, I have taken my stand, and looked forth; and behold a man riding on the clouds and he is very high, and his countenance is as the countenance of Angel, and his vesture as the brightness of piercing lightning; and he lifts his hand toward the East, and cries with a loud voice. His voice is like the voice of a trumpet; and round about Him is as it were a multitude of the Heavenly Host; and he saith, Today is salvation come unto the world, to that which is visible, and to that which is invisible. Christ is risen from the dead, rise ye with Him.[73]

The watchtower is thus not simply an elevated spot but the solid rock of faith which shall enable the faithful to push their gaze further and see the light of the Resurrection.

After Gregory of Nazianzus, Maximos also called Joppa "the watchtower of happiness" which Jonah abandoned for the "sea of sorrow".[74] Swallowed by the whale but not destroyed, the prophet was delivered on the third day, like Christ rising from the belly of Hades.[75] The Confessor identifies in the flight from the watchtower "the nature of human beings perpetually fleeing from Joppa, like Adam from paradise on account of his disobedience, fleeing, that is, from the stable habit of virtue and knowledge and the wisdom".[76] At this point, the gaze plunges from the safe height of the watchtower into the abyss:

> In this sea of sin, human nature preoccupies itself closely with the instability of material things, and thus it both bears and is borne about on the ever-shifting tides of deceit and confusion. Those who remain in this ocean of confusion gain nothing except to be dragged down into its depths and swallowed by the whale with water poured around them up

---

[73] Gregory of Nazianzus, *Second Oration for Easter* 1 Richardson. On the Byzantine reception of the prophecy, see Pentcheva 2000, 139–53; Papamastoraki 2001, 179–80, 232–35. In the first stanza of the fourth ode of the Easter Canon, John of Damascus invokes the passage to announce the Lord's Resurrection: Ἐπὶ τῆς θείας φυλακῆς, ὁ θεηγόρος Ἀββακοὺμ, στήτω μεθ' ἡμῶν, καὶ δεικνύτω, φαεσφόρον ἄγγελον, διαπρυσίως λέγοντα· σήμερον σωτηρία τῷ κόσμῳ ὅτι ἀνέστη Χριστὸς ὡς παντοδύναμος (Apostolikē Diakonia Ekklēsias Hellados 1960).

[74] According to Gregory of Nazianzus, when Jonah saw the falling away of Israel, "he left the watchtower of joy, for this is the meaning of Joppa in Hebrew, I mean his former dignity and reputation, and flung himself into the deep of sorrow: and hence he is tempest-tossed, and falls asleep, and is wrecked, and aroused from sleep, and taken by lot, and confesses his flight, and is cast into sea, and swallowed, but not destroyed, by the whale; but there he calls upon God, and, marvellous as it is, on the third day he, like Christ, is delivered" (Gregory of Nazianzus, *Oration* 2.109).

[75] The prophecy is read on Saturday morning of Holy Week.

[76] Maximos the Confessor, *Responses to Thalassios* 64.5 Constas.

to the soul, encompassed by the final abyss, with their heads submerged to the clefts of the mountains, and going down into the earth, whose bars eternal barriers.[77]

The 'sea of life', with its adversities and perils, was a recurrent topos in Patristic literature, especially in the writings of Gregory of Nazianzus, who, in his youth, risked his life in a storm while sailing from Alexandria to Athens.[78] Observed from an elevated spot, the sea (like the theatrical stage) metaphorically conveyed the utter instability of human life, as well as its many dangers, passions, and temptations. "I was walking alone, just as the sun was setting", writes Gregory, as he recounts one of his contemplative retreats in the wilds of Pontus.

> My path led me to a promontory [...] As my feet moved along, my gaze was fixed upon the sea. It was not a pleasant sight [...] some of the waves were raised up far out and crested for a moment, then broke and dispersed themselves quietly along the headlands; but others crashed against nearby rocks and were beaten into frothy foam and sprayed high in the air. Then pebbles and seaweed and trumpet shells and tiny oysters were churned up and scattered about; some of them were drawn back again, as the wave receded, but the rocks themselves were unshaken, immovable [...] Surely, I said to myself, is not the sea our life and all our human affairs—since so much about them is salty and unstable? And are not the winds the trials and unforeseen events that fall upon us? [...] When people undergo some trials, some always seem to me to be swept away like things without weight [...] Others seem like the rock, worthy of that Rock on whom we stand and whom we worship.[79]

As with the Scriptural city of Joppa, Gregory's firsthand contemplation of the marine scene from the height of the promontory reveals a spiritual map. It enables the hierarch to survey human life from a safe distance, or, in his own words, to "lift up [his] mind for a little, above changeable things". The metaphor was further elaborated by John Chrysostom as he described the righteous soul's departure from life. To the righteous, argued the hierarch, the transition from life to death is sweeter than life itself,

---

77   Ibid. 64.5.
78   See Gregory of Nazianzus, *On His Life*. Uses of sea metaphors are also found in *Oration* 42.20.
79   Gregory of Nazianzus, *Oration* 26.8.

> For as when one has climbed to the top of a cliff and gazes on the sea and those who are sailing upon it, he sees some being washed by the waves, others running upon hidden rocks, some hurrying in one direction, others being driven in another, like prisoners, by the force of the gale, many actually in the water, some of them using their hands only in the place of a boat and a rudder, and many drifting along upon a single plank, or some fragment of the vessel, others floating dead, a scene of manifold and various disaster; even so he who is engaged in the service of Christ drawing himself out of the turmoil and stormy billows of life takes his seat upon secure and lofty ground. For what position can be loftier or more secure than that in which a man has only one anxiety 'How he ought to please God?'[80]

Unlike Stoic *somnia*, the Patristic κατάσκοπος is not simply lifted up in the air, but is solidly stationed on "secure and lofty ground", on an unshakable watchtower; on the solid rock of faith.

This motif appears again centuries later in the life of Saint Basil the Younger (first half of the tenth century). This time, however, the κατάσκοπος is not set above the 'sea of life', but he is confronted with the even more frightening spectacle of Christ's Second Coming. Basil enabled his disciple and biographer Gregory to access the realm of the afterlife and explore its complex topographies in nocturnal visions.[81] In one of these visions, Gregory is led by an angel to a watchtower situated on the top of a lofty hill. From that privileged spot Gregory is offered nothing less than a bird's-eye view of the Second Coming in the fashion of Saint John's Revelation:

> Climbing up onto [the watchtower] and from there looking around [Rev. 21:10], to the east, we saw a most fearsome plain below the mountain, its surface strewn sevenfold with pure gold and adorned with incomparable splendour. [...] And the air was filled with a wondrous radiance and ineffable rejoicing, and we did not clearly see its upper regions as before.[82]

---

80 John Chrysostom, *Epistle 2 to Demetrius* Schaff & Wace.
81 While pre-iconoclast hagiographies hardly talked about the saints' lives after their deaths, in the tenth and eleventh centuries saints were conducted on 'tours' through hell, paradise, and the City of Christ, where they met biblical and contemporary figures. A notable example is the vision of tenth-century monk Kosmas (Angelidi 1983). See also Gerstel 2002 and Patlagean 1981.
82 *The Life of Saint Basil the Younger* 4.10 Sullivan et al.

At this point the gaze of the κατάσκοπος suddenly turns upwards. As the radiance dissolves, Gregory sees a giant awe-inspiring city, the Celestial Jerusalem, "its magnitude like the circumference of the firmament of the heavens".[83] Gregory's gaze shifts again, while scenes of salvation and damnation parade one after the other under his feet. Above the mobile eye of the κατάσκοπος is the all-seeing Lord, who "continued to gaze in His anger directly at the whole surface of the earth and saw it and observed all those upon it, and it was very defiled by the multitudinous sins of the sons of men".[84]

Everything is in flux, except for the solitary watchtower on which Gregory and the angel are standing: "Everything beneath us fled and it alone stood unshaken in the air".[85] The landscape is continuously transforming, like the waves tossing the coast of Joppa or the stormy waters Gregory of Nazianzus and John Chrysostom contemplated from the height of their promontories. The cosmic drama culminates with the creation of a new earth and a new heaven destined to the meek; an earth upon which "there were no mountains rising up, nor descending chasms, nor level plains, but that entire earth appeared in a uniform state and condition from one end to the other, and there was no concealed place in it".[86] At this point, Gregory's description turns into a sort of anti-*Hexaemeron*. As the Lord gazes at the smooth, translucent surface of this new earth, wondrous plants spring out one after the other, disclosing their sweetest aromas and beautiful features; as he gazes again, rivers of milk and honey bubble up; a further gaze results in the creation of sparrows, which fly in from the east singing beautiful melodies. The renewed earth becomes a giant Garden of Eden.

∙ ∙ ∙

The aerial view has historically held a unique appeal to the human senses and imagination as well as a unique capacity to produce moral spatialities. For generations of ancient thinkers, the displacement from the ground to look back at terrestrial life produced the detachment necessary to, literally, put the world into perspective and judge human conduct accordingly. There are, however, significant differences between the Stoic and the Patristic κατάσκοπος. To start with, the Christian κατάσκοπος of Patristic and Byzantine apocalyptic literature was usually not a detached master of space. From Basil the Great's

---

83   Ibid. 4.10.
84   Ibid. 5.3.
85   Ibid. 5.3.
86   Ibid. 5.12.

'amphitheatre of creation' to the apocalyptic visions in the life of Basil the Younger, the viewer was at once elevated over the scene and immersed in it. His gaze was not a gaze fixed on the worldly stage, but it was rather a mobile, participatory gaze turned upwards (whether to the starry vault of heaven or to the heavenly Jerusalem) as well as downwards. It was a dynamic gaze that always pushed to the horizon of eternal life.

Secondly, the stage on which the human play was enacted was no mere backdrop. The theatre of creation was intrinsically connected with the theatre of Salvation history. As God's handiwork, nature was inherently sacramental. Conversely, as incarnate spirit, humans were unable to grasp pure spirit; they had to use "the screen of a visible form", of symbols.[87] For the Greek Church Fathers and their Byzantine successors, nature was thus an interface, or a vast reservoir of familiar symbols through which the Creator revealed Himself to humans. God had spoken to the Hebrews through "the burning bush, the rock that gushed with water, the jar of manna, the fire from God that came down from the altar".[88] He continued to speak to humans through His works, which Basil called "visible memorials of His wonders", and it is within, this complex economy of spatialized symbols that Patristic views from above ought to be considered.[89] Read through the veiled language of Scripture and surveyed from the height of a sea promontory, or a lofty watchtower, landscape unfolded valuable spiritual maps to the Greek Fathers and their audience, as illustrated by the vivid topographic imagery employed by the Cappadocians and Maximos.

While in early Patristic literature κατασκοπή featured as an effective instrument for conveying different modes of spiritual insight (whether φυσική or γραφική), views from above are nonetheless conspicuously absent from medieval hagiographic accounts. The apocalyptic view from the watchtower in the life of Saint Basil the Younger is a very unusual instance. This does not mean that Byzantines had stopped enjoying elevated views. On the contrary, well into the tenth century, fortified towers were being used both as military defences and look-out points intended to provide aesthetic pleasure, and remarkable descriptions of views from these and other buildings have survived.[90] With

---

87   Staniloae 1981, 131. On the intrinsic link between human embodiment and space, see also the introduction to this volume.
88   John of Damascus, *On the Divine Images* Anderson.
89   Basil of Caesarea, *Oration* 8.8.
90   For example, John Geometres' poem on one of the towers on the walls of Constantinople, or Nicholas Mesarites' famous description of the Church of the Holy Apostles commanding wide views on the sea (Maguire 1994); Nicholas Mesarites, *Description of the Church of the Holy Apostles* Downey 864.

some rare exceptions, to holy men and women and to their biographers, however, scenic views would have probably appeared as mundane distractions from inner contemplation in a way not too dissimilar from Christ's view from the Mount of Temptation.[91] After all, on Sinai, Moses encountered God in darkness (Exod. 19:18)—beyond words and knowledge, beyond landscape and vision.

Bibliography

Primary Sources

Apostolikē Diakonia Ekklesias Hellados, *Triōdion*. Athens 1960.

Basil of Caesarea, *Hexaemeron*. Eds P. Schaff & H. Wace, *Nicene and Post-Nicene Fathers: Second Series*, vol. 8. Tr. B. Jackson. Buffalo, NY 1895.

Cicero, *Somnium Scipionis: The Dream of Scipio Africanus Minor, Being the Epilogue of Cicero's Treatise on Polity*. Tr. W. D. Pearman. Cambridge 1883.

Clement of Alexandria, *Exhortation to the Heathen*. Ed. A. Roberts et. al., *Ante-Nicene Fathers*, vol. 2. Buffalo, NY 1885.

Egeria, *Travels*. Ed. J. Wilkinson. Oxford 2006.

Gregory of Nazianzus, *Second Oration*. Eds P. Schaff & H. Wace, *Nicene and Post-Nicene Fathers: Second Series*, vol. 7. Tr. E. Richardson. Buffalo, NY 1894.

John Chrysostom, *Four Discourses, Chiefly on the Parable of the Rich Man and Lazarus*. Tr. F. Allen. London 1869.

John Chrysostom, *Homilies on the Gospel of St Matthew*. Ed. P. Schaff & H. Wace, *Nicene and Post-Nicene Fathers: First Series*, vol. 10. Tr. G. Prevost & M. B. Riddle. Buffalo, NY 1888.

John of Damascus, *On the Divine Images*. Ed. & tr. D. Anderson. Crestwood, NY 1997.

---

91 Or, in Maximos' words, "having broken all ties between his intellect and sensible objects" (*Ambiguum* 10.22 Constas). As a result, even saints' biographies signposted by mountain ascents, such as those of Lazaros of Galesion (of Mount Argeas), Maximos the Hutburner and Euthymios the Georgian (of Mount Athos) and Athanasios of Meteora (of Platys Lithos), are totally devoid of scenic views (see, for example, *Vita Lazari* 25 Greenfield). See also chapter 9 of the vita of Maximos the Hutburner by Theophanes (Greenfield & Talbot 2016). On Athanasios' ascent of Platys Lithos, see Lambros 1905, 72–73. Alice-Mary Talbot mentions some rare exceptions to the norm, but concludes that for the most part "the solitaries in search of spiritual tranquility deliberately disregarded the beauties of nature that surrounded them and turned inward in their search for conversation with God", though it is also possible that "it was their hagiographers who sought to emphasize holy men's focus on interior contemplation, rather than taking pleasure in the natural world" (Talbot 2019, 141–43).

Lucian, *Selected Dialogues*. Ed. & tr. C. D. N. Costa. Oxford 2005.
Marcus Aurelius, *Meditations*. Ed. & tr. M. Staniford. Harmondsworth 1964.
Maximos the Confessor, *On Difficulties in Sacred Scripture: The Responses to Thalassios*. Ed. & tr. Fr. M. Constas. Washington, D.C. 2018.
Maximos the Confessor, *On the Difficulties in the Church Fathers*, vol. 1. Ed. & tr. N. Constas. Washington, D.C. 2014.
Nicholas Mesarites, *Description of the Church of the Holy Apostles at Constantinople*. Ed. & tr. G. Downey, *Transactions of the American Philosophical Society, New Series* 47 (1957) 855–924.
Plato, *Phaedo*. Tr. D. Gallop. Oxford 1975.
Pliny the Younger, *The Letters of Pliny the Younger*. Tr. W. Melmoth. Cambridge, MA 1909.
Pseudo-Callisthenes, *The Greek Alexander Romance*. Tr. R. Stoneman. London & New York 1991.
Symboulai eis tēn istorian tōn monōn tōn Meteōrōn. Ed. S. Lambros, *Neos Ellēnomnēmōn* 2 1905.
The Life of Lazaros of Mt. Galesion: An Eleventh-Century Pillar Saint. Ed. & tr. R. Greenfield. Washington, D.C. 2000.
The Life of Saint Basil the Younger. Ed. & tr. D. Sullivan, A. M. Talbot & S. McGrath. Washington, D.C. 2014.
Theophanes, *Life of Maximos the Hutburner*. Tr. A. M. Talbot, *Holy Men of Mount Athos*. Ed. R. Greenfield & A. M. Talbot. Washington, D.C. 2016.

Secondary Sources

Angelidi, C. 1983. "La version longue de la vision du moine Kosmas", *Analecta Bollandiana Bruxelles* 101, 73–99.
Blowers, P. 2009. "'Entering This Sublime and Blessed Amphitheatre': Contemplation of Nature and Interpretation of the Bible in the Patristic Period", in S. Mandelbrote & J. van der Meer (eds), *Nature and Scripture in the Abrahamic Tradition*. Leiden, 148–76.
Christian, L. 1987. *Theatrum Mundi: The History of an Idea*. NY & London.
Constas, Fr. M. 2018. "Introduction", in Fr. M. Constas (ed. and trans.), *On Difficulties in Sacred Scripture: The Responses to Thalassios*. Washington, D.C., 3–60.
Cosgrove, D. 2001. *Apollo's Eye: A Cartographic Genealogy of the Earth in the Western Imagination*. Baltimore & London.
Cosgrove, D. 2003. "Globalism and Tolerance in Early Modern Geography", *Annals of the Association of American Geographers* 93, 852–70.
de Beer, W. 2015. "The Patristic Understanding of the Six Days (Hexaemeron)", *Journal of Early Christian History* 5, 3–23.
de Jong, I. 2012. *Space in Ancient Greek Literature: Studies in Ancient Greek Narrative*. Leiden & Boston.

Gerstel, S. 2002. "The Sins of the Farmer: Illustrating Village Life (and Death) in Medieval Byzantium", in J. Contreni & S. Casciani (eds), *Word, Image, Number: Communication in the Middle Ages*. Tavernuzze, FI, 205–17.

Hijmans, B. L. 1966. "Drama in Seneca's Stoicism", *Transactions and Proceedings of the American Philological Association* 97, 237–51.

Liddell, H. & R. Scott 1977. *Lexikou tēs Ellēnikēs glōssēs*. Athens.

Littlewood, A. R. 1992. "Gardens of Byzantium", *Journal of Garden History* 12, 126–53.

Maguire, H. 1994. "The Beauty of Castles: A Tenth Century Description of a Tower at Constantinople", *DChAE* 17, 21–24.

Maguire, H. 2000. "Gardens and Parks in Constantinople", *DOP* 54, 251–64.

Maguire, H. 2002. "Paradise Withdrawn", in A. Littlewood et al. (eds), *Image and Imagination in Byzantine Art*. Aldershot, 23–35.

Mavian, L. 1992. "Il ruolo della mitologia nella percezione della natura e nell'organizzazione delle sue risorse: luoghi mitici o illustri", in Y. Luginbuhl (ed.), *Il paesaggio mediterraneo*. Milan, 36–41.

McNeill, J. R. 1992. *The Mountains of the Mediterranean World: An Environmental History*. Cambridge.

Papamastorakē, T. 2001. *Diakosmos troulou*. Athens.

Patlagean, E. 1981. "Byzance et son autre monde: Observations sur quelques recits" *Faire Croire. Collection de l'École Françoise de Rome* 51, 201–21.

Pattenden, P. 1983. "The Byzantine Early Warning System", *Byzantion* 53, 258–99.

Pearsall, D. & E. Salter 1973. *Landscapes and Seasons of the Medieval World*. London.

Peatfield, A. 1983. "The Topography of Minoan Peak Sanctuaries", *Annual of the British School of Athens* 78, 273–79.

Pentcheva, B. 2000. "Imagined Images: Visions of Salvation and Intercession in a Double-Sided Icon from Poganovo", *DOP* 54, 139–53.

Purves, A. 2010. *Space and Time in Ancient Greek Narrative*. Cambridge.

Rossiter, J. 1989. "Roman Villas in the Greek East and the Villa in Gregory of Nyssa Ep. 20", *Journal of Roman Archaeology* 2, 101–10.

Rylaarsdam, D. 2014. *John Chrysostom on Divine Pedagogy: The Coherence of His Theology and Preaching*. Oxford.

Schmidt, V. 1995. *A Legend and Its Image: The Aerial Flight of Alexander the Great in Medieval Art*. Groningen.

Semple, E. C. 1932. *The Geography of the Mediterranean Region: Its Relation to Ancient History*. London.

Staniloae, D. 1981. *Theology and the Church*. Crestwood, NY.

Talbot, A. M. 2019. *Varieties of Monastic Experience in Byzantium, 800–1453*. Notre Dame, IN.

Thalmann, W. 2011. *Apollonius of Rhodes and the Spaces of Hellenism*. Oxford.

Theoktistos Docheiaritēs, Fr. 2006. "Archaios kosmos stē Monē Docheiariou", in Athanasiadēs (ed.), *Aghion Oros kai prōchristianikē archaiotēta*. Thessaloniki, 89–100.

Tolias, G. 2011. *Mapping Greece, 1420–1800: A History. Maps in the Margarita Samourkas Collection.* Houten.

Tozer, H. F. 1897. *A History of Ancient Geography.* Cambridge.

von Balthasar, U. H. 1988. *Theo-Drama: Theological Dramatic Theory*, vol. 1: Prolegomena. San Francisco.

von Humboldt, A. 1997 (1858). *Cosmos: A Sketch of the Physical Description of the Universe.* Tr. E. Otté, vol. 2. Baltimore & London.

Wallace-Hadrill, D. S. 1968. *The Greek Patristic View of Nature.* New York.

Space and Identity, a Located Negotiation
A Case Study on Mobile Bodies in Byzantine Hagiography

Myrto Veikou

"Every story is a travel story—a spatial practice", wrote Michel de Certeau in 1980, arguing that spatial practices involving mobility affect our everyday-life experience and our 'knowledge' of power structures.[1] Before him, Henri Lefebvre and Michel Foucault had already talked about purposeful creations and subjective experiences of human spaces through cultural practices, seen within a context of a critique of every-day life.[2] Various later spatial theories including Edward Soja's *thirdspace*, Doreen Massey's elusive *time-spaces* of power relations and Nigel Thrift's *non-representational theory* built on these notions of spatial productions and experiences by substantiating them as iterative and discursive processes.[3] Edward Soja explained how space hides power relations: "We must be insistently aware of how space can be made to hide consequences from us, how relations of power and discipline are inscribed into the apparently innocent spatiality of social life, how human geographies become filled with politics and ideology".[4] Doreen Massey widened this scope: "Space is the product of the intricacies and the complexities, the interlockings and the non-interlockings, of relations from the unimaginably cosmic to the intimately tiny. And precisely because it is the product of relations, which are active practices [...] space is always in a process of becoming. It is always being made".[5]

Several of these geographic issues and their relevance to the study of Byzantine cultures are discussed in the introduction of this volume. In this chapter, I argue that Byzantine texts allow us to believe that iterative makings of culture through spatial practices, as well as practices of "telling culture" by means of "spatial talking", both precede the explanation of such experiences by twentieth- and twenty-first-century thinkers.[6] With the aim of proving this

---

1 De Certeau 1984, 115.
2 Lefebvre 1947, 1961, 1974; Foucault 1975, 1984.
3 Massey 1995, 2005; Soja 1996, 1999; Thrift 2007.
4 Soja 1989, 6.
5 Massey 1999, 283.
6 Veikou 2018.

point, I base my arguments on the discussion of a Byzantine hagiographical text: the eleventh-century *Life of St Lazaros of Mount Galesion* by Gregory the Cellarer.[7] This work is part of a research project on Byzantine Saints' Lives, which analyses and interprets accounts of everyday-life spatial experiences, and to find ways in which Byzantine spatialities are both reflected in literature and used in narrative strategies.[8] Hagiographical texts encounter the sacred in a number of different locations such as the human body, the church, the cell, the pillar, open nature including the desert etc.; they contain large amounts of topographic definitions of an ever-changing locality of action.[9] One cannot, in fact, help wondering about the need for and the significance of this pronounced spatiality of human agency and its role in these narratives. In a way, asceticism comes as an experience of physical isolation—self-confinement within limited space and ample imagination—yet always in dialogue with the natural and social environment.

The main focus, in this chapter, is on a single narrative function of literary spatiality: in the hagiographical text discussed here, spaces are constantly being performed by the main character in ways as to allow him to negotiate his personal (holy) identity. My textual analysis involves two different tasks: firstly, an examination of how spaces are performed by human actants within the narrative, at the story level; and secondly, a discussion of how these literary 'performed spaces' are used as narrative devices in order to communicate performances and negotiations of identities to the reader.

1   Mobility and Walking

A first striking outcome of the research on spatialities of Byzantine Saints' Lives has been the outstanding amount of relocations and mobility, space constructions and re-constructions in hagiographical texts, as well as the attention drawn in definitions and accounts of spaces. The pages of the *Life of St Lazaros* provide a good visual impression of this mobility: the entire account of their early stages of life is an unending sequence of relocation verbs accompanied by spatial definitions.[10] In fact, the impression of mobility in the plot is

---

7   Gregory, *Life of Lazaros* (BHG 979); English translation by Greenfield 2000.
8   Veikou 2016, 2022.
9   See also chapters 13, 27, 28 of this volume.
10 See also Chapter 26, for a discussion of mobility and walking in Palladios' *Historica Lausiaca*.

so strong, that readers find themselves wishing these men would stay still for a second in the next sentence!

Evidently this was an important narrative device, but what was the purpose? A couple of books have been dedicated to this question. In 1959, Eleanor Ducket first suggested some mutual motives for the saints' wandering: "Release from the world; Solitude for the following of the ways of prayer; A lively seeking for knowledge; A passion for sacrifice and self-denial; A driving concern for the souls of their fellow-men; For these ends they wandered wherever their time called them".[11] More recently, Maribel Dietz named this wandering 'ascetic travel' and considered it as a transcultural feature, a common topos throughout the medieval Mediterranean; as to its significance, she interpreted it as a practical way of visiting living and dead holy people and as a means of religious expression of homelessness and temporal exile.[12] She distinguished one main metaphor in use throughout the texts:

> Monastic travel mirrored an interior journey or quest on both an individual level, the journey of the soul toward God and heavenly Jerusalem, and on the level of the church as a whole, as manifested in Augustine's notion of the City of God's journey on Earth. This mirroring quality of the inward journey attracted many early Christians. Travel was viewed as an imitation of the life of Christ, a literal rendering of the life of a Christian, a life only 'temporarily on this earth'.[13]

Dietz further observed that physical travel also served as a corporeal metaphor for spiritual progress and movement, with the journey itself reflecting the spiritual growth of the traveller.[14]

Here I will build on Dietz's thoughts in order to expand the perception of medieval hagiographical writing by suggesting a slightly different interpretation: that spatiality was employed by the specific *Vita*'s author, Gregory the Cellarer, not only in a metaphorical sense but also as a very efficient, direct link in order to connect with the reader's real-life experience and emotions. As I discuss below, Gregory seems to have used spatiality as a very important narrative method. The latter was intended to communicate typical 'saintly practices' within performances of holiness, in which a person's sanctification experience was built upon his constant discourse and negotiations with local

---

11   Ducket 1959, 27.
12   Dietz 2005.
13   Dietz 2005, 3.
14   Dietz 2005, 3–4.

social environments. On the other hand, becoming holy presupposed asceticism, i.e. an isolation of the ascetic from his social environment. This condition of being apart from—and at the same time in constant discourse with—a community is narrated in spatial terms within the texts. Relocation and spatial mobility of human bodies were used as narrative devices in two ways: firstly, they allowed constructing a process of holiness for the saint's body, by means of a constant selection of place of residence and subsequent construction of personal space. Secondly, they allowed all characters to perform iterative negotiations of identity and difference within the particular storyworlds.

I will now discuss these devices using examples from Lazaros' *Life*. St Lazaros was a famous monk on the Mount Galesion near Ephesos in the eleventh century, his life-story written by Gregory, his disciple and supporter. Born near Magnesia on the Meander, Lazaros set off on an adventurous journey to visit the Holy Land at the age of eighteen thus fulfilling his life-long dream. That was the beginning of twenty-five years of circular wandering across Asia Minor and the Holy Land before returning to his homeland, Ephesos. Despite what one would expect, a new phase of wandering around Ephesos and the nearby Mount Galesion awaited Lazaros back home. If his first, totally intentional, large-scale-wandering phase meant a process of personal education, spiritual improvement and making of a new identity as an ascetic in discourse with his fellow Byzantines, then the second, smaller-scale wandering of Lazaros around Mount Galesion involved a negotiation and performance of his identity as a holy man within the local social environment.

Starting from his first wandering phase, Lazaros travelled to the Holy Land and back, around Asia Minor, visiting renowned pilgrimage sites to worship local saints. And yet, he repeatedly came to places whose inhospitable inhabitants denied him food and water. In a way, relocating his body allowed Lazaros contact with people outside his own community network and offered him wider knowledge of the world. In this process, finding the right refuge for his wandering body was never an easy task for him. Gregory makes Lazaros' selection of place of residence emerge from divine instruction by means of signs associated with the availability of life resources (food, drink) and the attitudes of local people, as in the following passage:

> Ὡς δὲ ἡμέρα ἐγένετο, ἔκρινε μὴ ἐξελθεῖν τῆς κώμης τῇ ἡμέρᾳ ἐκείνῃ, μέχρις ἂν ἡ θεία λειτουργία τελεσθῇ διὰ τὸ τῆς ἡμέρας ἐπίσημον, ἦν γὰρ ἡ μνήμη τῶν τοῦ Χριστοῦ τεσσαράκοντα μαρτύρων, ἅμα δὲ καὶ πρὸς δοκιμὴν τῶν ἐκεῖσε ἀνελεημόνων ἀνθρώπων. Καὶ δὴ τοῦ καιροῦ τῆς λειτουργίας ἐφεστῶτος καὶ τῆς θείας ἱερουργίας τελεσθείσης, οὐδεὶς αὐτῷ κἂν κλάσμα ἄρτου εἰς τροφὴν δέδωκεν. Ὁ δὲ ἰδὼν τὸ τῆς γνώμης αὐτῶν ἀμετάδοτον, οὐκ ἠγανάκτησεν, οὐ

λόγον ὑβριστικὸν κατ' αὐτῶν ἀφῆκεν, ἀλλὰ χεῖρας ἅμα καὶ ὄμματα εἰς οὐρανὸν ἄρας πρὸς τὸν Θεὸν τοιαύτας φωνὰς εὐχαριστηρίους ἀφίει·Κύριε, λέγων, εὐχαριστῶ σοι· ἐὰν δέ με καταξιώσῃς ἐν τόπῳ, ὅπου δηλαδὴ τὸ σὸν θέλημά ἐστι, τὴν κατοίκησιν ποιῆσαι, οὐ μή μου τὸν ἄρτον, ὃν αὐτός μοι ἀποστέλλεις, μόνος φάγωμαι, ἀλλὰ πᾶσι τοῖς πρός με διὰ τὸ σὸν ὄνομα ἐρχομένοις, πλουσίοις τε καὶ πένησιν, εἰς τροφὴν παραθήσω. Καὶ ταῦτα εἰπὼν ἐξῆλθε τῆς κώμης. Μικρὸν δὲ εὐκτήριον ἐγγύς που ἰδών, πρὸς αὐτὸ ἦλθεν· ἐν ᾧ εὗρε μοναχήν τινα καθεζομένην· ἥτις ἰδοῦσα αὐτόν, ἀναστᾶσα καὶ ἄρτον καὶ ὕδωρ αὐτῷ προσκομίσασα ἐποίησεν αὐτὸν τροφῆς μεταλαβεῖν. Μεταλαβὼν οὖν τροφῆς καὶ τῷ Θεῷ εὐχαριστήσας, καὶ γὰρ πάντα εἰς δόξαν Θεοῦ ἐποίει καὶ εἴ τι ἂν συνέβαινε τούτῳ, εἴτε λυπηρὸν εἴτε χαροποιόν, ἀφορμὴ αὐτῷ τῆς πρὸς Θεὸν εὐχαριστίας ἐγίνετο, εἶτα καὶ τὴν μονάζουσαν εὐξάμενος τὴν ὁδὸν ἐστέλλετο τὴν αὐτοῦ.[15]

When daylight came, Lazaros decided not to leave the village that day until the divine liturgy had been celebrated, [partly] because of the solemnity of the day, as it was the feast of the Forty Martyrs of Christ, but at the same time as a test of the uncharitable people [who lived] there. When the time for the liturgy had come, however, and the divine service had been celebrated, [still] no one had given him even a crumb of bread to eat. Then Lazaros realized that they had no concept at all of sharing. He did not get angry or shout insults at them, but raised his hands and his eyes toward heaven and offered up some such words of thanks to God [as these]: "Lord, I give you thanks; and if you should consider me worthy to live in some place where it is clearly your will [for me to do so], I will not eat by myself the bread that you send me, but I will also serve it as food to all those, rich and poor, who come to me in your name". After he had said this, he left the village. As he saw a small chapel somewhere nearby, he went to it. He found a nun established in it who, when she saw him, got up and brought him bread and water and made him take some food. After he had partaken of [this] nourishment, he gave thanks to God (for he did everything to the glory of God and, if anything ever happened to him, whether happy or sad, it became an occasion for him to thank God) and then also blessed the nun, before setting off on his way.[16]

Lazaros in this passage is a special, holy person, but he is also a traveller. It goes without saying that, as such, he is also a hungry and thirsty man. Considering

---

15 Gregory, *Life of Lazaros* §28.
16 Greenfield 2000, 112–13.

this characterization of the main character in the story, the reader would expect that local people in the village would assist and protect the fragile—and in God's eyes precious—man. However, this does not happen, because Gregory wants to talk about the holy man's difficult training process. Lazaros' mission is to survive on his own and save humanity from its weak-mindedness and heartlessness. His only alternative to facing people's weaknesses is to pass them by and look for better Christians. In Gregory's entire biography of Lazaros, the latter does nothing else but relocate in order to encounter the optimal conditions for his process of sanctification. At the story level, Lazaros is shown as looking for the 'place which feels right' for his performance of holy identity within the context of a community. At the narrative level, departure symbolizes part of a spiritual journey toward a higher plane of understanding, and mental change, as David Westberg also shows in his discussion of Palladios' story of the monk, Pachon, in this volume.[17]

2   Setting Boundaries

Following Gregory's account to Lazaros' second phase of wandering around Ephesos and Mount Galesion, this pattern gets even clearer. Lazaros kept negotiating his identity as a holy man, among himself and with the locals, again by relocating himself on a smaller scale, by selecting his place for residence and by constructing his personal space.

Here, a very important aspect of this narrative strategy of space performance is the construction of his personal space on Mount Galesion. His status as a holy man was based chiefly on his extraordinary perseverance as a pillar ascetic or stylite. The outstanding feature of his ascetic practice was the confinement of his body on an open pillar for more than forty years, which was suitable for his performance of sanctification. He occupied a total of four pillars, all built to order and all similar in their basic features. They seem to have been constructed in a particular way so as to be liminal spaces between his body and the nature, the land and the heavens, himself and his community. So, a most interesting relocation strategy of Lazaros involved moving his pillar together with his body three times, higher and higher on Mount Galesion, always looking to escape from the attention of the community, which was simply following him on his way up, forming monastic settlements around him and his pillars. Every re-settling meant a re-construction of his own place

---

17   See Chapter 26.

within a process of re-negotiation of his identity. This renegotiation took place through his differences with his disciples and lay men and women, as shown in the following passage:

> Ἐπεὶ δὲ ὁ πατὴρ μετὰ τὸ πληρῶσαι εἰς τὸν Σωτῆρα χρόνους δώδεκα, ἀπάρας ἐκεῖθεν πρὸς τὸ ὑψηλότερον μέρος τῆς φάραγγος ἀνῆλθε, χρὴ κἀμὲ περὶ τούτου εἰπεῖν, τίς ἡ αἰτία, ὡς παρὰ τῶν εἰδότων μεμάθηκα, δι' ἣν συνέβη αὐτῷ ἐκ τοῦ Σωτῆρος ἀναχωρῆσαι καὶ ἐκεῖσε ἀπελθεῖν. Ὡς γὰρ ἡ προειρημένη μακαρία γυνὴ καὶ μετὰ τὸ ἀποκαρῆναι συχνοτέρως πρὸς αὐτὸν ἀπήρχετο, ἐν μιᾷ τῶν ἡμερῶν ἐκεῖσε αὐτῆς οὔσης καὶ ἔνδον τῆς ἐκκλησίας ἑστώσης, τοῦ δὲ πατρὸς ἐπάνω τοῦ στύλου ἱσταμένου καὶ τῶν ἀδελφῶν πέριξ τοῦ στύλου παρεστώτων, τινὶ τῶν ἀδελφῶν ὁ πατὴρ διά τι πταῖσμα ἦν ἐγκαλῶν· τὸ δὲ ἦν, ὅτι ὀπώραν φαγὼν τὴν αὐτῆς ὄψιν ὡς ἄχρηστον ἀποξύσας ἔρριψεν. Ἐκεῖνος δὲ ἀντὶ τοῦ ταπεινωθῆναι, ὅπερ ὤφειλε ποιῆσαι, καὶ βαλεῖν μετάνοιαν, ἵνα συγχώρησιν λάβῃ, ἰταμῶς ἐξ οὗ τόπου ἵστατο ἐκπηδήσας δρομαίως εἰς τὴν ἐκκλησίαν εἰσῆλθε καὶ τὴν μονάζουσαν ἐκ τῆς ἐπωμίδος δραξάμενος τῆς ἐκκλησίας ἐξάγει. Καὶ ἐξαγαγὼν ταύτην ἔμπροσθεν τοῦ πατρός· Αὕτη, φησίν, ἡ κἀμὲ καὶ τούτους βλάπτουσα ὑποδείξας αὐτῷ τοὺς ἐκεῖ ἑστῶτας ἀδελφούς, καὶ οὐχί, ἃ ἐγκαλῶν μοι φαίνῃ. Συνεμαρτύρουν δὲ αὐτῷ καὶ οἱ λοιποὶ ἀδελφοί, ὅτι οὕτως ἔχει. Ὁ δὲ πατὴρ μὴ ταραχθεὶς ἐπὶ τῇ τοῦ ἰταμοῦ ἐκείνου ἀναισχύντῳ παρρησίᾳ, ἀλλὰ μικρόν τι στυγνάσας, ἀταράχως καὶ ὁμαλῶς στυγνῇ τῇ φωνῇ ἀποκριθεὶς ἔφη πρὸς αὐτούς·Οὐκ ἔστιν ὑμᾶς ἡ βλάπτουσα αὕτη, ἀλλ' ἐγώ· καὶ γὰρ αὕτη οὐ δι' ἄλλον ἀνέρχεται ὧδε, ἀλλ' ἢ δι' ἐμέ. Καὶ ταῦτα πρὸς ἐκείνους εἰπὼν στραφεὶς πρὸς τὴν μονάζουσαν·"Ἄπελθε, φησίν, εἰς τὸ κελλίον σου καὶ μηκέτι ὧδε ἀνέλθῃς. Ἡ δὲ βάλλουσα μετάνοιαν, κλαίουσα καὶ ὀδυρομένη διὰ τὴν στέρησιν τοῦ πατρὸς κατῆλθε τοῦ ὄρους.[18]

After the father had spent twelve years at the [monastery of the] Saviour, he left there and went up to the higher part of the gorge. I must speak about this matter [now, and explain] the reason why he came to leave the [monastery of the] Saviour and go off there, as I have learned it from those who know. The aforementioned blessed woman [Irene] used to go up to Lazaros [even] more frequently after she had been tonsured. One day, when she was there and was standing in the church, the father was standing up on his pillar with the brothers standing round it, and he was rebuking one of them for some fault; this was that, when he was eating a piece of fruit, he had peeled off the skin and thrown it away as no good. But this man, instead of humbling himself as he should have done and

---

18   Gregory, *Life of Lazaros* §57.

prostrating himself so that he might receive forgiveness, dashed off brazenly from the place where he had been standing and went running into the church; there he seized the nun by her scapular and led her out of the church. He brought her before the father and said, "It is this woman who is hurting me and these [others]," indicating to Lazaros the brothers who were standing there, "and not the things for which you are apparently rebuking me". The other brothers backed him up [and confirmed] that this was the case. The father was not upset by that brazen fellow's shameless outspokenness, but grew a little sad, and replied to them calmly and coolly in a sad voice, "It is not this woman who is hurting you, but I, for she only comes up here on my account". After saying this to them, he turned to the nun and said, "Go back to your cell and don't come up here anymore". She prostrated herself and then went down the mountain, weeping and wailing at being deprived of the father.[19]

The spatial indicators of hierarchy are very clear in this passage. The father is giving order to his disciples from his high position on the pillar. The courtyard is the place of assemblage of the faithful and as such is a space controlled by the superior from his high position. Due to its public function, it exemplifies good and normative practice but also hosts disciplinary education. As such, the courtyard is also the perfect place for performing individual or collective acts of protest against authority and, in that context, is also perfect for dusting off the duties and responsibilities of different hierarchies in the monastery (the "brazen fellow" shown to be "first among equals") as well as negotiating the rules of cohabitation, such as the presence of a woman in the monastic facilities. Gregory continues by narrating the aftermath of this conflict, again stressing the spatial aspects of human agency:

Καὶ μεθ' ἡμέρας τινὰς προσκαλεσάμενος ὁ πατὴρ τινα τῶν μοναχῶν τῶν περὶ τὴν οἰκοδομικὴν ἐπισταμένων, προστάσσει αὐτῷ μετὰ καὶ ἑτέρων δύο ἀδελφῶν ἀπελθεῖν πρὸς τὸ ὑψηλότερον μέρος τῆς φάραγγος, διδάξας αὐτὸν καὶ τὸν τόπον, καὶ ἐκτεμεῖν τὸ ἐκεῖσε ἑστὼς ἀγριέλαιον δένδρον καὶ πλησίον αὐτοῦ λάκκον ποιῆσαι εἰς καῦσιν ἀσβέστου, ἐν ᾧ δὲ τόπῳ τὸ δένδρον ἵσταται, κτίσαι αὐτῷ στύλον παρεμφερῆ τῷ ἐν ᾧ ἦν, καὶ αὐτὸν ἀνώροφον καὶ ἄστεγον. Τελέσαντος οὖν τοῦ ἀδελφοῦ τὸν στύλον, καθὼς αὐτῷ ὁ πατὴρ προσέταξε, μιᾷ τῶν νυκτῶν ἐξελθὼν ἐκ τοῦ προτέρου στύλου, μηδενὸς τῶν ἐκεῖ ἀδελφῶν ἰδόντος ἀνελθὼν πρὸς τὸν νεοπαγῆ στύλον εἰσῆλθεν. Ὡς δὲ ἡ ὥρα τοῦ κρούματος τῆς ἐκκλησίας ἔφθασε καὶ εἰς γνῶσιν τοῦτο ἦλθε τοῖς ἀδελφοῖς, εὐθὺς πάντες

---

19   Greenfield 2000, 145.

πρὸς αὐτὸν ἀνῆλθον. Καὶ ἰδόντες αὐτὸν καὶ εὐχὴν καὶ παραγγελίαν, ὅπως δεῖ εἶναι αὐτούς, παρ' αὐτοῦ λαβόντες, κατῆλθον πάλιν πρὸς τὸν Σωτῆρα, μόνον αὐτὸν ἐκεῖσε καταλιπόντες. Καὶ ἦν ἐκεῖσε πάλιν ὡς στρουθίον μονάζον, φυγαδεύων καὶ αὐλιζόμενος ἐν τοῖς ἐρημοτέροις τόποις, προσδεχόμενός τε Θεὸν τὸν σῴζοντα αὐτὸν ἀπὸ ὀλιγοψυχίας καὶ ἀπὸ καταιγίδος τῶν πονηρῶν δαιμόνων καταποντίζοντά τε τὰς ἐκείνων κακοβουλίας καὶ κακομηχάνους τέχνας καὶ μεθοδείας, ἃς αὐτῷ καθ' ἑκάστην προσέφερον. Ὡς γὰρ ἡ πρώτη νὺξ ἐπέστη, παρέστησαν καὶ αὐτοί, ἐκ πρώτης οἰόμενοι ἐκφοβεῖν αὐτόν, καὶ λίθους κατ' αὐτοῦ ἔβαλλον· οὐκ ἐν αὐτῇ δὲ τῇ νυκτὶ μόνῃ ἢ καὶ τῇ ἐπιούσῃ τοῦτο ποιήσαντες ἐπαύσαντο, ἀλλ' ἐπὶ πολλαῖς, ἕως οὗ καὶ αὐτὸς τὰς εὐχὰς ὡς λίθους κατ' αὐτῶν ἀφιεὶς φυγάδας τούτους εἰργάσατο.[20]

Several days later the father summoned one of the monks who knew about construction and told him to go up to the higher part of the gorge with two other brothers; he indicated the place to him and [instructed him] to cut down the wild olive tree that stood there and to make a pit near it for burning lime. In the place where the tree stood Lazaros [told him] to build a pillar for him rather like the one on which he was, [that is] elevated and without a roof. When the brother had finished the pillar just as the father had ordered, [the latter] left his previous pillar one night, without any of the brothers there seeing him, climbed up to the newly built pillar, and got onto it. When the time came for hammering [the *semantron*] for church and the brothers realized what had happened, they all went straight up to him. They saw him and then went down again to the [monastery of the] Saviour, leaving him there alone. So Lazaros was once more *as a sparrow dwelling alone on a roof* there; he had wandered far off and had lodged in the wilder places, and was awaiting God Who would save him from faintheartedness and from the tempest of the wicked demons and Who would drown the malicious and ill-intentioned designs and contrivances with which they were attacking him every day. For as [soon as] the first night fell, they draw near too, intending to terrify him from the start, and began to throw stones at him; and they continued doing this not only on that night and the following one, but for many [nights] until he put them to flight by hurling prayers at them like rocks.[21]

Lazaros seems to have been, again, clearly disappointed by his disciples' weak-minded and heartless way of treating himself and the nun in this story. First of

---

20   Gregory, *Life of Lazaros* §58.
21   Greenfield 2000, 145–46.

all, he had to make his point, one way or another, by setting boundaries against such inappropriate behaviour. Second, he was also becoming rather impatient; dealing with this sort of 'low' matter, instead of teaching these disciples their way towards God, was becoming an obstacle between him and his own process of sanctification. A 'technical solution' is Gregory's narrative device: he uses physical distance in order to portray Lazaros' decision to establish his mental and social distancing from these problems. Lazaros relocates to another pillar, at a remote place on the mountain.

According to Richard Greenfield, despite Lazaros' astonishing reputation as a holy man, his endless visitors, and his repute as the intermediary or possessor of superhuman powers due to numerous stories of miraculous acts, it was the flourishing community of some three hundred monks who had sprung up around him on the barren and inhospitable mountain that was viewed by Gregory as the greatest miracle Lazaros ever performed.[22] Some monks even carried impressive reports of Lazaros' sanctity to Constantinople, bringing back recognition from the imperial court in the form of grants of land and money. Thus, at the story level, space transformation worked as a way to transform society. Gregory succeeds in giving this impression by narrating these iterative performances of the characters' identities. The audience would have received the message: 'This is how a saint acts'.

It has been argued that, in hagiographical texts, holiness is a performance.[23] In our case, performativity is encompassed by spatiality at two levels: first at the story level, through the character's spatial performances, and second at the textual level, through the author's spoken acts which work to create an impression about space in the audience.[24] With this narrative strategy, the full descriptions of spaces constantly function as the missing link between the characters' agency and the audience's own lived experience. Hence, the precise spatial descriptions create verisimilitude: they turn the author into a trustworthy narrator by proving than he was there when everything was happening.

This 'missing link', moreover, is not constructed as a precise representation (or imitation) of the (intended) readers' spatial experiences in real life. Instead, hagiographical narratives are built in such a way as to allow ordinary people's life experiences to connect to a wandering ascetic and a saint. In the *Life of Lazaros*, for example, Gregory uses full descriptions of spaces to construct 'symbolic landscapes', as defined and discussed by Darlene Brooks

---

22   Greenfield 2000, 28.
23   Constantinou 2005, 2014; Krueger 2004, 2014; Van Pelt 2018, 2019.
24   See Rose 1999.

Hedstrom, in this volume.[25] Gregory's 'symbolic landscapes', consisting of a series of places that allow Lazaros to spiritually escape the physical world and become a saint, work so as to make the reader understand a transition from ordinary life to holiness.

∙ ∙ ∙

To conclude, Gregory the Cellarer, author of the *Life of St Lazaros from Mount Galesion*, succeeds in communicating culture by describing Lazaros' body's spatial motion. How did that work? I have here tried to show that, first of all, the pronounced spatiality and mobility in Lazaros' story reflects the very own spatialities of Byzantine culture: Lazaros' character is relocating within the *Vita* because that is what a Byzantine holy man was supposed to do. Secondly, I am suggesting that this cultural practice worked in a bidirectional way, and here lies exactly the purpose of the narrative strategy under discussion: in one direction, becoming a holy person was practiced by bodily relocation; in the opposite direction, narrating on a mobile body was the way of recounting a mobile soul. In recent studies, walking has been shown to be much more than a destination-oriented, functional mode of transport. Within 'walking studies' in cultural geography and social anthropology, pedestrianism (as lived or practiced realities of walking) has been variously understood as being reflective of changing social forms and norms, and as expressive of diverse cultural meanings. These understandings open up a new set of possibilities for thinking about how wandering might have actually been working in hagiographical narratives, and how the authors of such texts directed their characters' movement through space in order to construct spatial stories, or forms of narrative understanding, for their audience.[26] Our mobilities create spaces and stories—spatial stories.[27]

Bibliography

Primary Sources

Gregory the Cellarer, *Life of Lazaros*. "Βίος καὶ πολιτεία καὶ ἄσκησις τοῦ ὁσίου πατρὸς ἡμῶν καὶ θαυματουργοῦ Λαζάρου τοῦ ἐν τῷ Γαλησίῳ" [Codex Athonensis, Lavra I. 127]. Ed. H. Delehaye, *Acta Sanctorum Novembris collecta digesta illustrata*, III, Brussels 1910,

---

25   See Chapter 13.
26   Tilley 1994, 28.
27   A phrase I borrow from Cresswell & Meriman 2010, 5.

508–88, dig. rep. Cambridge 2002. Tr. R. P. H. Greenfield, *An Eleventh Century Pillar Saint: The Life of Lazaros of Mt. Galesion*. Washington D.C. 2000.

Secondary Sources

Constantinou, S. 2005. *Female Corporeal Performances, Reading the Body in Byzantine Passions and Lives of Holy Women*. Uppsala.

Constantinou, S. 2014. 'Holy Actors and Actresses: fools and cross-dressers as the protagonists of saints' lives', in Efthymiadis, S. (ed.), 2014. *The Ashgate Research Companion to Byzantine Hagiography, vol. 2: Genres and Contexts*. Farnham, Surrey and Burlington VT, 343–62.

Cresswell, T. & P. Meriman 2010. "Introduction", in: Cresswell & Meriman (eds) 2010, 1–15.

Cresswell, T. & P. Meriman (eds) 2010b. *Geographies of Mobilities: Practices, Spaces, Subjects*. Farnham.

de Certeau, M. 1984. *L'invention du Quotidien*. Tr. S. Randall, *The Practice of Everyday Life*. Berkeley, Los Angeles & London.

Dietz, M. 2005. *Wandering monks, virgins, and pilgrims: ascetic travel in the Mediterranean world, A.D. 300–800*. University Park, PA.

Ducket, E. 1959. *The Wandering Saints of the Early Middle Ages*. New York.

Foucault, M. 1975. *Surveiller et punir: Naissance de la prison*. Paris.

Foucault, M. 1984. "Des Espaces Autres", *Architecture, Mouvement, Continuité* 5, 46–49.

Krueger, D. 2004. *Writing and Holiness: The Practice of Authorship in the Early Christian East*. Philadelphia: University of Pennsylvania Press.

Krueger, D. 2014. *Liturgical Subjects: Christian Ritual, Biblical Narrative, and the Formation of the Self in Byzantium*. Philadelphia: University of Pennsylvania Press.

Lefebvre, H. 1947. *Critique de la vie quotidienne*. Paris.

Lefebvre, H. 1961. *Critique de la vie quotidienne II, Fondements d'une sociologie de la quotidienneté*. Paris.

Lefebvre, H. 1974. *La Production de l'espace*. Paris.

Massey, D. B. 1995. *Spatial divisions of labour: Social structures and the geography of production*, 2nd ed. New York.

Massey, D. B. 1999. "Spaces of Politics", in Massey, Allen & Sarre (eds) 1999, 279–94.

Massey, D. B. 2005. *For Space*. London.

Massey, D., J. Allen & P. Sarre (eds) 1999. *Human Geography Today*. Cambridge.

Messis, Ch., M. Mullett & I. Nilsson (eds) 2018. *Storytelling in Byzantium: Narratological Approaches to Byzantine Texts and Images*, Uppsala.

Pelt, Van J. 2018. "Saints in disguise: Performance in the Life of John Kalyvites (BHG 868), the Life of Theodora of Alexandria (BHG 1727) and the Life of Symeon Salos (BHG 1677)", in Messis, Mullett & Nilsson (eds) 2018, 137–57.

Pelt, Van J. 2019. *Saints in Disguise: A Literary Analysis of Performance in Byzantine Hagiography*. PhD Diss., University of Gent.

Rose, G. 1999. "Performing Space", in Massey, Allen & Sarre (eds) 1999, 247–59.

Soja, E. W. 1996. *Thirdspace: Journeys to Los Angeles and Other Real-and-Imagined Places*, Oxford.

Soja, E. W. 1999. "Thirdspace: Expanding the Scope of the Geographical Imagination", in Massey, Allen & Sarre (eds) 1999, 260–78.

Soja, E. W. 1989. *Postmodern Geographies: The Reassertion of Space in Critical Social Theory*. London.

Tilley, C. 1994. *A phenomenology of landscape: places, paths, and monuments*, Oxford.

Thrift, N. 2007. *Non-Representational Theory: Space, Politics, Affect*. London.

Veikou, M. 2016. "Space in Texts and Space as Text. A new approach to Byzantine spatial notions", *Scandinavian Journal of Byzantine and Modern Greek Studies* 2, 143–75.

Veikou, M. 2018. "'Telling Spaces' in Byzantium: Ekphraseis, place-making and the 'thick' description", in Messis, Mullett & Nilsson (eds) 2018, 15–32.

Veikou, M. 2022. *Spatial paths to holiness: Literary 'Lived Spaces' in Byzantine Saints' Lives,* Studia Byzantina Upsaliensia 22. Uppsala.

PART 2

Experienced Spaces: Human Bodies within Their Natural Environments

∴

Editorial Note on Part 2

The environment shapes our experience of space in constant interaction with the human body. The five chapters of this section deal with the influences of natural environments upon Byzantine spatial experiences as well as with their impact on society and culture. They also consider the degree upon which such influences determined human thought and action. Adam Izdebski's theoretical study opens this series of chapters. Based on the Byzantine paradigm, Izdebski confronts a set of questions around the implications of natural environment in human history. Richard Hodges explores meanings of liminal spaces in a Balkan-Mediterranean context by means of developing a pertinent case study on the fluid forms of diachronic settlement around the site of Butrint in modern Albania. Robert Ousterhout offers another case study of Byzantine habitation in a completely different natural setting: Cappadocia, in the heartland of Eastern Anatolia. In an effort to understand a Byzantine spatial logic, Ousterhout explores strategies of adjustment to and practices of 'domestication' of a rocky environment. Joanita Vroom investigates Byzantine spatialities around the basic aspect of the human dependence on nature: sustenance. Vroom explores spatial practices around food storage, preservation, preparation and consumption; her discussion reveals profound changes in Byzantine culinary and dining cultures, inscribed within the general cultural transformation of the medieval Mediterranean world. Finally, Johannes Koder's chapter treats the relation between natural space and human identity. Koder discusses Byzantine conceptions of 'geographic belonging'—i.e. aspects of collective identity from a spatial perspective—and demonstrates that natural space served as a decisive landmark in Byzantine constructions of the (local) 'collective Self' against an (also local) 'collective Other'.

Space-environment as Historical Actor in Byzantium

Adam Izdebski

In this essay, I explore the ways in which the environmental historian conceives the role of space in human history. "Space" and "environment" are different concepts and each of them serves as a foundational notion for a different research tradition. Nevertheless, they do overlap in a significant way, as explained in this chapter. I here discuss the connection between them in order to show how the environmental history perspective can contribute to a collaborative effort aimed at understanding "Byzantine spatialities". Environmental history as a historical discipline focusing on the past interactions between societies and their environments —natural spaces of sort— brings in an important perspective to the "spatial debate" involving traditional history, archaeology, art history and literature, so well represented in this volume. In a way, compared to them, environmental history is materialistic and positive: it aims to connect in a way with past physical and biological realities, approximate or reconstruct them, and related them to human actions and human experience. Moreover, it treats humans as elements of these greater geological or biological wholes, going far beyond the traditional culture-bound perspective of the humanities.

Thus, for the purpose of this essay, I propose to think of the environment as an *enlivened* space; a busy space, filled with inorganic ("dead but dynamic") nature and living organisms ("life") of all kinds (including us, humans). All of them have their place in space; they adapt the space they live in to their needs, compete for space, occupy and transform it. From this point of view, every ecosystem is first and foremost a spatial formation, and such are also the social-ecological systems that (historical) human societies construct in tandem with the ecosystems they inhabit or rely on. All these elements—whether they are "alive or dead", "human or non-human"—have their agency, i.e. exert influence on the others and as a result make things happen. Therefore, we can think of not only human, but also nonhuman historical actors. They lived the present together, and if we are to do justice to our past, instead of just focusing on the human history in our historiography, we should also narrate it the way it actually was, that is the past lived together: taking the environment—enlivened space—as society's partner in shaping our shared history. This observation has long permeated environmental history, and it also provided the foundation of the Actor-Network Theory (ANT) (in particular in Bruno Latour's version), one of the most influential contemporary sociological theories. According to the ANT, when talking about a society, we should not only focus on humans, but on all kinds of nonhumans and the relationships between them. Together, these relationships form networks of (human and nonhuman) actors capable of exerting influence on the others and thus reshaping the network itself.[1] If we think of such a network as being (always?) embedded in a concrete space, it becomes easier for us to think of the environment as a space that can have a historical agency of its own. Space is one of the dimensions which we can use to describe the actors' relationships and thus the network itself. Hence, the peculiarities of the space in which the actors are active and where their relationships are played out can exert influence of its own on the course of what we call "history", thus making it into a historical actor of its own kind.

If we follow this way of thinking and relating the past, we can talk about the natural processes and natural space as actors in Byzantine history.[2] It is worth noticing that in this way we focus on a complex dynamic space which to a large extent exists independently of human perception and cultural activity. We go beyond the sphere of the "social and cultural" that is at the centre of spatial studies and also rightly occupies prominent place in this book. Even when a specific environment becomes completely anthropogenic, man-made, "nature" retains its autonomy. It can still actively influence human action, not only as a factor limiting opportunities available to human societies, or an agent that re-directs human activity in space (such as determining the choice of routes of communication, sites for habitation, etc.). In fact, the environment becomes an autonomous actor that can be regarded as pursuing its own aims, even "behaving", taking part in history in ways that are beyond human control. Indeed, environmental history's basic tenet is the deep conviction that the environment is one of the key actors in history. In that context, the notion of the "environment", of course, covers a number of phenomena, from energy flows and inorganic matter, through microorganisms, to plants and animals. Since the early years of the discipline in the late 1960s, practitioners of environmental history have felt the responsibility to stand for these different actors, hitherto absent from mainstream narratives of the past. The project of environmental history can thus be seen as being about "giving voice to the

---

1 For an introduction to the Actor-Network Theory, see for instance Latour 2005.
2 And such perspective has long been present in Byzantine Studies. See, for instance, Veikou 2012, 305–29.

voiceless", rendering "justice" to those who were kept on the margins of history, but whose role should actually be regarded as central.[3]

Given the fact that natural actors/processes operate across different timescales (ranging from days to centuries or millennia), Byzantine history—thanks to the longevity of the Eastern Roman Empire—offers in this context a particularly useful unit of analysis. Because Byzantine history covers well over a millennium (roughly speaking, 300–1500 CE), even the processes that take several (human) generations or hundreds of years to become visible can be studied in the context of Byzantine history, which makes it possible to embrace the Braudelian longue durée (even if we now know today that Braudel was too generous in placing all things environmental under this category, which he used to denote changes that take place over hundreds of years, in effect imperceptible to both the contemporaries and the modern historian).[4] These slow-paced changes (like sediment infilling of riverbeds, deltas and embayments; gradual desiccation of climate; soil exhaustion; or reforestation, which actually sometimes proceeds relatively quickly) occurred within the same empire and culture, and in theory the Eastern Romans themselves could draw on their cultural heritage to recall the previous state of the environment and apprehend these natural processes. At the same time, given the persistent availability of late antique ("early Byzantine") ecological know-how long into the Byzantine Middle Ages (be it through the continuity of managerial practice, be it through texts such as the legal or agrarian collections, copied again and again in every century), the eastern Romans could also (and often did) attempt to recreate long-lost ecosystems, for economic, political, or cultural reasons.[5]

At this point, one could mention a great number of classic works of environmental history.[6] Let me give just one more recent example that comes from the

---

3   For other, less historiography and theory-oriented introductory works, see: Hughes 2006; Winiwarter & Knoll 2007; and in the medieval context, Hoffmann 2014; Isenberg (ed.) 2014; For an introduction to the field of environmental history and environmental historiography in general, the reader would best be served by referring to Quennet 2014. It is important to note—as Quennet rightly observes—that even though French historiography from the early- and mid- Annales School was one of the sources of inspiration for the American historians who effectively founded the field of environmental history, there are major differences between the Annales and the environmental history approaches to this topic.

4   Also: Braudel 1958; for Braudel's notion of the longue durée, see Part I of Braudel 1966.

5   Beckh (ed.) 1895. Such collections included, for instance, the Farmer's Law and the *Geoponica* (Medvedev (ed.) 1984). For a brief discussion of their use throughout Byzantine history, see Izdebski 2018, 181–87.

6   The classic works of the first generation of environmental historians, which set the foundation for this historiographic tradition, include Crosby 1972; Worster 1979; Cronon 1983; Crosby 1986; Merchant 1989.

field of medieval studies. Paolo Squatriti's book on chestnuts in early medieval Italy moves to the front a plant, the chestnut tree, as the protagonist of a historical narrative.[7] This tree became a great companion and supporter of humans in the times of trouble. It was able to disguise itself as worthless in the eyes of invaders. It was strong and autonomous—hence, requiring little care. At the same time, it provided a great variety of resources, including precious calories. Seen in this way, the chestnut tree was a major actor in early medieval Italian history, an unrecognized hero which enabled the inhabitants of the peninsula to survive under unpredictable climatic and political conditions. In the Byzantine context, another such actor—apart from the chestnut tree, which must have also served as an important ally for many rural populations of the early Middle Ages—was the mastic (*Pistacia lentiscus* var. Chia) on the Greek island Chios: a resilient and simple tree, the source of a precious liquid that allowed for great economic development on an otherwise very poor island.[8]

After this introduction, I would now like to discuss three environmental phenomena that show how this approach applies to the Byzantine context: pathogens, climate, and landscape.

1 Space as Enabler: Pathogens

The success of various pathogens—be it bacteria, viruses, or parasites—in infecting large numbers of humans or animals depends on their access to these host populations.[9] To take the most famous example, if the plague bacterium *Yersinia pestis* had stayed in its Central Asian (or Caucasian) reservoir, there would have been no Justinianic Plague or Black Death—only some local plague events in Central Asia.[10] In other words, the activity of this pathogen would have remained restricted to a relatively limited, regional space, and this bacterium would have remained an important actor of nothing more than local

---

[7] Earlier works of Squatriti could also serve as a model: Squatriti 1992; 2002; 2010; 2013; see also his inspiring essay on the peculiarities of Mediterranean (which also includes Byzantine) environmental history: Squatriti 2014.

[8] Savvidis 2000. I would like to thank Myrto Veikou for suggesting this example.

[9] The argument presented in this section has been inspired by: McNeill 1976; Green 2017; Harper 2017; on some aspects of Harper's handling of the plague, see the discussion in: Haldon et al. 2018a, 2018b.

[10] The discussion on the geographical origin of the subsequent introductions of the plague bacteria to the Euro-Mediterranean sphere is still ongoing: Green 2015; Campbell 2016; Green 2018 (please also see the replies to this review, under the same link); Spyrou et al. 2019.

Central Asia history. However, once these different local spaces became connected in one Eurasian space in Late Antiquity, through trade, religious missions and empire-building, and then again in the later Middle Ages, *Yersinia pestis* was provided with the potential to become a major actor on the scene of global history.[11]

In the end, pandemics or large-scale epidemics are possible only in highly connected areas, when virgin populations of potential hosts are suddenly exposed to a new pathogen. We could even say that epidemic disease is a function of space: the more ecosystems that are "hospitable" to a specific pathogen are connected to each other (through trade, the movement of animals, armies, pilgrimage routes, etc.), the easier and quicker the pathogen can "jump" from one location to another. Thus, the demographic scale of past epidemics depended on the scale of existing interconnected spaces—political, economic, religious, cultural—that humans were creating. Byzantium, as the medieval continuator of the ancient Roman Empire, was at the very centre of such connected spaces. It was a hub for trade, empire-building, and culture—but also a hub for pathogen exchange between different parts of Eurasia.[12] In this sense, interaction between different places and the creation of a shared, interconnected space, a deeply cultural process that was central to Byzantine history and was one of the sources of Byzantium's vitality, also had major drawbacks. One could say the space was striking back. What used to be separate spaces, once connected, formed a new larger space that offered novel opportunities of long-distance movement not only for the activity of humans, but also for the activity of all other forms of life, including pathogens.

The Justinianic Plague or the Black Death is just one of several examples that can be mentioned in this context, and humans are just one species that suffered. Epidemics of domesticated animals were also to large extent a function of space. Epizootics took place primarily when man-made animal spaces, that is parts of the world that continuously exchanged their local stocks of animals but otherwise remained isolated from other similar areas, became temporarily connected. This could happen through war- or famine-related dislocation of humans and animals, which in turn created new spaces for pathogen activity.[13] Given the impact of epidemics and epizootics on the economy and all other related spheres of human activity, politics included, nobody could doubt that

---

11   For the emergence of the shared Eurasian space in Late Antiquity, see: Di Cosmo & Maas (eds) 2018.
12   On Byzantium's role as the "intermediary" between the Middle Eastern and European disease realms in the human and animal context: Dols 1979; Newfield 2015.
13   Again, the plague of ca. 940 CE is a good example: Newfield 2015.

through the ways in which pathogen activity depends on space, the space itself was becoming a major actor of history.

2 Space as Tele-Connector: Climatic Fluctuations

Let us now turn our attention to climate. Thanks to the growing body of palaeoclimate proxies, we are now able to identify several moments in Byzantine history when climatic conditions—temperature or precipitation—did change.[14] Climate is a major determining factor for vegetation cover in any area, including in the context of regional potential for agriculture. A specific climate could be said to "belong" or "characterize" a concrete location, creating along with the vegetation cover, animals, soils, and inorganic elements of the landscape the natural setting—or the natural space—in which humans live and where their history unfolds. At the same time, however, climate is probably the most dynamic of all these elements and the most interconnected: the succession of seasons with their characteristic weather depends on continental-scale or even global atmospheric processes, making climate and weather a highly unstable, fairly unpredictable, and somewhat external element of local space. As a result, even a subtle climatic change, if relevant for those vulnerable spheres of human activity that depend on very specific weather conditions, could alter the natural space in which humans live in significant ways. Such climatic change is always an outcome of a complicated interplay of a variety of factors: solar activity, changes in the Earth's orbit and axis, volcanic eruptions, and others. Thus, the experience of climate change extends to the actual space in which human life takes place in an astonishing way, connecting it to other parts of the globe and finally beyond the Earth, into the entire solar system.

Examples of such tele-connections abound. The fertility of the Nile valley depended on the Nile flooding, fed by monsoonal rains in Eastern Africa, which in turn could be suppressed by volcanic eruptions in the tropics.[15] Internal climate variability—that is, natural, ongoing processes in the atmosphere—could redirect substantial amounts of the winter rainfall from one Mediterranean region to another, or—on a yet larger scale—from the Mediterranean to Northern Europe.[16] A series of volcanic eruptions in other parts of the world could bring about a multi-annual or at times multi-annual

---

14 For a recent overview, see: Luterbacher et al. 2022.
15 Manning et al. 2017.
16 Roberts et al. 2012; Izdebski et al. 2016; Labuhn et al. 2018.

decrease in temperature in Europe, in particular during the summer months.[17] A slight decrease in solar activity could destabilize the succession of seasons and bring about cold, devastating winters, year after year, for a decade or more.[18]

Two examples from the Byzantine context will illustrate this point. The first one comes from Sicily: in the Late Roman period, under unusually wet conditions, the inhabitants of Sicily developed intensive, cereal-focused agriculture. After the island's reconquest during the early years of Justinian's rule, it became one of the bread baskets of the Eastern Roman Empire; eventually, the only one that remained in Roman-Byzantine hands after the Arab conquests. However, once these very humid conditions started to shift to drier ones in the later eighth and ninth centuries, cereal farming declined, undermining the economic basis for Byzantine power on the island.[19] Thus, the fate of Byzantine control over Sicily and the island's economic role was partly shaped by climatic variability. In other words, the situation of the entire Sicilian network of agro-ecosystems, landscapes, rural communities, landowners, merchants, and imperial officials managing the flow of goods, military units, etc., were influenced by yet another actor—the space that connects the air masses over Sicily with those over the Atlantic and the rest of the Mediterranean which determine the trends in precipitation variability over time. Through its climate, this fairly coherent regional space was opened up and extended all over the northern Atlantic-European area.

Another, less spectacular and somewhat speculative example comes from the Black Sea coast of Anatolia. The Sinope Peninsula, a major producer of olive oil in Late Antiquity, experienced a sudden collapse of its export economy and olive cultivation at some point during the seventh century.[20] While the political and socio-economic transformation of the Eastern Roman Empire that followed the seventh-century Arab conquests certainly had a strong influence on this development, there are areas on the coasts of Anatolia, in particular in the Aegean, where we have evidence of continuity of large-scale olive cultivation throughout the medieval period.[21] It is thus tempting to connect the disappearance of the olive cultivation and the shrinkage of the rural

---

17 Büntgen et al. 2016; Guillet et al. 2017.
18 For a well documented seventeenth-century case: Luterbacher et al. 2001; a less clear late medieval example from the early years of the Spörer Minimum, focusing on the societal impacts: Camenisch et al. 2016.
19 Sadori et al. 2016.
20 Doonan 2004, 93–118; Cassis et al. 2018.
21 Izdebski 2016.

settlement network on the Sinope Peninsula to the Late Antique Little Ice Age, the cooling that started in 536 CE and lasted a few decades.[22] The lower temperatures must have made it impossible or at least unreasonable to cultivate olives on one of the northernmost parts of Anatolia. The Late Antique Little Ice Age was triggered by a series of volcanic eruptions in the tropics, which emitted aerosols that dimmed the sun and brought the global temperature down. Again, we see a specific local space—the Sinope Peninsula—become part of a much larger and more powerful space through atmospheric connections. This climatic interconnection of distant places yet again shows space as an actor that influences the course of history.

3 Space as Partner: Anthropogenic Ecosystems and Landscapes

The previous two examples dealt with spatial connections that were either unintentionally created by humans or unfolded totally outside of human agency or even perception, even if in the end they did participate in and influenced the course of human history. This final example deals with the agency of natural spaces created purposely by humans themselves. Even before the Neolithic urbanization and plant-animal domestication, humans were re-shaping the ecosystems in which they lived in order to make them more productive and more fitting for their (human) ways of life.[23] Before they started cultivating specific plants and engineering completely new agro-ecosystems (e.g., cereal fields), they "domesticated" and managed entire "pristine" ecosystems. By the time Constantine founded Constantinople, this process had already been underway for thousands of years, its result being the profound transformation of Middle Eastern environments into an entirely anthropogenic landscape. This process continued in Late Antiquity and the Middle Ages, and the Eastern Romans, or Byzantines, were themselves efficient ecosystem engineers, transforming the Roman landscapes they inherited after Antiquity according to their needs.

One remarkable example of the ecosystem engineering that took place during Byzantine times is the early medieval rewilding of central-eastern Anatolia: the abandonment of fields and pastures and their subsequent transformation, through ecological succession, into a quasi-wild landscape.[24] The

---

22 Similar hypotheses on the impact of the cooler temperatures on cultivation are made in Haldon et al. 2014; Büntgen et al. 2016; Roberts et al. 2018.
23 Boivin et al. 2016; Scott 2017.
24 For the references to the relevant written sources, see: Haldon 2007. This process is reconstructed in detail in: Izdebski 2013; for the broader context, see: Haldon 2016.

new Anatolian wastelands that became the Byzantines' ally in the struggle with the Arabs, acting as a buffer that could absorb the first impetus of the invaders and make the defence of the more intensely cultivated lands lying in the west much easier. In this way, the Byzantines—through a combination of unintentional as well as deliberate processes—were creating a space that they wanted to become an actor on their side. The task of this new natural space, or—more precisely—of the post-anthropogenic vegetation that returned to a wild and inhospitable state, was to deter or at least discourage the enemy from moving to the core agricultural areas of Byzantine Anatolia. In general terms, through demographic change and (most probably) intentional action, humans (Byzantines) reshaped the human-natural networks (i.e. landscapes) of eastern Anatolia and made these networks in turn exert new type of influence on human actors (Arab invaders) who were interfering with it.

While the case of the Anatolian wastelands is perhaps the most spectacular, because of its scale and the role it played in ensuring the survival of the Byzantine Empire, examples of such man-made "partner" natural spaces are numerous, and gardens, parks (and game reserves), of course, should feature prominently on such a list.[25] If we include the broad category of turning nature into machine or economic device—in particular with regard to water energy, through dams, river rechanneling, etc.—the list would be even longer.[26] Byzantines constantly created natural spaces that protected them, sustained their lifestyles, and aided relaxation.

•••

This essay attempted to show how environmental history can broaden our understanding of the role that space played in Byzantine history. From a theoretical point of view, this was not an easy task: space is an abstract notion, and environment is always a concrete network of living and non-living entities. However, since spatial relations are inherent and essential to these eco-networks, we could start seeing how particular spatial characteristics—hence, space as such—could become a real actor shaping the course of Byzantine history. This we could observe in two ways.

First, they can be observed by focusing on concrete anthropogenic environments and the spatial configurations of human and nonhuman actors that

---

25 Maguire, Wolschke-Bulmahnm & Littlewood (eds) 2002.
26 The theme of river-as-machine has long been discussed within the field of environmental history: Steinberg 1991; White 1995; for the large number of such devices in Byzantine Epirus, see: Veikou 2012, 27–37.

build up these environments. Here, specific spaces were given role by humans and, by becoming part of the social-ecological network, acquired autonomy and historical agency of their own. Each of them—as a space—played a role in history. This was visible in particular in the case of our third group of examples, that is, the anthropogenic landscapes seen as the Byzantines' partners.

Second, we could observe the agency of space in history by demonstrating how natural processes created new spatial connections (atmosphere) or exploited spatial connections created by humans (pathogens). Changes in the spatial configuration of specific actors (bacteria, volcanoes, viruses, air masses, humidity) provided them with new opportunities and real historical agency. "Suddenly", thanks to emerging or already existing spatial connections, entities that used to be non-actors joined existing human-natural networks within the Byzantine world and started exerting powerful influence over entire human communities and ecosystems.

The role of space as such in all of these processes is somewhat elusive. At first, it is concrete human society and concrete "natural" environment that attracts our attention. However, once we realize they are all connected through spatial relationships that create a specific space, and it does matter for history what this space actually is, we start noticing that space does have its role in history and environmental history can help bring this realization to the fore. As we could see, space is actively inhabited and shaped by both humans and nonhumans. It is full of life and of chemical-physical processes. The environment has its own autonomous dynamic that changes the human experience of space. Through atmospheric, geological, and biological processes that are more or less independent from human activity, natural space becomes a true actor in what, from our perspective, is human history.

Bibliography

Primary Sources
Beckh, H. (ed.) 1895. *Geoponica: sive Cassiani Bassi scholastici De re rustica eclogae*, Lipsiae.

Medvedev, I. P. (ed.) 1984. *Nomos georgikos. Vizantiiskii zemledel'cheskii zakon*. Leningrad.

Secondary Sources
Belke, K. (ed.) 2007. *Byzantina Mediterranea: Festschrift für Johannes Koder zum 65. Geburtstag*. Wien.

Boivin, N. L. et al. 2016. "Ecological Consequences of Human Niche Construction: Examining Long-Term Anthropogenic Shaping of Global Species Distributions", *PNAS* 113, 6388–96.

Boivin, N., R. Crassard & M. D. Petraglia (eds) 2017. *Human dispersal and species movement: from prehistory to the present*. Cambridge.

Braudel, F. 1958. "Histoire et Sciences sociales : La longue durée", *Annales* 13, 725–53.

Braudel, F. 1966. *La Méditerranée et le monde méditerranéen à l'époque de Philippe II*, 2nd ed. Paris.

Büntgen, U. et al. 2016. "Cooling and Societal Change during the Late Antique Little Ice Age from 536 to around 660 AD", *Nature Geosci* 9, 231–36.

Camenisch, C. et al. 2016. "The 1430s: A Cold Period of Extraordinary Internal Climate Variability during the Early Spörer Minimum with Social and Economic Impacts in North-Western and Central Europe", *Clim. Past* 12, 2107–26.

Campbell, B. 2016. *The Great Transition: Climate, Disease and Society in the Late-Medieval World*. Cambridge.

Cassis, M., O. Doonan, H. Elton & J. Newhard 2018. "Evaluating Archaeological Evidence for Demographics, Abandonment, and Recovery in Late Antique and Byzantine Anatolia", *Hum Ecol* 46, 381–98.

Cronon, W. 1983. *Changes in the Land: Indians, Colonists, and the Ecology of New England*. New York.

Crosby, A. W. 1972. *The Columbian Exchange: Biological and Cultural Consequences of 1492*. Westport, CT.

Crosby, A. W. 1986. *Ecological Imperialism: The Biological Expansion of Europe, 900–1900*. Cambridge.

Di Cosmo, N. & M. Maas (eds) 2018. *Empires and Exchanges in Eurasian Late Antiquity: Rome, China, Iran, and the Steppe, ca. 250–750*. Cambridge.

Dols, M. W. 1979. "The Second Plague Pandemic and Its Recurrences in the Middle East: 1347–1894", *J Econ Soc Hist Orient* 22, 162–89.

Doonan, O. P. 2004. *Sinop Landscapes: Exploring Connection in a Black Sea Hinterland*. Philadelphia.

Green, M. 2015. "Taking 'Pandemic' Seriously: Making the Black Death Global", in Green (ed.) 2015, 27–61.

Green, M. 2018. "Review of Bruce M. S. Campbell, The Great Transition: Climate, Disease and Society in the Late-Medieval World (Cambridge: Cambridge University Press, 2016)", *Inference: International Review of Science* 4. https://inference-review.com/article/black-as-death.

Green, M. (ed.) 2015. *Pandemic disease in the medieval world: rethinking the Black Death*. Kalamazoo.

Green, M. 2017. "The Globalisations of Disease", in Boivin, Crassard & Petraglia (eds) 2017, 494–520.

Guillet, S. et al. 2017. "Climate Response to the Samalas Volcanic Eruption in 1257 Revealed by Proxy Records", *Nature Geoscience* 10, 123–28.

Haldon, J. 2007. "'Cappadocia Will Be given over to Ruin and Become a Desert'. Environmental Evidence for Historically-Attested Events in the 7th–10th Centuries", in Belke (ed.) 2007, 215–30.

Haldon, J. 2016. *The Empire That Would Not Die: The Paradox of Eastern Roman Survival, 640–740*. Cambridge, MA.

Haldon, J. et al. 2014. "The Climate and Environment of Byzantine Anatolia: Integrating Science, History and Archaeology", *Journal of Interdisciplinary History* 45, 113–61.

Haldon, J. 2018a. "Plagues, Climate Change, and the End of an Empire. A Response to Kyle Harper's *The Fate of Rome* (2): Plagues and a Crisis of Empire", *History Compass* 16, e12506.

Haldon, J. 2018b. "Plagues, Climate Change, and the End of an Empire: A Response to Kyle Harper's *The Fate of Rome* (3): Disease, Agency, and Collapse" *History Compass* 16, e12507.

Harper, K. 2017. *The Fate of Rome: Climate, Disease, and the End of an Empire*. Princeton.

Hoffmann, R. C. 2014. *An Environmental History of Medieval Europe*. Cambridge.

Horden, P. & S. Kinoshita (eds) 2014. *A companion to Mediterranean history* (*Wiley Blackwell companions to world history*). Chichester.

Hughes, J. D. 2006. *What Is Environmental History?* Cambridge.

Isenberg, A. C. (ed.) 2014. *The Oxford Handbook of Environmental History*. Oxford.

Izdebski, A. 2013. *A Rural Economy in Transition: Asia Minor from Late Antiquity into the Early Middle Ages*. Warsaw.

Izdebski, A. 2016. "Byzantine Miletus. Environmental History of the Hinterland" *Archäologischer Anzeiger* 2016, 270–80.

Izdebski, A. 2018. *Średniowieczni Rzymianie i Przyroda. Interdyscyplinarna Historia Środowiskowa*. Kraków.

Izdebski, A. et al. 2016. "The Environmental, Archaeological and Historical Evidence for Regional Climatic Changes and Their Societal Impacts in the Eastern Mediterranean in Late Antiquity", *Quaternary Science Reviews* 136, 189–208.

Izdebski, A. & M. Mulryan (eds) 2018. *Environment and Society in the Long Late Antiquity*. Leiden.

Izdebski, A. & J. Preiser-Kapeller (eds) 2022. *A companion to the environmental history of Byzantium*. Leiden.

Labuhn, I. et al. 2018. "Climatic Changes and Their Impacts in the Mediterranean during the First Millennium AD", in Izdebski & Mulryan (eds) 2018, 65–88.

Latour, B. 2005. *Reassembling the Social: An Introduction to Actor-Network-Theory*. Oxford.

Luterbacher, J. et al. 2001. "The Late Maunder Minimum (1675–1715)—A Key Period For Studying Decadal Scale Climatic Change in Europe", *Climatic Change* 49, 441–62.

Luterbacher, J. et al. 2022. "Palaeoclimatology of Byzantine Lands (300–1500 A.D.)", in Izdebski & Preiser-Kapeller (eds) 2022, 167–208.

Maguire, H., J. Wolschke-Bulmahnm & A. Littlewood (eds) 2002. *Byzantine Garden Culture*. Washington, D.C.

Manning, J. G. et al. 2017. "Volcanic Suppression of Nile Summer Flooding Triggers Revolt and Constrains Interstate Conflict in Ancient Egypt", *Nature Communications* 8, 900.

McNeill, W. H. 1976. *Plagues and Peoples*. Garden City, NY.

Merchant, C. 1989. *Ecological Revolutions: Nature, Gender, and Science in New England*. Chapel Hill.

Newfield, T. P. 2015. "Domesticates, Disease and Climate in Early Post-Classical Europe: The Cattle Plague of c.940 and Its Environmental Context", *Postclassical Archaeologies* 5, 95–126.

Quennet, G. 2014. *Qu'est-ce que l'histoire environnementale*. Seyssel.

Roberts, N., M. Cassis et al. 2018. "Not the End of the World? Post-Classical Decline and Recovery in Rural Anatolia", *Hum Ecol* 46, 305–22.

Roberts, N., A. Moreno et al. 2012. "Palaeolimnological Evidence for an East-West Climate See-Saw in the Mediterranean since AD 900", *Global and Planetary Change* 84–5, 23–34.

Sadori, L. et al. 2016. "Climate, Environment and Society in Southern Italy during the Last 2000 Years. A Review of the Environmental, Historical and Archaeological Evidence", *Quaternary Science Reviews* 136, 173–88.

Savvidis, Th. 2000. *Το Μαστιχόδεντρο Της Χίου*. Thessaloniki.

Scott, J. C. 2017. *Against the Grain. A Deep History of the Earliest States*. New Haven.

Spyrou, M. A. et al. 2019. "Ancient Pathogen Genomics as an Emerging Tool for Infectious Disease Research", *Nat Rev Genet* 20, 323–40.

Squatriti, P. 1992. "Marshes and Mentalities in Early Medieval Ravenna", *Viator* 23, 1–16.

Squatriti, P. 2002. *Water and Society in Early Medieval Italy, 400–1000*. Cambridge.

Squatriti, P. 2010. "The Floods of 589 and Climate Change at the Beginning of the Middle Ages: An Italian Microhistory", *Speculum* 85, 799–826.

Squatriti, P. 2013. *Landscape and Change in Early Medieval Italy: Chestnuts, Economy, and Culture*. Cambridge.

Squatriti, P. 2014. "The Vegetative Mediterranean", in Horden & Kinoshita (eds) 2014, 26–41.

Steinberg, T. 1991. *Nature Incorporated: Industrialization and the Waters of New England*. New York.

Veikou, M. 2012. *Byzantine Epirus: A Topography of Transformation. Settlements of the Seventh-Twelfth Centuries in Southern Epirus and Aetoloacarnania, Greece*. Leiden—New York.

White, R. 1995. *The Organic Machine*. New York.

Winiwarter, V. & M. Knoll 2007. *Umweltgeschichte: eine Einführung*, Köln.

Worster, D. 1979. *Dust Bowl: The Southern Plains in the 1930s*. New York.

In the Shadow of Virgil

The Significance of Butrint's Liminality in Deep Mediterranean History

Richard Hodges

> [...] We choose one story or variant over another for its superior interest. Minimally, we strive to tell stories that are at least relevant to our audience; optimally, we hope to make our stories compelling, if possible even gripping.
>
> MCHALE, 1992, 26

∴

The Unesco World Heritage site of Butrint, as I write, is in the process of being re-envisioned as a place in a new management plan (Figure 6.1).

With support from the Albanian Ministry of Culture, the Albanian-American Development Foundation (AADF) has taken over management of the archaeological site with a view to developing a pilot project for cultural heritage in the country. Such is the success of visitorship to Butrint that the few thousand visitors in 1992, when Albania became a democracy after fifty years of communist rule, now number about 300,000 visitors per annum. In the course of twenty-five years, this Graeco-Roman town has gone from being the seat of research excavations and selective tours for school-children and political visitors to becoming the face of Albania and its tourist economy. Quite who the visitors are today is the question being posed by the AADF. They want to use Butrint as a driver for economic development in southern Albania. Managing and, of course, protecting the asset—the ruins as well as the woodland canopy—is a fundamental aspect of the new plan, as it was in the Butrint Foundation's first management plan for Butrint in 2000.[1] Perceptions of Butrint as a place in terms of its spatial character are plainly changing and progressive. No longer is it perceived as ruins in a place once described by Virgil. It has a new identity.

---

1 Martin 2001, see below.

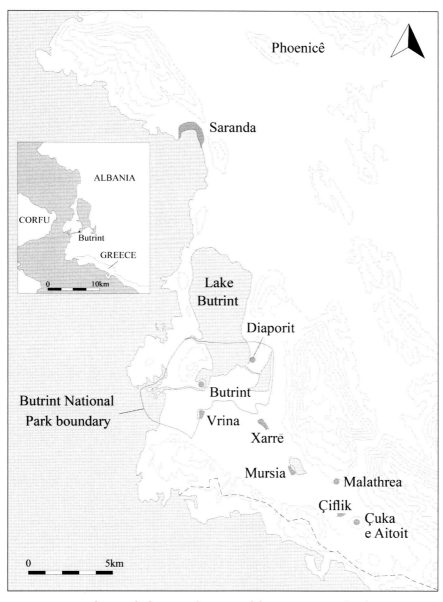

FIGURE 6.1 Map showing the location of Butrint and the Butrint National Park
© BUTRINT FOUNDATION ARCHIVES

FIGURE 6.2 Aerial view of Butrint and the Straits of Corfu, in the distance
PHOTOGRAPH BY ALKET ISLAMI. © BUTRINT FOUNDATION ARCHIVES

Now an emerging Balkan society, modern Albania, no longer a pariah state, has embraced this identity in the midst of seeking to enter the European Union. To do so, it needs not only cultural parks, but economic growth to make up for fifty years of communist isolation (Figure 6.2).[2]

This third millennium Butrint belongs to a globalized society. Releasing this patrimony to the care and protection of an NGO is unusual in the modern Mediterranean. No less unusual is the emphasis upon the archaeological site/ park—a legally defined if independently constituted space conceived as a cultural and economic driver. Finally, until 1992 Butrint was a liminal place which from 1945–91 was off-limits to visitors without permission. This progressive management approach to a modern archaeological space may seem obvious in a global society. Yet it is resisted by neighbouring countries like Greece or Italy. In both of Albania's neighbours, the Ministry of Culture continues to play a role as the arbiter of protection and preservation without seeking modern methods to define tourist supply chains and exploiting these to sustain archaeological assets. Their emphasis continues to be upon exceptional architecture

---

2 Hodges 2016.

and art—monumentalism—not on the changing historical spatial forms presented in a space managed for the modern visitor.

So why has this happened at Butrint and not at neighbouring Corfu (Palaiopolis, for example) or in Italy? In this chapter, I will review the history of Butrint through ancient, medieval and modern times with an emphasis upon the different spatial forms of each era (including Albania today) in an attempt to offer an answer to this question.

1   Albanian Thanks to Lord Grey

In early May 1923 Stewart Studdert Clarke (1897–1924), a fellow of Exeter College, Oxford, and student of archaeology at the British School at Athens, crossed the newly established Albanian-Greek frontier near Sagiada and began the first of three forays on foot into Albania, recording its then, largely unknown archaeology (Figure 6.3).[3]

Clarke's untimely death the following year in 1924 in a boating accident meant that his ground-breaking Albanian research was never published. Instead his diary-notes for a thesis on the "Historical Geography and Topography of Epirus" were to be used by N.G.L. Hammond in his thesis and later monograph on Epirus (1967), after he followed in Clarke's footsteps some seven years later in 1930. Clarke's initial visit, being the first recognized academic to survey the Butrint region in its disputed frontier setting after Albania was given nation status in August 1913, is interesting as much for what he did not do as for what he found. It also throws a little tangential light on why Luigi Maria Ugolini, the celebrated excavator of Butrint from 1928–36, chose after his first reconnaissance in 1924 to launch his Italian Archaeological Mission at nearby Phoinike in 1926–27 as opposed to Butrint (Figure 6.4).[4]

Any archaeologist travelling to northern Epirus in the early 1920s was taking a risk. The region had experienced much upheaval. The Second Balkan War in 1913 had ended with protracted diplomatic negotiations about exactly who might have control over Saranda and the region including Butrint. The British Foreign Secretary, Lord Grey, chairing the Great Powers committee designated to seek reparations from the Ottoman Empire initially proposed that this Greek-speaking area known as North Epirus should be designated to Greece. The Italian government objected and threatened to bombard Vlora

---

3   Hodges 2017.
4   cf. Gilkes 2003a; Gilkes & Miraj 2000.

FIGURE 6.3 Portrait of S.S. Clarke (1897–1924). Courtesy of the British School at Athens.
PHOTOGRAPH © BUTRINT FOUNDATION ARCHIVES

and Saranda, if this occurred. After several months Grey found a compromise which formed the basis of the Treaty of London, 1913.[5]

Grey's solution was that Saranda region (and Korça region of what is now south-east Albania) would be given to the new republic of Albania. Greece was compensated with islands in the eastern Aegean. The Greek minority in Saranda was greatly displeased and sought independence from Albania in 1914, christening itself the Autonomous Republic of Northern Epirus. The Republic lasted only six months before Greek troops were deployed until 1917 to safeguard the area after an agreement was made with the nascent state of Albania. Following the Greeks, there was an Italian peace-keeping force to protect the Greek minority community until the Armistice in November 1918. Butrint, in other words, was in a netherworld between Greece and Albania.

5 Kondis 1997.

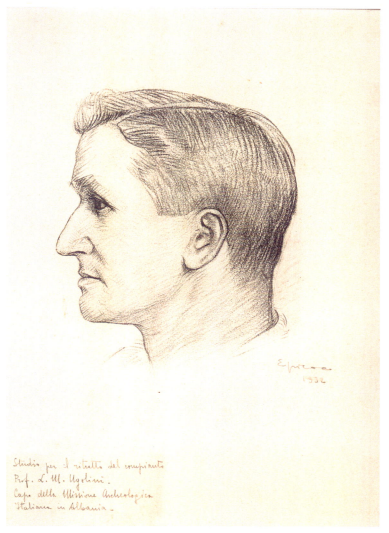

FIGURE 6.4 Portrait of Luigi Maria Ugolini (1896–1936)
PHOTOGRAPH © BUTRINT FOUNDATION ARCHIVES

The final southern border of Albania was ultimately fixed by the Conference of Ambassadors of the Great Powers in a decision released on 9 November 1921, but possession of southern Albania continued to be disputed even after Albania was admitted to the League of Nations in 1921. In this unsettled region, 10 years after the Ottomans had been expelled, S.S. Clarke was taking a risk in pursuing his fieldwork here.

Diligent in every way, Clarke records every element of his walking tour. Perhaps the most striking aspect is that he decided against visiting Butrint because the price of the boat to cross from the Triangular Castle to Butrint at 300 drachmas was too high. Clarke's diffidence towards Butrint—amazing at it seems now—is because his principal interest was to discover and survey Hellenistic sites. For this reason, the nearby hilltop settlement of Phoinike was of singular interest, primarily because Polybius in his *Histories* described it as the richest site in the region, and perhaps too because only a year earlier Bill Hill Hodge, Director of the American School of Classical Studies at Athens, had motored up to see it with a view to making an excavation there.[6] Butrint, notwithstanding Colonel Martin Leake's description of the ruins from 1805 (1835), and the palpably romantic lagoonal setting of the ancient town, was first and foremost considered to be a deserted medieval, Venetian and Ottoman town with alleged origins in the Roman and pre-Roman period. Clarke's decision helps to make sense of a bigger issue: why did Luigi Maria Ugolini initially choose to excavate at Phoinike on behalf of the Italian Archaeological Mission, and then change his mind two years later and launch the Butrint excavations with which his name will always be associated?

Ugolini first came this way in 1924, sailing from Saranda.[7] The road down the Ksamili peninsula was barely passable at this time and not to be a surfaced road until the occasion of Nikita Khrushchev's visit in May 1959 (Figure 6.5).[8]

Butrint, in short, was remote, as well as being located in dangerous border country. By selecting to excavate first at Phoinike, close to the Delvina-Saranda road, the Italian Archaeological Mission was also ensuring that the Americans would not change their minds and seek a permit to dig in this area. No less compelling a reason was Ugolini's unstated interpretation of Butrint in 1924. It appeared to be principally a post-Roman abandoned town with impressive fortifications. Whether in 1924 (as opposed to a decade later) Ugolini associated these defences with the Butrint of Virgil's Aeneid is not clear. Like Clarke he seems to have dismissed the archaeological potential of Butrint.

There was almost certainly a larger issue at stake here. Ugolini's letters to the Ministry of Foreign Affairs from 1924 express a concern that the Albanian authorities would not grant him a permit to excavate as the French authorities had signed a comprehensive agreement covering the issue of archaeological enquiries in the entire country.[9] In fact, the French archaeologists concentrated

---

6 Hodges 2017.
7 Ugolini 1927.
8 Hodges 2009.
9 Gilkes & Miraj 2000.

IN THE SHADOW OF VIRGIL 135

FIGURE 6.5   Nikita Khruschchev and Enver Hoxha at Butrint, May 1959
PHOTOGRAPH © BUTRINT FOUNDATION ARCHIVES

upon the Illyrian and Greek city site of Apollonia. Once Ugolini and the Italian plenipotentiaries had decided to test the resolve of the Albanians (and the French), it made sense to select a place for excavations which resonated with the academic ethos of the era in Italy, Greece, Great Britain, France and the United States. This was a quintessentially "Greek" site.

Only when the circumstances at Phoinike became difficult in 1927 did Ugolini recognize the opportunity for his mission presented by the prospect of the proposed two-thousandth anniversary of Virgil scheduled for 1930. More to the point, although Polybius championed the role of Rome in the history of Hellenistic Greece, there was a much greater story theoretically at stake at Butrint. Here Ugolini might lay claim to the archaeology of one of the celebrated places described in the *Aeneid*, thereby connecting Butrint to imperial Rome (and its Fascist new guise under Benito Mussolini). Only, after Ugolini returned to Butrint in early 1928 and began excavating what he assumed at first to be a Roman bathhouse that turned out to be a Hellenistic theatre, did the site begin to appear to be archaeologically interesting (Figure 6.6).

Ugolini proceeded with the support of the Italian Ministry of Foreign Affairs to artfully shape the story of Butrint as (Virgil's) Troy, consciously seeking to

FIGURE 6.6 Ugolini's excavations of the Butrint theatre, spring 1928
PHOTOGRAPH © BUTRINT FOUNDATION ARCHIVES

emulate Schliemann's skilful promotion of Mycenae.[10] As a result, he joined the pantheon of archaeological placemakers, shaping in his case Butrint to the myth of Aeneas, when much of its archaeology and history, in fact, relates not to classical antiquity but to its role in the Byzantine and Venetian ages.

2   The Butrint Foundation Project: Re-envisioning the Liminality of Butrint

In 1993, when the Butrint Foundation was formed, Butrint was the product of Ugolini's legacy.[11] Ugolini and his immediate successors, between 1928 and 1941, excavated many parts of the site and with a certain amount of creative self-publicity connected the ancient port to Virgil's account. Ugolini, for example, named one entrance the Scaean gate after the Virgil's description of Aeneas' visit to his fellow Trojan exile, Helenus, at Butrint. The gate in question

10   Ugolini 1937.
11   Hodges 2016.

FIGURE 6.7   Butrint's Sceaen Gate during clearance by Ugolini's team in ca. 1930
PHOTOGRAPH © BUTRINT FOUNDATION ARCHIVES

is Hellenistic in date, refurbished in Byzantine and possibly, Venetian times (Figure 6.7).

Ugolini found little or no evidence of any Bronze Age settlement that might have affirmed Virgil's story. Instead, Ugolini provides an unusual diachronic account (for the nineteen-thirties) of the Archaic Greek, Hellenistic, Roman, Byzantine, Venetian and Ottoman remains.[12] Virgil provided a motive for his work and his references to Mycenae, but this was no Mycenae. Post-war communist Albanian archaeologists embellished Ugolini's narrative, but with limited conviction. Being liminal and beyond the Illyrian heartlands, it was treated by a succession of Soviet-trained archaeologists as 'the Other'. Its maritime context, the opportunity to eat fish, which elsewhere in Albania was a luxury, and the growth of the woodland canopy lent Butrint a magical spirit. Albanian archaeologists embellished Ugolini's interpretation of the port, while publishing relatively little. However, by their actions they inadvertently created an exceptionally beautiful place that resonated strongly with the rise of

12   Ugolini 1937.

Mediterranean tourism in the 1990s and recent times. Virgil, in many respects, was to become irrelevant to the twenty-first-century success of Butrint once it was inscribed in 1992 into UNESCO's world heritage list.

It was the magic of Butrint which drew Lord Rothschild and Lord Sainsbury to create an NGO to protect and research the site. Of course, they hoped that new research might discover new classical statues, but their expectations were limited. The Albanian Institute of Archaeology, trapped in the confusing era of a sub-communist command economy, simply sought resources and support. In other words, the Butrint Foundation team had an opportunity to scrutinize Butrint as Ugolini had sixty years before. Between 1994 and 2009 active investigations proceeded alongside a major coordination effort to protect the special liminal spirit of the place and its setting. The success of the latter may be measured by the present government's recognition of the value of Butrint to the republic. The merits of the research project are actively being assessed.

Undertaking a new research project at Butrint in the 1990s was complicated and often dangerous. However, the first major innovation of the Butrint Foundation project was to reject the liminal thesis invented thanks to the modern political geography, and approach the site as a centre at the maritime ingress of a fluvial corridor reaching back into the mountains. With this in mind, a traditional field survey—the first in Albania—explored the coastal plain and the Pavlass river valley (Figure 6.8).[13]

The second major innovation was to comprehend the diachronic environmental history of this fluvial corridor.[14] Butrint clearly suffered from major tectonic changes throughout its history as a port. Not least, it was clear that the later Republican and early Imperial phases were once well above the modern water table.[15]

The third major innovation was to gather the archival information from Italian archives and Albanian archives, and with a survey made using a total station, begin to re-envision the topography of the place through time. In a pre-digital era, in woodland, and with regular flooding of sites, this was more challenging than it would be today. However, this showed that in Roman times a major road bridge led across the Vivari channel to a suburb of some size on the south-east side of the channel (Figure 6.9).[16] The scale and diachronic complexity of the suburb changing from a Roman colonial suburb, to a major later Roman villa, to a possible late Roman monastery, to a ninth- to

---

13   Pluciennik et al., 2004; Hodges et al., 2016.
14   Lane et al., 2004; see now, Morellón et al., 2018.
15   cf. Bescoby 2013; Hernandez 2017b.
16   Leppard 2013.

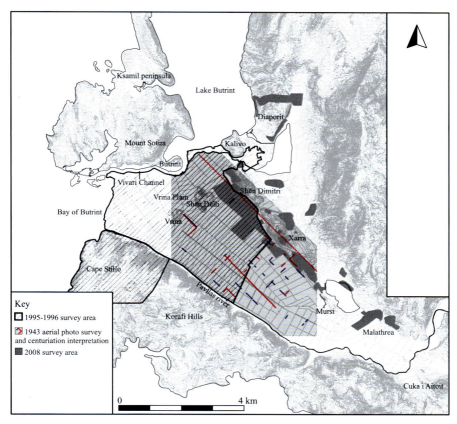

FIGURE 6.8 Beyond Butrint: field surveys by the Butrint Foundation
© BUTRINT FOUNDATION ARCHIVES

FIGURE 6.9 Reconstruction of the Roman bridge across the Vivari channel at Butrint
© BUTRINT FOUNDATION ARCHIVES

tenth-century administrative centre illustrated, if nothing else, that Ugolini's model was a diachronic topographical model that could be greatly refined. In so doing this, the topographical archaeology of Butrint provides a cornerstone for re-thinking Adriatic Sea ports from the Hellenistic to the later Byzantine era.

The deficiencies of the Butrint Foundation project (1994–2009) need to be considered, too. Too much trust in Ugolini's paradigm for Butrint is evident in the Butrint Foundation's earlier published interpretations. Only after a decade's, often politically complicated, research involving large-scale open-area excavations was it possible to develop a new model for the town's diachronic history. Even so, the limitations of this model are evident from David Hernandez's research following the Butrint programme.[17] Confronting the problems posed by the water table limited all excavations by Ugolini and his successors including the Butrint Foundation. With determination and logistical support, Hernandez brilliantly met this challenge. As a result, he has been able to re-interpret the Archaic to early Imperial topography of Butrint in a series of ground-breaking reports.

No less important are the analytical instruments that have gained currency after about 2005–7. In particular, the refinement of radio-carbon dating has made it possible to date levels today that were only approximately dated in the past on the grounds of ceramic typology and seriation methods. This enabled the Butrint Foundation to date the Mid Byzantine reoccupation of the western defences in the lower town.[18] A decade earlier this would have been impossible. Similarly, new dating and palynological tools have permitted a refinement of the town's evolving environmental context.[19] Further research, of course, might throw new light on the topographical history and evolving landscape contexts, especially if new analytical procedures were deployed to support the interpretations.

In summary, the Butrint Foundation's campaigns—with less than 5% of the city examined—have proposed the following history and intermittent urban sequence:[20]

– A mid to late Bronze Age homestead occupied the centre and probably the western reaches (now occupied by the Acropolis castle). Judging from the ceramics and the analogous excavated site at Cape Styllo, this was a small, enclosed hilltop refuge.[21] The ceramic assemblage contains no obvious evidence of connections with the Mycenaean world; instead, they indicate strong synergies with inland Epirote wares.

---

17   e.g. Hernandez 2017a and 2017c.
18   cf. Kamani 2013.
19   cf. Morellón et al. 2018.
20   cf. Hodges, Bowden & Lako 2004; Hodges 2006; Hansen & Hodges 2007; Bowden & Hodges 2011; Hansen Hodges & Leppard 2013.
21   Lima 2013.

- In the eighth to sixth centuries BCE the hilltop was reoccupied. The ceramics suggest the site was occupied with connections to the Corinthian colonists of Corfu. The remains of a major Archaic terrace wall on the south side of the hill, as well as an enclosure occupying the saddle of the acropolis and the Lion Gate sculpture suggest this was a modest sanctuary.[22]
- No evidence of the sixth to fourth centuries BCE has yet been discovered, though there is good reason to surmise that the putative sanctuary on the acropolis survived throughout this period and indeed into the Hellenistic and Roman periods.[23]
- The sanctuary of Asclepius probably dates from the era of King Pyrrhus in the early third century BCE. Judging from the manumission inscriptions as well as the excavations in the forum area, the sanctuary became a significant walled town incorporating the northern citadel by the second century BCE. It prospered under Roman republic hegemony.
- Roman Butrint prospered from the Augustan age until the third century. Investment in this era included a new civic centre as well as the creation of the Vrina Plain suburb,[24] connected by a road bridge to the old town,[25] and an associated centuriated landscape extending out as far as the old Hellenistic hilltop fortress of Çuka e Ajtoit.
- After a major seismic event in the fourth century,[26] Butrint enjoyed an economic revival based upon western Mediterranean connections until c. 470, and with eastern Mediterranean connections from c. 470–550. Before c. 470 major town houses were erected alongside both sides of the Vivari channel; then about 525 CE the town was refortified. At about the same time, a major triconch church was built on the eastern summit of the acropolis, and below it, a new cathedral was erected with an associated major baptistery.[27] By 550 CE, however, Butrint was in decline and little remained by the first quarter of the seventh century.
- The Byzantine kastron occupied two or more towers in the Western Defences that were destroyed by fire around 800 CE. The attackers may also have sacked the basilica on the Vrina Plain beside the southern, channel-side embarkation point to Butrint.

---

22 Hernandez 2017a.
23 Hernandez 2017c.
24 Greenslade 2013.
25 Leppard 2013.
26 Bescoby 2013.
27 Molla 2013.

- The archon of Butrint appears to have transferred from the old town to occupy a house made with a Vrina plain basilica in the period c. 840–950. From here, fishing and farming was probably managed on a limited scale, and embryonic trade with Byzantium and southern Italy was administered.[28]
- Butrint was reoccupied in the last quarter of the tenth century, with new defences defining the acropolis for the first time. The new defences refurbished the line of the earlier late antique walls. Evidence of landscaping and tenement divisions occurs in this period, as well as ubiquitous remains of urban revival instituted by families each with small chapels.[29]
- The defences of Butrint were repeatedly strengthened in the thirteenth and fourteenth centuries. New emphasis was placed upon an acropolis castle, as well as defending the northern citadel as water logging in the lower town made permanent occupation increasingly difficult.
- Butrint suffered terminal economic decline as an urban centre from the later fourteenth century, eclipsed as Corfu prospered. Under the Venetians, the old town was deserted and all efforts were invested in defending the fish traps in the Vivari channel (with the new Triangular Fortress and a major channel-side tower). The fishery supplied the needs of the Venetian fleet.[30]
- Ali Pasha strengthened the defensive elements of Butrint by building a new castle at the entrance of the Vivari channel.[31] Maintaining the fishing, focussed upon the triangular castle, the main market for these products was in Epirus, as this frontier area became separated from Adriatic Sea contacts.
- Butrint was created as a park after Khrushchev's visit with work beginning in the 1960s to fence the site, construct trails, undertake conservation works, and refurbish the acropolis museum.[32] The Butrint Foundation pursued and developed this park between 1993 and 2012.[33]

3　Space and Time at Butrint: From the Bronze Age until Today

The archaeology of Butrint essentially illustrates three very different spatial conditions for the port and its hinterland. The Bronze Age archaeology strongly point to an emphasis upon Epirote connections and little or limited emphasis

---

28   cf. Greenslade & Hodges 2013.
29   Hodges 2015.
30   cf. Gwynne, Hodges & Vroom 2014; Hernandez 2019.
31   Carvajal & Palanco 2013.
32   Hodges & Paterlini 2013.
33   Hodges 2016.

upon maritime Mediterranean connectivity. This regional picture is intriguing given the strong relations between the western Peloponnese and southern Ionian Islands with southern Italy. The archaeology from the age of Troy indicates an under-developed Bronze Age community that looked inwards rather than outwards.[34] The same picture emerges from the Ottoman archaeology.[35] Again, the emphasis, in an age of significant Mediterranean connectivity, was inwards with Ioannina, in southern Epirus, becoming a central point of reference.

By contrast, the Hellenistic, Roman, Byzantine and Venetian archaeology shows that there was Mediterranean connectivity with the port and the Pavlass fluvial corridor. Metaphorically the Venetian enclave, defined and mapped in detail on the ground, represents this model. A similar enclave probably existed from as early as the Archaic Greek period, defined by the Dema wall (apparently separating the Hellenistic territories of Butrint and Phoinike) which runs a kilometre from the Ionian Sea to the shore of Lake Butrint. The wall, it appears, was refurbished in the eleventh century as the northern extent of Butrint's hinterland, and remained a notional boundary until the Ottoman annexation of Butrint after 1797 (Figure 6.10).[36] The spatial footprint of this enclave is not very different today from the extent of the Butrint National Park, defined through the agency of the Butrint Foundation in 1999/2000, and the Ramsar area defined in 2002. Today, visitors are drawn to Butrint by its maritime context, coming in large numbers by ferries from Corfu, or by car from inland locations to enjoy the beaches near Butrint.

The third spatial condition was a north-south axis imposed on Butrint with the liminality created by the definition of the southern frontier of Albania just to the south (affirmed in 1921). This axis lasted from 1913 until the 1990s, and is responsible for the remote, natural spirit of the place, as noted above. When S.S. Clarke and Luigi Ugolini came here in the 1920s there was no road to the site. The construction of the road for Khruschchev's visit in 1959, masterminded by Butrint's archaeologist, Dhimosten Budina, provided access to the monument for selective visitors, and in time for collective farms in this liminal frontier zone.[37]

Butrint only prospered as an urban or quasi urban concept when it exploited its Mediterranean connectivity. The footprint of the Archaic and early Hellenistic settlements was small and essentially arranged around the

---

34 cf. Lima 2013.
35 cf. Carvajal & Palanco 2013.
36 Hodges 2014.
37 Hodges 2009.

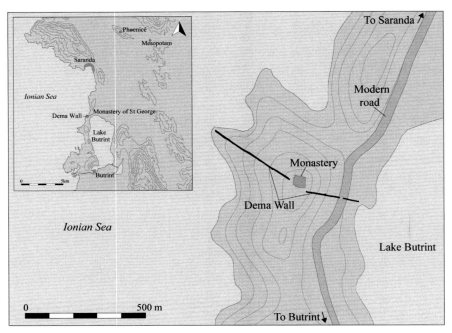

FIGURE 6.10   Map showing the location of the (archaic Greek) Dema Wall (refurbished in the 11th century and Venetian times)
© BUTRINT FOUNDATION ARCHIVES

low promontory of the isthmus around which the Vivari channel winds. The later Hellenistic town belonging to the Roman republican period enlarged this footprint and included civic amenities like the theatre. The first substantive fortifications belong to this time.

Butrint was transformed appropriately in the early Empire, the age of Virgil. While the epic story may be a misleading topographical guide, it is an approximate index of its sudden new significance. Following the battle of Actium in 31 BCE, the Roman colony envisaged under Julius Caesar was actually established in the 20s BCE by Augustus. This also involved a major new civic centre, as David Hernandez has shown, with civic amenities such as a bridge to connect the port to the coastal route through Epirus, and an aqueduct.[38] With this transformation came not only new fountains and internal roads, but the creation of residential blocks that included one on the south side of the Vivari channel.

---

38   Hernandez & Çondi, 2014; Hernandez 2017c.

This Augustan-era legacy was altered and transformed in later antiquity by new topographical elements, new defences and, most of all, by adaptation to a higher water table after seismic events in the 360s. The Augustan paradigm, except for two episodes, essentially defined the Butrint we see today. Thus, the eleventh-century Byzantine town architects used the Augustan concept; only the elements were different. This Middle Byzantine town then shaped the later Byzantine/Venetian topography until the town was abandoned in about 1533 (in the face of an Ottoman army advancing on Corfu).

The two episodes at variance with the Augustan footprint lay beyond the walled isthmus on the plain to the south of the Vivari channel. The first episode was approximately from the mid-ninth to the late-tenth century and nestled within the ruins of the Roman suburb. Here was located an administrative centre for the Byzantine region. Notably unfortified, and characterized by the presence of Byzantine seals and coin finds, it appears to have controlled trade with merchants from Italy or elsewhere in Byzantine Greece.[39] Conceivably, periodic trade occurred inside the ruined Roman town, close to the Vivari channel. The inversion of the topographical arrangement of the settlement is all the more intriguing because the conventional historical narrative lays emphasis upon how unsettled the ninth century was. The Vrina plain settlement appears to challenge this interpretation.

The second episode marks the end of residential occupation of the isthmus promontory. The passage of an Ottoman army to besiege Butrint in 1533 plainly called attention to the defensive costs involved in maintaining the old town while Corfu expanded as a Venetian hub in the lower Adriatic Sea region. The expedient solution, creating Corfu's 'right eye' was to build a compact fortress—today known as the Triangular Fortress—on the south side of the Vivari channel, at the entrance to the Pavlass river. This fortress offered security not only for the fishermen operating farms here, but also a robust military bulwark on the coast. Subsequently, after the fall of the Venetian empire, the Venetian fisherman's house on the very edge of the coast was transformed by Ali Pasha into a low castle to stop raids by the British navy on the Ottoman territory.[40] In these circumstances, the Venetian Triangular Fortress became the home of a local Ottoman official, one of his tasks being to provide fish for the court at Ioannina.

---

39   Greenslade & Hodges 2013.
40   Carvajal & Palanco 2013.

4 The Importance of Topography in Narrative

S.S. Clarke aborted his visit to Butrint because it appeared to not have fitted his positivistic historical narrative based on monumental archaeology. Luigi Ugolini initially did the same, but changed his mind with the aspiration of using his project for a larger political purpose. Both assumed history to be constructed from textual narratives in an age where stratigraphic archaeology and its promise was in its infancy. Today, just as the contemporary footprint of the Butrint National Park materially informs (and vice versa) a new history of post-Communist Albania, so we need to use the archaeology of this port, through its many topographical iterations, to help interpret the narrative history of this region.

Starting with the Bronze Age, this region appears to have been marginal as Mediterranean polities reached out to each other. No palace or similar settlement existed at Butrint; only a small hilltop encampment. Whether there was some memory of this encampment which gave rise to the Archaic and Classical sanctuary here is presently a matter of speculation. The size of this sanctuary settlement, too, merits further research. A strong case has been made by Hernandez for a proto-urban settlement that became the nucleus of the Hellenistic walled town.[41] Butrint before 30 BCE, however, was small in size, and plainly overshadowed in scale and significance by Corfu to the south-west, Gitani to the south-east and Phoinike to the north. Its stature was as a shrine rather than an urban community, a coastal, small version of Dodona, inland near Ioannina.

The colonial Roman town of the Augustan period was conceived on a new scale, thanks to the relations of the powerful, local family headed by Titus Pomponius. His agency, and especially his connections at court in Rome, coincided with the strong rise of Mediterranean trade, helping to advance the town in the face of its regional competitors. Phoinike attempted to revive its own status in the Mid Roman period as its community invested in a new theatre.[42] In reality, the old republican hilltop town lay too far from the sea, and needed an outport, Onchesmus (modern Saranda),[43] to participate in Mediterranean trade. The presence at Butrint in the second to fourth centuries of major villas alongside the channel suggests its wealth base was sustained in the recession of this era. Certainly, the archaeology shows it prospered in Late Antiquity

---

41 Hernandez 2017a.
42 De Maria 2007.
43 Hodges 2007.

FIGURE 6.11　View of the late antique settlement at Diaporit, showing the small chapel, residence, bath-house and, in the distance, the 6th-century basilica
PHOTOGRAPH © BUTRINT FOUNDATION ARCHIVES

with civic investment in new fortifications—the first since the Hellenistic era—and the presence of three major ecclesiastical communities: the bishop's large church inside the walls, a probable monastery stationed at the bridgehead in the old suburb, and another probable monastery at Diaporit on the shore of Lake Butrint (Figure 6.11).[44]

The zenith of Butrint in the sixth century, an economic barometer of the region and the port's hinterland, was followed imminently by its rapid contraction. There is no evidence of anything cataclysmic—a Slavic sack, or the Justinianic plague, for example. Instead, monumental and timber intra-mural buildings as well as the extra-mural monastic communities fell into ruin, and a new topographic feature, intra-mural random burial began to occur. Within a century classical Butrint became archaeologically invisible. Some settlement probably continued but where or on what scale is unclear.[45]

44　Bowden & Përzhita 2014.
45　Bowden & Hodges 2012.

The Middle Byzantine settlement comprised two tower-houses in the western defences. Small in scale, the material culture indicates that these belonged to a magnate official. Both towers were sacked and yet, paradoxically, their successor settlement lay outside Butrint on the Vrina plain. This ninth to tenth-century community, it has been proposed, was home to an archon, an official responsible for the region of Vagnetia. Expedient in architectural form, the material culture suggests moveable wealth of a certain status. From here, we might surmise, came the agency to re-fashion Butrint as a town in the late tenth and early eleventh centuries. Over two phases the old walls were refurbished before terraces were laid over the water-logged lower city and urban dwellings and family churches were constructed. The urban renewal, like that at neighbouring Himara and Rogoi, suggests an Adriatic Sea policy to promote Byzantine commerce as trade once again characterized connections within the central Mediterranean.[46] Again, Butrint is a barometer of this renewed connectivity.

Medieval expansion here, unlike other ports such as Dubrovnik, Kotor, and Stari Bar did not occur.[47] The eleventh-century bold investment was increased with the addition of an official's fortress on the acropolis but relatively little else. The limited presence of Middle Byzantine sites in the hinterland of Butrint, unlike the Hellenistic and Roman periods, may well reflect the new, entirely maritime and defensive emphasis of Butrint. Indeed, we must surmise that a reprise of its Augustan zenith was eclipsed by the rapid growth of Corfu as a Venetian hub. As a result, the steady contraction of the town to a few churches, fish-houses, and long defences made it very expensive to maintain. As the town gained an international status, thanks to the late medieval and Renaissance fascination with Virgil's *Aeneid*, paradoxically a succession of castellans lamented the costs of maintaining its fortifications. As the Albanians became a threatening presence beyond the Venetian enclave, so Butrint became de facto a place visited by educated tourists like Buondelmonti, Ciriaco d'Ancona,[48] Casanova, and later by Colonel Martin Leake (1835) and François De Pouqueville.

The stratigraphic evidence from many excavations small and large provides a new historical body for a long-nurtured textual narrative. The rise and fall of the ancient and medieval towns of Butrint each had differing spatial meanings for their respective inhabitants and, with the exception of the early Roman colony, mostly ephemeral impacts on their hinterlands. This episodic history simply accelerated in the twentieth century when the ruined town shifted

---

46   Hodges 2015.
47   cf. Gelichi 2008.
48   cf. Gwynne, Hodges & Vroom 2014.

from being an Ottoman to a liminal place and then became, in 1992, a Unesco World Heritage site. Today, its liminal spirit is celebrated, and is sometimes similar to that experienced by S.S. Clarke and Luigi Ugolini. At the same time, it is a quintessential Mediterranean port commanding a fluvial corridor that, given its new management in 2018 by an Albanian-American NGO, may lead it to become a progressive component in the re-making of southern Albania (a region that, as we have seen, Butrint only interacted with in Bronze Age and Ottoman times).[49]

Bibliography

Secondary Sources

Bescoby, D. 2013. "Landscape and environmental change; new perspectives", in Hansen, Hodges & Leppard (eds) 2013, 22–30.

Bowden, W. & R. Hodges 2011. *Butrint. Excavations at the Triconch Palace*. Oxford.

Bowden, W. & R. Hodges 2012. "An 'Ice Age settling on the Roman Empire': Post-Roman Butrint between strategy and serendipity", in Christie & Augenti (eds) 2012, 207–41.

Bowden, W. & L. Përzhita 2014. "The Roman villa and Early Christian complex at Diaporit'", in Përzhita et al. (eds) 2014, 469–84.

Carvajal, J. C. & A. Palanco 2013. "The castle of Ali Pasha at Butrint", in Hansen, Hodges & Leppard (eds) 2013, 288–307.

Christie, N. & A. Augenti (eds) 2012. *Urbes Extinctae*. Aldershot.

De Maria, S. 2007. "Butrinto e Fenice: a confront", in Hansen & Hodges (eds) 2007, 175–88.

De Pouqueville, F. H. C. 1820. *Travels in Epirus, Albania, Macedonia and Thessaly*. London.

Gelichi, S. 2008. *A Town through the Ages. The 2006–2007 archaeological project in Stari Bar*. Florence.

Gilkes, O. J. 2003a. "Luigi Maria Ugolini and the Italian Archaeological Mission to Albania", in Gilkes (ed.) 2003b, 3–23.

Gilkes, O. J. (ed.) 2003b. *The Theatre at Butrint*. London.

Gilkes, O. J. & L. Miraj 2000. "The myth of Aeneas, the Italian archaeological mission in Albania 1924–43", *Public Archaeology* 1, 109–24.

---

49   All the illustrations are courtesy of the Butrint Foundation archive, except for the portrait of S.S. Clarke which I obtained from the British School at Athens archive, to whom I am indebted. My thanks to Will Bowden and David Hernandez for discussions about Butrint, and to Sarah Leppard for the line drawings.

Greenslade, S. 2013. "The Vrina Plain settlement between the 1st–13th centuries", in Hansen, Hodges & Leppard (eds) 2013, 123–64.

Greenslade, S. & R. Hodges 2013. "The aristocratic oikos on the Vrina Plain, Butrint, c. AD 830–1200", *BMGS* 37, 1–19.

Gwynne, P., R. Hodges & J. Vroom 2014. "Archaeology and Epic: Butrint and Ugolino Verino's Carlias", *Papers of the British School at Rome* 82, 199–235.

Hammond, N. G. L. 1967. *Epirus*. Oxford.

Hansen, I. L. & R. Hodges (eds) 2007. *Roman Butrint. An Assessment*. Oxford.

Hansen, I. L., R. Hodges & S. Leppard (eds) 2013. *Butrint 4. The archaeology and histories of an Ionian town*. Oxford.

Hernandez, D. R. 2017a. "Bouthrotos (Butrint) in the Archaic and Classical Periods: The Acropolis and Temple of Athena Polias", *Hesperia* 86.2, 205–71.

Hernandez, D. R. 2017b. "Battling water: the frontiers of archaeological excavations at Butrint", *Annual of the British School at Athens* 116, 1–34.

Hernandez, D. R. 2017c. "Buthrotum's Sacred Topography and the Imperial Cult, I: The West Courtyard and Pavement Inscription", *Journal of Roman Archaeology* 30, 38–63.

Hernandez, D. R. 2019. "The abandonment of Butrint. From Venetian enclave to Ottoman backwater" *Hesperia* 88.2, 365–419.

Hernandez, D. & D. Çondi 2014. "The formation of Butrint: new insights from excavations in the Roman forum", in Përzhita et al. (eds) 2014, 285–302.

Hodges, R. 2006. *Eternal Butrint. An UNESCO World Heritage Site in Albania*. London.

Hodges 2007. *Saranda. Ancient Onchesmos. A Short History and Guide*, Tirana.

Hodges, R. 2009. "Nikita Khrushchev's visit to Butrint. May 1959", *Expedition* 51.3, 24–26.

Hodges, R. 2014. "Butrint's northern frontier in the 11th century: the Dema Wall", *Annual of the British School at Athens* 113, 1–5.

Hodges, R. 2015. "'A God-guarded city'? The New Medieval Town of Butrint", *BMGS* 39, 191–218.

Hodges, R. 2016. *The Archaeology of Mediterranean Placemaking. Butrint and the Global Heritage Industry*. London.

Hodges, R. 2017. "A colonial indifference to Butrint, 1923–24", in Σπείρα, Επιστημονική συνάντηση προς τιμήν της Αγγέλικας Ντούζουγλη και του Κωνσταντίνου Ζάχου. Πρακτικά (*Conference in honour of Angelika Douzougli and Konstantinos Zachos, Ioannina, 1st–3rd November 2012*), 411–20. Athens.

Hodges, R., W. Bowden & K. Lako (eds) 2004. *Byzantine Butrint: Excavations and Survey 1994–1999*. Oxford.

Hodges, R. & A. Paterlini 2013. "A short history of the Butrint Foundation's conservation programme at Butrint, Albania: 1994–2012", *Conservation and Management of Archaeological Sites* 15, 253–79.

Hodges, R., E. Carr, A. Sebastiani & E. Vaccaro 2016. "Beyond Butrint: the 'Mursi' survey, 2008", *Annual of the British School at Athens* 115, 1–29.

Kamani, S. 2013. "The Western Defences", in Hansen, Hodges & Leppard (eds), 245–56.

Kondis, B. 1997. "Epirus as part of the Greek state: the inter-war period", in M. B. Sakellariou (ed.) 1997, *Epirus*, 376–87. Athens.

Lane, A., D. Bescoby, O. Gilkes & S. O'Hara 2004. "The environs of Butrint 1: the 1995–96 environmental survey", in Hodges, Bowden & Lako (eds) 2004, 27–46.

Leake, W. M. 1835. *Travels in Northern Greece*. London.

Leppard, S. 2013. "The Roman Bridge of Butrint", in Hansen, Hodges & Leppard (eds) 2013, 97–104.

Lima, S. 2013. "Butrint and the Pavllas River Valley in the late Bronze Age and early Iron Age", in Hansen, Hodges & Leppard (eds) 2013, 31–46.

Martin, S. 2001. *The Butrint Management Plan*. London.

McHale, B. 1992. *Constructing Postmodernism*. London.

Molla, N. 2013. "The Great Basilica", in Hansen, Hodges & Leppard (eds) 2013, 202–14.

Morellón, M., G. Sinopoli, A Izdebski, L. Sadori, F. Anselmetti, E. Regattieri, B. Wagner, B. Brushulli, R. Hodges and D. Ariztegui 2018. "Environment, Climate and Society in Roman and Byzantine Butrint", *Late Antique Archaeology* 13, 3–17.

Përzhita, L. et al. (eds) 2014. *International Congress of Albanian Archaeological Studies*. Athens.

Pluciennik, M., K. Lako, L. Përzhita & D. Brennan 2004. "The environs of Butrint 2: the 1995–96 field survey", in Hodges, Bowden & Lako (eds) 2004, 47–63.

Ugolini, L. M. 1927. *Albania Antica*. Vol. 1: *Ricerche Archeologiche*. Rome.

Ugolini, L. M. 1937. *Butrinto. Il mito d'Enea, gli scavi*. Rome.

At Home in Cappadocia

The Spatialities of a Byzantine Domestic Landscape

Robert Ousterhout

Comfort, as Witold Rybczynski reminds us in *Home: A Short History of an Idea*, is a modern concept, at least as we understand the term.[1] Historically, the term connoted more about security than about physical ease; for most periods, comfort was provided by a firmly locked door, not an overstuffed chair. Our English word comfort derives from Latin verb *confortare*, meaning "to strengthen greatly", a derivative of *fortis*, or "strong". In our present-day usage, the word has come to connote physical or psychological ease. In fact, we are bombarded by advertisements for both types of comfort these days, such as security alarms with motion-activated cameras, operated from our digital phones; as well as endless designer recommendations for making our homes and domestic lives cozy—the Danish concept of the *Hygge* lifestyle is now ubiquitous.

Curiously, when historians look at daily life in an historical context, they often seek out those aspects that correspond to our own—that is, they look for comfort as we would understand the term today— something akin to the *Hygge* lifestyle. As I shall argue, daily life in the Byzantine period was rarely comfortable, in either sense of the word. For what follows, I draw my examples from the volcanic region of Cappadocia, in central Anatolia, while attempting to make some distinctions between the notions of comfort (in the modern sense) and security. At the same time, an examination of rock-cut residences raises questions about what is meant by "home" as a cultural concept within the expectations of a particular culture—in this case, the rock-cut dwellings of Cappadocia vis-à-vis those now vanished houses, villas, and *oikoi*, which they appear to have imitated, but which we know primarily from texts, written elsewhere, describing buildings that once existed elsewhere.

In fact, our best-preserved evidence for daily life in the Byzantine period comes from Cappadocia, where the rock-carved environment preserves countless architectural spaces representing all aspects of daily life, across a broad social spectrum.[2] The tenth-century historian, Leo the Deacon, noted that the

---

1 Rybczynski 1986.
2 For much of what follows see Ousterhout 2017; Idem 2011. Note also Kalas 2007.

inhabitants of Cappadocia used to be called "troglodytes": "They used to be called Troglodytes because they dwelt in caves, hollows, and labyrinths, as if in dens and holes. (Τρωγλοδῦται τὸ ἔθνος τὸ πρόσθεν κατωνομάζετο, τῷ ἐν τρώγλαις καὶ χηραμοῖς καὶ λαβυρίνθοις, ὡσανεὶ φωλεοῖς καὶ ὑπιωγαῖς, ὑποδύεσθαι)".[3] That is to say, they lived like animals. But his comment is made in passing, and it is unclear from his account whether he is imparting a first-hand observation or simply telling tales. Be that as it may, many of the myriad architectural spaces of the region are carefully carved and architectonically detailed, hardly to be confused with the lairs of moles or gophers. These range from houses, villages, monasteries, hermitages, churches, and chapels, to stables, storerooms, dovecotes, beehives, cisterns, irrigation systems, wine presses, and mills. For many of these elements, there is little to compare surviving from elsewhere in the Byzantine world. The wealth of physical evidence preserved from the region is only beginning to be studied, but its potential significance is undermined by the complete absence of texts, and the almost complete absence of stratigraphic archaeology. Along with an internal history, domestic assemblages and even a clear ceramic chronology are not to be found.

The abundant churches and chapels of the region have garnered much of the attention, as these replicate the standard architectural forms and painted programs of masonry churches. Many of the domestic spaces appear to do the same, at least for the upper level of Cappadocian society, and these deserve to be better known. In their forms and organization, the rock-cut houses of Cappadocia likely reflect their ephemeral urban counterparts, for which we have only limited evidence. All the same, assigning functions to architectural spaces remains a challenge—that is, how do we put people back into these spaces?

Another aspect of the Cappadocian housing relates more directly to the theme of this volume. The so-called Spatial Turn in historical scholarship marked a paradigm shift in outlook and perspective, offering new mean of analysis and new sets of questions to add to our scholarly toolbox.[4] Within the confines of the Byzantine Empire, Cappadocia provides a useful opportunity for discussions about space because of the direct and reciprocal relationship between the surviving rock-cut dwellings and the surrounding agricultural landscapes, all of which suggests a keen awareness of natural world. As the editors to this volume argue for Byzantium in general, the inhabitants of

---

3   Leo the Deacon, ed. Talbot and Sullivan 2005, 87; Leo Diaconus, *Historia*, III.α' 5–7, ed. K.B. Hase, *Leonis diaconi Caloënsis historiae libri decem* [Corpus scriptorum historiae Byzantinae, Bonn: Weber, 1828]: 35 (3–178).

4   See the comments in the Editors' Introduction to this volume.

Cappadocia surely had a strong sense of belonging to their land, and this sense must have affected both their personal and collective identities. Within the bewildering vastness of the landscape, the Cappadocians produced, constructed, or carved spaces on a relatable human-scape—what present-day theorists may regard as the translation of space to place.

That said, Byzantinists in general have been slow to theorize spatialities in dialogue with other fields of study. Rather than blame the stodginess of scholars, we may find one of the reasons for this under-theorization in the relative newness of Byzantine Studies. Too much of our critical evidence remains unpublished, unedited, un-translated, unexcavated, or undocumented. My own recent studies of Cappadocia alone have added or clarified dozens of sites; French and Italian scholars have added many others.[5] Frustratingly, beyond a few meagre inscriptions, internal textual evidence from the Byzantine period is absent. This requires the historian to use a very different approach from the traditional text-based studies, to rely on the spatial syntax of material remains to come to terms with the daily lives and attitudes of the inhabitants. This is no easy task, and alas, the evocative landscape with its myriad human interventions seems to demand a narrative, and scholars are often all too willing to leap into the void. Indeed, it is easy—and all too tempting—to make assumptions based on far too little evidence. With that caveat, please excuse my reticence in what follows, which I offer as a sort of prolegomena to the spatialities of Byzantine Cappadocia.

1   The Cappadocian House and Its Components

Rock-carved elite residences are scattered throughout the region—some are isolated, while others are associated with villages. Most commonly these centred on courtyards carved into the slope of the bedrock, with rooms organized around two, three, and occasionally four sides of the courtyard. The finer of these were likely the residences of the powerful, landowning families of the region. The residence now known as Hallaç Manastırı (the so-called Hospital Monastery) near Ortahisar, presents a good example, which we may take as a paradigm of a rock-cut mansion (Figures 7.1–3).

Initially published as a monastery, most scholars now view it instead as a secular residence.[6] Cut into the slope of the plateau facing south, the large

---

5   Ousterhout 2019, with extensive bibliography.
6   Rodley 1982; Mathews & Daskalakis-Mathews 1997.

FIGURE 7.1   Ortahisar (near), Hallaç Manastırı, view into courtyard, looking northeast
AUTHOR'S COPYRIGHT

complex had rooms organized around three sides of a courtyard, with the major spaces connecting to a broad vestibule, originally fronted by a portico, now fallen, which measured ca. 6 by 20 m. Lavishly detailed with pilasters and arcades, the vestibule was covered by a barrel vault. On axis is a three-aisled hall that terminates in a rectangular apse. Its walls are arcaded, and the aisles are separated from the barrel-vaulted nave by cylindrical piers. To either side are square rooms, their walls articulated with niches. These initially did not open to the exterior and were accessible only from the hall. From the west end of the vestibule another door connected to a centrally-planned hall, with a cross-in-square plan, its dome rising above four stout columns. Next to this, but not accessible from it, is a square room, originally with a conical vault, of a type identified as a kitchen. In the east range, somewhat removed from the portico, is an unfinished room with an upper level of dovecotes, and at the southern extreme, a church. The last has a cross-in-square plan and is tall in its proportions with much carved detail, but very little painted decoration. Large by Cappadocian standards, the naos measures ca. 7 x 8 m, extended to the south by a domed tomb chamber. All parts of the complex seem to have been carved at the same time, without evidence of a long period of use.

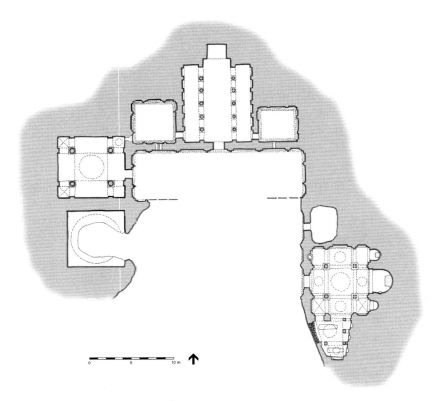

FIGURE 7.2   Ortahisar (near), Hallaç Manastırı, plan
AUTHOR'S COPYRIGHT, REDRAWN AFTER L. RODLEY

A date in the middle of the eleventh century or perhaps slightly later seems likely.[7]

Initially Hallaç was fronted by a carved façade, now fallen, but this would have formed a significant part of its language of power. Portions of the lateral façade are preserved, but we should imagine the carved façade to resemble those preserved elsewhere, as at Yaprakhisar (Figure 7.4).[8] An architectonically delineated façade would associate the complex with "real" (i.e., masonry) architecture and, in effect, advertise the elite status of the occupants. Assigning specific functions to the various spaces is problematic, however, as will be discussed below. At least from its organization—and from the many similar examples—we can suggest that the portico and hall were essential, primary

---

7   Rodley 1985, 24–26.
8   Ousterhout 2017, 351–53; Kalas 2000, 107–17.

FIGURE 7.3 Ortahisar (near), Hallaç Manastırı, interior of the hall, looking north
AUTHOR'S COPYRIGHT

features for the daily ceremonial life of a secular establishment of elite status, and while large, the church would have been secondary in importance, as it is situated at a distance from the core of the complex and does not communicate directly with it—perhaps to make it accessible for worship to those outside the household.

The types of rooms found at Hallaç are common throughout Cappadocia and neighbouring regions, as are the basic planning characteristics of the complex, although most were executed on a considerably smaller scale. The emphasis at Hallaç and similar complexes is on the formal or ceremonial spaces, and with the exception of the kitchen and the dovecote, all are elegantly detailed. But how were they used? The longitudinal hall, for example, could take on a variety of forms—three-aisled, single-aisled, set either axially or transversally, with a flat ceiling, terminating in a rectangular apse. Invariably, this was the most prominent space in the complex, given central position, and it must have been of central importance to the daily activities of the household. These halls may be the descendants of the Late Antique audience halls—ceremonial settings for the reception of visitors and retainers, where the daily business of the household was conducted. They might also be used similar to the western

FIGURE 7.4   Selime-Yaprakhisar, Area 11, façade
AUTHOR'S COPYRIGHT

European halls, a combination of audience hall and multi-functioned living space.[9]

Secondary, centrally-planned halls, such as the cross-in-square hall at Hallaç, are also common across Cappadocia, and many rock-cut complexes were equipped with both. These are often variations on the cruciform in plan, usually covered by a dome, as at Hallaç.[10] Various functions have been hypothesized, such as triclinia or bedchambers. One suggestion is that these were the women's quarters.[11] None of these suggestions makes sense. Formal dining as occurred in antiquity seems to have ended by the Byzantine Transitional Period (the so-called Dark Ages, ca. 680–850), and there is no evidence for beds or tables in these chambers. Moreover, gender segregation is the household seems unlikely.[12] Instead, it may have been a private hall for the use of the head of the household, but without further evidence, assignment of function

9   Ousterhout 2011, 170–74.
10   Ousterhout 2011, 174–76.
11   Mathews & Daskalakis-Mathews 1997.
12   Kazhdan 1998.

is entirely speculative. Also problematic are the two square rooms flanking the hall at Hallaç. Although neatly carved, they were initially accessible only from the hall and windowless. These might have been storerooms or treasuries, but they find no close comparisons in other Cappadocian domestic complexes.

Other, less elegantly carved spaces appear at some distance from the courtyard and are likely utilitarian or agricultural in function. These are more easily identified as to function. Kitchens, for example, usually have conical vaults to allow the smoke to evacuate.[13] The enormous kitchen at Selime may have served several households (Figure 7.5). Dovecotes are often included on an upper level, usually above the portico, with limited access.[14] At Hallaç, these are set off to one side (above the ladder in Figure 7.1), probably because of the limited elevation above the portico, which is now completely eroded. The settlement at Çanlı Kilise preserves several good examples, as well as evidence these were integral components of the complexes (Figure 7.6). On the interior, spaces are irregular and lined with pigeonholes. Guano collected from the dovecotes would have provided fertilizer for the kitchen gardens of the households.

At many sites, stables are also a common feature. In these, low-cut troughs or mangers, ca. 30 cm above floor level, may be used for sheep and goats, while mangers ca. 30–80 cm above floor level may be for cattle or donkeys; those higher were for different breeds of horses.[15] As ownership of horses was a sign of wealth, stables for horses were standard components of elite residences. Although situated separately from the main ceremonial spaces in the courtyard, they were given a more formal treatment than stables for other animals. Large rectangular spaces, their lateral walls are lined with rock-cut mangers, often with small holes for tethering the individual horses. The standard manger height for horses is ca. 90 to 110 cm, with a depth of ca. 50 cm.[16] A common type of stable appears in several examples at Açıksaray, a prosperous settlement whose economy may have been based on horse breeding (Figure 7.7). Covered by a longitudinal barrel vault, the space is extended to the sides by quadrant vaults above rock-cut mangers.

Winemaking facilities are ubiquitous in the rock-cut settlements of Cappadocia, and the region is well known today for wine production, as it was historically. In the thirteenth century, Cappadocian wines were famous, and the Greek communities continued to produce wine according to traditional

---

13 Kalas 2009.
14 Ousterhout 2011, 179–81; Demenge 1995.
15 Tütüncü 2008, esp. Figs. 8–17; Öztürk 2014.
16 Tütüncü 2008, esp. 44.

FIGURE 7.5 Selime, Kale complex, kitchen
AUTHOR'S COPYRIGHT

FIGURE 7.10 Keşlikköy, rock-cut beehive, interior
AUTHOR'S COPYRIGHT

2 Living in the Landscape

With a bit of on-site sleuthing, it is possible to say something about the status, social stratification, economic basis, and quality of life in the houses and settlements of Cappadocia, as I have attempted elsewhere.[22] At Hallaç, the courtyard complex sits on an elevated platform, facing south, overlooking the landscape—presumably the land holdings of the estate. Many isolated elite residences are similarly situated, to see and to be seen. Within settlements, as at Çanlı Kilise or Soğanlı Dere, similar establishments form parts of villages. For all, the basic organizational unit is the oikos, the household unit, as Paul Magdalino has discussed, as daily life centred on the household.[23] In all examples, at the core were the formal spaces, serving the ceremonial, spiritual, and material needs of the inhabitants. As one moves away from the core, the spaces become less well-organized, and more utilitarian, with stables and other agricultural installations separated from the core. Moving further away may be smaller, irregular dwellings or servants or retainers—those whose lives

22   Ousterhout 2017, 271–368.
23   Magdalino 1984.

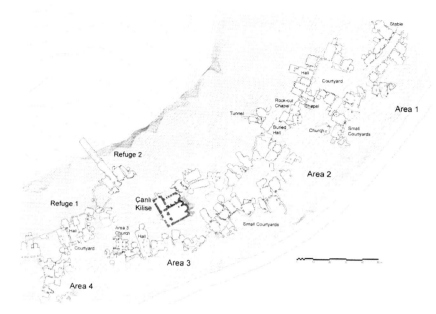

FIGURE 7.11   Akhisar (near), Çanlı Kilise settlement, plan of Areas 1–4
AUTHOR'S COPYRIGHT

depended on the primary inhabitants of the household. Still beyond lay the fields and grazing areas, the economic holdings of the oikos. The subsidiary spaces at Hallaç are not well preserved, but Area One at the Çanlı Kilise settlement gives some sense of the dependencies (Figure 7.11, right side).

One of the nagging questions for the analysis of such houses and settlements is the structure of the family and how we might situate its members into the spaces. First, what constituted a family?[24] Was it a nuclear family, or was it multigenerational? Did the families of siblings share the same spaces? Where were the servants housed? These are questions that have frustrated the Byzantine social historian. Even the question of gender segregation in the Byzantine household continues to be debated. What is clear, however, is that even at the upper levels of Cappadocian society, daily life for the household seems to have been limited to one or two formal spaces, with little evidence of privacy. It thus seems likely that the formally-carved spaces served multiple functions for many different family members.

24   See Patlagean 1987; Kazhdan 1998.

3 Finding Comfort in Cappadocia

Certain aspects of the rock-cut dwellings suggest a modicum of physical comfort. Large complexes like Hallaç are often oriented to the south or east, taking maximum advantage of natural daylight. Many are situated with spectacular views over the landscape, either as a visual manifestation of control and surveillance, or simply the aesthetic appreciation of natural beauty. The rock-cut spaces also came equipped with good natural insulation against the harsh climate of the region: the interiors retain the heat in the winter and stay cool in the summer time. The setting, living within the landscape, may also have provided a sense of place, a modicum of psychological comfort.

Although the interior spaces may have been improved with the presence of carpets and wall hangings, chairs and tables, physical comfort remained minimal, at least by modern standards. Unfortunately, evidence of furnishing is minimal in domestic spaces—something that stands in sharp contrast to monasteries or hermitages, many of which regularly feature rock-cut tables and benches in the refectories and rock-cut beds replete with rock-cut pillows in the dormitories or sleeping areas.[25] The latter might perhaps be taken as symbols of the asceticism of the monastic lifestyle. Nevertheless, it remains much easier to determine where monastics slept than where their secular counterparts spent the night.

Considering the architectural quality of interior spaces in the rock-cut residences, perhaps most surprising is the absence of natural light: in most rooms, no matter how finely carved, windows are rare, and most spaces opened to the exterior by a single door. The two halls at Hallaç each opened by a small door into the portico, so that the natural lighting was indirect; other spaces had no access to natural light at all (the small windows here represent more recent cuttings). In summer, the contrast between the brilliant, sunlit exterior and the dim interiors is particularly dramatic. Artificial illumination would have been necessary, provided by candles and lamps, and perhaps chandeliers in the more lavish spaces. During the winter braziers would have been necessary for heating the interiors spaces. All of these pose another problem: ventilation. With few openings to the exterior—most at ground level—and with low, flat or vaulted ceilings to many rooms, the interior spaces would have been filled with smoke. Nothing resembling a fireplace—i.e., a heating source with an accommodation for exhaust—appears in these houses, at least during the Byzantine period. Only the kitchens with their conical chimneys were provided with

---

25 Ousterhout 2017, 385–90, 402–11.

proper ventilation. The problem was exacerbated in later periods of habitation, as tandır ovens were cut into the floors of many poorly-ventilated spaces. Indeed, many interior surfaces remain blackened by centuries of accumulated soot. In short, while these spaces may have provided a welcome refuge from the heat of summer, year-round occupancy was much more challenging.

And what about aspects of psychological comfort—that is, security? Most large households, whether isolated or within a settlement, show little evidence of defence. Occasionally, courtyard complexes are four-sided, as at Eski Gümüş, with limited access from the exterior.[26] Some three-sided courtyards may have been provided with an outer barrier, closing off the fourth side, but there is no good evidence for this. Some settlements developed in relationship to existing fortresses: the settlement at Çanlı Kilise seems to have been founded in connection with the nearby fortress of Akhisar, which guarded the pass into the highlands.[27] At Selime, the extensive settlement appears below a fortress on the plateau above it.[28] On a more intimate level, many doorways preserve cutting for the insertion of wooden doors and locking mechanisms.

That said, evidence of insecurity abounds. The extensive "underground cities" of Cappadocia are often views as developing during the period of the Arab incursions of the 8th-9th centuries, as at Derinkuyu.[29] Extending deep underground, with access blocked by rolling-stone doors, the defensive character of these complexes is clearly evident. While they could have been used as storehouses or granaries, they could also have hidden village populations in times of danger. Smaller versions of the "underground cities" appear as refuges at many other sites. In our survey at Çanlı Kilise, for example, we discovered many of the courtyard complexes were equipped with small refuges, accessed from a back room by an inconspicuous tunnel, guarded by a rolling stone door (Figure 7.12).[30] While the settlement postdates the period of the Arab incursions, these refuges may respond to the increased insecurity of the post-Manzikert period, after 1071, as the Seljuks conquered the region.

All considered, life in Byzantine Cappadocia was likely no more and no less comfortable (in either meaning of the term) than elsewhere in the Empire, and the rock-carved environment provided certain natural amenities that other settings would not. We are left to wonder how the inhabitants of Cappadocia viewed their situation. Did they see their homes as "dens and holes", as Leo

26 Ousterhout 2017, 288–93.
27 Ousterhout 2011, 147–48.
28 Kalas 2006.
29 Ousterhout 2017, 346–49.
30 Ousterhout 2011; Idem 2017, 345.

FIGURE 7.6 Akhisar (near), Çanlı Kilise settlement, courtyard Area 13, view of dovecotes behind partially fallen façade
AUTHOR'S COPYRIGHT

FIGURE 7.7 Açık Saray, Area 1 stable, interior
AUTHOR'S COPYRIGHT

FIGURE 7.8   Erdemli, wine press
AUTHOR'S COPYRIGHT

practices into the twentieth century.[17] Wine was a standard part of the Byzantine diet.[18] The survey at Erdemli has yielded forty-four wine production facilities scattered throughout the southern portion of the settlement (Figure 7.8); the ongoing excavations at Mavrucan have identified more than thirty.[19] These may be identified by two interconnected basins, one the treading floor (ληνός) and the collecting vat. The higher and larger floor would drain into the vat.

Mills for grinding flour must have been standard features in villages, although few have been identified. At the village of Erdemli, the only mill adjoins the site's only elite residence, which presumably controlled it (Figure 7.9).[20] Elsewhere we have records of monasteries owning mills, and control of such necessary facilities must have been one aspect of status within the community. The mill has a central circular basin, into which the millstone

17   Vryonis 1971, 483; Balta 2008.
18   Kazhdan 1991. See also Kazhdan & Constable 1982, 55.
19   Çoraǧan Karakaya 2008, Figs. 4–7; Peker & Uyar 2011.
20   Çoraǧan Karakaya 2008, esp. Fig. 2.

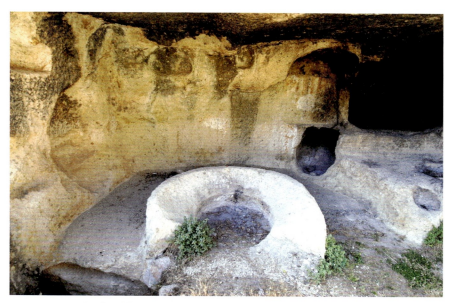

FIGURE 7.9 Erdemli, mill
AUTHOR'S COPYRIGHT

was set. A wooden rod anchored it to a depression in the ceiling. Poles were attached to the rod, which could be used to rotate the stone. A circular pathway surrounds the basin, where either humans or donkeys could walk to turn the stone.

There are also rare examples of rock-cut apiaries in Cappadocia that may be Byzantine in date, although the typologies of beehives continued into the Ottoman period and more recent times. Rock-cut beehives are distinguished on the exterior by a series of thin parallel vertical slits or rows of small holes to allow the bees to enter the hives, combined with a larger entrance, accessible by ladder, for the beekeeper to service the hives. Inside are tall compartments cut into the rock, ca. 30–40 cm wide and 90–100 cm deep. The hives could take two forms: tall cylindrical baskets could be set into the niches with the vertical slits; and the fixed cells opening to the holes had moveable stone slabs set into grooves to form shelves (Figure 7.10). More than 50 apiaries have been catalogued in the region.[21]

---

21   Bixio 2012, 17–18; 151–54; map p. 162; Roussel 2006; Idem 2008.

FIGURE 7.12   Akhisar (near), Çanlı Kilise settlement,
Area 4, rolling stone door to refuge
AUTHOR'S COPYRIGHT

the Deacon had pictured them? The many attempts to replicate "real" architecture suggest they may have taken issue with his assessment. Replete with finely-carved rooms, elegant façades and chapels, the replication of masonry forms must have provided the reassurance—at least in symbolic form—that the rock-cut house was indeed a home, and that a rock-cut home was indeed a house.

Bibliography

Primary Sources
Leo the Deacon, *The History of Leo the Deacon: Byzantine Military Expansion in the Tenth Century*. Ed. & tr. A.-M. Talbot & D. Sullivan. Washington, D.C. 2005.

Secondary Sources
Balta, E. 2008. "The Underground Rock-Cut Winepresses of Cappadocia", *Journal of Turkish Studies* 32, 61–88.

Bixio, R. (ed.) 2012. *Cappadocia: Schede dei siti sotterranei / Records of the underground sites*. Oxford.

Çorağan Karakaya, N. 2008. "Erdemli'de Ekmek ve Şarap", *Anadolu ve Çevresinde Ortaçağ* 2, 33–52.

Demenge, G. 1995. "Pigeonniers et ruchers byzantins de Cappadoce", *Archéologia* 311, 42–51.

Ellis, S. P. 1988. "The End of the Roman House", *AJA* 92, 565–76.

Jolivet-Lévy, C. & N. Lemaigre Desmenil 2009. "Un établissement monastique rural près de Bahçeli (Cappadoce)", in Vorderstrasse & Roodenberg (eds) 2009, 85–108.

Kalas, V. 2000. "Rock-Cut Architecture of the Peristrema Valley: Society and Settlement in Byzantine Cappadocia", unpublished Ph.D. diss., Institute of Fine Arts, New York University.

Kalas, V. 2006. "The 2004 Survey of the Byzantine Settlement at Selime-Yaprakhisar in the Peristrema Valley, Cappadocia", *DOP* 60, 271–93.

Kalas, V. 2007. "Cappadocia's Rock-Cut Courtyard Complexes: A Case Study for Domestic Architecture in Byzantium", in Lavan, Özgenel & Sarantis (eds) 2007, 393–414.

Kalas, V. 2009. "The Byzantine Kitchen in the Domestic Complexes of Cappadocia", in Vorderstrasse & Roodenberg (eds) 2009, 109–27.

Kazhdan, A. 1991. "Wine", *ODB* 3, 2199.

Kazhdan, A. 1998. "Women at Home", *DOP* 52, 1–17.

Kazhdan, A. P. & G. Constable 1982. *People and Power in Byzantium*. Washington, D. C.

Lavan, L., L. Özgenel & A. Sarantis (eds) 2007. *Housing in Late Antiquity: from Palaces to Shops*. Leiden.

Magdalino, P. 1984. "The Byzantine Aristocratic *Oikos*." In *The Byzantine Aristocracy IX–XIII Centuries*, M. Angold (ed). Oxford, 92–111.

Mathews, T. F. & A.-C. Daskalakis-Mathews 1997. "Islamic-Style Mansions in Byzantine Cappadocia and the Development of the Inverted T-Plan", *JSAH* 56, 294–315.

Ousterhout, R. 2011. *A Byzantine Settlement in Cappadocia*, rev. ed. Washington, D. C.

Ousterhout, R. 2017. *Visualizing Community: Art, Material Culture, and Settlement in Byzantine Cappadocia*. Washington, D.C.

Ousterhout, R. 2019. *Eastern Medieval Architecture: The Building Traditions of Byzantium and Neighboring Lands*. New York, Oxford.

Öztürk, F. G. 2014. "Açıksaray 'Open Palace': A Byzantine rock-cut settlement in Cappadocia", *BZ* 107, 785–810.

Patlagean, E. 1987. "Byzantium in the Tenth and Eleventh Centuries", in P. Veyne (ed.) 1987, *A History of Private Life I. from Pagan Rome to Byzantium*, 551–641. Cambridge, Mass.

Peker, N. & B. T. Uyar 2011. "Güzelöz-Başköy ve Çevresi Bizans Dönemi Yerleşimleri 2010", *Araştırma Sonuçları Toplantısı* 29.2, 251–65.

Rodley, L. 1982. "Hallaç Manastir. A Cave Monastery in Byzantine Cappadocia", *JÖB* 32.5, 425–34.

Rodley, L. 1985. *Cave monasteries of Byzantine Cappadocia*. Cambridge.

Roussel, G. 2006. "Découverte de vieux ruchers en Cappadoce", *Cahiers d'Apistoria* 5, 39–46.

Roussel, G. 2008. "Ruchers de Turquie", *Cahiers d'Apistoria* 7, 37–44.

Rybczynski, W. 1986. *Home: A Short History of an Idea*. New York.

Tütüncü, F. 2008. "The Land of Beautiful Horses: Stables in Middle Byzantine Cappadocia", M.A. thesis, Bilkent University, Ankara.

Vorderstrasse, T. & J. Roodenberg (eds) 2009. *The Archaeology of the Countryside in Medieval Anatolia*. Leiden.

Vryonis, S. 1971. *The Decline of Medieval Hellenism in Asia Minor and the Process of Islamization from the Eleventh through the Fifteenth Centuries*. Berkeley.

8
A Byzantine Space Oddity

The Cultural Geography of Foodways and Cuisine in the Eastern Mediterranean (700–1500)

Joanita Vroom

The moment I received the invitation by the organizers of the conference on "Spatialities of Byzantine Culture" to present on the spatial dimensions of Byzantine food provision, storage, preparation and dining (including ceramic vessels as spaces), I immediately thought of a scene in the Italian movie *Kaos* (1984). This film is directed by the brothers Paolo and Vittorio Taviani and is based on the novels of the Sicilian writer Luigi Pirandello (1867–1936). One of the stories in this movie is called *La giara*, or rather *A'giarra* in the Sicilian dialect of Agrigento. The title (which means "the vessel") refers to a large ceramic storage jar which is frequently used in the Mediterranean for the storage of grains and liquids (such as olive oil). The story in *Kaos* is in essence about a broken *giara* and about a jar maker who tries to fix the cracked pot. He is diligently working from inside the enormous pot, and indeed succeeds in fixing all the cracks, but then cannot get out of the vessel again. This leads, as one can imagine, to much commotion in the Sicilian rural community, where the story takes place.

But chaos is not limited to Italian cinema, not even chaos resulting from a person caught in a jar. It is well-known that in the Middle Ages people sometimes also got stuck in a ceramic or metal vessel. On wall paintings of Byzantine churches or in medieval sculptures one can, for example, detect saints (among whom St Vitus and St George), who ended up in a cauldron of hot oil. As one may notice in the pictures of St George in such a pot on Cretan church frescoes, it is not an environment in which human beings (not even Byzantine saints) feel comfortable (Figure 8.1).[1] This really looks like the last spatial context in which a medieval person would like to be, and perhaps even the ultimate Byzantine space oddity!

---

1 See for instance, the frescoes of St George in a cauldron at the Agios Nikolaos church in Mouri (ca. 1300) or the Agios Georgios church in Mourni (beginning of the fourteenth century).

FIGURE 8.1 Left above: Scene from the story 'La Giara' in the Italian movie *Kaos* (1984) (Wikimedia italia); Left below: Fresco of St George in a cauldron, Agios Nikolaos church, Mouri, ca. 1300; Right below: Fresco of St George in a cauldron, Agios Georgios church, Mourni, beginning of 14th century
AUTHOR'S COPYRIGHT

On the other hand, complete and broken vessels were used in hagiographic texts as positive metaphors, representing the human body, character and soul.[2] In this literary genre, utilitarian pots (made of earthenware) not only reflected the humble backgrounds of saints and their rural settings (often monasteries), but also their modest foodways and their communal eating and drinking habits with the use of one beaker and one plate for several diners.[3]

While keeping this in mind, the aim of this chapter is to trace general long-term developments and changes in food storage, in food preparation with various sources of heat and in food consumption in order to understand the

---

2 Gerstel 2007.
3 Gerstel 2007, 150.

physical remains and spatial aspects of Byzantine foodways and cuisine,[4] and use these as a window into past societies along with the purpose of this volume.[5] In this perspective I would like to discuss changing social and cultural practices related to food manners as a set of general ideas in a conceptualized Byzantine landscape. These social practices have no causal relation, but they influence each other and eventually make up the culinary *chaîne operatoire*. As I think that this approach forces archaeologists to think in different ways about their material, I will use some case-studies from archaeology to stress my point (including examples from my own archaeological projects in Albania, Greece and Turkey).[6] These case-studies range in date between circa the eighth and the fifteenth century. By using methods of quantification and middle-range theory (linking human behaviour and artefacts), I will discuss first the micro-geography of the Byzantine storeroom and of the Byzantine kitchen, followed by a closer inspection of the macro-geography of the Byzantine dining room.

1 Spatial Dimensions of Byzantine Food Preservation and Storage

The spatial aspects of Byzantine food preservation and storage are mainly technology driven, and facilities range from fixed storage areas (warehouses, granaries, barns, cellars) to portable containers (pithoi, amphorae). It is my intention to focus here on these last ones, and in particular on pithoi.[7] In fact, for my first case study I wish to present finds of large storage containers from excavations in the ancient Agora of Athens.

1.1 *Athenian Pithoi*

It is important to know that the excavated area of the Athenian Agora concerns in fact an industrial and commercial suburb west of the Byzantine fortification wall, and hence is not situated in the administrative core of the Byzantine city. Dense habitation was uncovered in this Byzantine suburb by the American

---

4 The term 'cuisine' is used here as an 'art of cooking and dining'; the term 'foodways' as 'a group's traditional food habits, encompassing feeling, thinking and behaviour towards food'; 'consumption' refers here rather to the spatial layout on the table of dining utensils.
5 The focus in this chapter is not on the food itself nor on historical recipes. For such an approach, see Vroom et al. 2017 and Vroom et al. 2018.
6 Given the complexity of 'spatiality' in Byzantine foodways and cuisine, I am aware that differences can occur from region to region in the eastern Mediterranean. Nevertheless, I think it is worthwhile to explore these practices in an as nuanced and realistic way as possible.
7 For an overview of Byzantine warehouses and granaries in the archaeological record, see Putzeys 2007, 75–76 with further literature.

School of Classical Studies at Athens (ASCSA) in the past 90 years.[8] Of the Agora pottery finds, I study, amongst other things, changes in shapes and sizes of glazed and unglazed utilitarian wares through various periods with one of the aims to distinguish long-term changes in Byzantine eating habits and dining manners.[9]

Within the Agora repertoire, the presence and the spatial distribution of ovens, wells and large storage jars (also known in Greek as a pithos, pitharion or pithopoulon) are studied as indicators for the function of spaces in a Byzantine house as kitchens or as storage rooms.[10] The area below many excavated Byzantine courtyard-style houses in the Athenian Agora had storage vessels of various sizes, which were most of the times dug into the ground.[11]

In order to get a glimpse of the spatial dimensions of food preservation and storage in Byzantine towns and in order to visualize the location of pithoi in domestic structures, a 2D map and a 3D reconstruction of three houses in one complex in the Athenian Agora were made, showing several interesting characteristics.[12] A number of installations can be identified in multiple phases of the complex, which included not only pithoi but also basins, cesspits (*bothroi*), wells, and funerary structures (*ostotheke*). Most pithoi were concentrated on the eastern side of the complex, and particularly in two rooms in the northwest part of the eastern house structure (Figure 8.2).[13]

The pithoi in this complex can be subdivided into two types: they are either built with ceramic sherds/tiles and fieldstones in hard lime mortar, or as a large earthenware vessel.[14] There are 17 masonry-built pithoi (63%) and 10 terracotta/ceramic pithoi (37%) in the complex. There seemed to have been a preference for the masonry-built pithoi, because they represent almost two-thirds

---

8   E.g. Frantz 1961.
9   For an earlier Agora study on Byzantine table wares, see Frantz 1938. At the moment ca. 40 unwashed sherds of coarse wares are prepared for organic residue analyses in the future.
10 According to Charalambos Bakirtzis (1989, 110–11 and 135), 'pithoi were large vessels stored in *pithones* and could not be moved once they had been placed in position, while pitharia, which were similar in shape but smaller in size, could be more easily moved and transported'.
11 Shear 1984, 52 and Figs. 17–18; 1997, 523, 531–32, Fig. 9, pl. 105:a; see also the pithoi on the Agora drawing of 'section MM': www.agathe.gr (Agora Drawing: PD 1169 (DA 132): Byzantine House; section MM, nb. 506).
12 This complex is located in section MM: Vroom & Boswinkel 2016, Figs. 4 and 5; see also in general, Vroom 2020.
13 Vroom & Boswinkel 2016, Fig. 6.
14 Vroom & Kondyli 2011, 34–35 and in particular Fig. 38, where one can distinguish clearly the two pithoi types in this Agora house complex.

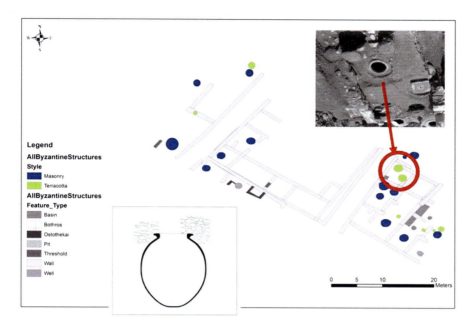

FIGURE 8.2 Athenian Agora, section MM, Distribution map of two types of pithoi (blue = masonry built and green = terracotta/ceramic), plus photograph of Byzantine terracotta/ceramic pithoi buried in the ground of the eastern building in this complex (after Vroom and Boswinkel 2016, Figures 6 and 7; photo number 2012.50-098 (x-72), ASCSA; cross-section drawing of a terracotta/ceramic pithos by A. Hoton, ASCSA)

of all the pithoi in the three houses (Figure 8.3).[15] This may have to do with the fact that these pithoi are, on average, larger than the ceramic ones.

Both pithoi-types were found throughout the three buildings, and in all the identified phases. Their bottoms were sometimes made flat to enable them to stand easily and to stabilize their weight;[16] handles sometimes occur on their external upper parts. The vessels had a wide flat rim in order to receive either a square stone slab, a broken tile or a lid (made of stone, wood or earthenware).[17]

---

15 See for a similar looking example, Bakirtzis 1989, pl. 53a. Apparently, there are also complete marble pithoi used in domestic and monastic contexts, as shown in Bakirtzis 1989, pl. 51a–b and Pitarakis 2010, 414–15, Fig. 16.12, who mentions that inscriptions on these marble vessels refer to measures of liquid capacity or *xestēs* (from the Roman *sextarius*), among which one of 'three hundred and fifty-five *xestai*".

16 Vroom 2003, 157; Grünbart 2007, 40.

17 Frantz 1961, 17; Vroom 2003, 157 and Fig. 6.13 (W 14.33). During the 1930s excavations in the Athenian Agora, pithoi were still recovered with such lids, tiles and stone slabs on top.

Both types were made impermeable, suggesting that they could have been used to store liquids (such as olive oil,[18] wine, vinegar or water) and solid foods (like grain, fruits, vegetables, legumes, salted fish and meat).[19] Chemical analyses carried out in Pergamon, for instance, showed distilled pine or cypress resin on the interior in order to seal these containers and as a preservative in wine storage and preservation.[20] Furthermore, surviving residues of food stored in these vessels can provide information about the diet of the people using them. Interesting in this respect is a pithos from Byzantine layers at Pessinous in central Turkey, which contained cereal grain, barley, triticum, peas and lentils, gallium and artiplex.[21]

Differences between the two pithoi types in the Agora complex can be distinguished in terms of quantity and size (Figure 8.3). The built stone pithoi have, on average, a 54% larger diameter and are 36% higher and therefore have more volume (the average volume for masonry pithoi is circa 1390 litres, for the ceramic ones circa 540 litres).[22] It is conceivable that it was easier to create larger pithoi with stone masonry than it was to create large ceramic ones. Many pithoi in the Agora are equal to or taller than human height.[23] Their height and diameter can indeed reach 2 meters, allowing them to contain up to circa 2000 litres.

The Athenian pithoi were all placed in the ground and sunk just below the house floor level with only the upper opening left outside (Figure 8.2). This provided not only an ideal dry, cool environment and a constant temperature for storage, but also protected their contents from harmful external effects (such as rodents or bugs). Pithoi were not only discovered in domestic contexts, but also in areas of industrial or commercial activities. Furthermore, written documents mention that pithoi were used in the houses of laymen or monks living in the countryside in order to store the year's harvest in this way.[24]

---

18   According to Evi Margaritis (2006, 26), archaeobotanical remains from Byzantine contexts in the Athenian Agora included several hundred complete and fragmented carbonized olive stones, suggesting that they represented 'the by-products of olive oil production'.
19   Bakirtzis 1989, 115; Rheidt 1990,199; 2002, 628; Grünbart 2007, 40, notes 7–8, who is even mentioning dried fruits such as figs and raisins for storage in pithoi; Giannopoulou 2010, 44 and Vroom 2018a, 178–82.
20   Rheidt 1990, 199 and n.23 (with further literature); 2002, 628 and figure 4.
21   Van Peteghem & Braeckman 2003, 165–68.
22   The volume is a rough estimate; see Vroom & Boswinkel 2016.
23   Vroom & Kondyli 2011, Fig. 38; cf. Rheidt 1990, 198 and Grünbart 2007, 40 for excavated pithoi in Pergamon and Corinth that can be up to 1,50 m. high and are able to hold ca. 100 to 1100 litres.
24   Oikonomides 1990, 211 and n.47.

Masonry	Max Diam (m)	Mouth Diam (m)	Height (m)	Volume (m)	Ceramic	Max Diam (m)	Mouth Diam (m)	Height (m)	Volume (m)
EP13	1,40	0,75	1,55	1,13	WP01	0,67	0,50	1,09	0,22
EP12	1,53	0,60	2,20	1,76	EP09	1,05	0,50	1,50	0,64
EP02	1,37	0,54	1,65	1,07	EP07	0,47	0,27	0,56	0,06
EP03	1,40	0,58	1,88	1,29	EP01	0,64	-	-	
EP04	1,80	0,60	2,08	2,21	EP14	0,70	-	-	
EP11	1,50	0,6	1,50	1,16	EP05	1,35	0,56	1,57	1,00
EP10	0,68	0,45	1,06	0,21	EP06	1,30	0,60	1,64	1,00
EP15	1,10	0,45	1,55	0,97	WP05	0,82	0,40	1,31	0,34
CP02	1,30	0,52	1,65	1,66	WP02	1,10	-	-	
CP01	1,65		1,85	1,51					
EP08	1,40	0,53	2,25	1,67	AVERAGE	0,90	0,47	1,28	0,54
WP04	2,00	-	1,67	-					
WP06	1,25	-	-	-					
WP03	1,30	-	-	-					
AVERAGE	1,39	0,56	1,74	1,39					

FIGURE 8.3 Athenian Agora, Dimensions of masonry built and terracotta/ceramic pithoi in section MM (after Vroom and Boswinkel 2016, tables 2–3; based on the excavation diaries of the ASCSA; cross-section drawing of a terracotta/ceramic pithos by A. Hoton, ASCSA)

1.2 *Pithoi in a Wider Context*

Ceramic pithoi (both complete ones and fragments) were recovered in urban and monastic centres, in fortresses, as well as in the countryside.[25] In Greece, for instance, they have been found until now at Corinth,[26] Argos,[27] Chalkis,[28] Panakton,[29] and on rural sites in surveyed areas such as Boeotia,[30]

---

25   Extra decorative elements were sometimes added to Byzantine and Medieval pithoi, including incised, painted, stamped or thumb-impressed decoration and applied bands. Although it remains difficult to create a typology of pithoi shapes due to their long period of use (mostly they are either ovoid or globular), an attempt has been made by identifying morphologically three main group shapes in the southern Crimea; cf. Teslenko 2009, 870–78.
26   Scranton 1957, pl. 18.2; Williams II & Zervos 1988, 101, Fig. 6.
27   Bouras 1983, 12, 14 and Fig. 8, mentioning a ground floor with 'large storage jars".
28   Vroom, personal observation.
29   Gerstel et al. 2003, 163–64, Fig. 11, n.19.
30   Vroom 2003, 157, Figs. 6.11–13 (W14.24–27, W14.29–31, W14.34), including a ceramic lid fragment for a pithos in Fig. 6.11 (W14.33).

Laconia,[31] Thessaly and on the islands of Kythera and Antikythera.[32] In Turkey, they were discovered amongst others at Pergamon,[33] Ephesos,[34] Hierapolis/Pamukkale,[35] Pessinous,[36] Amorion,[37] Avkat,[38] but also more eastwards in medieval settlements near the Euphrates River.[39] In regions around the Black Sea, pithoi were recovered at storerooms of houses in Chersonesos,[40] as well as in Gotsarnoe, Poliana and Sevastopol.[41] In Cyprus, they were very frequent in the late medieval and subsequent periods on the island, as shown by the fourteenth-century inventory of the goods of the Latin bishop of Limassol Guy d'Ibelin mentioning various cellars with *pitares* full of ruby red wine in his Nicosia lodge.[42]

That pithoi were used for a long period of time is also revealed by a reference in the 1247 will of the donor of the Theotokos Koteine Monastery in Greece. In this document "thirty ancient pitharia" were mentioned, showing that these storage jars were not replaced in this convent until they were completely useless.[43] From archaeological contexts we know of broken pithoi which were not discarded but repaired with lead clamps.[44] As such, these repaired jars could have been reused as containers for dry goods (such as grain), for burials (particularly for infants and young children), or as garbage cans filled with discarded objects.[45] In the Athenian Agora, Byzantine pithoi were occasionally recycled until Ottoman and even recent times. For example, each time a new house floor was built, the neck of a pithos was raised to match the higher floor level, so that the (new) owners could continue to use the jar. In other cases, new pithoi would be built in the same location as left by demolished older

---

31 Armstrong 1996, 138–40, Fig. 17.11–12.
32 Vroom, personal observation (for Thessaly, Kythera and Antikythera).
33 Rheidt 1990, 2002.
34 Vroom, personal observation.
35 Cottica 2007, 363, Fig. 12.
36 Devreker et al. 2003, Figs. 18–19.
37 Böhlendorf-Arslan 2010, 355, Fig. 9.5.
38 Vroom, personal observation.
39 Alvaro, Ballosi & Vroom 2004, Fig. 14 with further literature.
40 Yakobson 1979, 114–15, Figs. 70–71; see also Bakirtzis 1989, pls. 30.4 and 31.1–3; Teslenko 2009, 878.
41 Bakirtzis 1989, pl. 30.1–3.
42 Coureas 2014, 249–51. For the production and use of pithoi on Cyprus, see François 2016, 166–71.
43 Giannopoulou 2010, 45.
44 Giannopoulou 2010, 45.
45 Vroom & Kondyli 2011, 35; Giannopoulou 2010, 45.

ones—perhaps this was an optimal place in the house for food storage which allowed food to last longer.[46]

An important written source for the function of pithoi in Byzantine society is the *Geoponica*, a tenth-century collection on 'agricultural pursuits' compiled in Constantinople from earlier treatises for the Byzantine emperor Constantine VII Porphyrogennetos (905–59). Specifically, Book VI in this anthology gives valuable instructions on the making and distribution of pithoi, on their exact placement in storerooms and on their appropriate maintenance. The manuscript makes clear that pithoi should be kept in a dry environment, and placed in such a way that they do not touch each other.[47] In order to prevent humidity and dampness from the surrounding earth, pottery sherds or tiles were sometimes stuck in a kind of lime cement onto the outer surfaces of the pithos wall—like in the case of the aforementioned Agora examples.

Shapes of large storage jars (likely pithoi) can be observed in various Byzantine frescoes, mosaics and miniatures.[48] The most well-known examples in Byzantine art are the six jars represented on the "Wedding at Cana" vault mosaic in the Church of the Chora Monastery (Kariye Camii) in Istanbul (Figure 8.4).[49] This fourteenth-century mosaic depicts the storing and pouring of liquid for later consumption in large brown-coloured vessels with a short narrow neck and a distinct rim, of which the profiles look very similar to the excavated pithoi shapes in the Agora. Other scenes from the "Wedding at Cana" even show the drawing of wine or water from pithoi with implements such as a thin rod or reed for the testing and tasting of wine.[50]

2   The Spatial Dimensions of Byzantine Food Preparation with Heat

Having explored the micro-geography of Byzantine food storage, I will now discuss the spatial aspects of Byzantine food preparation with heat, or more

---

46   Vroom & Kondyli 2011, 35. In Swedish old houses, such an optimal place for food storage was always a dark, built-in cabinet occupying the northeastern corner of the building (I would like to thank Myrto Veikou for this information).
47   Bakirtzis 1989, 116; Teslenko 2009, 878–79; Giannopoulou 2010, 44; François 2016, 165–66.
48   E.g. Bakirtzis 1989, pls. 49–50; Anagnostakis & Papamastorakis 2005, Figs. 9–13; Giannopoulou 2010, 44 and n.263 with further literature.
49   Bakirtzis 1989, pl. 40a.
50   Anagnostakis & Papamastorakis 2005, 154–59, Figs. 8–15.

FIGURE 8.4 Istanbul, Chora Monastery, vault mosaic depicting the scene 'Wedding at Cana', 14th century
AUTHOR'S COPYRIGHT

precisely, the evolution of cooking infrastructure, architecture and utensils in the eastern Mediterranean.[51] Such an investigation will show on the one hand

---

51   Consequently, I will not discuss here the archaeological repertoire of cooking without heat, including grinding stones, mortars, strainers or sieves.

how food was cooked or eaten and, on the other, the changing forms of the pottery excavated. What do changes in kitchen architecture and cooking practices tell us about changes in utilitarian vessels, fuel and food, and about the society in which they were used? In order to answer some of these questions, I will introduce a few case-studies from the eastern Mediterranean—with a focus on Albania, Greece and Turkey.[52]

The last sixty years have seen a steady rise in anthropological and historical studies on the importance of food consumption and eating habits to society, some of which had a clear impact on archaeology (including cooking vessels).[53] Claude Lévi-Strauss introduced, for example, his famous "culinary triangle" on the human transformation of raw (nature) into cooked (culture), which included three cooking techniques: boiling, roasting, and smoking.[54] In fact, technology defines our food digestion; that is to say, what we eat depends on how we cook it.

The physical remains for Byzantine food preparation with heat range from permanent facilities (closed ones: ovens, furnaces, and open ones: hearths) to portable devices (chafing dishes, braziers). They can vary according to their function, their heat preservation capacity, their fuel resources, and their food processing. Although archaeologists usually do not tend to work with detailed recipes of a cookbook, they are nevertheless in the exceptional position to point out moments of change by showing the appearance of new forms of cooking techniques and their connected *batteries de cuisine* at different moments in time.[55]

2.1 The First Level: "A Designated Space for Cooking"

A first case-study of food preparation with heat is from a tower at Butrint (known as "Tower 1"), which shows "a designated space for cooking" with a central fire pit (made of wood) on the ground floor (Figures 8.5, 8.13 left, 8.14 left). The ceramics in this tower include, among others, wine jars (amphorae), painted vessels, locally made cooking pots, as well as two portable chafing

---

52 For the use of kitchens and bread ovens in Late Antique-Early Byzantine Egypt (especially in monastic communities), see Brooks Hedstrom 2017. For cooking and eating in (earlier) Roman households, see Ellis 1995, 1997; Salza Prina Ricotti 1978–80 and Dunbabin 2003.
53 Vroom 2015a.
54 Lévi-Strauss 1964.
55 I here focus rather on ceramic vessels—not on cooking utensils made in other materials (such as metal grids/grills or steatite/soapstone vessels). Furthermore, the three levels mentioned in this part can vary per region and do not necessarily have to be in a chronological order.

FIGURE 8.5 Butrint, Western Defences, Reconstructed drawing of Tower 1 with a selection of pottery finds from this tower
AUTHOR'S COPYRIGHT. DRAWING BY W.R. EUVERMAN. PHOTOGRAPHS
© BUTRINT FOUNDATION

dishes (vessels with a glazed bowl set on a hollow ventilated stand).[56] These pottery finds were recovered in a closed context, and can be dated to the 8th and the early-9th centuries.[57] In addition, some fragments of a circular-shaped hearth (to edge the fire) were found in the centre on the ground floor of Tower 1. These pieces are made of a soft, unbaked clay (that easily crumble in your hands), and have rows of impressed holes on the rim.

Next to the hearth, a cooking pot with a curved base was found, in combination with a chafing dish (Figures 8.5, 8.6). This last cooking device was totally burnt black on one side, with a very glossy lead glaze being over-vitrified on the interior.[58] It was clearly used near an open fire to get it quickly hot, or as a kind of movable mini-oven.[59] The amphorae on the ground floor were

---

56   See in general, Vroom 2014, 72–73.
57   E.g. Vroom 2008, 2012a, 2012b, 2017; see also Vroom 2018b for the ceramic finds in a second tower at Butrint.
58   Vroom 2008, 294–95 and Fig. 5.
59   Vroom 2008, 295.

FIGURE 8.6 Butrint, Western Defences, Photographs and drawings of a cooking pot (left) and a chafing dish (right) from Tower 1
DRAWINGS: AUTHOR'S COPYRIGHT. PHOTOGRAPHS © BUTRINT FOUNDATION

concentrated in the south-eastern corner of Tower 1 (Figure 8.5). A collection of recycled glass was further placed close to the door. From the way they were found it can be deduced that they must have been contained in a basket or some type of box which did not survive in the archaeological record.[60] Two tall bottle-shaped ceramic vessels were found towards the east wall, and some smaller jars closer to the door (Figure 8.5). A metal object, which was found in the collapsed layer of the tower, was probably part of a mechanism for opening a trap door between the ground and first floor.[61]

The number and variety of earthenware pottery found in the interior of the tower, as well as the predominance of household wares of a utilitarian nature suggest that Tower 1 was used as a dwelling in which storage of goods, preparation of food and cooking were all taking place at the same time (Figure 8.5). The tower might have been further associated to some minor industrial activity,

---

60 Jennings 2010; Jennings & Stark 2013.
61 An identical mechanism has been found, for instance, inside a contemporary tower at Amorion in Turkey; cf. Harrison et al. 1993, 161 and Fig. 3.

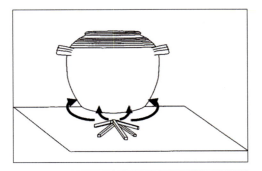

FIGURE 8.7 Drawing and photographs of culinary techniques of cooking vessels in a 'designated space' above a fire or on a tripod (after Dark 2001, colour plate 13; Papanikola-Bakirtzi 2002, no. 402; Pellegrino 2007, Fig. 3a). Left below: miniature of an angel with a cooking vessel on a tripod, Octateuch Manuscript, Vatopedi Monastery, Vatopedi cod. 802 (fol. 417a), Mount Athos, 13th century (after Bakirtzis 1989, Fig. 34a)

because of the presence of the recycled glass.[62] Apart from getting a better typology and chronology for pottery finds in this region, the tower context also permits a novel view on domestic life and food preparation at Butrint during the eighth and the early-ninth centuries.

Near the central fire-pit in the Butrint tower were several earthenware examples of the *batterie de cuisine* connected to this type of cooking, such as two transferable chafing dishes (one of which is discussed above; see Figure 8.6 left). These multi-functional utilitarian vessels (often covered with *tagine*-looking lids) were perhaps less efficient in size, but they provided a

---

62 We know, for instance, of well-known examples of industrial activities within a tower such as the case of a smithy in the Sadovsko Kale, a village in Bulgaria; see Curta 2004, 159.

more controlled way of cooking or of warming up food.[63] Furthermore, we can distinguish some cooking pots in gritty fabrics (with many non-plastic inclusions) that belonged to a designated space in direct contact with an open fire (Figure 8.6 right). These include locally made examples with a curved base (in Italy known as a *pentola Corinto/Apigliano*), being more resistant to high temperatures.[64] They were placed either within hot ashes/charcoal, or above the fire on a tripod or on a simple earthenware stand (such as a roof tile fragment) for more efficient cooking (Figure 8.7).[65] In fact, most of the pots from Butrint have a blackened or burnt exterior base showing such a cooking technique.

2.2   The Second Level: "A Special Space for Cooking"

The next phase of food preparation with heat is "a special space for cooking" in a separate room with permanent built-in structures (Figures 8.8, 8.13 centre, 8.14 centre). Apparently, stoves, fireplaces, and chimneys for cooking and heating were excavated in the Middle Byzantine village at Boğazköy (ancient Hattuša) in central Turkey.[66] Apart from pithoi buried in the ground, a few kitchens were also recovered in this tenth to eleventh-century village.[67] Within the settlement at Boğazköy, one monastery complex included, for instance, a kitchen with a stove, next to a small bakery. According to the excavators, another large farmstead ('Middle Byzantine Courtyard 1') yielded a kitchen with a low bench, a drain and a centrally-placed semicircular stove (made of broken millstones), as well as a small adjoining pantry and a slightly deepened basement room for storage.[68] A second farmstead ('Middle Byzantine Courtyard 2') could also have contained a kitchen (?), with a round hearth, ceramic vessels, and a drinking horn.[69]

More to the south, in Cappadocia, at least twenty-three kitchens were recorded in rock-cut courtyard complexes (in relation to other rooms, but

---

63   Vroom 2008, 295 and Fig. 4 for the distribution of chafing dishes in the Mediterranean.
64   Vroom 2017, 345 and n.11.
65   Pellegrino 2007, Fig. 3a; for the deposition of carbon on the surface of cooking vessels see Skibo 1992, 147–73.
66   Böhlendorf-Arslan 2017a, 364–65.
67   Apparently, a kitchen of an earlier Late Antique tradition (a *thermopolium*?) was also recognized in a large complex of Early Byzantine rooms (dated to the late fifth to seventh century) at Assos in western Turkey; cf. Böhlendorf-Arslan 2017b, 221–22, Fig. 16.1. This kitchen included a built-in oven and bench, and contained amongst others various types of pottery (both of a fine and coarse character), glass vessels, a marble mortar, weights and earthenware lamps.
68   Böhlendorf-Arslan 2017a, Fig. 34.2.
69   Böhlendorf-Arslan 2017a, Fig. 34.3.

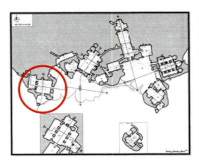
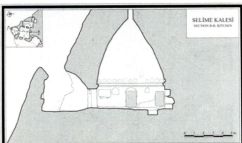
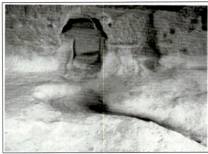
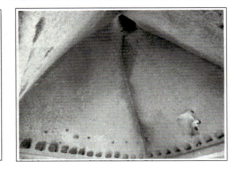

FIGURE 8.8 Cappadocia, Peristrema Valley, Drawings and photographs of the kitchen of Selime Kalesi with the remains of a *tandir* or *tabun* in the floor (left below) and a pyramidal chimney (right below). After Kalas 2009, Figures 2, 4–6

they were detached from living space).[70] Most have a square floor design and are dated to the Middle Byzantine period (ca. tenth to eleventh centuries).[71] The complex of Selime Kalesi seems to have the largest and most extensively detailed rock-carved kitchen in Cappadocia (Figure 8.8). In a suite of rooms (numbered 2–6), one large square kitchen even has "a sloping pyramidal ceiling that rises from an overhanging moulding and culminates in a smoke hole at the apex" (Figure 8.8 right above and below).[72]

Furthermore, this kitchen has all kind of built-in features, among which multiple spaces for food storage and for food preparation with heat (Figure 8.8 left below). There is an oven in a roughly-cut mushroom-like space in the north wall of the large kitchen as well as two circular pits carved into the floor that could have been used for a *tandir* (an enclosed structure, made of clay and heated from within, which is also known as a *tabun*) (Figure 8.9 above). This

---

70 Kalas 2009.
71 Kalas 2009, 111.
72 Kalas 2009, 112.

FIGURE 8.9 Drawing of four types of permanent fire-place installations. Left above: cylindrical, hollow clay installation (*tannur, tandoor*). Right above: smaller 'iglo-shaped' clay installation (*tabun*). Left below: domed metal pan (*saj*). Right below: domed cylindrical-shaped clay installation (*waqdiah*)
© J. VROOM AND S. VAN DER VLUGT

last type of built fire installation (for cooking and heating dishes, as well as for the baking of bread) is still used in traditional villages in eastern Turkey and in the Near East (Figure 8.9 below).[73]

According to ethno-archaeological research, four types of permanent fireplace installations could be discerned in Syrian villages: 1. a cylindrical, hollow clay installation, about one metre high and ca. 45–50cm wide with a small opening at the bottom for fuel (*tannur, tandoor*); 2. a smaller 'igloo-shaped' clay installation, partly dug into the floor, about 45cm high and ca 60cm wide at the bottom, with a small opening at the bottom for fuel (*tabun*); 3. a domed metal pan, placed on bricks with fuel in-between (*saj*); and 4. a domed cylindrical-shaped clay installation, ca. 80–100cm high, with a shelf and a large opening on the frontal side (*waqdiah*) (Figure 8.9).[74] Depending on the oven shape,

---

73 E.g., Mulder-Heymans 2002; Parker & Uzel 2007; Smogorzewska 2012; Vroom, personal observation (in eastern Turkey).
74 Mulder-Heymans 2002, 2.

different varieties of bread could be baked either on the inside or outside of the installation, while dishes could be cooked or meat roasted in the sintering fire. The fuel provision varied (e.g. wood, charcoal, animal dung, agricultural residues), but was always made of local sources.[75]

Medieval houses with a circular *tannur* embedded into the ground have been recovered at Erzincan-Kemah Castle (near the Upper Euphrates River) in eastern Turkey.[76] Their bottom diameter ranges between 65 and 85cm, and there are ventilation holes of 10cm in diameter near the bottoms.[77] Together with these *tannurs*, one- or two-handled ceramic cooking jars in various sizes were excavated, often in combination with flat-based lids with handles on top.[78]

With the introduction of a special space for cooking, we may thus notice the appearance of innovative cooking installations, such as (bread) ovens, domestic hearths or supports. Furthermore, we see in the archaeological repertoire the beginning of a larger variety in shapes and sizes of ceramic cooking implements, which were used in relation to these installations. Thick-walled cooking pots of a globular shape (dated to the eleventh to twelfth centuries) could be placed within hot embers/charcoal, on a metal tripod,[79] hanging from above on a pothook, or on a more permanent cooking installation (Figure 8.10).[80]

In pictures from Byzantine manuscripts one can, for example, notice such a wide round-bodied cooking pot placed on a metal stand/trivet above a fire or on a cooking installation; such placement ensured an equal and gentle distribution of heat from the open fire (Figures 8.7, 8.10).[81] Round-bottomed vessels are more appropriate for dispelling thermal stress during the cooking process, they cool more regularly, and they are resistant to cracks in the vessel's body (Figure 8.10 left above).[82]

---

75 See, for example, Smith 1998.
76 Özkul Fındık 2018, 305, Fig. 5.
77 Özkul Fındık 2018, 305, Fig. 6.
78 Özkul Fındık 2018, 305, Fig. 7.
79 See for a 13th-century example of a metal tripod/trivet from Sparta, Waywell & Wilks 1997, 404–5, Figs. 7–8, pl. 63; Papanikola-Bakirtzi 2002, 350, n.402.
80 According to Adrian Boas (2010, 123–25), more sophisticated cooking structures with ovens and traces of ash were found in various houses and castles in the Latin East. Excavations in the kitchen of the castle of Arsur yielded even an intricate system of domed ovens with heating chambers and holes on top, on which large cooking pots could be placed; cf. Yehuda 2011, 54, Figs. 4, 5 and 6.
81 E.g., Alexandre-Bidon 2005, Fig. 65 and pl. II; see also Bakirtzis 1989, pl. 34a.
82 Joyner 2007, 189 and n.34.

FIGURE 8.10 Drawings and photographs of cooking installations/techniques for food preparation with heat in a 'special space' (after Yehuda 2011, Fig. 6). Left below: miniature of the sorceress Medea, Venice Codex of Pseudo-Oppian's *Cynegetica*, Biblioteca Nazionale Marciana, cod. Gr. Z 479 (fol. 47r), ca. 1060 (after Spatharakis 2004, Fig. 99). Right below: detail from a miniature of the Alexander Romance made in Trebizond, Hellenic Institute of Byzantine and Post-Byzantine Studies, Cod. Gr. 5, Venice, 14th century (after Bakirtzis 1989, 35b)

This good distribution of the heat makes these pots ideal for the boiling of large portions of food or semi-liquids (such as soups, broth, and pottage) or other dishes for long stewing (for example, grain porridge). It has been suggested that the wide-mouthed shape "promoted the escape of moisture from a stew, and that the thicker walls helped retain and distribute heat during cooking".[83] Also the soaking or boiling of salted preserved meat and fish in much fresh water could have taken place in these large cooking jars. Furthermore, the wide rim allowed easy access for manipulating the content by stirring with a ladle or spoon, and the rounded or sagging base is suitable to tip from the fire without lifting, which is an advantage when pouring from a full vessel.

---

83   Joyner 2007, 190.

2.3 The Third Level: "A Specialized Space" for Cooking

From the thirteenth century onwards, we may notice "a specialized space" for food preparation with heat in the eastern Mediterranean, and the first appearance of a more technically advanced fireplace in a wall with a chimney to carry smoke away (Figures 8.13 right, 8.14 right). In Greece, one may distinguish this new phenomenon specifically in Crusader castles, palaces and fortresses. At Chlemoutsi Castle on the western coast of the Peloponnese, for example, the residential quarters on the first floor have large fireplaces of a northern European tradition.[84] In addition, a separate kitchen on the same floor communicates directly with these vaulted quarters. It contains an oven as well as twin chimneys over the hearths.[85] Below the kitchen is a blind vaulted basement (perhaps a water cistern) and space for storage.[86]

Such a specialized space for cooking (often in combination with an iron spit on which to roast meat over the fire) is not only to be seen in Crusader castles, but also in houses and towers of this period (Figure 8.11).[87] At Corinth, the sudden appearance of rectangular hearths and fireplaces, consisting of low, raised rectangular platforms, may be distinguished in buildings of the late thirteenth and early fourteenth centuries.[88] Furthermore, Frankish towers in Boeotia and on the island of Euboea (for instance at Vassiliko and Politika) have similar looking fireplaces on the highest floor, which is at the same time the domiciliary part of the building (Figure 8.11 right).[89]

It seems quite possible to relate this change in cooking infrastructure (a fireplace in the wall) to a different pottery repertoire in the 13th-century kitchen, such as a more frequent use of metal cauldrons for boiling and stewing as well as new pottery types. In fact, suddenly we start to see cooking pots of smaller dimensions with thinner walls and a flat bottom, which seem to be more adequate to be placed near or next to a fire or on a flat surface within a hearth or an oven. Placed in that way, the heat was applied to these vessels from one side, and their thinner walls facilitated its distribution over the entire content.[90]

---

84 Athanasoulis 2013, Fig. 27; for these features in North-Western Europe see van Oosten 2017, 197.
85 Athanasoulis 2013, 134.
86 Athanasoulis 2013, 134.
87 One may also distinguish elaborate fireplaces with stone chimneys in walls of Crusader castles and houses in the Latin East; cf. Yehuda 2011, 53 for examples in the villages of al-Kurum and Wadi Harramiye. Furthermore, fireplaces were also recognized in Byzantine houses in Mystras; cf. Orlandos 2000, 102–104.
88 See rectangular hearths at Corinth, Williams II & Zervos 1993, 7–8, pl. 3; Williams II & Zervos 1994, 35, Figs. 3 and 8; see also Vroom 2011, 422–23.
89 Vroom, personal observation.
90 Pellegrino 2007, Fig. 3b.

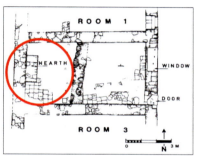

FIGURE 8.11 Drawings and photographs of hearths as a 'specialised space' for food preparation with heat in Crusader houses and towers in Greece and Israel (after Williams II and Zervos 1993, pl. 3; Yehuda 2011, Fig. 3)
PHOTOGRAPH: AUTHOR'S COPYRIGHT

Pictures from medieval manuscripts show that such cooking pots were indeed put next to the fire or near the fire, presupposing thus more formal kitchen architecture and stability of cooking areas (such as fixed built hearths).[91] Moving the cooking pot/jar to the edge of the heat (and away from the smoke) was often suitable for delicate dishes that required slow cooking with steam or moisture, or for keeping semi-liquids warm—even to the point that the substance was bubbling or boiling up to the rim.[92] These later thin-walled cooking pots (used for delicate dishes or semi-liquids; see Figure 8.12 left and right) were perhaps a useful addition in the kitchen to large cauldrons made of metal, which must have eventually replaced in function the thick-walled earthenware globular cooking pots of the 11th–12th centuries.

Furthermore, we can distinguish the introduction of various new shapes of cooking utensils in this period, among which one-handled jugs/jars (sometimes

---

91 Alexandre-Bidon 2005, Fig. 70.
92 See also Joyner 2007, 190.

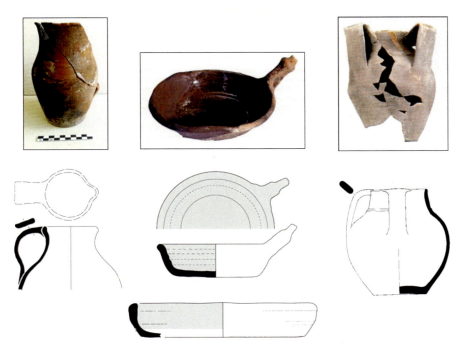

FIGURE 8.12   An overview of Late Byzantine/Crusader ceramic cooking vessels from Greece, Cyprus and Israel (after Yehuda 2011, Fig. 4; Gabrieli 2005, Fig. 4; Gabrieli et al. 2017, Fig. 7; PHOTOGRAPH LEFT ABOVE: AUTHOR'S COPYRIGHT)

with trefoil-shaped mouths),[93] frying pans,[94] baking dishes,[95] pots with double handles (two handles next to each other on one side),[96] which might be linked to a greater variety of cooking techniques and perhaps the development of an *haute cuisine* or at least a different type of cuisine (Figure 8.12).[97] Thin-walled fourteenth-century cooking pots with double handles from Lecce (known as

---

93   E.g., Gabrieli 2005, Fig. 4 (Paphos); Gabrieli et al. 2017, Fig. 7, BZY 627 and BZY 628 (Cyprus); François 2017, Fig. 5, n.3 (Nicosia); Vroom & Tzavella 2017, 152, Figs. 7, 8a–8b, n.7 and table 1 (Athens).

94   See for examples of such frying pans, Papanikola-Bakirtzi 2002, 349, no. 401 (Rhodes); Gabrieli et al. 2017, Figs. 3 and 5 (Beirut and Cyprus).

95   Gabrieli et al. 2017, Figs. 3 and 5 (Beirut and Cyprus); François 2017, Fig. 5, n.1–2, Fig. 6, n.5–8 (Nicosia).

96   Thin-walled cooking pots (also known as *pignatte*), dated to the fourteenth century, for instance, were found during excavations at Lecce (southern Italy) with organic finds, among which figs and grapes for the slow cooking of composts, confits or *defrutum* (reduced wine); cf. Güll 2007, 158, 164, Figs. 12–14 and graphs 2–3.

97   Vroom & Tzavella 2017.

A BYZANTINE SPACE ODDITY

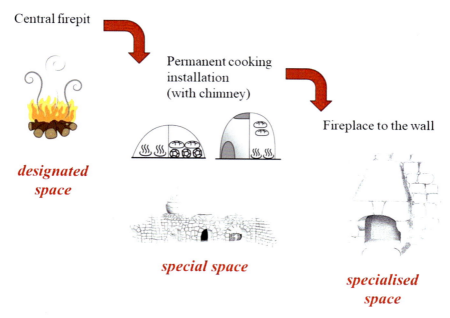

FIGURE 8.13   Three phases of food preparation with heat: left: a 'designated space', centre: a 'special space', and right: a 'specialized space' (Drawings centre below and right after Yehuda 2011)
© J. VROOM AND S. VAN DER VLUGT

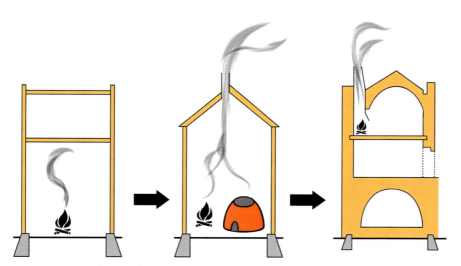

FIGURE 8.14   Architectural reconstruction of three phases of food preparation with heat. Left: a 'designated space'. Centre: a 'special space'. Right: a 'specialized space'
© J. VROOM & S. VAN DER VLUGT

pignatte) point, for instance, in this direction. They were found together with organic finds including grapes and figs.[98] Traces of use of these pots further suggest slow and long cooking of delicate vegetal dishes or semi-liquids near or next to a fire (while holding the side with the two handles most far away from the heat), perhaps for the preparation of composts, comfits (like jelly or marmalade) or *defrutum* (reduced wine).[99]

3 The Spatial Dimensions of Byzantine Consumption

A perspective for the 'spatiality' of Byzantine consumption will now be discussed with a focus on quantitative research on Byzantine tableware in relation to changing eating habits. Some general characteristics and long-term trends in the spatial layout of utensils on the table will be presented here, mostly based on various pottery assemblages from the eastern Mediterranean used for serving and eating. This will be done in combination with selected pictorial evidence in order to explore the macro-geography of the dining room.[100]

3.1 Changing Table Wares

In *After Antiquity*, I have discussed in detail the differences in table manners from Late Antiquity to late Ottoman times varying in date from ca. the mid-seventh century to the late-nineteenth century.[101] For that study, I measured, for example, the rim diameters and base diameters of table wares from various periods, concentrating in particular on open vessels from central Greece (Figure 8.15).[102] Noteworthy is the fact that in most excavated and surveyed ceramic assemblages in the eastern Mediterranean (and in particular, in the western Aegean), there are striking differences in pottery shape and technology of the table wares for each chronological phase. There are clear changes of shape from the Middle Byzantine to the Late Byzantine/Frankish and even post-medieval (or Post-Byzantine) times in all studied pottery assemblages.[103]

---

98 Güll 2007, 158, 164.
99 Vroom & Tzavella 2017.
100 A general synthesis of the available archaeological evidence of Late Antique-early Byzantine dining rooms in the eastern Mediterranean has been presented (Vroom 2007) and will therefore not be dealt with in this chapter.
101 Vroom 2003, 303–57 with further literature.
102 Vroom 2003, table 7.3.
103 The general designation 'Late Byzantine/Frankish' is used here for pottery types introduced, produced and used in the eastern Mediterranean from the thirteenth century to the fifteenth century, which are stylistically different from 'Middle Byzantine' wares.

A BYZANTINE SPACE ODDITY

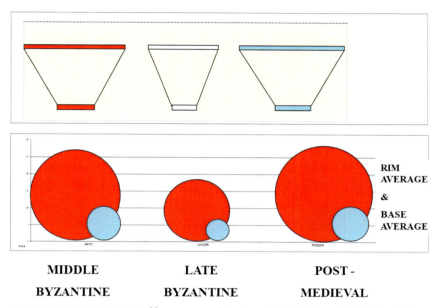

FIGURE 8.15 Rim average and base average diameters of Middle Byzantine (left), of Late Byzantine (centre), and of Post-Medieval tableware (right) (Drawings after Vroom 2003, table 7.3)

For instance, for the Middle Byzantine period (between circa the tenth and the twelfth to early-thirteenth centuries) more open shapes of large dishes with large rim diameters (sometimes up to 30cm) can be distinguished, while in the so-called Late Byzantine/Frankish period (between circa the thirteenth and mid-fifteenth centuries), much smaller bowls with smaller rim and base diameters form the larger part of diagnostic forms (Figure 8.15).[104]

The next step is to measure the volume of the Byzantine table wares. In order to do this, I have chosen twelve pottery assemblages from the eastern Mediterranean, preferably from single datable closed deposits (Figure 8.16). This study concerns approximately 900 individual vessels from Early Byzantine to Late Byzantine/Frankish times (circa mid-seventh century to fourteenth century). The studied pottery assemblages include material of the Early Byzantine period (Crypta Balbi excavations in Rome, Yassi Ada shipwreck, Alexandria/Cairo and the St Polyeuktos church in Istanbul), of the Middle Byzantine period (St Polyeuktos Church and St Irene church in Istanbul, Corinth), of the Middle Byzantine and Late Byzantine periods (Athenian Agora, the Alonissos

---

104   Vroom 2003, 229–39.

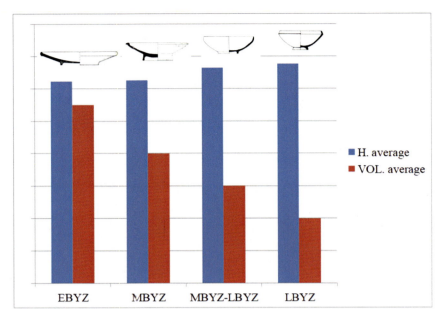

FIGURE 8.16 Average vessel height and volume of Byzantine tablewares (Drawing after Vroom 2016, Fig. 13.5 and table 13.C)

and Kastellorizo shipwrecks) and, finally, of the Late Byzantine/Frankish period (Maximianoupolis and Lagopesole).[105]

The vessel volumes of the table wares from these twelve assemblages have been calculated by means of information technology and weighing. For the mathematical calculation, I used the French software 'Archéo4'.[106] Furthermore, I checked volume results from the IT calculations (when possible) by weighing complete vessels filled with lentils, a common food source in Byzantine times.[107]

The total calculation of the volume of table wares from these twelve contexts brought interesting results from Early Byzantine to Late Medieval times. When looking at Figure 8.16, it is clear that the height of the vessels goes up throughout the centuries, while the volume becomes less over time. The same

---

105 See Vroom 2015b, 360, Fig. 2 and table 1 for the relevant literature. It is my intention to discuss the features of these twelve pottery assemblages in more detail in a forthcoming publication.
106 Meffre & Rigoir 2007.
107 See also Blake 1997 for such an approach.

trend from Early Byzantine to Late Medieval times can be distinguished in excavated examples in combination with the iconography of that period.

In Early Byzantine times, especially in the seventh century, one may distinguish one large flat low communal dish in the centre of a table on various dining scenes of this period (Figure 8.17). These large centrepieces were made in red-slipped varieties of high quality, descending from Roman pottery techniques (like *terra sigillata*).[108] The table wares consisted of fine textured and thin-walled vessels finished with a smooth reddish slip (not a glazed treatment) on the inside and outside. These Red Slip Wares were specifically intended for use on the dining-table and, therefore, the finish had to be of the best possible quality. However, both the fabric and the slip suggest that the vessels were not useful for very watery dishes, for which glazing would be a much more suitable finish.[109]

The shapes of Red Slip Wares were almost all open vessels, some with flat bases and quite steep sides that seem to have served as large bowls, dishes and plates.[110] The forms of ceramic table vessels changed during the seventh century: smaller bowls (of mixed shapes) for more individual use became less used on the dining table, whereas large platters on a ring foot became more common.[111] The rim diameters of open Red Slip vessels from Northern Africa could be quite large, ranging from 29cm to nearly a half-metre, and could cover the total surface of a semi-circular *sigma* table.[112]

The table setting on Early Byzantine dining pictures displays, in general, one large communal flat low dish of large dimensions in the centre.[113] The banquet scene on a late-sixth to early-seventh-century miniature depicting the story of St Joseph, for instance, shows a very large flat dish shared by all diners around the table, who grasp with their hands into the main dish.[114] This is a good example of communal dining without any cutlery or individual beakers or cups (Figure 8.17).

During the Middle Byzantine period, we start to see a more complicated situation (Figure 8.18). From the end of the eleventh century onwards, the practice of using decorated glazed pottery for table purposes became more widespread in the Byzantine world. The shapes of these decorative table wares

---

108 See in general, Hayes 1972, 160–71, 343–46, 377–83.
109 Vroom 2003, 229–30; Vroom 2007b, 342–45.
110 Vroom 2014, 32–41.
111 Vroom 2007, 343.
112 Hawthorne 1997, Figs. 5–6.
113 Vroom 2003, 309–13; Vroom 2007a, 193–95.
114 Vroom 2007b, 356 and Fig. 11.3 with reference.

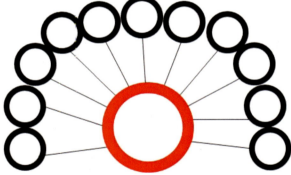

FIGURE 8.17 Dining scene and schematic table setting in Early Byzantine times. Miniature of Story of Joseph, Ahburnham or Tours Pentateuch, Bibliothèque Nationale de France lat. 2334, Paris, ca. late 6th-early 7th century (after Vroom 2016, Fig. 13.6)

are generally very simple. We see thick-walled dishes and shallow bowls, but jugs are unusual.[115] Looking from the perspective of dining habits, the size and proportions of most of these vessels must have been quite practical for communal rather than individual use. However, because of the porosity of their soft and coarse fabrics they were not very suitable for watery dishes.[116]

115 Vroom 2003, 231–33; Vroom 2014, 80–89.
116 Vroom 2003, 233.

FIGURE 8.18 Dining scene and schematic table setting in Middle Byzantine times. Miniature of Job's Children, St Catherine's Monastery gr. 3 (fol. 17v), Sinai, 11th century (after Vroom 2016, Fig. 13.7)

These table wares seem to have gone out of use in the thirteenth century, being superseded in the Late Byzantine/Frankish period by incised wares with sometimes two or more colours in the glaze. In addition to the vast improvement in the quality of the lead glaze (which became thicker and with a glossier appearance), a fine, thinly-potted ware replaced the previous thick, soft and coarse table wares. Noteworthy was also a change in shape: from the thirteenth century onwards we see deep small bowls instead of shallow large dishes (Figure 8.19).[117] These deep bowls could have been used in connection with fairly liquid mixtures, or perhaps were once drinking vessels. After all, the consumption of watery things clearly implies vessels with fairly high sides.

Recently, a Late Byzantine/Frankish ceramic assemblage of the Agora material (ca. late thirteenth century to fifteenth century) has been documented, containing vessels for dining, drinking, serving food and pouring liquids found

117 Vroom 2014, 108–25.

FIGURE 8.19   Composition image of Late Byzantine glazed and unglazed tablewares from the Athenian Agora (above: after Vroom and Tzavella 2017, Fig. 7, ASCSA) in relation to Late Byzantine dining scenes (below). Left below: Miniature of Job's Children, Ms. Grec. 135, fol. 18v, Bibliothèque Nationale de France Grec. 135 (fol. 18v), Paris, ca. 1361–1362 (after Vroom and Tzavella 2017, Fig. 9). Right below: Icon of the Hospitality of Abraham, Benaki Museum, Athens, 14th century (after Vroom 2003, Fig. 11.32)

in a well outside the Byzantine fortification wall (Figure 8.19 above).[118] Three imported vessels are noteworthy in this assemblage: a small bowl of so-called Roulette Ware from the Veneto region;[119] a painted dish of Spanish Lustreware from Valencia;[120] and a base fragment of Archaic Maiolica from Pisa painted with a heraldic pattern (coats-of-arms) on the inside.[121] These three imported vessels were of a small size (able to fit only one portion) thus probably for personal rather than communal use.[122]

118   Vroom & Tzavella 2017.
119   Vroom 2014, 132–33.
120   Vroom 2014, 134–35.
121   Berti & Tongiorgi 1977, 58–61.
122   A more detailed interpretation of this assemblage will be published; cf. Vroom & Tzavella 2017.

3.2 Changing Eating Habits

Were these technological and functional innovations in Late Byzantine/ Frankish table wares influenced by actual changes in dining habits or did they influence eating manners? How can we get a picture of this changing dining culture? Of course, textual sources could be explored and critical analysis of representations of pottery on Byzantine/Medieval icons, frescoes, and miniatures could perhaps offer some sort of insight in the use and social context of the objects.[123]

Comparing the table habits represented on eleventh-century frescoes and miniatures with those on fourteenth-century representations suggests what very well could be changing dining practices in the Byzantine world—at least for the well-to-do classes. If we look, for instance, at dining scenes of the Middle Byzantine period, we see most of the time one central wide-open dish on a high pedestal foot, suggesting a more careful presentation or display of food on the table (Figure 8.18).[124] This change is perhaps due to the gradual change from reclining to sitting at the table.[125] The centrally placed dish is indeed used for the main course by all diners, who are sitting around a semi-circular table. There are no knives, spoons or forks on the table, which implies that all guests used only their fingers to eat from the shared dish directly. Two cups or chalices were apparently also shared by all diners for drinking.

These scenes thus show a more complicated or elaborate type of communal dining with centrally placed communal dishes and two cups, which have many similarities with shapes of tenth to eleventh-century table wares found at excavations in the Aegean. An eleventh-century miniature of Job's Children from St Catherine's Monastery at Sinai in Egypt shows—apart from the one large communal plate and two communal cups—that five of the ten diners actually grasp with their hands towards and into the centrally-placed dish (Figure 8.18 above).[126] This seems to confirm that people were dining with their fingers in a communal way. We can, therefore, assume that as the well-to-do classes were apparently eating with their hands, the less wealthy were not doing otherwise.[127]

---

123 See Vroom 2003, 303–09; Vroom 2007a, 192; Vroom 2011, 420–21 for the discussion of using visual evidence from Byzantine art.
124 Vroom 2003, 313–15; Vroom. 2007a, 196–200.
125 Vroom 2012b, 362 and Fig. 7.
126 See also Vroom 2003, Fig. 11.17 with reference.
127 Nicholas Oikonomides published lists of household goods of middle- and lower-class households, living in the provinces. He suggested that, in contrast to the Byzantine court in Constantinople, eating procedures in the 11th century must have been rather simple in

Remarkable on most depictions of a later date (especially from the fourteenth century onwards) is the shift towards a greater variety and a larger amount of vessels, jugs, bread and cutlery spread over the table.[128] One can distinguish the separation of food into several smaller and higher bowls, which were apparently shared by three or four guests at the table (Figure 8.20). Glass beakers and glass jugs appear, as well as cutlery and a variety of vessels in different shapes, sizes and materials. A late twelfth- to thirteenth-century miniature in a *croce dipinta* in the Museo Nazionale di San Matteo in Pisa in Italy, for instance, shows five bowls on the Last Supper table (Figure 8.20), suggesting that Jesus and his Apostles were sharing one bowl between two or three men.[129] The diners were therefore expected to eat together from the same bowl with their immediate neighbours, and the food was eaten with their fingers and a knife.

Furthermore, one can notice in excavated ceramic assemblages a change in more wine consumption after the twelfth century (Figure 8.19 below). The dishes with food and vessels of wine or water were in dining scenes not placed regularly on the table. The guests were apparently expected to share the dishes and knives between three or four men, but it seems as if they had one individual bread roll each. All this suggests the spread of wealth, consumerism and thus a first start of more individual or a smaller group eating style with more food in several smaller and deeper bowls on the table.

The differences in vessel size may be interpreted as evidence for a change in specific types of food that required boiling and serving in suitable containers. This change to a different dining style in Late Byzantine/Frankish times may have been influenced by a progressive trend to more watery dishes cooked in their own juices which are known to have occurred also in north-western Europe.[130] The shift from an emphasis on roasting to an emphasis on stewing could perhaps explain the introduction of deeper containers during this era. As we have seen, the bowls of the Late Byzantine/Frankish period in most samples are notably deeper and glassier in appearance than the earlier dishes.

Various changes in table manners took place in the eastern Mediterranean in this period, as can be noticed in fourteenth- and fifteenth-century painted dining scenes from Late Byzantine art with diners sitting at tables and on chairs and benches (Figure 8.19 below).[131] We may conclude that the pictorial

---

the average Byzantine household. He concluded that "people often, if not always, ate with their fingers from a large serving plate and drank from a common cup or jar" (1990, 212).
128 Vroom 2003, 321–27; Vroom 2007a, 200–3.
129 See also Vroom 2003, Fig. 11.28 with reference.
130 Vroom 2003, 329.
131 Vroom 2003, 321–27; Vroom 2007b, 200–3, Figs. 17.14–17.

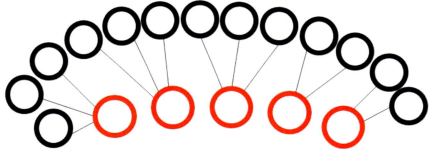

FIGURE 8.20 Dining scene and schematic table setting in Late Byzantine/Late Medieval times. Miniature in a *croce dipinta*, Museo Nazionale di San Matteo, Pisa, ca. 12th–13th century (after Vroom 2016, Fig. 13.8)

evidence, in combination with the actual artefacts (e.g. from the Agora excavations), shows a first start of more elaborate or small group dining in a western style in Athens from Late Byzantine/Late Medieval times onwards.[132] This transition took place at a different pace in different parts of the eastern Mediterranean, but it must have reached Greece and Athens by the fourteenth and fifteenth centuries.

∙ ∙ ∙

---

132   Vroom 2003, 329–31 and table 11.1.

What I have tried to present here is a cultural geography of Byzantine food practices and cuisine in the eastern Mediterranean while taking quantitative, archaeological, and iconographical perspectives of prospective research into account. Consequently, my focus was on the domestic micro-geography and macro-geography of the pantry, the kitchen, and the dining room. Furthermore, I have tried to understand the shifts in function of broken pottery fragments from archaeological projects in this region in conjunction with morphological features, with ergonomics, and with pictorial evidence (in particular to cooking techniques and schematic table settings). The combination of these factors leads to a kind of pattern, which apparently indicates shifts in Byzantine foodways and eating cultures. Perhaps both the strenuous process of dating pottery sherds and the use of challenging models to understand long-term developments in ceramic consumption make one thing clear: differences in Byzantine pottery use and shapes can be related to the spatial dimensions of food preservation and preparation (without and with heat), to new forms of cooking techniques and installations, and to changing eating manners (although these patterns can vary per region).

I have scrutinized the geography of food-associated domestic spaces with a focus on storage, on cooking infrastructure and architecture, and on dining habits in Byzantium, which might be linked to the introduction of new culinary trends and of new ceramic utensils. The spatial aspects of Byzantine foodways and cuisine are essential aspects of human interaction, and the tools (especially ceramic finds) involved in the storage, preparation and consumption of food are vital clues for understanding Byzantine society. The interrelation of these spatial aspects (location, size, capacity, scale, dimensions etc.) makes up the culinary *chaîne operatoire* of daily life practices.

As such, we may distinguish the perpetual change of social practices related to Byzantine foodways and cuisine in the eastern Mediterranean. Apparently, there is no causal relationship, but these practices are related and do influence each other. They force us to think and to look at our research material in different ways. By using quantitative methods and middle-range theory (the link between human behaviour and artefacts) we can examine the role of Byzantine households and their ceramic utensils within socio-economic, cultural and technological developments and in relation to wider contexts such as environmental conditions and subsistence practices. These range from the micro-geography of the storeroom and different kitchen-levels to the macro-geography of cyclical shifts from communal to more complicated small-group dining in Byzantine society.

Bibliography

Secondary Sources

Alexandre-Bidon, D. 2005. *Une archéologie du goût. Céramique et consummation*. Paris.

Alvaro, C., F. Balossi & J. Vroom 2004. "Zeytinli Bahçe: A Medieval fortified settlement", *Anatolia Antiqua* 12, 191–213.

Anagnostakis, I. & T. Papamastorakis 2005. "'…and radishes for appetizers': On banquets, radishes, and wine", in Papanikola-Bakirtzi (ed.) 2005, 147–73.

Armstrong, P. 1996. "The Byzantine and Ottoman pottery", in Cavanagh, J. et al. (eds) 1996, 125–204.

Ashbook Harvey, S. & M. Mullett (eds) 2017. *Knowing Bodies, Passionate Souls: Sense Perceptions in Byzantium*. Washington, D.C.

Athanasoulis, D. 2013. "The triangle of power: Building projects in the Metropolitan area of the Crusader Principality of the Morea", in Gerstel (ed.) 2013, 111–51.

Bakirtzis, C. 1989. *Βυζαντινά τσουκαλολάγηνα*. Athens.

Berti, G. & L. Tongiorgi 1977. *Ceramica pisana: secoli XIII–XV*. Pisa.

Blake, H., 1997. "Sizes and measures of later Medieval pottery in north-central Italy", in De Boe & F. Verhaeghe (eds), 221–50.

Boas, A. 2010. *Domestic Settings. Sources on Domestic Architecture and Day-to-Day Activities in the Crusader States*. Leiden—Boston.

Böhlendorf-Arslan, B. 2010. "Die Mittelbyzantinische Keramik aus Amorion", in Daim & Drausckhe (eds) 2010, 345–71.

Böhlendorf-Arslan, B. 2017a. "Boğazköy" in Niewöhner (ed.) 2017, 361–67.

Böhlendorf-Arslan, B. 2017b. "Assos", in P. Niewöhner (ed.) 2017, *The Archaeology of Byzantine Anatolia. From the End of Late Antiquity until the Coming of the Turks*, 216–25. Oxford.

Böhlendorf-Arslan, B., A. O. Uysal & J. Witte-Orr (eds) 2007. *Canak, Late Antique and Medieval Pottery and Tiles in Mediterranean Archaeological Contexts*. Istanbul.

Bonifay, M. & J.-C. Tréglia (eds) 2007. *LRCW 2. Late Roman Coarse Wares, Cooking Wares and Amphorae in the Mediterranean: Archaeology and Archaeometry*. Oxford.

Bouras, C. 1982–83. "Houses in Byzantium", *DChAE* 11, 1–26.

Brooks Hedstrom, D. L. 2017. "Monks baking bread and salting fish: An archaeology of early monastic ascetic taste", in Ashbook Harvey & Mullett (eds) 2017, 183–206.

Brubaker, L. & K. Linardou (eds) 2007. *Eat, Drink, and Be Merry (Luke 12:19)—Food and Wine in Byzantium*. Aldershot.

Cavanagh, W. G. et al. (eds) 1996. *Continuity and Change in the Greek Rural Landscape: The Laconia Survey*, vol. 2. London.

Cottica, D. 2007. "Micaceous white painted ware from insula 104 at Hierapolis/Pamukkale, Turkey", in Böhlendorf-Arslan, A. O. Uysal & J. Witte-Orr (eds) 2007, 255–72.

Coureas, N. 2014. "Pottery and its uses in the Latin church of Cyprus (ca. 1283–1367)", in Papanikola-Bakirtzi & Coureas (eds) 2014, 247–53.

Cutler, A. & A. Papaconstantinou (eds). 2007. *The Material and the Ideal. Essays in Medieval Art and Archaeology in Honour of Jean-Michel Spieser*. Leiden—Boston.

Curta, F. 2004. *The Making of the Slavs. History and Archaeology of the Lower Danube Region, c. 500–700*. Cambridge.

Daim, F. & J. Drauschke (eds) 2010. *Byzanz—Das Romerreich im Mittelalter*, vol. 2. Mainz.

Dark, K. 2001. *Byzantine Pottery*. Stroud, Gloucestershire—Charleston.

De Boe, G. & F. Verhaeghe (eds) 1997. *Material Culture in Medieval Europe. Papers of the 'Medieval Europe Brugge 1997' Conference 7 (I.A.P. Rapporten 7)*. Zellik.

Devreker, J. et al. 2003. "Fouilles archeologiques de Pessinonte: La campagne de 2001", *Anatolia Antiqua* 11, 141–56.

Drauschke, J. & D. Keller (eds) 2010. *Glass in Byzantium—Production, Usage, Analyses / Glass in Byzanz—Produktion, Verwendung, Analysen (RGZM Tagungen VIII)*. Mainz.

Dunbabin, K. M. D. 2003. *The Roman Banquet: Images of Conviviality*. Cambridge.

Düring, B. & T. Stek (eds) 2018. *The Archaeology of Imperial Landscapes: A Comparative Study of Empires in the Ancient Near East and Mediterranean World*. Cambridge.

Ellis, S. 1995. "Classical reception rooms in Romano-British houses", *Britannia* 26, 163–78.

Ellis, S. 1997. "Late Antique dining: Architecture, furnishing and behaviour", in Lawrence & Wallace-Hadrill (eds), 41–51.

François, V. 2016. "Des pithoi byzantins aux pitharia chypriotes modernes: Permanence des techniques de fabrication et des usages", in *Jarres et grands contenants entre Moyen Âge et Époque Moderne / Jars and Large Containers between the Middle Ages and the Modern Era* 2015, 163–73.

François, V. 2017. "Poteries des fosses dépotoirs du site de l'*Archiepiskopie* à Nicosie (fin XIIe–XIVe siècles): les vestiges d'une production locale sous les Lusignan", *BCH* 141.2, 821–59.

Frantz, A. 1938. "Middle Byzantine pottery in Athens", *Hesperia* 7, 429–67.

Frantz, A. 1961. *The Middle Ages in the Athenian Agora*. Princeton, N.J.

Gabrieli, R. S. 2005. "Specialisation and development in the handmade pottery industries of Cyprus and the Levant", in Vroom (ed.) 2005, 127–49.

Gabrieli, R. S. et al. 2017. "Cypriot and Levantine cooking wares in Frankish Cyprus", in Vroom, Waksman & Van Oosten (eds) 2017, 119–43.

Gelichi, S. & R. Hodges (eds) 2012. *From One Sea to Another. Trading Places in the European and Mediterranean Early Middle Ages, Proceedings of the International Conference Comacchio, 27th–29th March 2009*. Turnhout.

Gelichi, S. & C. Negrelli (eds) 2017. *Adriatico altomedievale (VI–XI secolo): Scambi, porti, produzioni*. Venice.

Gerritsen, F. & H. Van Der Heijden (eds) 2018. *Standplaats Istanbul. Lange lijnen in de cultuurgeschiedenis van Turkije*. Amsterdam.

Gerstel, S. E. J. 2007. "The sacred vessel and the measure of a man", in Cutler & Papaconstantinou (eds) 2007, 149–56.

Gerstel, S. E. J. (ed.) 2013. *Viewing the Morea: Land and People in the Late Medieval Peloponnese*. Washington, D.C.

Gonçalves, M.-J. & S. Gómez-Martinez (eds) 2015. *Actas do X Congresso Internacional A Cerâmica Medieval no Mediterrâneo*. Silves.

Gretel, S. E. J. et al. 2003. "A late Medieval settlement at Panakton", *Hesperia* 72, 147–234.

Giannopoulou, M. 2010. *Pithoi. Technology and History of Storage Vessels Through the Ages* (BAR I.S. 2140). Oxford.

Grünbart, M. 2007. "Store in a cool and dry place: Perishable goods and their preservation in Byzantium", in Brubaker & Linardou (eds) 2007, 39–49.

Güll, P. (ed.) 2007. "Lecce, ex convento del Carmine. Un'associazione di reperti ceramici, vitrei, faunistici e botanici in un silo del XIV secolo", *Archeologia Medievale* 34, 147–68.

Haldon, J., H. Elton & J. Newhard (eds) 2018. *Archaeology and Urban Settlement in Late Roman and Byzantine Anatolia: Euchaita-Avkat-Beyözü and its Environment*. Cambridge.

Hansen, I. L., R. Hodges & S. Leppard (eds) 2013. *Butrint 4: The Archaeology and Histories of an Ionian Town*, 257–59. Oxford.

Harrison, R. M. et al. 1993. "Excavations at Amorion: 1992 interim report", *Anatolian Studies* 43, 147–62.

Hawthorne, J. W. J. 1997. "Post processual economics. The role of African Red Slip Ware vessel volume in Mediterranean demography", in K. Meadows, C. Lemke & J. Heron (eds) *TRAC 96: Proceedings of the Sixth Annual Theoretical Roman Archaeology Conference Sheffield 1996*. Oxford, 29–37.

Hayes, J. W. 1972. *Late Roman Pottery*. London.

Jarres et grands contenants entre Moyen Âge et Époque Moderne / Jars and Large Containers between the Middle Ages and the Modern Era. 2015. Aix-en-Provence.

Jennings, S. 2010. "A group of glass ca. 800 A.D. from tower 2 on the western defences, Butrint, Albania", in Drauschke & Keller (eds) 2010, 225–35.

Jennings, S. et al. 2013. "Appendix: The glass from tower 1 in the Western Defences", in Hansen, Hodges & Leppard (eds) 2013, 257–59.

Joyner, L. 2007. "Cooking pots as indicators of cultural change. A petrographic study of Byzantine and Frankish cooking wares from Corinth", *Hesperia* 76: 183–227.

Kalas, V. 2009. "The Byzantine kitchen in the domestic complexes of Cappadocia", in Vorderstrasse & Roodenberg (eds) 2009, 109–27.

Laiou, A. E. (ed.) 2002. *The Economic History of Byzantium: From the Seventh through the Fifteenth Century*. Washington, D.C.

Lavan, L., E. Swift & T. Putzeys (eds) 2007. *Objects in Context, Objects in Use. Material Spatiality in Late Antiquity*. Leiden—Boston.

Lawrence, R. & A. Wallace-Hadrill (eds) 1997. *Domestic Space in the Roman World*. Portsmouth.

Lemaître, S. (ed.) 2007. *Céramiques antiques en Lycie (VIIe S..a.C.—VIIe S. p.C.)*. Bordeaux.

Lévi-Strauss, C. 1964. *Mythologiques I: Le cru et le cuit*. Paris.

Margaritis, E. 2006. "Archaeobotanical remains from the Agora's Byzantine contexts", *Akoue* 56: 26.

Meffre, J.-F. & Y. Rigoir 2007. "...Faire bonne contenance ...", in Bonifay & Tréglia (eds) 2007, 65–9.

Metheny, K. C. & M. C. Beaudry (eds) 2015. *The Archaeology of Food: An Encyclopedia*, vol. 1. New York & London.

Morrisson, C. (ed.) 2010. *Trade and Markets in Byzantium*, 399–426. Washington D.C.

Mulder-Heymans, N. 2002. "Archaeology, experimental archaeology and ethnoarchaeology on bread ovens in Syria", *Civilisations* 49, 1–22.

Niewöhner, P. (ed.) 2017. *The Archaeology of Byzantine Anatolia. From the End of Late Antiquity until the Coming of the Turks*. Oxford.

Oikonomides, N. 1990. "The contents of the Byzantine house from the eleventh to the fifteenth century", *DOP* 44, 205–14.

Orlandos, A. 2000. *Τα παλάτια και τα σπίτια του Μυστρά*. Athens.

Özkul Fındık, N. 2018. "Ceramics recovered in some excavations in east and south Anatolia", in *XIth Congress AIECM3 on Medieval and Modern Period Mediterranean Ceramics Proceedings / XI. AIECM3 Uluslararası Orta Çağ ve Modern Akldeniz Dünyası Seramik Kongresi Bildirileri, 19–24 October/Ekim 2015 Antalya*, 301–8.

Papanikola-Bakirtzi, D. (ed.) 2002. *Everyday Life in Byzantium*. Athens.

Papanikola-Bakirtzi, D. (ed.) 2005. *Food and Cooking in Byzantium*. Athens.

Papanikola-Bakirtzi, D. & N. Coureas (eds) 2014. *Cypriot Medieval Ceramics: Reconsiderations and New Perspectives*. Nicosia.

Parker, B. J. & M. B. Uzel. 2007. "The tradition of tandır cooking in southeastern Anatolia: An ethnoarchaeological perspective", in Takaoğlu (ed.) 2007, 7–43.

Pellegrino, E. 2007. "Présentation des céramiques à pâte rouge orangé sableuses de Xanthos. Une production de céramique culinaire locale sur le long terme", in Lemaître (ed.) 2007, 225–59.

Pitarakis, B. 2010. "Daily Life at the Marketplace, Late Antiquity and Byzantium", in Morrisson (ed.) 2010, 399–426.

Putzeys, T. 2007. "Productive space in Late Antiquity", in Lavan, Swift & Putzeys (eds) 2007, 63–80.

Rheidt, K. 1990. "Byzantinische Wohnhäuser des 11. bis 14. Jahrhunderts in Pergamon", *DOP* 44, 195–204.

Rheidt, K. 2002. "The urban economy of Pergamon", in Laiou (ed.) 2002, 623–29.

Salza Prina Ricotti, E. 1978–80. "Cucine e quartieri servili in epoca romana", *Rendiconti della Pontificia Accademia Romana di Archeologia* 51–52, 237–94.

Scranton, R. L. 1957. *Medieval Architecture in the Central Area of Corinth*, Vol. 16. Princeton.

Seyer, M. (ed.) 2012. *40 Jahre Grabung Limyra*. Vienna.

Shear, Jr. T. L. 1984. "The Athenian Agora: Excavations of 1980–1982", *Hesperia* 53, 1–58.

Shear, Jr. T. L. 1997. "The Athenian Agora: Excavations of 1989–1993", *Hesperia* 66, 520–48.

Sibbesson, E., B. Jervis & S. Coxon (eds) 2016. *Insight from Innovation: New Light on Archaeological Ceramics*. St Andrews.

Skibo, J. M. 1992. *Pottery Function. A Use-Alteration Perspective*, New York & London.

Smith, W. 1998. "Fuel for thought: Archaeobotanical evidence for the use of alternatives to wood fuel in Late Antique North Africa", *Journal of Mediterranean Archaeology* 11.2, 191–205.

Smogorzewska, A. 2012. "Fire installations in household activities: Archaeological and ethnoarchaeological study from Tell Arbid (North-East Syria)", *Paléorient* 38, 227–47.

Spatharakis, I. 2004. *The Illustrations of the Cynegetica in Venice. Codex Marcianus Graecus Z 139*. Leiden.

Takaoğlu, T. (ed.) 2007. *Ethnoarchaeological Investigations in Rural Anatolia*, vol. 4. Istanbul.

Teslenko, I. 2009. "Vessels for wine-storage from archaeological complexes of the 14th–15th centuries in the Crimea", in Zozaya et al. (eds) 2009, 869–80.

van Oosten, R. 2017. "A Medieval cooking revolution: Changing ceramic cookware ca. 1300 as a window into cooking infrastructure, fuel, and food transitions", in Vroom, Waksman & Van Oosten (eds) 2017, 193–219.

Van Peteghem, A. & K. Braeckman 2003. "Pessinonte 2001, recherché paleobotanique: Etude des grains et des fruits", *Anatolia Antiqua* 11, 165–68.

Vorderstrasse, T. & J. Roodenberg (eds) 2009. *Archaeology of the Countryside in Medieval Anatolia*. Leiden.

Vroom, J. 2000. "Byzantine garlic and Turkish delight. Dinging habits and cultural change in Central Greece from the Byzantine to Ottoman times", *Archaeological Dialogues* 7, 199–216.

Vroom, J. 2003. *After Antiquity. Ceramics and Society in the Aegean from the 7th to the 20th centuries A.C. A Case Study from Boeotia, Central Greece*. Leiden.

Vroom, J. (ed.) 2005. *Medieval and Post-Medieval Ceramics in the Eastern Mediterranean—Fact and Fiction: Proceedings of the International Conference on Byzantine and Ottoman Archaeology*. Turnhout.

Vroom, J. 2007a. "The archaeology of Late Antique dining habits in the eastern Mediterranean: A preliminary study of the evidence", in Lavan, Swift & Putzeys (eds) 2007, 313–61.

Vroom, J. 2007b. "The changing dining habits at Christ's table", in Brubaker & Linardou (eds) 2007, 191–222.

Vroom, J. 2008. "Dishing up history: Early Medieval ceramic finds from the Triconch Palace in Butrint" *Mélanges de l'Ecole française de Rome—Moyen Âge* 120.2, 291–305.

Vroom, J. 2009. "Medieval ceramics and the archaeology of consumption in Eastern Anatolia", in Vorderstrasse & Roodenberg (eds) 2009, 235–58.

Vroom, J. 2011. "The Morea and its links with southern Italy after AD 1204: Ceramics and identity", *Archeologia Medievale* 38, 409–30.

Vroom, J. 2012a. "Tea and ceramics: New perspectives on Byzantine pottery from Limyra", in Seyer (ed.) 2012, 341–55.

Vroom, J. 2012b. "From one coast to another: Early Medieval ceramics in the southern Adriatic region", in Gelichi & Hodges (eds) 2012, 337–52.

Vroom, J. 2013. "Digging for the 'Byz': Adventures into Byzantine and Ottoman archaeology in the eastern Mediterranean", *Pharos* 19, 79–110.

Vroom, J. 2014. *Byzantine to Modern Pottery in the Aegean: An Introduction and Field Guide*. Turnhout.

Vroom, J. 2015a. "Food and dining as social display", in Metheny & Beaudry (eds) 2015, 184–87.

Vroom, J. 2015b. "The archaeology of consumption in the Eastern Mediterranean: A ceramic perspective", in Gonçalves & Gómez-Martinez (eds) 2015, 359–67.

Vroom, J. 2016. "Pots and pies: Adventures in the archaeology of eating habits of Byzantium", in Sibbesson, Jervis & Coxon (eds) 2016, 221–44.

Vroom, J. 2017. "The Byzantine Web: Pottery and connectivity between the southern Adriatic and the eastern Mediterranean", in Gelichi & Negrelli (eds) 2017, 285–310.

Vroom, J. 2018a. "The ceramics, agricultural resources and food", in Haldon, Elton & Newhard (eds) 2018, 134–84.

Vroom, J. 2018b. "On the edge: Butrint on the Western frontier of the Byzantine Empire", in Düring & Stek (eds) 2018, 272–98.

Vroom, J. 2020. "Eating in Aegean lands (ca 700–1500). Perspectives on pottery", in S.Y. Waksman (ed), *Multidisciplinary Approaches to Food and Foodways in the Medieval Eastern Mediterranean (Archéologie(s) 4)*, Lyon, 275–93.

Vroom, J. & F. Kondyli 2011. *Life Among Ruins. Greece and Turkey between Past and Present / Leven tussen brokstukken. Griekenland en Turkije tussen verleden and heden*, Utrecht.

Vroom, J. & Y. Boswinkel 2016. "New dimensions in archaeology: 2D and 3D visualisations of Byzantine structures and their contents in the Athenian Agora", *Pharos* 22.1, 87–114.

Vroom, J. & E. Tzavella 2017. "Dinner time in Athens: Eating and drinking in the Medieval Agora", in Vroom, Waksman & Van Oosten (eds) 2017, 145–80.

Vroom, J., M. van Ijzendoorn, M. van Nieuwkoop & K. Post 2017. "A matter of taste: The experiment of a 'Byzantine food-lab' placed in socio-historical context", in Vroom, Waksman & Van Oosten (eds) 2017, 323–52.

Vroom, J., A. Everts & S. van den Brand 2018. "De smaak van het verleden: Proefexperimenten met Byzantijnse en Osmaanse gastronomie", in Gerritsen & Van Der Heijden (eds) 2018, 272–79.

Vroom, J., Y. Waksman & R. Van Oosten (eds) 2017. *Medieval MasterChef. Eastern Cuisine and Western Food Customs: An Archaeological and Historical Perspective.* Turnhout.

Waywell, G. B. & J. J. Wilks 1997. "Excavation at Sparta: The Roman Stoa, 1988–1991, part 3", *ABSA* 92, 401–34.

Williams, II Ch. K. & O. H. Zervos 1988. "Corinth 1987: South of Temple E and East of the Theater", *Hesperia* 57, 100–6.

Williams, II Ch. K. & O. H. Zervos 1993. "Frankish Corinth: 1992", *Hesperia* 62, 1–52.

Williams, II Ch. K. & O. H. Zervos 1994. "Frankish Corinth: 1993", *Hesperia* 63, 1–40.

XIth Congress AIECM3 on Medieval and Modern Period Mediterranean Ceramics Proceedings / XI. AIECM3 Uluslararası Orta Çağ ve Modern Akldeniz Dünyası Seramik Kongresi Bildirileri, 19–24 October/Ekim 2015 Antalya. 2018. Ankara.

Yakobson, A. L. 1979. *Keramika I keramicheskoe proisvodstvo srednevekovoi Tavriki*, Leningrad.

Yehuda, L. 2011. "Cooking and food in the Latin Kingdom of Jerusalem", in Ziffer & Tal (eds) 2011, 52–61.

Ziffer, I. & O. Tal (eds) 2011. *The Last Supper at Apollonia: The Final Days of the Crusader Castle in Herzliya.* Tel Aviv.

Zozaya, J. et al. (eds) 2009. *Actas del VIII Congreso de Cerámica Medieval en el Mediterráneo*, vol. 2, 869–80. Ciudad Real.

Space and Identity

Byzantine Conceptions of Geographic Belonging

Johannes Koder

Identity is strongly connected with the twin terms auto-stereotype and hetero-stereotype*. As the self-sight of individual or collective identity becomes clear-cut only by comparison with the "other", be it in similarities or in contrasts, a consequent separation of auto- and hetero-stereotypes would be rather difficult. Identity is formed in reaction to the behaviour or policy of the other.[1] This paper is focussed on collective identity. Collective identity can be defined as a combination of the similar goals, ideas and views that unite a group of people and are often at least in part formed by subconsciously developed stereotypes.

The formation of a collective identity is in many cases initiated and controlled from the top of the society, from political or religious leaders, but it may also be developed by individuals within a group, against or at least apart from the actual peer group. As a possible result, a new leading group may emerge, or a regional ruler, who acts largely independent from or even against the emperor. Examples of this are the Paulicians or the legendary Digenis Akrites.[2]

1 Terms and Paraphrases for Identity

The notions *tautotes* ('identity") and its opposite *heterotes* ("otherness") were discussed by pagan philosophers since Aristotle,[3] at least until the sixth century, when the Neoplatonist Damaskios stated that identity and otherness are rather more established and divine (καθολικωτέρη τίς ἐστιν καὶ θεία ἡ ταυτότης καὶ ἡ ἑτερότης).[4] In a traditional sense both terms also existed in the medieval philosophical vocabulary of Byzantium. For example, Michael Psellos speaks

---

* I would like to express my sincere thanks to the editors for their help with the translations and careful editing of the article.
1 See Browning 1989a.
2 See Hoffmann 1974.
3 Aristotle, *Metaphysics* 1018a and passim Ross.
4 Damaskios, *De Principiis* 310 Ruelle.

about the contrast between *tautotes* and *heterotes* as a subdivision of *genos* (Πέντε τὰ γένη κατὰ Πλάτωνα, οὐσία, ταυτότης, ἑτερότης, κίνησις, στάσις, οὐχ ὡς τὰ παρὰ τοῖς φιλοσόφοις ὑπάλληλα, ἀλλ' ὡς πανταχοῦ διήκοντα),[5] as also does John Italos (Τὸ γὰρ ὂν οὐκ ἔστιν οὐσία, καθ' ὃ τῶν ἄλλων ἔρημόν ἐστι, κινήσεως, στάσεως, ἑτερότητός τε καὶ ταυτότητος, ἡ δὲ οὐσία μετὰ τούτων, καὶ ὄν· ἔστι γὰρ ταῦτα οἱονεὶ στοιχεῖα αὐτῆς, ἢ μᾶλλον εἰπεῖν παθήματα καὶ ἐνέργειαι, διὸ καὶ ἐν αὐτῇ λέγεται εἶναι).[6] Since the church fathers *tautotes* was equated with *homoiotes*, "likeness" (ὁμοουσιότης· ταυτότης κατὰ τὸ ὑποκείμενον, καὶ τὸ ἀπαράλλακτον κατὰ τὴν οὐσίαν),[7] and *heterotes* with *anomoiotes* ("unlikeness"). In the fourteenth century, Theodoros Dexios explained the contrast of God's identity and simplicity and likeness (ταυτότης καὶ ἁπλότης [...] καὶ ὁμοιότης) versus otherness, unlikeness and difference which exist among the humans (ἑτερότης καὶ ἀνομοιότης καὶ διαφορά, ἅπερ ἐν τοῖς πολλοῖς).[8]

When Christian authors discussed the relation between *soma* and *psyche*, they ascribed the *tautotes* to the soul; we dispose of two examples. Niketas Choniates explains that while the body is susceptible to decay, the soul remains unaffected within the *tautotes*: [...] τὴν μὲν ψυχὴν ἐν ταὐτότητι μένουσαν καὶ τροπῆς ἀπαράδεκτον, ἀλλοιωτὸν δὲ τὸ σῶμα καὶ πάθεσιν ὑποκείμενον.[9] And, in the late fourteenth century, Theophanes of Nicaea says that the heart and all parts of the entire body are unified in a single substance through the *tautotes* and harmony of the soul: Ἡ καρδία καὶ πάντα τὰ μέρη καὶ μέλη τοῦ σώματος φυσικῶς ἀλλήλοις ἐν μιᾷ ὑποστάσει ἥνωνται τῇ τῆς ψυχῆς ταυτότητι καὶ ἁρμονίᾳ.[10]

Obviously these authors do not use the term *tautotes* exactly with the meaning of 'identity', which is given in current identity research. Though the social and political meaning of identity was discussed indirectly, Byzantine scholars reflected on other terms. David of Thessaloniki equates *genos* with *patris* and *pater*: Καὶ γὰρ ἡ πατρὶς ἀρχή τίς ἐστι τῆς ἑκάστου γενέσεως, ὥσπερ καὶ ὁ πατήρ. [...] Ὥσπερ γὰρ ὁ πατὴρ γένος λέγεται, οὕτω καὶ ἡ πατρίς. Ἐδείξαμεν δὲ ὅτι καὶ κρεῖττον γένος ὑπάρχει τὸ τῆς πατρίδος ἤπερ τὸ τοῦ πατρός.[11] Later, Nikephoros Blemmydes came to a similar conclusion about the meanings of *genos* which he considers as the agent of birth, deriving either by one's father or by one's homeland. Hence, one's birth agency is double—both natural and local:

---

5   Michael Psellos, *Philosophica minora* 38 O'Meara.
6   Ioannes Italos, *Quaestiones* 72 Ioannou.
7   Hesychios, Lexicon, omicron 780 Latte.
8   Theodoros Dexios, *Appellatio versus Cantacuzenum*, ch. 53 Polemis.
9   Niketas Choniates, *Epistle* 7.210 van Dieten.
10 Theophanes Nicaenus, *In Sanctissimam Deiparam* 11.140 Jugie; see Polemis 1996, 185–90.
11 David, *In Porphyrii isagogen* 128 Busse.

Τὰ σημαινόμενα τοῦ γένους διάφορα. Γένος γὰρ λέγεται καὶ ἡ ἑκάστου τῆς γενέσεως ἀρχή, εἴτε ἀπὸ τοῦ τεκόντος, εἴτε ἀπὸ τῆς πατρίδος. [...] Διττὴ τοίνυν ἡ τῆς γενέσεως ἀρχή, φυσική τε καὶ τοπική [...] Λέγεται γένος καὶ αὐτὸ τὸ πλῆθος τῶν ἀπὸ μιᾶς ἀρχῆς, καθὸ σχέσεως ἔχουσι πρός τε τὴν πρώτην ἀρχὴν καὶ πρὸς ἀλλήλους αὐτούς· ὡς ὅταν λέγωμεν τὸ γένος τῶν Ἰουδαίων.[12]

We conclude that some Byzantines were aware of the relation between biological and local identity, specified in the terms of *genos* and *patris*.

2   Identity and Space

Primary markers for a better understanding of collective identity in Byzantium, for the feeling of belonging, were, for the majority of the Romaioi, a religious commitment[13] (in close proximity to the state as political factor),[14] their language[15] (in many cases including ethnic[16] and probably also cultural factors)[17] and their spatial references.[18] The dimension of space belongs to the most obvious and deeply rooted ones for the collective and the individual.[19] The understanding of spatial reference has mental and material facets. In particular, the mental facets are mainly related to ideology, social ties, culture, religion, the material facets to land use, economy, travel, traffic.

As for spatial identity, a basic distinction of three levels is helpful: local, regional and supra-regional. These three levels cannot be strictly separated. For historians, collective identity is of particular interest in the context of the mythical *ethnogenesis* of many nations and their states before the very beginning of their 'history'.[20] Byzantium is one of the rare exceptions.[21] In the context of the spatial dimension of identity, historians initiated some time ago the research topic 'sites of memory'; it referred originally to real places, but was

---

12   Nikephoros Blemmydes, *Epitome logica* 753 Migne.
13   See Dunn (ed.) 2015.
14   See Chrysos 1996; Dagron 2005.
15   See Fussenegger 2012.
16   See Tielker 2003; Wagner 2006.
17   See Delanty 1995; Assmann 2007.
18   Comparing language and space, I think that—at least in Byzantium—language acts stronger as a hetero-stereotype identifier and space as an auto-stereotype identifier, but this aspect will be discussed in another paper.
19   For Byzantium see Stouraitis 2014, 2017, 2018.
20   See Geary 2002; Gillett (ed.) 2002.
21   See Koder 1990, 2000, 2003, 2011a, 2018, 2019b.

soon widened to include any phenomenon which directs our attention to a certain aspect of the past.[22] The most prominent Byzantine example of a *real* site of memory is the second church of Hagia Sophia in Constantinople, built by the Emperor Justinian I, an anonymous hymnographer praises the church on the occasion of its second inauguration (after the partial collapse of the main dome). He suggests that the dome is meant to be viewed and taught as a heaven on earth due to its appearance and to the worship of God who has chosen the latter as His residence:

Οὐρανός τις ἐπίγειος καὶ ὁρᾶται καὶ κηρύσσεται
καὶ μορφώματι καὶ λατρείᾳ θεοῦ·
ὃν ᾑρετίσατο ἑαυτῷ εἰς κατοικεσίαν.[23]

Since then, Hagia Sophia has been praised in a similar manner inside and outside the frontiers of Byzantium. In Kievan Rus', for example, an ambassador of the Grand Prince, after his returning from Constantinople reported the following words in 987 to Vladimir and the *družina*:

> The Greeks led us to the edifices where they worship their God, and we knew not whether we were in heaven or on earth. For on earth there is no such splendour or such beauty, and we are at a loss how to describe it. We know only that God dwells there among men, and their service is fairer than the ceremonies of other nations. We cannot forget that beauty.[24]

Hagia Sophia remained a site of memory in the post-Byzantine period—an anonymous Greek chronicle of the sixteenth century, mourning the fall of Constantinople, asks:

Καὶ παρεδόθημεν εἰς χεῖρας ἐχθρῶν ἀνόμων ἐχθίστων ἀποστατῶν καὶ βασιλεῖ ἀδίκῳ καὶ πονηροτάτῳ παρὰ πᾶσαν τὴν γῆν διὰ τὰς ἁμαρτίας ἡμῶν. Πῶς κατεδέξατο ἡ ἐπ' ὀνόματι τοῦ Θεοῦ λόγου κτισθεῖσα Σοφία, ὁ ἐπίγειος παράδεισος, ἡ νέα Σιών, τὸ καύχημα πάσης τῆς οἰκουμένης, τὸ ἄγαλμα τῶν ἐκκλησιῶν, ἡ ὑπερέχουσα πάντων τῶν τῆς γῆς κτισμάτων; Ὢ τοῦ θαύματος· ὁ τοῦ Θεοῦ περιώνυμος ναὸς γέγονε νῦν ναὸς τῶν Ἰσμαηλιτῶν. Φρῖξον, ἥλιε· στέναξον ἡ γῆ καὶ κλονουμένη βόησον· ἀνεξίκακε Κύριε, δόξα Σοι.

---

22 See Assmann 2006; Nora 1990; Riedel 2009.
23 *Akathistos* stanza 5.5s. Trypanis. See also Koder 2011b.
24 Povest'vremennikh let, 6, ad annum 6495 (987), quoted from http://pages.uoregon.edu/kimball/chronicle.htm. For other examples see Majeska 1984, 199–236.

So we were delivered into the hands of lawless foes and most hateful apostates, into the hands of an unjust and most wisked emperor, throughout the entire earth, on account of our sins. How could the Church of Hagia Sophia endure it? Named after God's Word, it was the earthly paradise, the new Zion, the boast of the world, the delight of churches, and the most proud building on the earth. What a marvel: the famous church of God now became a temple of the Ismaelites. Shudder, O Sun; groan, O Earth; shake and cry out: Glory to you, enduring Lord.[25]

So, this church was (and is) a focus of *belonging-to* for the Byzantines, the Greeks, and the major part of orthodox Christians, a central site of memory (like Constantinople, the *Polis*, as a whole).

When speaking about the spatial dimension of identity, one realizes soon that it is closely linked to varying feelings of belonging-to. In the fifteenth century, Bessarion offered appropriate key-words related to these feelings, by writing that they are citizens, they are soldiers, they are generals, and they simply defend their city, land, homeland, children, ancestors' tombs, and every other honorable asset: Ἡμεῖς πολῖται, ἡμεῖς στρατιῶται, ἡμεῖς ἐσμεν στρατηγοί, πόλεως, χώρας, πατρίδος, τέκνων, τάφων πατρῴων καὶ πάντων ἁπλῶς τῶν τιμιωτάτων ὑπερασπίζοντες.[26] Nearly self-evident, the central terms of spatial belonging in Bessarion's text are *polis, chora,* and *patris*. Important in our context is the term *patris*,[27] especially when connected with *soma*, the body. This relation was interpreted differently in differing contexts. In a reference to the 'pagan' past, Eustathios of Thessaloniki refers to Achilles, who sits crying on the shore, being with his *soma* in Troy, but in his *phantasia* in Phthia, and Eustathios comments that Achilles understandably dreams of his *patris*: Ἀχιλλεὺς ἐνταῦθα ἐκάθητο παρὰ τὸν αἰγιαλὸν ὁρῶν ἐπὶ πόντον καὶ ἀποπλέων οἷον τῇ θέᾳ εἰς τὴν πατρίδα καὶ σώματι μὲν ἐν τῇ Τροίᾳ παρών, τῇ φαντασίᾳ δὲ τὴν Φθίαν ὁρῶν. ἔχει δὲ καὶ ἄδειαν οὕτω πενθεῖν.[28] In the early Christian period, John Chrysostom confirms that, on the contrary to the mind, the body is grounded on the *patris*: Τὸ μὲν γὰρ σῶμα ἐπὶ τῆς πατρίδος ἵδρυτο· ὁ λογισμὸς δὲ καὶ ὁ νοῦς ὥσπερ ὑπό τινων πτερῶν κουφιζόμενος τῆς τοῦ Πνεύματος χάριτος, καὶ διὰ παντὸς ὑμῖν ἐπιχωριάζων, ἅπαντα τοῦτον τὸν δῆμον ἐν τοῖς ἐκείνου περιέφερε σπλάγχνοις.[29] And John of Damascus, finally, asks: Πλούτῳ κομᾷς; καὶ ἐπὶ προγόνοις μέγα φρονεῖς, καὶ ἐπαγάλλῃ πατρίδι,

---

25 *Anonymous Greek Chronicle* 34.3–9 Philippides 51.
26 Bessarion, *In calumniatorem Platonis* 14.6.15–18 Mohler.
27 Fort the development of the meaning of πατρίς (πατρίδα) see Moutafidou 2001, 183–84.
28 Eustathios, *Commentarii ad Iliadem* 1.180 van der Valk.
29 Ioannes Chrysostomos, *De S. Meletio Antiocheno* 517 Migne.

καὶ κάλλει σώματος, καὶ ταῖς παρὰ πάντων τιμαῖς; πρόσεχε σεαυτῷ, ὅτι θνητός.[30] Later, Theodore Stoudites describes the exemplary heroism of the monks as witnesses for Christ: they left the world, their parents, their family, their *patris*, and exposed their *soma* to the stress of obedience: Καταλελοιπότες κόσμον καὶ τὰ τοῦ κόσμου, γονεῖς τε καὶ ἀδελφούς, γένος καὶ πατρίδα, αὐτό τε τὸ σῶμα ἐκδεδωκότες εἰς ἄθλησιν διὰ τῆς ὑπακοῆς.[31]

3 Local Identity: The *Patris*

For many of us, the spatial feeling of belonging-to is related to a homeland (a region) or a hometown (home-settlement). The Byzantines understood the term *patris* normally not as a landscape, but nearer to its original sense as the native city, town or village.[32] This is the first of the mentioned three levels, the local identity, everybody's immediate neighbourhood of interpersonal relations. It may be described as a place with its surrounding countryside, within one-or-two-days' walking distance for its inhabitants, though larger in the case of nomadic or semi-nomadic pastoral tribes or populations. This first level may be defined as a sense of belonging to the place of birth and origin of the family, to the main place of residence, to a local language or dialect, or to local religious and other customs. It may also be understood through sensual impressions that are familiar since childhood; in short, the home-place in its narrowest sense.

Accordingly, Roman and Byzantine law provides the possibility of deportation and exile from the *patris*, though sometimes also in a wider sense: [...] ἐξορίζεται τῆς πατρίδος αὐτοῦ καὶ ἐπαρχίας.[33] Generally speaking, narrative sources identify *patris* with a settlement, though it must be admitted that as an exception, mainly in hagiographical texts, a province (*eparchia*) as such also may be a *patris*, e.g.: Πατρὶς μὲν γὰρ τοῦ ἐν ἁγίοις τούτου πατρὸς Πάταρα τῆς Λυκῶν ἐπαρχίας καὶ μητροπόλεως τῆς Μυρέων Ἐκκλησίας.[34]

---

30 Ioannes Damaskenos, *Sacra Parallela* 1121 Migne.
31 Theodoros Studites, *Parva catechesis* 75.21–23 Auvray.
32 See Liddell & Scott & Jones 1966, 1349a.
33 *Basilika* 50.28.1 Scheltema & van der Wal.
34 Neophytos Enkleistos, *Panegyrike A'* 26.57s. Giagkou & Papatriantafyllou-Theodoridi.— Cf. also *Vita Euaristi* 2.4s. van de Vorst, or *Synaxarium ecclesiae Constantinopolitanae* Day 26, 5.2s. Delehaye.

3.1 Polis and Politeuma

In the majority of cases the hometown-function was assigned to the *polis* and its community, the *politeuma*. The origin of this importance of the *polis* can be explained by the Greek political tradition of *polis*-states and their development in the Roman Empire;[35] it is later confirmed by Roman and Byzantine legislation stating that a villager's patris is the city to which the village is subjected: Ὁ ἀπὸ κώμης ὁρμώμενος ἐκείνην τὴν πόλιν ἔχει πατρίδα, ὑφ' ἣν ἡ κώμη τελεῖ.[36] The narrative sources demonstrate that this distinction was not restricted to legal regulations, but rather was widespread in other texts. A striking example is the *Life of Alypios Stylites*, where the saint's *patris* is the *polis* Adrianoupolis in the *chora* (the land) of Paphlagonia: [...] πατρίδα μὲν ἔσχεν, εἰ δεῖ πατρίδα λέγειν τὴν ἐπὶ γῆς, τὴν Ἀδριανοῦ πόλει ὁμώνυμον, ἢ μία τῆς Παφλαγόνων καθέστηκεν χώρας.[37]

In Byzantium, the term *polis* is a special case insofar as it has a twofold meaning. It is not only a city in general, but also specifically Constantinople, "the city" (ἡ Πόλις). This special meaning developed since the early Middle Ages and was unequivocally used in this sense also in colloquial Greek probably since the reign of the emperor Herakleios (610–641).[38] The second prooemium of the *Akathistos Hymnos*, which likely was composed by Sergios (Patriarch 610–638),[39] uses the term *polis* (consciously or unconsciously) in both senses:

Τῇ ὑπερμάχῳ στρατηγῷ τὰ νικητήρια
ὡς λυτρωθεῖσα τῶν δεινῶν εὐχαριστήρια,
ἀναγράφω σοι ἡ πόλις σου, Θεοτόκε.

Unto you, O Theotokos, invincible Champion,
your City, in thanksgiving ascribes the victory
for the deliverance from sufferings.[40]

---

35 See Zanker 2000; Rapp 2011, with bibliography.
36 *Basilika* 54.1.30 Scheltema & van der Wal.
37 *Vita prior Alypii Stylitae* 2.4 Delehaye.—Belonging together to a *polis* could be expressed by the term συμπολίτευσις, Trapp et al. (eds) 1994–2017, 1660a; Lampe 1961 1289b: "fellow citizenship"; see also προέλευσις.—I just mention, that larger cities could be divided in *geitoniai* ("neighbourhoods"; [...] πόλις μεγάλη ἔχῃ γειτονίας πολλάς, Makarios, *Homily* 8.4.1 Berthold); but these quarters had not the quality or function of *patrides*.
38 See Koder 2019a.
39 So the prevailing opinion, but see Speck 1981, 170–71, who proposes Germanos (Patriarch 715–30) as author.
40 *Akathistos* second prooimion Trypanis. English translation by Papadeas 1980.

Soon the term was understood quite naturally as Constantinople, not only until 1453, but also during the Ottoman period[41]—the first verses of the *Anakalema tes Konstantinoupoles*, an anonymous song of mourning for the loss of the holy City, are just one example:

Θρῆνος κλαυθμὸς καὶ ὀδυρμὸς καὶ στεναγμὸς καὶ λύπη.
Θλίψις ἀπαραμύθητος ἔπεσεν τοῖς Ῥωμαίοις.
Ἐχάσασιν τὸ σπίτιν τους, τὴν Πόλιν τὴν ἁγία,
τὸ θάρρος καὶ τὸ καύχημα καὶ τὴν ἀπανταχήν τους.[42]

However, one should keep in mind that the term *Byzantion* always could also have the meaning "Constantinople"— Timarion was welcomed as citizen of Constantinople: Ἐπὶ τούτοις ἦλθε καὶ ὁ Βυζάντιος σοφιστὴς καὶ τοῖς μὲν φιλοσόφοις προσιὼν ἡδέως ἠσπάζετο παρ' αὐτῶν καὶ τὸ "χαῖρε, Βυζάντιε", πυκνὸν ἐλέγετο.[43]

3.2 *Chorion and Kome*

The meaning of *polis* had a dominant position, but in non-legal texts *chorion* and *kome*, both terms meaning a settlement of basically agricultural character, often had the function of *patris*.[44] The term *chorion* originally was used in the sense of "lot of land" or "landed property", and it changed its meaning— chronologically varying from region to region—between the fifth and the seventh century, to "village"; already in the fifth century a *chorion* in Cappadocia is mentioned as the *patris* of Saint Longinos: [...] ἦλθεν εἰς τὴν ἰδίαν πατρίδα, ἐν τῇ Καππαδοκίᾳ τῇ δευτέρᾳ, ἐγγὺς Τυάνων, εἰς χωρίον καλούμενον Ἀνδραλές.[45] This meaning became dominant in medieval texts, except those whose authors wrote *attikizontes*, for example Niketas Choniates, also traditional lexica, which defined *chorion* as *oikopedon* and *gepedon*, like the Suda.[46] In some instances, a Byzantine writer felt that *chorion* needs a complementary explanation: Theophanes Continuatus relates about the origin of the empress Theodora, the spouse of the emperor Theophilos: Ἀλλὰ πατρίδα μὲν ἡ Θεοδώρα .τοῦτο γὰρ ὄνομα τῇ Αὐγούστῃ. Παφλαγονίαν ἐσέμνυνεν, καὶ χωρίον Ἔβισσαν.[47]

---

41 Not to forget that the modern Turkish name of the city derives from *polis*.
42 *Anakalema Kpl* l. 1–4 Kriaras. Even the film "A Touch of Spice" (2003) has in its original Greek title the pun *Polítiki / Politikí kouzina* ("Cuisine from Constantinople" / "Political Cuisine").
43 *Timarion* l. 1123–25 Romano.
44 See Koder 2011c, 47.
45 Hesychios, *Homilia* 20, 17.9–11 Aubineau.
46 *Suda*, Iota 74 and Gamma 244 Adler.
47 Theophanes Continuatus, *Chronographia* 89.15s. Bekker.

The term *kome* during late antiquity and the early Byzantine centuries was used in the sense of a big village, often with administrative and marketing functions. Procopius refers to some *komai*, which were turned into *poleis* by protecting them with a circuit wall, e.g. Dara and Theodosioupolis: [...] βασιλεὺς μὲν Ἀναστάσιος [...] κώμην ἄδοξόν τινα τὰ πρότερα οὖσαν, Δάρας ὄνομα, τείχει περιβαλεῖν διὰ σπουδῆς ἔσχεν, πόλιν τε αυτὴν [...] ἐργάσασθαι.[48] Later *kome* was common only in the works of authors who wrote in a pretentious sophisticated style, for example Niketas Stethatos, in the *Life of Symeon The New Theologian*,[49] and the patriarch Photius, who gives the following explanation for the apostle Paul's *patris*: Παῦλος ὁ θεῖος ἀπόστολος [...] τὴν ἐκ παλαιῶν προγόνων καὶ τῆς σωματικῆς γενέσεως τὰ Γίσχαλα (κώμη δὲ νῦν τὸ χωρίον, τῆς Ἰουδαίας πάλαι πολίχνιον χρηματίσαν) πατρίδα λαχὼν εἶχε.[50]

In this example, both *chorion* and *kome* are used in their antiquated meanings. Aside from these by far dominant possibilities to refer to a *patris*, others were occasionally used as well. A striking example is the "Armenian History" (attributed to Agathangelos); the author relates that in Armenia after the conversion of King Trdat, εἰς πάντα τὰ ὅρια Ἀρμενίων τῆς μεγάλης χώρας, ᾠκοδόμησεν ἐκκλησίας ἐν πάσαις ταῖς ἐπαρχίαις (provinces) καὶ πατρίσι (homelands) καὶ μέρεσιν (parts), ἐν ταῖς πόλεσί (cities) τε καὶ κωμοπόλεσιν (towns), κώμαις τε καὶ χωρίοις (big and little villages) καὶ ἐποικίοις (hamlets).[51] Obviously, the hierarchical order of *patris*-related terms in Agathangelos' text is similar to middle-Byzantine fiscal terminology: *polis—kome—chorion—agridion—proasteion—stasis*.[52]

Quite different to the mentioned types of settlement, a monastery or any other place of monastic life could not be a worldly *patris*, because the monk has to leave home and family behind, like Porphyrios[53] or Theodoros.[54] Through ascetic exercise he has to earn heaven as his *patris*,[55] whereas a monk who, seduced by Satan, fails to live an *angelikos bios* returns in shame to his worldly *patris* like a dog returns to its vomit:

---

48   Prokopios, *De Aedificiis* 2.1.4 Wirth; see also Prokopios, *Bella* 1.10.18s. Wirth, for Theodosioupolis. See Zanker 2000.
49   Niketas Stethatos, *Vita Symeonis* 2. 3–5 Hausherr.
50   Photius, *Epistle* 246, 2–6. Laourdas & Westerink.
51   Agathangelos, *Version grecque ancienne*, ch. 150.1–4 Lafontaine.
52   Lefort et al. (eds) 1991.
53   Markos Diakonos, *Vita Porphyrii*, ch. 4.10s. Grégoire & Kugener.
54   Georgios Sykeotes, *Vita Theodori*, ch. 62.7s. Festugière.
55   *Synaxarium Cpl.*, Day 15 ch. 3.5s. Delehaye.

Ἀφ' οὗ δὲ τοῖς οἰκείοις θελήμασι, μᾶλλον δὲ τοῖς τοῦ Σατὰν βουλεύμασιν, ἀκολουθεῖν ἤρξατο, εἰς τὸν τῆς πορνείας καὶ αὐτὸς κρημνὸν ὤλισθε. Διὸ καὶ τῆς μονῆς λάθρα τοῦ πατρὸς ἐξελθών, πρὸς τὴν ἑαυτοῦ πατρίδα ὡς κύων ἐπὶ τὸν ἴδιον ἔμετον αὖθις ὑπέστρεψε.

But, from the moment he began to follow his own wishes, or rather the counsels of Satan, he too slid into the abyss of fornication. As a result, he left the monastery without letting the [spiritual] father know, and went back to his homeland like a dog to its vomit.[56]

3.3 *Chora*

Finally, we come to the term *chora*, meaning "land", "landscape", or "region". Sometimes it is used—in the pre-Byzantine tradition—as the territory belonging to a *polis*: ἡ δὲ πόλις, χώραν τε πολλὴν ἔχουσα καὶ πολίχνια ὑπ' αὐτήν.[57] Yet aside from its general meaning, *chora* also expresses a very special feeling of familiarity and closeness to "one's own land". Kekaumenos makes this relation clear when he says:

Ἐὰν εἰς ἰδίαν χώραν κάστρα τυχὸν ἢ χωρία ἔχῃς [...], μή σε πλανήσῃ πλοῦτος ἢ ἀξιώματα ἢ ὑποσχέσεις μεγάλαι τῶν βασιλέων καὶ δῴης τὴν χώραν σου βασιλεῖ καὶ ἀντ' αὐτῆς λάβῃς χρήματα καὶ κτήματα, εἰ καὶ τετραπλασίονα μέλλεις λαβεῖν, ἀλλὰ ἔχε τὴν χώραν σου κἂν μικρὰ καὶ οὐδαμινὴ ἐστι.

If you own fortresses, or perhaps villages, on your own land, [...] don't let wealth or titles or big promises from the Emperors lead you astray, and give your land to an emperor, and get money and possessions in exchange for it, even if you are going to get four times as much, but own your land, even if it is small and insignificant.[58]

---

56 *Vita Lazari in monte Galesio* 569 col. 2.48–54 Delehaye. The author quotes Septuaginta, *Proverbs* 26.11. English translation by Greenfield 2000, 294, with Author's addition.
57 Michael Attaleiates, *Historia* 80 Bekker.
58 Kekaumenos, *Strategikon* 218 Roueché. The term *kastron* (originally "fortress") is in this text an equivalent to a fortified *polis*; this meaning is witnessed since the early byzantine period, e.g. in Agathangelos, *Martyrium S. Rhipsimae* 118 Garitte (5th century).

4 Regional Identity

The second and larger geographical dimension, the regional identity, is often defined by the terms *klima* and *epeiros*. Both have regional and supra-regional meanings.

4.1 Klima

The term *klima* and its plural *klimata* have the basic meaning "inclination", and later, mainly in cosmographical and geographical texts, "latitude", "latitudinal strip", and "region".[59] In the Middle Ages, a variety of related meanings appear depending on the literary genre and the text's chronological classification. Especially the plural *ta Klimata* was, since the early ninth century, the original name of the western thema Cherson (the fortress-town Cherson being capital of *ta Klimata*).[60] Later, in ecclesiastical texts, the plural corresponds to the directions of the compass and describes the geographical extensions of the patriarchates; so for example Matthaios Blastares, quoting Balsamon, notes that (in his time) the five traditional patriarchates cover the four klimata of the Ecumene.[61]

In texts of the late period, *klima* is also used to define more limited regions, often administrative territories.[62] Many examples are to be found in the chronicle of Ephraem, which speaks not only in general about the *klimata tes Romaïdos* (the territories of the Roman state) or about the *pros hesperan klima* (the western, European part of the empire), but in many cases uses the term as the equivalent of a geographic region (*Isauria, Pelopos, ton Illyrion, Albanon hapan, ton Ausonon*) or simply a province (*Smolenon, Nauplion, Prespa, Deabolis, Achris*).[63]

The regionally limited meanings of *klima(ta)* may in part be enforced by the biblical distribution of land after the Flood to the descendants of Noah: ἐκ τούτων ἀφωρίσθησαν νῆσοι τῶν ἐθνῶν ἐν τῇ γῇ αὐτῶν, ἕκαστος κατὰ γλῶσσαν ἐν ταῖς φυλαῖς αὐτῶν καὶ ἐν τοῖς ἔθνεσιν αὐτῶν.[64] This narrative was often repeated by Byzantine authors, who substituted the biblical terms with geographical ones. The chronographer George the Monk, for example, says that after the Flood

---

59   Liddell, Scott & Jones 1966, 960b.
60   *Constantine Porphyrogennetos, De Thematibus 182s*. Pertusi. See Papageorgiou 2008.
61   Matthaios Blastares, *Collectio alphabetica*, Epsilon 11.150–55 Potles & Rhalles.
62   Lampe 1961, 758a: *region*, hence *district* in a city.
63   Ephraim, *Historia* 245, 3995, 6592, 6602, 7238, 7280, 7319, 8091s. Lampsides.
64   Septuaginta, Genesis 10.5.

the descendants of the sons of Noah took possession of the *topoi, klimata, chorai, nesoi* and *potamoi*, each of them to which they were entitled.[65]

Corresponding to ancient Greek sources, *klima* sometimes encompasses the tilt of the Earth's axis; in this case the term expresses a supra-regional meaning. It derives at least indirectly from the view of the world in ancient cosmographical theories. Anna Komnene tells her public that for people living in famous Thoule, in the northern *klima*, the *boreios polos* stands above them.[66] In greater detail, Michael Psellos explains in his *De omnifaria doctrina* that for those, who live in the *boreion klima*, the North Pole may always be seen appearing as floating over them, whereas the South Pole is hidden by the Earth:

[…] παρὰ τὴν διάφορον τῶν κλιμάτων θέσιν οἱ πόλοι νῦν μὲν ἐπὶ τοῦ ὁρίζοντος κύκλου ἑστήκασι καὶ ἀμετάθετον τὸ πᾶν συντηροῦσι, τοῖς δὲ τὸ βόρειον κλίμα λαχοῦσιν οἰκεῖν ὁ μὲν ἐκεῖσε πόλος μετέωρος φαίνεται καὶ ἀειφανής, ὁ δὲ νότιος ὑπὸ τὴν γῆν κρύπτεται.[67]

My last example for *klima* comes from Pseudo-George Sphrantzes. Quoting from the Old Testament,[68] he equates the four wind directions (the directions of the compass) with the four great empires, the Chaldaean, the Persian, the Macedonian, and the Roman. These four empires, he says, ruled over the two copper mountain ranges, which represent the two *klimata tes Oikoumenes*, namely Asia and Europe:

Καὶ διὰ μὲν οὖν τῶν τεσσάρων ἀνέμων τὰς μεγάλας τέσσαρας βασιλείας ὁ μέγιστος διδάσκει Ζαχαρίας καὶ Δανιὴλ ὁ θεῖος, τὴν Χαλδαίων λέγω, τὴν Περσῶν καὶ τὴν τῶν Μακεδόνων καὶ Ῥωμαίων. Τὰ δὲ δύο ὄρη τὰ χαλκᾶ τὰ δύο κλίματα τῆς οἰκουμένης εἶναί φασιν· εἰς δύο γὰρ τέμνεται, εἴς τε Ἀσίαν καὶ Εὐρώπην.[69]

In this case it is evident that the term *klima* means what the majority of Byzantine historians and geographers traditionally called *epeiros*.

---

65 See e.g. Georgios Monachos, *Chronicon* 55 de Boor, Ioannes Malalas, *Chronographia* 13s. Dindorf and similar Symeon Logothetes, *Chronographia* 14 Bekker.
66 Anna Komnene, *Alexias* 6.11.3 Kambylis & Reinsch.
67 Michael Psellos, *De omnifaria doctrina*, § 160 (title: Τίς ἡ αἰτία τοῦ τὸν κόσμον ἐγκλιθῆναι) Westerink.
68 Septuaginta, Zacharias 2.10, 6.1 a d 6.5, cf. *Daniel* 7.2.
69 Ps.-Georgios Sphrantzes, *Chronikon* 464 Grecu; similar already Georgios Monachos, *Chronicon* 432s. de Boor and Georgios Kedrenos, *Historia* 1.423 Bekker.

4.2 Epeiros

Aside from the traditional name of the landscape in north-western Greece and southern Albania,[70] the term *epeiros* had both a regional and a supra-regional meaning, the broadest being 'continent'. Geographers and historians discussed the number of *epeiroi*—two or three—known in their time, but many took Africa (Libye) for a part of Asia. Procopius, for example, explains in the Vandal War the extension of the Roman Empire in the two continents Asia and Europe, which are surrounded by the *Okeanos*. In this passage Procopius avoids to mention Libye,[71] though later, in his Gothic War, he is himself not sure: first he refers to other authors who discuss the number of continents, and finally he tends to the opinion of Herodotus and his theory of three continents.[72]

Sometimes the contrast between Asia and Europe is scaled down to the straits and their hinterlands. An extreme example is the *Breviarium* of Nikephoros. In the Propontis, he asserts, the distance between *Thrake* and *Asiatís* near Abydos is so small that one nearly would not need a ship but could walk on foot from one side to the other: [...] συστραφέντα δὲ πρὸς ἑαυτὰ κατὰ τὸν αὐτόθι στενὸν πόρον, τὸν μεταξὺ πορθμὸν πληρώσαντα τὰς ἑκατέρωθεν ἠπείρους, τήν τε Θράκην καὶ τὴν Ἀσιάτιδα, ἀλλήλαις συνήνωσαν, ὡς ἐξ ἑκατέρας πρὸς θατέραν πεζῇ μᾶλλον ἢ πλοῖ διαπεραιοῦσθαι ἐξεῖναι τῷ βουλομένῳ.[73] Characteristically, the maritime space between Constantinople and Abydos was called *ta esabyda*.[74]

If one considers the extensive interdependence between land and sea in many parts of Byzantium, it is not surprising that the contrasting pair "land and sea" appears in many texts in order to express their distinction.[75] A special case is Michael Psellos, who makes general observations in *De omnifaria doctrina*, in "About the changing of the parts of the Earth". He explains that certain changes may be to the drier or to the more humid, with the effect that in a hot summer the sea becomes land or in a harsh winter the land becomes sea:

Μεταβάλλει τὰ μέρη τῆς γῆς κατὰ τὸ ξηρότερον καὶ ὑγρότερον, ἀπὸ μὲν ὑγροῦ ξηρότερα γινόμενα καὶ ἀπὸ ξηροῦ ὑγραινόμενα· συμβαίνει δὲ καὶ τὴν θάλασσαν ἠπειροῦσθαι καὶ τὴν ἤπειρον θαλαττοῦσθαι. καὶ ἐν μὲν τῷ μεγάλῳ χειμῶνι ἡ

---

70 See Soustal 1981.
71 Prokopios, *Bella* 3.1.4–7 Wirth.
72 Prokopios, *Bella* 8.6.12s. Wirth, see also *Bella* 8.6.1–3 and 12–15.
73 Nikephoros I., *Breviarium* 68 Mango, similar also Prokopios, *De Aedificiis* 1.5.5–7 Wirth.
74 See Trapp 1994–2017, 603a, s. v. ἐσάβυδα, τά.
75 See e.g. Anna Komnene, *Alexias* 3.12.2 and 7.8.8 Kambylis & Reinsch.

ἤπειρος θαλαττοῦται, ἐν δὲ τῷ μεγάλῳ θέρει ἡ θάλασσα ἠπειροῦται. αἴτιοι δέ εἰσι καὶ οἱ ποταμοὶ [...].[76]

5 Supra-regional Identity

What was the highest level of Byzantine collective identity for the Byzantines, especially in relation to *patris*? On this supra-regional, political level the spatial—as also the ethnic, religious, linguistic and cultural identifiers—were always shifting, sometimes in subtle ways that accounted for the timeless Roman claim to ecumenical power, and sometimes more overtly, as in the often-changing reality of the geographic extension of the empire's territory. Dominant key terms are *oikoumene* and the derivatives of the word root **roma(n)*, in contrast to the *barbarikon*.

5.1 *Oikoumene*

Since Julius Caesar,[77] the idea of *oikoumene* is essential for the spatial self-conception of Roman and Byzantine emperors and their spatial claims to power. It permeated all areas of the ideological, religious, political, and cultural thought of the ruling classes. In short,[78] the ecumenical claim encompassed the entire then known world from Late Antiquity and the early Byzantine centuries. This claim was, for well-known historical reasons, spoiled and subject to substantial changes, which led to something like schizophrenia. On the one hand, the political theory of a total domination of the world survived[79] and on the other hand, foreign policy had to become more and more realistic—first indications may already be found in the peace treaty between Rome and Persia in 298 AD. Partner (or better: opponent) was the Sasanian empire until its demise,[80] followed by the Arab caliphate.[81] But still Michael Psellos appeals to the emperor Constantine IX Monomachos to rule the *oikumene*: Σὺν θεῷ, κράτιστε, τῷ σκέποντί σε, / ἄνασσε, βασίλευε τῆς οἰκουμένης![82] Since he knows that this is (in his time) a reduced *oikoumene*, he scales in other texts the Byzantine

---

76   Michael Psellos, *De omnifaria doctrina* § 163 (163. Περὶ μεταβολῆς τῶν τῆς γῆς μερῶν) Westerink.
77   See Cassius Dio, *Historiai* 43.14.6 Boissevain.
78   For details see Koder 2000 and 2005, both with bibliography.
79   See Constantine Porphyrogennetos, *De Administrando Imperio* Prooem 20–23 and 38s., ch. 1.4–15, ch. 13.195–200, ch. 48.22–27 Moravcsik.
80   For the 6th century see e.g. Prokopios, *De aedificiis* 2.8.4–5 Wirth.
81   Schmalzbauer 2004.
82   Michael Psellos, *Poemata* 17.448 Westerink.

political *oikumene* down through restrictive wording like "the belonging to us *oikoumene*" or "our *oikoumene*" (καθ' ἡμᾶς οἰκουμένη or ἡμετέρα οἰκουμένη).[83]

5.2 Terms Related to Romania

For the word root *roma(n)* and its derivatives, the most important term is the already mentioned: *Romania*.[84] It appears in Greek narrative sources quite often in the context of political geography and as a special label for the Roman Empire from at least the second century CE and until the post-Byzantine period. There are only ten Greek narrative references to *Romania* from before the seventh century;[85] the most detailed may be found in Epiphanios' *Panarion*:

> [...] καὶ τὰ ἀπὸ τῆς Ἰνδικῆς ἐρχόμενα εἴδη ἐκεῖσε τῇ Θηβαΐδι διαχύνεται ἢ ἐπὶ τὴν Ἀλεξανδρέων διὰ τοῦ Χρυσορρόα ποταμοῦ, Νείλου δέ φημι, [...] καὶ ἐπὶ πᾶσαν τῶν Αἰγυπτίων γῆν καὶ ἐπὶ τὸ Πηλούσιον φέρεται· καὶ οὕτως εἰς τὰς ἄλλας πατρίδας διὰ θαλάσσης διερχόμενοι οἱ ἀπὸ τῆς Ἰνδικῆς ἐπὶ τὴν Ῥωμανίαν ἐμπορεύονται.

> Goods are brought to the Thebaid by way of this port called Bernice, and the various kinds of merchandise from India are either distributed there in the Thebaid or to Alexandria by way of the river Chrysorroes—I mean the Nile, which is called Gihon in the scriptures—and to all of Egypt as far as Pelusium. And this is how merchants from India who reach the other lands by sea make trading voyages to the Roman Empire.[86]

An interesting early example comes from a *non*-narrative source, a *sgraffito* tile from Sirmium (Srmska Mitrovica). Its inscription is evidently not related to the production of the tile. It reads:

> † Χριστέ Κύριε. Βοήτι τῆς πόλεος κ' ἔρυξον τὸν Ἄβαριν κὲ πύλαξον τὴν Ῥωμανίαν κὲ τὸν γράψαντα. Ἀμήν. †

---

83 Michael Psellos, *Orationes panegyricae* 6.222 et passim, Dennis; *Philosophica minora* 45.40 Duffy.
84 See Kaldellis 2019, 81–120, with bibliography.
85 Arrianos, *Fragmenta* 49a Jacoby; Epiphanios, *Panarion* 3.17, 3.25, 3.159 Holl; Athanasios, *Historia Arianorum*, ch. 35.2 Opitz; *Oracula Tiburtina* 139 Alexander; Kosmas Indikopleustes, *Christianike Topographia* 2.75, 11.23 Wolska-Conus; Ioannes Malalas, *Chronographia* 407 Dindorf ; *Chronikon Paschale* 610 Dindorf; see TLG (downloaded November 2015).
86 Epiphanios, *Panarion* 3.17 Holl. Translation by Williams 2013, 228.

Christ Lord. Help the city and and fend off the Avar [sic] and protect Romania and the scribe. Amen.[87]

This inscription, similar to a quick prayer, expresses the fear of the imminent capture of the fortress-city by the Avars. Without discussing the manifold aspects of this inscription, I would like to point out that the text combines *Romania* and *polis*. Thus, the inscription refers to the double identity of its author: his belonging to the entire Roman state and specifically to the *polis* Sirmium.

Unlike *Romania*, the nominal adjective *Ta Romaïka* does not describe primarily the political dimension of the Byzantine Empire, but rather its particular territorial extension. John Malalas was the first Byzantine chronographer to use it, mainly in Book 18,[88] and from him it was quoted by Theophanes.[89] Both writers understood τὰ Ῥωμαϊκά as an abridged expression for τὰ Ῥωμαϊκὰ μέρη and similar wordings,[90] which rarely appear in later texts.

The adjective *romaïkos* as such appears in the special periphrase of Roman imperial identity *Romaïkos axon*. The first reference is found in Synesios' *Dion*.[91] Michael Psellos used *Romaïkos axon* several times in order to describe the accession of Byzantine emperors to the throne with wordings like τὸν Ῥωμαϊκὸν ἐπιπεφόρτισται ἄξονα, εἰς τὸν Ῥωμαϊκὸν ἀναβεβηκὸς ἄξονα.[92] *Romaïkos axon* expresses Byzantium's ecumenical claim to power. The meaning of *axon* is crucial: this "axis" is connected with the mythical Titan Atlas, who had to bear the weight of the "celestial spheres"[93] with his hands and his head in the heavens and his feet on the earth; hence John Galenos' allegory: [...] ἐπὶ τῷ ἄξονι προσαγορεύει ὁ λόγος, τὰς μὲν χεῖρας καὶ τὴν κεφαλὴν ἐς τὸν οὐρανὸν ἔχοντα καὶ διὰ τούτων ἐρείδοντα αὐτόν, τοὺς δὲ πόδας ἐπὶ τῆς γῆς.[94] In a similar manner,

---

87   Noll 1989, 145. English translation by M. Veikou. For details see Koder & Wedenig 2018.
88   Ioannes Malalas, *Chronographia* 12.47 and 18.2, 14, 16, 26, 44, 59, 60, 66 and 76 Dindorf.
89   Theophanes, *Chronographia* 175, 254, 274, 281 and 291 de Boor.
90   Ioannes Malalas, *Chronographia* 18.70 Dindorf, Theophanes, *Chronographia* 247, 265 and 147 de Boor (Ῥωμαϊκὴ [...] γῆ); cf. also Theophylaktos Simokattes, *Historiae* 1.5.11 and 7.7.5 de Boor & Wirth: τὸ Ῥωμαϊκὸν ἔδαφος.—For the "Romaic language" see Kaldellis 2019, 97–106.
91   Synesios, *Dion* 16.14–18 Terzaghi.
92   Michael Psellos, *Chronographia* 4.14.3, 6.140.10s., 6.177.6, 7.57.6s. Renauld; *Orationes forenses* 1650s. Dennis; *Encomium in Constantinum Leichudem* 8s. Sathas.
93   Liddell, Scott & Jones 1966, 172b, Lampe, *Patristic Greek Lexicon* 168b (Plural: "tablets of laws").
94   Ioannes Galenos, *Allegoriae* 333s., similar 347.20–22 Flach.

Eustathios of Thessaloniki relates: Ἄλλοι δὲ Ἄτλαντα τὸν νοητὸν ἄξονα νοοῦσι τὸν διὰ μέσης τῆς γῆς ἐληλαμένον καὶ ἀπὸ τοῦ βορείου εἰς τὸν νότιον πόλον καθήκοντα.[95]

By analogy to Atlas, the Byzantine emperor was bearing the burden of the axis of the Ecumene.[96] Michael Psellos refers only to contemporary emperors, but it is evident that this imperial Roman rule—with regard to Roman political ideology—encompasses a super-temporal claim. This aspect is confirmed by introductory passages in the legislation of the Macedonian dynasty: The Prooemium of the *Epitome legum* (dated to 913/914) claims the rule over the Ecumene for the *Romaioi*, who rule "as fair legislators": ὅπλοις καὶ νόμοις Ῥωμαῖοι τῆς οἰκουμένης ἐκράτησαν, [...] δικαίως νομοθετοῦντες.[97] It justifies the legality of the ecumenical identity of the Romans, whereas in the proem of the *Eisagoge* (dated to 885/886), the author—probably the patriarch Photius—claims its legitimisation by the will of God as the creator of the universe: Ὁ ποιήσας πάντα θεὸς καὶ κύριος [...] εἰσάγων δὲ τὴν τῆς μιᾶς δεσποτείας καὶ ἑνιαίας μοναρχίας κυριότητά τε καὶ ἐξουσίαν.[98] Both texts call upon the subjects, namely all inhabitants of the Ecumene, to accept this universal and trans-temporal dimension of Roman identity.

5.3 Terms Related to Barbaroi

A strong distinction is made between the Romans (and their state *Romania*) and the *barbaroi*.[99] Following Stephanos' *Ethnika*, the *barbaroi* are defined by a language and a region, not by the tribe or nation (*ethnos*): Βάρβαρος, οὐκ ἐπὶ ἔθνους, ἀλλ' ἐπὶ φωνῆς ἐλαμβάνετο.[100] The Barbarians often are enemies (*echthroi*) who threaten the Roman realm. Kosmas Indikopleustes, e.g., reflects in his *Christianike Topographia* in general upon the confrontations with Barbarian tribes, and explains hostile threats of them as divine *paideia* (correction) for the sins which were committed by the Romans: Εἰ καὶ διὰ τὰς ἡμετέρας ἁμαρτίας πρὸς παιδείαν ὀλίγον ἐχθροὶ βάρβαροι τῇ Ῥωμανίᾳ ἐπανίστανται, ἀλλὰ τῇ δυνάμει τοῦ διακρατοῦντος ἀήττητος διαμένει ἡ βασιλεία, ἐπὶ τὸ μὴ στενοῦσθαι τὰ τῶν χριστιανῶν, ἀλλὰ πλατύνεσθαι.[101] Conforming to Byzantine political ideology,

---

95 Eustathios, *Commentarii in Odysseam* 17.29–30 Stallbaum.
96 One time the term is also used by Nikephoros Kallistou Xanthopoulos, *Historia ecclesiastica* 1.17.6–11 Migne, when he tells about the emperors Augustus visit at the oracle of Delphi: Καῖσαρ δὲ Αὔγουστος [...] Πυθῶδε παραγίνεται. Ἑκατόμβην δὲ τῷ δαίμονι θύσας, διεπυνθάνετο τίς δὴ μετ' αὐτὸν τοὺς Ῥωμαϊκοὺς ἄξονας διιθύνειεν.
97 See Schminck 1986, 112.
98 *Eisagoge* (885/886), prooem Zepos.
99 See e.g. Gillett (ed.) 2002, with bibliography.
100 Stephanus Byz., *Ethnica* 158 Meineke.
101 Kosmas Indikopleustes, *Christianike Topographia* 2.75 Wolska-Conus.

Indikopleustes insists that independently from ἡμετέρας ἁμαρτίας the kingdom will remain undefeated: ἀήττητος διαμένει ἡ βασιλεία.

The latter conviction is confirmed by the sixth-century narrative in Alexandros' *Inventio crucis*: Ἐν πολλῷ οὖν κινδύνῳ καὶ ἀκαταστασίᾳ τῶν πραγμάτων ὑπαρχόντων, καὶ βαρβάρων τινῶν ἐπικειμένων τῇ Ῥωμανίᾳ, [...] ἐξαίφνης τὰ Ῥωμαίων αὖθις ἐπανωρθώθη, τοῦ Δομετιανοῦ ἐξολοθρεύσαντος τοὺς ἐπανισταμένους βαρβάρους.[102] Danger and uncertainty, caused by the Barbarians may be great, but in the end a good emperor will always raise up again *ta Romaion*. Michael Psellos confirms this attitude towards the Barbarians: [...] ἐντεῦθεν ἡμῖν καὶ τὸ ἑῷον καὶ τὸ ἑσπέριον ἐξημέρωται καὶ δεδούλωται. ἢ πόθεν τὰ τῆς οἰκουμένης τμήματα τὴν δούλωσιν συνωμολόγησε καὶ βάρβαρος χεὶρ τὴν εἰρήνην ἠσπάσατο.[103]

If the Byzantines wanted to define the territorial dimension of Barbarian lands, they used mainly two names: *to barbarikon* and *barbaria*. The first term, τὸ βαρβαρικόν, was used by historians and in legal texts to designate in general a foreign (and often enemy) country,[104] sometimes with the specification τὸ πέριξ or τὸ κύκλῳ βαρβαρικόν,[105] also contrasting τὸ Ῥωμαϊκόν.[106] The second term, Βαρβαρία, was particularly restricted to the region near the Horn of Africa and its hinterland, the λιβανωτόφορος γῆ τῆς καλουμένης Βαρβαρίας,[107] which παράκειται τῷ Ὠκεανῷ and lies near the μεσόγειος Αἰθιοπία (or corrupted Θεοπία).[108]

---

102 Alexandros, *Inventio crucis* (6 CE?) 4041 Migne.

103 Michael Psellos, *Oratoria minora* 1.88–91 Littlewood.

104 Examples: Ioannes Malalas, *Chronographia* 12.22 Dindorf, Ioannes Lydos, *De magistratibus* 24 Bandy, Theophylaktos Simokattes, *Historiae* 2.5.10 de Boor & Wirth, *Basilika* 19.1.85, 60.7.8 Scheltema & van der Wal, Ioannes Kantakouzenos, *Historiai* 1.328, 2.530, 3.123,128,327 Schopen, Nikolaos Lampenos, *Enkomion* 47 Polemis.

105 Michael Psellos, *Chronographia* 1.31, 2.2 Renauld, Niketas Choniates, *Historia*, 401 and 432 van Dieten, Ephraim, *Historia* 4021 Lampsides.

106 Nikolaos Lampenos, *Enkomion* 50 Polemis.

107 Kosmas Indikopleustes, *Christianike Topographia* 2.30,45,50,64, 6.12 Wolska-Conus, see also Stephanus Byz., *Ethnica* 158 Meineke, and Dellaportas 1.1252 Manoussacas.—Cf. also : ... ἔστι δὲ χώρα παρὰ τὸν Ἀράβιον κόλπον Βαρβαρία, ἀφ' οὗ καὶ Βαρβαρικὸν πέλαγος, Stephanus Byz., *Ethnica* 158 (Meineke).

108 Kosmas Indikopleustes, *Christianike Topographia* 2.26,29,48,49,64 Wolska-Conus, *Historia Alexandri Magni* 48.8 and 49.29 Konstantinopulos, and Lolos, *Historia Alexandri Magni Vind.* 56 and 62 Mitsakis. See also *Historia Alexandri Magni* 47.2 Konstantinopulos & Lolos, *Historia Alexandri Magni Vind.* 54 Mitsakis.

6   Soma and Space

Finally, a central term in considering spatiality is the body (*soma*): Did the Byzantines, or at least some educated members of the intellectually or the politically leading classes, see these two issues as linked, the *basileia ton Romaion* and the spatial concept of an organic body? I found two examples. The first, a passage in the *Alexiad*, is remarkable for its terminological concentration. Anna Komnene reflects in general on the fate (*tyche*) of the empire (*basileia*):

> Καὶ ἔγωγε στοχάζομαι ἀπὸ τῶν πραγμάτων αὐτῶν τὴν Τύχην τῆς βασιλείας, ὅτι πανταχόθεν συνέρρευσε τὰ δεινὰ καὶ ἐτετάρακτο αὐτό τε τὸ σῶμα τῆς πολιτείας καὶ πᾶν ἀλλότριον ἐμεμήνει κατὰ τῆς βασιλείας Ῥωμαίων, ὡς εἴ τις οὕτως ἔχοι κακῶς, ὥστε καὶ ὑπὸ τῶν ἀλλοδαπῶν πολεμεῖσθαι καὶ ὑπὸ τῶν οἰκείων κατατρύχεσθαι τὰς σάρκας διαμασσώμενον, τοῦτον δὲ ἀνεγεῖραι τὴν Πρόνοιαν, ἵνα πρὸς τὰ πανταχόθεν κακὰ ἀντιμηχανῷτο, ὥσπερ δὴ καὶ τὸ τηνικαῦτα συνιδεῖν ἔδει.

> From all these things I infer the Fate of the kingdom because dangers accumulated from every direction, and the body politic was disturbed, and every foreign nation was raging against the Roman Empire; it was as if a man were so unfortunately placed as to be attacked by enemies from without, whilst he was being exhausted physically by cruel pains, and yet Providence roused him up to make a stand against these manifold ills; as was to be observed in this case.[109]

The body of the polity (*to soma tes politeias*) may be in a state of confusion, and all the "others" (*pan allotrion*) may threaten the *basileia ton Romaion*. Not only do foreigners (*allodapoi*) wage war against it, but so do their own people (*oikeioi*). Only divine providence (*pronoia*) may rouse what is in such a bad state.

The second example is Theophanes Continuatus' chronicle. He describes the state of the empire at the time of the rebellion of Thomas the Slav as a body: Οὐκ ἔμελλε δὲ ἄχρι τούτων ἡ φορὰ στήσεσθαι τῶν κακῶν, ἀλλὰ τῶν δύο ἠπείρων, Ἀσίας φαμὲν καὶ Εὐρώπης, ἐν θυμῷ κυρίου οἷόν τινος κεφαλῆς καὶ οὐρᾶς, [...] τέλος καὶ ταῖς ταλαιπώροις νήσοις οἷόν τινα μέσην, ἵν' ὁλόσωμος εἴη ἡ πληγή.[110]

---

109   Anna Komnene, *Alexias* 12.5.3. Kambylis & Reinsch. English translation by Daws 2000, 220.
110   Theophanes Continuatus, *Chronographia* 73 Bekker, cf. Ioannes Skylitzes, *Synopsis* 41 Thurn.

The two mainlands, the head *Asia* and the tail *Europe* already face the wrath of God, and finally the catastrophe hits also the *talaiporoi nesoi*, the *mese*. Thus the blow struck the entire body (ὁλόσωμος).

This hierarchy of (1) Asia and (2) Europe corresponds to that of *De thematibus*. Constantine describes first the Asian themes, beginning with *Anatolikon* (Πρῶτον μὲν οὖν τοῦ καλουμένου Ἀνατολικοῦ, εἰ δοκεῖ, μνημονεύσωμεν· ἐνταῦθα τῆς Ἀνατολῆς θέματα ἤγουν τῆς μικρᾶς Ἀσίας. Πρῶτον θέμα τὸ καλούμενον Ἀνατολικόν [...]),[111] followed by the other themes in Asia Minor up to *Kibyrraiotos* (The island themes *Kypros*, *Samos* and *Aigaion Pelagos* also belong to Asia). In the second place the "western" European themes are ranked, beginning with *Thrakoon* and including *Kephalenia* (as the head of all the Ionian Islands), *Sikelia* and *Longibardia*. The last "western" thema is *Cherson*.[112] Thus Theophanes Continuatus' image of Asia Minor as the dominating *kephale* (of a *soma*) is also an illustrative description for the hierarchical perception of the political geography of Byzantium since the post-ancient period.

Bibliography

Primary Sources

Agathangelos, *Martyrium S. Rhipsimae*. Ed. G. Garitte, "La vie grecque inédite de saint Grégoire d'Arménie (ms. 4 d'Ochrida)", *Analecta Bollandiana* 83 (1965) 257–90.

Agathangelos, *Version grecque ancienne*. Ed. G. Lafontaine, *La version grecque ancienne du livre Arménien d'Agathange* (Publications de l'institut orientaliste de Louvain 7). Louvain-la-Neuve 1973.

Akathistos. Ed. C. A. Trypanis, *Fourteen Early Byzantine Cantica* (Wiener Byzantinistische Studien 5). Vienna 1968, 29–39. Tr. Fr. George Papadeas, *The Akathist Hymn Preceded by the Brief Compline*. Daytona Beach, Florida 1980.

Alexandros, *Inventio crucis*. Ed. J. P. Migne,, PG 87/3, 4015–76.

Anakalema Kpl. Ed. E. Kriaras, *Τὸ ανακάλημα της Κωνσταντινόπολης* (Παλιότερα κείμενα της νεοελληνικής λογοτεχνίας 4). Thessalonike 2012.

Anna Komnene, *Alexias*. Ed. A. Kambylis & D. R. Reinsch, *Annae Comnenae Alexias* (CFHB 40/1). Berlin & New York 2001. Tr. E. A. S. Daws, *Anna Comnena, The Alexiad*. Cambridge, Ontario 2000.

Anonymous Greek Chronicle. Ed. M. Philippides, *Emperors, Patriarchs and Sultans of Constantinople, 1373–1513. An Anonymous Greek Chronicle of the Sixteenth Century*

---

111 *Constantine Porphyrogennetos, De Thematibus*, end of the prologue, Pertusi.
112 *Constantine Porphyrogennetos, De Thematibus*, Asia 1 and Europe 12 Pertusi.

(The Archbishop Iakovos Library of Ecclesiastical and Historical Sources 13). Brookline, Mass. 1990.
Aristotle, *Metaphysics*. Ed. W. D. Ross, *Aristotle's metaphysics*, 2 vols., Oxford 1924.
Arrianos, *Fragmenta*. Ed. F. Jacoby, *Die Fragmente der griechischen Historiker*. Leiden 1923–1958.
Athanasios, *Historia Arianorum*. Ed. H. G. Opitz, *Athanasius Werke*, vol. 2.1. Berlin 1940.
Basilika. Ed. H. J. Scheltema & N. van der Wal, *Basilicorum libri* LX. Series A, vols. *1–8*. Groningen 1955–1988.
Bessarion, *In calumniatorem Platonis*. Ed. L. Mohler, *Bessarionis in calumniatorem Platonis libri* IV (Kardinal Bessarion als Theologe, Humanist und Staatsmann. Funde und Forschungen, vol. 2). Paderborn 1927.
Cassius Dio, *Historiai*. Ed. U. P. Boissevain, *Cassii Dionis Cocceiani historiarum Romanarum quae supersunt*, 3 vols. Berlin 1895–1901.
Constantine Porphyrogennetos, *De Administrando Imperio*. Ed. G. Moravcsik, *Constantine Porphyrogenitus, De Administrando Imperio* (CFHB 1). Washington, D.C. 1967.
Constantine Porphyrogennetos, *De Thematibus*. Ed. A. Pertusi, *Constantino Porfirogenito, De Thematibus*. Città del Vaticano 1952.
Chronikon Paschale. Ed. L. Dindorf, *Chronicon paschale*, 2 vols. (CSHB). Bonn 1832.
Damaskios, *De Principiis*. Ed. C. É. Ruelle, *Damascii successoris dubitationes et solutiones*, 2 vols. Paris 1889–1899.
David, *In Porphyrii isagogen*. Ed. A. Busse, *Davidis in Porphyrii isagogen commentarium*. Berlin 1904.
Eisagoge. Ed. P. Zepos (post C.E. Zacharia von Lingenthal), *Leges Imperatorum Isaurorum et Macedonum* (Jus Graecoromanum 2). Athens 1931.
Ephraim, *Historia*. Ed. O. Lampsides, *Ephraem Aenii Historia Chronica* (CFHB 27). Athens 1990.
Epiphanios, *Panarion*. Ed. K. Holl, *Epiphanius*. 3 vols. (Die griechischen christlichen Schriftsteller 25, 31, 37). Leipzig 1915–1933. Tr. F. Williams, *The Panarion of Epiphanius of Salamis, Books ii and iii. de Fide: Second, Revised Edition*, Leiden 2012.
Eustathios, *Commentarii ad Iliadem*. Ed. M. van der Valk, *Eustathios von Thessalonike, Commentarii ad Homeri Iliadem pertinentes*. Leiden 1987.
Eustathios, *Commentarii in Odysseam*. Ed. G. Stallbaum, *Eustathii archiepiscopi Thessalonicensis Commentarii ad Homeri Odysseam*, 2 vols. Leipzig 1825–1826.
Georgios Kedrenos, *Historia*. Ed. I. Bekker, *Georgius Cedrenus Ioannis Scylitzae ope*, 2 vols. (CSHB). Bonn 1838–1839.
Georgios Monachos, *Chronicon*. Ed. C. de Boor, *Georgii monachi chronicon*. Leipzig 1904.
Georgios Sykeotes, *Vita Theodori*. Ed. A.-J. Festugière, *Vie de Théodore de Sykeôn*, vol. 1 (Subsidia hagiographica 48). Brussels 1970.

Hesychios, *Homilia*. Ed. M. Aubineau, *Les homélies festales d'Hésychius de Jérusalem, vol. 2. Les homélies xvi–xxi* (Subsidia hagiographica 59). Brussels 1980.

Hesychios, *Lexicon*. Ed. K. Latte, *Hesychii Alexandrini lexicon*, vols. 1–2. Copenhagen 1953–1966.

Historia Alexandri Magni. Ed. V. L. Konstantinopulos & A. C. Lolos, *Ps.-Kallisthenes. Zwei mittelgriechische Prosa-Fassungen des Alexanderromans*, Vols. 1–2 (*Beiträge zur klassischen Philologie* 141 & 150). Meisenheim am Glan 1983.

Historia Alexandri Magni Vind. Ed. K. Mitsakis, *Der byzantinische Alexanderroman nach dem Codex Vind. Theol. gr. 244* (*Miscellanea Byzantina Monacensia* 7). Munich 1967.

Ioannes Chrysostomos, *De S. Meletio Antiocheno*. Ed. J. P. Migne, PG 50, 515–20.

Ioannes Damaskenos, *Sacra Parallela*. Ed. J. P. Migne, PG 95, 1040–588.

Ioannes Galenos, *Allegoriae*. Ed. H. Flach, *Glossen und Scholien zur hesiodischen Theogonie*. Leipzig 1876.

Ioannes Italos, *Quaestiones*. Ed. P.-P. Joannou, *Joannes Italos. Quaestiones quodlibetales* (Ἀπορίαι καὶ λύσεις) (Studia patristica et Byzantina 4). Ettal 1956.

Ioannes Kantakouzenos, *Historiai*. Ed. L. Schopen, *Ioannis Cantacuzeni eximperatoris historiarum libri IV*, vols. 1–3 (CSHB). Bonn 1828–1832.

Ioannes Lydos, *De magistratibus*. Ed. A. C. Bandy, *Ioannes Lydus. On powers or the magistracies of the Roman state*. Philadelphia 1983.

Ioannes Malalas, *Chronographia*. Ed. L. Dindorf, *Ioannis Malalae Chronographia* (CSHB). Bonn 1831.

Ioannes Skylitzes, *Synopsis*. Ed. J. Thurn, *Ioannis Scylitzae synopsis historiarum* (CFHB 5). Berlin 1973.

Kekaumenos, *Strategikon. Consilia et Narrationes* (Sharing Ancient Wisdoms / SAWS, 2013) http://www.ancientwisdoms.ac.uk/folioscope/greekLit:tlg3017.Syn0298.saws Grc01. Tr. Ch. Roueché, http://www.ancientwisdoms.ac.uk/folioscope/greekLit:tlg3 017.Syn0298.sawsEng01.

Kosmas Indikopleustes, *Christianike Topographia*. Ed. W. Wolska-Conus, *Cosmas Indicopleustès. Topographie chrétienne*, 3 vols. (Sources chrétiennes 141, 159, 197). Paris 1968–1973.

Leonardos Dellaportas. Ed. M. Manoussacas, Λεονάρδου Ντελλαπόρτα Ποιήματα (*1403/ 1411*). Athens 1998.

Makarios, *Homily*. Ed. H. Berthold, *Makarios/ Symeon Reden und Briefe*, 2 vols. Berlin 1973.

Manuel Gabalas, *Epistle*. Ed. D. R. Reinsch, *Die Briefe des Matthaios von Ephesos im Codex Vindobonensis Theol. Gr. 174*. Berlin 1974.

Markos Diakonos, *Vita Porphyrii*. Ed. H. Grégoire & M.-A. Kugener, *Marc le Diacre. Vie de Porphyre, évêque de Gaza*. Paris 1930.

Matthaios Blastares, *Collectio alphabetica*. Ed. M. Potles & G.A. Rhalles, Σύνταγμα τῶν θείων καὶ ἱερῶν κανόνων τῶν τε ἁγίων καὶ πανευφήμων ἀποστόλων, καὶ τῶν ἱερῶν οἰκουμενικῶν καὶ τοπικῶν συνόδων, καὶ τῶν κατὰ μέρος ἁγίων πατέρων. Athens 1859.

Michael Attaleiates, *Historia*. Ed. I. Bekker, *Michaelis Attaliotae Historia* (CSHB). Bonn 1853.

Michael Psellos, *Chronographia*. Ed. É. Renauld, *Chronographie ou histoire d'un siècle de Byzance (976–1077)*. Paris 1926–1928.

Michael Psellos, *De omnifaria doctrina*. Ed. L. G. Westerink, *Michael Psellus, De omnifaria doctrina*. Nijmegen 1948.

Michael Psellos, *Encomium in Constantinum Leichudem*. Ed. K. N. Sathas, Ἐπιτάφιοι Λόγοι, vol. 4 (Bibliotheca Graeca Medii Aevi). Paris 1874.

Michael Psellos, *Orationes forenses*. Ed. G. T. Dennis, *Michaelis Pselli orationes forenses et acta*. Stuttgart 1994.

Michael Psellos, *Orationes panegyricae*. Ed. G. T. Dennis, *Michael Psellus Orationes panegyricae*. Stuttgart 1994.

Michael Psellos, *Oratoria minora*. Ed. A. R. Littlewood, *Oratoria minora*. Leipzig 1985.

Michael Psellos, *Philosophica minora*. Ed. D. J. O'Meara, *Michael Psellus Philosophica minora*. Leipzig 1992.

Michael Psellos, *Poemata*. Ed. L.G. Westerink, *Michaelis Pselli poemata*, Stuttgart 1992.

Neophytos Enkleistos, "Panegyrike A". Ed. Th. Giagkou & N. Papatriantafyllou-Theodoridi, "Πανηγυρική Α", in D. G. Tsames, C. Oikonomou, I. Karabidopoulos & N. Zacharopoulos, Ἁγίου Νεοφύτου τοῦ Ἐγκλείστου Συγγράμματα, vol. 3. Paphos 1999.

Nikephoros I., *Breviarium*. Ed. C. A. Mango, *Nikephoros Patriarch of Constantinople, Short History: Text, Translation and Commentary* (CFHB 13). Washington, D.C. 1990.

Nikephoros Blemmydes, *Epitome logica*. Ed. J. P. Migne, PG 142, 685–1004.

Nikephoros Kallistou Xanthopoulos, *Historia ecclesiastica*. Ed. J. P. Migne, PG 145–47.

Niketas Choniates, *Epistle*. Ed. J. van Dieten, *Nicetae Choniatae orationes et epistulae* (CFHB 3). Berlin 1972.

Niketas Choniates, *Historia*. Ed. J. van Dieten, *Nicetae Choniatae historia, pars prior* (CFHB 11.1). Berlin 1975.

Niketas Stethatos, *Vita Symeonis*. Ed. I. Hausherr, *Un grand mystique byzantin. Vie de Syméon le Nouveau Théologien par Nicétas Stéthatos* (Orientalia Christiana 12). Rome 1928.

Nikolaos Lampenos, *Enkomion*. Ed. J. Polemis, Ο λόγιος Νικόλαος Λαμπηνός καὶ τὸ ἐγκώμιον αὐτοῦ εἰς τὸν Ἀνδρόνικον Β' Παλαιολόγον (Διπτύχων Παράφυλλα 4). Athens 1992.

Oracula Tiburtina. Ed. P.J. Alexander, *The oracle of Baalbek. The Tiburtine Sibyl in Greek dress* (Dumbarton Oaks Studies 10). Washington, D.C. 1967.

Photius, *Epistle*. Ed. B. Laourdas & L. G. Westerink, *Photii patriarchae Constantinopolitani Epistulae et Amphilochia*, 6 vols. Leipzig 1983–1988.

Prokopios, *De Aedificiis*. Ed. G. Wirth (post J. Haury), *Procopii Caesariensis opera omnia*, vol. 4. Leipzig 1964.

Prokopios, *Bella*. Ed. G. Wirth (post J. Haury), *Procopii Caesariensis opera omnia*, vols. 1–2. Leipzig 1962–1963.

Ps.-Georgios Sphrantzes, *Chronikon*. Ed. V. Grecu, *Georgios Sphrantzes. Memorii 1401–1477* (Scriptores Byzantini 5). Bucharest 1966.

Ps.-Makarios, Homily. Ed. H. Dörries, E. Klostermann & M. Krüger, *Die 50 geistlichen Homilien des Makarios* (Patristische Texte und Studien 4). Berlin 1964.

Stephanos Byz., *Ethnica*. Ed. A. Meineke, *Stephan von Byzanz, Ethnika*. Berlin 1849.

Suda. Ed. A. Adler, *Suidae lexicon*, 4 vols. Leipzig 1928–1935.

Symeon Logothetes, *Chronographia*. Ed. I. Bekker, *Leonis Grammatici chronographia* (CSHB). Bonn 1842.

Synaxarium ecclesiae Constantinopolitanae. Ed. H. Delehaye, *Synaxarium ecclesiae Constantinopolitanae* (Acta Sanctorum 62). Brussels 1902.

Synesios, *Dion*. Ed. N. Terzaghi, *Synesii Cyrenensis opuscula*. Rome 1944.

Theodoros Dexios, *Appellatio versus Cantacuzenum*. Ed. J. Polemis, *Theodori Dexii Opera Omnia* (Corpus Christianorum. Series Graeca 55). Turnhout 2003.

Theodoros Studites, *Parva catechesis*. Ed. E. Auvray, *Theodori Studitis Parva Catechesis*. Paris 1891.

Theophanes, *Chronographia*. Ed. C. de Boor, *Theophanis chronographia*, vol. 1. Leipzig 1883.

Theophanes Continuatus, *Chronographia*. Ed. I. Bekker, *Theophanes Continuatus, Ioannes Cameniata, Symeon Magister, Georgius Monachus* (CSHB). Bonn 1838.

Theophanes Nicaenus, *In Sanctissimam Deiparam*. Ed. M. Jugie, *Theophanes Nicaenus, Sermo in Sanctissimam Deiparam*. Rome 1936.

Theophylaktos Simokattes, *Historiae*. Ed. C. de Boor & P. Wirth. Stuttgart 1972.

Timarion. Ed. R. Romano, *Pseudo-Luciano, Timarione*. Naples 1974.

Vita Euaristi. Ed. Ch. van de Vorst, "La vie de s. Évariste, higoumène à Constantinople", *Analecta Bollandiana* 41 (1923) 295–325.

Vita Lazari in monte Galesio. Ed. H. Delehaye, *Acta Sanctorum (Novembris)*, vol. 3. Brussels 1910. Tr. R. P. H. Greenfield, *An Eleventh Century Pillar Saint: The Life of Lazaros of Mt. Galesion*. Washington D.C. 2000.

Vita prior Alypii Stylitae. Ed. H. Delehaye, *Les saints stylites*. Brussels 1923.

Secondary Sources

Assmann, A. 2006. *Erinnerungsräume: Formen und Wandlungen des kulturellen Gedächtnisses*. Munich.

Assmann, J. 2007. *Das kulturelle Gedächtnis. Schrift, Erinnerung und politische Identität in frühen Hochkulturen*. Munich.

Avramea, A., A. Laiou & E. Chrysos (eds) 2003. *Byzantium State and Society. Memory of Nikos Oikonomides*. Athens.

Browning, R. 1989a. "Greeks and Others from Antiquity to the Renaissance", in Browning (ed.) 1989b, 257–77.

Browning, R. 1989b. *History, Language and Literacy in the Byzantine World*. Northampton.

Chrysos, E. 1996. "The Roman Political identity in Late Antiquity and Early Byzantium", in Fledelius (ed.) 1996, 7–16.

Chrysos, E. (ed.) 2005. *Το Βυζάντιο ως Οικουμένη*, Institute for Byzantine Research, International Symposia 16. Athens.

Dagron, G. 2005. "L'œcuménicité politique: droit sur l'espace, droit sur le temps", in Chrysos (ed.) 2005, 47–57.

Delanty, G. 1995. *Inventing Europe: Idea, Identity, Reality*. London.

Drauschke, J. et al. (eds) 2018. *Lebenswelten zwischen Archäologie und Geschichte. Festschrift für Falko Daim zu seinem 65. Geburtstag*. Mainz.

Dunn, G. (ed.) 2015. *Christians shaping identity from the Roman Empire to Byzantium. Studies inspired by Pauline Allen*. Leiden.

Fledelius K. (ed.) 1996. *Byzantium. Identity, Image, Influence. XIX. Int. Congress of Byz. Studies, Major Papers*. Kopenhagen.

Fentress, E. (ed.) 2000. *Romanization and the City: Creation, Transformation, and Failures*. Portsmouth, RI.

Fussenegger, H. 2012. *Sprachidentität—Identität durch Sprache*. Vienna.

Geary, P. J. 2002. *The Myth of Nations. The Medieval Origins of Europe*. Princeton NJ.

Gillett, A. (ed.) 2002. *On Barbarian Identity. Critical Approaches to Ethnicity in the Early Middle Ages*. Turnhout.

Hoffmann, J. 1974. *Rudimente von Territorialstaaten im byzantinischen Reich (1071–1210). Untersuchungen über Unabhängigkeitsbestrebungen und ihr Verhältnis zu Kaiser und Reich*. Munich.

Kaldellis, A. 2019. *Romanland. Ethnicity and Empire in Byzantium*. Cambridge, Mass.

Karamanolaki, Eu. et al. (eds) 2019. *Έλλην, Ρωμηός, Γραικός: Συλλογικοί προσδιορισμοί και ταυτότητες*. Athens.

Katerelos, K., A. Glavinas & G. Larentzakis (eds) 2011. *ΣΚΕΥΟΣ ΕΙΣ ΤΙΜΗΝ. Festschrift zum 25-jährigen Jubiläum der Bischofsweihe und 20-jährigen Jubiläum der Inthronisation von Dr. Michael Staikos*. Athens.

Koder, J. 1990. "Byzanz, die Griechen und die Romaiosyne—eine ‚Ethnogenese' der Römer?", in Wolfram & Pohl (eds) 1990, 103–11.

Koder, J. 2000. "Anmerkungen zu γραικόω", in *Byzantina* 21 (*Mneme Ioannes E. Karagiannopoulou*), 199–202.

Koder, J. 2002. "Die räumlichen Vorstellungen der Byzantiner von der Ökumene (4. bis 12. Jahrhundert)", *Anzeiger der philosophisch-historischen Klasse der Österreichischen Akademie der Wissenschaften* 137.2. Vienna, 15–34.

Koder, J. 2003. "Griechische Identitäten im Mittelalter. Aspekte einer Entwicklung", in Avramea, Laiou & Chrysos (eds) 2003, 297–319.

Koder, J. 2005. "Η γεωγραφική διάσταση της βυζαντινής οικουμένης", in Chrysos (ed.) 2005, 25–45.

Koder, J. 2011a. "Byzantium as seen by itself—Images and mechanisms at work", in *Proceedings of the 22nd International Congress of Byzantine Studies Sofia, 22–27 August 2011, Plenary Papers*, Sofia, 69–81.

Koder, J. 2011b. "Der Hymnus auf die zweite Kirchweih der Hagia Sophia im Jahr 562", in Katerelos, Glavinas & Larentzakis (eds) 2011, 421–436.

Koder, J. 2011c. "Überlegungen zur ländlichen Siedlungsterminologie der Byzantiner, insbesondere zu chorion, kome und verwandten Termini", in *Bulgaria Mediaevalis* 2 (Studies in honor of Professor Vassil Gjuzelev), 3–14.

Koder, J. 2018. "Remarks on the Linguistic Romanness in Byzantium", in Pohl & al. 2018, 111-121.

Koder, J. 2019a. "Byzantion wird Konstantinupolis: Anmerkungen zu Ortswahl und Namen", in Morrisson et al. (eds) 2018, 21–33.

Koder, J. 2019b. " Ῥωμαϊστί· Παρατηρήσεις για τη γλωσσική *Romanitas* των Βυζαντινών", in Karamanolaki & al. (eds) 2018, 73–84.

Koder J. & R. Wedenig 2018. "Anmerkungen zum Awaren-Sgraffito von Sirmium. Mit einem archäologischen Kommentar von R. Wedenig", in Drauschke et al. (eds) 2018, 733–40.

Lampe, G. W. H. 1961. *A Patristic Greek Lexicon*. Oxford.

Lefort J. et al. (eds) 1991. *Géométries du fisc byzantin*. Paris.

Liddell, H. G., R. Scott, R. & H. St. Jones (eds) 1966. *Greek-English Lexicon*, Oxford.

Majeska, G. P. 1984. *Russian Travellers in Constantinople in the Fourteenth and Fifteenth Centuries (Dumbarton Oaks Studies*, 19), Washington, D.C.

Morrisson, C. et al. (eds) 2019. *Constantinople réelle ou imaginaire. Autour de l'œuvre de Gilbert Dagron*. Paris.

Moutafidou, A. 2001. Von der „aufgeklärten Vaterlandsliebe" zum „privilegierten Patriotismus": Zur Entwicklung und Veränderung politischer Begriffe im Griechenland des 19. Jahrhunderts. Mit einem Anhang von S. E. Katsikas, *Anzeiger der philosophisch-historischen Klasse der Österr. Akademie der Wissenschaften*, 136, 177–98.

Noll, R. 1989. "Ein Ziegel als sprechendes Zeugnis einer historischen Katastrophe. Zum Untergang Sirmiums 582 n. Chr.", *Anzeiger der philosophisch-historischen Klasse der Österreichischen Akademie der Wissenschaften* 126, 139–54.

Nora, P. 1990. *Zwischen Geschichte und Gedächtnis: Die Gedächtnisorte* (Kleine kulturwissenschaftliche Bibliothek, 16). Berlin.

Papageorgiou, A. 2008. "Theme of Cherson (Klimata)", in *Εγκυκλοπαίδεια Μείζονος Ελληνισμού, Εύξεινος Πόντος,* http://www.ehw.gr/l.aspx?id=11973.

Pohl, W. et al. (eds) 2018. *Transformations of Romanness in the Early Middle Ages: Regions and Identities*. Berlin & Boston.

Polemis, D. I. 1996. *Theophanes of Nicaea: His Life and Works* (Wiener Byzantinistische Studien 20). Vienna.

Rapp, C. 2011. "The Christianization of the Idea of the *Polis* in Early Byzantium", in *Proceedings of the 22nd International Congress of Byzantine Studies, 1. Plenary Papers*, Sofia, 263–84.

Riedel, K. 2009. *Europabegriffe und Europas Grenzen bei mittelalterlichen Autoren*. Munich.

Schmalzbauer, G. 2004. "Überlegungen zur Idee der Oikumene in Byzanz", in W. Hörandner (ed.), *Wiener Byzantinistik und Neogräzistik: Beiträge zum Symposion Vierzig Jahre Institut Byzantinistik und Neogräzistik der Universität Wien im Gedenken an Herbert Hunger, Wien, 4.—7. Dezember 2002*. Vienna, 408–419.

Schminck, A. 1986. *Studien zu mittelbyzantinischen Rechtsbüchern* (Forschungen zur byz. Rechtsgeschichte 13). Frankfurt / Main.

Soustal, P. 1981. *Nikopolis und Kephallenia*, unter Mitwirkung von J. Koder (Tabula Imperii Byzantini 3, Denkschriften der phil.-hist. Klasse der Österr. Akademie der Wissenschaften 150). Wien.

Speck, P. 1981. *Artabasdos, der rechtgläubige Vorkämpfer der göttlichen Lehren. Untersuchungen zur Revolte des Artabasdos und ihrer Darstellung in der byzantinischen Historiographie* (Poikila Byzantina 2). Bonn.

Stouraitis, Y. 2014. "Roman Identity in Byzantium: A critical approach", *BZ* 107, 175–220.

Stouraitis, Y. 2017. "Reinventing Roman Ethnicity in High and Late Medieval Byzantium", in W. Pohl & A. Gingrich (eds), *Comparative Studies on Medieval Europe* (medieval worlds: comparative & interdisciplinary studies 5), Vienna, 71–94.

Stouraitis, Y. 2018. "Byzantine Romanness: From Geopolitical to Ethnic Conceptions", in Pohl et al. (eds) 2018, 123–139.

Tielker, W. 2003. *Der Mythos von der Idee Europa. Zur Kritik und Bedeutung historischer Entwicklungsgesetze bei der geistigen Verankerung der europäischen Vereinigung*. Münster.

Trapp, E. et al. (eds) 1994–2017. *Lexikon zur byzantinischen Gräzität*, I–II. Vienna.

Wagner, H. 2006. *Bezugspunkte europäischer Identität. Territorium, Geschichte, Sprache, Werte, Symbole, Öffentlichkeit—Worauf kann sich das Wir-Gefühl der Europäer beziehen?* Münster.

Wolfram H. & W. Pohl (eds) 1990. *Typen der Ethnogenese unter besonderer Berücksichtigung der Bayern* 1 (Denkschriften der philosophisch-historischen Klasse der Österreichischen Akademie der Wissenschaften 201). Vienna.

Zanker, P. 2000. "The City as Symbol. Rome and the Creation of an Urban Image", in Fentress (ed.) 2000, 24–41.

PART 3

Anthropogenic Spaces: Byzantine Landscapes

∴

Editorial Note on Part 3

This section concerns the concept of landscape as the human appropriation of natural space through social practices. The chapters present five different examples of Byzantine appropriations of space resulting in very different landscapes with their own social, political, cultural, and symbolic implications. Together, the chapters vocalize the theoretical and methodological diversity in Byzantine studies, by demonstrating the variety of conceptual approaches to the term 'landscape' as: (a) a common word in history and archaeology; (b) a visual term in archaeology and art studies; (c) a geographical term in post-processual archaeology (meaning the wider context for social practices relationally constituted by spaces and places, thus integrating all natural and anthropogenic environment together with human agency).

Michael Decker offers a theoretical discussion of previous uses of the term and its associations with the environment, settlement, geography, politics, economy, and culture. Decker also makes an effort to reconstruct what a Byzantine 'landscape' (a and c) would have been as seen through Byzantine eyes and sensorial experiences. Nick Kardulias employs modern geographical and archaeological conceptions of landscape (c) to discuss located and diachronic strategies of adaptation and development within an insular context of the Eastern Mediterranean: Cyprus. Kardulias demonstrates the role of peripheries in activating intense political, cultural and economic interactions, as well as the importance of locality and the persistence of local social practices, in an effort to identify a spatial ecology of the past. Enrico Zanini offers an innovative, experimental study of pairing a Late Antique (Dara) and a modern city (Littoria), in order to comment on meanings and aspects of human appropriations of 'new' (i.e. uninhabited) space. Zanini discusses the political and economic background of such practices, as well as their cultural and symbolic implications, defining the dynamic of the relationship between city and hinterland as a research field of great potential. Darlene Brooks Hedstrom explores the symbolic and cultural landscapes of monasticism in yet another part of the Byzantine Empire: Egypt. While her case study deals with the still and void Byzantine space (the 'humble' desert), Brooks Hedstrom—with the help of her geographical conception of landscape (c)—symbolically 'inhabits' the desert. She unfolds the great complexity and constant transformation of anthropogenic spaces, comprehending them as manifold expressions of cultures. In the last chapter, Georgios Pallis employs 'landscape' both as a common word and by its historical and archaeological conceptions (a and b) in a study of the transformation of settlement in the Athenian countryside from Late Antiquity into the Middle Ages. He demonstrates the significance of cultural, political and economic change for the human appropriation of the same natural space (the plain that surrounds Athens) in the long duration.

What Is a Byzantine Landscape?

Michael J. Decker

The question of landscape continues to be an important one in Byzantine Studies. In what follows I will offer a brief overview of some ways we currently understand landscapes and discuss some thoughts on what one might think of as a conceptual framework for approaching the study of landscape. It is helpful, I think, to note some of the textual boundaries established for us, particularly in the early period of Byzantine history, in the fifth and sixth centuries. As Johannes Koder stresses, technical terms like *kōmē* (κώμη), *chōra* (χώρα), and *chōrion* (χωρίον) were not mere legal baubles, but widely employed in religious and vernacular life in expressing the nature of settlement and real categories of living arrangements as people lived and perceived them.[1] However, in other ways, Byzantine views of the interactions of space and place challenge and perhaps elude us.

Here we will explore aspects of two constructions of Byzantine landscapes. There is the view of the ordering of space of the Byzantines themselves. There is the matter, too, of how scholars today order and arrange the landscapes of Byzantium via their own studies. Key to our understanding of these arrangements are the use of some terms like 'space', 'place', 'landscape', 'environment', 'urban' and 'rural'. What do we mean by these?

Let us begin with notions of 'rural' and 'urban'.[2] A convenient way to see rural space is as an anthropogenically shaped area beyond the boundaries of the city. Problems arise mainly from our acceptance of formalist notions of the city based on an imagined paradigm of the classical polis as comprising a large population (typically more than 5,000 residents) which lives in densely-organized space defined by central planning, often in the form of an orthogonal grid and a street system. Other essential elements of the classical city include monumental buildings, clear architectural markers of public and private, as well as architecturally expressed boundaries limiting production to non-core areas, or better still, from the urban fabric altogether. These are accidental features of the city. Of Louis Wirth's venerable but still relevant major

---

1 See the contribution by Johannes Koder in the present volume.
2 For discussion of alternatives to the rural-urban dichotomy, see Veikou 2009, 43–54.

characteristics, it seems to me that the city must possess a relatively dense population, some degree of social heterogeneity, and permanence.[3]

For several reasons, urban spaces are not the focus of this discussion. Early Byzantium was certainly an empire of cities, but for the bulk of its existence, the empire was not one of large-scale urban settlement when one considers Byzantium in the context of its neighbours in the Islamic world. The Byzantine city is also a specialist subject of its own, with a particularly rich and growing body of scholarship devoted to it. Finally, in most times and places in the course of the history of the empire, about ninety per cent of people lived in villages, hamlets, or other kinds of settlements, not in cities.

The classical city is but one expression of urban life, and an anomalous one at that. It would be useful to reframe the discussion of Byzantine rural life by stressing that, as everywhere in pre-industrial societies—the boundaries between city and country were blurred by the conduct of domestic, manufacturing, and agricultural activities throughout the cities of the medieval world. Once we shed centrally planned, possessing monumental architecture, defined by strict spatial delineations bounding public from private we begin to make progress. I would also jettison the focus on monumental architecture and central planning, for example, with an orthogonal grid and street system, as well other characteristics of classical Mediterranean cities which Byzantine cities simply do not fit. A functional approach to cities, derived from the experience of New World archaeologists, affords us a much more useful framework within which to organize ourselves. In one such approach, cities are best identified by their role within the landscape with which they interact, for example their role as religious centres, markets, or administrative places.[4] The issue of scale is a particular pitfall in Byzantine Studies, as early medieval cities were generally less populous than their late antique predecessors. Certainly, by the seventh century it seems that only a handful of settlements would have met the 5,000 persons' population threshold defining a city held by many anthropologists and archaeologists.[5] Rather here it behooves us to consider the functionalist view that what makes cities should be recognized via analysis of how important these places might have been compared to their regional settlement neighbours. This perspective greatly mitigates, if not removes entirely the problem of 'ruralization' from the discussion of the essence of the city, a myopic focus inherited by Byzantinists from classical archaeologists

---

3   Wirth 1938.
4   Smith 1989; Smith 2008, 454–60.
5   Osborne & Cunliffe 2005; in many instances the English word 'town' may have utility in describing a certain order of settlement.

and historians. In this view, the essential *polis* (πόλις) is marked by what the anthropologist Kwang-Chi Chang would identify as its capacity to be wasteful, as expressed in monumental architecture and cultural markers.[6] I am ready to admit that many Middle Byzantine cities were modest affairs to say the least; Cappadocian Mokissos would be comfortable among the villages of late antique central- and northern Syria, and I have little doubt that the sixth- to seventh-century *kome* of Androna (al-Andarin) hosted a greater population than did tenth-century Mokissos. However, the latter has claims to city status on the criteria of settlement hierarchy: to our knowledge it is one of the largest settlements in western Cappadocia. Perhaps it would be better to describe such medieval places as 'towns', especially in the (rare) instances when authors use *polichne* (πολίχνη) or *komopolis* (κωμόπολις) to describe sites. However, we also can consider, apart from textual descriptions, material traces which indicate the relative importance of settlements in local religious life. In the case of Mokissos, local prominence is demonstrated by its multiple churches and its inclusion among the bishoprics of the east in Byzantine *Notitiae*.[7]

While they lack many of the markers of the larger classical poleis, urban landscapes in Middle and Late Byzantium may be viewed as 'cities' if we accept many aspects of the medieval city as differing from their classical predecessors. Indeed, differentiation between city and village is not one of specific action, but also of degree, of intensity, and relative hierarchy. Thus, while we might find villages with clergy, elites, or soldiers present or manufacturing or market activity, these functions alone do not make such settlements cities; it is rather the relationship of these activities in aggregate on a regional level and, in comparison with other regional competitors, and, if known, the views of the Romans themselves. As the seat of the bishop was by definition a polis, this basic concept is a good departure point if we adopt a more expansive approach to settlement and rural life in Byzantium (we will also consider the special role played by the church in defining cities via symbolic hierarchies, though this is not a focus here). Since the ecclesiastical *Notitiae* most likely reflect changes in the landscape, as a number of ancient settlements disappear and new sees are added, the ecclesiastical *Notitiae* should be weighed alongside other information—and perhaps even privileged, all other factors being equal.[8] After the eighth century, when *kastron* (κάστρον) became generally synonymous with fortified *polis* in the literature,[9] the functionalist characteristics

---

6 Chang 1980, 364–67.
7 Berger 1995, 1996, 1997 and 1998; Cooper & Decker 2012, 18 and 24.
8 Ostrogorsky 1959, 59–60.
9 Brandes 1989, 40–41.

noted above will help us separate settlements that were largely administrative or defensive in nature from those which had grown organically from the requirements of the local population.

Since it is unlikely that scholars will cease to use the word 'rural' to describe certain features of the landscape, it seems more desirable if we agree that the word 'rural' be used in neutral fashion, to connote space that is not densely populated and not heterogenous. If we mean, for example, that many Middle- and Late-Byzantine cities possessed certain features like agricultural work spaces, and were therefore 'rural' as matters of fact, without asserting these later settlements to be the inferior to classical poleis that such centres may or not have replaced, then 'rural' is appropriate and perhaps the least-undesirable description.[10]

What do we mean by terms like 'space', 'place', 'environment', and 'landscape'? While these terms are often used interchangeably, clearly it would be desirable if we could agree to employ them in a somewhat consistent fashion. As is well known, there are a number of fields which have developed theories of these terms, and while all are not applicable to the case of Byzantium, some clearly are.[11] For the purpose of this discussion, 'landscape' means a human-organized space, or 'active surface' in which human cognition and relationships unfold over time, both changing, and changed by power relationships. Space must be more than a social product, in other words.[12] Landscapes are not necessarily green or 'country' spaces, but may include urban areas, sacred areas created by social and cultural expressions, and other sorts of spaces.[13] 'Places' are also created by humans assigning meaning to a given point of geography; while in the system I am proposing all landscapes are places, not all places are landscapes. It may be useful to apply 'environment' to non-anthropogenically conditioned spaces, as would environmental scientists. This is possible only insofar as we remove notions of social or cultural elements from our understanding of these spaces, and this seems a fraught proposition.

Landscapes are human-organized spaces. The landscapes of Byzantium, then, are not to be likened to those from which the modern Anglo-Saxon world has inherited its understanding, which is essentially the product of both the Classicism of the seventeenth century and the Romanticism of the eighteenth century.[14] In the former, the landscape is objectified, an ordered arena made

---

10   Decker 2016; Veikou 2009 and 2010.
11   See Dawson, Zanotti & Vaccaro 2014 for additional bibliography.
12   Lefebvre 1958.
13   Wall 1999.
14   Lothian 1999.

harmonious by humans and natural law. Later generations reacted by seeing the landscape as a rather more dangerous, emotional state whose mysteries cannot be known by reason and are therefore the discovery of the individual who is likewise a force of nature.[15] Increasingly, discourse is returning to some of these concepts where, instead of a human drama with God amongst the stage-hands and spectators and managers, we have a purely people-driven theatre in which the landscape is a tableau into which are etched unmistakable signs of the past exercise of power.[16] This trend has been especially prevalent in scholarship since the 1920's, and the use of the term 'landscape' has become so common that it has taken on the meaning of 'natural environment' or 'settlement pattern'. While these are quite broad, such concepts could benefit from refinement within the specific context of Byzantine Studies so that perhaps we can agree upon a more defined set of categories and shared vocabulary of expression as we advance our discussion.

If we think simply in terms of 'environment', then the Byzantine landscape could be as small as a single settlement and its environs, or as large as the territory fenced in by Byzantine political boundaries at a given date. But are we then bound to cut off discussion of Byzantine landscapes in the Peloponnese, for example, after 1204 when the region was under Frankish control? This would be simpler, but it also, I think, flies in the face of what we recognize about Byzantium, that its cultural influence, borders, and life dwelled far beyond areas under the political control of Constantinople. Thus, for comfort's sake, we often employ the term 'medieval' to these landscapes. Archaeologists are equipped to handle some of these questions, if not resolve them to the satisfaction of all. Although the notion has been put forward that the settlement hierarchy of Byzantium in the eleventh century was dominated by the *polis* in a constellation of villages, hamlets, and estates, as I have just noted, this notion of the organization of the countryside is not unproblematic. Indeed, the notion of the city as the focal point of the Byzantine landscape is especially questionable during the seventh through ninth centuries when urban life in its classical Graeco-Roman manifestations largely receded from imperial territory.

In English, 'environment' can connote something as large as the entire biosphere—basically the whole of planet earth, especially in material relationships. Yet there are other environments as well, often examined through ecological niches, as in the disease matrix of the Justinianic and later plagues,

---

15   Labbe 1998, 37.
16   Witness, for the example, the determinist writings of Jared Diamond: Diamond 1998 and 2005.

or the ecology of disease in Byzantium generally. This matrix is bound in time and space by the vision of the investigator, who both accesses these different environments and reifies them. To me, rather than using the word 'environment' synonymously with 'landscape', one should be more specific and think of the environment as the overall immersive space in which humanity is present through time. Landscapes are therefore part of the environment, and environments are likewise not fixed, but part of a dialectic mediated in part by humans.

1 Byzantine Views

Byzantine landscapes must be viewed from the vantage of how the Romans themselves might have perceived them—as discussed in the case of monasteries above, and in reference, as some recent studies have suggested, through religious and vernacular placemaking. This is difficult to accomplish. Such construction may be viewed rather as a by-product of organizing the land for different purposes. This sort of organizing is a mental as well as a physical activity; imperial bureaucrats could and did physically measure the land, but they also ordered it in their ledgers, as did estate managers of all stripes. Power is certainly a central element in the organizing of landscapes. Beyond viewing landscapes, as Lefebvre did, as social products and not simply as either mental or physical ones, it would be useful to look at how the Byzantines conceived of and organized various kinds of landscape.[17] We gain insights into how the peoples of the empire viewed their physical world not only from practical texts such as the *Geoponika* but from the work of imperial officials who divided and reckoned the land, its people, and their usufruct. This can be viewed in early documents like the Syro-Roman Lawbook and in later tax treatises such as the Marcian Treatise of the tenth century (see below).[18] In these texts, we can view the landscape through its division, labour input and output, and, crucially, in its surplus passed on to owner, market, or collector. In other words, one could make the argument that a Byzantine landscape to a Roman person of most places and times in their own history was the immediate inhabited environment and its usufruct. In the Novels of Justinian I, the *chōrion* means more than simply "free village", though it does have this sense in certain instances. Often the legal theorists of Justinian viewed *chōria* as fiscal units, which are

---

17 Lefebvre 1958.
18 Vööbus 1982; Brand 1969.

not terribly abstract, pinned as they are in the divisions ascribed by the state and thus tied to units of land, labour, and money (produce).[19] The scribes of the later empire, often *anagrapheis* (ἀναγραφείς) who wrote the *praktika* (πρακτικά) recorded the assessment of lands belonging to the church, the state, or individuals.[20] In creating this record of the land, its furnishings, and its labour, these recorders created landscapes in a way analogous to those of earlier fiscal codices—that is, in notional units which were removed from the organizer of that space. This is a remote landscape, imposed by the mind ('notional' or perhaps 'imagined') and determined by boundaries of ideas—of ownership, production, and power.

Landscapes are not simply geological, environmental, or spatial; in other words, human exertion must be present. Landscapes are therefore constructed in reference to people and, like others, the Byzantines rendered landscapes in reference to themselves (see below). The Germanic 'Landschaft', with its notions of total spatial and visual comprehension and interaction with the total environment, is useful in helping us distil a more functional understanding of 'landscape'.[21] We might therefore consider landscapes as interlocking nodes or surfaces that can also sometimes function independently of one another. For example, a monastic farm may, in addition to serving as a place of agricultural production as a primary purpose, house an important sacred space. Then as now, landscapes may be sometimes defined visually and by proximity, created from the eye of the human observer on the ground today or proximate but notional only, as in the case of the *praktika* or cadastral records. Researchers today may define a landscape based on a picture of a picture—for example an archaeologist may delineate a survey area dependent on what is considered a major place, usually an ancient city.[22] In many instances, regional survey does not reveal the chronological markers that we would like; in the cases of installations and rock cut features, the absence of diagnostic pottery requires spatial analysis to embed such features within the Byzantine-era environment. I would also add that I would like to think of Byzantine landscapes as interconnected vessels of human activity, and these could in theory be reassembled for rather broad chronologies into a giant quilt of overlapping landscapes via the tools of spatial analysis, as movement cost, or viewshed analysis, or more abstractly, via network analysis.[23]

---

19 *Novellae* CXXVIII, 7, 8.
20 Bartusis 1991.
21 Naveh & Lieberman 2013, 4.
22 Bintliff et al 2007; Bintliff 2013, 127.
23 Knappett 2013; Wheatley & Gillings 2000.

Throughout the history of the empire, the village was the principal, but not the only, node around which the rural landscape was organized and understood. Villages, which can typically be described as having more than 100 persons, are generally referred to in the sources as *chorion*. In the early Byzantine period, *kōme* frequently signified a village, especially the free villages of the late antique east, such as the large settlement of Androna (al-Andarin) in the steppe desert territory of Apameia, as well as many from the Limestone Massif comprising portions of the territories of Antioch and Apameia.[24] Some villages were clearly owned by individual landowners, whether private persons or corporate entities such as the church of monasteries. In the early period, in Syria, *chorion* may have indicated such dependent villages, but the question requires more investigation and likely varied substantially through space and time.

In medieval Byzantium, villages were the physical nodes to which the landscape was tethered.[25] With the changes of urbanism which occurred by the seventh and eighth centuries at the latest (and earlier over much of the Balkans), the village gained further administrative functions (which some likely had during Late Antiquity in places like Syria, for example, where some very large villages had taken over many functions of the city).[26] The *chorion* of the Middle Byzantine era was a generic term for a rural settlement as well as a district accounting to the fisc.[27] But the village is also a mentality, a particular way of relating to the world, a certain sort of hierarchy and structure of power in which it differs from larger settlements.[28] Ideally, in our understanding of the village landscape as well as a landscape of villages, we would be able to take into account certain elements of these mentalities and relations, as Gerstel has recently conducted for villages in Late Byzantine Greece.[29]

One basic aspect is the creation of a landscape, in part, through the human gaze. It is easy, though, to lose track of the ways in which humans interacted with the landscape in constructing spaces into landscapes. One of the ways they did so was through the sensory act of seeing. One may easily see, for example, how the castle of Kastamon in northern Paphlagonia where the Turkish-period castle of Kastamonu today rests atop (and likely expands) the

---

24 Tchalenko 1953–58, I. 312; III, 8 c, 9.
25 The literature on the village in the empire is vast: seminal works include Lefort, Morrisson & Sodini 2005, but see also Taxel 2013; Tchlaneko 1953–58; Rautman 2005; Bintliff 1997; Hirschfeld 1997; Delattre & Heilporn 2008; Varinlioglu 2008; Kaplan 1992.
26 Gerritsen et al. 2008, 241–314.
27 Neville 2004, 94.
28 Zadora-Rio 1995.
29 Gerstel 2015.

Byzantine era stronghold of the Komneni dominates the upper Amnias River (Gökırmak) Valley. While the view from the castle walls today is very different from the eleventh century, it is easy to see how, from such a vantage, the military and aristocratic family of the Komneni understood the land around them; they were with little doubt literally the lords of all they surveyed from such a vantage. Such a node, or central place, offers us a marker whence to understand a landscape from multiple perspectives, from the 'interior' one just noted, which may well be a mental one, in this case the possible application of theories of power. To go further, places that dominate their physical environment like Kastamon, whether churches, monasteries, villages, or cities, are as much creators of landscape as they are the products of it. Certainly, by virtue of the choice to erect such structures and select their positions in the terrain and fortify them, the Byzantine builders of these fortified centres demonstrate an understanding similar to our own: that these places were visible from many, if not all directions, and that they protected not only the family or garrison emplaced there, but the surrounding terrain and inhabitants as well. This protection was of course, not free, with increasing control and a sense of ownership exerted over peasants and others around these fortified dwellings, referred to variously as *kastra*, or as *phrourion*, "fortified refuge". Certainly, by the Komnenian era it would not be entirely wrong to refer to these places as 'castles', although this term is freighted with a number of 'f' words, including Franks and feudalism that are among the bugbears of medievalists.

But we move beyond the simply physical when we look at descriptions of an idealized landscape in the early Byzantine account of Basil of Caesarea. The family estate of Annisa (probably modern Uluköy) in Pontus to which Basil retreated for spiritual contemplation, a place he called "perfectly suited to my character" and one which he recalled fondly to his close friend Gregory of Nazianzus:

> Ὄρος γάρ ἐστιν ὑψηλὸν βαθείᾳ ὕλῃ κεκαλυμμένον, ψυχροῖς ὕδασι καὶ διαφανέσιν εἰς τὸ κατ' ἄρκτον κατάρρυτον. Τούτου ταῖς ὑπωρείαις πεδίον ὕπτιον ὑπεστόρεσται, ταῖς ἐκ τοῦ ὄρους νοτίσι διηνεκῶς πιαινόμενον. Ὕλη δὲ τούτῳ αὐτομάτως περιφυεῖσα ποικίλων καὶ παντοδαπῶν δένδρων μικροῦ δεῖν ἀντὶ ἔρκους αὐτῷ γίνεται, ὡς μικρὰν εἶναι πρὸς τοῦτο καὶ τὴν Καλυψοῦς νῆσον, ἣν δὴ πασῶν πλέον Ὅμηρος εἰς κάλλος θαυμάσας φαίνεται. Καὶ γὰρ οὐδὲ πολὺ ἀποδεῖ τοῦ νῆσος εἶναι, ἕνεκά γε τοῦ πανταχόθεν ἐρύμασι περιείργεσθαι. Φάραγγες μὲν γὰρ αὐτῷ βαθεῖαι κατὰ δύο μέρη περιερρώγασι· κατὰ πλευρὰν δὲ ἀπὸ κρημνοῦ ὁ ποταμὸς ὑπορρέων τεῖχός ἐστι καὶ αὐτὸς διηνεκὲς καὶ δυσέμβατον· ἐκ δὲ τοῦ ἐπὶ θάτερα τεταμένον τὸ ὄρος, δι' ἀγκώνων μηνοειδῶν ταῖς φάραγξιν

ἐπιζευγνύμενον, τὰ βάσιμα τῆς ὑπωρείας ἀποτειχίζει. Μία δέ τις εἴσοδος ἐπ' αὐτῆς, ἧς ἡμεῖς ἐσμεν κύριοι. Τήν γε μὴν οἴκησιν αὐχήν τις ἕτερος ὑποδέχεται [...]

> There is a high mountain covered with thick forest, watered from the north by clear, fresh streams. At its base, there lies an inclined plain, perennially watered by the streams issuing from the mount. A wood grows on this plain, with all manner of trees, and almost fences in the place [...] indeed it is not far from being an island, because it is surrounded by defenses on all sides. Deep ravines cut off two sides of it; on its side the river plunges down the escarpment and forms a continuous, impassable wall. The mountain extends on two sides, joining to the ravines with crescent-shaped spurs, and thus blocks access at the foot. These have only one passage, and it is we who are its masters. Our home is sheltered in another gorge.[30]

Saint Basil defines the landscape of Annisa in several complex, interlocking ways, all of which contribute to his mental picture of the estate as a 'place' and as a 'landscape'. The landscape of Annisa is paradisiacal, a mirror of the bounty of nature and, ultimately, of God the creator of nature. The estate was a microcosm of God's 'wonderfully wrought' landscape of creation as a reflection of the divine, a theme of which the Cappadocian Fathers were especially fond. More importantly, this landscape is one of peace, for the future bishop states that the greatest bounty that Annisa provided him was quiet, a refuge away from the bustle of the city. Pleasure was the primary feature Basil associated with the landscape of the estate—the pleasure of solitude, partaking of the bounties of the land, including fishing and hunting, the wild resources of the parklands.

In his homilies on the six days of creation, the *Hexaemeron*, Basil of Caesarea most clearly elaborates his views of nature, and the relationships between human beings, nature, and the divinity. Nature is, first and foremost, a wondrous reflection of the Creator. "Therefore, when you see the trees in our gardens, or those of the forest [...] recognize even in small objects the grandeur of God [...] redoubling your love of the Creator". (Σὺ δὲ ὅταν ἴδῃς τὰ ἥμερα, τὰ ἄγρια, τὰ φίλυδρα, τὰ χερσαῖα, τὰ ἀνθοφοροῦντα, ἢ τὰ ἀνάνθη, ἐν μικρῷ τὸν μέγαν ἐπιγινώσκων, πρόσθες ἀεὶ τῷ θαύματι, καὶ αὔξησόν μοι τὴν ἀγάπην τοῦ κτίσαντος.)[31]

---

30 Basil of Caesarea, *Epistles*, 14 (43 Courtonne).
31 Basil, *Hexaemeron* 5.9 (320–21 Giet).

His praise of the landscape of Annisa demonstrates the aesthetic value that Basil assigned to natural beauty; he lauds the loveliness of the scenery, its flowers, and its birdsong. He speaks admiringly of the abundance of fish in the river and of game in the field and forest—clearly these fruits were particularly attractive to the priest who was himself an elite landowner and who still enjoyed aristocratic pursuits. While the Cappadocian was happy to laud the environment for its intrinsic beauty and for the way that beauty pointed to the Creator, another strong argument Basil of Caesarea makes is that of utility; nothing is created without a purpose, and part of the way we see God in nature is through the usefulness of each animal and plant in some form or fashion. Plants and animals had a purpose beyond reminding us of God, and Basil sees that purpose as nested in their productive relationship to humans. Nature is not complete in and of itself, its fecundity and productivity, in fact, complete the circle: "The right form of the earth is its own beauty and suitable to its nature: harvests waving in the valleys, green meadows green with grass embellished with all kinds of flowers" (οἰκεῖος αὐτῇ καὶ κατὰ φύσιν κόσμος, λήϊα μὲν ταῖς κοιλότησιν ἐγκυμαίνοντα, λειμῶνες χλοάζοντες καὶ ποικίλοις ἄνθεσι βρύοντες, νάπαι εὐθαλεῖς [...]);[32] this is a landscape imagined and brought into existence by God but seen and experienced only through people.

The views expressed by Basil, whose works on creation continued to be read and were influential throughout the history of the empire, were reified in the art of Late Antiquity. Prior to Iconoclasm, scenes of the natural world, especially animals, trees, and other plants were all considered appropriate in the decorative schema of sacred spaces, and they appeared often. While these scenes may be read as reminders, as Basil articulated, of the wonders of God's handiwork in created matter (and thus a positive view of it), these depictions also reflect the notion of a mastery of creation by human beings which is the second major theme expressed in Basil's work. In some ways, we can see the approach to landscape in the late Roman imperial projects, especially of Justinian I whose monumental buildings left indelible marks on cities throughout the empire and who attempted, through the building of large-scale fortifications, to place visible stamps of Roman authority over whole regions or populations.

32 Basil, *Hexaemeron* 2.3 (152–53 Giet).

2 Sacred and Religious Landscape

Sacred landscapes have drawn some attention from scholars of Byzantium; Sharon Gerstel is one of a number of scholars to have recently worked on this area.[33] One important question is how sacred centres, especially monasteries, fit into these organized arenas. Are they part of the landscape or somehow removed from it by virtue of their unique socially constructed role as 'not of the world', as distinct entities where men and women went to pray, labour for their salvation and die ultimately in isolation from 'the world'. In considering monasteries in the landscape, my mind was drawn to the stories of *Pratum Spirituale*, where monasteries and hermitages comprise the main places where action occurs. Cities and villages are not really part of the narrative, rather John and his companions travel from monastery to monastery as if navigating through a sanctified mirror image of the secular road network, with its *mitata* (sg. μιτᾶτον) and *stathmoi* (sg. σταθμός).[34] Perhaps a better approach is to see the hermit cells and monasteries of Byzantium as isolated redoubts of spiritual warfare, renewal, and divine activity set aside from the baser physical space of the unsanctified. Notions of a simple dichotomy of secular and sacred, as these are post-Enlightenment concepts that, while they may useful when addressing a twenty-first century audience, do not seem to convey much if we are trying to understand the people of Byzantium in ways that at least approximate their self-perceptions.

In any century of Byzantine history, there were thousands of sacred landscapes embedded within the topography of the empire. How might we understand such spaces? The notion of the physical field of view of the individual as a crucial part of the culturally conditioned act of seeing as essential to conceptualizing 'sacred landscapes' is useful, but limited.[35] In towns and cities, liturgical processions and local martyr's shrines sanctified many spots in a tangible, but ultimately ephemeral way which we cannot today measure or understand. In the countryside, roadside shrines, local martyria, hagiasmata, and other sites of veneration are now mostly inaccessible to us. Large, transregional sites of pilgrimage which frame what we may appropriately call 'sacred landscapes' existed of course in places like Athos, Meteora, Ephesos, Myra, Chonai, and many others.

---

33 Gerstel 2015; Horster 2010, 435–58; Crumley 1999; Della Dora 2016; Nixon 2006; Kalas 2009; Soustal 2010.
34 PG 87.3.3036–43.
35 Crumley 1999.

Apart from Athos and other remote important monasteries which served as the visually and physically dominant, central places of their districts, such as Sumela in Trebizond, St Catherine's on Mount Sinai, or the Judean Desert Monasteries, it would be easy to dismiss the utility of thinking of broad swathes of rural territory as 'sacred' lands, and certainly not in the classical sense where cultic sites, often spread over multiple loci of worship and practice, held significant tracts of land. However, Byzantium received directly from the Greeks and Romans the notion of the sacred landscape. For example, the temple precincts and cult sites of antiquity were clearly marked, and were, legally, 'sacred lands' which often had an economic function, as attested in the Byzantine era by *praktika* and sometimes in the *typika* (sg. τυπικόν). The sacred nature of these spaces is underscored by their boundary stones, which marked them as spaces belonging to God, as in the case of the marker at Çandir Yayla (Galatia) which declares "the boundaries of St John have been established by the power of God and by the hand of the emperor".[36] Yet it is useful further to consider the "religious landscape"[37] as something apart from the formal, physical confines of the monastic compound, the major pilgrim shrine, like the Martyrion of Philip at Hierapolis, or hundreds of more modest, largely anonymous foci of religious travel and prayer.[38]

3   Contemporary Views

A second view is a contemporary perspective conditioned by scholars, especially historians and archaeologists. The latter, often with the aid of remote sensing tools, dissect an area of interest with transects and survey grids, collecting pottery, carefully noting 'sites' and 'offsite' or 'non-sites'. Such surveys are anchored in the physical reality of the moment in which they occur, but they seek to reconstruct slices of the landscape in geological and cultural time, to create a frozen image, so to speak, often of centuries far distant from our own. This approach views the landscape not as a passive backdrop, as was once the case, but as both a creation of human interaction with their environments and natural processes. In doing so, the aim of landscape study is an exercise in decoding. After all, pottery gets eroded from hillslopes; forests grow up and cover ancient remains or disappear and expose them. Monumental buildings crumble through erosion, the action of wind and rain, and are dissolved

---

36   Cosentino 2016.
37   Horster 2010.
38   Gümgüm 2012.

chemically by aerosol pollutants. The images we decode from surveys are therefore processed and constructed to the best of our knowledge based on the diagnostic tools available: greater or lesser detailed ceramic chronologies, an evolving knowledge of geomorphology, reference to climate change data, and artefactual evidence of human-made objects still visible in the environment. One of the benefits gained from the adoption by archaeologists of methods from geomorphology in the study of past environments is the notion that, while topography and terrain might in some sense serve as a 'canvas' of human activity, an understanding of relief or the natural environment is only one piece of the larger mosaic that moulds our notion of landscape today.

Survey areas are often quite arbitrary, as is establishing the relationship of one site to another; it can thus be quite difficult to establish the hierarchic and network features which knit together the environment into a landscape through human interaction. Regional surveys are based on modern regions, constrained by bureaucracy, property rights, housing and industrial development, environmental change, and the difficulty of applying methodologies consistently across a wide area. The creation of archaeological landscape through site recording is still often dependent on notions of sites and hierarchies which may not reflect the realities of a millennium ago.[39] One recent discussion of data from three systematic surveys conducted in Anatolia by researchers without an interest in Byzantine history yielded interesting results from the investigation of a huge area of former Byzantine Cappadocia. Substantially different research methods, variation in coverage, and problems of artifact collection and interpretation mean that our ability to reconstruct the spatial relationships of sites in communication with one another and which interacted with one another in the way I am employing the dynamic notion of 'landscape' here, is difficult to say the least. Results like these are not uncommon, hindered as we are by a general lack of tools, especially local ceramic chronologies, and blind spots in our view of diagnostic material culture which, if overcome, would make identification and dating of loci of human activity more streamlined and less open to doubt.

Remote sensing methods, which involve the use of satellite imagery, LIDAR, aerial reconnaissance photographs (or photographs from drones) are tools which often dictate how we approach the construction of landscapes. In most instances, the data we glean from remote sensing sources are themselves the products of our interventions, and investigators are often at the mercy of bureaucrats or others who determine the limits of their archaeological permits,

---

39   Banning 2002.

while realities such as international borders, massive changes in the landscape due to terraforming and the accompanying total obliteration of cultural heritage which accompanies it, further constrain us. Archaeologists, naturally, operate using data which they consider relevant to their study areas; in many instances those who record and publish information about past Byzantine landscapes do not have a research interest in the empire and are thus unlikely to consider, for example, the likely *territorium* of a late antique or medieval settlement as derived from texts or material markers.

4 Space and Placemaking

Perhaps more basic is the creation of a landscape through the human gaze. Human vision is generally capable of a 210°-degree field of view and this field of view lends certain visible areas to be organized mentally and physically into landscapes. While field of view of course varied from one person to another, as well as one location to another, there are certain clear examples whereby the human field of view formed the building block for organizing landscape.

Were we to approach the landscape of Athos or Sabas or any other region with Byzantine monastic elements, we would surely not view these structures as something apart from, but rather embedded, within the landscape. Thus, it would be unthinkable for us today to extract the remains of an eleventh-century monastery from amongst a scatter of contemporary artefactual remnants. That rural landscapes of Byzantium may be partially read and perhaps constructed through minor relics of social and economic activities embedded in the landscapes has yet to receive the full attention of scholars. Many non-architectural features, such as sherd scatters, banal ceramics, roads, paths, wells, ditches, field boundaries, and terrace walls, remain understudied. Temporary pastoral campsites, sheepfolds, shepherd's- and forester's huts used seasonally, water- and windmills, clay pits, kilns, mines, and ore-processing sites as well as rural shrines and cemeteries are but a few of the micro-environments which in aggregate can provide a picture of Byzantine landscapes but which are largely absent from the landscapes of Byzantium as currently constructed. Architectural remains of rural towers, isolated farmhouses, hamlets, and villages are more visible and have received somewhat fuller treatment, though less, it seems, than 'urban' features.

Using landscape as an approach through which to view the former spaces of the empire is, to my mind, exceedingly challenging. In order to foster better analysis, it seems imperative to move beyond some of the rather simplistic views we have held regarding the dichotomous nature of the production of landscapes and to enact our shared vocabulary with more consistency. In addition to the difficulty of the basis of judgement of what constitutes a landscape, one must ask what constitutes a particular Byzantine version of landscape, understanding that this is going to vary depending on the markers of time and place. In fact, our access to the artefacts and features which allow us to construct Byzantine era landscapes are quickly receding to the vanishing point as economic development and urban growth continues at an astonishing pace. We have to admit that within twenty years' time many Byzantine landscapes will be completely obliterated without having been recorded, and our need to refine our tools and apply them is perhaps more acute than ever before.

Bibliography

Primary Sources

Basil of Caesarea, *Epistles*. Ed. Y. Courtonne, *Lettres 1*. Paris 1957.
Basil of Caesarea, *Hexaemeron*. Ed. S. Giet, *Homélies sur l'Hexaéméron*. Paris 1968.
John Moschus, *Spiritual Meadow* in PG 87/III, 2851–3112. Paris 1865.
Novellae, Corpus Iuris Civilis, vol. 3, Ed. R. Schoell & W. Kroll, *Novellae*. Berlin 1904.

Secondary Sources

Ashmore, W. & A. Bernard Knapp (eds) 1999. *Archaeologies of Landscape: Contemporary Perspectives*. Malden, MA.
Banning, E. B. 2002. *Archaeological survey*. New York.
Bartusis, M. 1991. "Praktikon", in Kazhdan (ed.) 1991, 1711.
Berger, A. 1995. "Survey in Viransehir (Mokisos)", *Arastirma Sonuçkaru Toplantisi* 13.2, 109–29.
Berger, A. 1996. "Survey in Viransehir (Mokisos)", *Arastirma Sonuçkaru Toplantisi* 14.1, 27–41.
Berger, A. 1997. "Survey in Viransehir (Mokisos)", *Arastirma Sonuçkaru Toplantisi* 15.2, 219–37.
Berger, A. 1998 "Viransehir (Mokisos), eine byzantinische Stadt in Kappadokien", *Istanbuler Mitteilungen*, 48, 349–429.
Bintliff, J. L. 1997. "The archaeological investigation of deserted medieval villages in Greece", in De Boe and Verhaeghe (eds.) 1997, 21–34.
Bintliff, J. L. 2013. "The Contribution of Regional Surface Survey to Byzantine landscape History in Greece", in Poblome (ed.) 2013, 127–39.
Bintliff, J. L. et al. 2007. *Testing the Hinterland: The Work of the Boeotia Survey (1989–1991) in the Southern Approaches to the City of Thespiai*. Cambridge.
Brand, C. M. 1969. "Two Byzantine Treatises on Taxation", *Traditio* 25, 35–60.

Brandes, W. 1989. *Die Städte Kleinasiens im 7. und 8. Jahrhundert*. Berlin.
Chang, K.-C. 1980. *Shang Civilization*. New Haven.
Cooper, J. E. & Decker, M. J. 2012. *Life and Society in Byzantine Cappadocia*. London.
Corner, J. (ed.) 1999. *Recovering landscape: Essays in contemporary landscape architecture*. Princeton.
Cosentino, S. 2016. "Boundary Marks and Space Organization in Early Byzantine Epigraphy", in Stavrakos (ed.) 2016, 95–110.
Crumley, C. L. 1999. "Sacred landscapes: constructed and conceptualized", in Ashmore & Bernard Knapp (eds) 1999, 269–76.
Dawson, A. C., Zanotti, L. & I. Vaccaro 2014. *Negotiating Territoriality: Spatial Dialogues Between State and Tradition*. London.
De Boe, G. & F. Verhaeghe (eds) 1997. *Rural Settlements in Medieval Europe*. Brugge.
Decker, M. J. 2016. *The Byzantine Dark Ages*. London.
Delattre, A. & P. Heilporn (eds) 2008. *Et maintenant ce ne sont plus que des villages: Thèbes et sa région aux époques hellénistique, romaine et byzantine: actes du colloque tenu à Bruxelles les 2 et 3 décembre 2005*. Brussels.
Della Dora, V. 2016. *Landscape, Nature, and the Sacred in Byzantium*. Cambridge.
Diamond, J. M. 1998. *Guns, Germs and Steel: The Fate of Human Societies*. New York.
Diamond, J. M. 2005. *Collapse: How Societies Choose to Fail or Succeed*. London.
Gates, C., J. Morin, & T. Zimmermann (eds) 2009. *Sacred Landscapes in Anatolia and Neighbouring Regions*. Oxford.
Gerritsen, F. et al. 2008. "Settlement and landscape transformations in the Amuq Valley, Hatay: A long-term perspective", *Anatolica* 34, 241–314.
Gerstel, S. E. J. 2015. *Rural Lives and Landscapes in Late Byzantium: Art, Archaeology, and Ethnography*. Cambridge.
Gümgüm, G. 2012. *Il Martyrion di Hierapolis di Frigia (Turchia): analisi archeologica e architettonica*. Oxford.
Hirschfeld, Y. 1997. "Farms and Villages in Byzantine Palestine", *DOP* 51, 33–71.
Horster, M. 2010. "Religious landscape and sacred ground: relationships between space and cult in the Greek world", *Revue de l'histoire des religions* 4, 435–58.
Kalas, V. 2009. "Sacred Boundaries and Protective Borders: Outlying Chapels of Middle Byzantine Settlements in Cappadocia", in Gates, Morin & Zimmermann (eds) 2009, 79–91.
Kaplan, M. 1992. *Les hommes et la terre à Byzance du VIe au XIe siècle: propriété et exploitation du sol*. Paris.
Kazhdan, A. P. (ed.) 1991. *The Oxford Dictionary of Byzantium*. Oxford.
Knappett, C. 2013. *Network analysis in archaeology: New approaches to regional interaction*. Oxford.
Labbe, J. 1998. *Romantic Visualities: Landscape, Gender and Romanticism*. London.
Lefebvre, H. 1958. *La Production de l'espace*. Paris.

Lefort, J., C. Morrisson, C. & J.-P. Sodini (eds) 2005. *Les villages dans l'Empire byzantin, IVe–XVe siècle*. Paris.

Lock, G. (ed.) 2000. *Beyond the Map: Archaeology and Spatial Technologies*. Amsterdam.

Lothian, A. 1999. "Landscape and the philosophy of aesthetics: is landscape quality inherent in the landscape or in the eye of the beholder?", *Landscape and Urban Planning* 44.4, 177–98.

Mornet, E. (ed.) 1995. *Campagnes médiévales. L'homme et son espace. Etudes offertes à Robert Fossier*. Paris.

Naveh, Z. & A. S. Lieberman 2013. *Landscape Ecology: Theory and Application*. New York.

Neville, L. 2004. *Authority in Byzantine provincial society, 950–1100*. Cambridge.

Nixon, L. 2006. *Making a Landscape Sacred: Outlying Churches and Icon Stands in Sphakia, Southwestern Crete*. Oxford.

Osborne, R. & B. Cunliffe 2005. *Mediterranean Urbanization 800–600 BC*. Oxford.

Ostrogorsky, G. 1959. "Byzantine Cities in the Early Middle Ages", *DOP* 13, 45–66.

Poblome, J. (ed.) 2013. *Exempla Gratia: Sagalassos, Marc Waelkens and Interdisciplinary Archaeology*. Leuven.

Rautman, M. 2005. "The Villages of Byzantine Cyprus", in Lefort, Morrisson & Sodini (eds) 2005, 453–63.

Smith, M. E. 1989. "Cities, Towns, and Urbanism: comment on Sanders and Webster", *American Anthropologist* 91.2, 454–60.

Smith, M. E. 2008. *Aztec City-State Capitals*. Gainesville, FL.

Soustal, P. 2010. *Wirtschaft und Handelsleben auf dem Heiligen Berg Athos*. Vienna.

Stavrakos, C. (ed.) 2016. *Inscriptions in the Byzantine and Post-Byzantine History and History of Art: Proceedings of the International Symposium "Inscriptions: Their Contribution to the Byzantine and Post-Byzantine History and History of Art"* (Ioannina, June 26–27, 2015). Wiesbaden.

Taxel, I. 2013. "Identifying social hierarchy through house planning in the villages of Late Antique Palestine: the case of Ḥorvat Zikhrin", *Antiquité Tardive* 21, 149–66.

Tchalenko, G. 1953–58. *Villages antiques de la Syrie du Nord: le massif du Bélus à l'époque romaine*, 3 vols. Paris.

Varinlioglu, G. 2008. *Rural Landscape and Built Environment at the End of Antiquity: Limestone Villages of Southeastern Isauria*. Philadelphia.

Veikou, M. 2009. "'Rural Towns' and 'In-Between' or 'Third' Spaces. Settlement Patterns in Byzantine Epirus (7th–11th c.) from an interdisciplinary approach", *Archaeologia Medievale* 36, 43–54.

Veikou, M. 2010. "Urban or Rural? Theoretical Remarks on the Settlement Patterns in Byzantine Epirus (7th–11th c.)", *BZ* 103.1, 171–93.

Vööbus, A. 1982. *The Syro-Roman Lawbook*. Stockholm.

Wall, A. 1999. "Programming the urban surface", in Corner (ed.) 1999, 233–49.

Wheatley, D. & M. Gillings 2000. "Vision, perception and GIS: developing enriched approaches to the study of archaeological visibility", in Lock (ed.) 2000, 1–27.

Wirth, L. 1938. "Urbanism as a Way of Life", *American Journal of Sociology* 44.1, 1–24.

Zadora-Rio, E. 1995. "Le village des historiens et le village des archéologues", in Mornet (ed.) 1995, 145–53.

Adapting to the Cypriot Landscape
A Study of Medieval to Modern Occupation of the Malloura Valley

P. Nick Kardulias

Humans have always been situated in the natural environment. What distinguishes people from other animals that share this basic fact is that we use the artifice of culture to mediate our interaction with our physical surroundings, and this is true for societies at all levels of technological complexity. A review of the archaeological and historical records reveals the various ways in which people have augmented that cultural buffer to insulate themselves from the vagaries of climate and terrain through the use of tools, shelters, clothing, different subsistence practices, etc. The dependence of hunters and gatherers on wild food resources, combined with their rudimentary artifact inventory, contrasts with the complex agricultural systems of premodern states, which often involved irrigation and intensive terracing. However, both the forager and the peasant farmer had to create mental categories of their respective environments in order to deal effectively with individual and social needs. These groups at opposite ends of the subsistence spectrum had to map out their activities on a daily, weekly, monthly, and annual schedule that imposed meaning on the features of the space they occupied.

In the introductory chapter to this volume, the editors note that the Spatial Turn formed an important shift in orientation for the social sciences and humanities beginning some 50 years ago. In archaeology specifically, prehistorians had traditionally incorporated a more explicit examination of the locational or spatial facet of the remains they examined than had their classical counterparts, though the latter by no means ignored this aspect. In the 1950s, American archaeologists formulated a hierarchical spatial model that encompassed the largest domain (culture area) down to the site and the individual discreet stratigraphic layers (components) that comprise the stratigraphic record in an effort to define the spatial units of study.[1] Much of that terminology has become standard in archaeology across the board, along with the attendant critiques that have attempted to refine the system. The efforts to

---

1 Willey & Phillips 1958, 18–24.

clarify the various terms (e.g., what exactly constitutes a site?) are on-going, and are relevant to the study of the Byzantine past.

While there has been considerable scholarship concerning the use of space in Byzantine art, architecture, urban layout, and religion, the topographic or spatial dimension has received less attention at the level of secondary or tertiary settlements, both in terms of their internal organization and the relationship between sites. A key goal of archaeological survey is to determine the patterning of human dispersal over a given terrain. Since essentially all survey work is multi-period by default, such research provides a comparative database to explore how settlement patterns have evolved in a region over time. In this way, we can track the evolution of settlement dispersal and land use. Data on Byzantine settlement benefits our understanding of spatial logistics by placing it in a framework that includes prehistoric and other historic periods, allowing us to assess the factors that make for both settlement stability and variation. Byzantine occupants of the Mediterranean countryside, no less than the people before and after them, conceived of their surroundings in particular ways that are reflected in where they positioned themselves and what they did in those locations. The material record of survey thus provides an avenue to explore how Byzantine people thought about, exploited, and attempted to manipulate their environment. We can think of this work as an effort to identify a spatial ecology of the past. Among the projects over the past several decades that have carefully investigated Late Antique, Byzantine, and post-medieval settlement systems as part of all-period surveys are the Ancient Cities of Boeotia Project,[2] the Eastern Korinthia Archaeological Project,[3] and the Western Argolid Regional Project[4] in Greece, and the Pyla-*Koutsopetria* Archaeological Project,[5] and the Settled and Sacred Landscapes of Cyprus Project[6] in Cyprus. These projects focus on landscape as a key unit of analysis.

The landscape concept has become a key means by which archaeologists try to make sense of the complex interactions between humans and their surroundings.[7] The approach suggests that people subdivided their living space along a series of dimensions that largely overlapped. The physical attributes of a region along with its climate form the baseline. These elements include the terrain on which people build structures, from which they extract food, and

---

2 Bintliff et al. 2004; Vionis 2008, 2017.
3 Tartaron et al. 2006; Pettegrew 2007.
4 Caraher et al. 2020.
5 Caraher et al. 2014.
6 Papantoniou & Vionis 2017.
7 Ashmore & Knapp 1999; Athanassopoulos & Wandsnider 2004a.

over which they move; the geological and geomorphological features (bedrock, soils, and hydrological system) are constituent parts of the terrain and provide the raw materials for construction, and the matrix for foraging and agricultural subsistence patterns. The economic landscape can also encompass the location of raw materials for tools (e.g., chert, obsidian, metal ores); it may develop into an industrial landscape as pyro-technologies develop through the extraction of ores and their transformation into metals through the burning of various organic or fossil fuels (e.g., wood, charcoal, coal). Transportation routes and built features that facilitate trade alter the physical terrain in the form of roads, paths, and harbours, which form a dynamic part of the landscape. Shrines and sanctuaries can form part of the religious landscape that may relate to a mortuary landscape with designated locations for disposal of the dead. Borders, often flexible and movable, mark the political landscape; these may be in the form of physical features such as rivers or mountains, but can also be more arbitrary demarcations. All of these factors together form the categories that people create to impose a sense of order and meaning on their surroundings. Determining the intersite and intrasite spatial relationships reflected in the material record is a key focus of archaeological research of all periods. To do so requires an understanding of landscape taphonomy, which Athanassopoulos and Wandsnider argue "focuses on the evolution of the landscape as it participates in necessarily interlinked cultural and natural processes."[8] The particular spatial structure of Byzantine settlements/sites is part of the ongoing process of human adaptation to the environment, and thus reveals some commonalities that crosscut time.

1 Theoretical Perspective

The present work employs several key concepts in examining how the residents of the Malloura Valley in central Cyprus interacted with their neighbours and people outside the locale. Collectively, the notions are part of world-systems theory, today more commonly referred to as world-systems analysis (WSA).[9] World-systems theory originated some 50 years ago in the work of scholars concerned with the economic, political, and social mechanisms that have created deep linkages between modern states. Immanuel Wallerstein provided some of the key concepts and structure through his analysis of how

---

8 Athanassopoulos & Wandsnider 2004b, 10.
9 See Hall et al. 2011.

the capitalist system came to exist, beginning in the sixteenth century.[10] His approach suggested a tripartite system with cores (primarily European states) extracting raw materials from peripheries in an exploitative fashion. Semi-peripheries were societies that could mediate between the other two, providing access to resources and labour (e.g., slaves). A. G. Frank contributed important elements to this formulation, noting that cores practiced the "development of underdevelopment" as they exploited the peripheries in a manner that perpetuated their inferior status.[11] One process that has received substantial attention recently is globalization, the process by which linkages are created between groups so that certain elements become universal.[12] In common parlance, this is discussed in economic terms, but we should not ignore the political and social implications. What the current discussion fails to understand is that globalization is not just a phenomenon of the modern world; it extends back minimally to the origins of civilization, and probably much earlier.[13] Another key concept is that of incorporation, which refers to the process by which certain areas identified as cores (with complex political, economic, and military institutions) engulf other groups referred to as peripheries (usually with simpler, less hierarchical institutions), pulling the latter into a network of interconnected societies in a subservient status. While this original approach by Wallerstein fit the situation of early capitalism,[14] I suggest that ancient and medieval states lacked the apparatus to dominate outsiders for long periods of time.

I argue that WSA represents the type of approach we need in archaeology and history. That is, a generalizing perspective that does two things. First, it allows us to speak in broad terms. By stressing certain commonalities among cultures over space and through time, WSA is one approach that permits, in fact demands, comparison. While individual historical trajectories are certainly important, I fear that various disciplines have fallen into a historical particularism that blinds us to features that pervade all societies. I would argue that WSA can be a basis for a science of culture along the lines advocated by Leslie White and Marvin Harris.[15] It is through comparison that we can legitimately draw lessons from the past to understand and act intelligently in the present and future. Second, as the label states, WSA espouses a systemic approach to

10   Wallerstein 1974.
11   Frank 1966.
12   Gills &Thompson 2006.
13   Chase-Dunn & Hall 1997; Jennings 2011.
14   Wallerstein 1974.
15   White 1943 and 1949; Harris 1979.

societal and intersocietal interaction. As an anthropologist, I find appealing the holistic emphasis in a systems approach. Even internally, the various components of a society do not stand in isolation. Political, economic, social, and religious institutions regularly intersect in a web of mutual activity that reinforces all of the components.

Such a holistic approach does not necessarily obscure the role of individuals, as some have argued. Individuals and groups or institutions operate in a cultural context in which there is a dynamic series of dyadic relationships.[16] WSA forces us to identify linkages beyond the local, and in this way explore globalization from a long-term chronological perspective as a phenomenon that has characterized many cultures at different times, not just recently. Justin Jennings argues for such an evaluation by looking at the ways in which cultures in three different periods and geographical regions (Uruk Mesopotamia; Mississippian culture in late prehistoric North America; Huari Empire of South America) developed extensive external contacts through trade and other means.[17] He notes that the cultural sequences worked out by archaeologists and historians demonstrate a cyclical pattern in which there are what he calls "surges of interaction" followed by collapse and decentralization. Cities played an important role with impacts on the long-distance movement of people, goods, and ideas in a cascading effect that simultaneously expanded the system and accelerated the interactions between urban dwellers, people in the hinterland, and those from more distant regions. The cycling of such expansion and contraction seems an apt way to think about events during the Byzantine period on Cyprus. Archaeological survey, with its regional focus, provides the means to examine the shifting tides of such globalization on sites and the use of space. Settlements expand and contract, shift the location of specific features, acquire goods locally or through long-distance trade networks, thus revealing the ebb and flow of the forces that constitute globalization. Acculturation occurs as different groups interact, often in the form of trade, both local and interregional. From Late Antiquity through the Byzantine and into the late medieval periods, trade at these various levels persisted, as indicated by various shipwrecks among other evidence,[18] and linked Cyprus to the neighbouring mainland and more distant locales.

16   See Frederik Barth (1959) on the Swat Pathans.
17   Jennings 2011.
18   Bass & van Doorninck 1982.

2 The Athienou Archaeological Project on Cyprus

The geographic region on which I have focused my research over the past three decades is the Eastern Mediterranean, with a particular emphasis on Greece and Cyprus. In order to gain a comprehensive understanding of the complex mosaic of life in the environs of Athienou, Cyprus, the Athienou Archaeological Project (AAP) from the outset adopted an interdisciplinary approach (Figure 11.1). Excavation has concentrated on the site of Athienou-*Malloura*, and archaeological survey has examined the settlement distribution in a project area of 20 km² around *Malloura*.[19] In addition, project personnel also examine aspects of both ancient and modern life in the immediate vicinity of Athienou itself; these efforts have included study of traditional agricultural practices,[20] and integration of the local economy into national and international market systems.[21] The goal is to expand our understanding of human occupation in the region up to and including the present, and to provide analogues for the ancient and medieval past.

Methodologically, the data with which I deal comes largely from survey. Because of its inherent emphasis on regions, survey complements WSA well. Taken together, survey and excavation can help us address some of those key questions about how people interacted across broad areas. In the present study I discuss some of the results from the AAP that pertain to the late Medieval to Modern periods.

The specific goal of this chapter is to emphasize the role of peripheries as locations where cultural contact is often at its most intense.[22] These margins afford opportunities for direct interaction between indigenous people and the members of cores who seek various raw materials, and often markets for their industrial products. In one case study, I examined the fur trade frontier of North America where native Indian groups provided animal pelts, especially beaver, in exchange for a range of goods, including firearms, a range of metal objects (e.g., cooking pots, knives, hatchets), blankets, beads, and other items manufactured in European factories.[23] Major trade centres emerged in various places visited by Europeans, creating a cosmopolitan mix. Thus, peripheries can be zones of considerable ferment where people encounter new practices, ideologies, and material culture. Innovation in all of these facets is evident in

---

19 Kardulias & Yerkes 2004 and 2011.
20 Kardulias 2008; Kardulias & Yerkes 1996.
21 Kardulias 2007.
22 Hall 2001.
23 Kardulias 1990.

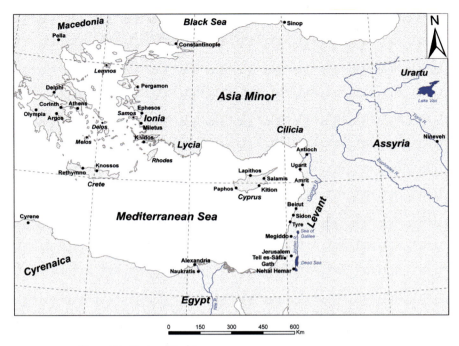

FIGURE 11.1 Map of the Eastern Mediterranean
© DAVID MASSEY; AAP ARCHIVES

these areas as people adopt and modify what they encounter. The amalgamation of items from different societies is the direct result of their availability, but equally important is the openness of people on the margins to innovation. The effect of such cultural entrepreneurs is to create a basis for reformulation of social identity. Critical to this process is negotiation, which may lead a group to radically alter some essential elements of its lifestyle, such as subsistence, settlement location, and house structure.

In some periods, change took place at times because new elements were introduced by direct contact between groups. For example, metal artifacts obtained from Europeans at major trade fairs radically altered the material culture of Native American groups beginning in the sixteenth century.[24] However, the contact zone could also be a thick buffer through which items travelled well before groups actually faced each other. In North America, European glass beads and metal artifacts reached deep into the interior before the indigenous

---

24   Kardulias 1990.

people in those regions ever encountered the English, French, or Dutch who manufactured these items in their home countries and transported them to the New World. In many instances, other native groups acted as the middlemen connecting the groups on either side, often carefully guarding access to the interior and its resources.

A similar series of trade relations almost certainly existed in the ancient and medieval Mediterranean;[25] Gunder Frank argues that an extensive network existed as early as the Bronze Age.[26] In the prehistoric period, the copper that was mined and smelted on Cyprus by native workers found its way to many sites in the eastern, and as far as the central Mediterranean through a trade network that involved transport ships (e.g., the Ulu Burun wreck),[27] local merchants, and other personnel.[28] Similarly, in the medieval/Byzantine period, it is likely that pottery found in domestic settings, particularly elaborate fine wares, made its way to the AAP study area in the Malloura Valley by means of a series of intermediaries who connected the production sites in Anatolia or elsewhere on Cyprus with those who utilized these items in the southern Mesaoria. Colin Renfrew has described a number of exchange systems, including down-the-line trade and entrepots, in which intermediaries were essential components.[29] Several of the trade systems he discusses would be appropriate for explaining the nature of exchange in the Eastern Mediterranean during the Medieval and Early Modern periods. In addition, the great caravan routes that terminated at Aleppo, Cairo, and other cities contributed to the prosperity of the merchants in the region. The Venetians facilitated the system of international trade by establishing trading outposts in many cities,[30] including on Cyprus. Horden and Purcell provide another take on the nature of the Mediterranean with their emphasis on several factors.[31] Rather than consider the basin as having a unified culture, they argue it is a collection of micro-regions that are not constant over time. In addition, the uncertainty introduced by variable weather and tectonics offers both problems and opportunities, which in turn influenced the development of diversified economic strategies to spread out risk, as is evident in the traditional multi-cropping in several local niches to provide options in the case of catastrophic failure of any

---

25   LaBianca & Scham 2006.
26   Frank 1993.
27   Pulak 1998.
28   Knapp & Cherry 1994.
29   Renfrew 1975.
30   Braudel 1966, 548–49.
31   Horden & Purcell 2000.

one food source. Connectivity is another key feature of the area, made possible by sea travel along a highly dissected coastline that offers multiple landing points where a string of exchanges can occur. More recently, Broodbank has suggested more overtly the element of agency, stating

> [...] that the ancient Mediterranean as a human world was not a given, but came into being as a consequence of actions over time, that in this sense it was long in the process of becoming. If such 'mediterraneanization' was therefore a dynamic process, it necessarily involved change, often conflictual, and so produced winners and losers.[32]

At some level, each of these approaches suggests that the sea acts as a major route for communication and the transporting of goods and people, while at the same time composed of somewhat isolated pockets that impose certain limitations to connectivity and foster variable adaptations to local conditions.

The feature of WSA that is of greatest interest in the present study is incorporation, by which is meant the process of integrating the triad of cores, peripheries, and semi-peripheries. As originally defined by Wallerstein, incorporation involved the exploitation of peripheries by cores, where industries with specialized division of labour and other complex economic and political structures transformed the raw materials derived from the former.[33] This process siphoned resources from the margins and accumulated wealth in the cores. The expansion of European influence through exploration and colonization that defines the emergence of the modern world created many contact zones where incorporation took place. It is in these contact zones that cultural exchange occurred. Negotiation played a major role in the dynamic interchange along these frontiers. In the initial stages of incorporation, marginal areas have the ability to retain a degree of autonomy in their relations with intrusive cores through a process that I have called negotiated peripherality, defined as "the willingness and ability of individuals in peripheries to determine the conditions under which they will engage in trade, ceremonial exchange, intermarriage, adoption of outside religious and political ideologies, etc. with representatives of expanding states".[34]

Peripheries exhibit variation. In general, they tend to have decentralized political and economic systems, especially when compared to core regions. Furthermore, there are several types of peripheries. One type is an extraction

---

32 Broodbank 2013, 53.
33 Wallerstein 1974.
34 Kardulias 2007, 55.

zone that supplies raw materials to core states. Second, a fully incorporated periphery will have evidence of foreign installations that indicate the incursion of a core state, complete with administrative structures and central storage facilities. A third type is the contested periphery between competing cores.[35] Some areas are coveted by cores because of raw resources they possess, while others may provide access to routes that facilitate trade and communication. Cyprus offered both features, and thus was often the object of imperial ambitions. Its proximity to southwest Asia led to numerous mainland influences passing to the island, and also made it a target of contention. For example, in the medieval period, Cyprus experienced control by the Byzantine Empire, the western Lusignan dynasty, the Venetians, and the Ottoman Empire, ending in the nineteenth century as a British colony. Another important point is that peripheries are not permanent fixtures; they move back and forth over time, in tune with the expansion and contraction of world-systems, a process that Christopher Chase-Dunn and Thomas Hall refer to as pulsation.[36] The multiple foreign powers that occupied the island at various times reflect this oscillation. For example, the Venetian control of Cyprus gave way to the expanding Ottoman Empire in 1570–1572, as it did also somewhat later in the Aegean at places such as Crete. Beihammer (this volume) provides a detailed discussion of the fluctuating nature of the boundaries between the regions controlled by the Byzantines and Seljuk Turks in western Anatolia over a period of several centuries. His argument that the "entire region from Bithynia and Phrygia down to Lycia and Caria turned into a contested zone of border warfare, nomadic migratory movements, and population displacements" parallels the development of Cyprus as such a zone, with the added dimension of Frankish and Venetian intrusion and control in the late medieval period. For the earlier era, Rautman has noted the transition of Cyprus from "a prosperous Late Roman province to an unstable frontier territory" took place over a relatively short period of several generations in the seventh century. Arab attacks on the coastal cities had an impact on the rural interior, where settlements declined or moved to less accessible sectors.[37]

Another important issue is the strength of incorporation. This varies along a continuum from weak to strong. At the weak end, peripheries have great latitude in selecting the degree of interaction (i.e., maximum ability to negotiate), while at the strong end are the fully incorporated peripheries mentioned above in which the core dictates the conditions of interaction. As the degree of

---

35   Allen 1997.
36   Chase-Dunn & Hall 1997.
37   Rautman 2003, 259, 262.

incorporation increases, the ability of the periphery to negotiate declines; the contact zone becomes less interactive in some ways.

The Eastern Mediterranean provides an excellent venue to examine the nature of contact zones. Abundant written documents complement a rich material record, at least for some periods. Many scholars have discussed aspects of trade and connections in the region. The efforts have included the large-scale diffusionist model of Gordon Childe, later countered by Colin Renfrew, whose *The Emergence of Civilisation* looked to internal forces as most telling in the development of early Aegean states.[38] I believe that WSA permits a more nuanced explanation of intersocietal contacts in the region over time. For the Bronze Age Aegean, I have suggested that connections existed on three tiers: local, regional, and international.[39] The materials exchanged within and between the different units varied, with low to medium value bulk goods (e.g., obsidian for tool production)[40] concentrated in the internal and intermediate levels, and high value preciosities (and perhaps some bulk goods such as timber) the focus of trade between the Aegean and the Near East, including Egypt.

The world-systems model is also useful for explaining interactions in other periods. Alan Greaves skillfully adapts some important world-systems concepts to the study of Ionia in the Archaic period (ca. eighth to fifth centuries BC), a time of significant innovations in material culture, intellectual pursuits (philosophy and science in particular), and sociopolitical structure throughout the Aegean world.[41] Greaves makes subtle use of WSA, identifying the network types[42] that correspond with various phases: information network with pre-colonization, prestige goods network with *emporion* (trading post), political-military network with *apoikia* (settlement), and bulk goods network with full assimilation (rarely if ever happened in antiquity).

My work in Cyprus has involved survey and excavation in a valley near the centre of the island.[43] The survey identified 31 sites, ranging in date from Aceramic Neolithic to Early Modern. Athienou-*Malloura* (Site 1) in the centre of the Malloura Valley contains the most evidence for occupation/site use in the project area (Figure 11.2). It was the location of a rural sanctuary from the Archaic through Early Roman periods, followed by a farming village (Early Roman to Early Byzantine), a hiatus in occupation of three centuries, and a

---

38   Childe 1957; Renfrew 1972.
39   Kardulias 1999a.
40   Kardulias 1999b; Parkinson & Cherry 2003.
41   Greaves 2010.
42   Hall 2006.
43   Kardulias & Yerkes 2004; Toumazou et al. 2011.

revived settlement in Frankish through Ottoman times. A number of tombs and small sites are scattered elsewhere in the valley. The nature of negotiation, and thus the degree of incorporation, varied over time in this zone. Initially, the Malloura Valley was exploited by Neolithic farmers only as a source of chert for the production of basic tools necessary for a wide range of tasks. A series of hills running north to south that form the western boundary of the valley contain significant outcrops of good quality chert that was easily accessible on the surface. Prehistoric inhabitants of the region shaped cores and a few other basic tools at several quarry locations, but transported those items to locations outside the valley since we have no evidence of Neolithic settlements. The material does fit the general style found at other Neolithic sites to the west and south. Cyprus developed its own unique forms in various things from architecture to stone tool assemblages in this early period, distinguishing it from the well-known Neolithic cultures of the Levant and Asia Minor, despite the fact that the early farmers clearly migrated from the mainland as attested by the range of domesticated plants and animals on the island of mainland origin. It seems the people of the Malloura Valley and surrounding regions, and to a significant extent the whole island, modified portions of the Neolithic lifestyle to fit their particular interests.

Later in time, the process of incorporation involved differential acquisition and display of religious symbolism by elites and shifts in agricultural strategies by farmers to take advantage of certain opportunities. Material from a religious sanctuary and some tombs in the centre of the Malloura Valley dating to the Archaic period provide a clear indication of culture contact that is both insular and international in nature, especially noticeable in artistic motifs that demonstrate connections with the Phoenician Levant, Pharaonic Egypt, and the Hellenized Aegean. This connection is perhaps most clearly seen in a number of ceramic and stone figurines retrieved from the Classical and Hellenistic levels in a religious sanctuary at *Malloura*. These items include representations of Astarte, Zeus Ammon, and Pan, made of local materials, thus demonstrating a significant level of stimulus diffusion. The valley residents adopted certain elements from each area, creating a unique mixture of features that reflects the cultural variability available at such contact zones. In other periods, major empires intruded on Cyprus, and incorporation took on a more overtly exploitative form. Cyprus fits well the definition of a contested periphery under these conditions. Because of its strategic position close to the Levant and Anatolia and its extensive coastline, the island offered an excellent location for intermediate stops along sea trade routes, making it a tempting target of ancient, medieval, and modern empires. In such times, negotiation could take the form of resistance; for example, despite the long periods of foreign domination of

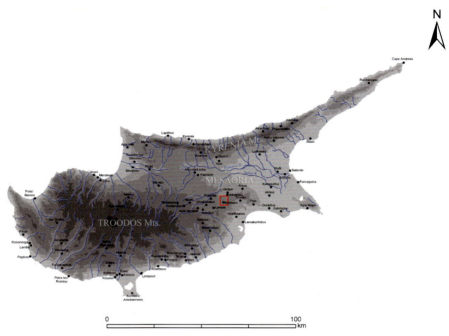

FIGURE 11.2　Map of Cyprus showing location of Athienou Archaeological Project survey area in red rectangle
© DAVID MASSEY; AAP ARCHIVES

the central political system by the Venetians, Franks, Ottomans, and British, Cypriots largely retained their allegiance to Orthodox Christianity as a key element of national identity, while adopting certain features of the hegemonic culture, from a variety of Turkish words to the English practice of driving on the left side of the road.

The role that islands such as Cyprus play in major events of a period should not be overlooked. In the ancient and medieval periods, movement by ship, while quite common, was still a potentially perilous exercise. Islands provided way stations as beacons to mark locations, offered safe harbours during storms, resupplied with fresh water and food, and sold or traded goods brought from other regions, as well as loading new commodities for commerce further along the line of travel. Fernand Braudel opines that "The events of history often lead to the islands. Perhaps it would be more accurate to say that they make use of them".[44] For Cyprus, this meant incorporation into the Roman Empire in the

---

44　Braudel 1966, 154.

late first century BC, as clearly seen at major sites such as Paphos and Kourion, but also reflected in the rural hinterland. In our project area, this transition is most clear at Athienou-*Malloura* where a village was established to the east of the sanctuary where there was no earlier settlement. Excavations revealed several houses with substantial walls ca. 1m in thickness, containing an array of ceramic wares. The survey collected many Roman ceramics both near these structures and across a broad swath of the eastern and northern part of the site. Chronologically, the diagnostic fine wares from these investigations cover a span of some 600 years and include Cypriot Red Slip (imitating imported forms—an interesting indication of the degree to which artifact styles were copied to facilitate local needs and support indigenous production that one might call an example of ancient glocalization). However, the ceramic assemblage also includes Phocaean Red Slip Ware from Asia Minor, and African Red Slip Ware, although in a limited range of forms.[45] The Late Roman period in particular is also represented by isolated collections of such material elsewhere in the Malloura Valley that probably indicate the locations of individual farmsteads. The ceramic evidence thus indicates that Athienou-*Malloura* and its satellite small sites in a rural backwater were still linked to the broader Roman commercial system up through the seventh century AD, clear evidence that incorporation extended beyond the major coastal centres. On the coast south of our project area and east of Larnaka, the Pyla-Koutsopetria Archaeological Survey retrieved substantial quantities of Late Roman Phocaean Ware and African Red Slip at and around the silted-in ancient harbour, leading the team to argue that the site enjoyed more intensive links to the production centres in western Anatolia and North Africa than major cities in western Cyprus despite the latter sites being closer to the sources of the ceramics.[46]

As noted above, the Malloura Valley seems to have been devoid of permanent settlements from the late seventh through the middle of the tenth century AD, and perhaps as late as the twelfth century. On Cyprus, the phase AD 647–965 is usually identified with the Arab Raids, and it has been suggested that residents abandoned many sites to seek refuge in more protected areas. Whatever the reasons may have been for this decline in occupation in the valley, it is reflected in site data and ceramic evidence in other parts of Cyprus as well.[47] What this period may reflect is one of those periods of oscillation in a world-system that can lead to the reorientation of incorporation as new players come on the scene. As mentioned above, Arab attacks on major coastal

---

45   Moore & Gregory 2011, 207.
46   Caraher, Moore & Pettegrew 2014, 295.
47   Gregory 2003, 283–84.

cities (Amathous, Constantia/Salamis, Lapithos, Paphos, Soloi) led to a reorientation of settlement in the interior of the island, as well as enhanced urban fortifications.[48]

The fluctuating fortunes of the Byzantine state throughout much of the medieval period meant that Cyprus retained its status as a contested periphery. In the latter half of the first millennium AD, the empire confronted the advances of Arab forces. From the late eleventh to the end of the thirteenth century, the Crusades initiated by western Europeans in an effort to wrest control of the Holy Land from Islamic rule introduced a new set of challenges. Cyprus was drawn directly into these clashes when Richard I defeated Isaac I Komnenos and took possession of the island in 1191, subsequently ceded it to the Knights Templar, from whom Guy de Lusignan bought it and established there a Frankish dynasty that lasted until the fifteenth century.[49] Venice controlled the island from 1473 until they were ousted by the Ottomans in 1571. Despite this turbulent political history, Cyprus did enjoy a level of prosperity in the Frankish period, with Famagusta renowned for its wealth, and the countryside providing an abundant agricultural bounty. In her discussion of the concept of insularity, Veikou makes the case for the complex relationship of regions on Cyprus clear:

> Being on the boundaries of the Eastern Mediterranean and at times changing hands between the Byzantines, the Arabs, the Franks and the Venetians, it [Cyprus] hosted not only violence and separation but also ethnic contacts, cultural interpenetration and a remarkable flexibility of adjustment to political change with concurrent preservation of internal stability and economic sustainability.[50]

The Frankish and Venetian periods represented in excavation and survey material from *Malloura* indicate a strong degree of incorporation into the respective world-systems of the western powers. For Cyprus as a whole, the historical documents demonstrate how western knights thoroughly dominated the indigenous rulers and then pursued certain economic interests by turning many areas to the production of sugar cane, which Braudel states originally came to Cyprus from Egypt in the tenth century.[51] Archaeological work has investigated the Cypriot sugar industry that was concentrated in the southwestern part of

---

48   Rautman 2003, 260; Stewart 2013.
49   Hill 1940, 22, 35–7; Wallace and Orphanides 2005, 45–7.
50   Veikou 2015, 362.
51   Braudel 1966, 154.

FIGURE 11.3   Late medieval Frankish sugar mill at Kolossi Castle, Cyprus
AUTHOR'S COPYRIGHT

the island. The evidence from Kouklia, Kolossi, and Episkopi includes the structures where the cane was processed, with the milling done with both water and animal power in the Frankish and Venetian periods.[52] Cyprus remained an important source of sugar for Europe until the development of the massive sugar plantations on Caribbean islands took over the market. While we have found no evidence of sugar production in the Malloura Valley, there are a significant number of large millstones that reflect agricultural abundance that may have exceeded local needs (Figure 11.3). In addition, excavation revealed a house from the Venetian period with an elabourately paved floor, indicating a level of affluence in this rural setting.

Braudel also notes that the Lusignan dynasty on the island was important in the spread of silkworms and elaborate garments made of the fine thread they produced to western Europe; the transmission also included clothing styles that had been fashionable during the T'ang dynasty in China centuries earlier.[53] The Malloura Valley witnessed a significant resurgence of occupation

---

52   von Wartburg 2001; Jones 2016, 49–54.
53   Braudel 1966, 154.

during these periods after a decline in the seventh through tenth centuries also noted in other parts of Cyprus, as indicated above. The settlement at Athienou-*Malloura* contains a number of houses dated to the twelfth to sixteenth centuries. At least one is built directly over the remains of a Late Roman house, but others indicate the settlement expanded to the west and south, away from the areas of major residence in the first half of the first millennium AD.[54] Excavation in the western half of the settlement revealed the foundations of an unusual structure with a series of narrow parallel stone walls that may have supported a wooden floor (Figure 11.4). The building may have served as a granary, with the floor raised above ground level in order to prevent moisture from damaging the stored crop. The surface survey collected a substantial amount of Late Medieval sgrafitto glazed fine ware and various coarse pottery, both at *Malloura,* especially in the area around this structure, and in the project area as a whole. This late medieval pottery (n=470) is second in quantity only to Roman material (n=487) throughout the project area; the former is found at eight of the 31 sites identified during the survey.[55]

In this period, as in several previous ones, political incorporation preceded and facilitated economic incorporation. Under the Venetians, Cyprus became an entrepôt, a major base for their commercial empire. These efforts filtered into the hinterland at Malloura in the form of a resurgent village. Clearly, though, the ancient pattern of nucleated settlement remained in place. Once again, *Malloura* became one local node in an international system that produced substantial wealth in the village. The amount of grain processing represented by the number of large millstones suggests production at a level capable of providing a surplus that may have subsidized the purchase of fine ceramics for domestic and funerary uses. Near the centre of the late medieval/Venetian settlement at *Malloura*, we have excavated several burials from the period with sgraffito bowls placed between the legs of individuals laid out in extended fashion with the head facing east (Figure 11.5). Such fine wares have also been found in several houses from this period and on the surface both within the confines of the settlement and scattered intermittently throughout the valley. Since we have no evidence for pottery production on site, all of the ceramics were imported from at least another part of the island or further afield. The small number of early medieval sherds derive from the Aegean or Asia Minor, while the late medieval/Frankish assemblage was almost exclusively Cypriot

---

54 Toumazou & Counts 2011, 81–84.
55 Moore & Gregory 2011, 204, 208–9.

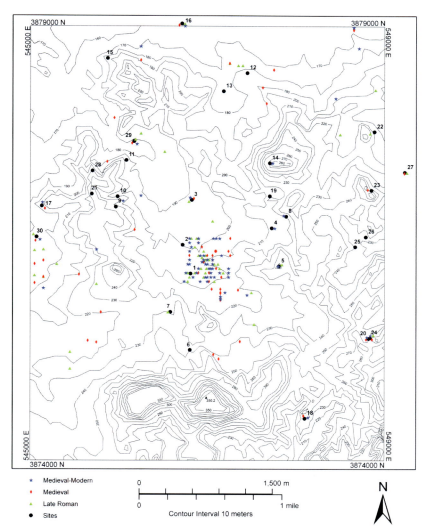

FIGURE 11.4 Map of AAP survey area showing locations of sites and distribution of pottery by period
© AAP ARCHIVES

in manufacture with just a handful of imports. The Venetian to early Ottoman period witnessed a significant rise in imports, in particular from Italy.[56]

---

56   Moore & Gregory 2011, 208–9.

FIGURE 11.5   Millstone at Athienou-*Malloura*
© AAP ARCHIVES

We have identified as lookout posts four sites from the Roman and later periods; we believe these reflect the continuing status of Cyprus and the Malloura Valley as a contested periphery. Located on prominent hills that border the valley on several sides, the locations along the southern edge offer unimpeded views to the coast near Larnaka, an important port from antiquity to the modern era; from several of the hill sites on the northern margin one can see all the way across the flat Mesaoria to the Kyrenia Range. In part, these sites may reflect the clash of imperial giants (e.g., Venetians vs. Ottomans), and probably also the concern with raids by pirates or corsairs at various times. While the valley probably never offered the kind of concentrated wealth found in urban centres, its location on the route between the port of Larnaka and the major city of Nicosia in the centre of the island would have placed its residents and their agricultural produce at risk from marauders. Pirates both raided settlements on the island, and also set up bases there, in particular under the Venetians.[57]

---

57   Jennings 1993, 345–46.

The decline of *Malloura* (Site 1) and the development of the village of Petrophani[58] at the northern end of the valley were probably linked events, especially in the past 125 years. The scatter of isolated farmsteads and lithic workshops from the modern period represent local management of resources and production of certain agricultural implements, such as threshing sledges,[59] within the context of a truly global world-system. Cypriot products of all types, including olives, oil, carobs, and today milk and cheese, moved from small villages to regional centres, and then into overseas markets via the British imperial system. The town of Athienou grew into a local market centre that serviced both Greek and Turkish hamlets, such as Petrophani, and we suspect Malloura lost its residents to the emerging town. The map prepared by Kitchener in the early 1880s after the British acquired Cyprus shows Malloura, with the parenthetical description of "ruins."[60] The village that had been founded in the Early Roman period, was abandoned in the late seventh century, and revived in the twelfth, had been deserted again; today, no structural evidence of those remains exists above ground. The culmination of many of these processes came in the 1970s when Cyprus, ever the contested periphery, was invaded by Turkish forces. The people of Athienou who lost access to their farmland north of the town turned to the former Turkish-held land in the Malloura Valley and converted large tracts of land to barley production. The grain feeds large herds of milk cattle that, along with large herds of sheep and goats, have made the region one of the most productive dairy areas in that part of the Mediterranean. The people now market milk and cheese throughout Cyprus and the Levant; exported Athienou halloumi can even be purchased at stores in Columbus, Ohio. The people of the Malloura Valley rethought the nature of their agricultural and herding pursuits and modified their use of the landscape accordingly. Modern machinery has made it possible to transform slopes comprised of soft limestone into planted fields by breaking up the bedrock, and large combines make it possible to harvest the extensive fields of barley that have taken the place of a more diverse agricultural regime over the past 50 years. Despite the fractious political situation, the bulk-goods network has become a key component of the economic system. Here is yet another example of the people of the Athienou/Malloura region taking an active part in defining their destiny and reshaping their landscape.

∙ ∙ ∙

58   Yerkes 2011.
59   Kardulias & Yerkes 1996.
60   Kitchener 1885.

Underlying all archaeological interpretations either explicitly or implicitly is an assumed set of similarities in the items under study that crosscut time and space. Otherwise, we are left with describing unique objects with little hope of making any sense of the data. To say anything meaningful about the past material record, generalization, which is based on such comparisons, is a central concern. In turn, generalizing models, such as world-systems analysis, provide the opportunity to explore the past in ways that can make sense in the present. The world-systems approach forces us to view the dynamic interaction of societies over time as played out over an evolving landscape.

The AAP has examined these social forces as they relate to a peripheral area in the central part of Cyprus from antiquity through the medieval and into early modern times. Our investigations reveal that even rural hinterlands participated actively in local, regional, and international networks that brought new products, ideas, and people even to relatively isolated portions of the island. In this process, residents defined and redefined space to meet the circumstances they confronted, from where they placed their houses, to the internal layout of the structures, and the orientation of bodies in cemeteries (Figures. 11.6 and 11.7).

In each of these instances, people had to reimagine the local setting and their place within it. The Late Medieval and Early Modern periods seem to have been particularly active in this respect. As control of Cyprus changed hands from Byzantium to the Franks, then the Venetians, and finally the Ottomans, residents of the Malloura Valley adapted by altering utilization of their space, which almost certainly affected community structure; the social network in the village in turn probably influenced the placement of buildings and their internal designs, among other aspects of settlement organization. As their modern descendants do, the medieval people of the region probably adhered to a mental geography that conceived of the landscape as a place to be valued both for its extant features and its future potential.[61]

---

[61] The work of the AAP has been undertaken through permits from the Department of Antiquities, Republic of Cyprus. I thank Ellie Howell, Archaeology Labouratory Research Assistant at the College of Wooster, for help with formatting the manuscript. My AAP colleagues and I are grateful to the people of Athienou who have provided immense support to our efforts since the beginning of the project in 1990.

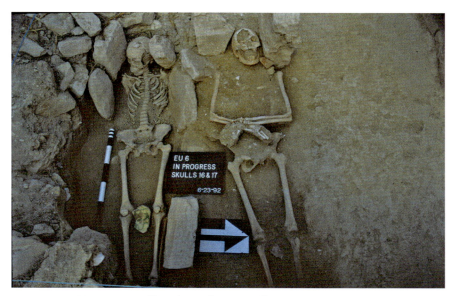

FIGURE 11.6   Venetian period burials at Athienou-*Malloura*
© AAP ARCHIVES

FIGURE 11.7   Cattle in pen in AAP project area
AUTHOR'S COPYRIGHT

Bibliography

Secondary Sources

Allen, M. 1997. "Contested Peripheries: Philistia in the Neo-Assyrian World-System" Unpublished PhD diss., UCLA.

Ashmore, W. & A. B. Knapp 1999. *Archaeologies of Landscape: Contemporary Perspectives*. Malden, MA.

Athanassopoulos, E. & L. Wandsnider (eds) 2004a. *Mediterranean Archaeological Landscapes: Current Issues*. Philadelphia.

Athanassopoulos, E. & L. Wandsnider 2004b. "Mediterranean Landscape Archaeology Past and Present", in Athanassopoulos & Wandsnider (eds) 2004, 1–13.

Barth, F. 1959. *Political Leadership among Swat Pathans*. London.

Bass, G. F. & F. H. van Doorninck, Jr. 1982. *Yassı Ada 1: A Seventh-Century Byzantine Shipwreck*. College Station, Texas.

Bintliff, J., E. Farinetti, K. Sbonias, K. Sarri, V. Stissi, J. Poblome, A. Ceulemans, K. De Craen, A. K. Vionis, B. Music, D. Kramberger, & B. Slapsak 2004. "The Tanagra Project: Investigations at an Ancient Boeotian City and in its Countryside (2000–2002)", *Bulletin de Correspondance Hellénique* 128 (2.1), 541–606.

Braudel, F. 1966. *The Mediterranean and the Mediterranean World in the Age of Philip II*, 2nd rev. ed. New York.

Broodbank, C. 2013. *The Making of the Middle Sea*. Oxford.

Caraher, W., R. S. Moore & D. K. Pettegrew 2014. *Pyla-Koutsopetria I. Archaeological Survey of an Ancient Coastal Town*. Boston.

Caraher, W., L. Hall & R. S. Moore (eds) 2008. *Archaeology and History in Roman, Medieval and Post-Medieval Greece: Studies on Method and Meaning in Honor of Timothy E. Gregory*. Aldershot.

Caraher, W., S. Gallimore, D. Nakassis & S. A. James 2020. "Survey and the 7th century in the Western Argolid", *Journal of Greek Archaeology* 5, 377–405.

Chase-Dunn, C. & T. D. Hall 1997. *Rise and Demise: Comparing World-Systems*. Boulder, CO.

Childe, V. G. 1957. *New Light on the Most Ancient East*. New York.

Frank, A. G. 1993. "Bronze Age World System Cycles", *Current Anthropology* 34, 383–429.

Frank, A. G. 1966. "The Development of Underdevelopment", *Monthly Review* Sept, 17–31.

Gills, B. K. & W. R. Thompson (eds) 2006. *Globalization and Global History*. London.

Given, M. & A. B. Knapp (eds) 2003. *The Sydney Cyprus Survey Project. Social Approaches to Regional Archaeological Survey*. Los Angeles.

Greaves, A. M. 2010. *The Land of Ionia. Society and Economy in the Archaic Period*. Malden, MA.

Gregory, T. E. 2003. "The Byzantine Problem", in Given & Knapp (eds) 2003, 283–4.

Hall, T. D. 2001. "Using Comparative Frontiers to Explore World-Systems Analysis in International Relations", *International Studies Perspectives* 2, 252–68.

Hall, T. D. 2006. "[Re]periphalization, [Re]incorporation, Frontiers and Non-State Societies", in Gills & Thompson (eds) 2006, 96–113.

Hall, T. D., P. N. Kardulias & C. Chase-Dunn 2011. "World-Systems Analysis and Archaeology: Continuing the Dialogue", *Journal of Archaeological Research* 19, 233–79.

Harris, M. 1979. *Cultural Materialism: The Struggle for a Science of Culture*. New York.

Hill, G. 1940. *A History of Cyprus*. Volume 2. *The Frankish Period*. Cambridge.

Horden, P. & N. Purcell 2000. *The Corrupting Sea: A Study of Mediterranean History*. Oxford.

Jennings, J. 2011. *Globalizations and the Ancient World*. Cambridge.

Jennings, R. C. 1993. *Christians and Muslims in Ottoman Cyprus and the Mediterranean World, 1571–1640*. New York.

Jones, R. 2016. *Sweet Waste. Medieval Sugar Production in the Mediterranean Viewed from the 2002 Excavation at Tawahin es-Sukkar, Safi, Jordan*. Glasgow.

Kardulias, P. N. 1990. "Fur Production as a Specialized Activity in a World System: Indians in the North American Fur Trade", *American Indian Culture and Research Journal* 14, 25–60.

Kardulias, P. N. 1999a. "Multiple Levels in the Aegean Bronze Age World-System", in Kardulias (ed) 1999c, 179–201.

Kardulias, P. N. 1999b. "Flaked Stone and the Role of the Palaces in the Mycenaean World-System", in Parkinson & Galaty (eds) 1999, 61–71.

Kardulias, P. N. (ed) 1999c. *World-Systems Theory in Practice: Leadership, Production, and Exchange*. Lanham, MD.

Kardulias, P. N. 2007. "Negotiation and Incorporation on the Margins of World-Systems: Examples from Cyprus and North America", *Journal of World-Systems Research* 13.1, 55–82.

Kardulias, P. N. 2008. "Interpreting the Past through the Present: The Ethnographic, Ethnoarchaeological, and Experimental Study of Early Agriculture", in Caraher, Hall & Moore (eds) 2008, 109–26.

Kardulias, P. N. & R. W. Yerkes 1996. "Microwear and Metric Analysis of Threshing Sledge Flints from Greece and Cyprus", *Journal of Archaeological Science* 23, 657–66.

Kardulias, P. N. & R. W. Yerkes (eds) 2003. *Written in Stone: The Multiple Dimensions of Lithic Analysis*. Lanham, MD.

Kardulias, P. N. & R. W. Yerkes 2004. "World-Systems Theory and Regional Survey: The Malloura Valley Survey on Cyprus", in Athanassopoulos & Wandsnider (eds) 2004, 143–64.

Kardulias, P. N. & R. W. Yerkes 2011. "The Malloura Valley Survey", in Toumazou, Kardulias & Counts (eds) 2011, 87–105.

Kitchener, H. H. 1885. *A Trigonometrical Survey of the Island of Cyprus*. London.

Knapp, A. B. & J. F. Cherry 1994. *Provenience Studies and Bronze Age Cyprus: Production, Exchange and Political-economic Change*. Madison, WI.

LaBianca, Ø. S. & S. A. Scham (eds) 2006. *Connectivity in Antiquity. Globalization as a Long-Term Historical Process*. London.

Moore, R. S. & T. E. Gregory 2011. "Athienou Archaeological Project Survey Pottery", in Toumazou, Kardulias & Counts 2011, 203–13.

Papantoniou, G. & A. K. Vionis 2017. "Landscape Archaeology and Sacred Space in the Eastern Mediterranean: A Glimpse from Cyprus", *Land* 6, 40: 1–18. https://doi.org/10.3390/land6020040.

Parkinson, W. A. & J. F. Cherry 2003. "Lithic Artifacts from Surveys: A Comparative Evaluation of Recent Evidence from the Southern Aegean", in Kardulias & Yerkes 2003, 35–57.

Parkinson, W. & M. Galaty (eds) 1999. *Rethinking Mycenaean Palaces: New Interpretations of an Old Idea*. Los Angeles.

Pettegrew, D. K. 2007. "The Busy Countryside of Late Roman Corinth: Interpreting Ceramic Data Produced by Regional Archaeological Survey", *Hesperia* 76, 743–84.

Pulak, C. 1998. "The Uluburun Shipwreck: An Overview", *The International Journal of Nautical Archaeology* 27.3, 188–224.

Rautman, M. 2003. *A Cypriot Village of Late Antiquity. Kalavasos-Kopetra in the Vasilikos Valley*. Portsmouth, RI.

Renfrew, C. 1972. *The Emergence of Civilisation*. London.

Renfrew, C. 1975. "Trade as Action at a Distance: Questions of Integration and Communication", in Sabloff & Lamberg-Karlovsky 1975, 3–61.

Sabloff, J. & C. C. Lamberg-Karlovsky. 1975. *Ancient Civilization and Trade*. Albuquerque.

Stewart, C. A. 2013. "Military Architecture in Early Byzantine Cyprus", *Cahier du Centre d'Études Chypriotes* 43, 285–304.

Tartaron, T. F., T. E. Gregory, D. J. Pullen, J. S. Noller, R. M. Rothaus, J. E. Rife, L. Tzortzopoulou-Gregory, R. Schon, W. R. Caraher, D. K. Pettegrew, and D. Nakassis 2006. "The Eastern Korinthia Archaeological Survey: Integrated Methods for a Dynamic Landscape", *Hesperia* 75, 453–523.

Toumazou, M. K., P. N. Kardulias & D. B. Counts (eds) 2011. *Crossroads and Boundaries: The Archaeology of Past and Present in the Malloura Valley, Cyprus*. Cambridge, MA.

Toumazou, M. K. & D. B. Counts 2011. "Excavations at Malloura (1990–2010). Context, Methods, and Results", in Toumazou, Kardulias & Counts (eds) 2011, 67–86.

Veikou, M. 2015. "One Island, Three Capitals. Insularity and the Successive Relocations of the Capital of Cyprus from Late Antiquity to the Middle Ages", in Rogge & Grünbart (eds) *Medieval Cyprus. A Place of Cultural Encounter* 2015, 357–87. Münster.

Vionis, A. K. 2008. "Current Archaeological Research on Settlement and Provincial Life in the Byzantine and Ottoman Aegean: a Case-Study from Boeotia, Greece," *Medieval Settlement Research* 23, 28–41.

Vionis, A. K. 2017. "Understanding Settlements in Byzantine Greece. New Data and Approaches for Boeotia, Sixth to Thirteenth Century." *Dumbarton Oaks Papers* 71, 127–173.

von Wartburg, M-L. 2001. "The Archaeology of Cane Sugar Production: A Survey of Twenty Years of Research in Cyprus", *The Antiquaries Journal* 81, 305–35.

Wallace, P. W. & A. G. Orphanides (eds). 2005. *George Boustronios. A Narrative of the Chronicle of Cyprus 1456–1489*. Sources for the History of Cyprus. Volume XIII. Nicosia.

Wallerstein, I. 1974. *The Modern World-System 1: Capitalist Agriculture and the Origins of the European World-Economy in the Sixteenth Century*. New York.

White, L. 1943. "Energy and the Evolution of Culture", *American Anthropologist* 45, 335–56.

White, L. 1949. *The Science of Culture, a Study of Man and Civilization*. New York.

Willey, G. R. & P. Phillips 1958. *Method and Theory in American Archaeology*. Chicago.

Yerkes, R. W. 2011. "Viewing the Past through the Present: Ethnoarchaeological Studies of Population and Ancient Agriculture", in Toumazou, Kardulias & Counts (eds) 2011, 321–39.

Constructing New Cities, Creating New Spatialities
An Ethnoarchaeological Experiment

Enrico Zanini

The most important way—or at least the most archaeologically visible one—in which a public power can transform a natural landscape is by establishing of a new human settlement; among the wide variety of human settlements, new cities certainly make the most impact, since they not only change the landscape image, but also construct a whole range of new spatialities within it. From this perspective, a new city interacts with the natural/human landscape in many different ways, for instance creating the spaces of new local economy, a new network of pathways for human mobility, a new road system to connect the single territory to the rest of the "new" world in which it is now inserted. These multiple new spatialities transform the previous landscape in a durable way, and, once established, can survive also beyond the lifespan of the city itself.

The discussion about the so-called 'new cities' is not a new one in historical and archaeological studies of the Early Byzantine world. Yet, from the earliest to the more recent studies,[1] the discussion has focused quite exclusively on the foundation phase of the single cities, and this was for at least two reasons, possibly defined as 'heuristic convenience'.

The first point of heuristic convenience resides in the nature of the available archaeological data, since, normally, the phase of the foundation is the most neatly identifiable one, or, at least, the most frequently investigated until recent years, like in the most famous cases of Caričin Grad—*Prima Iustiniana*, in the Balkans, modern Serbia,[2] and Dara, in ancient Mesopotamia, now a small village located near the border separating Turkey from Syria.[3] In both these cases, the foundation phase is marked by a unitary design and by the adoption of homogeneous building techniques, as well as, obviously, being clearly visible in the archaeological levels between the earlier natural landscape and the later deposits. The second point of heuristic convenience resides

---

[1] See Zanini 1994, 2007; Arce 2000; Rizos (ed.) 2017.
[2] Ivanišević 2017.
[3] Keser-Kayaalp & Erdogan 2017.

in the extra-archaeological sources too, since the foundation phase is often well attested in textual records due to the ideological and propagandistic value that a new foundation always had in its contemporary society. The convergence of these two reasons mean that the archaeology of Early Byzantine new cities has essentially been conceived as an "archaeology of production" of the cities themselves: that is a study of the reasons, the procedures and the practices related to the building up of a very complex, but substantially unitary artifact, as a newly-founded city really is.

Far less travelled was the road of the "contextual analysis" of this complex phenomenon. The importance of this approach goes without saying; in some ways, the impact of a new city on a certain landscape could be metaphorically paralleled with that of a meteorite falling in a territory. The impact of the meteorite onto a natural and human landscape which, until that moment, preserved its equilibrium, inevitably upset that equilibrium, transforming the surrounding landscape with short-, medium-, and long-term effects. Drawing an extreme synthesis, this impact can be read as the moment when a new structural relationship is established between a local micro-ecology and/or micro-economy (the local historical landscape in the way it was defined until that moment) and the macro-economy—or, better, the whole set of many different macro-economies—of the more or less complex state system that decided the birth of the new city.[4]

In most cases, the foundation of an Early Byzantine 'new city' didn't respond to the specific needs of the micro-territory in which it was erected, but largely to several "external" needs, like state administration and defence, religious administration, imperial propaganda, and/or manifestation of different authorities and power-relations. Each of these external needs connects the new city to one of the many infrastructural networks that are the bases of the administration of a complex state. This is obviously true also for the long-lasting cities, which (following the change of the macro-economic systems) experienced, over time, ascending or descending trajectories. But this is theoretically more visible in the case of the 'new' cities, where the relationship between pre-existing local micro-ecology and new macro-economy/economies is much more neatly expressed.

The creation of a new city represents a relevant change in the economic and social geography of a specific territory, since it involves a concentration of money, knowledge, and workforce which that territory had not experienced until that moment. This first impact will be a short-term economic factor, since

---

4 Zanini 2019.

the creation of a new city is a process that is basically continuous but brief. But this initial phase will be followed by a second one, with a more extended chronological horizon. Following its construction, a new city must play the role it was conceived for, and this, in the medium term, can be done in just two ways: a) by continuing to be fed by external (state) resources, for instance in the case of cities conceived to be directing and organizing centres of the state's defensive system; or b) by creating a stable network of economic and social relationships with the surrounding territory.

In most cases, probably, the economic system of our theoretical new city will be a mixture of state and local economic networks in proportions that can easily vary over time. From this point of view, a new city will tend to become progressively similar to a long-lasting city. This process will go ahead for a relatively long time, depending on the continuity of interest in the new city by central administration. The more extemporary the demands that have caused its foundation (e.g. celebrating the name of a single sovereign), the shorter the length of the city's life will be. The more its foundation has been connected with the structural needs of a single micro-territory, the higher the probability that our city will survive.

However, at the end of the day, a new city could continue to exercise its function inside a micro-territory even when in decline, and several centuries after that. The reason is that the construction of a new city involves a sensible and permanent (or, at least, semi-permanent) alteration to the natural landscape: the concentration of manpower connected with the building operations involves the transportation of natural resources (stone, bricks, wood) from their original place to a new part of the landscape (the site). After the collapse and abandonment of the city, that place will become a privileged part of the old landscape: a place where it is easier to find residual building materials, ready to be reused, or even, *extrema ratio*, a quarry where pre-cut stones can be recovered.

The infrastructural networks connected with the construction and the functioning of the new city—for instance the road system or the urban water system—will become new structural elements of the landscape, reshaping the distribution map of natural resources (for instance, in the case of aqueducts) or the map of accessibility to the different parts of the landscape itself, in the case of the road network.

Seen from this perspective, the foundation of a new city is a more complex and interesting phenomenon; although a problem in reading the material traces evidently arises, given the limits of available extra-archaeological sources and given the objective narrowness of our archaeological datasets. The heuristic convenience principle appears here radically reversed, and the objective lack of a knowledge base should advise against our going any further on this path, at least by practising a "traditional" approach based on the comparison between archaeological and literary sources.

A small place for further development of the research could open instead if we were to apply to our hypothesis those approaches which we normally use to study similarly complicated items such as those connected with the archaeology of complex human behaviour in deep history. In this case too, our desire for knowledge is impacted by a desperate lack of sources and we have to turn to more sophisticated approaches, like ethnoarchaeology.

1 Dara vs Littoria: A Bizarre or Useful Idea?

The perhaps bizarre idea I shall develop in this paper is to conduct a very small experiment of 'ethnoarchaeology'—or, if preferred, of cross-cultural comparison—as applied to a new city of the sixth century by trying to observe some 'parallel' phenomena in a case we can study more easily, since it was founded much more recently and it is contemporaneous with us. It will offer some ideas about the relationship between a newly founded city and its surrounding territory, albeit in a very different context in time and space.

In the following pages, I will use some ideas derived from the analysis of the impact that the foundation of the new city of Littoria (presently Latina, a medium size city, ca. 70km south of Rome) had on the surrounding territory in the short, medium and medium-long term, with a view to evaluating the applicability of this 'model' to a completely different context: the city of Dara, in northern Mesopotamia (today a small Kurdish village, close to the border between Turkey and Syria), that is perhaps the best prototype of a new city of the sixth century.

Dara and Littoria are evidently very far from each other in terms of time, space, and general context. But they have at least something in common: both of them were cities founded *ex novo*, by the will of the highest expression of the state system to which they belonged, the Early Byzantine emperor and the Duce of Italian fascism. In both cases, the new city was located in a territory where no urban centre was previously attested; therefore, we have two particularly fitting cases of that image of a "meteorite" impacting a fairly deserted land (as noted above).

In the case of Dara, the physical landscape where the meteorite, conceived in Constantinople, landed was not precisely empty and unstructured. In that portion of the Syrian plain immediately adjacent to the steep slopes of the Anatolian plateau, the precise location that was chosen (and the ultimate reason for the choice, is related to a small but important, then perennial river—the Kordes—which represents one of the few water resources in a semi-arid region.

The Kordes River was a double-sided coin: at a local and micro-ecological scale, its presence was the reason for the birth, in ancient times, of a small human settlement, that the contemporary literary sources describe as an insignificant rural village.[5] Conversely, at a larger and macro-economic scale, such as the defensive system of the Early Byzantine Empire, the same river represented a risk, because it was one of the few possible water points for Sassanian armies marching from the east to attack the heart of the empire in Constantinople.

The landscape in which Dara was erected was, therefore, a marginal frontier territory with little economic appeal tied to a local micro-economy of mere subsistence: an 'empty' space, destined to be crossed rather than inhabited, where the imperial army could not find any resting point either. Most probably, the appearance of this space has changed very little since antiquity, and what we could observe until the 1980s can be assumed to be a largely intact relic of the ancient natural landscape where the Dara meteorite impacted in the very first years of the sixth century CE (Figure 12.1).[6]

In the case of Littoria, the physical space was more radically 'empty' since it was a portion of land that only a very few years before had emerged from the deepest part of the Pontine marshes, after a process of integral land reclamation that was not completely accomplished even at the moment when the new city was founded.[7] In this case, the decision to place a new settlement at that exact location was dictated by the presence of a small medical centre, a sort of advanced 'frontier post' in the struggle against malaria. This facility appeared to the fascist regime as a good opportunity to underline the change determined by the integral land reclamation, from a 'frontier point' against an invisible but dangerous enemy to a central place in the so called 'wheat battle', intended to ensure food for the entire State.[8]

---

5   The entire process of foundation of the new city of Dara, after a decision by the emperor Anastasios I, at the very beginning of the sixth century CE, is described in the Ps.-Zachariah *Historia Ecclesiastica*, VII, 6 and the *Chronicle of Joshua the Stylite* (ed. Wright 1870, 70); see Zanini 1990.
6   Zanini 2018.
7   Before the fascist land reclamation, the Pontine marshes were actually not an empty space since they were inhabited by a relatively large community of people who exploited its natural resources (Gruppuso 2014), but the place where the new town of Littoria was placed was previously named "Piscinara," which literally means something resembling a large water-pool.
8   Mariani 1976.

FIGURE 12.1   The plain of Dara in 1980
AUTHOR'S COPYRIGHT

In both cases, the meteorite took the shape of a military settlement. At Dara, this intention was explicitly declared: the entire city-foundation process was related to the creation of a new large stronghold—with the spatial dimension and the services and facilities of a medium size town—to host a permanent garrison to control one of the most important routes connecting the Syrian plain to the Anatolian plateau. At the same time, it established a base to host the mobile army during the military campaigns against the Sassanids that followed one another with great frequency in that area.

In the case of Littoria, the connection with the military dimension is less direct, but not less strong. In this case, there was no frontier to defend against an external enemy, but there was the idea to create a colony that adopted the shape of a Roman legionary camp. This choice was explicitly intended to have a strong communicative effect in that historical moment. So, it was not by chance that the first settlement had the shape and even the dimensions of a Roman *castrum*, since the entire project of land reclamation was under the control of the 'Opera Nazionale Combattenti e Reduci' (National Body of Veterans), an institution created immediately after the end of the First World War to sustain people coming back from the front.[9] The relationship with the

---

9   Liguori 2012; Antonelli 2017.

military power is explicit in the first emblem of the new city: a lictor's *fasce* associated with two rifles and one axe surrounded by two bundles of rods; an ideal image of a company of *limitanei*, the peasants-soldiers settled on the frontier separating civilization from the barbarity of hostile nature.[10]

A second and very important common point between our case studies is that both of them are the product of remote design that followed predefined principles. In the case of Dara, this aspect is reported in great detail by literary sources. At the time of the original foundation around 505 CE, under Anastasios I, after an initial topographic evaluation completed directly on the site by the military commanders, the project was conceived in its essential outline at Constantinople; then, it was sent to Dara to be adapted to the terrain during the building process. After that, a second phase of construction, under Justinian, changed the original structure in many ways: the defensive value was enhanced, reinforcing and elevating towers and curtain walls; at the same time, the city received a more definite "urban" shape, with the construction of new infrastructure (aqueduct, dam, reservoirs, streets, bridges) and new civil and religious monuments (Figure 12.2).[11] The case of Littoria was similar: the architect, charged with the overall design, took a standardized project for a new rural settlement and adapted and enlarged it. Doing this, he created an entity very different in many respects from that originally expected: a new city instead of a large rural village (Figure 12.3).

Last but not least, a third common element is represented by the complexity of relationships that the new city developed with the surrounding society. At Dara as at Littoria, the foundation of the new city responds to the interests of a strongly centralized state—the Early Byzantine Empire in the age of Anastasios I and Justinian I on the one hand and fascist Italy on the other— but also to the interests of several other secondary but important stakeholders.

In the case of Dara, a main stakeholder was clearly the Church, from two different points of view. On the one hand, the secular clergy—specifically the bishop of Amida (modern Diyarbakir, in southern Turkey)—has to be counted among the protagonists of the entire foundation process of the new city. The land on which the city was to be erected was the property of the Church of Amida, and the state had to buy it. The bishop was charged with overseeing the

---

10   It is perhaps worth remembering the slogan created by Mussolini during the inauguration ceremony of the newly built Littoria: "It is the plough that traces the furrow, but it is the sword that defends it".
11   Justinian's intervention at Dara is reported by Procopius (*De Aedificiis*, II, 2.1.11–27; 2.2.1–15); for a debate about the reliability of this source, see Crow & Croke 1983; Whitby 1986; Zanini 1990.

CONSTRUCTING NEW CITIES, CREATING NEW SPATIALITIES   295

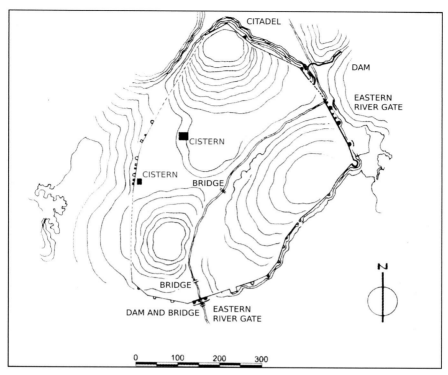

FIGURE 12.2   Sketch-plan of the archaeological site of Dara
AUTHOR'S COPYRIGHT, REDRAWN BASED ON DIFFERENT SOURCES

entire building process and he had the responsibility of managing the money provided by the state. At the end of the process, a deacon of the same Church, charged with direct oversight of the construction site, was rewarded with the position of first bishop of the newly created bishopric of Dara.

In the case of Littoria, on the other hand, the institutional stakeholders are not so clearly identifiable,[12] but the interest of at least two social groups emerges. The first stakeholders were the people originally intended as beneficiaries of the new foundation: they were poor rural families, mainly coming from north-eastern Italy, who were experiencing difficult living conditions in the economic crisis that affected their homeland after the end of the First World War.[13] A second, and perhaps unexpected, interested group was

---

12   It is worth noting, however, the "political" interest in the foundation of Littoria expressed by some parts of the Italian Church; see Ciammaruconi 2005.
13   Alfieri 2018.

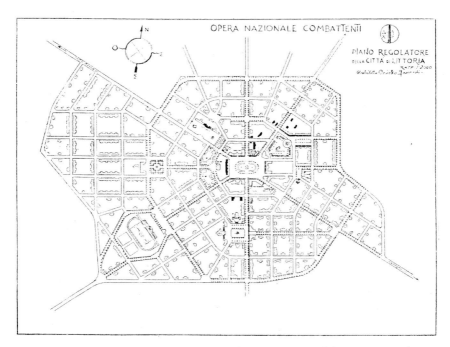

FIGURE 12.3   First zoning plan of Littoria by architect O. Frezzotti (after Mariani 1976)

represented by the rural people that lived in the healthy areas surrounding the Pontine marshes: as we will discuss later, after the structuring of Littoria as a proper city, they largely moved towards the settlement, which was transforming into a new economic centre with proper 'urban' facilities.

The latter is, to my mind, a very interesting phenomenon, since a similar one could have reasonably occurred at the new city of Dara too, mainly after the Justinian's reshaping, even if it remains virtually invisible to us due to the lack of specific archaeological or literary sources.

2   Circles in the Water: The Economic Impact of a New City's Building Site

The first way in which the building up of a new city interacts with a landscape is evidently connected with the economy of its construction. The creation of a totally new urban organism means concentrating economic resources on a territory, so changing its economic structure, at least for the period practically needed for the building operations.

In the case of Dara, this element is underlined by literary sources attesting that a massive recruitment of workforce—both specialized masons and simple workers—was operated in the surrounding regions, to ensure that the city would be completed in the due time, as imposed by the defensive needs. To do that, the imperial administration used a double economic lever: the workers engaged in the building site received a salary equal to twice the normal wage and were simultaneously exempted from taxes. In other words, they received a net pay of three or four times a normal salary.[14]

During the timespan required for the construction of the city—more or less three years—the macro-economic system of the Early Byzantine state was able to concentrate imposing resources on that remote frontier: a very rough estimate of the simple material cost of construction for a fortress of that size—just counting the building material and the workers wage—can easily reach a figure between 50,000 and 100,000 golden *solidi*.[15] This was a really massive investment that was turned into a great economic benefit for a relatively large community. With this amount of money and paying the workers twice their normal wage, 2,500 or 3,000 people could be recruited—this figure fitting well with the short time recorded by literary sources for the completion of the building works. If every worker had a family behind it, the construction of Dara produced a three-year period of "anomalous" well-being for a social group of some 10,000 to 15,000 people.

If we add to this the positive economic effect related to non-taxation, the impact of the Dara meteorite on that community will have been even more relevant: it was an important wealth re-distribution exercise that operated in the subsequent years, generating a new chain of micro-economic effects. In other words, such a larger construction site represented a sort of small and localized 'new deal', able to change the everyday life of a significant number of people.

A further effect related to such a large construction site would have consisted in micro-migration phenomena,[16] and in the birth of small service activities connected to the primary needs of such a large group of people. Something very similar to that happened just around a newly founded legionary *castrum*

---

14   The entire process is reported by Ps.-Zachariah, *Historia Ecclesiastica*, VII, 6.
15   This rough appraisal of the construction cost is conducted on the basis of the so called "DeLaine method" (DeLaine 2006). A more detailed analysis of the economic impact of the construction of Dara is presented in Zanini, 2021.
16   Ps.-Zachariah (*Historia Ecclesiastica*, VII, 6) refers of a large-scale recruitment that extended to the "whole region", whatever really was the significance of this expression.

FIGURE 12.4 Arrival of the settlers at Littoria (after Mariani 1976)

or even around a famous pilgrimage site; as it happens today around temporary settlements of workers engaged in large construction sites located far away from the nearest urban centres.

In the case of Littoria, perhaps the economic impact of the physical construction of the city was of a more modest scale, if compared with the overall volume of a modern economy, even that of Italy in the years between the two world wars. The social impact was anything but negligible, because the first-generation 'builders' of the new city belonged, in this case too, to a very low band of the Italian socio-economic scale. So, that large building site surely acted as a temporary attraction for workers—that were significantly named as *legionari* in the fascist rhetoric—which then went back to their original regions only to be replaced by a second migratory 'wave': the groups of *coloni* that had the task of cultivating the reclaimed land (Figure 12.4).

'Archaeological' evidence of this second migration remains today in the network of *poderi* (single-family agricultural units), distributed following a regular grid in the countryside that surrounded the new city, and in a second network of very small rural villages (*borghi*), designed to offer basic services (everyday commerce, tools and seeds for cultivation, primary schools, churches) to the rural families.[17]

In the absence of a specific landscape archaeology project, we cannot know if something similar occurred at Dara, too. In any case, if there weren't virgin lands to be cultivated, it seems quite probable that in the sixth-century Mesopotamia the city assumed—together with its principal defensive function—a whole series of secondary functions, acting as a new central place of the surrounding territory.

3   New Socio-economic Spatiality in the Surrounding Countryside

At this point of our reasoning, it is worth noting that—on the basis of present archaeological and historical knowledge—we are quite well-informed about the initial moments of the relationship between a new Early Byzantine city and its surrounding territory. By contrast, we are very poorly informed about the way this relationship evolved in the subsequent period.

Generally speaking, once a new city is built, its system of relationships with its surrounding socioeconomic environment could evolve in some independent way, if compared to the original intentions of the authority that planned its construction. When landing on a specific landscape, the meteorite thrown by the central authority begins to interact with that landscape in a relatively free way. It becomes a sort of point of contact between the local society and the general system that can be used in both directions: from centre to periphery (i.e. for administrative duties or tax collection) and from periphery to centre (i.e. to obtain new services and/or financial resources).

One could reason here in terms of heterogenesis of intents. A new city, born for a specific purpose (in the case of Dara, a defensive one), can interact with the surrounding territory also at a completely different level after the end of its foundation phase, even if this possibility was initially unintended.

Here again, a comparison with Littoria is maybe useful. Let's look at the history of Littoria, in brief: Mussolini's original new settlement idea (part of a network of three, together with Pontinia and Sabaudia) was conceived as a large hamlet for some 5,000 people. It was intended to offer the surrounding countryside several services (administration, justice, commerce, banks, schools, large churches) at a higher level than those offered by the other smaller rural villages. Only at the moment of the laying of the first stone, at the beginning

---

17   Alfieri 2018.

FIGURE 12.5 Aerial view of Littoria's first monumental setting, a few years after the foundation (after Mariani 1976)

of 1932, Mussolini himself realized that the architect and the other people responsible for the 'large hamlet' construction had gone well beyond his directive, designing a true city, decidedly larger and more structured than originally expected (Figure 12.5). Mussolini was really disappointed by this, he deserted the ceremony and was on the point of cancelling it; yet he radically changed his mind, after seeing the great interest in the new foundation by the international press. Just a few months later, he was the absolute protagonist of the Littoria inauguration ceremony, glorifying the large monumental spaces, the monumental buildings erected to host the public offices, and actively encouraging a rapid population growth (Figure 12.6).[18]

Mutatis mutandis, something very similar could have happened in the case of Dara, imagined and designed to be a fortress, large enough to host the Byzantine army during a military campaign, but soon transformed into a proper city. We are informed of that both from literary sources and archaeology, at least within the limits of our present material knowledge of that city's urban fabric. The whole long and detailed report by Procopius,[19] apart from

18   Mariani 2006; Muntoni 2006.
19   *De Aedificiis*, II, 2.1.11–27; 2.2.1–15.

FIGURE 12.6 Mussolini depicted as an urban planner in a lost wall mosaic, originally in Pomezia (after Mariani 1976)

any discussion about the reliability of this source, is clearly focused on this aspect: the transformation of a fortress born as point of border control into a fortified city that managed the whole frontier area. This is implied not only by the strength of the defensive walls, but also the strong enlargement of urban infrastructure (dam, aqueduct, water reservoirs, granaries), the new definition of the spaces and places of religious and civil power, and the management of everyday living spaces.[20]

Archaeology seems to go in the same direction. Two main elements have to be considered: the overall extension of the city surface, and the number and dimension of the water reservoirs. Both of them are good proxy indicators to give us a first idea about the population the city had been designed and re-designed to host.

The physical dimensions of the city require some reflection. Dara has a walled perimeter of approximately 2.5km, with an enclosed area of just under forty hectares. If we rapidly compare these numbers with those of some other sixth century "new cities", they emerge as significant. A very important fortress of the same defensive line, Zenobia-Halebiyye, has a walled perimeter

20 Furlan 1984, 1988, 1995; Keser-Kayaalp & Erdogan 2017; Zanini 1990, 2003.

of less than 1.5km, with an internal area of just ten hectares.[21] A fortified city like Resafa, to which no one can deny a properly urban status, has a perimeter of 1,900m with an internal area of some twenty-three hectares.[22] Prima Iustiniana—Caričin Grad itself, after the recent research that has considerably extended the previously estimated area, has more or less the same surface of Resafa, while the reconstruction of the city walls perimeter is more complicated.[23]

In general, Dara seems to be two-to-four times larger than other settlements of similar typology: it is not a "pure" fortress like Zenobia-Halebiyye and it is decidedly larger than its 'sister' cities.

It goes without saying that the extension of the urban perimeter depended only in part on the architects' will, since they were conditioned by strategic reasons such as the opportunity to best use the terrain shape and to control the natural resources. But it seems equally evident that the precise dimensions of Dara were the result of a deliberate choice. Trying to calculate the number of a city's inhabitants based only on its size is notoriously complicated, given the number of possible variables and their interactions. Although adopted only to provide a very rough approximation, the "traditional" figure of 100/200 people per hectare[24] would suggest a range from 4,000 to 8,000 inhabitants. It would be a figure that cannot be defined as too small if compared with the demographic scenario of the Mediterranean in the sixth century. As a quick comparison, a medium-size provincial capital like Gortyn on Crete, where the population can be calculated on the basis of different and independent sources, probably had a population of some 20,000 or 25,000 distributed on an urban area that was more or less four times that of Dara.[25]

Once again, one can believe that such oversized spaces inside the fortress have been envisaged in the initial design to respond to the need of hosting an entire army—and really the walled perimeter remained the original one after Justinian's intervention too—, but this did not take anything away of the properly 'urban' image that Dara had acquired at least by the middle of the sixth century.

The same urban image is strengthened by our second indicator, the drinkable water-storage system. The archaeological site of Dara is rich in water reservoirs, and further research could again improve this image. The three already-known reservoirs offer a highly significant image. The largest one,

---

21 Blétry 2017; Lauffray 1983.
22 Gussone & Sack 2017; Konrad 2001.
23 Ivanišević 2017.
24 Hassan 1981, 66–7.
25 Giorgi 2016, 60.

located near the physical centre of the city, consists of a ten-nave structure and could have an overall extension of some 3,000 square meters (excluding the internal walls), normally equivalent to a reception of 21,000/24,000 cubic meters of water (Figure 12.7). If we add to this amount the water contained within the large underground cistern recorded in the southern part of the city, as well as that in the vaulted cistern located near the western gate, we can easily reach a total of some 30,000 cubic meters.

This was certainly an important site for water storage, although we have to consider it not in terms of "real" and measurable quantities. In fact, when speaking about water storage, we must be aware of a great number of variables (ratio between reservoirs and feeding aqueducts, seasonality of hydraulic supply etc.). So, it would be better to discuss this point rather in terms of orders of magnitude. From the latter point of view, assuming an average use of some 25 litres per person per day, a quite normal consumption in antiquity and the modern pre-industrial world, such an amount of water would mean a reserve of some 1,200,000 people/days. Returning to a figure of 4,000/8,000 inhabitants, that would mean a reserve for the city ranging from a minimum of 120 days to a maximum of many more than 300 days, even with a total absence of atmospheric precipitation and with the aqueduct (and river) dried up. Assuming that the real number of citizens was close to the estimated minimum, say 5,000 people, this would have meant a hydraulic autonomy of

FIGURE 12.7   The main cistern of Dara
AUTHOR'S COPYRIGHT

some eight months or even longer if the water use was more strictly controlled. Beyond mere numbers, it is very interesting to note that, combining the two different approaches towards measurement estimations, the inhabitants' order of magnitude—estimated on the basis of urban surface area—is fully consistent with the real availability of such a vital resource as drinking water.

Therefore, based on all the above one can conclude that with Justinian's intervention—if we trust Procopius' narrative—or, in any case, after an extensive reorganization of the city, Dara acquired the size, shape, and infrastructure of an average city of its time. This inevitably suggests that the city really acquired the quite large population it was designed for; so our perspective has to move from the material shape of the city to the nature of its citizens. Who were the 5,000 to 8,000 people who populated Dara? Where did they come from? And what socio-economic relationships did this new urban group establish with its hinterland?

These questions once again connect Dara with our small ethno-archaeological or cross cultural experiment based on Littoria. In the latter case, too, the birth of a new city activated new dynamics in the relationships with the surrounding landscape that inevitably ended up creating a new urban social class consisting of administrators, merchants, and public officials. As in antiquity, those "urban" people needed to be fed, and the satisfaction of these basic needs led to the establishment of new economic relationships with the immediate countryside.

One can ask if similar dynamics could have been active in the case of Dara as well; the answer to this question is not certain, but the possibility that this might also have happened in that corner of sixth-century Mesopotamia is high. Two hypotheses can be advanced. The first one is that the foundation of Dara triggered a real transfer into the new city of people coming from far away—either soldiers or civilians—following a decision by a higher authority. This certainly occurred, but only for some members of the urban elites coming from neighbouring cities: some literary sources state that the city became the seat of at least two main authorities—the *dux Mesopotamiae* and a suffragan bishop—and their respective offices. But this was not enough to make Dara a city with a durable relationship with the surrounding country: the region was too sparsely populated to support the weight of a medium-sized 'parasitic' city populated with a social group of 'pure' citizens who were fed by the surplus of the adjacent countryside.[26] As a matter of fact, when the defensive role of the city ended, the financial support directly coming from the central administration was lost and the settlement inevitably ceased its 'urban' life.

26   On such a complex item, which we obviously cannot discuss here, see Horden & Purcell 2000, 105–8.

A second hypothesis that at present seems decidedly more sustainable is that the construction of a new fortified nucleus generated the mobilization of people from surrounding regions. This external intervention would have triggered a sort of 'induced' synoecism ending in the movement of some people from small villages dispersed in the countryside towards the new city. From this perspective, the new economic relationship between the city and the surrounding countryside would be automatically solved: the new inhabitants of Dara would have been the same people that already lived in the region. These people would have now found life in the fortified city more convenient, since they would have evaluated the benefits of urban life as greater than the energetic expenditure required by the necessity of commuting every day in order to reach and cultivate their fields.

From a certain point of view, the analysis of the evolution of Littoria can be useful in this respect too. Originally conceived to be populated by allogeneic peoples arriving in the Pontine plain following a plan of encouraged and controlled immigration, Littoria soon became something completely different: a central socio-economic place for the surrounding countryside, mainly populated by families coming from the neighbouring territories with a very rapid increase in the number of residents.[27] Within the span of less than a decade, Littoria, originally conceived as a 'colony' of the poor rural areas of northeastern Italy, was turned into a quite large 'agro-town': a knot of intensification of a territory that, after the completion of land reclamation, had progressively been changing its nature (Figure 12.8).[28]

In a completely different scenario, it is not impossible that a quite comparable process can be detected in the case of Dara, where a large fortress was turned into a 'defended agro-town'.[29] This centre represented a contact point between two distinct worlds: that of the macro-economic system of the empire of Constantinople and that of the micro-economic local system based on a dense weave of relationships among the city, its citizens, the countryside, and the rural population that lived there.

4   After the End: A New Micro-ecological Spatiality

A further interesting perspective is represented by the analysis of occurrences after the end of a new city's lifespan. Theoretically speaking, assuming that a

---

27   Antonelli 2017; Liguori 2012.
28   Curtis 2013.
29   Cf. Arthur 1991.

FIGURE 12.8 Littoria shaped as a full-size city in 1940
© AEROFOTOTECA DEL MINISTERO DELLA CULTURA

new city is the product of a punctuated impact by an external macro-economic system on a specific territory, the phenomenon should be completely reversible: when the specific necessities of the macro-economic system (defence, administration, etc.) end, the city should disappear and its site should be, in turn, reverted more or less to its initial state.

This could appear a purely theoretical issue, but in some well-known cases things went more or less in this way. This is, for instance, the case of Prima Iustiniana—Caričin Grad, the new city built to celebrate Justinian's birthplace, which did not survive the Avaro-Slavic migrations into the Balkans. This was also more or less the case of Resafa, in Syria, where the collapse of the defensive system of the eastern *limes* caused the definitive abandonment of the city and its transformation into ruins. Upon closer inspection, however, both cited cases call for a more reflective and nuanced approach. The image of a sudden abandonment of Caričin Grad immediately after the Avaro-Slavic invasion could be the product more of a contemporary perspective than of a deep archaeological analysis. The reason for this is that the reading of that site in a purely monumental perspective is largely related to an excavation strategy intended to exalt the "imperial" image of the city itself. It is worth noting that this image is now largely challenged by the new extensive archaeological research which is based on accurate micro-stratigraphical excavations and adopts a landscape-archaeology approach. As a result of this recent research, we now have a less stereotypical image of a "monumental" city and a more interesting perspective on everyday life, where the chronological horizons also appear to be much more nuanced than in the past.[30] The case of Resafa could be in some way similar, since we have some sure indicators of an "afterlife" in Ummayyad times, albeit still awaiting proper investigation.[31]

From this perspective, the case of Dara looks emblematic because it is not deniable that, after a long phase of alternate control by Byzantines and Sasanids, the city-fortress lost its strategic significance after the Arab conquest of Syria and the withdrawal of the southern-eastern border of the empire of Constantinople. However, when Dara disappeared from the historical and literary sources only means that the "old" new city—that is the only one registered in those sources—disappeared from the macro-economic Early Byzantine system. Dara did not really disappear from the micro-economic local system because the construction of the city, along with the re-organization of its major infrastructure in the age of Justinian, had transformed the landscape in a permanent way, *de facto* creating a new local micro-ecology.

These micro-ecological transformations were long lasting. Indeed, some of them are still visible today, as, for example, the hydrology. The Kordes River valley, which runs from immediately north of the archaeological site and then through it from the north-east and which was perhaps the most important reason for the establishment of the new city in the sixth century, appears in today's satellite images as a green oasis in a semi-arid context. It also has a relatively large strip of gardens which are easily cultivated during the summer when the river is completely dry. This is largely due to the presence of the invisible ruins of the dam built up in the age of Justinian, according to Procopius; the stone enclosure still creates a small basin where the water stops when the river is full, preserving the soil moisture during the hottest months.[32]

We have much less evidence about possible prolonged use of the aqueduct that collected spring water a few miles upstream after the end of the fully urban life in Dara. A field-survey demonstrated that the aqueduct itself had been fully excavated into the bedrock, which suggests that it probably remained functional for a considerable time. Such a simple channel was, by its very nature, less subject to structural failures and able to function for centuries without specific maintenance. In this case, too, artificial infrastructure—the

---

30   Ivanišević 2016.
31   Konrad 2001.
32   Furlan 1984.

aqueduct originally conceived for feeding the largest water tanks—could have been converted into a part of the hydrographic structure of that landscape.[33]

A similar argument could be extended to the city walls that, as we have seen, represent the more effective image of the impact of imperial macro-economy on that territory. In this case too, the concentration of economic resources operated by the imperial administration caused a structural change of the landscape, with some hundred thousand cubic meters of rock quarried out to be cut and transformed into defensive walls. After the end of the city's life, the half-ruined walls were in turn transformed into low-cost quarries and/or extemporary shelters.[34]

In conclusion, the remains of the city walls, the availability of fresh drinking water, and the opportunity to cultivate vegetable gardens in the immediate vicinity of dwellings made Dara a privileged place for human settlement in the *longue durée*. They created favourable conditions for the birth and longevity of a village which has remains inhabited uninterrupted to this day.

The vicissitudes of Littoria obviously look very different, first of all, because our temporal scale of observation is very different. Notwithstanding that, in this case too, we can find some interesting parallels. Littoria never became a 'dead' new city: it was attacked by some heavy aerial bombings in the last years of the Second World War, but it was not abandoned. The most concrete risk of disappearance was represented, after the end of the war, by the wish for a sort of *damnatio memoriae*, expressed by some political groups. These groups were determined to erase from the maps a city that was the most explicit manifestation of fascism, starting with its name. The city escaped this risk precisely thanks to the structural changes that its construction had caused in the social and anthropic landscape of the micro-territory in which it had been inserted. Although ideologically compromised with the past regime, after the end of the war the city was still physically present. It had spaces, infrastructure, and buildings that looked precious to the new ruling classes who had to reorganize civil life after the void of twenty-years' fascist dictatorship and military devastation. Some large buildings, which had been 'compromised' by fascism, escaped demolition, and this happened precisely due to their re-usability in these new conditions. The most evident example was a large building designed with an M-shaped plan—to recall the initial letter of the name of the Duce—which had been partially destroyed during bombing and was rebuilt in its original form and transformed into a school.

33 For a similar approach to the water collecting in ancient Resafa, see Beckers & Schütt 2013.
34 The same occurred at Resafa, as clearly recorded by the first aerial photos by A. Poidebard (Mouterde & Poidebard 1945).

The same happened with some essential infrastructure such as the water distribution network, the sewage system, and the street grid: they were the product of an urban design completely extraneous to the new post-bellum city; nevertheless, their presence deeply conditioned the development of the city in subsequent decades. Littoria became Latina and the buildings and infrastructure inherited from the fascist period served as the physical basis for the maintenance of its status as the district capital and for its very rapid demographic and socio-economic development in the roaring years of the Italian economic boom. In those years, the 'agro-town' (un)wanted by Mussolini at the very centre of Pontine marshes was transformed into an important directional centre for the surrounding territory despite its location far away both from the great communication facilities and the sea. Mainly in the 1960s (before the large and largely uncontrolled urban development in the 1970s), Latina took on the aspect of a new 'vertical' city—with a skyline of medium-high buildings—that replaced the fascist 'horizontal' city, using the already existing spaces and infrastructure more intensively.

5   Concluding Remarks: Evaluation of the Experiment

Despite the self-evident difficulties of comparing two realities so different in space, time, and historical reality, this small experiment in the "ethnoarchaeology" of a new city seems to have paved the way for some interesting reflections on a number of different issues. The first one concerns the relationship between the imperial macro-economy and local micro-economies. The new cities of the sixth century appear more and more clearly as points of contact and interaction between two deeply different economic spheres, the general one and the local one. This means that they are the physical spaces in which the concentration of important state resources leads to significant changes in the local economic structures of their territories. These changes occur in different moments: immediately in real time when the new city is built, later during its lifespan, and, finally, after the end of its life as a "new" foundation (whether followed by the end of the urban experience in that territory or by a different form of urbanism). The second relevant element is represented by the physical and economic dimensions of building activities, both in terms of structures and infrastructure. These changes cause permanent or semi-permanent transformations of the local micro-ecological system, thus creating a somehow 'new' natural landscape. The third element is the lack of a direct relationship between the original intentions of the authority that decided to build a new city and the effects that this decision really had over the natural and human landscape, where the new city was located, in the short-, medium-, and long-term. Looking at these three points, the dynamic of the relationship between city and hinterland emerges as a research field of great complexity and interest in re-defining the spatiality of the Early Byzantine world. The cities which emerge as new foundations constitute undoubtedly an extraordinarily important field of study that deserves to be developed with the help of different approaches and research perspectives, and through the conduct of "unorthodox" experiments.

Bibliography

Secondary Sources

Alfieri, G. 2018. *Questo piatto di grano. La colonizzazione nell'Agro Pontino. Nomi, volti, origini delle famiglie che si insediarono*. Latina.

Antonelli, P. 2017. *Littoric-Latina. La città di nessuno*. Latina.

Arce, J. 2000. "La fundaciòn de nuevas ciudades en el Imperio romano tardìo: de Diocletiano a Justiniano (s. IV–VI)", in Ripoll & Gurt (eds) 2000, 31–62.

Arthur, P. 1991. "Naples: a case of urban survival in the early Middle Ages?" *Mélanges de l'Ecole Française de Rome, Antiquité* 103, 759–84.

Barsanti, C., A. Guiglia Guidobaldi & A. Iacobini (eds) 1988. *Atti della giornata di studio del Gruppo Nazionale di Coordinamento C.N.R "Storia dell'arte e della cultura artistica bizantina*. Roma.

Beckers, B. & B. Schütt 2013. "The elaborate floodwater harvesting system of ancient Resafa in Syria - Construction and reliability", *Journal of Arid Environments* 96, 31–47.

Bevilacqua, L. & G. Gasbarri (eds) 2018. *Picturing a Lost Empire*. Istanbul.

Blétry, S. 2017. "L'urbanisme et l'habitat de la ville de Zénobia-Halabiya: résultats de la mission franco-syrienne (2006–2010)", in Rizos (ed.) 2017, 137–52.

Cau Ontiveros, M. A. & C. Mas Florit (eds) 2019. *Change and Resilience. The Occupation of Mediterranean Islands in Late Antiquity*. Philadelphia.

Ciammaruconi, C. 2005. *Un clero per la «città nuova». I Salesiani da Littoria a Latina*. I. 1932–1942. Roma.

Crow, J. & B. Croke 1983. "Procopius and Dara", *JRS* 73, 143–59.

Curtis, D. 2013. "Is there an 'agro-town' model for Southern Italy? Exploring the diverse roots and development of the agro-town structure through a comparative case study in Apulia", *Continuity and Change* 28/3, 377–419.

DeLaine, J. 2006. "The cost of creation: technology at the service of construction", in Lo Cascio (ed.) 2006, 236–52.

de' Maffei, F., C. Barsanti & A. Guiglia Guidobaldi (eds) 1990. *Costantinopoli e l'arte delle province orientali*. Roma.

Freeman, P. & D. Kennedy (eds) 1986. *The Defence of the Roman and Byzantine East*. Oxford.

Furlan, I. 1984. *Accertamenti a Dara*. Padova.

Furlan, I. 1988. "Oìkema katàgheion. Una problematica struttura a Dara", in Barsanti, Guiglia Guidobaldi & Iacobini (eds) 1988, 105–29.

Furlan, I. 1995. "Cisterne a Dara", in Iacobini & Zanini (eds) 1995, 51–64.

Giorgi, E. 2016. *Archeologia dell'acqua a Gortina di Creta in età protobizantina*. Oxford.

Gruppuso, P. 2014. *Nell'Africa tenebrosa alle porte di Roma. Viaggio nelle Paludi Pontine e nel loro immaginario*. Roma.

Gussone, M. & D. Sack 2017. "Resafa/Syrien. Städtebauliche Entwicklung zwischen Kultort und Herreschaftssiz", in Rizos (ed.) 2017, 117–36.

Hassan, F. A. 1981. *Demographic Archaeology*. New York.

Horden, P. & N. Purcell 2000. *The Corrupting Sea. A Study on Mediterranean History*. Oxford.

Iacobini, A. & E. Zanini (eds) 1995. *Arte profana e arte sacra a Bisanzio*. Roma.

Ivanišević, V. 2016. "Caričin Grad (Justiniana Prima). A New-Discovered City for a 'New' Society", in *Proceedings of the 23rd International Congress of Byzantine Studies (Belgrade, 22–27 August 2016)* 2016, 107–26.

Ivanišević, V. 2017. "Main Patterns of Urbanism in Caricin Grad (Justiniana Prima)", in Rizos (ed.) 2017, 221–32.

Keser-Kayaalp, E. & N. Erdogan 2017. "Recent Research on Dara/Anastasiopolis", in Rizos (ed.) 2017, 153–76.

Konrad, M. 2001. *Der spätrömische Limes in Syrien. Archäologische Untersuchungen an den Grenzkastellen von Sura, Tetrapyrgium, Cholle und in Resafa*. Mainz.

Lauffray, J. 1983. *Halabiyya-Zenobia place forte du Limes oriental et la Haute Mésopotamie au VIe siècle 1. Les Duchés frotalier de Mésopotamie et les fortifications de Zenobia*. Paris.

Lavan, L. & W. Bowden (eds) 2003. *Theory and Practice in Late Antique Archaeology*. Leiden & Boston.

Lavan, L., E. Zanini & A. Sarantis (eds) 2007. *Technology in Transition A.D. 300–650*. Leiden & Boston.

Liguori, A. 2012. *Luce su Littoria 1932–1944. Aspetti sociali della bonifica nell'Agro pontino*. Latina.

Lo Cascio, E. (ed.) 2006. *Innovazione tecnica e progresso economico nel mondo romano*. Bari.

Mariani, R. 1976. *Fascismo e città nuove*. Milano.

Mariani, R. 2006. "Città nuove pontine", *Architettura* 14, 17–25.

Mouterde, R. & A. Poidebard 1945. *Le limes de Chalcis: organisation de la steppe en Haute-Syrie romaine documents aériens et épigraphiques*. Paris.

Muntoni, A. 2006. "Urbanistica e Architettura nelle città dell'Agro Pontino", *Architettura* 14, 26–35.

Ripoll, G. & J. M. Gurt (eds) 2000. *Sedes Regiae*. Barcelona.

Rizos, E. (ed.) 2017. *New cities in Late Antiquity: documents and archaeology*. Turnhout.

Whitby, M. 1986. "Procopius and the Development of Roman Defences in Upper Mesopotamia", in Freeman & Kennedy (eds) 1986, 717–35.

Zanini, E. 1990. "La cinta muraria di Dara. Materiali per un'analisi stratigrafica", in de' Maffei, Barsanti & Guiglia Guidobaldi (eds) 1990, 229–64.

Zanini, E. 1994. *Introduzione all'archeologia bizantina*. Roma.

Zanini, E. 2003. "The Urban Ideal and Urban Planning in Byzantine New Cities of the 6th Century A.D.", in Lavan & Bowden (eds) 2003, 196–223.

Zanini, E. 2007. "Technology and ideas: architects and master-builders in early Byzantine world", in Lavan, Zanini & Sarantis (eds) 2007, 381–405.

Zanini, E. 2018. "Doğu Sınırında Gezmek / Traveling Along the Eastern Border", in Bevilacqua & Gasbarri (eds) 2018, 143–72.

Zanini, E. 2019. "Macro-economy, Micro-ecology, and the Fate of Urbanized Landscape in Late Antique and Early Byzantine Crete", in Cau Ontiveros & Mas Florit (eds) 2019, 139–62.

Zanini, E. 2021. "Cost, value and wealth redistribution: micro- and macroeconomy in Early Byzantine evergetism", *PCA—Post Classical Archaeologies* 11, 137–62.

'The Humility of the Desert'

The Symbolic and Cultural Landscapes of Egyptian Monasticism

Darlene L. Brooks Hedstrom

In the late seventh century, Isaac of Alexandria fled his home to reside in the desert he loved. He wanted to find solitude. He did not do this because of the recent Arab conquests which disrupted his life in the city, but rather because he was frustrated by constant contact with his biological family and his Christian community. The desert (Coptic ⲁⲁⲓⲉ; Greek ἔρημος) he fled to was never fully described in his biography. The physical desert was not the subject of his affection. It was rather the *symbolic* desert he desired—a space that fostered greater spiritual connection to God and an arena to battle demons.[1] The place also provided emotional and physical distance from family and the non-monastic world.[2] The desert dissolved from the perfect place for solitude to a place for continuous engagement with other monks and Christian visitors. The entanglements with people, conversations, and social obligations weighed on Isaac. Now when he needed time alone, he slipped away from his monastic home to a dwelling place outside the monastery, further into the desert, often called the "Inner Desert" (ἐνδότατῳ ἔρημος), where he could escape the noise and obligations of being in community with others.[3] He was not really looking for a physical place of quietude, but rather a *symbolic* place—a place that would allow him to spiritually escape the physical world—the imagined desert.[4]

In the introduction to this volume, Veikou, Nilsson and James highlight the ambiguity that surrounds some of our terminology in discussing space and in particular the concept of landscape.[5] The term is one that is not used by our ancient authors, but they do discuss the physical and imagined world that is

---

1 Brakke 2006, 15–16; Lane 1993; Goehring 1993, 281–96.
2 On the mindscape of the desert, see the contribution by David Westberg (Chapter 26) in the present volume.
3 The Coptic word for his private residence is *ma nshōpe*, which literally means the "place of dwelling". Edition of the Coptic text: Amélineau 1890; English translation in Bell 1988, 57.
4 Goehring 1993, 2003. See Westberg, Chapter 26, on the importance of using movement to traverse a spiritual and physical desert as expressed in the story of Pachon in the *Historica Lausiaca*.
5 See Introduction, in this volume.

shaped by the environment and by place-making activities. In what follows I provide a theoretical framework for examining the monastic landscape as a bipartite space. It comprises a *symbolic* landscape, which is a space created by monastic authors as an idealized or mythologized space for monastic living, and the *cultural landscape*, which includes the natural environment, anthropogenic structures, and artifacts. Drawing upon archaeological evidence of monastic settlements, I survey how the physical desert was redesigned and ordered to serve the purposes of monastic living.[6] The evidence for the cultural landscape of monasticism differs significantly from the symbolic desert described in monastic literature.[7] In order to examine the cultural landscape of monasticism, I use theoretical models that help shift our attention away from what monks desired of the desert—the symbolic landscape—to look at the cultural landscape, which includes new evidence for how monks actually inhabited the desert and modified their environments to create new settlements.[8]

Recent papyrological work on excavated monastic archives reveals the complexity of the cultural landscape of monastic life and offers a corrective to examine the life of monks like Isaac in greater detail.[9] New reading strategies also provide fruitful avenues for reassessing hagiography for historical frameworks that may enhance our understanding of the natural environment, anthropogenic structures, and the artifacts that comprise a monastic site. In order to explore the cultural landscape of the monastic desert, I will first present the theoretical frameworks for reading the cultural landscape and then turn to the physical evidence that will build a more robust portrait of Egyptian monasticism.

---

6 One way to consider monastic communities is as a form of niche dwelling, which is part of the marginal environment, much like communities that adapt to the environment in creating new zones of habitation in earlier eras. See Spengler 2014; Bendrey 2011.
7 See Westberg's chapter #26 where he examines how physical movement within a desert landscape is coded as spiritual development within a monk's spiritual journey.
8 Niche Construction Theory (NCT) could be applied to the earliest monastic settlers who, like pastoralists, are often cast as being dependent upon the environment and initially itinerant, but greater analysis of the anthropogenic landscape illustrates the "cultural change toward cultural practice and acknowledges a reciprocal interaction between humans and the environment" (Spengler 2014, 818). Brooks Hedstrom 2017a, 106–9; Brooks Hedstrom 2007; Wipszycka 2009, 2018.
9 Krueger 1999. A fourth-century Melitian Hathor Monastery's archive in the Heracleopolites is part of a larger discussion of the wide variety of monasticism not found in literary accounts. For a discussion of the archive, see Kramer & Shelton 1987.

1   Why Study the Cultural Landscape? Theoretical Models

The field of Byzantine monastic archaeology has focused primarily on locating monastic settlements and offering a descriptive account of them, but with little analysis of the meaning of these components to those who inhabited the land.[10] The field of Byzantine archaeology in general has lagged behind other fields in embracing robust archaeological theory and was rather antiquated in its approach to material and landscape until now.[11]

One area of development in the 1990s was landscape archaeology, which evolved to encompass a much wider array of attributes and shifted our attention away from subsistence, exploitation, and adaptation of land to a relational view of the land with human experiences and emotions.[12] One way to consider the monastic landscape of Egypt is to adopt an archaeology of place as a lens for reading both archaeological material *and* literary sources as mutually informative for reconstructing the natural and cultural landscape—a space often neglected in the elite or high texts of hagiographers, biographers, and monastic leaders, who seek to create the symbolic landscape.[13]

The focus on the cultural meaning of archaeological material stems from the seminal work of Ian Hodder and fellow postprocessual archaeologists, who call for a "turn to things" in which one "explore[s] how the objectness of things contributes to the ways things assemble us" and not vice versa.[14] The call to take "things" seriously is not just a phenomenological or semantic exercise; the objective is an engaging path forward to reevaluate how we understand the relationship between materials and humans with the aim to treat them equally or at least symmetrically.[15] Using theoretical models for reading artifacts, texts, and sites, we can investigate how monks "conceptualized these spaces and actively created and modified them in culturally specific ways".[16] In this view landscape and humans have equal importance and reflect what is

---

10 Larger issues of cultural bias against Coptic Christianity and monastic remains are part of a larger problem facing Byzantine archaeology in general and in Egypt specifically. Brooks Hedstrom, 2017, 20–24.
11 See the contribution by Decker in the present volume. For comparative material from other monastic communities outside of the Byzantine world see Bowes 2011; Dailey 2013; Fogelin 2010.
12 David and Thomas 2016a.
13 David & Thomas 2016a, 38.
14 Hodder 2012, 14.
15 Hodder 1991; Nativ 2014; Webmoor & Witmore 2008, 53–70; Webmoor 2007.
16 Torrence 2002, 766.

called symmetrical archaeology.[17] This means one does not separate the cultural landscape from the symbolic landscape; rather the two landscapes are needed to understand the other and to build a more complete picture of how monks inhabited space.[18] Thus, this discussion will illustrate not only how the built environment changed the landscape of Byzantine Egypt but also how monks interacted with the natural world as they experienced it.[19]

In order to build the cultural landscape of monasticism, we need to look at neglected or overlooked materials that were not traditionally considered as informative for writing a history of life in the desert. Architecture of monastic communities is one component of the cultural landscape that has been described in a cursory manner but has not significantly challenged the perception that monks lived in caves or in the desert without any form of habitation. According to Cynthia Baker, objects and architecture are discursive things. They are not merely transparent things or objects that only require description.[20] Baker suggests that architecture reflects communities and that architecture, like smaller objects or even the larger landscape, can be overlooked. By turning a spotlight on the architecture of the monastic built environment, for example, we can intentionally assemble the cultural landscape of Egyptian monasticism.

The next step in constructing the cultural landscape of monasticism is to look at the other things of monastic life that have been disregarded. It seems counterintuitive to state that we would undervalue the artifacts of monastic life found through excavation, but the reality is that little has been recovered in Byzantine archaeology that has penetrated the historical narratives. In the case of Egyptian monasticism, if we adopt the frameworks of Bill Brown, Daniel Miller and Bjørnar Olsen, who call for a focus on things—both remarkable and mundane—we will set aside the stories of monastic men and women

---

17 Latour outlines the symmetrical values of things and attributing agency to things, which has equipped archaeologists with new language for discussing how non-human things may impact and act upon others. See Latour 2005, 106–8; Webmoor 2007, 563–78.

18 The study of cultural landscape is now linked to discussions of heritage management and the protection of various areas whose history and culture are under threat. In many ways the cultural landscape of Christian Egypt has been marginalized, along with Islamic Egypt, for a preferential landscape of Pharaonic Egypt. It is also important to note that post-colonial readings of landscape have highlighted the dominance of Western views of landscape that do not account for indigenous perspectives. For some communities, "the relationship between communities and landscapes is first and foremost cerebral and spiritual rather than visual" (Sinamai 2017, 400). Doyon 2018.

19 Taylor & Lennon 2011.

20 Baker 2002, 25.

FIGURE 13.1 Private kitchen from a monastic residential building in Wādī al-Naṭrūn, Egypt
AUTHOR'S COPYRIGHT

as the centre of stories in order to see the space and things around the famous monks.[21] For too long monastic sermons, hagiographies, and sayings of famous monks, both men and women, diminished the presence of the natural world and the built environment as the cultural landscape of monasticism. The cultural landscape, therefore, does not appear in the literary sources in ways that make it an object of admiration or even of interest, unlike the monks who are the main characters for emulation and edification. Coptic and Greek personal letters, financial records, and bequests found in excavated archives and middens allow us to see how monks regarded the desert and the things within it. Additionally, the discovery of private kitchens, leather shoes, and fishing nets provide new evidence to enrich the history of monastic life that is not immediately apparent in reading the literary sources (Figures 13.1–3).

21 Brown 2010; Miller 1987, 2005; Olsen 2003, 2010; Goldhill 2015; Webmoor & Witmore 2008; Brooks Hedstrom 2017a, 70–74; Brooks Hedstrom 2017b.

FIGURE 13.2 Leather sandal (#870-1903) from Byzantine Egypt showing punchwork, incising, and foot straps
COURTESY OF THE VICTORIAN AND ALBERT MUSEUM

FIGURE 13.3 Fishing net (14.1.560) found at the Topos of Apa Epiphanius in Western Thebes
COURTESY OF THE METROPOLITAN MUSEUM OF ART

2 The Physical Environment of the Cultural Landscape of Monasticism

Egypt's topographical features created the conditions for a desert monasticism that was very near and equally visible to nonmonastic communities.[22] Since the Nile served as the main avenue for transportation, most travellers could see monastic settlements while sailing. The natural landscape of Egypt offered a very rich and dynamic physical space for Byzantine Christians to begin building homosocial communities. The natural, tripartite landscape of Egypt includes the Nile, the expansive floodplains, and the near desert, whose cliffs and terraces rise vertically to frame the Nile valley below (Figure 13.4).

The cultural landscape of monastic Egypt is one shaped in large part by Byzantine monastic literature, which constructed a symbolic desert. The monastic movement introduced more people, primarily men, into abandoned

FIGURE 13.4   The proximity of the Nile, cultivated fields and desert cliffs
AUTHOR'S COPYRIGHT

---

22   For considerations of the landscape and other Byzantine monastic settlements, see Ashkenazi & Aviam 2012; Bar 2003, 2005; Brenk 2004; Patrich 2004. A study of later developments of monastic landholdings in a rural landscape is Kondyli 2010.

spaces such as caves, quarries, and tombs, along with visitors, to new settlements. The reclamation of the Egyptian deserts for habitation ushered in a new period of Byzantine expansion into areas previously used only for the extraction of natural resources, burials, and temporary shelters. In most cases, only limited documentary evidence was found in such encampments, perhaps reflecting a lower level of literacy among the miners, soldiers, and guards who were required to live at outposts in the near desert. The presence of temporary workers and of travellers making their way along well-worn tracks did not merit the attention of earlier scholars, who were more interested in literate populations.[23] As monks repurposed natural spaces for monastic living, visitors quickly followed and their residences became places for continued connections with the "inhabited world" (Figure 13.5).

Elevated as the stage for divine encounters and a space for temptation, the desert became a Christian place (*topos*) for spiritual performances of tragedy, comedy, and history.[24] It was as if the demons and temptations outnumbered the monks and the desert might engulf the little islands of devout souls.[25] This place, as it appears in the ancient and medieval monastic literature, was not a space based in the reality of Egypt's natural environment.[26] Rather, the monastic desert was conceptualized as a place devoid of people, buildings, and things.[27] Jacques Van der Vliet describes the landscape in monastic sources as "a palimpsest, both in its physical and in its ideological dimensions".[28] He acknowledges that the landscape has both a symbolic and cultural value, but that its symbolic or ideological component often overrides the story of monastic history.

When the desert did appear, it was as a one-dimensional character of its own, to indicate the place that was not the city. And thus, the desert was placed in opposition to the city. At times it became necessary to further divide the natural environment even further into the Inner and Outer deserts. Writers referred to the Inner Desert, which was more remote, and the Outer Desert, which was closer to non-monastic settlements and visible to others.[29] The admirable heroes of asceticism lived in the Inner Desert and only rarely encountered others. In contrast, the majority of monastic communities were

---

23 Bloxam 2011.
24 Øistein Endsjø 2008; Guillaumont 1975.
25 Brakke 2006.
26 Thomas 1998.
27 Brooks Hedstrom 2017a, 76–85.
28 Van der Vliet 2006.
29 Brooks Hedstrom 2017a, 82–83; Goehring 1993, 280–81; Vivian 1999, 15–21.

FIGURE 13.5 Thin border walls provided visual markers of settlements for travellers and residents of the desert in Middle Egypt near Dayr al-Bala'yzah
AUTHOR'S COPYRIGHT

integrated into the fabric of Byzantine life and their settlements are well attested in the archaeological record throughout Egypt.

The desire to relocate to the outskirts of the cultivated regions and to subject oneself to more dangers in the forms of animals, limited water, and questionable shelter might have appeared reckless to Egyptians who lived in the villages, towns, and cities of Egypt. Why would one seek the heat and endless sand, when one could retire to a comfortable home and be protected from animals and insects? Some of the dangers came from the environment's residents, who were displaced from their natural habitats by human construction.

Snakes, scorpions, gazelles, crocodiles,[30] hyenas, and rodents were equally at home in Byzantine Egypt as they were in pharaonic Egypt.[31]

Less present, but clearly evident in the archaeological record, is the presence of insects in monastic landscapes.[32] Shenoute, the archimandrite of the White Monastery in Upper Egypt, used insects as an allegory for the presence of heretics as pests in the church. Writing in *As I Sat on a Mountain*, Shenoute recognizes that some pagans elevate insects such as the dung beetle found in traditional Egyptian religion. He says: "Every fly is rejected, and they are hated, except by some of your sort (pagans), who consider them honorable [...] Justly hated are the flies that dwell on all unclean things (ⲁϥ ⲙⲉⲛ ⲛⲓⲙ ⲥⲧⲏⲩ ⲉⲃⲟⲗ ⲁⲩⲱ ⲥⲉⲙⲟⲥⲧⲉ ⲙⲙⲟⲟⲩ ⲉⲓⲙⲏⲧⲉⲓ ⲟⲛ ⲉϩⲟⲉⲓⲛⲉ ⲛⲧⲉⲧⲛϩⲉ ⲉⲩⲙⲉⲉⲩⲉ ⲉⲣⲟⲟⲩ ϫⲉ ⲥⲉⲧⲁⲉⲓⲏⲩ)".[33] Although Michael Psellos used the flee, louse, and bedbug as subjects for humorous and educational encomia,[34] few monks found insects to be subjects for appreciation or wonder. One evening a monk let a woman into his cell because she was being attacked by insects only to find himself tempted by her beauty. In response he burned each of his fingers off so he would not touch her.[35] Insects were a reality of daily life and made only rare appearances in monastic literature as elements to highlight the ascetic virtue of the monk. Despite their limited importance in the symbolic landscape, insects were very important in the cultural landscape of desert monasticism.

Archaeoentomological studies of mummies illustrate that Egyptians long contended with infestations of bed bugs, lice, and weevils.[36] Bed bugs were a reality of daily life and could be used as a natural method for training monks to ignore bodily discomfort.[37] Monks were instructed to "Let not another's hand approach you or caress you and never tell anybody to remove lice from your beard, your head or your clothing. (Μνδὲ προσεγγίσῃς χεῖρα ἀλλοτρία, μνδὲ προσκυνήσῃ σε, μνδὲ εἴπῃς ποτὲ τινὰ ἆραι φθεῖρα ἀπὸ τοῦ πώγονος ἢ τῆς κεφαλῆς σου ἢ ἐκ τοῦ ἱματίου σου)".[38] During Lent, one monk practiced self-confinement and

---

30 Nr. 295 recounts a story of a monk being licked by a crocodile, but not harmed. Wortley 2013, 198–99. Crocodiles could also protect monks from harm by attacking their assailants, such as a robber, for which, see Wortley 2013, 488–89 (Nr. 610).
31 See Allen 2005, 9–14 Hoath 2003.
32 Beavis 2002.
33 Coptic edition with French translation is Amélineau 1911, 338; English translation is Brakke & Crislip 2015.
34 Michael Psellos, *Encomium for the Louse* 15 (*Or. Min.* 26–28) as quoted in Hawhee 2017, 103–8.
35 Wortley 2013, 134–35 (Nr. 190).
36 Papagiotakopulu 2000, 2001.
37 Laiou 2010, 252.
38 Greek text and Enlgish translation is Wortley 2013, 426–27 (Nr. 592.65).

refused to see anyone for forty days. The devil's only response to this asceticism was to fill the monk's living quarters with bugs that infested his food, his water, and all his things.[39] The monk's discipline was rewarded when an army of ants, sent by God, came and battled the insects and carried each of the pests away. In rereading these accounts of monastic heroes, we can now see the insects as part of the cultural landscape of monks living and residing in a real, physical environment—one that was certainly infested.

Little work has been carried out on monastic burials to assess the impact of insect infestation on monastic individuals after burial, although new excavations present pathologies of various individuals and lives of monks involving their diet, health, and the presence of other organisms.[40] Evidence from the monastic site of Kom el-Nana, for example, at Amarna, suggests that the community had several infestations of insects in its gardens, pools, and complex water storage systems.[41] All of these anthropogenic structures created environments that attracted insects to live in new monastic settlements. Kom el-Nana's evidence illustrates how an attention to Egypt's cultural landscape provides important context for understanding the reality of living in a monastic desert that was now equipped with gardens for vegetables, pools for fish, and storage systems for water conservation.

Another example of the interplay between insects and water in the physical desert is found around the marshes and salt lakes in Wadi al-Natrun (ancient Sketis). The salt lakes provide ample ground for mosquitoes to thrive and they, like the wild animals, also appear as actors in monastic stories (Figure 13.6).[42] Makarios of Alexandria was human enough to detest mosquitoes and killed one after it had bitten him. As a form of penance for this violent act he elected to expose himself entirely to mosquitoes for six months. Sitting naked in the great desert (πανέρημος), Makarios suffered so many bites and swellings he was left unrecognizable to those who knew him.[43] His self-imposed punishment was a lesson in how to not be affected by pain by creating a pain so extreme that it led to his temporary disfigurement from welts and swelling. This story, often used to illustrate the horrible conditions of the symbolic desert, actually represents the real, physical environment of Wadi al-Natrun and the physical welts that a person might acquire while exposed to mosquitoes. It is

---

39   Wortley 2013, 628–29 (Nr. 763).
40   Dunand 2007; Dziezbicka & Ozarek 2012; Lösch, Hower-Tilmann & Zink 2013; Muc 2009; Piasecki 2000; Zych 2008.
41   Panagiotakopulu 2001, 1244.
42   Vivian 2003.
43   *Hist. Laus.* 18.4.

FIGURE 13.6   Accumulation of natron salt deposits at one of the four lakes in Wādī al-Naṭrūn
AUTHOR'S COPYRIGHT

not an unrealistic portrait, as many individuals can experience severe allergic reactions to insect bites. Like the insects or even the landscape, animals were not the main focus of the literary stories as the emphasis was upon the symbolic landscape. Despite this fact, we can reread well known sources to offer greater context to understand the presence of the cultural landscape embedded within these stories.

3   The Anthropogenic Structures of the Cultural Landscape of Monasticism

In moving our focus away from the physical environment of the desert to the built environment of the cultural landscape, we can see how much monastic builders modified and adapted the desert to facilitate their new ways of life. Egypt's riverine landscape had a significant impact on monastic settlements and spatial configurations. While monastic literature does not address the importance of canals, dikes, and waterwheels we learn from documentary evidence, excavated from numerous monastic sites, that monastic estates were equally concerned and invested in maintaining water pathways.[44] Unlike the pools and gardens associated with the monastery or monastic dwelling proper, the dikes lay in the agricultural lands, away from many of the monastic settlements proper. But this distance does not mean that the fields or the associated canals were not also part of the monastery. In fact, if we extend our spatial definition of the monastery to include the cultivated estates, the dikes, and the management of the fields by monks, then the built environment extends even further, and the edge of the desert is blurred. The desert's boundaries were permeable, much like the cultural landscape, which allows monastic and non-monastic people to interact regularly.

The cultural landscape of Byzantine Egypt is most evident with the advent of monasticism as new building projects appear in areas not previously used for long-term domestic habitation.[45] Monastics built many new, purpose-built settlements, and in some cases, they also used remodeled abandoned caves, tombs, and temporary shelters of those who once lived on the fringes. From the fifth to ninth centuries, monks participated in a process of desert reclamation by electing to use areas on the borderline between the densely-settled areas of the cultivated valley and the Delta.[46]

The intentionality of monastic construction to meet the needs of the resident and the challenges of the environment are apparent at several sites. Naqlun, in the Fayyum, is an example of site design in which monastics used the very contours of the cliffs to create spatial divisions within their large community.[47] In terms of construction of the residences, these too show a sensitivity to the natural environment as the rooms enhance morning and midday light to come into the large communal areas on the south side of the complex (Figure 13.7). Low afternoon indirect light is given to the dwelling areas on the north side of the complex as well as a kitchen.[48] Windows often align with

---

44   Bagnall 2007, 18.
45   The previous significant jump in settlement and urban development occurs in the Hellenistic period under the Ptolemies. Butzer 1960.
46   In part, the difficulty with looking at Egypt's rural landscape or countryside stems from the limited regional survey work that is possible in Egypt; thus, "While some regions such as Syria and Italy have been extensively surveyed over several decades, few surveys exist for Asia Minor or Egypt. Thus the heterogeneity of available information makes it impossible to give a complete or fully balanced picture of the state of the countryside in every region during late Antiquity" (8). For a discussion of the countryside as a physical and theoretical entity in archaeological studies in other areas of the late Roman and Byzantine Empire, see Chavarria & Lewit 2004.
47   Godlewski 2008; Dobrowolski 1992.
48   Mossakowska-Gaubert 2000.

FIGURE 13.7 One of over eighty monastic dwellings in the hills around Gebel Naqlun in the Fayyum Oasis
AUTHOR'S COPYRIGHT

ventilation shafts on opposite walls to allow for airflow through rooms as seen at the dwellings in Wadi al-Natrun and at Kellia.[49] The arid climate and the intensity of the heat in the summer months in Egypt required dwellings to have thick walls to retain the cool from the desert evenings. A similar feature exists in the dwellings at Esna, much further south in Upper Egypt, in which the residences were carved down into the sand plain. Steeply sloping window sills that extend almost to the floor provide the widest area for light to reflect down into the dwelling.[50] At Esna we see the use of short walls in front of doorways to prohibit wind-blown sand from entering into the rooms.[51] This feature is particularly important as the open courtyards are sunk into the desert floor and thus the depressions would naturally accumulate significant amounts of drift sand compared to buildings that were built level with the rest of the desert escarpment and terraces.

49 Nenein & Wuttmann 2000.
50 Sauneron & Jacquet 1972, 42–46, Fig. 17.
51 Sauneron & Jacquet 1972, 50–51, pl. XVIII.

Monastic letters recorded on papyrus and pottery sherds report on the activities of deliveries from monastic estates and the payment for services rendered in tending to the fields that lay adjacent to the desert's edge.[52] We also learn of goods and raw materials moving into and out from monastic communities with the help of non-monastic merchants. Sometimes monks required stones for building or sent out cakes to be distributed to the local communities. At other times, monks sent orders to each other to gather supplies for making nets, fetching food, or settling disputes.

In the fifth century, Shenoute, for example, told his monastic community:

ⲞⲨϨⲀⲘϢⲈ ⲆⲈ ⲞⲚ Ⲏ ⲞⲨϨⲀⲘⲔⲀⲖⲈ Ⲏ ⲞⲨⲈⲔⲰⲦ Ⲏ ⲞⲨⲤⲀⲈⲒⲚ ⲈⲨϢⲀⲚⲢⲞⲨϨⲰⲂ
ⲚⲀⲚ Ⲏ ⲈⲨϢⲀⲚϪⲒ ⲚⲦⲞⲞⲦⲞⲨ ⲚϨⲈⲚⲤⲔⲈⲨⲞⲤ ⲚⲂⲀⲖϪⲈ Ⲏ ϨⲈⲚⲤⲞⲦⲂⲈϤ ⲘⲂⲈⲚⲒⲠⲈ
Ⲏ ϨⲈⲚϨⲚⲀⲀⲨ ⲚϢⲈ Ⲏ ⲈⲨϢⲀⲚⲔⲰⲦ ⲚⲀⲚ ⲚⲞⲨⲘⲀ ⲈϨⲈⲚⲈⲔⲰⲦ ⲚⲈ ⲚⲢⲈϤⲔⲈⲦⲎⲒ
Ⲏ ⲈⲨϢⲀⲚⲢⲠⲀϨⲢⲈ ⲈⲨⲠⲖⲎⲄⲎ ⲈⲀⲤϢⲰⲠⲈ ϨⲒⲞⲨⲀ ⲚϨⲎⲦⲚ ⲚⲀⲒ ⲀⲨⲰ ⲚⲈⲒⲔⲞⲞⲨⲈ
ⲈⲚⲚⲀⲤⲘⲚⲠⲈⲨⲂⲈⲔⲈ ⲚⲘⲘⲀⲨ

And also, if a carpenter or smith or builder or doctor does some work for us; or if ceramic vessels or iron tools or wooden things are received from them; or if being house builders they build us a place; or if they treat a wound that one of us has gotten—we shall agree with them one and all on their wages.[53]

Shenoute offers a unique window into the cultural landscape in which monks worked with others for pay and that payments should be agreed upon and not altered. Such behaviours seem to be at odds with the portrait of the monks in the symbolic desert. It seems that the longer the monks resided in the monastic desert the greater value their built environments had. By the early eighth-century, Apa Helias was taken to task by another monk, Pinoute, for not making repairs to a monastic building under his charge. Writing in Coptic (*P.Bal.* 241), Pinoute relates his concerns for the structure and his displeasure with Helias' neglect of it and he complains that Apa Helias has not completed any work for three years at his small "dwelling-place (ⲘⲀ ⲚϢⲰⲠⲈ)".[54] Helias failed to make any bricks and did not place a necessary roof beam at the dwelling found at the site of Dayr al-Bala'yzah in Middle Egypt. In this letter we learn of Pinoute's personal ties and concerns about his building and his desire to ensure its maintenance by a fellow monk. For this monastic writer, the desert

---

52 Richter 2009, 210–12; Schenke 2019.
53 Coptic text and English translation is Layton 2014, 192–93 (Nr. 247).
54 *P.Bal.* 241. Kahle 1954, trans. 667–68.

was not devoid of things, but rather filled with things, and with the expectation for house maintenance that was not being followed by another.

The tension in the sources emerges when we read the difference between didactic materials for monks about the power of a place or space to shape one's asceticism and the documentary evidence illustrating that monks were fully participating in activities that brought them back into the relationships they sought to escape. For example, a list of payments (*P.Mich.* inv. 3935a) from the late fourth-century Oxyrhynchus papyri lists a monk receiving a payment consisting of two double jars. He is paid the same wages as a whitewasher and a brickmaker —both professions needed in construction of buildings.[55] The list does not seem to have a particular order, but Neel suggests the listing may reflect that the monk and skilled builders "worked together (i.e. in the same building) or close by".[56] Being in the workforce seems at odds with the monks who struggled to remain away from the world as described in the *Sayings of the Desert Fathers*.

Perhaps the most striking evidence to contradict the symbolic landscape of monasticism was the discovery of the monastic community at Kellia, otherwise known as the Cells in monastic literature. Excavations conducted since the late 1960s recovered a settlement that at its apex had over 1500 multi-roomed complexes in close proximity to each other.[57] Most dwellings had latrines, private kitchens, rooms for two monks, and a central room decorated for prayer. In many ways the residences resemble small villas in providing a full set of accommodations for comfortable living. Due to the location of the site in the wet Delta region, very little documentary evidence survives from Kellia to reveal the daily interactions monks had at the site. Painted and inscribed graffiti provide some clues to social expectations for monks to pray for others and the use of curses to damn anyone who might steal even a cup from another monk's residence. In a settlement with little documentary evidence, the architecture and its spatial configuration offer a vivid portrait of the cultural landscape of monasticism in Lower Egypt.

Further south at the Monastery of Apa Thomas, at Wadi Sarga, archaeologists were able to recover a treasure trove of letters along with extensive mud brick remains of anthropogenic strictures (Figure 13.8). The letters document how monks built new rooms and paid each other for their special services. The excavations at the monastery at Wadi Sarga, primarily unpublished until

---

55 Neel 2015; Choat 2002.
56 Neel 2015, 55.
57 Nenein & Wuttmann 2000; Kasser et al. 1967; Kasser, Favre & Weidmann 1972; Grossmann 2002.

FIGURE 13.8 The Monastery of Apa Thomas at Wadi Sarga. The North Building was built into and against the bed rock of the wadi with a combination of small boulders, mud brick, and plaster
COURTESY OF THE TRUSTEES OF THE BRITISH MUSEUM

now, included extensive physical remains of monastic housing, monastic correspondence, and a plethora of objects.[58] One set of rooms, the North Buildings, were engineered to integrate the physical bed rock into the rooms. Such planning is a testament to the community's planning in how to use the natural landscape as a component of the buildings. At another monastery the Archimandrite Daniel contracted Apa Paul, a carpenter, to complete a project on behalf of the monastery (P.Bal. 161).[59] The carpenter monk was paid with corn and wine as a payment in kind for services rendered.

The reality of the cultural landscape was not always accepted by monks. Some preferred the idea of the desert over the reality. A Coptic graffito at Aswan recounts a monk complaining that he hated his cell and wished to

[58] O'Connell 2014; Brooks Hedstrom 2017a, 33–36, 245–52. A more extensive publication is underway sponsored by the British Museum under the project direction of O'Connell. "Wadi Sarga at the British Museum", http://www.britishmuseum.org/research/research_projects/all_current_projects/wadi_sarga.aspx.

[59] P.Bal. 161. Kahle 1954, trans. 667–68.

leave.[60] A more permanent way of dealing with unhappiness in the desert was by divesting of one's monastic property. In the sixth century (*P. Princ.* II 84), a deed of sale presents a female monk named Euphemia selling the house that she co-owned with a male named Serenos.[61] Like other monastic men and women, Euphemia was able to sell her property as long as it was legally hers to sell or bequeath. Monks, just like their non-monastic counterparts, were property owners, thus illustrating that monks, male and female, were active in the buying, selling, and transfer of property.[62] Such earthly matters run counter to the narratives put forward in the stories of the symbolic landscape in which monks were free from the obligations of ownership. Yet, documentary evidence and the physical buildings of monastic communities reveal that the cultural landscape was far more complex and interconnected with the world outside of the desert.

4   The Things of the Cultural Landscape of Monasticism

New excavations and recent publications of sermons, papyri, and ostraca from late antique archives create a monastic landscape that is much closer and integrated into Byzantine life than previously thought. The evidence fills gaps left in the symbolic landscape by grounding monks within a very specific landscape.[63] For example, monks supervised deliveries, demanded a host of things from each other, made books, taught grammar, and moved across the landscape with goods. Texts from the Monastery of Epiphanius describe property they owned, non-monastic labour they hired, and payments to other monks for work (Figure 13.9).[64] When possible they used locally available materials to construct their buildings such as stone, mud, plaster, and wood and complained when deliveries were late.[65] The archaeological evidence for these communities exists and demonstrates that monks were engaged with

---

60   No. 29. Delattre, Dijkstra & Van Der Vliet 2015, 302.
61   Bagnall & Worp, 2003.
62   Choat 2009, 129–40; Wilfong 2003.
63   For differences between the generalized and specific landscape see Lars Fogelin's work on the Buddhist homosocial communities and the crafting of idealized landscapes. Fogelin 2006; Brooks Hedstrom 2017a, 72.
64   Brooks Hedstrom 2007.
65   Bricks from monastic sites include items found in animal dung with small pellets from sheep or goats, who were eating vegetation from wet or riverbank areas along with desert vegetation. Marinova et al. 2011.

FIGURE 13.9 Documentary source from the Topos of Apa Epiphanius, Western Thebes (*P.Mon.Epi.* 198)
PHOTOGRAPH © METROPOLITAN MUSEUM OF ART

the world and even with the very mundane objects of construction and modifications to the land.

Reading both monastic and non-monastic documentary evidence together helps build a picture of how monks lived and moved with each other and with animals. Domesticated animals served many functions. They provided milk, meat, clothing, fuel, and transportation of goods and people.[66] Several papyri and ostraca record the sale of animals between monastic and village members.[67] Account lists of goods found at monastic sites reveal a variety of animal skins (ox, goat, and sheep) that were traded.[68] Rooms with animal dung and pens at monasteries led archaeologists to identify some sites as spaces for animal husbandry. And a few monks have titles that demonstrate they were in charge of the dung, meaning they were working with camels, donkeys, and cattle. Dung patties were an essential fuel sources for the various kitchens at the monastery.[69] Domesticated animals therefore were an essential part of monastic life, and regardless of how many a community had, part of its built environment would have features designed for the care of these animals as part of the new anthropogenic landscape.

As we look at the cultural landscape, it is important to remember that monastic literature was more concerned to describe the symbolic landscape of the desert—the mindscape— than the actual, physical landscape inhabited by Egyptian monks. The purpose of the hagiographic literature was not to capture the lived experience of monastic life, but rather its ideal for the edification of readers and their audiences.[70] Fortunately archaeology offers new paths of

---

66   Bagnall 2007, 38–40.
67   *P.Bal.* 119 records how Peilitheos agreed to a price of one solidus for the sale of his ass and foal to Abraham, a resident at the monastery of Apa Mena. Kahle, 1954, 525–26.
68   *P.Bal.* 332. Kahle 1954, 768; *Clackson* 35. Clackson & Clackson 2009.
69   See *P. Louvain Lefort* copt. 9/4 in Clackson 2008, 27–42. Eighth-century tax receipts from Middle Egypt speak of monks who worked as dung-men being paid with garum and fish, food—goods commonly referenced in monastic diets.
70   Cain 2016; Goehring 2006; Frankfurter 2006.

inquiry that sometimes run entirely counter to the literary portrait of monasticism. The archaeology of monasticism consists of built structures, material objects, and also excavated archives consisting of papyri and ostraca intersect through spatial theories to build a more complex landscape of Byzantine monastic life.

Monastic authors consciously avoid focusing on the mundane aspects of monastic life. Rather than seeing the physical mud bricks, animals, and buildings that comprised the cultural landscape of monasticism, they crafted an imagined, symbolic landscape in which the realia of daily life were opaque.[71] The desert was not a quiet and remote topos. The desert may have contained demons, but it also included labourers, animals, disputes, and family visitors who accompanied monks on journeys and participated in their economic activities. While Athanasios was correct that "there were monasteries in the mountains, and the desert was made a city by monks", he was not accurate in stating monks left their people far behind when they moved into the desert.[72] In reality, monks brought the world with them and a study of the cultural landscape offers a richer portrait of actual spaces of Byzantine monasticism in Egypt.

Bibliography

Primary Sources

Amélineau, E. (ed. and trans.) 1890. *Historie du partiarche copte Isaac: Étude critique, texte et traduction.* Paris.

Bell, D. N. (trans.) 1988. *Mena of Nikiou: The Life of Isaac of Alexandria and the Martyrdom of Saint Macrobious.*

Brakke, D. & A. Crislip. 2015. *Selected Discourses of Shenoute the Great: Community, Theology, and Social Conflict in Late Antique Egypt.* Cambridge.

Clackson, S. (trans.) 2003. *It is Our Father Who Writes: Orders from the Monastery of Apollo at Bawit.* Cincinnati.

Kahle, P. E. (ed.) 1954. *P.Bal: Bala'izah: Coptic Texts from Deir el-Bala'izah in Upper Egypt,* 2 vols. London.

Kramer, B. & J. C. Shelton. 1987. *Das Archiv des Nepheros und Verwandte Texte.* Mainz am Rhein.

---

71 Sadek 1993.
72 *Life of Antony* 14; Vivian & Athanassakis 2003.

Vivian, T. and A. N. Athanassakis (trans.) 2003. Athanasius of Alexandria. *The Life of Antony: The Greek Life of Antony and the Coptic Life of Antony, and an Encomium on Saint Antony by John of Shmûn, and a Letter to the Disciples of Antony by Serapion of Thmuis.*

Wortley, J. (trans.) 2013. *The Anonymous Sayings of the Desert Fathers: A Select Edition and Complete English Translation.* Cambridge.

Secondary Sources

Allen, J. 2005. *The Art of Medicine in Ancient Egypt.* New York.

Ashkenazi, J. & M. Aviam 2012. "Monasteries, Monks and Villages in Western Galilee in Late Antiquity", *JLA* 5, 269–97.

Bagnall, R. (ed.) 2007. *Egypt in the Byzantine World, 300–700.* Cambridge.

Bagnall, R. S. & K. W. Worp 2003. "P. Princ. II 84 Revisited", *The Bulletin of the American Society of Papyrologists* 40, no. 1/4, 11–25.

Baker, C. M. 2002. *Rebuilding the House of Israel: Architectures of Gender in Jewish Antiquity.* Palo Alto.

Bar, D. 2003. "The Christianization of Rural Palestine during Late Antiquity", *Journal of Ecclesiastical History* 54.3, 401–21.

Bar, D. 2005. "Rural Monasticism as a Key Element in the Christianization of Byzantine Palestine", *Harvard Theological Review* 98.1, 49–65.

Beavis, I. C. 2002. *Insects and Other Invertebrates in Classical Antiquity.* Exeter.

Bendrey, R. 2011. "Some Like It Hot: Environmental Determinism and the Pastoral Economies of the Later Prehistoric Eurasian Steppe", *Pastoralism* 1.8, 1–16.

Bloxam, E. 2011. "Ancient Quarries in Mind: Pathways to a More Accessible Significance", *World Archaeology* 43.2, 149–66.

Boud'hors A., J. Clackson, C. Louis & P. Sijpesteijn (eds) 2009. *Monastic Estates in Late Antique and Early Islamic Egypt: Ostraca, Papyri, and Essays in Memory of Sarah Clackson (P. Clackson).* Cincinnati.

Brenk, B. 2004. "Monasteries as Rural Settlements: Patron-Dependence or Self-Sufficiency?", in Bowden, Lavan & Machado (eds) 2004, 447–78.

Brown, B. 2010. "Objects, Others, and Us (The Refabrication of Things)", *Critical Inquiry* 36.2, 183–217.

Bowden, W., L. Lavan & C. Machado (eds) 2004. *Recent Research on the Late Antique Countryside.* Leiden.

Bowes, K. 2011. "Inventing Ascetic Space: Houses, Monasteries and the 'Archaeology of Monasticism'", in Dey and Fentress (eds) 2011, 315–51.

Brakke, D. 2006. *Demons and the Making of the Monk Spiritual Combat in Early Christianity.* Cambridge.

Brooks Hedstrom, D. L. 2007. "Divine Architects: Designing the Monastic Dwelling Place", in Bagnall (ed.) 2007, 368–89.

Brooks Hedstrom, D. L. 2017a. *The Monastic Landscape of Late Antique Egypt: An Archaeological Reconstruction*. Cambridge.

Brooks Hedstrom, D. L. 2017b. "Reconsidering the Emerging Monastic Desertscape", in Van Doorn (ed.) 2017, 205–17.

Butzer, K. W. 1960. "Remarks on the Geography of Settlement in the Nile Valley during Hellenistic Times", *Bulletin de la Société de Géographie d'Égypte* 33, 5–36.

Cain, A. 2016. *The Greek Historia monachorum in Aegypto: Monastic Hagiography in the Late Fourth Century*. Oxford.

Chavarria, A. & T. Lewit 2004. "Archaeological Research on the Late Antique Countryside: A Bibliographic Essay", in Bowden, Lavan & Machado 2004, 3–51.

Choat, M. 2002. "The Development of the Usage of Terms for 'Monk' in Late Antique Egypt", *JAC* 45, 5–23.

Choat, M. 2009. "Property ownership and tax payment in fourth-century monasticism", in Boud'hors et al. (eds.) 2009, 129–40.

Clackson, J. & S. Clackson 2009. "*P. Clackson* 35: A Greek-Coptic Glossary from the Beinecke Collection", in Boud'hors et al. (eds.) 2009, 52–59.

Dailey, E. T. 2013. "Introducing Monastic Space: The Early Years, 250–750", in Dailey & Werronen 2013, 5–25.

Dailey E. T. and S. Werronen (eds) 2013. *Monastic Space through Time*. Leeds.

David, B. & J. Thomas 2016a. "Landscape Archaeology: Introduction", in Bruno and Thomas (eds.) 2016, 27–43.

David, B. & J. Thomas 2016b. *Handbook of Landscape Archaeology*. London.

Delattre, A., J. Dijkstra & J. Van Der Vliet 2015. "Christian Inscriptions from Egypt and Nubia 2 (2014)", *The Bulletin of the American Society of Papyrologists* 52, 297–314.

Delattre, A., M. Legendre & P. Sijpesteijn (eds) 2019. *Authority and Control in the Countryside: From Antiquity to Islam in the Mediterranean and Near East (sixth-tenth century)*. Leiden.

Dey, H. & E. Fentress (eds) 2011. *Western Monasticism Ante Litteram: The Spaces of Monastic Observance in Late Antiquity and the Early Middle Ages*. Turnhout.

Dijkstra, J. H. F. & M. van Dijk (eds) 2006. *The Encroaching Desert: Egyptian Hagiography and the Medieval West*. Leiden.

Dobrowolski, J. 1992. "The Monastic Complex of Naqlun—Topography of the Site", in Scholz (ed.) 1992, 309–25.

Doyon, W. 2018. "The History of Archaeology through the Eyes of Egyptians", in Effros and Lai (eds) 2018, 173–200.

Dunand, F. 2007. "Between Tradition and Innovation: Egyptian Funerary Practices in Late Antiquity", in Bagnall (ed.) 2007, 163–84.

Dziezbicka, D. & M. Ozarek 2012. "Two Burials from Cemetery A in Naqlun: Archaeological and Anthropological Remarks", *Polish Archaeology in the Mediterranean (Research 2009)* 21, 233–43.

Effros, B. & G. Lai (eds) 2018. *Unmasking Ideology in Imperial and Colonial Archaeology: Vocabulary, Symbols, and Legacy.* Los Angeles.

Endsjø, D. Ø. 2008. *Primordial Landscapes, Incorruptible Bodies: Desert Asceticism and the Christian Appropriation of Greek Ideas on Geography, Bodies, and Immortality.* New York.

Fahmy A. G., S. Kahlheber & A. C. D'Andrea (eds) 2011. *Windows on the African Past: Current Approaches to African Archaeology.* Frankfurt.

Fogelin, L. 2006. *Archaeology of Early Buddhism.* Lanham, MD.

Fogelin, L. 2010. "Material Practice and the Metamorphosis of a Sign: Early Buddhist Stupas and the Origin of Mahayana Buddhism", *Asian Perspectives* 51.2, 278–310.

Frankfurter, D. 2006. "Hagiography and the Reconstruction of Local Religion in Late Antique Egypt: Memories, Inventions, and Landscapes", in Dijkstra & van Dijk (eds.) 2006, 13–37.

Froschauer, H. & C. Römer (eds) 2008. *Spätantike Bibliotheken: Leben und Lesen in dem frühen Klöstern Ägyptens.* Wien.

Godlewski, W. 2008. "Naqlun: Monastery Never to Be Forgotten", in Froschauer & Römer (eds.) 2008, 71–80.

Goehring, J. E. 1993. "The Encroaching Desert: Literary Production and Ascetic Space in Early Christian Egypt", *Journal of Early Christian Studies* 1.3, 281–96.

Goehring, J. E. 2003. "The Dark Side of Landscape: Ideology and Power in the Christian Myth of the Desert", *Journal of Medieval and Early Modern Studies* 33.3, 437–51.

Goehring, J. E. 2006. "Remembering Abraham of Farshut: History, Hagiography, and the Fate of the Pachomian Tradition", *Journal of Early Christian Studies* 14, 1–26.

Goldhill, S. 2015. *The Buried Life of Things: How Objects Made History in Nineteenth-Century Britain.* Cambridge.

Grossmann, P. 2002. *Christliche Architektur in Ägypten.* Leiden.

Guillaumont, A. 1975. "La conception du désert chez les moines d'Égypte", *Revue de l'histoire des religions* 188, 3–21.

Hawhee, D. 2017. *Rhetoric in Tooth and Claw: Animals, Language, Sensation.* Chicago.

Hoath, R. 2003. *A Field Guild to the Mammals of Egypt.* Cairo.

Hodder, I. 1991. "Interpretive Archaeology and Its Role", *American Antiquity* 56.1, 7–18.

Hodder, I. 2012. *Entangled: An Archaeology of the Relationships between Human and Things.* Oxford.

Kasser, R. et al. 1967. *Kellia 1965 1. Topographie générale, mensurations et fouilles aux Qouçour 'Isa et aux Qouçour el-'Abid, mensurations aux Qouçour el 'Izeila.* Genève.

Kasser, R., S. Favre & D. Weidmann (eds) 1972. *Kellia. Topographie. Recherches suisses d'archéologie copte*, vol. 2. Genève.

Kondyli, F. 2010. "Tracing Monastic Economic Interests and Their Impact on the Rural Landscape of Late Byzantine Lemnos", *DOP* 64, 129–50.

Krueger, D. 1999. "Hagiography as an Ascetic Practice in the Early Christian East", *Journal of Religion* 79, no. 2, 216–32.

Laiou, A. 2010. *Gender, Society, and Economic Life in Byzantium*. Brooksfield, VT.

Lane, B. C. 1993. "Desert Catechesis: The Landscape, and Theology of Early Christian Monasticism", *Anglican Theological Review* 75, 292–314.

Latour, B. 2005. *Reassembling the Social: An Introduction to Actor-Network-Theory*. Oxford.

Lösch, S., E. Hower-Tilmann & A. Zink 2013. "Mummies and Skeletons from the Coptic Monastery Complex Deir el-Bachit in Thebes-West, Egypt", *Anthropologischer Anzeiger* 70.1, 27–41.

Manyanga, M. & S. Chirikure (eds) 2017. *Archives, Objects, Places and Landscapes: Multidisciplinary Approaches to Decolonize Zimbabwean Pasts*. Mankon.

Marinova, E. et al. 2011. "Plant Economy and Land Use in Middle Egypt during the Late Antique/Early Islamic Period: Archaeobotanical Analysis of Mud Bricks and Mud Plasters from the Area of Dayr al-Barshā", in Fahmy, Kahlheber & D'Andrea 2011, 119–36.

Mayerson, P. 2010. "The Pharanitai in Sinai and in Egypt", *The Bulletin of the American Society of Papyrologists* 47, 225–29.

Miller, D. 1987. *Material Culture and Mass Consumption*. Oxford.

Miller, D. 2005a. "Introduction", in Miller (ed.) 2005, 1–50.

Miller, D. (ed.) 2005b. *Materiality*. Durham, NC.

Mossakowska-Gaubert, M. 2000. "Question d'éclairage: ermitage no 44 à Naqlun (Fayyoum)", *Annales islamologiques* 34, 335–57.

Muc, A. 2009. "Some Remarks on the Egyptian Monastic Dress in the Context of Literary Sources and Funerary Finds", *Studies in Ancient Art and Civilization* 13, 183–88.

Nativ, A. 2014. "Anthropocentricity and the Archaeological Record: Towards a Sociology of Things", *Norwegian Archaeological Review* 47:2, 180–95.

Neel, J. 2015. "List of Payments (P.Mich. Inv. 3935a)", *The Bulletin of the American Society of Papyrologists* 52, 43–58.

Nenein, N. H. & M. Wuttmann 2000. *Kellia II. L'ermitage copte QR 195. 1. Archéologie et architecture*. Cairo.

O'Connell, E. 2014. "R. Campbell Thompson's 1913/14 Excavation of Wadi Sarga and Other Sites", *British Museum Studies in Ancient Egypt and Sudan* 21, 121–92.

Olsen, B. 2003. "Material Culture after Text Re-Membering Things", *Norwegian Archaeological Review* 36.2, 87–104.

Olsen, B. 2010. *In Defense of Things: Archaeology and the Ontology of Objects*. Lanham, MD.

Panagiotakopulu, P. 2001. "New Records for Ancient Pests: Archaeoentomology in Egypt", *Journal of Archaeological Science* 28, 1235–46.

Panagiotakopulu, P. 2000. *Archaeology and Entomology in the Eastern Mediterranean: Research into the History of Insect Synanthropy in Greece and Egypt*. Oxford.

Patrich, J. 2004. "Monastic Landscapes", in Bowden, Lavan & Machado (eds) 2004, 413–46.
Piasecki, K. 2000. "The Skulls from Naqlun", *Polish Archaeology in the Mediterranean* 12, 173–80.
Richter, T. S. 2009. "The Cultivation of Monastic Estates in Late Antique and Early Islamic Egypt: Some Evidence from Coptic Land Leases and Related Documents", in Boud'hors et al. (eds) 2009, 205–215.
Sadek, A. I. 1993. "Du désert des pharaons au désert des anachorètes" *Le Monde Copte* 21–22, 5–14.
Sauneron, S. & J. Jacquet. 1972. *Les ermitages chrétiens du désert d'Esna*, I. Cairo.
Schenke, G. 2019. "Monastic Control over Agriculture and Farming: New Evidence from the Egyptian Monastery of Apa Apollo at Bawit Concerning the Payment of APARCHE", in Delattre, Legendre & Sijpesteijn (eds) 2019, 420–31.
Scholz, P. O. (ed.) 1992. *Orbis Aethiopicus: Studia in honorem Stanislaus Chojnacki ntali septuagesimo quinto dicata, septuagesimo septimo oblate*. Albstadt.
Sinamai, A. 2017. "Myths as Metaphors: Understanding Narratives in Sustaining Living Cultural Landscapes in Zimbabwe and Australia", in Manyanga & Chirikure (eds.) 2017, 399–420.
Spengler, R. N. 2014. "Niche Dwelling vs. Niche Construction: Landscape Modification in the Bronze and Iron Ages of Central Asia", *Human Ecology* 42, no. 6: 813–21.
Taylor, K. & J. Lennon. 2011. "Cultural Landscapes: A Bridge between Culture and Nature", *International Journal of Heritage Studies* 17.6, 537–54.
Thomas, T. K. 1998. "Topoi: Investigations into Some Social and Spiritual Geographies of Post-Pharaonic Egypt", *The Bulletin of the American Society of Papyrologists* 35, no. 1/2, 9–16.
Torrence, R. 2002. "Cultural Landscapes on Garua Island, Papua New Guinea", *Antiquity* 766–76.
Van der Vliet, J. 2006. "Bringing Home the Homeless: Landscape and History in Egyptian Hagiography", *Church History and Religious Culture* 86.1/4, 39–55.
Van Doorn-Harder, N. (ed.) 2017. *Copts Revisited: Pharaohs, Caliphs and iPods. Theories, Methods and Topics in Coptic Studies*. Columbia.
Vivian, T. 1999. "Mountain and Desert: The Geographies of Early Coptic Monasticism", *Coptic Church Review* 12.1, 15–21.
Vivian, T. 2003. "The Peaceable Kingdom: Animals as Parables in the Virtues of Saint Macarius", *Anglican Theological Review* 85.3, 477–91.
Webmoor, T. 2007. "What About 'One More Turn After the Social' in Archaeological Reasoning? Taking Things Seriously", *World Archaeology* 39, 563–78.
Webmoor, T. & C. L. Witmore 2008. "Things Are Us! A Commentary on Human Things Relations under the Banner of a 'Social' Archaeology", *Norwegian Archaeological Review* 41.1, 53–70.

Wilfong, T. G. 2003. "Women's Things and Men's Things: Notes on Gender and Property at Jeme", *The Bulletin of the American Society of Papyrologists* 40. 1/4, 213–21.

Wipszycka, E. 2009. *Moines et communautés monastiques en Égypte (IVe–VIIIe siècles)*. Varsovie.

Wipszycka, E. 2018. *The Second Gift of The Nile, Monks and Monasteries in Late Antique Egypt*. Varsovie.

Zych, I. 2008. "Cemetery C in Naqlun: Preliminary Report on the Excavation in 2006", *Polish Archaeology in the Mediterranean* 18, 230–46.

From the Ancient Demes to the Byzantine Villages

Transformations of the Landscape in the Countryside of Athens

Georgios Pallis

Athens is a place rather favourable for a multi-layered reading of its historical landscape. Especially for the Byzantine period, one has the opportunity to look into the processes that altered the countryside as a result of the change from the ancient system of *demes* to a medieval mode of organisation with small settlements alongside scattered monastic communities. Both of these new modes contributed in the subsequent period to changing the identity of the space. In particular I will trace this transformation of the landscape of the plain that surrounds Athens and forms diachronically its direct and vital hinterland (Figure 14.1). This region supplied the city with manpower and material resources, affected its security, and composed the very scenery of its history. My research combines information from published archaeological evidence and historical sources, a traditional historiographical approach that will comprise a historical narrative regarding the role of Athenian and Attic landscapes in their inhabitants' diachronic development. I will begin with a synopsis of the evolution of the space based on the available historical and archaeological evidence. Thereafter, I will proceed to a definition of the stable and the mutable principles of this evolution within a period spanning the third to twelfth centuries CE.[1]

The Athenian plain is roughly triangular in shape, defined on the one hand by the Saronic Gulf whose coasts stretch from Perama to Kavouri and, on the other, by a mountain range with variated altitudes: Egaleo, Poikilon, Parnitha, Penteli and Hymettus.[2] The enclosed terrain formed and contained within this triangle is mostly lowland with few elevations mainly met at the west of

---

[1] Two recent theses pertain to a thorough historical and archaeological exploration of Attica during the period under discussion; the first is by Chryssa Kontogeorgopoulou (Kontogeorgopoulou 2011 and 2016) and the second by Elli Tzavella (Tzavella 2013). The present study focuses on the Athenian plain only, which has long been among my research interests, in terms of its monumental topography during the Middle Byzantine and the Ottoman periods, for which see Pallis 2007, 2009 and 2013.

[2] Nezis 2002.

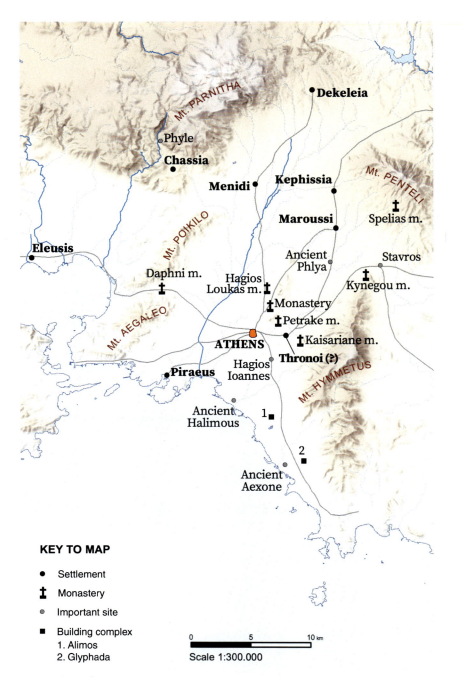

FIGURE 14.1 The Athenian plain and the sites under examination (Map: Eleutherios Tsouris)

Hymettus from the Tourkovounia hills to those of the Nymphs and the Muses. A large river, the Cephissus (modern Kifisos) crosses diagonally the plain and in doing so it is being fed by several tributaries and streams. This landscape is open to the sea with the natural harbour of Piraeus and the smooth shore of Phalerum (modern Faliron) and at the same time protected from the continental hinterland by a wall of mountains rising in almost every direction. The mountain passes designated the traffic routes leading to the neighbouring areas.

Human settlement in the Athenian plain dates back to the prehistoric period, when the first road trails were actually laid.[3] However, the turning point to all settlement and residential planning of the space was the *synoikismos* by Kleisthenes who in 508 BCE organised the deme of the *asty* and the rest of the settlements of the plain into forty-five *demes* of varying sizes.[4] These comprised of agricultural in their majority communities of free citizens who maintained their local cult as their cohesive element and participated actively in the functions and decision-making processes of the Athenian polity. In topographical terms, the *demes* were located in sites with natural attractions such as arable land and water resources or proximity to the coast. Despite the fact that this organisation gradually lost all of its political content, it remained alive until the third quarter of the third century CE, although it differed periodically either in the number of *demes* or in the tribal division of the settlements.[5]

The collapse of this system was the result of historical changes that were underway at both wider and local levels. The great crisis of the Roman Empire during the third century CE economically crushed many of the ancient cities and their traditional model of municipal self-government.[6] The Heruli sack of Athens in 267/8 struck a serious blow to its infrastructure and ancestral administrative models and marks its transition into Late Antiquity.[7] During the next centuries, the city and its surroundings followed the general developments that have been observed for settlements in the rest of Attica.[8] The countryside now acquired a more intense agricultural character and many of the rural agglomerations were either weakened and impoverished or disintegrated completely due to the transfer of the farming or pastoral activities to large agricultural manor houses and other secluded settlements. However, the

---

3   See cursorily, Pantelidou-Gofa 1997.
4   Traill 1975; Traill 1986; Whitehead 1986.
5   Traill 1975, 87–96; Sironen 1994.
6   Bowman, Garnsey & Cameron 2005, passim.
7   Frantz 1988, 1–15.
8   Fowden 1988.

foundation of Early Christian churches at sites once occupied by ancient *demes*, for example in Halimous (modern Alimos),[9] Aexoni (modern Glyfada),[10] and probably Athmonon (modern Amaroussion/Maroussi),[11] combined with other evidence,[12] suggests that several of these ancient localities were still active and flourishing. Additionally, these churches attest to the transition from Paganism to Christianity, a course of events that profoundly affected the identity of the landscape.[13]

The period between the seventh and ninth centuries, also known as "Dark Centuries" or as a period of transitions and transformations, is characterised by the scarcity of both the textual sources and material evidence that could be used to explore the conditions prevailing in the Athenian countryside. Yet it can be assumed that, while the city continued to be alive notwithstanding that it had shrunk within its Late Roman walls,[14] the countryside seemingly had been denuded of its manpower and rural settlements. The Slavic invasions were not followed by any resettlement, the only meagre evidence of which is a few toponyms.[15] Besides, the destruction of the basilica churches of Halimous and Aexoni verifies that the coastal area had turned into a dangerous place for the population living there. The coastal settlements were abandoned at around the time of the Arab conquest of Crete at the latest.

At the beginning of the Middle Byzantine period, an effort at reorganisation was undertaken, according to the archaeological data, in the countryside of the city. This has been traced at sites where natural conditions such as arable land and water resources were available at hand or at spaces located a safe distance from the coastline. For instance, at Maroussi, an inscription of 850/1 testifies to the inauguration of a church consecrated to the Virgin by Niketas the bishop of Athens (Figure 14.2), while various architectural and sculptural pieces and numismatic finds of the next century from the same site hint at the presence of an active community living there.[16] Similar evidence has been gathered from

---

9   Soteriou 1929, 195, Fig. 28; Orlandos 1933, 155–56, Fig. 203.
10 Orlandos 1930; Savvidou 2006.
11 Pallis 2004.
12 Especially the presence of early Christian spolia reused in churches of the Ottoman era.
13 On the process of christianisation of Attica and the role of the foundation of churches, see Tzavella 2014.
14 Karapli 2020, with references and bibliography.
15 Vasmer 1941, 120–23. The recent research on this matter does not acknowledge Slavic origin in some of the 18 toponyms that Vasmer included in his catalogue for Attica, such as the cases of Rentis or Mpala; hence the extent of any Slavic presence in the Athenian plain seems rather meagre.
16 Pallis 2013, 126–29, Fig. 4, with previous literature.

FIGURE 14.2   The inscription of 850/1 from Maroussi, squeeze of the now lost stone (after Orlandos 1933, 202, Fig. 272)

recent excavation reports of a chapel in Kephissia (modern Kifisia) containing burials in the nave, the earliest of which dates to the ninth century.[17] A little later, perhaps from the second half of the tenth century, monasticism was established in the vicinity of Athens in a systematic way, as suggested by the foundation of monasteries not only in the suburbs but also on the slopes of the neighbouring mountains too. Among the latter group, only their *katholika* survive today.

The city and its country prospered from the eleventh to the middle of the twelfth century. The rural agglomerations at Dekeleia, Chassia, Menidi, Kephissia, Maroussi, Thronoi, and Piraeus, and probably the *villages* Iskios and Lakkoi, which are named in the sources,[18] showcase a demographic growth which accords with the general developments seen elsewhere in the lands of the Byzantine Empire at the same time. Land use is organized through agriculture, animal husbandry, and other activities. These even expand into the coastal areas, which had not been considered secure until the middle of the tenth century. There, an isolated farmhouse and two large building compounds with possible agricultural functions were unearthed.[19] This period ends in 1204; the Frankish conquest followed a recession and period of decline over the last decades of the twelfth century. During the latter period, heavy taxation, abuse of power by local authorities, and shortages in foodstuffs afflicted

17   Andreadaki-Vlazaki 2012, 37.
18   Pallis 2013, 155–57. It should be stressed here that some of the unidentified, yet, settlements could also be contained within the borders of the area under discussion.
19   Pallis 2013, 150–55, 157, Fig. 7–9.

the population of the Athenian countryside, as suggested by the writings of its bishop, Michael Choniates.[20]

In what way did the landscape of Athens transform in this period, which spans approximately into nine centuries? How durable was the "canvass" of the ancient scenery onto which all these changes took place? Taking the settlement network as our starting point, we might observe that the system of *demes*, which survived for eight centuries, actually sealed the fate of the Athenian landscape. As John Travlos has long noted, the vast majority of Early Christian churches in Athens were founded at the sites of the ancient *demes*, hence the former can be used as means for tracking the latter,[21] as already mentioned in the cases of Halimous and Aexoni. Furthermore, the majority of the Byzantine villages, either archaeologically or textually attested in the sources of the eleventh and twelfth centuries, seem to have successively occupied the sites of ancient *demes*. Quite often they retained the same toponyms; two representative examples of this are Dekeleia and Kephissia. The names of ancient sanctuaries once consecrated to local cults – like the Pagrateion (Παγκράτειον) of Apollo Pagrates,[22] the Herakleion (Ἡράκλειον) of the Hephaistiads,[23] or the Amaryssion (Ἀμαρύσιον) of the Athmoneis[24] – continue even today to be used as landmarks of topographic importance around Athens, e.g. the districts of Pagrati, Arakli (modern Herakleion), and Amaroussion/Maroussi.

Critical factors for the population's attachment to the exact same sites were natural environment, as already mentioned, and historical circumstances. The abandonment of the coastline due to the dangers lurking from the sea, which presumably started after the sixth or seventh centuries, desolated flourishing *demes* such as Aexoni, Halimous, and Piraeus. In contrast, *demes* located on the safer midlands, such as Kephissia, Acharnai, and Dekeleia, continued to attract people from the plain. Evidence of agricultural and pastoral exploitation[25] and some chapels[26] seems to suggest that only after the recovery of the eleventh to twelfth century, when Athens had expanded to the south of the

---

20 The information given by Choniates has been assessed analytically in Herrin, 1975.
21 Travlos 1974.
22 Travlos 1980, 278–79, Fig. 356–61.
23 Klaffenbach 1926, 21–24, Abb. 1.
24 Pikoulas 1992–98.
25 Two large Middle Byzantine complexes of this kind have been unearthed at Alimos and Glyphada (Pallis 2013, 152, Fig. 8 and 154–155, Fig. 9, with references and bibliography).
26 The Early Christian basilicas of Alimos and Glyphada were rebuilt in smaller scale during the Middle Byzantine period (Soteriou 1929, 195, Fig. 28; Orlandos 1930, 260–61, Fig. 2). There is no evidence for settlements of this era near the two churches, which probably were serving as simple countryside chapels.

Acropolis and towards the sea,[27] did the population return to the coast; nevertheless, as far as we can tell, this come-back never really took the form of a permanent establishment.

The phenomenon of the ancient background's durability in regard to the location of certain settlements changes when we turn to the plain's road network, which seems to have been more stable. With the city of Athens as point of reference, the road axes radiated out in all directions from the coastline to the hinterland of Attica following the course that had already been cut in antiquity.[28] Their diachronic use has been verified both by the fact that they remain in use even nowadays and by the excavations of major highways such as the Sacred Way (Ἱερὰ Ὁδός) connecting Eleusis to Thebes and the Peloponnese, which has brought to light several layers of its paving. These could be regarded as testimonies of an enduring and constant use of the same logistic network from at least the Late Roman to the Middle Byzantine period.[29] Conversely, the ancient roadside temples that once existed were replaced by the small chapels built along those arteries. This is suggested by the church of Hagios Ioannis located on Vouliagmenis Avenue (Figure 14.3),[30] which runs along the eastern coast to the cape of Sounion.

A major concern of the Athenian polity during antiquity was the security of the villages and road network of the Athenian plain. This was accomplished by a system of fortifications, walls, and towers that were built in places and passages of strategic importance.[31] In the period under consideration, however, the countryside was left unattended, since the city of Athens was not the city-state it once had been but the centre of a periphery, albeit of secondary importance in a vast empire. According to all evidence, the Acropolis' castle and the walls of the lower city offered adequate refuge to the citizens of the nearby settlements and hamlets.[32] In case of invasion, the rest of population would probably have to run to the mountains. During the Early Christian period, there is evidence of resettlements in some ancient fortresses such as at Phyle in Parnitha, which controlled a pass to Boeotia and a few watchtowers,[33] but the evidence is inconclusive as to whether that was the result of military planning. Elli Tzavella underlines that Plyle fort underwent a systematic,

---

27 Bouras 2010, 85–94, Figs. 44–50.
28 Korres 2009.
29 E. Baziotopoulou-Valavani, CE 40 (1985) Chronicles, 32.
30 Bouras 2010, 191, with earlier bibliography.
31 McCredie 1966; Ober 1985; Munn 1993.
32 Bouras 2010, 29–40, Figs. 2–12.
33 Fowden 1988, 55–56, with references and bibliography.

FIGURE 14.3 The surviving part of Hagios Ioannis church at modern Vouliagmenis avenue
AUTHOR'S COPYRIGHT

masterly refurbishment,[34] but it is still uknown whether this work served the wider defence of Athens or just the safety of the small settlements in the fort and near it. Quite recently, the ruins of a building at Stavros of Agia Paraskevi were attributed to a watchtower dated to the third century CE or later, which would have overlooked the passage from the Athenian plain to the Mesogeia.[35]

In the following centuries the image of the defenceless countryside did not change drastically. Perils from the sea were dealt with by abandoning the entire coastal zone, although the presence of some form of a tower warning system cannot be excluded.[36] Only in the middle of the eleventh century was a measure adopted in order to control the main land route to the region. The foundation of the fortified monastery of Daphni (Figure 14.4) in the ancient Sacred Way, on the entrance of the pass to Eleusis, secured the main gate to the Athenian plain. The fortified monastic complex has only recently been proven not to have had an Early Christian phase as had previously been assumed.[37]

34 Tzavella 2021, 158–59, Fig. 3.
35 Christodoulou 2008. Tzavella (2021, 163) suggests that the chronology may be moved at least one century later, redating several small finds (glass vessels and a lamp).
36 Pallis 2012.
37 Delinikolas-Miltiadou-Fezans 2013.

FIGURE 14.4 The fortified monastery of Daphni, inner view of the north wall
© S. TOPOUZI

It has been suggested by Tonia Kiousopoulou that the great provincial monasteries were founded in a pre-determined location because they had other functions besides their religious ones.[38] To such a context probably belongs the compound of the monastery of Daphni, the only and biggest Middle Byzantine fortress in the whole of Attica. This twofold role – religious as well as military – can only be supported by its architectural layout, since literary or epigraphic evidence has been lost and its foundation still remain obscure. Maria Panayotidi-Kesisoglou has recently proposed that the founder could be ascribed to Gregory Kamateros, a high-rank official of the eleventh-twelfth centuries, who served as praetor of the adjacent themes of Hellas and the Peloponnese and owned land properties in the Athenian countryside.[39]

In a lowland such as the Athenian plain, agricultural activity marked its character in a decisive manner. The established cultivation of olives trees and vines, practiced since antiquity, was a factor of continuity during the medieval period. The great olive grove dating back to Peisistratus' time, which even on the eve of the twentieth century was still covering at length both sides of

38 Kiousopoulou 2009, 97.
39 Panayotidi-Kesisoglou 2019.

FIGURE 14.5 The central part Athenian olive grove as it was preserved in 1908 (after D. Aiginites, Τὸ κλίμα τῆς Ἀττικῆς, Athens 1908, 88–89)

the Cephissus river (Figure 14.5), must have flourished in the period under discussion, as we can indirectly presume from both written and archaeological sources.[40] Olive trees as a source of income were subject to taxation during the twelfth century. Besides, the survival of the ancient toponyms in the vicinity attest to a constant human presence, e.g. the case of Academia, which lived on until the nineteenth century as Akathemia or Kathemia.[41] Viticulture was equally important, as can be inferred by the newly discovered Middle-Byzantine wine-presses found on Piraeus street in Athens and in the suburb of Drossia.[42] We are informed by the sources that resin and a local variety of wine were produced in Attica, the last one in the ancient *deme* of Dekeleia and its eponymous medieval successor, located in the foothills of Parnitha; this wine was called Dekeleian (δεκελεικός οἶνος).[43] Apart from olive-growing and viticulture, other economic activities were husbandry, timber, and apiculture, all of which must have turned the mountainous regions into income resources for a great part of the population.[44]

The religious factor was also crucial for the landscape in a most meaningful way. The broader area of Athens always had a powerful pagan background consisting of different cults, which were rather widespread as each *deme* had a number of municipal temples. New cults and deities of Eastern origin were added to the latter during Late Antiquity. However, a lack of sufficient

---

40 Ropaitou-Tsapareli 2006, 43–45; Pallis 2013, 139–41, 160, with references and bibliography.
41 Biris 1971, 16.
42 Andreadaki-Vlazaki 2012, 35–36, Figs. 12–13 and 37, Figs. 19–20.
43 Pallis 2013, 160–61, with literature.
44 Pallis 2013, 161–62, 164, with literature.

evidence challenges our understanding of the ways in which this transition from Paganism to Christianity took place. The foundation of the basilica churches in the former *demes* of Halimous and Aexoni and the abundant presence of *spolia* around the site of Amaryssion, Artemis' temple in Maroussi,[45] are tokens of the penetration of the new religion within the ancient landscape of Athens and, with reference to the last case, in their own cult centres. It could be postulated that due to the geographical contiguity of the plain to the city of Athens, where the old pagan cults were on solid ground, the Christianisation of the region was a slower process compared to the rest of the Attica. The three taurobolic altars from Flya (modern Chalandri), which were dated to the end of the fourth century CE,[46] suggest that the local mystical cults continued to be practised and preserved their power in spite of the changing and increasingly hostile environment around them. Worthy of mention are the cases of the pagan cult of Omvrios Zeus, whose temple at the peak of Hymettus was probably still in use by the end of the fourth or the beginning of the fifth century,[47] or the worship of Pan in grottos such as those in Vari[48] and Parnitha,[49] which continued up to the fifth century. According to Garth Fowden, these isolated and sacred places attracted both the literate ethnic population of Athens and the local pastoral one; the latter who lived far away from the *asty* presumably continued worshipping the old gods for a long time.[50] Alongside the shifting religious synthesis of population, the landscape was slow to lose its pagan character.

The foundation of the monasteries at the foothills of the city and at the slopes of the nearby mountains[51] from the middle of the tenth century and onwards was decisive in reshaping the Athenian landscape on its religious basis. The first monastery of Kaisariani on Hymettus,[52] the so-called "Frankish church" (Frankoklissia),[53] and the compound of Spelia at Penteli[54] (Figure 14.6),

---

45 See above n.11.
46 Skaltsas 2001, 368–69, no. 784, with previous literature; Saradi & Eliopoulos 2011, 285–87.
47 Langdon 1976, 73–74, 76, 95, pl. 28.
48 Schröner & Goette 2004, 100–6, 108–10, T. 58–64.
49 Skias 1918.
50 Fowden 1988, 57.
51 On the scepticism upon the geographical placement of the monasteries see Kiousopoulou 2009, 95–97. The relevant testimony from the hagiographical sources has collected and evaluated Michel Kaplan (Kaplan 2001a).
52 Orlandos 1933, 164, Figs. 219–20. On the literature regarding to the excavations on the site see Pallis 2013, 147–48, Fig. 6.
53 Orlandos 1933, 194, Fig. 259; Dimitrokallis 1991. See more explicitly Pallis 2013, 124–26.
54 Major bibliographical titles for the architecture and painting of the monastic complex: Moutsopoulos 1960; Mouriki 1973–74. See in detail also Pallis 2013, 122–24.

FIGURE 14.6   The church complex at Penteli cave
AUTHOR'S COPYRIGHT

all dated to the second half of tenth century, point to an organised anchoritic movement. A part of their contemporary "suburban" monasteries are the surviving churches of the Asomatoi Petraki,[55] or the church of the Taxiarchs at the Pedion tou Areos.[56] It would, thus, seem that the city was surrounded by two distinct monastic circles creating a sacred-and-protective ground around it: a central one within its direct circumference, and a peripheral one located in the mountains.[57] These institutions, due to their prominent liturgical life and important economic activities, flourished in the following two centuries and were considered the new landmarks of the Athenian plain, reaffirming in a way its spiritual and metaphysical dimensions which had been long lost since its pagan past died out.

According to the above evidence, the image put together so far from the third to the twelfth century for the landscape of the Athenian plain has elements of both continuity and transformation that are either independent or

---

55   Bouras 2010, 223–29, Figs. 210–15, with earlier literature.
56   Orlandos 1929–30, 582, T. 6; Orlandos 1933, 132, Figs. 168–69; Pallis 2013, 135–36.
57   On the importance of the mountains for the byzantine monasticism see Talbot 2001.

interwoven with other phenomena. The crystallized ancient urban network seems to have survived at those sites where natural resources and historical conditions allow it, preserving original toponyms. Furthermore, the process of the abandonment of the coastal zone and the withdrawal of habitation into the safer midlands did not cease except sporadically, and only during the zenith of the eleventh century. Nonetheless, the preservation of the road network suggests that it was being used throughout this whole era, even probably during the somewhat obscure, transitional period. The loss of Athens' political importance might have left the countryside defenceless against invasions and even limited the city's ability to protect itself. But the same is true for the routes by land and sea, which were left uncontrolled, with the coincidental exception of the fortified monastery of Daphni. On the one hand, the productive cycle of agricultural activities with a key emphasis on olive-growing and viticulture kept the human landscape unchanged and bonded it to its natural environment. On the other hand, through the processes of abandonment, reoccupation, and oblivion, the transition from Paganism to Christianity released all those sites that were of importance to the ancient cult and helped recreate a new religious identity that was forged by the monasteries of the countryside. In short, the picture of the Athenian landscape matches that of a place where the past has designated its principal features in terms of habitation and logistics, where the feeling of security was usually at stake in perilous times, and where ancient productive activities were retained, but whose religious identity re-emerged completely anew.[58]

Bibliography

Secondary Sources

Andreadaki-Vlazaki, M. (ed.) 2012. *2000–2010. Από το ανασκαφικό έργο των Εφορειών Αρχαιοτήτων*. Athens.

Biris, K. H. 1971. *Αι τοπωνυμίαι της πόλεως και των περιχώρων των Αθηνών*. Athens.

Bouras, Ch. 2010. *Βυζαντινή Αθήνα, 10ος–12ος αι., Mouseio Benaki, Supplement*, 6. Athens.

Bowman, A. K., P. Garnsey & A. Cameron (eds) 2005. *The Cambridge Ancient History, Second Edition, v. XII. The Crisis of Empire, AD* 193–337. Cambridge.

Castrén, P. 1994. *Post-Herulian Athens*. Helsinki, 15–62.

---

[58] I would like to thank my colleagues Myrto Veikou for her precious remarks on this paper, Sophia Topouzi for the picture of the Daphni monastery wall as well the geographer, Lefteris Tsouris, for designing the map of the area.

Christodoulou, D. N. 2008. "Ογκώδες κτίσμα Ρωμαϊκής περιόδου στο Σταυρό Αγίας Παρασκευής: Το πέρασμα στα Μεσόγεια κατά την ύστερη αρχαιότητα", Πρακτικά ΙΒ' Επιστημονικής Συνάντησης ΝΑ Αττικής (Παλλήνη 30 Νοεμβρίου – 3 Δεκεμβρίου 2006). Kalyvia Thorikou Attikis, 309–26.

Delinikolas, N. & A. Miltiadou-Fezans. 2013. Ο μεγάλος περίβολος της μονής Δαφνίου, Τριακοστό Τρίτο Συμπόσιο Βυζαντινής και Μεταβυζαντινής Αρχαιολογίας και Τέχνης (Αθήνα, 17–19 Μαΐου 2013), Πρόγραμμα και περιλήψεις εισηγήσεων και ανακοινώσεων. Athens, 45–46.

Dimitrokalles, G. 1991. Η Φραγκοκκλησιά της Πεντέλης, Ενδέκατο Συμπόσιο Βυζαντινής και Μεταβυζαντινής Αρχαιολογίας και Τέχνης (Αθήνα, 31 Μαΐου – 2 Ιουνίου 1991), Πρόγραμμα και Περιλήψεις Ανακοινώσεων. Athens, 40–41.

Fowden, G. 1988. "City and Mountain in Late Roman Attica", *Journal of Hellenic Studies* 108, 48–59.

Frantz, A. 1988. *Late Antiquity: AD 267–700. The Athenian Agora, XXIV*. Princeton, NJ.

Gratziou, O. & Ch. Loukos (eds) 2009. Ψηφίδες. Μελέτες Ιστορίας, Αρχαιολογίας και Τέχνης στη μνήμη της Στέλλας Παπαδακη-Oekland. Herakleion.

Herrin, J. 1975. "Realities of Byzantine Provincial Government: Hellas and Peloponnesos, 1180–205", *DOP* 29, 253–84.

Kaplan, M. 2001a. "Le choix du lieu saint d'après certaines sources hagiographiques byzantines", in Kaplan 2001b, 183–98.

Kaplan, M. (ed.) 2001b. *Le sacré et son inscription dans l'espace à Byzance et en Orient, Byzantina Sorboniensa 18*. Paris.

Karapli, K. 2020. "Athènes et les «siècles obscures»", Βυζαντινός Δόμος 28, 683–700.

Kiousopoulou, T. 2009. "Η γεωγραφία των βυζαντινών μοναστηριών. Παρατηρήσεις για μια τυπολογία", in Gratziou and Loukos (eds) 2009, 95–106.

Klaffenbach, G. 1926. "Zwei neue Horossteine aus Attika", *Mitteilungen des Deutschen Archäologischen Instituts, Athenische Abteilung* 51, 21–25.

Kontogeorgopoulou, Ch. 2011. Η Αττική κατά την πρώιμη και μέση βυζαντινή περίοδο (324–1204), Διατριβή επί διδακτορία. Athens.

Kontogeorgopoulou, Ch. 2016. Η βυζαντινή Αττική. Athens.

Korres, M. (ed.) 2009. Αττικής οδοί. Αρχαίοι δρόμοι της Αττικής. Athens.

Langdon, M. K. 1976. *A Sanctuary of Zeus on Mount Hymettos, Hesperia Supplement XVI*. Princeton.

Lavan, L. & M. Mulvyan (eds) 2011. *The Archaeology of Late Antique Paganism*. Leiden.

McCredie, J. R. 1966. *Fortified Military Camps in Attica, Hesperia Supplements XI*. Princeton.

Mouriki, D. 1973–74. "Οι βυζαντινές τοιχογραφίες των παρεκκλησίων της Σπηλιάς της Πεντέλης", *DChAE*, ser. 4, v. 7, 79–119, pl. 20–44.

Moutsopoulos, N. 1960. "Το ασκηταριό της Σπηλιάς του Νταβέλη", Ζυγός 50, 34–42.

Munn, M. H. 1993. *The Defence of Attica. The Dema Wall and the Boeotian War of 378–375 B.C.* Berkeley.
Nezis, N. 2002. *Τα βουνά της Αττικής. Γεωγραφία – φύση – μνημεία – τοπωνυμία – βιβλιογραφία*. Athens.
Ober, J. 1985. *Fortress Attica. Defense of the Athenian Land Frontier, 404–322 B.C.* Leiden.
Orlandos, A. K. 1929–30. "Eine unbeachtete Kuppelform", BZ 30, 577–82.
Orlandos, A. K. 1930. "La basilique paléochretienne de Glyphada", *Praktika tis Akademias Athenon* 5, 258–65.
Orlandos, A. K. 1933. *Μεσαιωνικά μνημεία της πεδιάδος των Αθηνών και των κλιτύων Υμηττού-Πεντελικού-Πάρνηθος και Αιγάλεω, Ευρετήριον των Μεσαιωνικών Μνημείων της Ελλάδος*, τ. 3. Athens, 123–230.
Pallis, G. 2004. "The Early Christian Attica: The Area of Marussi", *The Eastern Mediterranean in the Late Antique and Early Byzantine Periods. Papers and Monographs of the Finnish Institute at Athens* 9. Helsinki, 59–73.
Pallis, G. 2007. "The Topography of the Athenian Plain Under the Ottoman Rule (1456–1821)", *The Historical Review/La Revue Historique* 4, 33–58.
Pallis, G. 2009. *Τοπογραφία του αθηναϊκού πεδίου κατά την μεταβυζαντινή περίοδο. Οικισμοί, οδικό δίκτυο και μνημεία*. Thessaloniki.
Pallis, G. 2012. "Μεσαιωνικοί πύργοι στα παράλια της Αθήνας", *Πόλη και ύπαιθρος στη Μεσόγειο. Diachronia, Supplement* II, Athens, 145–60.
Pallis, G. 2013. "Τοπογραφικά του αθηναϊκού πεδίου κατά τη μέση βυζαντινή περίοδο (9ος–12ος αι.)", *Byzantina Symmeikta* 23, 105–82.
Panayotidi-Kesisoglou 2019. "Αναζητώντας τον ιδρυτή της μονής Δαφνίου", *DChAE*, ser. 4, v. 40, 193–222.
Pantelidou-Gofa, M. 1997. *Η νεολιθική Αττική*. Athens.
Pikoulas, G. A. 1992–98. "Ἀμαρυσία Ἄρτεμις Ἀθμονῆσι", ΗΟΡΟΣ 10–12, 205–14.
Ropaitou-Tsapareli, Z. E. 2006. *Ο Ελαιώνας της Αθήνας. Ο χώρος και οι άνθρωποι στο πέρασμα του χρόνου*. Athens.
Saradi, H. G. & D. Eliopoulos. 2011. "Late Paganism and Christianization in Greece", in Lavan and Mulvyan (eds), 263–310.
Saradi, H. 2021 (ed.). *Byzantine Athens. Proceedings of a Conference* (Athens, May 21-23, 2016, Byzantine and Christian Museum). Athens.
Savvidou, Ch. 2006. "Βασιλική της Γλυφάδας", *Εικοστό έκτο Συμπόσιο Βυζαντινής και Μεταβυζαντινής Αρχαιολογίας και Τέχνης* (Αθήνα 12–14 Μαΐου 2006), *Πρόγραμμα και Περιλήψεις Εισηγήσεων και Ανακοινώσεων*. Athens, 76–77.
Schröner, G. & H. R. Goette. 2004. *Die Pan-Grotee von Vari*. Mainz am Rhein.
Sironen, E. 1994. "Life and Administration of Late Roman Attica in the Light of Public Inscriptions", in Castrén (ed.), 15–62.
Skaltsas, N. 2001. *Εθνικό Αρχαιολογικό Μουσείο. Τα γλυπτά. Κατάλογος*. Athens.

Skias, A. 1918. "Το παρά την Φυλήν άντρον του Πανός κατά τας ανασκαφάς των ετών 1900 και 1901", *Αρχαιολογική Εφημερίς*, 1–28.

Soteriou, G. 1929. "Αι παλαιοχριστιανικαί βασιλικαί της Ελλάδος", *Archaeologiki Ephemeris*, 161–248.

Talbot, A. M. 2001. "Les saint montagnes à Byzance", in Kaplan (ed.) 2001b, 263–75.

Traill, J. S. 1975. *The Political Organization of Attica. A Study of the Demes, Trittyes, and Phylae, and their Representation in the Athenian Council.* Princeton.

Traill, J. S. 1986. *Demos and Trittys. Epigraphical and Topographical Studies in the Organization of Attica.* Toronto.

Travlos, I. 1974. "Νέα στοιχεία για τον προσδιορισμό της θέσεως των αρχαίων δήμων της Αττικής", *Επιστημονική Επετηρίς Πολυτεχνικής Σχολής Αριστοτελείου Πανεπιστημίου Θεσσαλονίκης* 6.2, 187–92.

Travlos, J. 1980. *Pictorial Dictionary of Ancient Athens*. New York.

Tzavella, E. 2013. *Urban and Rural Landscape in Attica in the Early and Middle Byzantine Period (4th–12th c.).* Ph.D. Thesis, University of Birmingham.

Tzavella, E. 2014. "Christianization of Attica. The topography of Early Christian churches", *Pharos* 20.2, 121–158.

Tzavella, E. 2021. "Defence in Early Byzantine Attica (4th–7th Centuries): Fortified Towns, Forts, and Guard Posts", in Saradi (ed.), 154–169.

Vasmer, M. 1941. *Die Slaven in Griechenland.* Berlin.

Whitehead, D. 1986. *The Demes of Attica, 508-7-ca. 250 B.C. A Political and Social Study.* Princeton.

PART 4

Empowered Spaces: Byzantine Territories

∴

Editorial Note on Part 4

This section deals with space as a power device. The concept of territory serves well relevant discussions, because it offers the conception of a space as physical container and support of the body politic organized under a particular governmental structure. The five chapters consider very different spaces as territories: the capital city; a city (Venice); a small province (Peloponnese); entire geographical areas (the Northern frontier, i.e. the Balkan peninsula, and the Eastern frontier in Asia Minor). They focus upon connections between spatiality, political power, and identity.

With a case study on Late Byzantine Constantinople, Tonia Kioussopoulou elaborates on the close connection between the exertion of political power and the urban space as a bearer of social relations. Kiousopoulou works towards two ends. She seeks to understand the ways in which the building policy of the Palaiologoi was connected to their exertion of power, but she also explores the image of the capital through the prism of the emperor's understanding of the organisation of space. Konstantinos Moustakas discusses the transformation of Byzantine perceptions of geographic regions in the Balkan Peninsula between the sixth and the ninth centuries. Through a scrutiny of the interplay between geography, shifts in the exertion of power, and constructions of collective identity, Moustakas demonstrates that Byzantine authors' background and distance from the core land of Byzantium informed their understanding of Byzantine geography. Ilias Anagnostakis and Maria Leontsini reflect on the interplay between space and politics and present ways in which political events change perceptions of geography and place. In their case study about Byzantine Peloponnese, they present connections between the physical features of that space, the human agency and mobility that it hosted, and the the long-term transformation of both. Alexander Beihammer's chapter on the fluid Byzantine-Turkish frontier, in Asia Minor, showcases the permeability of these borderlands during the twelfth century. Beihammer demonstrates the direct reciprocation between political administration and space as landscape through this representation of Asia Minor as a political 'mosaic' constituted by an assembly of fragmented regional powers and mobile groups. Sauro Gelichi concludes this section with his study on a 'formerly Byzantine' city, Venice, reflecting on the formation of Venetian identity and its relationship to Byzantium in the Early Medieval period. Gelichi relies for his inquiry upon material indicators (ceramics, sarcophagi, *spolia*) in order to trace the Venetian elite's 'material' ways of exerting power in the city and transforming citizens' collective identities.

L'inscription du pouvoir impérial dans l'espace urbain constantinopolitain à l'époque des Paléologues

Tonia Kiousopoulou

Resumé

The starting point for the analysis attempted here is the question as to whether the first Palaiologoi, with their rise to the throne and the ushering in of a new period in the governance of the state, sought to reshape Constantinople. Given this question, the image of the city in the early 14th century is not in itself what interests us here. What *is* of interest are the implications for the relationship between (imperial) power and (urban) space, understood, of course, as a bearer of social relations. In other words, the aim is to examine to what extent the building policy of the Palaiologoi reflects their understanding of the exercise of power, and vice versa: to explore the image of the capital through the prism of the emperor's understanding of the organisation of space.

L'historiographie de Constantinople est très riche, surtout en ce qui concerne sa fondation et son histoire jusqu'à l'époque des Comnènes. Les informations fournies par les sources écrites ainsi que les résultats des récentes fouilles archéologiques nous permettent d'apercevoir l'évolution du paysage urbain et la transformation de la capitale de l'Empire Romain de l'Orient en ville médiévale. En revanche, on dispose de peu d'études traitant de la période tardive, dont plusieurs se consacrent à quelques bâtiments de cette époque ayant survécu, d'églises, dans la plupart des cas, considérées comme des exceptions dans cette période de "décadence". Il s'agit d'une lacune de l'historiographie, souvent signalée, et due entre autres causes à l'absence de données archéologiques.[1]

En dépit de la carence des informations topographiques, je vais tenter par la suite de répondre à la question suivante : dans quelle mesure les premiers Paléologues en introduisant une nouvelle ère dans l'histoire de Byzance ont-ils

---

[1] Cf. Necipoglu 2011, 133–41 et plus récemment Agoritsas 2016.

voulu transformer l'espace de Constantinople reconquise ? L'objet de mon enquête débouche moins sur la topographie de la ville au début du 14e siècle en soi que sur la relation entre le pouvoir impérial et l'espace urbain. Étant donné que la puissance constituée doit se montrer parce que c'est sa monstration même qui l'institut, mon propos est notamment d'examiner la politique ékistique de Michel VIII et d'Andronic II Paléologue et leur présence personnelle dans la ville comme indices de leur conception du pouvoir. Inversement, en m'appuyant sur le principe que la présence du souverain structurait la ville, je suggère que l'aspect de Constantinople peut nous aider à appréhender comment l'organisation de l'espace urbain correspondait aux besoins des empereurs.

La prise de Constantinople par les Croisés en 1204 a entraîné une coupure dans l'histoire de son espace. Une grande partie des quartiers de l'ouest de la ville ainsi qu'au nord de la Mésè a été détruite à la suite d'incendies,[2] tandis qu'il y avait une grande diminution de sa population. En outre, des bâtiments publics ont été pillés et des œuvres d'art ont été ramené à l'Occident. Lorsqu'en 1261 Michel Paléologue reprit la ville, il a dû d'abord rétablir ses fonctions essentielles. Une des premières tâches de l'empereur a été de la repeupler et d'installer des habitants dans les maisons abandonnées ainsi que de réparer les églises endommagées.[3] Selon Pachymérès, qui veut évidemment faire allusion à la piété de l'empereur, le plus important était qu'il a aidé des anciens monastères à retourner à leur état premier.[4] Afin d'assurer l'approvisionnement en vivres de la population et des monastères l'empereur alloua aux monastères et à des particuliers des terres ἐκτός τε καὶ ἐντὸς τῆς πόλεως τόπους εἰς γεωργίαν.[5] Nous ne connaissons pas l'étendue des terres cultivables allouées à l'intérieur des murs ; il est cependant certain qu'une grande partie du territoire intra-muros n'était pas construit et qu'elle englobait des terres cultivables. En outre, l'empereur a pris soin de réparer le palais des Blachernes dont l'état ne lui permettait pas de s'y établir dignement.[6]

Michel VIII en tant que nouvel empereur, et en plus usurpateur du trône, devait s'approprier symboliquement l'espace urbain pour légitimer son pouvoir. C'est ainsi qu'il a fait son entrée dans la ville par la Porte Dorée renouant

---

2 Selon Grégoras (Greg. I, 87–8), quand on est arrivé à Constantinople, on a trouvé la Ville πεδίον ἀφανισμοῦ, μεστὴν ἐρειπίων καὶ κολωνῶν, οἰκίας τὰς μὲν κατεσκαμμένας, τὰς δὲ πυρκαιᾶς μεγάλης μικρὰ λείψανα. Sur les incendies voir Madden (1991–1992, 72–93).
3 Greg. I, 87–8.
4 Pach. II, 223.
5 Pach. II, 221.
6 Pach. II, 219.

avec le mode des triomphes romains.[7] Dans le même but, une de ses décisions a consisté à ériger devant l'église des Saints Apôtres une colonne avec un ensemble qui montrait l'empereur offrant à l'Archange Michel, son patron, la représentation symbolique de la ville.[8] En se présentant comme le nouveau Constantin, refondateur de la ville,[9] un motif reproduit sur les inscriptions et les sceaux et répété par la rhétorique de la cour,[10] Michel VIII voulait légitimer son pouvoir non seulement face à ses adversaires, mais aussi aux yeux de ses partisans. Dans le cadre de cette politique il a procédé à la restauration de Sainte Sophie et de l'Orphelinat et il a fondé le monastère familial de Saint Dèmètre à la gloire de sa lignée.[11] Pendant le règne de Michel VIII il ne semble pas que la topographie urbaine ait été modifiée profondément, car ses interventions se sont limitées à des actions nécessaires au bon fonctionnement de la ville ou bien elles concernaient des lieux d'un grand poids symbolique pour le pouvoir impérial, tels que les murailles, le port de Kontoskalion, le palais des Blachernes, Sainte Sophie, les Saints Apôtres etc.[12] Cependant comme son but principal consistait à confirmer son rôle de garant de la continuité avec le passé glorieux,[13] Michel VIII a fourni la base idéologique aux interventions de son successeur Andronic II dans l'espace urbain.

Tout d'abord il faut remarquer que pendant son long règne Andronic II a dû faire face aux catastrophes naturelles ou d'origine humaine, des tremblements de terre et des incendies.[14] Il a donc entretenu à plusieurs reprises les murailles de Constantinople et réparé l'église des Saints Apôtres, tandis qu'il a restauré Sainte Sophie grâce à l'argent, hérité de son épouse Irène de Montferrat. Entre autres travaux il a relevé et consolidé la colonne de Justinien qui était tombée lors du tremblement de terre de 1317.[15] Grégoras loue l'empereur pour son absence de vanité, puisqu'il a préféré restaurer les églises existantes au lieu de les abattre ou de construire des nouvelles, même si cette dernière option lui aurait coûté moins cher. En agissant de la sorte Andronic II voulait selon Grégoras perpétuer la mémoire des fondateurs des anciennes églises (τῶν

---

7   Pach. II, 217–19.
8   Talbot 1991, 243–61.
9   Macrides 1980, 13–41.
10 Angelov 2007, 98ff ; Hilsdale 2014, 27–30, 99 ff ; Macrides 1980, 23–4.
11 Hilsdale 2014, 92–94, 100.
12 Talbot 1991, 261 ; Agoritsas 2016, 72 ff.
13 Macrides 1994, 269–82.
14 Agoritsas 2016, 91–95.
15 Greg. I, 273. Grégoras considère la statue de Justinien τὸ κάλλιστον […] τοῦτο θέαμα τῆς βασιλευούσης ὃ μόνον ἐξ ὁμοίων καὶ ἰσορρόπων μυρίων ἐλλέλειπται, διαφυγὸν τῶν τε πυρκαϊῶν τὰς ἐπιβουλὰς καὶ τὴν τῶν Λατίνων πλεονεξίαν.

οἰκοδομησάντων).[16] Nicéphore Kallistos Xanthopoulos loue aussi l'empereur pour la beauté des églises qu'il a fait construire.[17]

En effet, sous Andronic II il y a eu une grande activité de construction ou de rénovation d'églises et de monastères, qui a transformé le paysage urbain. On estime qu'au moins dix nouveaux monastères ont été élevés, et vingt-deux ont été rénovés. Selon les mêmes estimations entre 1261 et 1328 vingt-huit nouvelles églises ont été édifiées et au moins dix autres ont été restaurées.[18] Les plus grands des monastères connus de cette époque sont les monastères de Lips, de Chora, de Bebaia Elpis, de Pammakaristos, de Christos Philanthropos, de la Panagia Mouchliotissa (des Mongols).

Les informations fournies par Pachymérès et Grégoras, déjà mentionnées, ainsi que les louanges de Nicéphore Kallistos Xanthopoulos[19] qu'Andronic II avait fait couler ses pas dans ceux de ses contemporains (dans la construction des églises anciennes et des bâtiments publics) convergent et attestent une implication des Paléologues directe, – c'est le cas des couvents de Chora, de Christos Philanthropos[20] et de Lips –, ou indirecte dans la construction d'autres monastères. Le fait que ceux qui ont fondé ou rénové les grands monastères appartenaient à la famille impériale étendue ou à son proche entourage peut être attribué, à première vue, à la politique de conciliation avec l'Église poursuivie par Andronic II après la brouille de l'époque de son père, qui était entré en conflit avec les dignitaires ecclésiastiques en raison de sa politique concernant l'Union des Églises et son attitude face aux Arséniates. Cependant, je pense que l'empereur voulait avec la fondation de certains monastères s'approprier indirectement l'espace et surtout les lieux sacrés.[21] Rappelons-nous à cet égard les paroles de Théodore Métochite selon lesquelles l'édification du monastère de Chora était l'expression de la piété du fondateur et en même temps la reconnaissance envers l'empereur qui lui avait octroyé l'emplacement.[22] La relation

---

16 Greg. I, 274–75.
17 PG 145, 584.
18 Talbot 2001, 330 ; basée sur une catalogue dressée par Kidonopoulos 1994.
19 PG 145, 585.
20 Irène Choumnaina, membre de la famille impériale par alliance, est la fondatrice du monastère de Christos Philanthropos. La bibliographie sur Constantinople acceptait que ce monastère fut fondé dans le quartier des Manganes. Or, N. Melvani (2016, 361–84) dans un article récent a montré qu'il s'agit de la restauration du double monastère fondé par Alexis I Comnène et son épouse Irène Doukaina (Christos Philanthropos et Théotokos Kécharitôménè). Le monastère de Choumnaina donc était situé près de la citerne d'Aspar, sur les pentes de la cinquième colline.
21 Kioussopoulou, à paraître.
22 Magdalino 2011, 171–73, 175.

de réciprocité décrite par Métochite existe aussi entre les fondateurs des autres monastères et Andronic II Paléologue. Dimiter Angelov a observé qu'Andronic II avait cherché à établir son autorité sur la réciprocité entre l'empereur qui octroyait des privilèges à ses sujets en récompense de leurs services.[23] A mon avis cette relation réciproque est visible dans l'espace urbain. L'empereur, en soutenant financièrement le rétablissement des monastères ou en octroyant les chrysobulles qui réglaient leur fonctionnement, obtenait en contrepartie la protection symbolique ou réelle que ces monastères offraient du fait de leur volume à lui-même et à son palais. C'est plus particulièrement le monastère de Chora, dont la clôture atteignait pratiquement les murailles terrestres, qui suggère une fonction défensive par rapport au palais des Blachernes. Ceci est d'autant plus probable que le monastère était dédié à Notre Dame, la protectrice de la ville.[24]

La restauration des monastères, dont la fondation remontait à l'époque des Comnènes, par des membres de la famille impériale semble être un choix délibéré. C'est la mémoire des Comnènes, τῶν οἰκοδομησάντων, que l'empereur voulait perpétuer. Le souci des Paléologues de s'associer à la mémoire des Comnènes s'est exprimé par d'autres moyens aussi, surtout symboliques,[25] comme il est manifeste dans les textes rhétoriques.[26] En témoigne surtout leur décision de s'installer dans le palais des Blachernes. Nous connaissons que pour Alexis I Comnène l'édification de ce palais à l'extrémité de la ville faisait partie d'un plan plus large de remodelement de Constantinople, signale du début d'une nouvelle ère pour l'empire.[27] Selon la description d'Eudes de Deuil (1147) le palais se distinguait par sa hauteur et il offrait à ceux qui y résidaient le plaisir d'une triple vue, sur la mer, sur la campagne et sur la ville.[28] Les informations disponibles indiquent que le palais des Blachernes formait un complexe immobilier entouré d'une muraille ayant à son centre un bâtiment à plusieurs étages avec une grande cour intérieure. Il ressemblait davantage à un château fort et il était d'une conception totalement différente de celle de l'ancien Grand Palais qui s'étalait plutôt au même niveau au milieu de la ville.[29] La conception du palais des Blachernes correspondait à la concentration du pouvoir et elle reflétait les origines militaires des Comnènes. Mais à leur époque

---

23 Angelov 2007, 150 ff.
24 Ousterhout 2000, 241–50.
25 Macrides 1994, 272–73.
26 Angelov 2007, 107.
27 Magdalino 1993, 116. Voir aussi Magdalino 1996, 68–70.
28 Eudes de Deuil, 65.
29 Sur l'agencement du palais de Blachernes et la fonction de sa cour intérieure voir Macrides 2013, 277–304. Voir aussi *Pseudo-Kodinos,* 367–78.

le Grand Palais, Sainte Sophie et l'église des Saints Apôtres étaient encore des lieux chargés d'un sens politique et ils constituaient selon Paul Magdalino "le lien visible avec les empereurs du lointain passé".[30] Or, avec l'établissement des Paléologues aux Blachernes le centre politique s'est déplacé vers le nord-ouest de la ville.

Si Michel VIII a réparé les dégâts subis par le palais lors de la conquête latine, celui qui a effectué les interventions les plus radicales dans le complexe immobilier des Blachernes est Andronic II, si on en juge par les louanges de Nicéphore Kallistos Xanthopoulos.[31] Sous son règne a été construite la terrace sur la quelle prenait place l'empereur lors des fêtes de Noël et de l'Épiphanie et lors de la cérémonie de prokypsis. Il est caractéristique que Grégoras considérait la cérémonie de prokypsis comme une réplique des anciens triomphes impériaux.[32] Dans la cour intérieure du palais, qui selon Ruth Macrides remplissait les fonctions politiques de l'Hippodrome d'autre fois,[33] avaient lieu les cérémonies officielles en présence de la « foule » ($\pi\lambda\hat{\eta}\theta$ος), dont les sources nous laissent dans l'ignorance de sa composition et de son importance.

Les sorties officielles de l'empereur dans la ville étaient peu nombreuses. Il sortait pour se rendre à l'église de la Théotokos des Blachernes et au monastère de Saint-Jean Prodrome de Pétra qui était proche, ainsi que pour participer selon Pseudo-Kodinos aux fêtes des saints patrons d'autres églises et monastères.[34] Pourtant on ne sait pas s'il allait à ses festivités et à Sainte Sophie ou au Grand Palais, dans les rares occasions où il devait s'y rendre, à cheval en traversant la ville jusqu'à l'ancien centre administratif, ou s'il la contournait par la Corne d'Or en utilisant une embarcation depuis l'embarcadère des Blachernes. De toute façon, on ne connaît pas quel itinéraire terrestre il choisissait pendant ces sorties officielles, qui aurait pu marquer la ville. D'Andronic II sont rapportés les déplacements qu'il effectuait dans la ville pour résoudre des conflits religieux qui étaient fréquents à son époque. Ses efforts répétés de se concilier avec les Arséniates montrent son intention de dominer le jeu politique. Du récit de Pachymérès il parait que sa présence aux actes publics

---

30   Magdalino 1993, 112.
31   PG 145 : 585–88. Magdalino 2007, 13–14 fait la traduction du récit de Xanthopoulos concernant le palais.
32   Greg. II, 616.
33   Macrides 2011, 230–35. Eadem 2015, 263–66 : la différence selon Macrides consistait au fait qu'à l'époque des Paléologues les cérémonies officielles avaient lieu dans l'espace limité de la cour intérieure du palais tandis que dans le passé elles étaient déployées dans l'espace ouvert de l'Hippodrome ou dans les espaces étendus du Grand Palais.
34   Magdalino 2007, 8–9.

était déterminée par la tactique qu'il suivait dans chaque circonstance particulière.[35] Il a assisté par exemple à l'accueil des reliques du patriarche Arsénios et il a participé à côté d'une grande foule à leur transfert au monastère de Saint André ἐν τῇ Κρίσει.[36] D'autres sorties de l'empereur en ville rapportées par Pachymérès, surtout celles pendant le patriarcat d'Athanase I, obéissaient au même souci d'inscrire dans l'espace le fait que c'était lui qui gardait l'initiative politique et non les dignitaires ecclésiastiques. Ces mouvements s'effectuaient ad hoc avec pour objet des buts politiques et ils ne faisaient pas partie d'un cérémonial impérial. Pachymérès parle avec mépris des processions qu'organisait toutes les semaines le patriarche Athanase, accompagné seulement par les higoumènes des monastères, les moines et les croyants.[37]

Au cours du 14ème siècle l'empereur semble vouloir se retirer progressivement de la vie de la ville, alors que dans les siècles passés en entrant dans la ville par la Porte Dorée ou lors de ses sorties du Grand Palais il conférait du sens aux lieux qu'il traversait lors des triomphes et d'autres défilés rituels.[38] Il convient de signaler à cet égard qu'aussi bien Andronic III[39] et Jean Cantacuzène,[40] après leur couronnement, ils sont sortis pendant la nuit pour visiter le monastère des Hodègoi afin de remercier la Théotokos de leur accession au trône. Une remarque de Grégoras va dans le même sens : Andronic III était ἀνομίλητος [...] καὶ μισῶν περὶ ἑαυτὸν πλῆθος ὁρᾶν.[41] Bien que Grégoras présente la réticence de l'empereur d'organiser ou de participer aux cérémonies et aux défilés traditionnels comme le résultat d'un trait de son caractère, je crois que le rapport d'Andronic III avec l'espace urbain était plutôt le résultat d'un choix politique comme nous laisse penser le texte de Pseudo-Kodinos. C'est ainsi qu'on peut interpréter le silence du texte sur les déplacements de l'empereur hors du palais. Or, si les mots ne décrivent pas seulement l'état statique des choses, mais ils évoquent le processus de leur transformation, la désignation du palais comme φρούριον par Cantacuzène[42] indique le confinement progressif du détenteur du pouvoir impérial dans le palais au fur et à mesure de son affaiblissement politique et économique, du rétrécissement de l'appareil administratif et de la montée des tensions sociales en ville.

---

35   Voir p.e. Pach. IX, 261 ; X, 401, 419.
36   Greg. VI, 167.
37   Pach. XIII, 639, 675, 693.
38   Berger 2001, 73–87.
39   Greg. I, 541–42.
40   Kant. II, 607.
41   Greg. I, 565.
42   Kant. II, 611.

Dans le voisinage du palais se trouvaient plusieurs monastères datant, on l'a déjà remarqué, de l'époque des Comnènes et rétablis après 1261 ou fondées au 14ème siècle. Ces monastères ensemble avec le plus grand monastère de Saint-Jean Prodrome de Pétra formaient une sorte de ceinture qui délimitait le centre administratif et l'isolait du quartier commercial et du centre religieux que constituait Sainte Sophie et les monastères de la première colline. En même temps des monastères de la ceinture hiérarchisaient l'espace urbain en marquant celui de l'empereur et de ses proches. C'est aussi dans les quartiers marqués par ces monastères que se trouvaient les hôtels de l'aristocratie comme celui de Métochite dont le terrain semble avoir été proche du palais.[43] Dans le quartier des Blachernes et les quartiers voisins, Pétra, ou Kynégoi[44] se situaient d'autres demeures aristocratiques comme celles de Jean Cantacuzène[45] et d'Andronic Asan, la dernière étant près de la Vierge des Mongols.[46] Ces maisons représentaient des petites enclaves fortifiées complétant la ceinture de protection du palais. A l'instar des Comnènes, le cercle familial des Paléologues qui entourait l'empereur s'inscrivait aussi dans l'espace urbain. Le repeuplement du quartier des Blachernes, qui avait souffert des incendies, obéissait à un plan politique comme le laisse penser un petit fragment d'un document de l'époque qui mentionne également l'existence de trois hôtels de dignitaires dans le quartier.[47]

...

On a déjà remarqué que c'était la Ville qui conférait à l'empereur sa légitimité.[48] Par la reconquête de 1261 les Paléologues avaient conquis le droit au pouvoir impérial. Ce qui leur manquait était la preuve qu'ils étaient les continuateurs d'une tradition glorieuse. Le discours Βυζάντιος de Métochite souligne ce besoin de reconnaissance, quand, entre autres, il considère les ruines comme preuves de la gloire passée et en observant l'activité de construction, qui se

---

43   Sur le οἶκος de Métochites, voir Magdalino 2011, 176–77 ; Kiousopoulou 2014, 328–32.
44   Kidonopoulos 1994, 171–81.
45   Kant. II, 164–65.
46   *Register*, 66–68. Voir Kidonopoulos 1994, 179–81 et Agoritsas 2016, 196–97, où d'autres cas des maisons aristocratiques dans ces quartiers.
47   Schreiner 1998, 273–83 : κατὰ τὴν ιʹ ἰνδικτιῶνα ἀνῆλθον εἰς Βλαχέρνας ἐξ ὁρισμοῦ βασιλικοῦ καὶ ἐδόθη τόπος διὰ τοῦ μεγάλου δρουγγαρίου ὑπὸ Γαβαλᾶ πλησίον τοῦ δομεστίκου Καλοειδᾶ. ἐδόθη μου καὶ χάριν ἐξόδου ὑπερπύρων ϛʹ. ἐκτίσθησαν δὲ τὰ ὁσπήτια ἀρχὴ ἀπριλλίου [...].
48   Magdalino 1993, 109.

déroulait autour de lui, il présente le recyclage des matériaux de construction comme l'occasion d'élever de nouveaux bâtiments prestigieux.[49]

Les signes de la tradition impériale dans le vieux centre administratif autour du Grand Palais et de Sainte Sophie étaient visibles et les Paléologues ont réparé ceux dont ils avaient besoin pour montrer leur autorité. De l'autre côté du fait qu'ils ont choisi de se présenter comme les continuateurs de la tradition et que leurs ressources économiques étaient limitées, ils ne s'intéressaient pas à laisser leur empreinte propre sur la Ville en la remodelant. Même si Andronic II Paléologue avait un plan ékistique, il est clair qu'il avait chargé les aristocrates de le mettre en œuvre en construisant des monastères. D'un certain point de vue, la construction de plusieurs monastères à l'époque d'Andronic II, qui ont modifié l'aspect de l'espace urbain, doit être mise en relation avec les disputes religieuses de l'époque.[50] Cependant grâce à leur volume ces bâtiments tranchaient sur l'image urbaine et certains d'entre eux ont à long terme constitué une frontière entre l'espace de l'empereur et de ses proches et le reste de la Ville, dans laquelle se produisaient des rééquilibrages entre les groupes sociaux.

Constantinople n'a jamais retrouvé sa splendeur d'avant, les voyageurs qui la visitent la décrivent appauvrie, habitée d'une manière éparse et avec des grandes étendues de terres cultivées. La Ville en tant que centre de l'Œcumène existait seulement dans les textes des rhéteurs. Pour eux le symbole œcuménique n'était plus l'empereur, mais Constantinople elle-même.[51]

Bibliographie

Sources primaires

Βυζάντιος = Θεοδώρου Μετοχίτου Βυζάντιος. ἡ περί τῆς βασιλίδος μεγαλοπόλεως. Ed. I. D. Polemis. Athens 2015.

Eudes de Deuil = Odo of Deuil, *De profectione Ludovici VII in orientem*, Tr. V. C. Berry. New York 1948.

Pach. = *Georges Pachymérès. Relations historiques*. Ed. A. Failler, CFHB 24, 5 vols, Paris : Belles Lettres et Institut Français d'Études Byzantines 1984–2000.

Kant. = *Ioannis Cantacuzeni eximperatoris historiarum libri IV*. Ed. L. Schopen, 3 vols. Bonn : Impensis Ed. Weberi 1828–32.

---

49   Βυζάντιος 2015, 272–85. Voir aussi Magdalino 2012, 113–15.
50   Kiousopoulou, à paraitre.
51   Angelov 2007, 109–11.

Greg. = *Nicephori Gregorae Ῥωμαϊκὴ ἱστορία*. Ed. L. Schopen and I. Bekker 3 vols., Bonn : Impensis Ed. Weberi 1829–35.

Pseudo-Kodinos = *Pseudo-Kodinos and the Constantinopolitan Court: Offices and Ceremonies,* Eds. R. Macrides, J. A. Munitz, D. Angelov. Ashgate 2013.

Register = *Das Register des Patriarchats von Konstantinopel.* Eds. J. Koder, M. Hinerberger, O. Kresten. Wien 2001.

Notiz = Schreiner, P. 1998. "Die Topographische Notiz uber Konstantinopel in der Pariser Suda-Handschrift. Eine Neueinterpretation", in I. Ševčenko & I. Hutter (eds), *AETOS. Studies in Honour of Cyril Mango.* B.G. Teubner.

Sources secondaires

Agoritsas, D. 2016. *Κωνσταντινούπολη. Η πόλη και η κοινωνία της στα χρόνια των πρώτων Παλαιολόγων (1261–1328)*, Thessaloniki.

Angelov, D. 2007. *Imperial Ideology and Political Thought in Byzantium 1204–1330*, Cambridge.

Berger, A. 2001. "Imperial and Ecclesiastical Processions in Constantinople", in N. Necipoglu (ed.), *Byzantine Constantinople. Monuments, Topography and Everyday Life*, Leiden – Boston – Köln, 73–87.

Hilsdale, Cecily J. 2014. *Byzantine Art and Diplomacy in the Age of Decline*, Cambridge.

Kidonopoulos, V. 1994. *Bauten in Konstantinopel 1204–1328*, Wiesbaden.

Kiousopoulou, T. 2014. "Demeures aristocratiques à Constantinople au cours de l'époque byzantine tardive", in *AUREUS. Τόμος αφιερωμένος στον καθηγητή Ευάγγελο Κ. Χρυσό*, Athens, 328–32.

Kiousopoulou, T. à paraitre. "Political power and urban space: Constantinople during the Palaiologan period", *51st Spring Symposium of Byzantine Studies, Edinburg*.

Macrides, R. 1980. "The New Constantine and the New Constantinople – 1261?", *Byzantine and Modern Greek Studies* 6, 13–41.

Macrides, R. 1994. "From the Komnenoi to the Palaiologoi: Imperial Models in Decline and Exile", in P. Magdalino (ed.), *New Constantines. The Rhythm of Imperial Renewal in Byzantium 4th–13th Centuries*, Aldershot.

Macrides, R. 2011. "Ceremonies and the City. The Court in Fourteenth-Century Constantinople", in J. Duindam, T. Artan, M. Kunt (eds), *Royal Courts in Dynastic States and Empires. A Global Perspective*, Leiden, 217–35.

Macrides, R. 2013. "The Citadel in Medieval Constantinople", in S. Redford, N. Egin (eds), *Cities and Citadels in Turkey: from the Iron Age to the Seljuks*, Louvain – Paris – Walpole – Mass, 277–304.

Macrides, R. 2015. "Processions in the 'Other' Ceremony Book", in D. Boschung, K. J. Hollkeskamp, Claudia Sode (eds), *Raum und Performanz. Rituale in Residenzen von der Antike bis 1815,* Stuttgart, 261–78.

Madden, T. F. 1991–1992. "The Fires of the Fourth Crusade in Constantinople, 1203–1204: A Damage Assessment", *BZ* 84–85, 72–93.

Magdalino, P. 1993. *The Empire of Manuel I Komnenos, 1143–1180*, Cambridge.

Magdalino, P. 1996. *Constantinople médiévale. Études sur l'évolution des structures urbaines*, Paris.

Magdalino, P. 2007. "Pseudo-Kodinos' Constantinople", *Studies on the History and Topography of Byzantine Constantinople*, Aldershot 2007, no. XII.

Magdalino, P. 2011. "Theodore Metochites, the Chora, and Constantinople", in H. A. Klein, R. Ousterhout, B. Pitarakis (eds), *The Cariye Camii Reconsidered*, Istanbul.

Magdalino, P. 2012. "The Beauty of Antiquity in Late Byzantine Praises of Constantinople", in P. Odorico, Ch. Messis (eds), *Villes de toute beauté, l'Ekphrasis des cités dans les littératures byzantine et byzantino-slave*s, Paris, 101–21.

Melvani, N. 2016. "The dublication of the Double Monastery of Christ Phhilanthropos in Constantinople", *RÉB* 74, 361–384.

Necipoglu, N. 2011. "The Social Topography of Late Byzantine Constantinople: The Evidence from the Patriarchal Register", in C. Kafadar, N. Necipoglu (eds), *Journal of Turkish Studies 36 (In Memoriam Angeliki E. Laiou, Harvard University)*, 133–41.

Ousterhout, R. 2000. "Contextualizing the Later Churches of Constantinople: Suggested Methodologies and a Few Examples", *DOP* 54, 241–50.

Talbot, A.-M. 1991. "The Restoration of Constantinople under Michael VIII", *DOP* 47, 243–61.

Talbot, A.-M. 2001. "Building Activity under Andronikos II. The Role of Women Patrons in the Construction and Restoration of Monasteries", in N. Necipoglu (ed.), *Byzantine Constantinople. Monuments, Topography and Everyday Life*, Leiden – Boston – Köln, 329–43.

Byzantine Notions of the Balkans

Symbolic, Territorial and Ethnic Conceptions of Space, Sixth to Ninth Centuries

Konstantinos Moustakas

Even though the Byzantine Empire did not incorporate the whole of the Balkan peninsula up to its conventional northern geographic limit of the lower Danube (then the Sava or Drava rivers) except for a few decades from the mid to the late sixth century, it did include large tracts of it for long periods of time within the long period from the sixth to the late twelfth century. In this respect, the Balkans can be considered, from a modern viewpoint, as one of the major lands that formed the imperial territory. The question that arises in the following discussion is whether the period's contemporaries had a similar view and also how they conceived of the space we now call the Balkans.

With the sea setting the obvious limits of the peninsula on its three sides, the northern limit is left to uncertainty and convention, a fact of our modern age and certainly of older times. Strabo's view of the Danube can be described as ambiguous; on the one hand, he seems to have regarded the big river as a geographic limit. In introducing the fifth chapter of the seventh book of his *Geography*, he places at the Ister (i.e. the lower Danube) the geographic limit that separates this part of Europe from the rest of the continent. That part of Europe is delineated by the Ister and the surrounding sea, "[…] running from the head of the Adriatic gulf to Hieron at the mouth of the Ister (ἀρξαμένη ἀπὸ τοῦ μυχοῦ τοῦ Ἀδριατικοῦ, μέχρι τοῦ Ἱεροῦ στόματος τοῦ Ἴστρου)" and had no single name to describe it; in fact it included the lands of Greeks, Macedonians and Epirotes, as well as of Illyrians and Thracians.[1] On the other hand, we can again deduce from Strabo that the Danube could not be considered a real border, since it did not separate anything. In his account, the peoples who settled in the lands along the river, the Getae and the Mysi, equally occupied both banks of it.[2]

---

1 Strabo, *Geography* VII §5.
2 Strabo, *Geography* VII §3.

Strabo emphasises another landmark of the peninsula, the mountain chain that was formed by the Haemus Mountains in the east and their supposed continuation to the west, the mountains that reached the Adriatic Sea. In this respect, Strabo is critical of older authors such as Theopompus and Polybius who had considered the Haemus so central and tall a mountain that one could see both seas, the Black Sea and the Adriatic, from its peak. Even though it is not directly stated, those older authors could have considered the Haemus as the limit of the peninsula to the north, conforming to the traditional Greek view of mountains as more important landmarks than rivers. This view can be interpreted in relation to the rough mountainous terrain of Greece that led to political fragmentation between city-states, which were centred on valleys, basins and plateaus, and their territories, which were delimited by mountains. In Roman times rivers gained in prevalence over mountains in geographic conceptions, probably due to the fact that the frontiers of the empire were placed on big rivers such as the Rhine, the Danube, and the Euphrates. In late Roman and early Byzantine times, rivers were considered to be the borders between continents.[3]

Nevertheless, in the map of Kosmas Indikopleustes (sixth century), the Balkans appear in a rounded peninsular form delimited to the north in some manuscripts by the sketch of a mountain chain, with the Danube completely absent in all surviving copies of his map.[4] This should not be interpreted as a regeneration on the part of Kosmas of the older Greek concept that gave priority to mountains rather than to rivers, but his deliberate decision not to put on his map any rivers, irrespective of their size and importance, other than the four rivers of Paradise: Tigris, Euphrates, Gihon (identified as the Nile) and Phison (identified as the Indus). Kosmas adhered to the theological conception of space that had become common with the ascendance of Christianity,[5] which he tried to rationalize with respect to the earthly space. He shared the view of a flat earth surrounded by the ocean, which in his version had a roughly rectangular shape. He identified Paradise as a land beyond the ocean to the

---

3 Kordosis 1996, 31. There was a common agreement between contemporary scholars about the Nile being the border between Asia and Africa (see for instance Isidore of Seville's account: Isidorus Hispalensis Episcopi, *De Natura Rerum* Migne, *Patrologia Latina*, LXXXIII, cols. 1016–17). As for the border between Europe and Asia, Ammianus Marcellinus, Livanius and the same Isidore placed it on the Tanais River (Don), while Procopius placed it on the Phasis: Kordosis 1996, 31
4 E.g. in *Sinaiticus Graecus* 1186, fol. 66v, or in *Vaticanus Graecus* 600, f. 40v.
5 Saradi 2010, 88–92.

east. The four rivers sprang there and followed submarine and subterranean courses before they reemerged in the parts of the earth they actually lay.

The Christian discourse about the four rivers came out of the notion of a symbolic quadripartition, which conceived the world to be distinguished into four parts. In Kosmas' rationalizing view, the four parts of the earth are described in purely geographic terms, as the north, south, east and west. Others considered that the four parts corresponded to the rivers of Paradise, with each river running along a respective part of the earth. While there was a more or less common agreement of the identification of the Gihon with the Nile, the Phison River was the subject of numerous different identifications. The Phison was mostly identified with one of the great rivers of India, the Indus or the Ganges, as was the case with Kosmas' geography; however, there were some notable exceptions from authors who identified the biblical river as the Danube. Such an identification of the Phison appears in the sixth-century writings of Pseudo-Kaisarios,[6] while Leo the Deacon acknowledged in his late tenth-century *Histories* that for some the Phison was identified as the Danube for others as the Ganges.[7] Those scholars who opted to identify the Phison as the Danube probably had in mind that Europe and the Balkans were too large and significant a part of the earth not to be watered by one of the Paradise rivers.

The logic of quadripartition is also present in the seventh-century *Apocalypse* by Pseudo-Methodius, but its geographic relevance is far more abstract and transcendental. The earthly space of the *Apocalypse* is symbolically conceived of as consisting, on the one hand, of the settled earth (οἰκουμένη γῆ) and, on the other hand, of the desert. The former, which is also described as the Promised Land, is inhabited by the "chosen people", first the Jews then the Christians/Romans. The latter is distinguished as the southern desert, inhabited by the Ismaelites who constitute the reverse image of the chosen people, and the northern desert, inhabited by the "impure nations". The settled earth of the *Apocalypse* is identical to the Roman Empire, which is shown to have been established by the union of four pre-existing empires, through conquest or dynastic marriage, those being the Greek empire of Byzas, the Macedonian empire of Philip, the Aethiopian Empire of Pil and the original Roman Empire of Romulus.[8] It is unnecessary to stress the historic and geographic inaccuracy of this account, which combines myths with religious symbolism. If one makes an effort to actually put on a map the geography of the *Apocalypse*, the

---

6 *MPG*, XXXVIII, col. 985.
7 Leonis Diaconi Caloënsis, *Historiae Libri Decem* 129–30 Hase.
8 *Die Apokalypse des Ps.-Methodios* I, 83–88 Lolos & Meisenheim.

Greeks are centred on Byzantium (and Asia Minor?) rather than in Greece proper, whereas Aethiopia represents Egypt too and Africa in general. In this respect, the Balkan part of the Roman Empire is more likely to correspond to the "Macedonian Empire" among the preceding ones.

A single name is not known to have existed for the whole of the Balkan peninsula before the nineteenth century. This does not mean that a sense of the peninsular shape of this broad area had not existed, but that the need to describe the whole of it with a specific name had not emerged, especially since there never had been a political entity to fully incorporate the entire peninsula in its territory (with the exception of the Roman Empire between roughly the second and sixth centuries), in conjunction with its intense geophysical, ethnic and political fragmentation. Even in Roman times, a single name had not emerged to be consistently used for the description of the whole area. Then, the names of Graecia or, more commonly, Illyria or Illyricum were occasionally used in order to describe a broad part of the land to an unspecified extent. With the re-organization of the provincial administration by Constantine I (306–37) and the creation of the prefectures, the areas of the Balkan peninsula were incorporated into two major administrative units, the prefecture of Illyricum and the diocese of Thrace, the latter being part of the prefecture of the Orient. The diocese of Thrace included what can be described as the eastern Balkans, from the shores of the Propontis and the Aegean to the Danube. In this respect, most of the Balkans was incorporated into the prefecture of Illyricum, which always included the central Balkan area (the Roman provinces of Dacia Fluvialis, Dacia Ripensis, Dardania, and Macedonia Secunda), part of the western Balkans (the provinces of Praevalitana and Epirus Nova), and the southern Balkans (the provinces of Macedonia Prima, Thessalia, Epirus Vetus, Graecia or Achaia, and Crete). Yet, the north-western part of the peninsula, mostly identical to the province of Dalmatia, was from time to time included in the prefecture of Italy, through the shifting of prefectural boundaries between Illyricum and Italy.

The distinction of the Balkan territories into the two major administrative units, Thrace and Illyricum, may be regarded as having "institutionalized" the absence of a single appellative mark for the whole region. Most references to the Balkan lands of the empire either specified Thrace or Illyricum, or both, according to the context and circumstances. That was true even in cases where the writer apparently had a view of the peninsula as a whole. An exemplar case can be noticed in a well-known passage by Procopius, referring to enemy attacks on the Balkans during the reign of Justinian I: "Almost every year, Huns, Sclaveni and Antes made inroads over the Illyrians and the whole of Thrace, from the Ionian gulf to the outskirts of Byzantium, including Hellas and the land of Chersonesos ('Ιλλυριοὺς δὲ καὶ Θράκην ὅλην, εἴη δ' ἂν ἐκ κόλπου τοῦ 'Ιονίου μέχρι ἐς τὰ Βυζαντίου προάστεια, ἐν τοῖς Ἑλλάς τε καὶ Χερρονησιωτῶν ἡ χώρα ἐστίν, Οὖννοι τε καὶ Σκλαβηνοὶ καὶ Ἄνται σχεδόν τι ἀνὰ πᾶν καταθέοντες ἔτος) [...])".[9]

At the beginning of the passage, Procopius makes it clear that he refers to the territories of Illyricum and Thrace as adhering to contemporary terms of administrative geography. By using the ethnic term of "Illyrians" (meaning the land of Illyrians) instead of Illyricum, he demonstrates his antiquarianism as well as the literary mode, common among ancient and medieval writers, to denote a geographic area by using the ethnic term that pertained to its contemporary or historic (as in this case) inhabitants. Then, he also set the geographic demarcation of the land: "from the Ionian (i.e. the Adriatic) gulf to the outskirts of Byzantium (i.e. Constantinople)", making clear that he had in mind the whole of the Balkan peninsula, which he could not describe by a single name but rather had to use both the official names of the two administrative units that incorporated it.

However, a few authors seem to have adopted a view of the Balkan part of the empire as a single geographic entity and describe it accordingly. In this respect, the most characteristic record comes from an author outside Byzantium. In a well-known quotation from the chronicle of Isidore of Seville (d. 636), it is stated that in the fifth year of Herakleios' reign (615): "[...] the Sclaveni—Slavs—took Greece from the Romans (Sclaveni Graeciam Romanis tulerunt)[...]".[10] The exact meaning of the term Graecia is a puzzling point. It could be claimed that what is meant is the early Byzantine province of Hellas (or Achaia), which was confined to the lands south of Thermopylas, or the historic Greek land in a broad sense that also was identified as the parts of central and southern Greece, including the Peloponnese. Indeed, as Peter Charanis has demonstrated, most references to Graecia or Hellas in sources of the sixth to the early ninth centuries pertain to a notion of the name that identifies it with either the province and the theme of Hellas, established late in the seventh century over the same territories, or with the historic Greek lands, that were placed on the same territories more or less.[11] Nevertheless, there are some exceptions. The same Charanis has dedicated a study to the use of the term Graecia by Isidore of Seville.[12] He pointed out that, apart from the passage

---

9   Procopii Caesariensis, *Anecdota*, XVIII 20–21 Haury.
10   Isidori Hispalensis Episcopi, *Chronicon*, Migne, *Patrologia Latina*, LXXXIII, col. 1056.
11   Charanis 1955. In the title of his study Charanis sets its limits to sixth- and eighth-century sources, nevertheless, as he includes the chronicle of Theophanes in his source repertoire, we have to slightly correct him and, when discussing his study, expand its time-span to include the early ninth century.
12   Charanis 1971.

from the *Chronicon* cited above, Isidore uses the same term in another of his works, the *Etymologies*, in which Graecia is explicitly stated to mean Illyricum:

> Graecia a Graeco rege vocata, qui cunctam cam regionem regno incoluit. Sunt autem provinciae Graeciae septem, quarum prima ab Occidente Dalmatia, inde Epirus, inde Hellas, inde Thessalia, inde Macedonia, inde Achaia, et duae in mari, Crete et Cyclades. Illyricum autem generaliter omnis Graecia est.

> Greece is called after king Graecus, who included every part of it in his kingdom. However, there are seven provinces in Greece, Dalmatia being the first among them from the west, then Epirus, then Hellas, then Thessalia, then Macedonia, then Achaia, and two at sea, Crete and Cyclades. Therefore, Illyricum is generally identical with Graecia.[13]

Isidore apparently had a confused idea about Illyricum, since his list of the prefecture's provinces is partial and imprecise. He took no account of the Dacian diocese of Illyricum; moreover, he did not distinguish between the two provinces with the name Epirus, Vetus and Nova, and also regarded Achaia as a distinct province from Hellas. In stating a total number of seven provinces, he probably dealt with the religious symbolism of the number seven, even though the actual adding up of his list makes a sum of six mainland provinces, totaling eight with the two insular ones. In any case, what is important is that he used the terms Graecia and Hellas with different meanings, the former describing the whole prefecture of Illyricum the latter the province of Hellas in a strict sense, and also that he used the term Graecia as a synonym for Illyricum.

Isidore was not alone in describing Illyricum with the term Graecia. We can notice other authors too of the late sixth to early seventh century, from inside and outside the Byzantine Empire, who appear to use the names Hellas or Graecia in order to describe the lands of Illyricum in a wider sense, all when referring to the Avaric and Slavic raids. In the first case, John of Ephesus relates in a surviving fragment of his *Ecclesiastical History*: "In the 3rd year from the death of emperor Justin and the reign of victorius Tiberius a cursed people attacked all Hellas and run over the regions of Thessaloniki and the whole of Thrace. (Anno 3° mortis Iustini regis et regni victoris Tiberii populus maledictus egressi Hellada totam et regions Thessalonicae et totius Thraciae

---

13   Isidori Hispalensis Episcopi, *Etymologiarum sive originum libri xx*, Lindsay 4.7 (cited in Charanis 1971, loc. cit., 22–23).

percurerunt) [...]".[14] The general context of those events points to the assertion that the reference to "Hellas" should not be related to Greece proper, but to areas further north. Being distinguished from Thrace, John's "Greece" should rather be identified with Illyricum in general, even though there is a distinct reference to the areas of Thessaloniki which was a part of the Illyricum prefecture. This is made clearer in a similar passage written by John of Biclar when he refers to the events of c. 579: "The Avars are repulsed only at the ends of Thrace and occupy parts of Greece and Pannonia as well (Avare a finibus Thraciae pelluntur et partes Graeciae atque Pannoniae occupant.)" For some slightly later events he states: "The race of Sclaveni—Slavs—lay waste Illyricum and Thrace (Sclavinorum gens Illyricum et Thracias vastat)".[15] The second reference leaves little doubt about what is meant in the first one, i.e. that Graecia stands as a synonym for Illyricum.

In any case, both John of Ephesus and John of Biclar adhere to the norm of viewing the Balkans as distinguished into the major administrative units of Thrace and Illyricum (or "Greece" in their cases) and not as a single entity. The importance of their testimony lies in their demonstration of the use of the term Graecia as a synonym of Illyricum in a geographic—administrative logic. Turning back to Isidore of Seville and his reference to Graecia in his *Chronicon*, Charanis suggests that Isidore probably used the name with a similar meaning as in the *Etymologies*, that by Graecia he meant Illyricum.[16] Yet, a careful reading of the relevant passage of the *Chronicon* may provide grounds for a modified view. The whole caption reads: "[A.M. year] 5814.[17] Herakleios was then in fifth year of his reign. In its beginnings the Slavs took Greece from the Romans, and the Persians Syria and Egypt, and numerous provinces (Heraclius dehinc quantum agit imperii annum. Cujus initio Sclavi Graeciam Romanis tulerunt. Persae Syriam et Aegyptum, plurimasque provincias)".[18] At that point Isidore not only mentions the loss of "Graecia" to the Slavs, but also the loss of Syria

14 Ioannis Ephesinus, *Historiae Ecclesiasticae*, (ed.) E.W. Brooks, Louvain 1952², III, 29. The Latin translation belongs to the editor as John wrote in Syriac.
15 Ioannis Biclarensis Chronicon, *Monumenta Germaniae Historica, Auctores Antiquitas*, XI, 215, 216.
16 Charanis 1971, 23–24.
17 Similar to other late ancient and medieval scholars in the West, Isidore followed the prototype of Eusebius of Caesarea in setting the *anno mundi* chronology, which was calculated to have taken place 5198 years before Jesus Christ. Thus, the chronology cited correctly gives the year 615/16 as the fifth year of Heraclius' reign. However, the more commonly followed protype was that of Sextus Julius Africanus that had the world created around 5500 years before Christ.
18 MPL, LXXXIII, col. 1056.

and Egypt to the Persians. The reference to Syria and Egypt does not seem to have a strictly administrative sense, but rather relates in a wider sense to two of the major countries, or geographic regions, that constituted the Roman Empire then. Other such countries were Asia (i.e. Asia Minor), Italy and Africa. In this respect, Isidore's reference to "Graecia" is more likely to relate to the whole Balkan part of the empire, albeit in a vague sense, than strictly to Illyricum as opposed to Thrace.

In a similar way, the same meaning of the term "Hellas" can be suggested for its use by Menander the Guardsman some decades earlier, relating to events of the year 578, i.e. that it referred to the Balkans in general and in an abstract sense: "Due to Hellas being ravaged by the Sclaveni–Slavs–, and suffering their continuous threat everywhere, Tiberius … sends an embassy to Baianos (Ὅτι κεραϊζομένης τῆς Ἑλλάδος ὑπὸ Σκλαβηνῶν, καὶ ἀπανταχόσε ἀλλεπαλλήλων αὐτῇ ἐπηρτημένων τῶν κινδύνων, ὁ Τιβέριος [...] πρεσβεύεται ὡς Βαϊανὸν [...]).[19] Vaguely referring to "Hellas", Menander is unlikely to mean the lands of Greece proper in his account. The context of the events described in this passage points to the northern areas of the Balkans as the lands under consideration, without any specification as to whether Illyricum or Thrace is included. Again, the Balkans in general, with an emphasis on its northern parts, have to be meant by the reference to the same "Hellas" in the *Ecclesiastical History* by Evagrius, relating to events of the 580s: "The Arabs <sic> twice advanced up to the so-called Long Wall, besieging and enslaving Siggidon, Anchialus and the whole of Hellas, as well as other towns and fortresses. (Οἱ Ἄραβες <sic> δὶς μέχρι τοῦ καλουμένου Μακροῦ Τείχους ἐλάσαντες, Σιγγηδόνα, Ἀγχίαλόν τε καὶ τὴν Ἑλλάδα πᾶσαν καὶ ἑτέρας πόλεις τε καὶ φρούρια ἐξεπολιόρκησαν καὶ ἠνδραποδίσαντο.)"[20]

To summarize the preceding discussion, a number of late sixth to early seventh century authors deviated from the norm of properly dividing the Balkan part of the empire into the major administrative units of Illyricum and Thrace and instead used the term "Graecia" or "Hellas" either as a synonym for Illyricum (John of Ephesus, John of Biclar, Isidore of Seville in the *Etymologies*), or in order to abstractly describe that Balkan part in a vague sense (Menander the Guardsman, Evagrius, Isidore of Seville in the *Chronicon*). With regard to the latter, it can be suggested that their need to refer to the Balkan part of the empire in a simple way and distinguish it as one of the major regions or countries of the empire (such as Syria, Asia, Italy, Egypt, Africa), in conjunction with their limited familiarity with the administrative arrangements in

---

19   Blockley 1985, 192.
20   Evagrius Scholasticus Epiphaniensis, *Ecclesiasticae Historiae* VI §10 Valesius.

that part, probably drove them to the use of the term "Greece" in a vague and abstract territorial sense. Moreover, it may not be chance that those authors mostly were not Byzantine or originated from lands remote from the core-land of Byzantium. Isidore of Seville and John of Biclar were westerners, while John of Ephesus and Evagrius were Syrians. One could suggest that they had a limited familiarity with administrative arrangements in the Balkan parts of the empire. Nevertheless, such an idea has to be treated cautiously, for Evagrius and John of Ephesus had lived enough time in Constantinople, while Isidore is known to have travelled in Illyricum and his descriptions in the *Etymologies* reflect whatever knowledge of the land he gained on that occasion.

Territorial names in early Byzantium most commonly had an ethnic background and etymology derived from the names of the peoples who once occupied those particular areas. That fact was generally known to the inhabitants of the empire. In the passage discussed above, Procopius employed the literary mode of using the name of a people, the Illyrians, in order to describe the land he was referring to, i.e. Illyricum.[21] From time to time, the norm of naming the land after the name of the people that occupied it was updated in response to ethnological developments and changes. In this respect, such a change in the ethnic conception of the Balkans can be observed in the eighth-century *Hodoeporicon* of St Willibald.

As a young monk, St Willibald, an Anglo-Saxon, had embarked on a pilgrimage journey from Italy to the Holy Land and back through Constantinople, lasting from 721 to 729, in the days of Leo III the Isaurian. The *Hodoeporicon*, an itinerary text describing his journey, was processed and composed by the nun Huneberc of Heidenheim late in the eight century based on his dictations. Sailing from Syracuse, Willibald's ship crossed the Adriatic and first reached the port of *Manafasia* (Monemvasia): "[...] *in Slawinia terra*".[22] Evangelos Chrysos suggests that the word Slawinia here is an adjective and the strict meaning of the *Slawinia terra* is "Slavonian land".[23] It could be. Yet, Willibald's Slawinia can also be a substantive, in which case the meaning would be "the land of Slawinia". In any case, whatever use the term Slawinia may have in the *Hodoeporicon*, an adjective or a substantive, its meaning is practically the same. Critical approaches to the account arise from the misconception that the "*Slawinia terra*" is referring to the area of Monemvasia strictly speaking, or

21 Supra, 372-73.
22 "[...] et inde navigantes venerunt Syracusam urbem in ipsa regionem, et inde navigantes venerunt ultra mare Adria ad urbem Manafasiam in Slawinia terra": Willibaldis *Hodoeporicon*, in *Monumenta Germaniae Historica, Scriptores*, XI 1, 93.
23 Chrysos 2007, 130.

even to the town itself, or to the Peloponnese in general.[24] There has even been some effort to devalue Willibald's account on the grounds of his supposedly poor geographical knowledge. In this respect, Karl Hopf followed by Dionysios Zakythinos claimed that the *Hodoeporicon* should not be taken into serious account, as it confusedly placed the cities of Tyre and Sidon in the Adriatic.[25] Nevertheless, it is these modern scholars who misinterpreted the text due to inattentive readings. Indeed, especially in its descriptions of the Holy Land and surrounding areas, the *Hodoeporicon* is plentiful in detail and shows no significant errors. It does place Sidon and Tyre in the Adriatic, but by the "Adriatic" the *Hodoeporicon* means the eastern Mediterranean in general. It is important to add here that no common name existed then for the Mediterranean Sea and different authors described it with different names (e.g. for Kosmas Indikopleustes it was the Roman Gulf).

Using the term "Slawinia" the *Hodoeporicon* has rather to be interpreted as meaning the Balkans in general and in a vague and imprecise sense. It is more likely that the Slavic settlement in large tracts of the Balkan peninsula changed the conception of the land in ethnic terms. From the seventh century already, Slavic raiders crossed the Adriatic and attacked Italy.[26] On the other hand, the eighth-century *Life of St Pancratius of Taormina* reflects on campaigns of the Byzantine governor of Sicily against the pagan "Avars" (i.e. Slavs) across the Adriatic.[27] Therefore, we can deduce that for many in Italy and Sicily the lands on the opposite side of the Adriatic would no longer be "Graecia", or "Illyria" or "Illyricum" etc., they would have become Slavinia, the land of the Slavs. There is a strong probability that Willibald came to describe those lands as such in line with what he heard in Italy and Sicily. Willibald's view, in the way it is interpreted here, can be regarded as a Byzantine view in some respect, since a considerable part of the Italian peninsula still made part of the Byzantine Empire at the time of his sojourn there, and that was especially true for Sicily.

It is quite clear that the use of "Slawinia" in Willibald's *Hodoeporicon* refers to the Balkan lands in general, in reflection of contemporary views in Italy, which acknowledged their new ethnological realities. Whether such a view of the Balkans had arisen in Byzantium proper in the same period is a matter that is open to question. There is a puzzling point in the chronicle of Theophanes in the sections where the campaign of Constans II against the Slavs and the one of Justinian II against Slavs and Bulgars are described. First, Theophanes

---

24 Charanis 1971, 25.
25 Zakythinos 1945, 44.
26 Curta 2001, 110.
27 *Life of St Pancratius of Taormina*, 1, 269–72, Stallman.

reports about Constans II's (642–68) campaign of 657/8: "this year the emperor campaigned against Sclavinia and captured and subdued many (τούτῳ τῷ ἔτει ἐπεστράτευσεν ὁ βασιλεὺς κατὰ Σκλαυινίας καὶ ἠχμαλώτευσε πολλοὺς καὶ ὑπέταξεν)".[28] In the second relevant section, Justinian II is reported to have gathered a thematic army from Asia Minor in the year 687/88 with the purpose of conquering the Bulgarians and the *sclavinias*.[29] The last point is not problematic, as Theophanes clearly refers to the several distinct *sclavinias*, i.e. the areas in the Balkans where the Slavs had settled since early in the seventh century and where they lived outside any effective control by the Byzantine state up to some time.

Nevertheless, in following up his narration, Theophanes goes on to describe the facts of the campaign in the next year 688/89, in which case he presents Justinian to have campaigned against "Sclavinia" and Bulgaria: "this year Justinian campaigned against Bulgaria and Sclavinia ([...] τούτῳ τῷ ἔτει ἐπεστράτευσεν Ἰουστινιανὸς κατὰ Βουλγαρίας καὶ Σκλαβινίας)".[30] In this case, similarly to his earlier report about Constans II's campaign, if one is to translate the clause literally, Theophanes has to be interpreted as meaning one single land of the Slavs. It can be proposed that Theophanes might have made a grammar error in those points, by fitting the preposition κατὰ with the accusative case, in which case his Σκλαβινίας is plural accusative and not singular genitive (as would fit correctly with the preposition), thus he means several distinct Slavic areas in a similar way to his previous phrase and not a single land of the Slavs.[31] However, such a point is weakened by his parallel reference to Bulgaria. As he places the two terms, Sclavinia and Bulgaria, side by side in the same form, it is more logical to interpret him as to mean the same thing for both, i.e. a single land for each of the respective peoples. In such a case, Theophanes would be inconsistent in his conception of Slavic settlement, as he gives two different views about it. Further down in his narrative, Theophanes refers to the *sclavinias* once again, at the point where he describes the introduction of Byzantine transferees into them, as part of the policies of Nicephorus I (802–11).[32] In the last case, in which Theophanes relates events contemporary to his own

---

28   Theophanis, *Chronographia*, 347 De Boor.
29   Ibid. 364: [...] καὶ κελεύει περᾶσαι ἐπὶ τὴν Θρᾴκην τὰ καβαλλαρικὰ θέματα βουλόμενος τούς τε Βουλγάρους καὶ τὰς Σκλαυινίας αἰχμαλωτίσαι (and he ordered the cavalry units (themes) to pass to Thrace wishing to conquer the Bulgarians and the sclavinias).
30   Ibid. 364.
31   Lemerle 1981, 130–31.
32   Theophanes, *Chronographia*, 486 De Boor.

lifetime, the *sclavinias* are many and can be properly interpreted as the several areas of Slavic settlement then under the imperial authority.

With respect to the earlier puzzling references of Theophanes to a single Sclavinia, Florin Curta in commenting on Constans II's campaign of 657/8 suggests that the emperor campaigned against one particular Slavic polity in the hinterland of Constantinople, while for the later campaign by Justinian II he uses the plural form *sclaviniai* without considering the one case of singular used by Theophanes.[33] Evangelos Chrysos interprets the use of Sclavinia or sclavinias by Theophanes through the discursive trope of metonymy, discarding the relation of the term in these cases with particular areas or polities, either one or many, and suggesting that it means several groups of Slavs wherever they were to be found, i.e. the substance of the metonymy here is the use of a term that would properly have a territorial meaning in order to refer to a people.[34]

Chrysos' interpretation can be sustained to some extent, especially if the argument remains one of discursive style. In this respect, one can bear in mind the relative entries of Patriarch Nicephorus' *Short History* on the events discussed previously, who is known to have shared a common lost source with Theophanes, and also of later chronicle writers who reproduced the account of Theophanes in describing those events. They all wrote not of Sclavinia or sclavinias but of Slavs, opting for a wording that was more proper for the particular context.[35] In the point of view of the present study the importance lies in the inconsistency of Theophanes in the use of the singular or the plural as he referred to Sclavinia. It can be suggested that his lost source related to Sclavinia in singular, and Theophanes' inconsistencies reflect his confusion vis-à-vis what he read in his source as opposed to his contemporary realities, when several sclavinias were under proper imperial authority by then. However, the Sclavinia that was probably related in Theophanes' source, is reflective of an earlier Byzantine conception of the Balkan lands, corresponding to the waning Byzantine control over most of the Balkans during the seventh and eight centuries, when in most of the Balkan lands the Byzantine authority was non-existent or precarious at the most. In this respect, Sclavinia would have a notion of abstract territoriality pertaining to all areas of Slavic settlement throughout the Balkans.

A similar interpretation can be supported for Theophanes' use of Bulgaria in the same context. This too can have derived from his lost source. In his

---

33   Curta 2001, 110–12.
34   Chrysos 2007, 127–30.
35   Nikephoros Patriarch of Constantinople, *Short History*, 92 Mango; Chrysos 2007, 129.

campaign of 688/89, Justinian II is rather unlikely to have attacked Asparuh's Danubian Bulgaria, and thence to have descended down to Thessaloniki where the campaign concluded. He had rather ventured to locate and fight groups of Bulgars that could be found in the areas between Constantinople and Thessaloniki, the same as he did with Slavs. In this respect, there is a strong plausibility in the suggestion that, in so far as the Bulgars are concerned, the target of the campaign were those Bulgars who reportedly were present in the vicinity of Thessaloniki around those times under the leadership of Kuver.[36] Therefore, in a similar way to Sclavinia, Bulgaria as used by Theophanes in this context can be interpreted either as a metonymy for Bulgars, as proposed by Chrysos, or as a term of a geographic notion albeit of abstract and relative territoriality, as proposed here.

In the Byzantine worldview of the early and middle periods, it was very common to conceive of geographic space in ethnic terms, and that was especially true for the lands outside of the confines of imperial authority. If the Byzantine territories were thought of in terms of administrative divisions or as an ensemble of cities,[37] the foreign lands were mostly designated as the lands of the respective peoples. Even lands within the imperial territory could be distinguished through the ethnic criterion, in the case that some particularities of theirs had to be emphasized. The case of the Peloponnese makes a good example, as local realities in the middle Byzantine years were conceived in the logic of bipartition, with the ethnic criterion being a major indicator of this logic. It seems that the Peloponnese was broadly thought to consist of two distinct parts, the eastern and the western, and the idea of this distinction was present in different fields, either practical (ecclesiastical administration, antagonisms between Corinth and Patras for supremacy), or symbolic (the contradiction of a "pure" eastern part with an "impure" western), and certainly ethnic, as the eastern part was considered to be "Greek" and the western part "Slavic".[38]

The evidence of the period sixth to ninth centuries, which is of interest in this study, shows that in the mind of the period's contemporaries the land we today call the Balkans was considered as a distinct geographic area that constituted one of the major geographic areas, or countries, of the empire, albeit

---

36 Fine 1983, 72.
37 Saradi 2010, 73–74.
38 See the contribution by Ilias Anagnostakis and Maria Leontsini in the present volume (Chapter 17). Moreover, Anagnostakis and Leontsini support that the facets of that bipartitional logic, including the ethnic, were consequences rather than causes, and they determined on underlying factors such as the geography of the land and the level of capacity to exercise control.

in a vague and rather imprecise sense. However, its official distinction into two major administrative units, the *prefecture* of Illyricum and the *diocese* of Thrace prompted contemporaries to take into account this distinction and describe the land accordingly by using the names of both territories (John of Ephesus, John of Biclar), even in cases when they apparently conceived the whole Balkan land as a single geographic entity (Procopius). Yet, some examples of authors can be noticed, who not only conceived of the Balkans as a single entity but also described them with a single name (Isidore of Seville in the *Chronicon*, Menander the Guardsman, Evagrius probably). Moreover, recent ethnic changes did leave their imprint on the conception of the Balkans, as demonstrated by Willibald's account, according to which the land across the Adriatic opposite Italy and Sicily was no longer "Illyria" or "Graecia" but the *Slawinia terra*. On similar grounds, the two instances of Theophanes' reference to Sclavinia in the singular, probably deriving from his lost source, are proposed to mean an abstractly conceived land of the Slavs extending over unspecified large tracts of the Balkan peninsula. With the restoration of firm Byzantine rule over the southern part of the Balkans by the late eighth—early ninth centuries, no thought could be made of a Sclavinia as a single entity. Then the Balkan territories of the empire were conceived as an ensemble of Byzantine *themes*, which would incorporate several s*clavinias* as special administrative subdivisions.

Bibliography

Primary Sources

Evagrius Scholasticus Epiphaniensis, *Ecclesiasticae Historiae*. Ed. H. Valesius. Oxford 1844.

Ioannis Biclarensis *Chronicon, Monumenta Germaniae Historica, Auctores Antiquitas*. Ed. T. Mommsen, vol. 11. München 1981.

Isidore of Seville, *Isidorus Hispalensis Episcopi, De Natura Rerum*. Ed. J.-P. Migne. Paris 1878–90.

Isidore of Seville, *Isidori Hispalensis Episcopi, Chronicon*. Ed. J.-P. Migne.

Isidore of Seville, *Isidori Hispalensis Episcopi, Etymologiarum sive originum libri XX*. Ed. W. A. Lindsay. Oxford 1911.

John of Ephesus, *Ioannis Ephesinus, Historiae Ecclesiasticae*. Ed. E. W. Brooks. Louvain 1952.

Leonis Diaconi Caloënsis, *Historiae Libri Decem*. Ed. C. B. Hase. Bonn 1828.

Life of St Pancratius of Taormina, II vols. Ed. C.J. Stallman, DPhil Thesis, University of Oxford 1986.

Nikephoros Patriarch of Constantinople, *Short History*. Ed. C. Mango. Washington DC 1990.

Pseudo-Methodios, *Die Apokalypse des Ps.-Methodios*. Ed. A. Lolos. Meisenheim 1976.

Procopius, *Anecdota*. Ed. J. Haury *Procopii Caesariensis Opera Omnia*, vol. 3. Leipzig 1913.

Strabo, *Geography*. Tr. H. L. Jones. *Geography*, vol. 3. Cambridge 1924.

Theophanis, *Chronographia*. Ed. C. De Boor. Leipzig 1883.

Willibaldis, *Hodoeporicon, Monumenta Germaniae Historica, Scriptores*, XI 1.

Secondary Sources

Belke, K. (ed.) 2007. *Byzantina Mediterrannea. Festschrift für Johannes Koder zum 65 Geburtstag*. Wien.

Blockley, R. C. (ed.) 1985. *The History of Menander the Guardsman. Introductory Essay, Text, Translation and Historiographical Notes*. London.

Charanis, P. 1955. "Hellas in the Greek Sources of the Sixth, Seventh and Eighth Centuries", in K. Weitzmann (ed.) 1955, 161–76. [reprinted in Charanis, P. 1972. *Studies on the Demography of the Byzantine Empire*. London 1972].

Charanis, P. 1971. "Graecia in Isidore of Seville", *BZ* 64. 1, 22–25.

Chrysos, E. 2007. "Settlements of Slavs and Byzantine Sovereignty in the Balkans", in Belke (ed.) 2007, 123–35.

Curta, F. 2001. *The Making of the Slavs. History and Archaeology of the Lower Danube Region, c. 500—700*. Cambridge.

Ćurčić S., Hadjitryphonos, E. (eds) 2010. *Architecture as Icon: Perception and Representation of Architecture in Byzantine Art*. New Haven CO.

Fine, J. V. A. 1983. *The Early Medieval Balkans. A Critical Survey from the Sixth to the Late Twelfth Century*. Ann Arbor MI.

Kordosis, M. S. 1996. Ιστορικογεωγραφικά πρωτοβυζαντινών και εν γένει παλαιοχριστιανικών χρόνων. Athens.

Lemerle, P. 1981. *Les plus anciens recueils des miracles de Saint Démétrius et la penetration des Slavs dans les Balkans*, II. *Commentaire*. Paris.

Saradi, H. G. 2010. "Space in Byzantine Thought", in S. Ćurčić—E. Hadjitryphonos (eds) 2010, 73–111.

Weitzmann, K. (ed.) 1955. *Late Classical and Medieval Studies in Honor of Albert Mathias Friend Jr*. Princeton.

Zakythinos, D. 1945. Οι Σλάβοι εν Ελλάδι. Athens.

The Partitioned Space of the Byzantine Peloponnese

From History to Political and Mythical Exploitation

Ilias Anagnostakis and Maria Leontsini

The space of the Peloponnese has always had its own particularity: it is, in fact, almost an island, a *paene insula*, in other words, a peninsula that has since mythical times taken its name as a whole from its north-western part, and this designation remained consistent up to the Middle Ages. This area of land, almost completely surrounded by water except for an isthmus connecting it with the mainland, was named Peloponnese, 'the island of Pelops', after the ancient king of Pisa, a town in the northwestern part of the peninsula. It became the dominant name, although, as appropriate, it was also called the *land of the Argives*.[1] From Hellenistic and Roman times onwards, the northwest part was also known as Achaia and came under the administration of the Roman province of Achaia, which included further territories in the Hellenic Peninsula.[2] During the Byzantine period, it bore both names, the Peloponnese and Achaia, and from the thirteenth century onwards the appellation Morea prevailed, a name originating most probably from Elis, an area in the western Peloponnese.[3] This introductory remark on the peninsula's naming in relation to its spatial partitioning is an essential supplement to what we shall discuss below concerning the formulation of the concept about the two separate Peloponnesian parts during the Middle Byzantine era, which recognized the eastern part as pure (καθαρεῦον) and the western one as Slavic-occupied, commixed (σύμμικτον), and thus implicitly alleging that, in contrast to the eastern part, this was the "impure" one. As nomenclature signifies, a section of the partitioned space of the peninsula, specifically the northwest, over time gave its

---

1 Strabo, 8.1, 2, 6–7; 8.5, 5, 134–37; 8.6, 5, 154–55; Stephanos Byzantios, letter P 95, 52–3; *De thematibus*, 6.7–13, 90; *Chrestomathie*, 8.117, 294; Eustathios, 338.8; 608.35–609.9; 684.5; Pseudo-Zonaras, *Lexicon*, letter alpha, 362.11; Anagnostakis et al. 2002, 67, 78–9; Jeffreys 2013, 9–12.
2 *De Administrando Imperio*, 49.43, 230–31; *De thematibus*, 6.2–3, 90; Bon 1951, 61, 108–10.
3 Bon 1951, 117, 137, 158–59; Diller 1954, VIII. 337A, 38; Laurent 1962; Bon 1969, 306–26; Gregory 1991; Nesbitt & Oikonomides 1994, 88–9 n. 32 (with commentary); della Dora 2013, 459–61; Gerstel 2013, 1–2.

name to the whole, with whatever that entailed in each era as a political, economic, or cultural dynamic of this part in relation to the entirety of the region.[4] This study intends to assess how some special attributes were employed to project the Peloponnese as a space divided into two parts, leading subsequently to a reevaluation of accepted notions on population movement and space drawn from ancient literature.

The resilient designation of the spatial partition of the Peloponnese emanated from environmental, geographical, and ethnological features that formed the setting for movements, exchanges, and communication. The morphology and the topography of the terrain, with its mountain ranges and promontories stretching far out into the sea and its bays, create indeed a very distinctly east-west partitioned space in the Peloponnese. Over time this partitioned space shaped ethnological and cultural-historical divisions and determined communicability. Suffice it to say that Peregrine Horden and Nicholas Purcell speak of physically distinct landscapes, such as the Peloponnese, and discuss the liaisons developed between its micro-regions and the centres of major authority that formed distinctive communication dynamics from ancient to modern times.[5]

Communication lines clearly existing during the Early Byzantine period became difficult after the seventh century; at that time, according to certain sources, a different reality of subdividing the Peloponnese into two distinct parts was established through the restructuring of the regional, ecclesiastical, civil, and military organization. This segmentation of the Peloponnese was attributed invariably to the raids of the Avars and Slavs[6] and was transmitted with some novel denotations concerning the spatial fragmentation of the Peloponnese. The individuality of the Peloponnesian space and the formation of particular regions and units had already been highlighted by historians and geographers in antiquity. Herodotus described seven geographically separate peoples, indigenous and settlers; Strabo spoke of the western and eastern parts, measuring the length and breadth of the peninsula; while Pausanias divided it into coherent, self-contained sections. In other words, the divided character of the landscape was not unknown in antiquity[7] (Figure 17.1).

---

4 Pausanias, 5.8, 2, 420–21; Anagnostakis et al. 2002, 67.
5 Horden & Purcell 2000, 130; see also Avramea 1997, 107–8; Stewart 2013, 81–2.
6 Anagnostakis et al. 2002, 76–7, with sources; Koder 2020, 85, 90–3.
7 Herodotos, 8.73, 70–71; Strabo 8.2, 1–2, 12–15; Pausanias, 5.1, 1–2, 380–81; Baladié 1980, 2–4 n. 8; Anagnostakis et al. 2002, 66–7; for a general assessment of the one-sided valuations of the Peloponnese in the textual sources and their influence in archaeological analysis, see Stewart 2013, 15–17. On the new conceptions on space influenced by theology and politics and introduced in Late Antique historiography, see van Nuffelen 2019, 1–12.

During the Middle Byzantine period the peninsula's division into eastern and western parts was again presented in terms of communicability, ethnic purity, and administratively partitioned space. From the seventh century onwards, this reoccurring concept of spatial partitioning acquired a novel political, administrative, and ethnological peculiarity. It is indeed strange, if not provocative, for example, that the vertical axis proposed by Strabo and other geographers for measuring the length of the Peloponnese – a line running from Aigion to Cape Maleas and dividing the peninsula into eastern and western parts – coincides perfectly with the dividing line between the western and eastern sections of the Peloponnese put forward by the Byzantines.[8] This spatial partition was considered to have been brought about by Slavic settlement, which determined the later applications of portioned space and coincided with the logic of the ecclesiastical and administrative arrangements in the Byzantine era[9] (Figure 17.2).

The reprocessed formation of this spatial shaping, voiced along with concepts of population dynamics, could be a simple coincidence, although it is not; yet, even if it were a coincidence, it is highly revealing. Cape Tainaron and the Taygetos mountain range could have been the dividing line. We have to wonder why the western part of the Peloponnese, in this case Patras, was not united politically to Cape Tainaron but to the Laconian Helos and Cape Maleas, although the last two could form the end or the beginning of another section in the eastern part of the Peloponnese. Aspects of this differentiation have been discussed with regard to geomorphology, ethnic diversity, and communicability.[10] We shall simply point out that the north-west part, which, as we said above, gave the name to the peninsula over time, although presented as being vulnerable and exposed, was also occupied and separated and ended up having no political or administrative contact with the rest of the Peloponnese during two historical changeover periods: the Slavic invasion and the Frankish rule. The criteria of spatial partition acquired new dimensions during the Byzantine era and mainly concerned the livelihoods of the local populations and the strategies aimed at their subordination to state structures. This reality was concurrent with the decline of the urban centres in the Early Byzantine period and the increasing role of the countryside. Changes became obvious from the end of the sixth century, probably following the Slavic incursions

---

8   Strabo 8.2,1, 12–3; Bon 1951, 16, 18, 19–1; Lambropoulou 2000, 95–113; Anagnostakis et al. 2002, 67.
9   Yannopoulos 1993; Kislinger 2001, 35; Anagnostakis 2012, 104–5, 107–8 with references to documentation; Stewart 2013, 97–8; Anagnostakis & Kaldellis 2014, 109.
10 Anagnostakis et al. 2002, 67, 73–8, see also n. 6 above.

FIGURE 17.1   The longitudinal division of Peloponnese (after Jones 1968, Book VIII, vol. 4, map n. 8)

and settlement, when the eastern and western units of the Peloponnese again came to determine space.[11] Slavic settlement contributed to reshaping the dynamics of urban-rural relations and at the same time created the ground for power claims among the urban centres, where state structures were traditionally established, primarily in Corinth, the metropolis and capital city of the theme of the Peloponnese, and then in Patras and Lakedaimon (Sparta), while creating at the same time antagonism with regard to their bonds with

11   Bon 1951, 89; Nesbitt & Oikonomides 1994, 78; Avramea 1997, 111–12. Literature has dealt extensively with the policies of integration of the Slavs, see below and nos. 19 and 33. More on the resuming of the repressive strategies to subdue the Slavic populations in the 10th c. can be found in Zuckerman 2014.

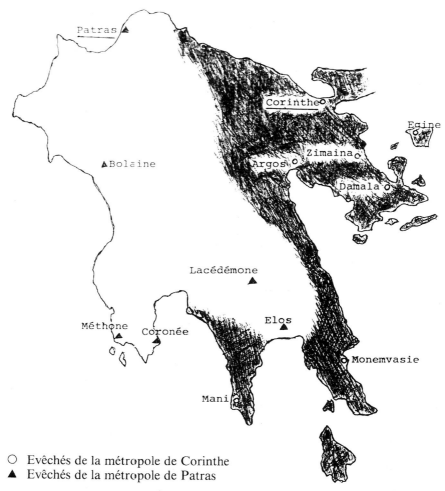

○ Evêchés de la métropole de Corinthe
▲ Evêchés de la métropole de Patras

En couleur foncée, le territoire approximatif de la métropole de Corinthe.

FIGURE 17.2   Metropolitan sees of Middle Byzantine Peloponnese (after Yannopoulos 1993, 390)

Constantinople. Therefore, the division of the Peloponnese according to Byzantine textual sources was no longer defined by mathematical, geographical, and geomorphological standards, but only in terms of communication and control.[12] The spatial distribution of Slavic settlements located elsewhere in

---

12   Konstantakopoulou 1989; Koutava–Delivoria 1993, 98; Anagnostakis & Kaldellis 2014, 105–6.

the interior of the Peloponnese, and not only in the eastern and western parts, has been well attested on the basis of numismatic material, especially coin hoards, pottery, metal objects, and burial practices.[13]

So far, the distribution of these findings and the material from sites with Slavic names, designating the tools used for land clearing and cultivation, suggest a wide spread of the Slavic establishment.[14] However, allusions to the formation of the two separate geographical units of the Peloponnese presented in the sources are projected as a result of Byzantine efforts to take control of the territories where the Slavs had settled. Such state policies point clearly to the changes of power relations in the peninsula which introduced the setting of new spatial boundaries into areas under the jurisdiction of bishoprics, cities, and fortified settlements. It is even evident that the sources' narratives were invested with historical and mythical explanations so as to illustrate and vindicate the partition of the Peloponnese in relation to the rivalries that emerged after the claims of superiority among different centres of power.[15]

The transformation of the Peloponnesian space into a divided territory with an eastern and a western section is set out in the *Chronicle of Monemvasia*, a tenth-century text, probably written by Arethas, the bishop of Kaisareia, a native of Patras (ca 850–after 932). The western part of the Peloponnese is mentioned as a specific unit which differs in population and culture from the eastern part. The *Chronicle* describes the eastern part as rugged and inaccessible.[16] This landscape morphology was obviously projected in this text as influencing the formation of the political, military, and ecclesiastical division and as having an impact on the subjugation and control of the populations. From this perspective, the *Chronicle* outlines the rise of Patras to a metropolis, exercising its jurisdiction over the bishoprics not only of the western part but also over Lakedaimon in the southern part, previously under the metropolitan see of Corinth.[17] Thus, the western part, due to state

---

13   Fougères 1898, 596–99; Bon 1951, 51 n.2, 57, 60, 62–3, 165; Konti 1985, 107–8, 116; Weithmann 1996; Anagnostakis 1997, 288–89, passim; Anagnostakis 2009; Avramea 1997, 72–81; Anagnostakis & Poulou 1997, 232–33, 292–303, 309–17; Kislinger 2001, 96–8; Vroom 2003, 141–43; Veikou 2012, 200–5; Metaxas 2018, 689–700, especially 692 n. 32, 693 n. 37.

14   Malingoudis 1981; Anagnostakis 2009 passim; Curta 2011, 210–11; Anagnostakis 2012, 106–8 and passim; Veikou 2012, 184–88.

15   These issues are clarified in Anagnostakis 2009; and Anagnostakis 2012.

16   *Chronicle of Monemvasia*, 10.55–8 (Lemerle), 12, 18 (Dujčev); Avramea 1997, 68–70; Kislinger 2001, 18–25; 101–4, 106; Anagnostakis et al. 2002, 74; Anagnostakis & Kaldellis 2014, 107–10. On the text see also Charanis 1950, 142–44, 161–64; Anagnostakis 2012, 106–7; Neville 2018, 130–31.

17   *Chronicle of Monemvasia*, 10.70–11.76 (Lemerle), 18, 20 (Dujčev); *Notitia* 4.493; *Notitia* 5.42; *Notitia* 7.32.549–55; *Notitia* 8.34; *Notitia* 9.410–15; *Notitia* 10.492–75, Darrouzès 1981, 261,

policies, was reinforced with regard to administration, while, however, it soon became more impure and commixed after Lakedaimon's repopulation with a mixture of people (Kapheroi, Thrakesians, Armenians, and others). The *Chronicle* also presents the western part as being exposed to the Slavs and threatened by their uprisings, but, on the other hand, it makes clear that it was well-strengthened by the measures taken after the suppression of the revolts by the thematic armies heading from Constantinople and Corinth, the capital of the Peloponnese's *thema*.[18] Similar arguments regarding the spatial partition were expressed by Constantine VII Porphyrogennetos when Byzantine control had been regained over the entire area of the Peloponnese. His account of the military operations carried out for the subjugation of the Slavic tribes, the Melingoi and the Ezeritai, is framed by narratives comparable to the *Chronicle*'s reports on the morphology and accessibility of the lands where these populations settled.[19] Constantine segregates the Slav incomers of the western part from the people in the southeastern Peloponnese (namely the Mani, the Maleas peninsula, and probably including also the region of Monemvasia), claiming that the inhabitants there were descendants of the ancient Greek and Romaioi:

> Οὐκ εἰσὶν ἀπὸ τῆς γενεᾶς τῶν προρρηθέντων Σκλάβων, ἀλλ' ἐκ τῶν παλαιοτέρων Ῥωμαίων, οἳ καὶ μέχρι τοῦ νῦν παρὰ τῶν ἐντοπίων "Ἕλληνες προσαγορεύονται [...] κατὰ τοὺς παλαιοὺς "Ἕλληνας [...] Διάκειται δὲ ὁ τοιοῦτος τόπος εἰς ἄκραν τοῦ Μαλέα, ἤγουν ἐκεῖθεν τοῦ Ἐζεροῦ πρὸς τὴν παραθαλασσίαν.

> The inhabitants of the castle of Maïna are not of the race of Slavs, but of ancient Romaioi and even to this day they are called Hellenes-Greeks after the ancient Hellenes [...] and the place where they live (i.e. all the

---

265, 271, 284, 291, 303, 326–27; *De thematibus*, 6.4,6, 90; Charanis 1950, 154–57, 163–64; Bon 1951, 44, 106, 109–10; Kresten 1977; Yannopoulos 1993; Weithmann 1996, 18; Živković 1999; Kislinger 2001, 43–4, 102–3; Turlej 2001, 55–57, 60–70, 87–90, 112–14; Anagnostakis et al. 2002, 72; Curta 2011, 136–37, 251–52; Moulet 2011, 107–8 and n. 360; Anagnostakis 2012, 103–4.

18 *Chronicle of Monemvasia*, 10.45–58 (Lemerle), 20, 22 (Dujčev); *De Administrando Imperio*, 49.4–18, 39–59, 65–75 228–32, 50.9–15, 63, 232–33, 234–35; Kislinger 2001, 42–44, 50, 54, 104; Turlej 2001, 101–4; Anagnostakis & Kaldellis 2014, 110. On the creation of an axis of alliances between Peloponnesian Slavs and other invaders during these revolts, see Anagnostakis 2015.

19 *De Administrando Imperio*, 50.1–5, 15–32, 40–70 232–35; Bon 1951, 61, 73; Kalligas 1990, 43, 45; Kislinger 2001, 53; Zuckerman 2014.

Hellenes) is situated on the tip of Maleas, that is beyond Ezeron towards the coast.[20]

He also relates how the *strategos* who had his seat in Corinth, in the eastern extremity of the *thema* of the Peloponnese, was expected to send aid to Patras, in the west, when besieged by the Slavs, that is, to the part that is presented in the *Chronicle* as unclean or impure. In the same way Strabo's tenth-century *Chrestomathy* refers to Slavs only in the western Peloponnese.[21] This elucidative commentary confirms the general tendency prevailing in the tenth-century sources to present us with the partitioned reality of the Peloponnesian space by exploiting mythological and geographical themes from ancient writers, especially Strabo and Pausanias.[22]

What is particularly interesting in this case is that a historical reality, such as the Slavic settlement and the spatial partition of the Byzantine Peloponnese, was subjected to political and mythical exploitation, adapting and appropriating old patterns of spatial partitioning to official written testimonia on the Peloponnese coming from the state and church authorities. Ancient mythology and medieval legends were used in the fabrication of propaganda and etiological narrative to serve political and ecclesiastical interests and were purported to explain the Peloponnesian particularity. This partitioned space also served to create identities and to generate or justify administrative innovations. The author of the *Chronicle of Monemvasia* reveals an antiquarian cast of mind, and we know that he used Pausanias in extenso: autochthony in a Greek context was precisely the concern of Pausanias.[23] The narratives in relation to the Peloponnese of both Pausanias and the *Chronicle* inaugurated periods that historians have called the Dark Ages, one with the coming of the Dorians, and the other with the coming of the Avars and Slavs.[24] In Pausanias' general account of the peoples of the Peloponnese, at the beginning of Book v,

---

20 *De Administrando Imperio*, 50.1–5, 13–4, 71–6, 232–33, 236–37; *De thematibus*, 6.36–40, 91; Bon 1951, 33 n. 2–3, 72–3 n. 2, 116–18; Kalligas 1990, 43, 45–54; Anagnostakis 1992; Avramea 1997, 89; Avramea 1998; Kislinger 2001, 41–2; Curta 2011, 187; Anagnostakis 2012, 107–9; Anagnostakis & Poulou 1997, 300–2; Anagnostakis 2012, 107; Anagnostakis & Kaldellis 2014, 125, 129. For this original reading of the passage in the *De Administrando Imperio*, 50.71–82 see Anagnostakis 1992; Anagnostakis 1993, 27–30 and n. 6.
21 *Chrestomathie*, 7.47, 288, 8.108, 293; Bon 1951, 39 n.2, 43–44, 63 n. 1; Diller 1954, X.449C, 38–9, 48–50; Anagnostakis et al. 2002, 74; Anagnostakis & Kaldellis 2014, 11.
22 Anagnostakis & Kaldellis 2014, 111–14.
23 Pausanias, 5.1, 1, 380–81; on further documentation and comments see Anagnostakis & Kaldellis 2014, 111–14.
24 *Life of Nikon*, 31.4–5, 108, 283; Kalligas 1990, 48–49; Curta 2011, 187; Anagnostakis 2012, 118.

we find a narrative that presents all the basic structural elements of the tale of migrations and division of the Peloponnese, which were reiterated in the *Chronicle*. State measures taken and rearrangements applied in political and ecclesiastical administration and the supervision of populations in certain areas were invested in the *Chronicle* with contrasting notions that valued space with antithetical properties like continuity versus rupture, and assessed ethnicity likewise (καθαρεῖον, pure versus impure: i.e. 'pure' Patras versus 'impure' Lakedaimon; ἐγγενής, autochthonous, 'indigenous' versus σύμμικτος, mixed).[25]

The *Chronicle* does not refer directly to the 'impurity' of the western or central Peloponnese, but simply presents the eastern part as rugged and inaccessible and as being controlled by the Byzantines. It is this part which is pure *kathareuon* (καθαρεῦον); consequently, the other part is impure, apart from Patras with the newly established metropolitan see.[26] We are faced with the most blatant formulation, perhaps unique, of a partitioned space in terms of difficulty of access and control but also of population diversity and purity. The meaning of the 'purity' and 'impurity' of a space attributed to the partitioned Byzantine Peloponnese had implications associated with population mobility. It is evident that the "purity," of *the kathareuon* space, a Byzantine hapax, was juxtaposed to "commixture," of the *symmikton* (σύμμικτον) part; the term *kathareuon* was attributed to the pure part, while *symmikton* or with Slavs was used in the *Chronicle* to describe populations settled in the western and consequently "impure" part.[27] These terms, used to provide the image of contrasting distinct spatialities, were associated with mobility, transfers or deportations, exiles, and population movements, as well as to rivalries among cities (Corinth, Patras, and Lakedaimon), which in several ways were initiated by political motives.[28]

Kathareuein, meaning to be pure, was used by the Byzantines exclusively for matters of morality, to be clean from bad thoughts, passions, pleasures, sins, or crimes, and hardly ever for the ethnic purity of a country or a region. In ancient writers, we come across the use of *kathareuein* for a place, but not corresponding to its sense articulated in the *Chronicle*, mainly with the meaning of a road

---

25 Pausanias, 5.1, 1–2, 380–81; *Chronicle of Monemvasia*, 10.57 (Lemerle), 12 (Dujčev); Mazaris, 76.17–26; Bon 1951, 63 n.3, 73–4; Westerink 1972, 241; Koder 1976; Kalligas 1990, 16–8, 48–54; Kislinger 2001, 37–8, 55; Curta 2011, 279–80; Anagnostakis 2012, 105–6, 107–8, 111–13 and passim; Anagnostakis & Kaldellis 2014, 111–12, 115 with analysis.

26 *Chronicle of Monemvasia*, 10.56–58, 62–70 (Lemerle), 12, 18 (Dujčev); Anagnostakis & Kaldellis 2014, 109, 111.

27 *Chronicle of Monemvasia*, 10.58, 71 (Lemerle), 12, 22 (Dujčev).

28 *Chronicle of Monemvasia*, 9.36–11.76 (Lemerle), 12, 22 (Dujčev); Curta 2011, 279–80; Anagnostakis 2012, 105–6, 107–8.

or a region being free from dangerous beasts, poisonous plants, lepers, unclean people, or thieves. The closest examples to the *Chronicle*'s use of *kathareuein* exist in the *Roman History* of Appian, referring to a street or space that is clear or free of enemies (ὁδὸν καθαρεύουσαν πολεμίων),[29] and in Pausanias, who speaks of the island of Sardinia being free of poisonous plants except for the Sardinian plant (καθαρεύει καὶ ἀπὸ φαρμάκων ἡ νῆσος ὅσα ἐργάζεται θάνατον).[30] Similarly, an early twelfth century text states that after the grazing herds and the Vlachs were expelled, Mount Athos was cleared, *ekatharisthē* ("Ὅτι μετὰ τὸ ἀπελασθῆναι τὰ ζῶα καὶ τοὺς Βλάχους [...] ἐκαθαρίσθη τὸ ἅγιον ὄρος).[31]

We believe, however, that the issues referring to purity in the *Chronicle*, regardless of any purposes they may have served, while also having a pronounced ethnic character (control of the western part by Slav conquerors), were ultimately exploited quite differently and conceived of in a completely 'physical' and 'administrative' way. We could say that it is something similar to dealing with the wild, savage nature on the one hand and the subjugated, tamed nature on the other. In the first case intervention is not easily allowed, while in the second it is subjugated to the state. The concepts of occupation and control of space are close to equivalent considerations concerning the taming of the wilderness and its transformation into managed landscapes, a process practiced by saints and monks in the Byzantine countryside with the establishment of monasteries.[32] Spatial control and the management of the Peloponnese seems to have been a central element in Byzantine state strategy and ideology in the tenth century. There seems to be also a paradoxical correlation between Byzantine domination and the open areas (lowland areas), where physical contacts allowed the development of administrative activities, compared to areas that are difficult to obtain and therefore controlled only by military operations (mountainous areas and inaccessible areas). Porphyrogennetos described certain regions of the Peloponnese where populations tended to revolt (like the Melingoi and the Ezeritai) as maintaining separate identities but still subject to state taxation.[33]

The exploitation of another kind of spatiality appeared again with the restructuring of the partitioned Peloponnesian space, this time with reference to fiscal and political claims, settled by the granting of privileges on the

---

29 Appian, 3.9, 67, 80–81; 4.12, 99, 306–7.
30 Pausanias, 10.17, 13, 644–45.
31 Meyer 1894/1965, 163.10–13.
32 Anagnostakis & Kaldellis 2014, 128–29; della Dora 2016, 120, 139–40, 148, 170.
33 *De Administrando Imperio*, 49.1–8, 40–44, 65–71, 229–31, 50.1–82, 232–37; Anagnostakis & Kaldellis 2014, 128–31.

eve of and shortly after the Frankish conquest. A type of this administratively partitioned spatiality was extant during the following centuries, but without any reference to purity or to other spatial discriminations: the chrysobull of Alexios III Angelos, dated 1198 and preserved in Latin, refers to *orion* (ὅριον, regional delimitation): the 'Orion Patron et Methonis', which included the western parts of the Peloponnese, and the 'Orion Corinthii, Argus et Nauplii'.[34] In the *Partitio Regni Graeci* a third part, from Lakedaimon to Kalavryta, was put forward as a reasonable complement to the restoration of spatiality and filled the gap between the other two sides of the peninsula.[35] During this period the north-south axis created earlier and being further exploited in the alliance between the Bulgarians and Slavs in the tenth century, corresponded to different operational needs and combined actions which aimed at dealing with the realities that had arisen with the Frankish conquest of the Peloponnese. The Peloponnesian Slavs of the western part, independent to some degree, take on – despite their isolation on Taygetos – the important role of mercenaries and were employed by both the Frankish lords of the *Principality* of Achaia and by the Greeks of the *Despotate* of the Morea. In 1205, at the famous battle in the Olive Grove of Koundouros, they sided with, or were employed by, the Byzantines, and thus found themselves, for the first time, on the opposite side of their traditional alliances in the north-south axis.[36] Thus, the demarcation of the partitioned administrative space of the Peloponnese in the *Partitio Regni Graeci* appears completely official and adjusted to the physical features of the landscape. The problem of control related to purity, as encountered in the sources of the Middle Byzantine period, separating the Peloponnese in two parts, was no longer a fundamental issue. Challenges regarding spatial control strongly re-emerged with the Frankish conquest and the partitioning yet again of the Peloponnese, this time into a *Despotate* and a *Principality*.[37]

So, from the Roman era up to the period of Frankish rule, the partition of the eastern section centred on Corinth and the western one centred on Patras was based primarily on the formation of territorial and power relations, as well as on the capacities of control and communication. The study of the spatial division of the Peloponnese during the Middle Byzantine period bears out the contention that the ethnological, cultural, or other administrative particularities

---

34 *I trattati con Bizanzio*, 130; Tafel & Thomas, 264–65, 468–70; Kordosis 1981, 94; Anagnostakis et al. 2002, 79; Anagnostakis 2012, 104.
35 Zakythinos 1941, 248–52; Bon 1951, 100–2; Bon 1969, 120–25.
36 Anagnostakis 2015, 138–39, 141–44, 156–57; see also above n. 18.
37 Jacoby 1973, 874–75, 877–78; Kalligas 1990, 70–9, 96–7; Anagnostakis 2012, 104; Jeffreys 2013, 11–2; Ragkou 2018.

of each section constituted the consequences and not the causes of the partitioned space of the Peloponnese.[38]

Bibliography

Primary Sources

Appian, *Roman History. The Civil Wars*. Ed. H. White, vol. 4. Cambridge, Mass 1913 (repr. 1968).

Chronicle of Monemvasia. Ed. P. Lemerle, "La chronique improprement dite de Monemvasie. Le contexte historique et légendaire", *RÉB* 21 (1963) 5–49. Ed. I. Dujčev, *Cronaca di Monemvasia*, Palermo 1976.

Chrestomathie. Ed. St. Radt, *Epitome und Chrestomathie. Strabons Geographika*, vol. 9. Göttingen 2010.

De Administrando Imperio. Ed. Gy. Moravcsik & R. J. H. Jenkins *Constantine Porphyrogenitus De Administrando Imperio*, CFHB 1. Washington 1967.

De thematibus. Ed. A. Pertusi, *Costantino Porfirogenito De Thematibus*. Introduzione, testo critico, commento. Studi e Testi 160. Vatican City 1952.

Eustathios. Ed. M. van der Valk, *Eustathii archiepiscopi Thessalonicensis, Commentarii ad Homeri Iliadem pertinentes ad fidem codicis Laurentiani editi*, vol. 1. Leiden 1971.

Herodotos. Ed. A. D. Godley, *Herodotus. Books VIII–IX*, vol. 4. London & Cambridge, Mass. 1925 (repr. 1969).

Life of Saint Nikon Metanoeite. Ed. D. F. Sullivan, *The Life of Saint Nikon. Text, Translation and Commentary*. The Archbishop Iakovos Library of Ecclesiastical and Historical Sources 14. Brookline, Mass. 1987.

Mazaris. *Mazaris' Journey to Hades or, Interviews with dead men about certain officials of the imperial court*. Ed. J. N. Barry, M. J. Share, A. Smithies & L. G. Westerink. Arethusa Monographs 5. Buffalo, Department of Classics, State University of New York, 1975.

Meyer Ph. 1894/1965. *Die Haupturkunden für die Geschichte der Athosklöster*. Amsterdam.

Notitiae. Ed. J. Darrouzès, *Notitiae episcopatuum Ecclesiae Constantinopolitanae*. Texte critique, introduction et notes. Géographie ecclésiastique de l'empire byzantin 1. Paris 1981.

Pausanias. Ed. W. H. S. Jones & H. A. Ormerod, *Pausanias Description of Greece. Books III–V*, vol. 2. London & Cambridge, Mass. 1926 (repr. 1966).

---

38 We want to express our gratitude to Myrto Veikou for the instructive amendments to this paper.

Pausanias. Ed. W. H. S. Jones, *Pausanias Description of Greece. Books VIII.22–X*, vol. 4. Cambridge, Mass. & London 1935 (repr. 1965).

Pseudo-Zonaras. Ed. J. A. H. Tittmann, *Ioannis Zonarae Lexicon ex Tribus Codicibus Manuscriptis*, vol. 1. Leipzig 1808 (Amsterdam 1967).

Strabo. Ed. H. L. Jones, *The Geography of Strabo. Book VIII*, vol. 4. London & Cambridge, Mass. 1927 (repr. 1968).

Stephanos Byzantios. Ed. M. Billerbeck & A. Neumann-Hartmann, *Stephani Byzantii Ethnica*, vol. IV: Π–Υ. CFHB – Series Berolinensis 43/4. Berlin & Boston 2016.

Tafel G. L. & G. M. Thomas. *Urkunden zur älteren Handels- und Staatsgeschichte der Republik Venedig mit besonderer Beziehung auf Byzanz und die Levante*, vol. 1. Vienna 1856 (Amsterdam 1964).

I trattati con Bizanzio. Ed. M. Pozza & G. Ravegnani, *I trattati con Bizanzio 992–1198*. Pacta Veneta 4. Venice 1993.

Secondary Sources

Anagnostakis, I. 1992. "Η Μάνη και οι οικήτορές της κατά τον Πορφυρογέννητο. Μία ακόμη ερμηνεία," *5th Symposion of History and Art*, Monemvasia 1992 (communication manuscript).

Anagnostakis, I. 1993. "Η θέση των ειδωλολατρών στο Βυζάντιο. Η περίπτωση των «Ελλήνων» του Πορφυρογέννητου," in Maltezou 1993, 25–47.

Anagnostakis, I. 1997. "Η χειροποίητη κεραμική ανάμεσα στην Ιστορία και την Αρχαιολογία," *Βυζαντιακά* 17, 285–330.

Anagnostakis, I. 2009. "Μετονομασίες – μετοικεσίες. Η περίπτωση της βυζαντινής Κορώνης," in *Πρακτικά επιστημονικού συνεδρίου (5–7 Αυγούστου). Ομηρική Αίπεια – Αρχαία Κορώνη – Πεταλίδι*. Petalidi, 45–69.

Anagnostakis, I. 2012. "Μονεμβασία – Λακεδαίμων. Για μια τυπολογία αντιπαλότητας και για την Κυριακή αργία στις πόλεις," in Kioussopoulou (ed.) 2012, 101–37.

Anagnostakis I. & A. Kaldellis 2014. "The Textual Sources for the Peloponnese, A.D. 582–959. Their Creative Engagement with Ancient Literature," *Greek, Roman and Byzantine Studies* 54, 105–35.

Anagnostakis, I., V. Konti, A. Lambropoulou & A. Panopoulou 2002. "Χώρος και ενότητα της δυτικής Πελοποννήσου," in Themelis & Konti (eds), 65–81.

Anagnostakis, I. & N. Poulou 1997. "Η πρωτοβυζαντινή Μεσσήνη (5ος–7ος αιώνας) και προβλήματα της χειροποίητης κεραμικής στη Πελοπόννησο," *Symmeikta* 11, 229–319.

Anagnostakis, I. 2015. "'From Tempe to Sparta': Power and Contestation prior to the Latin Conquest of 1204," in Simpson 2015, 135–57.

Avramea, A. 1997. *Le Péloponnèse du IVe au VIIIe siècle. Changements et persistances*. Paris.

Avramea, A. 1998. "Le Magne byzantin. Problèmes d'histoire et de topographie," in Balard et al. 1998, vol. 2, 49–62.

Balard M., J. Beaucamp, J.-Cl. Cheynet, C. Jolivet-Lévy, M. Kaplan, B. Martin-Hisard, P. Pagès, C. Piganiol & J.-P. Sodini (eds.) 1988. Εὐψυχία. Mélanges offerts à Hélène Ahrweiler. Paris.

Baladié, R. 1980. Le Péloponnèse de Strabon. Étude de géographie historique. Paris.

Belke, K., F. Hild, J. Koder & P. Soustal (eds) 2000. Byzanz als Raum. Zu Methoden und Inhalten der historischen Geographie des östlichen Mittelmeerraumes. Denkschriften der philosophisch-historischen Klasse283. Veröffentlichungen der Kommission für die Tabula Imperii Byzantini 7. Vienna.

Bon, A. 1951. Le Péloponnèse byzantin jusqu'en 1204. Changements et persistances. Paris.

Bon, A. 1969. La Morée franque. Recherches historiques, topographiques et archéologiques sur la principauté d'Achaïe (1205–1430). Texte. Paris.

Charanis, P. 1950. "The Chronicle of Monemvasia and the Question of the Slavonic Settlements in Greece," *DOP* 5, 141–66. [Charanis P. 1972. *Studies on the Demography of the Byzantine Empire*. Collected Studies. London].

Curta, F. 2011. *The Edinburgh History of the Greeks, c. 500 to 1050*. Edinburgh.

della Dora, V. 2016. *Landscape, Nature, and the Sacred in Byzantium*. Cambridge.

della Dora, V. 2013. "Mapping 'Melancholy-Pleasing Remains'. Morea as a Renaissance Memory Theater," in Gerstel (ed.) 2013, 455–75.

Diller, A. 1954. "The Scholia on Strabo," *Traditio* 10, 29–50.

Dimitriadis, E. P. & A. Karadimou-Gerolymbou (eds) 1989. *Space and History. Urban, architectural and regional space. Proceedings of the Scopelos Symposium*. Thessaloniki.

Fougères, G. 1898. *Mantinée et l'Arcadie orientale*. Paris & Athens.

Gerstel, S. E. J. (ed.) 2013. *Viewing the Morea. Land and People in the Late Medieval Peloponnese*. Washington D.C.

Gerstel, S. E. J. 2013. "Introduction," in Gerstel (ed.) 2013, 1–9.

Gregory, T. E. 1991. S.v. "Morea," *ODB* 2, 1409.

Horden, P. & N. Purcell 2000. *The Corrupting Sea. A Study of Mediterranean History*. Oxford.

Jacoby, D. 1973. "The Encounter of Two Societies. Western Conquerors and Byzantines in the Peloponnesus after the Fourth Crusade," *The American Historical Review* 78, 873–906.

Jeffreys, E. 2013. "The Morea through the Prism of the Past," in Gerstel (ed.) 2013, 9–22.

Kalligas, H. 1990. *Byzantine Monemvasia, The Sources*. Monemvasia.

Kazhdan, A. P. (ed.) 1991. *The Oxford Dictionary of Byzantium*. 3 vols. New York.

Kioussopoulou, T. (ed.) 2012. Οι βυζαντινές πόλεις, 8ος–15ος αιώνας. Προοπτικές της έρευνας και νέες ερμηνευτικές προσεγγίσεις. Rethymno.

Kislinger, E. 2001. *Regionalgeschichte als Quellenproblem. Die Chronik von Monembasia und das sizilianische Demenna. Eine historisch-topographische Studie*. Österreichische Akademie der Wissenschaften, philosophisch-historische Klasse.

Denkschriften 294. Veröffentlichungen der Kommission für die Tabula Imperii Byzantini, 8. Vienna.

Koder, J. 1976. "Arethas von Kaisareia und die sogenannte Chronik von Monembasia," *JÖB* 25, 75–80.

Koder, J. 2020. "On the Slavic Immigration in the Byzantine Balkans," in Preiser-Kapeller, Reinfandt & Stouraitis (eds), 81–100.

Konstantakopoulou, A. 1989. "Χώρος και εξουσία στο έργο του Κωνσταντίνου Πορφυρογέννητου. 'Περί τῶν θεμάτων' και 'Πρὸς τὸν ἴδιον υἱὸν Ρωμανόν'," in Dimitriadis & Karadimou-Gerolymbou (eds) 1989, 113–29.

Konti, V. 1985. "Συμβολή στην ιστορική γεωγραφία της Αρκαδίας (395–1209)," *Symmeikta* 6, 91–124.

Kordosis, M. S. 1981. *Συμβολή στὴν ἱστορία καὶ τοπογραφία τῆς περιοχῆς Κορίνθου στοὺς μέσους χρόνους*. Athens.

Koutava-Delivoria, V. 1993. *Ὁ γεωγραφικός κόσμος Κωνσταντίνου του Πορφυρογέννητου*, vol. 1. *Τα 'Γεωγραφικά'*. Athens.

Kresten, O. 1977. "Zur Echtheit des σιγίλλιον des Kaisers Nikephoros I. für Patras," *Römische Historische Mitteilungen* 19, 15–78.

Lambropoulou, A. 2000. "Le Péloponnèse occidental à l'époque protobyzantine (IVe–VIIe siècles). Problèmes de géographie historique d'un espace à reconsidérer," in Belke et al. (eds) 2000, 95–113.

Laurent, V. 1962. "L'évêché de Morée (Moréas) au Péloponnèse," *Revue des études byzantines* 20, 181–89.

Malingoudis, P. 1981. *Studien zu den slavischen Ortsnamen Griechenlands. 1. Slavische Flurnamen aus der messenischen Mani*. Mainz.

Maltezou, Ch. .A. (ed). 1993. *Πρακτικά ημερίδας Οι περιθωριακοί στο Βυζάντιο*. Athens.

Metaxas, S. 2018. "Νέα αρχαιολογικά στοιχεία για την οικιστική δραστηριότητα στο Παλλάντιον στην πρωτοβυζαντινή εποχή," in Zymi, Karapanagiotou & Xanthopoulou (eds) 2018, 689–700.

Moulet, B. 2011. *Évêques, pouvoir et société à Byzance (VIIIe–XIe siècle). Territoires, communautés et individus dans la société provinciale byzantine*. Paris.

Nesbitt, J. & N. Oikonomides 1994. *Catalogue of Byzantine Seals at Dumbarton Oaks and in the Fogg Museum of Art*, vol. 2. *South of the Balkans, the Islands, South of Asia Minor*. Washington D.C.

Neville, L. 2018. *Guide to Byzantine Historical Writing*. Cambridge.

van Nuffelen, P. 2019. "Introduction: From Imperial to Post-Imperial Space in Late Ancient Historiography," in Van Nuffelen (ed.) 2019, 1–12.

van Nuffelen, P. (ed.) 2019. *Historiography and Space in Late Antiquity*, Cambridge.

Preiser-Kapeller J., L. Reinfandt & Y. Stouraitis (eds) 2020, *Migration Histories of the Medieval Afroeurasian Transition Zone. Aspects of mobility between Africa, Asia and Europe, 300–1500 C.E.*, Studies in Global Social History 39/13, Leiden & Boston.

Ragkou, K. 2018. "The Economic Centrality of Urban Centres in the Medieval Peloponnese. Late 11th–Mid-14th Centuries," *Land* 7.4, 153.

Reinhard, L. R. & P. Schreiner (eds) 1996. *Die Kultur Griechenlands in Mittelalter und Neuzeit*. Göttingen.

Simpson, A. (ed.), *Byzantium, 1180–1204: 'The Sad Quarter of a Century'?* [International Symposium 22], Institute of Historical Research, National Hellenic Research Foundation, Athens 2015.

Stewart, D. R. 2013. *Reading the landscapes of the rural Peloponnese. Landscape Change and Regional Variation in an Early 'Provincial' Setting*. Oxford.

Themelis, P. G. & V. Konti (eds) 2002. *Πρωτοβυζαντινή Μεσσήνη και Ολυμπία. Αστικός και αγροτικός χώρος στη Δυτική Πελοπόννησο. Πρακτικά του Διεθνούς Συμποσίου*, Αθήνα 29–30 Μαΐου 1998. Athens.

Turlej, W. 2001. *The Chronicle of Monemvasia. The Migration of the Slavs and Church Conflicts in the Byzantine Source from the Beginning of the 9th Century*. Cracow.

Veikou, M. 2012. "Byzantine Histories, Settlement Stories. Kastra, 'Isles of Refuge' and 'Unspecified Settlements' as In-between or Third Spaces," in Kioussopoulou (ed.) 2012, 159–206.

Vroom, J. 2003. *After Antiquity. Ceramics and Society in the Aegean from the 7th to the 20th century A.C. A Case Study from Boeotia, Central Greece*. Leiden.

Weithmann, M. W. 1996. "Politische und ethnische Veränderungen in Griechenland am Übergang von der Antike zum Frühmittelalter," in Reinhard & Schreiner (eds) 1996, 13–30.

Westerink, G. 1972. "Marginalia by Arethas in Moscow Greek Ms. 231," *Byzantion* 42, 196–244.

Yannopoulos, P. 1993. "Métropoles du Péloponnèse mésobyzantin. Un souvenir des invasions avaro-slaves," *Byzantion* 63, 388–400.

Zakythinos, D. A. 1941. "Μελέται περὶ τῆς διοικητικῆς διαιρέσεως καὶ τῆς ἐπαρχιακῆς διοικήσεως ἐν τῷ βυζαντινῷ κράτει," *Ἐπετηρὶς Ἑταιρείας Βυζαντινῶν Σπουδῶν* 17, 248–52.

Živković, T. 1999. "The Date of the Creation of the Theme of Peloponnese," *Symmeikta* 13, 141–55.

Zuckerman, C. 2014. "Squabbling Protospatharioi and Other Administrative Issues from the First Half of the Tenth Century," *RÉB* 72, 193–233.

Zymi, E., A.-B. Karapanagiotou & M. Xanthopoulou (eds) 2018. *Το αρχαιολογικό έργο στην Πελοπόννησο (ΑΕΠΕΛ 1). Πρακτικά του Διεθνούς Συνεδρίου. Τρίπολη*, 7–11 Νοεμβρίου 2012. Kalamata.

Spatial Concepts and Administrative Structures in the Byzantine-Turkish Frontier of Twelfth-Century Asia Minor

Alexander Beihammer

The Turkish penetration of Byzantine Asia Minor from the 1040s onwards and the ensuing collapse of the imperial government's administration in the eastern provinces resulted in a complete and, for the most part, irreversible reconfiguration of political landscapes.[1] Byzantium's eastern territories turned from a politically integrated and centrally controlled realm into an assembly of fragmented regional powers of Muslim, Byzantine, Armenian, or Frankish identity. The fragmentation of Asia Minor was to last for centuries, going hand in hand with constantly changing constellations in the adjacent regions of the Levant and the Middle East up to the rise of the Ottoman Empire.

For the Byzantine state these developments meant huge losses of territories, economic resources, tax revenues, and subject populations. Social, political, administrative, and military structures, which had begun taking shape in the wake of the Arab expansion in the seventh century, once again underwent a profound transformation. One of the most remarkable changes in terms of spatial arrangements was the gradual emergence of a new frontier zone between Byzantium and the nascent Muslim-Turkish realm that started to crystallize in the second half of Alexios I Komnenos' (1081–1118) reign, running along the intersections of the fringes of the Anatolian plateau and the mountain ranges and fertile riverine lands of western Asia Minor.[2] The system of advanced military districts based on a network of *katepanata* and *doukata*, which had made its appearance in the time of the Byzantine eastward expansion, collapsed in the 1070s.[3] Romanos IV Diogenes (1068–1071) and his successors failed to assert control over the access routes across the Armenian highlands and the Anti-Taurus Mountains. As a result, Armenian local lords carved out independent lordships in Cilicia and the Euphrates region, while Turkish warrior groups

---

1 For the traditional narrative, see Vryonis 1971 and Cahen 2001.
2 For geographical details, see Vryonis 1975, 43–44.
3 For a detailed discussion, see Leveniotis 2007.

pushed into the interior and the western coastland of Asia Minor.[4] Turkish lords holding sway over the western ports and towns of Asia Minor are a relatively short-lived phenomenon between about 1080 and the arrival of the First Crusade.

Yet from 1097 onwards the Byzantines and newly arriving crusading hosts were facing Turkish warrior groups who began establishing rudimentary lordships in the Anatolian plateau and Cappadocia.[5] The eastern frontier had shifted some 500–600 miles westwards and the entire region from Bithynia and Phrygia down to Lycia and Caria turned into a contested zone of border warfare, nomadic migratory movements, and population displacements. The Byzantine imperial government faced the challenges of readjusting its concepts of territorial control to the new situation and of strengthening its grip over the remaining provinces. The western Anatolian frontier persisted with various alterations until the time of the Palaiologan emperor Andronikos II Palaiologos (1282–1328). For more than one-and-a-half centuries, it constituted a conspicuous political, cultural, and religious divide and contact zone between the remnants of Byzantine-Christian Asia Minor and an increasingly Islamized sphere, which was dominated by the elites of the Seljuk sultanate of Rum and interspersed with groups of semi-independent nomadic pastoralists.[6]

1   Frontier Studies and Scholarly Debates on Byzantium's Eastern Borderland

Modern scholars paid much more attention to the classical Islamic-Byzantine borderlands along the Taurus and Anti-Taurus mountain ranges.[7] Thus, it comes as no surprise that many of the assumptions, concepts, and explicatory models developed on the basis of the latter reappear in a slightly modified version in the context of western Asia Minor. Asa Eger's recent monograph on the Islamic-Byzantine frontier, the first systematic attempt to configure archaeological and textual evidence in an analysis of settlement patterns, economic activities, and land-use, proposes a useful distinction between physical and ideological visions of the frontier as superimposed layers referring to different levels of human activities from handling specific ecological and environmental conditions up to promoting collective images and perceptions

---

4 Beihammer 2017, 133–68, 285–303.
5 Beihammer 2017, 307–32.
6 Vryonis 1971, 143–286.
7 See, for instance, Honigmann 1935, Lilie 1976, and other works cited below.

of borderlands and their inhabitants for political and ideological purposes.[8] Interpretations of Byzantium's Anatolian frontiers can certainly benefit from the broader scholarly debate about the notion of boundaries, borders, frontiers, or borderlands in pre-modern and modern times.[9] Attempts have been made to develop a generally applicable terminology across linguistic and disciplinary divides and to distinguish different types and sets of boundaries, which taken together represent a continuum of boundary dynamics and illustrate the interaction of boundary processes.[10] In terms of internal power dynamics it is important to distinguish between political centres or core polities and frontier populations along with their local elites, institutions, and other particularities (core-periphery relationships).[11] The cultural and ethnic processes in frontier regions are marked by various levels of communication, confrontation, and interpenetration between different population groups, their ideologies, and symbolic universes. Post-colonial theory defines this sphere of interaction as a "Third Space", ascribing to it certain characteristics, such as hybridity and constant dialogue.[12] With respect to historical evolution, one has to be aware of the structural and organizational differences between the static linear boundaries of modern territorial states and the much more porous or fluid zonal frontiers of medieval state formations.[13] Settler-colonialist versions of frontier narratives, such as Jack Turner's American frontier in the wilderness as "the meeting point between savagery and civilization" and its European counterpart relating to the expansion of Latin Christendom through conquest, mission, and colonization, are still referred to and impinge upon modern imagination. More recent narratives premised upon the idea of frontier as a "middle ground" or upon concepts of frontier ethnogenesis and acculturation provide a much more balanced and accurate portrayal of frontier realities, replacing fantasies of emptiness and uncivilized savages with ethnically and culturally distinct population groups living side by side and interacting with one another in equilibrium.[14]

Some of the interpretive frameworks used in modern narratives of Byzantium's eastern frontier apparently have their roots in these romanticized

---

8 Eger 2015, 2–3.
9 Baud & Van Schende 1997, 213–21; Berend 1999, 55–72; Power & Standen (eds) 1999, 1–31; Curta (ed.) 2005, 1–9; Parker 2006, 77–83; Naum 2010, 101–08.
10 Power & Standen (eds) 1999, 6–9; Parker 2006, 82–91.
11 Power & Standen (eds) 1999, 21–22; Parker 2006, 91–94; Naum 2010, 104–105.
12 Naum 2010, 105–107.
13 Parker 2006, 81, 83–85.
14 Power & Standen (eds) 1999, 9–12; Brather 2005, 39–71; Curta 2005, 173–204; Naum 2010, 107.

cultural-clash images of medieval Europe and colonial America. Notions of a highly militarized space, a devastated no-man's land, a primitive frontier culture, and an incessant threat of warlike barbarians need to be scrutinized and re-evaluated under the light of more accurate theories.[15] We may discern three thematic subfields that prevail in scholarly debates: (1) the administrative structures and military organization through which power elites exerted control and integrated frontier zones into the state apparatus;[16] (2) the practices and institutions of border warfare as they became manifest in Muslim raids, jihad concepts, Byzantine defensive measures, and counterattacks;[17] (3) the mental and cultural particularities of border societies with a special emphasis on local elites and their mixed identity as reflected, for instance, in the Byzantine epic cycle of Digenis Akrites and Arabic heroic tales.[18] It was mainly Paul Wittek and Speros Vryonis who, on the grounds of the aforementioned themes, developed their own theories about the nature and historical role of the Byzantine-Turkish frontier.[19]

Wittek sees the most powerful element of the Anatolian borderland society in a community of ghazis or Muslim marcher warriors, who in his view came to be the driving force in the formation and expansion of the Ottoman state. He places their origins in post-1071 Asia Minor, in which the decline of the Byzantine military organization and the overall anarchy in the provinces encouraged Seljuk warriors and independent nomadic groups to deeply penetrate the interior of Asia Minor.[20] Wittek perceives the new borderland as a culturally and politically fluent strip of no-man's land situated between the Byzantine-held territories of western Asia Minor and the sultanate of Rum in Konya.[21] Perpetual warfare carried out by marcher warriors striving for booty and a linguistically and ethnically mixed society are its most salient characteristics. The people living there were devoted to chiefs of warrior clans, were at odds with the central power in the hinterland, and stood in constant contact with the other side. Wittek distinguishes between a quickly vanishing Byzantine varnish and a strong local substrate of Anatolian traditions that fused with the incoming ghazis and thus contributed to the crystallization of a distinct borderland civilization. The Turkish population consisted mainly of Turkmen

---

15 Eger 2015, 2–12.
16 Lilie 1976; Haldon & Kennedy 1980.
17 Bonner 1996.
18 Beaton & Ricks (eds) 1993; Lyons 1993, 147–61.
19 Wittek 2012; Vryonis 1971, 1975.
20 Wittek 2012, 43–48.
21 Wittek 2012, 50–51.

nomads who operated in the frontier zone as both shepherds and robbers and adopted ghazi traditions from the Danishmend dynasty in Malatya and other regions.[22] The terminological convergence between the Turkish word *uc*, i.e., "extremity, end, frontier", which also designates the Turkmen population in the frontier zone, and its Greek equivalent *akra* points to the cultural uniformity of borderland populations and the similarities between Muslim ghazis and Byzantine *akritai*.[23] In sum, Wittek conceptualizes the Anatolian border society as a belligerent, but vigorous and progressive, force, which eventually gained the power to oust the old elites and to create a new empire.

Speros Vryonis shares many of Wittek's assumptions, such as the overwhelmingly nomadic character of the Muslim-Turkish frontier population, the prevalence of ghazi ideology, and the distinction between a mixed frontier culture and a high culture centred in the core regions of Byzantium and the Seljuk sultanate.[24] His conclusions, however, differ quite sharply with respect to the cultural identity of the indigenous population and the historical role of the nomads. In Vryonis' view, the cultural fundament of Asia Minor is Orthodox Hellenism.[25] Hence, the change Turkmen nomads set into motion is tantamount to destroying a flourishing civilization. The presence of Turkmen in the borderland constituted a disruptive threat to the Christian-Roman cultural sphere that over centuries had been shaped by Constantinopolitan imperial and ecclesiastical institutions. By taking the descriptions and figures provided by primary sources at face value, Vryonis construes the image of nomadic hordes flooding the frontier zones and rural areas of the Byzantine hinterland.[26] Vryonis also highlights the violent nature of Turkish expansion, which in his view was mainly based on burning, killing, pillaging, enslaving, and defiling holy places. The sedentary population enduring in fortified cities found itself rapidly encircled by a nomadic belt posing a constant threat to their harvests, sources of income, and lifestyle.[27] Nomadic activities are thus conceived of as an ethnic migration causing the partial destruction of the local society and eliciting a process of Islamization and Turkification.[28] The decay of ecclesiastical structures, the spread of Islamic institutions relying on the material and moral support of the sultanate, and the activities of dervish

---

22 Wittek 2012, 48–49.
23 Wittek 2012, 50.
24 Vryonis 1975, 48–60.
25 Vryonis 1971, 1–68.
26 Vryonis 1971, 43–47; Vryonis, 1975, 143–94.
27 Vryonis 1975, 50–57.
28 Vryonis 1975, 49–50.

groups were factors accelerating a multi-layered process of conversion and religious change.[29] Hence, the borderland was primarily a deadly threat to the Byzantine state and culture.

In a recent article, Andrew Peacock challenged Wittek's assumptions about the characteristics of the western Anatolian frontier zone, arguing that it "formed an integral part of the Seljuk state" and had close economic, political, and cultural ties with the court of Konya.[30] In other words, he rejects the notion of a politically and culturally distinct border zone or no-man's land, adducing evidence for the frontier's integration in economic networks, Seljuk patronage, and political structures. The thirteenth-century Seljuk ruling elite, Peacock's argument goes, was able to keep a grip on the borderland by pursuing a policy of accommodation with the Byzantines through treaties and by fostering trade through the erection of caravanserais and commercial exchanges with the local pastoralists.[31] The Seljuk elites further strengthened their presence by erecting religious monuments and by forging administrative links with the Turkmen nomads through governors and garrisons in important strongholds like Sozopolis/Uluborlu, for instance, or through the appointment of a local *shiḥna* or chief commander.[32] The investments of the Byzantine landed aristocracy in the Maeander Valley and signs of economic growth in Bithynia point to similar trends on the other side of the border.[33]

Overall, it is fair to say that modern reconstructions of borderland life in medieval Anatolia and its dynamics are still controversial and, in many respects, unsatisfactory. They largely depend on how scholars imagine the extent and nature of political authority exerted by the central governments in Constantinople and Konya. Other aspects of this debate concern the relations between capital-based power elites and provincial populations; those between sedentary groups and nomads; as well as the crystallization of cultural and religious hybridity through cross-border contacts. Frequently, ideas of cultural and ethnic superiority/inferiority appear as explicatory models for the rise and fall of social structures or political entities. The written and material evidence is sparse, unevenly distributed, and frequently ambiguous in its informative value. Studies on Byzantine fortifications brought to light a number of sites related to the erection or rebuilding of fortresses from the Komnenian period onwards and thus attest to a centrally governed reorganization of defensive

---

29 Vryonis 1971, 94–216, 288–402; Vryonis 1975, 60–71.
30 Peacock 2014, 273.
31 Peacock 2014, 275, 278–79.
32 Peacock 2014, 279–80, 281–84.
33 Peacock 2014, 275–77.

structures, but many details of this process need further research.[34] The bulk of written information has to be extrapolated from Byzantine, Muslim, or Latin chronicles, which all have a different thematic and geographic focus and refer to the Anatolian borderlands only circumstantially. These texts mostly reflect outside perceptions and imaginations which are closely related to the ideologies and visions of imperial centres and foreigners. Borderland realities thus remain shrouded in the borderland memories of distant observers.

Modern historians, therefore, should refrain from generalizations about what borderland life was like. The disparate and frequently contradictory pieces of information mostly relate to specific areas and moments of the frontier and have to be contextualized within specific spatial and structural settings. These are shaped by a variety of factors, such as geographic features, road networks, settlements patterns, forms of land-use, and institutions of central control. We may assume that deserted and uncultivated zones, strips of no-man's land affected by nomadic movements, and prosperous settlement areas protected by defensive structures existed side by side, yet in different parts of the borderland. Neither Byzantium nor the Seljuk sultanate had the means to set up a hermetically sealed shield of border protection. They rather focused on certain core areas in western Asia Minor which stood out for their economic and strategic significance, were accessible through rifts, plains, or river valleys, and were connected to the coastland. Lineal border concepts gave way to a flexible control system in which the power of the central government rested upon certain key points and was fading out towards the fringes.

2 Ideological Expressions and Political Realities

In diplomatic contacts and treaties, the Byzantine ruling elite repeatedly expressed its readiness to accept the state of affairs that had resulted from expansionist movements and military encounters and conceded extensive territorial rights to the new rulers. Ideologically, however, it tenaciously refused to forfeit its patrimonial rights to suzerainty over the whole of Asia Minor. Inevitably, this caused a discrepancy between territorial realities and political claims. Indicative of this attitude is the way in which Niketas Choniates describes the succession arrangements made by the Seljuk Sultan Mas'ūd of Konya in view of his imminent death in 1155: "He distributed among his sons the cities and provinces which had once been included within the boundaries

---

34 Foss 1985, 1986.

of the Romans and now were under his rule;" and, in a similar vein, "Mas'ūd's sons divided the major regions of the lordship, or to be more exact, the territories of the Romans, into three parts". (διανέμει τοῖς ἐκείνου παισὶ τὰς ποτὲ μὲν Ῥωμαίων ὅροις κληρουχουμένας, τότε δὲ ὑπ' ἐκείνῳ ταττομένας πόλεις καὶ χώρας [...] οἱ δ' οὖν τοῦ Μασοὺτ τριχῇ δασάμενοι τὰ κεφαλαιώδη τῆς ἀρχῆς ὁρίσματα, ἢ τὸ νητρεκὲς εἰπεῖν τὰ τῶν Ῥωμαίων σχοινίσματα).[35] These statements tally with what Anna Komnene had her father, Alexios I Komnenos, say in the peace negotiations with the Seljuk ruler Shāhinshāh in 1116: He should submit to the empire of the Romans and content himself with the lands the Turks had ruled in the time prior to Romanos III Argyros' defeat at Manzikert.[36] In about 1070, Turkish groups had already deeply penetrated Byzantine territory, but they did not yet possess permanent footholds.[37] Fifty years later the imperial government was no longer able to negotiate the restoration of the old borderline. Yet Anna Komnene and Niketas Choniates agree that in terms of political legitimacy the empire had to perpetuate its claims to hold sway over the whole of the eastern lands.

The agreements between Emperor Alexios I and the leaders of the First Crusade stipulated among other things that they restore to imperial rule whatever they would seize on their way to Jerusalem and formerly had belonged to Byzantium.[38] It remains, perhaps deliberately, obscure which territories were actually meant by this agreement, but the underlying claims and ambitions of the imperial government are clearly recognizable. Armenian lords in Cilicia and the Euphrates region continued to receive Byzantine court titles long after the administrative bonds with Constantinople had been severed.[39] In a similar vein, Alexios I considered bestowing the title of *domestikos in the East*, a position that at times had been granted ad hoc to powerful commanders in the borderlands, upon the Norman chief Bohemond during his sojourn in Constantinople.[40] The arrival of the crusading hosts in late 1096 and early 1097 prompted the emperor to negotiate the future status of the Euphrates frontier. It should not be forgotten, however, that at that time the Turks had spread over most parts of the western coastland of Asia Minor while military and administrative structures in the interior were rapidly disintegrating. The

35   Niketas Choniates, *Historia* 116–17 van Dieten.
36   Anna Komnene, *Alexias* 15.6.5 (478 Reinsch).
37   Vryonis 1971, 80–96.
38   Anna Komnene, *Alexias* 10.9.11 (313 Reinsch).
39   Pryor & Jeffreys 2012, 35–39, 67–70, 80–82.
40   Anna Komnene, *Alexias* 10.11.7 (320 Reinsch); for a recent discussion of this issue, see Pryor & Jeffreys, 2012, 31–35, 44–48, 57–67, 76–79.

emperor may have placed great hopes in the binding force of the crusaders' oath of allegiance and their willingness to serve as his mercenaries.[41] But, at least since the Seljuk conquest of parts of Cilicia and Antioch in late 1085, the Constantinopolitan government must have been aware of its inability to exert any effective control over the east.[42] Norman propaganda presented Alexios' failure to advance to Antioch in 1098 as an act of treason, while modern scholars ascribe it to political miscalculations. Another important factor, however, seems to have been the highly insecure conditions in central Anatolia.[43]

After Alexios' death in 1118, his successors John II Komnenos (1118–1143) and Manuel I Komnenos (1143–1180) took pains to substantiate their claims to the east by launching a number of military campaigns that aimed at ousting the Turks from certain areas and strongholds in the frontier zone.[44] In addition, the imperial government made ample use of well-established diplomatic tools, such as the bestowal of titles, invitations to Constantinople, or face-to-face meetings, through which Turkish emirs were integrated into the Byzantine court hierarchy and thus could formally be considered subjects and allies of the emperor. Imperial rhetoric, as articulated, for instance, in the works of court rhetoricians and poets, such as Euthymios Malakes, Eustathios of Thessaloniki, and Theodore and Manganeios Prodromos, provided an ideological frame for these endeavours.[45] These authors frequently evoked the historical model of the Roman-Persian wars in antiquity by equating the Turks with the Persians and by transferring the lands of an imaginary Persian Empire to the banks of the Halys River in central Anatolia. The Komnenian emperors' wars against the Turks thus appeared as the ultimate stage of the Romans' perennial heroic struggle against an overwhelming eastern threat.

The political realities in the borderland differed sharply from court rhetoric. As soon as the imperial government managed to restore a certain amount of control over western Asia Minor in the wake of the crossing of the First Crusade in 1097/1098, it made efforts to adjust the local administrative and military structures to the new political constellations and to respond to the challenges posed by Turkish warrior groups who had been pushed back to the Anatolian plateau.[46] Simultaneously, the conflicts with the Normans in Antioch and the

---

41 For a new interpretation of this issue, see Kaldellis 2017, 280–301.
42 Vryonis 1971, 114–15.
43 Beihammer 2017, 317–18.
44 Angold 1997, 181–90, 192–200, 221–25.
45 Stone 2003, 183–99; Stone 2004, 125–42; Beihammer 2011, 23–25.
46 Frankopan 2012, 145–46 (dates the beginning of the expedition to the summer of 1097); Beihammer 2017, 315–18.

activities of Pisan and Genoese fleets prompted Constantinople to strengthen its naval power and its hold over the southern littoral of Asia Minor along with a maritime extension to the island of Cyprus.[47] The spatial arrangement in this new frontier zone, however, differed quite sharply from what had been in place in key areas of the old borderland. There were no clearly defined boundaries demarcating Byzantine and Turkish territories, as was the case, for instance, at the border of the ducate of Antioch vis-à-vis the adjacent emirate of Aleppo.[48] Rather, we are dealing with a soft and highly permeable frontier that consisted of some advanced outposts and patrol units of scouts monitoring roads and river valleys. Denser networks of fortified places were confined to the hinterland at a rather long distance from the front.

The emergence of this system was closely related to a new phase of military conflicts that occurred in the time span 1109–1116. In these years, Turkish hosts made their last large-scale incursions into the western coastland while the Byzantine army fathomed its limits in pushing into the Anatolian plateau.[49] Access to water, fodder, and food supplies largely determined the movements and actions of both invaders and defenders. Invading hosts typically split up into smaller units spreading out in a fan-shaped manner so as to widen their radius of action for raiding purposes.[50] In so doing, the invaders organized their advances and retreats by following the river valleys running from east to west, such as the Hermos/Gediz, the Kaystros/Küçük Menderes, and the Maeander/Menderes, and by concentrating on certain nodal points in the local road network for rallying purposes.[51] Accordingly, Byzantine defensive measures focused on the fortification of key strongholds blocking access routes along or across the river valleys, such as Pergamon/Bergama, Poimanenon/Manyas, Chliara/Kırkağaç, Philadelpheia/Alaşehir, and Akroinon/Afyonkarahisar. The configuration of contact and combat zones in the conflict areas was closely intertwined with logistical considerations about the proximity and accessibility of roads, waterways, fertile pastureland, and agricultural zones. Mishaps and miscalculations in this respect could have fatal consequences for the supply situation and health condition of troops. For instance, the effects of seasonally changing weather conditions immediately caused precarious

---

47   Lilie 1993, 61–72.
48   Dölger & Müller 2003, no. 728a.
49   Beihammer 2017, 363–73.
50   For instance, Anna Komnene, *Alexias* 14.1.5–7 (426–27 Reinsch) and 14.5.3 (443–44 Reinsch).
51   For instance, Anna Komnene, *Alexias* 14.3.1 (434–35 Reinsch), 14.3.7 (437 Reinsch), 14.5.3 (443–44 Reinsch); for roads in Western Asia Minor, see Külzer 2018, 83–95.

shortages of foodstuff or water supplies. A case in point is what happened to the army of John II Komnenos, when in the late fall of 1135 it pitched its winter camp in the Rhyndakos valley after an unsuccessful siege of the Pamphylian city of Gangra/Çankırı.[52] The protracted hostilities apparently had prevented the soldiers from preparing themselves appropriately for the winter season. Thus, they endured severe starvation in a region that under normal conditions proved perfectly suitable for accommodating large gatherings of soldiers over longer time periods. Just as Konstantinos Moustakas, Ilias Anagnostakis, and Maria Leontsini have demonstrated in their respective chapters on the Balkan Peninsula and the Peloponnese, in Byzantine Asia Minor, too, it was the convergence of various factors, such as administrative structures, military needs, geographic configurations functioning as barriers or corridors, communications, and road networks, which determined conceptions of space in the empire's provinces and peripheries.

3 The Main Sections of the Byzantine-Turkish Frontier

The consolidation of the new defensive structures was contingent upon a number of key strongholds that were easily accessible from the seaside and the major port cities and were connected with existing road networks and riverine systems. On the basis of landscape and connectivity characteristics we may single out three distinct sections: (1) a northern zone stretching from the western banks of the Sangarios River to the Propontis littoral; (2) a central zone straddling the Phrygian highlands from the region around Dorylaion/Eskişehir to the Sultan Mountains; (3) a southern region extending from the springs of the Maeander Valley as far as the south-western coastland. Each of these areas evinced its particularities in its relations with the Byzantine central government and the surrounding Muslim-Turkish entities and thus developed separately over the twelfth century.

The nodal points of the Byzantine defensive system in Bithynia and the Propontis region were situated in the Gulf of Nicomedia (Kibotos, Aer, Helenoupolis); the city of Nicaea and the Askanian Lake; the castle of Metabole and the plain of Malagina, which Clive Foss located in an area between the modern cities of Mekece and Geyve close to the westernmost bench of the Sangarios River; the heights of the Bithynian Olympus; and the area of Lake Lopadion and the Rhyndakos Valley with the city of Poimanenon

---

52   John Kinnamos, *Histories* 1.6 (15 Meineke).

further south.[53] Anna Komnene's detailed account of Byzantine military operations fending off Turkish attacks in 1116 makes plain that Alexios I Komnenos invested much energy and manpower in building up an extensive network of fortifications, observation posts, and garrisons. Nicomedia and Lopadion are depicted as places offering rich water and food supplies and thus were especially suitable for prolonged encampments of military units, rallying troops, and training fresh recruits.[54] The region in question was easily accessible by sea from Constantinople and the ports of the European Propontis shores so that troops from Thrace could be quickly transferred.[55] Even in the time before 1097, when large sections of this region were still under Turkish control, the coastland of the Gulf of Nicomedia was intermittently exposed to Byzantine incursions and military presence.[56] Near-contemporary Crusader accounts refer to a Greek-Christian rural population and its agricultural activities in the villages of the region.[57] There seems to have been some fierce pillaging and ransacking in the rural areas of Bithynia as far as the Propontis coastland in the years preceding the revolt of Nikephoros III Botaneiates, but the agreements with the latter and Alexios I indicate that the Turkish takeover in the towns of Bithynia in about 1080 was carried out in a largely peaceful manner. Apart from some uprisings of Byzantine aristocrats, the region hardly witnessed any serious disruptions before the arrival of Peter the Hermit's crusader hosts in late 1096.[58] Apparently, there was a strong continuity in terms of demographic, institutional, and economic structures, and the Turkish presence was mostly confined to a ruling elite and garrisons in Nicaea and some fortresses in its vicinity.

Accordingly, the imperial government restored its authority after the surrender of Nicaea in May 1097 without serious obstacles while a considerable number of Turkish commanders switched sides and entered the emperor's service.[59] Immediately after the re-conquest, Alexios I appointed Manuel Boutoumites, who had played a leading role in the preceding military

---

53 Anna Komnene, *Alexias* 10.6.1–2 (299–300 Reinsch) (Helenoupolis), 14.5.3, 15.1.3 (443, 462 Reinsch) (Kibotos), 15.1.5–6 (462–63 Reinsch) (Aer), 15.1.5 (462–63 Reinsch) (Malagina and Olympus, 14.5.1–2, 15.1.3 (443, 462 Reinsch)(Nicaea and Lake), 15.1.3, 15.1.5 (462–63 Reinsch) (Lopadion), 15.1.5 (462–63 Reinsch) (Poimanenon); for the position of Malagina, see Foss 1990.
54 Anna Komnene, *Alexias* 15.2.6–7 (465–66 Reinsch) (fertility of Nicomedia).
55 Anna Komnene, *Alexias* 15.2.6 (465–66 Reinsch) (easy transport of provisions).
56 Anna Komnene, *Alexias* 3.11.1–4 (114–16 Reinsch).
57 Albert of Aachen, *Journey to Jerusalem* 1.16 (32 Edington).
58 Frankopan 2006, 153–84.
59 Anna Komnene, *Alexias* 9.11.1–10 (325–29 Reinsch).

operations and diplomatic contacts, *doux* of the city and thus made it the administrative and military centre of Bithynia.[60] A challenge from a strategic point of view resulted from the fact that the Turks maintained their dominance in the regions east of the Sangarios River and in Paphlagonia. Alexios I Komnenos sent detachments from Nicaea to Sagoudaous/Söğüt to safeguard the connection between the Sangarios Valley and Dorylaion.[61] Naturally, the major rallying point of the Byzantine army for local defensive purposes and expeditions to the east was transferred further west to the well-protected area around Lopadion and the Rhyndakos Valley. Alexios I used the area as his headquarters during his 1116 expedition and John II Komnenos set off from there for his campaigns to Paphlagonia in the 1130s.[62] In the event of Turkish counterattacks, the imperial army adopted a similar strategy: When in 1139 Turkish invaders appeared in the Sangarios Valley, John II immediately took up a position in Lopadion.[63] Being an ideally situated harbour closely linked with Constantinople, Nicomedia, too, maintained great significance as a secondary base and starting point for military operations, as is exemplified by Manuel I's 1180 campaign to free Klaudioupolis from a Turkish siege.[64] The strongholds close to the Sangarios Valley were certainly much more exposed to hostile attacks. Thus, in 1143 Manuel I rebuilt and refortified the castle of Malagina after an attack of Sultan Mas'ūd.[65] Overall, the Bithynian section of the Byzantine-Turkish frontier, due to its proximity to the capital and the western provinces, was the region with the strongest Byzantine military presence and enjoyed a high degree of safety and prosperity up to the time of the internal unrest during the reign of Andronikos I Komnenos (1183–85).[66] Byzantine territorial control apparently fizzled out towards the Sangarios Valley, and the imperial government's influence in Paphlagonia and the northern parts of the Anatolian plateau around Ankara sharply declined after 1140.[67] Yet the Turkish emirs in the said region were increasingly embroiled in the power struggles of

---

60   Anna Komnene, *Alexias* 11.2.7 (329 Reinsch); see also Ragia 2007, 228.
61   Anna Komnene, *Alexias* 15.2.4 (465 Reinsch); for the significance of Söğüt, see Lindner 2007, 35–56.
62   Anna Komnene, *Alexias* 15.1.3, 15.2.5 (462, 465 Reinsch); Niketas Choniates, *History* 20 van Dieten.
63   Niketas Choniates, *History* 33 van Dieten.
64   Niketas Choniates, *History* 197 van Dieten.
65   Niketas Choniates, *History* 52 van Dieten.
66   Niketas Choniates, *History* 280–89 van Dieten (revolt of Nicaea, Lopadion and Prousa in 1184).
67   Belke & Restle 1984, 128; Niketas Choniates, *History* 116 van Dieten (the Danishmend emir Yaghī Basān ruler over Ankara, Amaseia and northern Cappadocia).

the Seljuk sultanate of Rum under Qilij Arslan II and thus rarely exerted any serious pressure on the Byzantine-held regions.

The city of Dorylaion (near Eskişehir) was an excellently situated nodal point in the road network connecting Bithynia with the Phrygian highlands and served in the time before the Turkish expansion as a military base for expeditions to the east. The area around the city was the battlefield of two major clashes between crusader armies and the Seljuk Turks in 1097 and 1147, which illustrates the site's strategic significance as a central access point to the Anatolian plateau.[68] During the 1116 expedition, Alexios I Komnenos' army was still able to camp there despite Turkish attacks,[69] but in the following decades the Byzantines seem to have gradually lost control of the site, as is evidenced by the events of the Second Crusade and the skirmishes fought by Manuel I against various Turkish groups in the late 1150s.[70]

The route leading from Dorylaion southeast to Polybotos (near Bolvadin) and Philomelion/Akşehir north and south of Lake Tessarakonta Martyron (Eber and Akşehir) respectively and thence towards the highlands north of Konya demarcated the outermost contact zone between Byzantine and Turkish spheres of influence.[71] Neither side exerted any durable control over this area. Political constellations were permanently shifting and the local strongholds frequently changed hands. In Alexios I's 1116 campaign, imperial troops took hold of Polybotos, Amorion (near Emirdağ), Philomelion, and other fortresses east of Akroinon (Afyonkarahisar). This does not imply, however, that in the years prior to the Byzantine advance all territories east of this line were firmly held by the Turks. For instance, Anna Komnene describes the town of Tyragion/Ilgın east of Philomelion as a Byzantine enclave exclusively inhabited by *Romaioi* or Greeks, who were well disposed towards the Seljuk lord Saisan (Shāhinshāh) and afforded him protection against his internal opponents.[72] This goes a long way towards explaining why the Byzantines were able to seize the fortresses so easily. The nascent Seljuk sultanate reacted efficiently to major threats, such as the onslaught of the crusader armies, but it was unable to sustain an impervious defensive line running along the fringes of the Anatolian plateau.

Nevertheless, it seems also misleading to assume that the region had fallen into the hands of recalcitrant nomadic groups wandering about and raiding at

---

68 Belke & Mersich 1990, 238–42.
69 Anna Komnene, *Alexias* 15.2.5, 15.3.6 (465, 469 Reinsch).
70 John Kinnamos, *Histories* 4.22, 23 (191, 194–95 Meineke).
71 For a detailed description, see Belke & Mersich 1990, 143–46.
72 Anna Komnene, *Alexias* 15.6.9 (480 Reinsch); Belke & Mersich 1990, 409–11.

their heart's yen. The aforementioned case of Tyragion as well as the Greek communities at Lake Pousgouse/Beyşehir, which at the time of John II Komnenos' arrival in 1142 maintained close commercial links with the inhabitants of Konya,[73] indicate that the local population enjoyed a fair amount of security and stability while disruptive nomadic incursions were rather the exception to the rule of largely peaceful coexistence. The Byzantine troops retreating in 1116 transferred inhabitants of the area elsewhere,[74] but this measure does not necessarily indicate that the region had become permanently uninhabitable. Most probably, the emperor took this decision in response to the perils of that specific period. Moreover, population transfer also served other purposes, such as securing tax revenues or forestalling the estrangement of the frontier population from the Byzantine central government, as apparently had happened to the inhabitants in the Lake Pousgouse region. Seemingly, both Byzantine and Turkish units moved relatively freely in these marches and took turns in entrenching themselves temporarily in accessible strongholds. This would explain why the sources hardly provide any evidence for stable defensive lines in this area while we hear about Byzantine and Seljuk groups penetrating deeply into the other side's hinterland without creating any permanent footholds.

The region stretching from the western coastland as far as the lower courses of the Kaikos, Hermos, and Kaystros Rivers formed the core area of Byzantine rule in the central section of western Asia Minor ever since its recovery in 1097/1098. The imperial troops first re-conquered Smyrna and Ephesos, which had been the power bases of the Byzantine-Turkish ruler Tzachas and a Turkish emir called Tangripermes respectively.[75] Thereafter they seized a number of major strongholds in the Hermos and Maeander Valleys, manned the conquered places with fresh contingents and expelled most Turkish groups settling in this area. There are indications that the old theme of Thrakesion was restored in the early 1100s and Anna Komnene reports appointments of commanders to key strongholds in the re-conquered areas.[76] We cannot say with certainty whether the terminology she uses in each case reflects the establishment of distinct military and administrative districts, but it seems that the seaports of Smyrna and Ephesos quickly turned into key positions in the reorganized

---

73 John Kinnamos, *Histories* 1.10 (22 Meineke); Niketas Choniates, *History* 37–38 van Dieten.
74 Anna Komnene, *Alexias* 15.7.1–2 (481 Reinsch).
75 Anna Komnene, *Alexias* 11.5.1–5 (335–37 Reinsch).
76 Ahrweiler 1965, 124–127; Ragia 2007, 227–28 (seal of an *archon tou Thrakesiou* that may have belonged to Epiphanios Kamateros, ca. 1100); Anna Komnene, *Alexias* 11.5.4–5 (337–38 Reinsch).

administrative structures as seats of *doukes*. Sardis and Philadelpheia became strongholds for garrisons commanded by Michael Kekaumenos and protected the entire upper course of the Hermos River and the adjacent Kogamos Valley. Similar attempts were made at about the same time in the Maeander Valley.[77] The imperial government thus restored a relatively well-protected area of direct control inhabited by a largely homogenous and loyal population. Being situated at a safe distance from the outer frontier zone, the region was relatively well defended.

As Turkish nomads and marauders found hardly any obstacles in crossing the fringes of the Anatolian plateau, the Byzantines concentrated their efforts on strengthening the inner chain of fortified places that stretched from the coastland of Mysia to the Upper Maeander Valley. This new line of defensive structures came into being for the most part in the later years of Alexios I Komnenos' reign. An indispensable precondition was Constantinople's holding sway over the coastland. Adramyttion, an important seaport in the northern section of the Aegean coastland, had been pillaged and destroyed by the fleet of Tzachas. In 1109 the Byzantine general Eumathios Philokales repaired and repopulated the city.[78] His expedition aimed more broadly at rebuilding towns and fortresses along the Aegean coastland from Smyrna to Attaleia and at offering incentives to the indigenous population to return to their hometowns.[79] The crucial significance of Adramyttion throughout the twelfth century is evidenced by the fact that the port appears as part of two different administrative units, namely the theme of Neokastra, which was established by Manuel I between 1163 and 1172 and included the fortresses of Chliara and Pergamon, and later the theme of Opsikion.[80] Attaleia seems to have endured Turkish attacks but was never conquered or destroyed. It gained paramount importance for protecting the Pamphylian coast and its hinterland and for maintaining lines of communication with the Byzantine strongholds further east and the naval base in Cyprus.[81] The city thus formed the link between the mountainous hinterland of Lycia and the newly established maritime network along the southern shores of Asia Minor. The seaports of Adramyttion, Smyrna, Ephesos, and Attaleia formed the backbone of the Byzantine administrative

---

77   Ragia 2007, 228–29, assumes the establishment of four distinct *doukata* in the years after 1097.
78   Anna Komnene, *Alexias* 14.1.4 (425 Reinsch); Ragia 2007, 229.
79   Anna Komnene, *Alexias* 14.1.2–3 (424–25 Reinsch).
80   Ahrweiler 1965, 133–37.
81   Hellenkemper & Hild 2004, 305.

and military presence in western Asia Minor and secured the communication between the central government and the fertile lower parts of the river valleys.

The defensive structures further inland were closely linked with the local rivers and east-west connections: Pergamon and Chliara blocked the routes leading across the Kaikos River into north-western Asia Minor.[82] Garrisons in Philadelpheia and Kelbianon curbed forays through the Hermos, Kogamos, and Kaystros Valleys and thus afforded additional protection to the precarious region around the Gulf of Smyrna, the centre of the Thrakesion theme.[83] In about 1110/1111 military units were transferred from Thrace to this area in order to monitor the hostile movements of Turkish invaders subject to the Seljuk sultan of Konya. Once again, Philadelpheia loomed large in this strategy as a base defending the region between Sardis and Kelbianon.[84] Due to the lack of defensive lines in western Phrygia, the Turks advanced relatively unhindered as far as Kotyaion/Kütahya, but Byzantine resistance stiffened as soon as they reached the Hermos Valley.[85]

The proximity of the Upper Maeander Valley to the Seljuk centre of power in Konya may explain why the Maeander Valley remained a favourite invasion route for Turkish westward advances throughout the twelfth century. The *Via Sebaste* provided a connection between Antioch of Pisidia/Yalvaç and Apameia/Dinar near the Maeander sources in southern Phrygia and afforded the Turks easy access to the entire river valley.[86] Its fertile agricultural areas, towns, and villages offered ample opportunities for economic interactions between sedentary people and pastoralists but also easy targets for raids. The imperial government launched a number of campaigns in this area but was unable to block it against intruding nomads and Seljuk troops or to create a stable defensive line. The region can be more properly described as a large Byzantine-Turkish transit zone, in which Byzantine troops, Seljuk regular forces, and nomadic elements took turns in temporarily expanding over certain areas, while the local population was constantly exposed to threats from all sides and had to interact with all these groups.

The stationing of a garrison in Lampe near the Acıgöl under Eustathios Kamytzes in 1098 was the Byzantine army's first attempt to strengthen the

---

82 Anna Komnene, *Alexias* 14.1.6, 14.3.1 (427, 434–35 Reinsch).
83 Anna Komnene, *Alexias* 14.3.1 (434–35 Reinsch); for the Kaystros valley, see Külzer 2017, 195–213.
84 Anna Komnene, *Alexias* 9.5.6., 14.3.1, 7 (338, 435, 437 Reinsch).
85 Belke & Mersich 1990, 313.
86 Belke & Mersich 1990, 152–53; for the river system in the region of Apameia/Kelainai along with the adjacent Dombay ovası and Lake Aulutrene, see Thonemann 2011, 57–75.

defence of the Upper Maeander Valley. Some Turks in the region seem to have forged closer ties with the indigenous population and submitted to imperial rule, as was the case with the Turks in and around Laodikeia on the Lykos (near Denizli),[87] which is situated between the episcopal see of Hierapolis and the fortress of Chonai with the nearby pilgrimage church of St Michael at Kolossai.[88] Already in 1110, however, Turkish nomads threatened the region of Lampe so that a detachment of the troops commanded by Eumathios Philokales mounted an attack on them.[89] Despite the peace treaty Emperor Alexios I Komnenos reached with the Seljuk ruler Shāhinshāh in 1116, a Turkish garrison soon took hold of Laodikeia.[90] Byzantine counter-attacks in 1119–1120 restored Byzantine control as far as Sozopolis and thus blocked the *Via Sebaste* coming from Antioch in Pisidia. They also succeeded in seizing strongholds in the mountainous area north of the Gulf of Attaleia.[91] At about the same time (*terminus ante quem* is 1128), the imperial government administratively reorganized the lower part of the Maeander Valley from Miletus to Antioch on the Maeander/Yenişer near Kuyucak, along with the province of Caria in the south into a new theme of Mylasa and Melanoudion.[92] It is not clear how this district is related to the theme of Maeander, which is attested in the late twelfth century and seems to have been situated further upstream around Antioch on the Maeander and Laodikeia.[93] Irrespective of these intricacies, it is evident that the imperial administration was aware of the military and economic particularities of the region and took pains to consolidate its defensive and administrative structures as a separate unit headed by its own *doux*. However, these endeavours did not result in any tight control of the region, as is evidenced by the clashes between the crusading army of the French King Louis VII and the Turks in the winter of 1147–1148. The French chronicler of the Second Crusade, Odo of Deuil, gives a detailed description of the army's advance from Ephesos to Laodikeia:[94] The Turks had occupied the foothills of the Messogis Range north of the river and harassed the French soldiers on both banks until the latter reached Antioch on the Maeander. This place is described as a "small

---

87 Anna Komnene, *Alexias* 11.5.1–6 (335–38 Reinsch), esp. 11.5.6 (338 Reinsch) for Laodikeia.
88 Thonemann 2011, 75–88; Külzer 2018, 89.
89 Anna Komnene, *Alexias* 11.5.5 (338 Reinsch) and 14.1.4 (425–26 Reinsch) for the situation around 1110.
90 John Kinnamos, *Histories* 1.2 (5 Meineke).
91 John Kinnamos, *Histories* 1.2–3 (6–7 Meineke).
92 Ahrweiler 1965, 127–129; Ragia 2007, 229–230 and 232–34 for a detailed discussion regarding the location of Melanoudion somewhere around the Lake of Herakleia (Bafa Gölü).
93 Thonemann 2011, 5.
94 Odo of Deuil, *Crusade of Louis VII*, 64–66 Waquet.

town of the emperor" (*civitatula imperatoris*) that opened its gates to fleeing Turkish soldiers.[95] Odo considers this behaviour as proof of the emperor's treacherous intentions vis-à-vis the crusaders, but the overall situation in the region suggests that the imperial government was hardly in a position to give orders to the local population. Apparently, the townspeople merely continued to collaborate with the Turks according to their customary interactions. This also explains Odo's observation that "along our way the Turks and the Greeks had boundaries of lands" (*in nostra via habebant Turci cum Grecis terrarum terminos*).[96] It is highly improbable that there was an actual borderline between Byzantine and Turkish territories in the region. The phrase only makes sense if we take it as a description of an overlapping contact zone in which Byzantine subjects and Turks were living side by side and maintained close economic and social relations.

In the 1160s, Turkish troops once again roamed about the region of Laodikeia. Niketas Choniates, our only source for these events, does not go into further details but he makes a clear distinction between troops of Sultan Qilij Arslān II and Turkish nomads "who were pouring like large herds into the Roman territories" (τοὺς ὡς πώεα πλατέα διεκκεχυμένους τοῖς Ῥωμαϊκοῖς σχοινίσμασι Τούρκους).[97] The emperor is said to have stopped their invasions by attacking the Turks in the Pentapolis region (Sandıklı Ovası and Kuru Çay/Hamam Çayı Valley), where he acquired rich booty of captives and animals.[98] The imperial troops, according to the author, successfully advanced as far as the headwaters of the Maeander River, but nothing indicates the existence of Byzantine outposts or a stable borderline.

Choniates' report about Manuel I's 1176 campaign that ended with the disaster of Myriokephalon and its consequences gives us further insight into the spatial arrangement of the Byzantine defence system in the Maeander Valley.[99] The Byzantine military presence in terms of effective territorial control seems to have been fizzling out east of Laodikeia and Chonai (Honaz). The latter formed the easternmost point affording protection to the survivors of the battle.[100] Laodikeia provided a safe connection to Philadelpheia in the Kogamos Valley through the basin of Hierapolis so that Manuel retreated there to recover

---

95   Odo of Deuil, *Crusade of Louis VII*, 65–66 Waquet.
96   Odo of Deuil, *Crusade of Louis VII*, 66 Waquet.
97   Niketas Choniates, *History* 124–25 van Dieten.
98   Belke & Mersich 1990, 358.
99   Niketas Choniates, *History* 175–91 van Dieten.
100 Niketas Choniates, *History* 191 van Dieten.

from the hardships of his campaign.¹⁰¹ When in the late 1170s Turkish raiders penetrated the region west of Akroinon as far as Lakerion (Dazkırı north of Acıgöl) and Panasion (Banaz) it was again the garrison of Laodikeia that curbed their advance.¹⁰² At about the same time, Turkish nomads penetrated the Maeander Valley and pitched their camp at a fortress called Charax, which was situated somewhere east of Chonai.¹⁰³ Overall, Laodikeia stands out as a nodal point at the east-west connections between the southern Anatolian plateau and the western coastland and was one of the most important strongholds in the southern section of the Byzantine defensive system. As for the region farther west, we hear of another defensive position at a bridge near the villages of Hyelion and Leimmocheir. These places cannot be accurately located but there is reason to believe that they were situated at a close distance to Antioch on the Maeander.¹⁰⁴ The lower section of the Maeander Valley down to Tralleis (Aydın) and the coastland enjoyed a relatively high degree of safety and was rarely exposed to hostile attacks. It was only in the post-1176 period that the Turks managed to invade the said area around Antioch, Tralleis, Louma, and Pentacheir.¹⁰⁵

Just as in the borderland's central section, the central government's sway was fading towards the east, but it took pains to maintain some limited military presence through isolated fortresses monitoring the upper Maeander course as far as the headwaters around Apameia/Kelainai (Dinar) and Sozopolis.¹⁰⁶ The best-known example is the deserted castle of Siblia/Soublaion situated at an unknown location west of Apameia (probably near Evciler). Emperor Manuel restored the stronghold in 1175 but it had to be dismantled at the sultan's demand shortly after the defeat of Myriokephalon.¹⁰⁷ Yet there were no coherent defensive structures preventing Turkish soldiers and nomads from moving westwards. This is manifest in the 1176 advance of Manuel's army, which seems to have had a considerable size of about 25,000 troops. The Turkish military seriously harassed it, the soldiers ran short of food and water supplies, and many of them suffered from dysentery due to the Turks' successful scorched earth strategy.¹⁰⁸ Apparently, the local garrisons were far too weak to afford

101 Niketas Choniates, *History* 191 van Dieten; for the road connection between the Hermos and Maeander Valleys, see Belke & Mersich 1990, 150–51; Külzer 2018, 89.
102 Niketas Choniates, *History* 195 van Dieten; Belke & Mersich 1990, 321, 355.
103 Niketas Choniates, *History* 197 van Dieten; Belke & Mersich 1990, 221.
104 Niketas Choniates, *History* 193 van Dieten.
105 Niketas Choniates, *History* 192 van Dieten.
106 Belke & Mersich 1990, 188–89, 387–88.
107 Niketas Choniates, *History* 177, 189, 192 van Dieten; Belke & Mersich 1990, 382.
108 Niketas Choniates, *History* 179–81 van Dieten.

any effective protection. Sixty years after Alexios I's retreat, the region around the Sultan Mountains and the main route leading towards the Anatolian plateau continued to be a barely controllable no-man's land. Accordingly, the fortress of Myriokephalon, which was most probably situated at the entrance of a narrow valley called Tzybritze close to the north-western edge of the Sultan Mountains, is described as an old deserted place (τῷ Μυριοκεφάλῳ ἐφίσταται· φρούριον δὲ τοῦτο παλαιὸν καὶ ἀοίκητον).[109] The destruction of Manuel's army in the pass of Tzybritze may be primarily due to fatal tactical mistakes in the Byzantine march order. That the Turks so successfully encircled Manuel's troops, however, has certainly to do with the geographical space of the Upper Maeander Valley and the inability of either side to maintain permanent control over it.

4   Conclusions

To sum up, the Byzantine-Turkish borderland in twelfth-century western Anatolia was no well-organized frontier, nor was it a remote wilderness dominated by marcher lords, outlaws, and nomads. Unsurprisingly, a long strip of land extending from the Gulf of Attaleia to the Black Sea exhibits a broad variety of living conditions and geographical features. Hence, social groups, economic relations, administrative institutions, and military structures developed differently in each section of the borderland. As regards the Byzantine side of the borderland, we may distinguish between a loosely controlled outer frontier, which consisted of remote outposts, Greek enclaves, and mobile military units curbing the movements of Turkish nomads and raiders, and a well-defended inner frontier, which rested upon a chain of well-fortified strongholds stretching from the Gulf of Adramyttion over Philadelpheia in the Kogamos Valley to Laodikeia and Chonai in the Maeander Valley. The Byzantine defence system, rather than encompassing large territorial units, concentrated on the protection of specific key zones consisting of agricultural areas, roads, and towns. A well-defended region in Bithynia stretching from the Sangarios to the Rhyndakos Valleys stood under close surveillance of the imperial government and comprised the major rallying points of the Byzantine army in Asia Minor. The coastland from Adramyttion to Ephesos secured the connection between the fertile riverine valleys of western Anatolia and the Aegean Sea. While

---

109   Niketas Choniates, History 178 van Dieten; Belke & Mersich 1990, 343–44, 411.

the lower parts of the river valleys were well integrated into the Byzantine administrative and military system, there were hardly any stable structures along the outer frontier in Phrygia from Dorylaion to Tessarakonta Martyron Lake and the Sultan Mountains. The Maeander Valley again was divided into a well-defended lower section between the delta region and Laodikeia and a Byzantine-Turkish contact zone running along the upper course as far as the headwaters around Apameia. Rather than referring to a distinct Byzantine-Turkish borderland, it seems more appropriate to speak of a set of different frontier zones and hinterland sections each of which had its structural particularities and its own spatial organization.

In the realm of military action and defensive structures, the spatial organization of the individual frontier zones was contingent upon strategic and logistical considerations regarding the accessibility of water and food supplies, the suitability of deployment areas and observation posts, or the location of invasion routes. These issues, in turn, were largely determined by natural or man-made geographical features, such as river valleys, fertile plains, well-positioned hills, and road networks. In terms of administrative structures, Emperor Alexios I Komnenos and his successors restored certain elements of the pre-existing thematic system within smaller territorial units (Opsikion and Aigaion Pelagos, Thrakesion) and created new thematic units (Neokastra, Mylasa-Melanoudion) in accordance with the requirements of the new spatial configuration in the frontier zones. As regards the daily life of the provincial population, commercial relations, and cultural influences, all regions of the Byzantine-Turkish frontier evinced a high degree of mutual permeability. While killing, ransacking, and violent displacements inevitably formed part of the harsh living conditions in times of war, there were numerous instances in which local population groups negotiated a *modus vivendi* with the authorities on both sides. People living a short distance from the Seljuk capital of Konya profited from trade relations with their neighbours and exhibited signs of cultural and linguistic assimilation. In regions like western Phrygia and the Upper Maeander Valley, there seem to have been regular contacts between nomads and sedentary groups. Ideologically speaking, the Constantinopolitan elites continued to claim the territories farther east as integral parts of the Roman Empire. All in all, we may distinguish between three different levels of spatial conceptualization in the Byzantine-Turkish frontier of the twelfth century, which were related to the needs of military organization, the exigencies of daily life, and the dreams of Byzantine imperial ideology.

Bibliography

Primary Sources

Albert of Aachen, *Journey to Jerusalem*. Ed. & tr. S. B. Edgington, *Albert of Aachen, Historia Ierosolimitana. History of the Journey to Jerusalem*. Oxford 2007.

Anna Komnene, *Alexias*. Ed. D. R. Reinsch & A. Kambylis, *Annae Comnenae Alexias*. Berlin & New York 2001.

John Kinnamos, *Histories*. Ed. A. Meineke, *Ioannis Cinnami Epitome rerum ab Ioanne et Alexio Comnenis Gestarum*. Bonn 1886.

Niketas Choniates, *History*. Ed. I. A. van Dieten, *Nicetae Choniatae Historia*. Berlin & New York 1975.

Odo of Deuil, *Crusade of Louis VII*. Ed. H. Waquet, *Eudes de Deuil, La croisade de Louis VII roi de France*. Paris 1949.

Secondary Sources

Ahrweiler, H. 1965. "L'histoire et la géographie de la région de Smyrne entre les deux occupations turques (1081–1317) particulièrement au XIIIe siècle", *Travaux et Mémoires* 1–204.

Angold, M. 1997. *The Byzantine Empire, 1025–1204: A Political History*. London & New York.

Baud, M. & W. Van Schendel 1997. "Toward a Comparative History of Borderlands", *Journal of World History* 8, 211–242.

Beaton, R. & D. Ricks (eds) 1993. *Digenes Akrites: New Approaches to Byzantine Heroic Poetry*. Aldershot.

Beihammer, A. D. 2011. "Orthodoxy and Religious Antagonism in Byzantine Perceptions of the Seljuk Turks (Eleventh and Twelfth Centuries)", *Al-Masāq* 23, 15–36.

Beihammer, A. D. 2017. *Byzantium and the Emergence of Muslim-Turkish Anatolia, ca. 1040–1130*. London & New York.

Belke, K. & M. Restle 1984. *Tabula Imperii Byzantini 4: Galatien und Lykaonien*, Vienna.

Belke, K. & N. Mersich 1990. *Tabula Imperii Byzantini 7: Phrygien und Pisidien*, Vienna.

Berend, N. 1999. "Medievalists and the Notion of the Frontier", *The Medieval History Journal* 2, 55–72.

Bonner, M. 1996. *Aristocratic Violence and Holy War: Studies in the Jihād and the Arab-Byzantine Frontier*. New Haven, CT.

Brather, S. 2005. "Acculturation and Ethnogenesis along the Frontier: Rome and the Ancient Germans in an Archaeological Perspective", in Curta (ed.) 2005, 139–171.

Cahen, C. 2001. *The Formation of Turkey: The Seljukid Sultanate of Rūm: Eleventh to Fourteenth Century*. Tr. & ed. P. Holt.

Curta, F. (ed.) 2005. *Borders, Barriers, and Ethnogenesis: Frontiers in Late Antiquity and the Middle Ages*. Turnhout.

Curta, F. 2005. "Frontier Ethnogenesis in Late Antiquity: The Danube, the Tervingi, and the Slavs", in Curta (ed.) 2005, 173–204.

Dölger, F. & A. E. Müller 2003. *Regesten der Kaiserurkunden des oströmischen Reiches. 1. Teil, 2. Halbband, Regesten von 867–1025*. Munich.

Eger, A. A. 2015. *The Islamic-Byzantine Frontier: Interaction and Exchange among Muslim and Christian Communities*. London & New York.

Foss C. 1985. *Survey of Medieval Castles of Anatolia*. Oxford.

Foss C. 1986. *Byzantine Fortifications: An Introduction*. Pretoria.

Foss C. 1990. "Byzantine Malagina and the Lower Sangarios", *Anatolian Studies* 40, 161–83.

Frankopan, P. 2006. "The Fall of Nicaea and the Towns of Western Asia Minor to the Turks in the Later 11th Century: The Curious Case of Nikephoros Melissenos", *Byzantion* 76, 153–84.

Frankopan, P. 2012. *The First Crusade: The Call from the East*. Cambridge, MA.

Haldon, J. & H. Kennedy 1980. "The Arab and Byzantine Frontiers in the Eighth and Ninth Centuries: Military Organisation and Society in the Borderlands", *Zbornik Radova Vizantoloshkog Instituta* 19, 79–116.

Hellenkemper, H. & F. Hild 2004. *Tabula Imperii Byzantini 8: Lykien und Pamphylien*. Vienna.

Honigmann, E. 1935. *Die Ostgrenze des byzantinischen Reiches von 363 bis 1071*. Brussels.

Kaldellis, A. 2017. *Streams of Blood, Rivers of Gold: The Rise and Fall of Byzantium, 955 A.D. to the First Crusade*. Oxford.

Külzer, A. 2017. "Streifzüge durch das Tal des Kaystrios (Küçük Menderes): Historisch-geographische Impressionen aus Westanatolien", in Külzer & Popović (eds) 2017, 195–213.

Külzer, A. 2018. "The Late Antique and Byzantine Road Network in Western Asia Minor: Some Additions to a Widely Ramified System", *Sanat Tarihi Dergisi* 27.1, 83–95.

Külzer, A. & M. Popović (eds) 2017. *Space, Landscapes and Settlements in Byzantium: Studies in Historical Geography of the Eastern Mediterranean*. Vienna & Novi Sad.

Leveniotis, G. 2007. *Η πολιτική κατάρρευση του Βυζαντίου στην Ανατολή. Το ανατολικό σύνορο και η κεντρική Μικρά Ασία κατά το β΄ ήμισυ του 11 αι*. Thessaloniki.

Lilie, R.-J. 1976. *Die byzantinische Reaktion auf die Ausbreitung der Araber: Studien zur Strukturwandlung des byzantinischen Staates im 7. und 8. Jh*. Munich.

Lilie, R.-J. 1993. *Byzantium and the Crusader States 1096–1204*, tr. J. C. Morris & J. E. Ridings. Oxford.

Lindner, R. P. 2007. *Explorations in Ottoman Prehistory*. Ann Arbor.

Lyons, M. 1993. "The Crusading Stratum in the Arabic Hero Cycles", in Shatzmiller (ed.) 1993, 147–61.

Naum, M. 2010. "Re-emerging Frontiers: Postcolonial Theory and Historical Archaeology of the Borderlands", *Journal of Archaeological Method and Theory* 17, 101–131.

Parker, B. J. 2006. "Toward an Understanding of Borderland Processes" *American Antiquity* 71, 77–100.

Peacock, A. C. S. 2014. "The Seljuk Sultanate of Rūm and the Turkmen of the Byzantine Frontier, 1206–1279" *Al-Masaq* 26, 267–87.

Power, D. & N. Standen (eds) 1999. *Frontiers in Question: Eurasian Borderlands, 700–1700*. London & New York.

Pryor, J. H. & M. J. Jeffreys 2012. "Alexios, Bohemond, and Byzantium's Euphrates Frontier: A Tale of Two Cretans", *Crusades* 11, 31–86.

Ragia, E. 2007. "Η αναδιοργάνωση των θεμάτων στη Μικρά Ασία τον δωδέκατο αιώνα και το θέμα Μυλάσσης και Μελανουδίου", *Symmeikta* 17, 223–238.

Shatzmiller, M. (ed.) 1993. *Crusaders and Muslims in Twelfth-Century Syria*. Brill.

Stone, A. F. 2003. "Dorylaion Revisited. Manuel I Komnenos and the Refortification of Dorylaion and Soublaion in 1175", *RéB* 61, 183–99.

Stone, A. F. 2004. "Stemming the Turkish Tide: Eustathios of Thessaloniki on the Seljuk Turks", *ByzSlav* 62, 125–42.

Thonemann, P. 2011. *The Maeander Valley: A Historical Geography from Antiquity to Byzantium*. Cambridge.

Vryonis, S. 1971. *The Decline of Medieval Hellenism in Asia Minor and the Process of Islamization from the Eleventh through the Fifteenth Century*. Berkeley.

Vryonis, S. 1975. "Nomadization and Islamization in Asia Minor", *DOP* 29, 41–71.

Wittek, P. 2012. *The Rise of the Ottoman Empire: Studies in the History of Turkey, Thirteenth-Fifteenth Centuries*. London & New York.

The Other Than Self

Byzantium and the Venetian Identity

Sauro Gelichi

Byzantine Venice represents an age-old problem. Basically, this is a problem of identity. The concept of identity is closely related to a sense of belonging by means of which social groups (or individuals) both perceive and compare themselves with others. Since being part of a group encourages competition, identity is not something static; it is a continuous process.[1] Archaeology, "through its expertise at dealing with material culture", is capable of adding a material dimension to the understanding of social dynamics as well as through some of these items (such as clothing, the organisation of space, architecture, etc.) and the *habitus*[2] "can detail how the material world used to engage, and is still engaged, in the articulation of social identity of both the individual and the group".[3] Precisely because archaeology is a dynamic process, it is capable also of chronologically monitoring identity.

With regards to Venice, attention has been paid to its political and institutional aspects;[4] its architecture and artwork; and, finally on materials, touching upon aspects regarding everyday life. Naturally, we are well aware of the political ties between Venice and Byzantium and it is common knowledge how these bonds were often formalised during important moments of public life, such as during court ceremonies or when official titles that dukes and members of their families demanded from Byzantium were handed down, and then flaunted.[5] However, is this enough to sustain, as has also been authoritatively endorsed, that for a long time Byzantium was seen as a model of perfect life for Venice, even beyond the constraints of political submission?

---

1 Hall 1996.
2 On the concept of *habitus,* see Bourdieu 1990, 53 (translated as *Les sens pratique*, Paris, 1980).
3 Díaz-Andreu & Lucy 2005, 9.
4 There is a wealth of literature on the political and institutional history of Venice. With regards to the most ancient stages, it could prove helpful to refer to Cessi 1963; Carile & Fedalto 1978; Ortalli 1992.
5 Ravegnani 1992, 829.

In this specific circumstance, it is important to pursue a similar path, or rather to tackle the same problem (with regards to the relations the Venetian community had with Byzantium, on the one hand, and the mainland communities, on the other) by examining it from an archaeological perspective. This shall be carried out by focusing attention on certain specific aspects of both private (at the dinner table, in the home) and public life (the use of the past, funeral rites): aspects that, always studied from a diachronic perspective, reflect, more or less explicitly, yet clearly voluntarily, the image that the emerging Venetian society (or rather its elite class) intended to give of itself.

This paper discusses the identity created by the community of Venice during the early Middle Ages (8th-10th century) and does so using material indicators: ceramics, sarcophagi, *spolia*. Through the analysis of these indicators, I will try to demonstrate the distance between Venice and Byzantium, with a view to enhancing cultural relations with inland counties.

1   Water and Golden Forks

In 1066, Pier Damiani wrote a long letter to a certain Bianca *comitissa*, who was about to enter a convent. Pier Damiani provided a couple of examples while suggesting the kind of behaviour the widow should adopt once she entered the convent.[6]

One of these examples makes specific reference to Venice. More specifically, it concerns an incident involving the wife of Duke Giovanni Orseolo (984–1006),[7] a woman named Maria who originated from Constantinople. Maria lived in such a sophisticated manner that, in order to have a wash, she asked the servants to collect, wherever possible, "dew from heaven" (*eius servi rorem coeli stagebant undecumque colligere*) so that "with this water, a bath fit for her could be prepared (*ex quo sibi laboriosum satis balneum procurarent*)"; in

---

6 The text is very famous: S. Petri Damiani, *Opp. Tomus seu Pars III—Opuscula Varia, Opusculum Quinquagesimum, Institutio Monialis. Ad Blancam ex comitissa sanctimonialem*, cp. XI, col. 743–44 Migne; Ortalli 2005, 309–11.

7 The identity of this woman is definitely not certain, as the name does not appear in the text. Pertusi identify her as Teodora Ducas, sister of Emperor Michael VII, who married the Venetian duke Domenico Silvio (Pertusi 1965, 143–46), who held the Dogado (or Duchy) of Venice between 1071 and 1084. However, the same Ortalli, who also accepts such juxtaposition, expresses a few justified perplexities, given that Pier Damiani's death (1072) would have been too close to the occurrences mentioned in the story. Another option is that it could refer to Maria Argyropoulina, daughter of the Byzantine patrician Argyropoulos, of imperial lineage (*Istoria Veneticorum*, IV, 71, 73 and 75) and the wife of Duke Giovanni Orseolo (984–1006): just as in Frugoni 2001, 114; Ravegnani 2006, 71; and La Rocca 2015.

the meantime "she would never use her hands to eat, yet after ordering her eunuchs to cut the food up into small pieces, she would bring the food to her lips using a gold, two-pronged fork (*Cibos quoque suos manibus non tangebat, sed ab eunuchis eius alimenta queque minitius concidebantur in frusta; quae mox illa quibusdam fascinulis aureis atque bidentibus ori suo, liguriens, adhibebat)*".

Beyond the rhetorical resonance coming from a letter with clear educational functions, the tale appears to be accurate. The example of water is both plausible and rather intriguing. There are no known natural springs in Venice and thus the water used was most likely rainwater opportunely collected in water cisterns.[8] Furthermore, there are no known water cisterns dating back to the historical period specified in Pier Damiani's account,[9] though their existence was indirectly mentioned in a few written texts[10] as well as by a substantial number of decorative wellheads representing a truly outstanding phenomenon on the Italian scene at that time (Figure 19.1).[11] Among the known

---

8   The procurement of water was a necessity of paramount importance for the city that did not have its own sources of drinking water: Costantini 2007. The need for water in medieval and modern times seems to have been guaranteed by the collection of rainwater in cisterns or, as documented with certainty only in the late Middle Ages, by means of transport with boats along the rivers flowing through inland areas: Gelichi, Ferri & Moine 2017, 111–12.

9   A very famous collection system and which was used in Venice, consists of the so-called "Venetian water wells" (Penzo 1995, 1–4). These are complex water collection, purification and storage systems, the construction of which regarded both the elevation of buildings (that had to be equipped with eaves and drainpipes) and the actual collection structure itself (a kind of large, generally quadrangular or rectangular-shaped hydraulic cistern full of filtering sand). This type of structures is known both in medieval and modern times, also with archaeological attestations yet which, in the lagoon area, are not known to date back prior to the 12th century. In the most ancient cases of archaeologically-known containers used for the collection and storage of water, it is not possible to establish whether these are just simple cisterns or more sophisticated collection systems, such as the "Venetian water wells" (see Gelichi, Ferri & Moine 2017, 113–14, for both a critical discussion of this information and with regards to the relevant bibliography). During a recent excavation carried out on the island of Murano, some wells dating back to the 11th century were discovered and, at least some of which could originate from around the same time as Pier Damiani's story was written. One of these had a kind of 2.5 m diameter sand-filled circular crown around its shaft, interpreted as "a sort of filtering device and collection basin", a forerunner of the more sophisticated water collection systems, or rather the "Venetian water wells": Cozza & Valle 2014, 34–35, Fig. 38.

10   The oldest documents referring either to wells or wellheads date back to the 11th century (even if it is necessary to consider the lack of Venetian maps dating back to before the year 1000 A.D.): see, once again, Gelichi, Ferri & Moine 2017, 114. From these texts (the oldest is dated 1038) it can be assumed that the wells could already be found on private properties, as shown also in the abovementioned case in Murano (Cozza & Valle 2014).

11   Ongania 1911; Rizzi 1981, 1992, 2007.

Venetian wellheads, those which are particularly worthy of note traditionally date back to the later centuries of the Early Middle Ages (or rather between the ninth and the tenth centuries). This timeline is based on the decorative elements that often accompany them,[12] and is thus rather uncertain, given the long-term use of certain motifs. Even though there is an objective problem of dating and therefore many examples (excluding fakes) could even date back to historical periods later than those indicated by traditional studies, the phenomenon of the Early Medieval Venetian wellheads is still rather unique, both in terms of quantity and quality. Moreover, their presence gave strength to the idea of the central and even symbolic role that water played in the everyday life of the Venetians. However, despite this, the water collected from the Venetian cisterns in Pier Damiani's days could not have been of the best quality, even if, in his opinion, this was not sufficient to justify the princess' demand for water collected directly from heaven.

The other example, concerning the gold fork, is just as interesting. Forks were already known and used in Roman times, and a number of Byzantine archaeological and iconographic references date as far back as the tenth and eleventh centuries.[13] Naturally, there is little archaeological and iconographic evidence prior to that period.[14] Moreover, those of an iconographic nature have to be subjected to strong critical analysis that directly regards the greater or lesser adherence to reality, the uniqueness of the subject matter, the social environment to which the subject refers, and the iconographic transmission.[15] In the western context, for example, a representation of the fork appears in a couple of illustrations that accompany *De Universo* (otherwise known as *De Rerum Naturis*) (Figure 19.2), a text written by Rabano Mauro (780–865), in a code created in Montecassino in the days of abbot Theobald (1022–1035).[16]

---

12 However, none of these (twenty-four of them were identified and listed) is in its original position and also it was a stroke of luck that these were on the antiques market in the 19th century where both the dispersal and the imitation of such must have been brought about: thus, it is suspected that many of these are fakes (see once again Gelichi, Ferri & Moine 2017, 115–16, listed in Fig. 14).

13 Vroom 2007a.

14 Parani 2010.

15 Vroom 2003, 303–4; Vroom 2007b, 192–95; Parani 2010, 139–41. In any case, I agree with Joanita Vroom (although with a certain amount of caution) when she writes: "does the pictorial and written evidence indicate a clear development in the portrayal of dining scenes? And if so, do the depicted and described artefacts make anything clear about the cultural changing of dining manners?" (Vroom 2003, 304).

16 With regards to the code in general: Rabano Mauro, *De Rerum Naturis Cod. Casin. 132/ Archivio dell'Abbazia di Montecassino* Cavallo; as for the representations, see D'Onofrio,

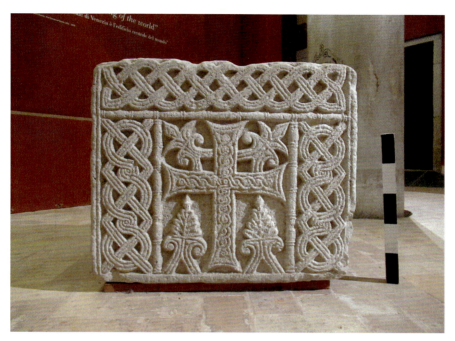

FIGURE 19.1   Venice, Museo Archeologico Nazionale, medieval wellhead
© MARTINA SECCI

However, there is a great deal of uncertainty with regards to the composition of the illustrated part of that code.[17] Furthermore, a representation of the fork appears precisely in Venice, on a tile in the Pala d'Oro in the presbytery in St Mark's Basilica (or better, there are two of them, always appearing together with a knife), in a scene depicting the Last Supper (Figure 19.3).[18] However, as

"Per una filologia delle illustrazioni del 'De rerum Naturis'" di Rabano Mauro", in Rabano Mauro, *De Rerum*, 99–176. The images that portray two table companions are in XVI.4 *De civibus* and in XXII, 1 *De mensis et escis*", (respectively referring to D'Onofrio 1995, 161 and 172).

17   D'Onofrio 1995, 102–3 and 107–8. The scholar, who recalls the theories studied by previous researchers, believes that the illustrations of the code could have possibly originated from a Carolingian model, even if they could have been developed on-site (where the Cassinese code was created). However, she also believes that the miniatures derived from examples dating back to the Late Antiquity period, were divided into types that deriving from the Carolingian *scriptoria*. Therefore, one could ask whether the image of the two forks must be attributed to the potential prototype dating back to the Late Antiquity period, to the Carolingian re-elaboration or even to the possibility of being inserted by the miniaturist who worked in Cassino towards the beginning of the 11th century.
18   Volbach 1994, 56, 29, Tab. 31.

FIGURE 19.2   Forks (after Rabano Mauro, *De Rerum Naturis*: XVI.4 *De civibus*; XXII, 1 *De mensis et escis*)

far as is known, the Pala D'Oro is a combined work of art composed of enamels dating back to different historical periods: the one of interest can be found in the lower panel, attributed, along with another twenty-six of them, to the early years of the twelfth century.[19]

This lack of documentation (of archaeological, written, and iconographic nature) has led scholars to suppose that in the Byzantine area, the use of the fork had been totally abandoned, in favour of picking up food from a shared plate in the centre of the dining table using one's hands.[20] This could be true for the social classes residing in the provinces, perhaps originating from important cities in the Empire, though not necessarily for the Constantinople elite.[21]

19   Lorenzoni 1965, n.31, 6; Volbach 1994, 3. This refers to a panel belonging to the second pall, commissioned by Doge Ordelaffo Falier (1102–18), moreover, explicitly portrayed in another enamel. Scholars consider this to be a stylistically homogeneous part, even if it has been carried out by several artists. The main artist is believed to be a Byzantine master.
20   Oikonomides 1990, 212.
21   A series of forks, dating back to between the 9th and the 12th centuries, coming from the excavations in Corinth (Parani 2010, 157, Fig. 13).

FIGURE 19.3 Venice, presbytery in St Mark's Basilica, Pala d'Oro: the Last Supper (after Lorenzoni 1965, p. 6, n. 31)

Despite a certain variety of behaviours that also make the Byzantine world a subject to be analysed by paying attention to particulars rather than generalities, one can reasonably sustain that the fork, in those areas, must still have been a widely-used utensil in the period between the ninth and the tenth centuries. In any case, its use must have been perceived as an expression of sophistication within the banquet context. The episode featuring the Venetian princess, therefore, seems to emphasise a cultural distance that was fully perceived at the time and, as such, deliberately written down and highlighted in stories with conspicuous didactic content.

Briefly, the Byzantine princess' affectation, her sophisticated habits and customs, used specifically in this case to represent 'the other', someone different, was outlined by two examples referring to both private and public spheres (respectively bathing and eating).[22] By way of these two examples, it could be assumed that the Venetians, even at the highest levels of power (the entourage referred to is of a ducal nature), led a definitely spartan life in their mealtime rituals. Thus it can also be assumed that their behaviour was significantly different to what was customary in the Byzantine world. Therefore, according to Pier Damiani, the behaviour of the Venetians in the eleventh century no longer resembled that of their "cousins" from Constantinople. They still referred to themselves as dignitaries (*ypati*), noble Patricians (*patrizi*), and notables (*protospatari*)[23] yet they did not eat with a fork!

2 At the Dinner Table

From an archaeological point of view, the likelihood of being able to capture the presence of certain items, that must have been present on the table, is limited by the perishable nature of the products themselves. Metal objects are rarely found during excavations (as they have either been recycled or are recyclable), those made of glass (also potentially recyclable) are generally found in highly fragmented conditions while wooden items can only be found in particular types of soil (and depending on its conditions).[24] A few comments can indeed be made on the basis of ceramic findings, as they are present, with a certain continuity, in stratigraphic sequences (however, with the risk that their role is overestimated). Through ceramic artefacts (just as much through their

---

22 The event has been recently analysed also from another perspective, that of highlighting the different perception given of the 'foreign woman', within a socially-changeable context in the Early Middle Ages (La Rocca 2015). Moreover, both cases referred to by Pier Damiani (the one regarding the Duke's bride must be added to the episode relating to Marchioness Sofia, set in a different environment) would help to emphasise the perception of danger (and misfortunes) that the presence of female figures unrelated to the family entourage could bring. Should she be identified as the princess Maria Argyropoulissa, in fact, she would have died together with her husband Giovanni Orseolo, after a terrible plague had struck all areas of Italy and Venetian territories (as recalled in *Istoria Veneticorum* IV, 75); while Sofia, the other key figure in Pier Damiani's stories, would have belonged to the same group of relatives as Waldrada, the first foreign wife of the Venetian duke, Pietro Candiano, killed during an uprising in 976 (La Rocca 2015, 412). In any case, in this circumstance, the most important aspect to highlight refers to the examples that are given to express the distance and separation, not so much as to their nature or why they took place.

23 With regards to the Byzantine titles held by Venetian dukes, see Ravegnani 1992, 838–46. More specifically, with reference to *Istoria Veneticorum*, see Berto, 2001, 60–65.

24 Other household objects from textile, lead/tin alloys, horn, leather and parchment are also underrepresented in the soil: Gilchrist 2012, 115.

presence as their absence), it is possible to gain an idea of dietary habits (to the extent that these can be reflected by certain objects) as well as how food was eaten during mealtimes. A comparison made between the information gained from written sources (when these exist) and those from iconographic representations (with all the limitations that this kind of source can entail) can help reconstruct the behaviour associated with conviviality with a certain degree of reliability, even if only in a rather general sense.

Unfortunately, with regards to Venice, there is no quantitative data relating to well-explored and, above all, socially diversified excavations.[25] Only from the tenth to eleventh centuries are there a few contexts in which it is possible to make a comparison between certain social categories.[26] However, the analysis of the ceramic artefacts, coming from the lagoon, is sufficient enough to roughly outline the sort of domestic equipment existing between the eighth and tenth centuries. At this level, a specific comparison with what occurred in the Byzantine world is possible.

We can start from pottery such as the well-known ceramics called "Early Plain Glazed Ware" and "Glazed White Ware" (Class II–IV), a category of products which was coated in a monochromatic glazing, often with incised and impressed decorations.[27] These were from the Byzantine world dating back to between the eight and the eleventh centuries from both Constantinople and the other areas of Greece, the Aegean Sea, and Asia Minor.[28]

Formally, the "Early Plain Glazed Ware" and the "Glazed White Ware" include chafing dishes and a number of open forms such as cups, possibly glasses and, above all, large dishes for communal eating.[29] These large dishes were, perhaps, used as central table pieces and made up a variation in the table settings that increasingly appeared from Late Antiquity onwards. The production of "Plain Glazed Ware" (and "Glazed White Ware"), therefore, testify to a continuation of sorts of these customs. A chafing dish is a rather particular vessel and is considered to be the most elaborate kind of Byzantine pottery known to

---

25 As for a summary on these problems, see Gelichi et al. 2017.
26 Monastery of St Hilary of Gambarare: Ferri 2017, 158–68. In particular for the episcopal context of Equilus (Jesolo) Gelichi & Sabbionesi 2018
27 Talbot Rice 1958a, 110–13; and more recently Dark 2001, 63–65; Vroom 2005, 64–65 and 72–77.
28 The initial stages are still uncertain and, at the moment, also the timelines are based on the few well-dated contexts available. A context that is particularly rich in this type of pottery and which is used as a date-based standard is the Saraçhane excavation in Constantinople: Hayes 1992; in the most ancient type, here defined as "Glazed White Ware I", "the fabric is really not white" (15).
29 Hayes 1992, Figs. 4, 7, 8 and so on; Vroom 2005, Figs. 3.3. and 4.3.

FIGURE 19.4 Athens, Stoà of Attalus, Museum, photograph of a "Glazed White Ware" chafing dish
© GIOVANNI DALL'ORTO

date (Figure 19.4).[30] This is a container consisting of two connecting, yet separate parts, the use of which has been interpreted in several ways, even if the most plausible hypothesis is that it could have been used to prepare and serve hot sauces, in particular fish sauce (also known as *garum*).[31] Moreover, it can be rather interesting to notice how the chafing dish was associated by some scholars with the use, at the table, of the two-pronged type of fork.[32] In this case, it would be used as an actual fondue pot, where someone would stick a piece of meat or bread onto the tip of their fork and dip it into the warm sauce contained in the upper part.

The chafing dish, depending also on its distribution, was interpreted as a means of identification of a kind of Byzantine cultural or culinary koine.[33] In fact, the distribution map omits North Africa, the Syrian-Palestinian coast and most of the Adriatic and Tyrrhenian area above Rome (Figure 19.5), or

30 Vassiliou 2016.
31 Vassiliou 2016, 252–55. With regards to the hypothesis that it was used for the preparation of mulled wine, see Arthur 1997, 538 (upon suggestion by Mark Whittow).
32 Vassiliou 2016, 254–55, n.21 (with bibliography).
33 Arthur 2007, 15–16, Fig. 1; Vroom 2008, 293–96, Fig. 4 (taken from Arthur 2007, with a few slight variations).

regards pottery, the findings in the Venetian Lagoon clearly indicate that, in the Early Medieval Age, there was an absence of open-shaped receptacles used to cook food (typical for the Byzantine area), while the most-documented shape within Early Medieval Age is the olla.[41]

Going back to table habits, further confirmation that, in this area, no need was felt to either import or locally produce chafing dishes and trays or large shared glazed pottery dishes is given by the fact that a category of glazed pottery was documented in the Venetian Lagoon during the same period. This is the so-called *ceramica a vetrina pesante* (mono-fired pottery covered by a plain, thick, monochrome glaze) and *ceramica invetriata* (Sparse glazed ware):[42] a type that is very similar to the "Forum Ware" found in the areas of Rome and Lazio[43] (Figure 19.6). Based on archaeometric analysis, such pottery could possibly have also been produced in the north of Italy.[44] The prevalent shapes found in north Italy, dating back to between the ninth and eleventh centuries, were jugs and, in later periods, also small cups with handles. None of this can be found in the Byzantine world where, on the contrary, closed glazed pottery shapes are either rare—if not totally unknown—in this period or they date to a later period than the one under analysis (Figure 19.7).[45] However, at the same time, this category of products does not include any kind of open shaped vessels (neither small nor large), unlike those found in Byzantium.

Therefore, the presence of forks (mentioned previously), individual and communal serving dishes, and possibly other kinds of containers like chafing dishes, were not in use in Venetian dining halls—let us not forget that between the ninth and tenth centuries Venice qualified as a city.[46] All this is not much different from what took place in the same period on the mainland, where we find the same type of associations within urban contexts.

---

41   Up-to-date summaries on this topic are currently lacking. Thus, please refer to Ardizzon & Bortoletto 1996. In this type of context, it would be interesting to explain the function of some of the open shapes that are generally defined as bowls and/or basins and which are used for cooking on an open fire as well as for serving purposes. In any case, the functional and morphological overviews of excavations conducted in the Venice Lagoon refer to similar situations found on the mainland.

42   For a recent summary on this kind of glazed pottery, see Gelichi 2016b (with previous bibliography); Gelichi 2014.

43   Whitehouse 1965, 1968; Mazzucato 1972; Paroli 1992a.

44   The precise location or locations have not been identified as yet. However, based on its distribution pattern, these appear to have been found in the north-eastern area of the peninsula, more specifically in the Ravenna-Ferrara area (on the one hand) and the Venice Lagoon (on the other): Gelichi 2016b, 299–300.

45   For example, see Hayes 1992, 29 (after 10th century?) and 33–34 (late 11th–12th centuries?).

46   Gelichi 2015a, 2015b.

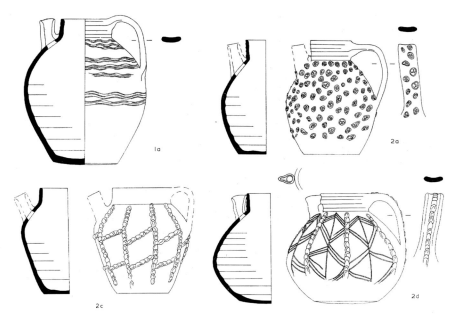

FIGURE 19.6   "Forum Ware" from Rome (after Whitehouse 1965, p. 57, Fig. 16)

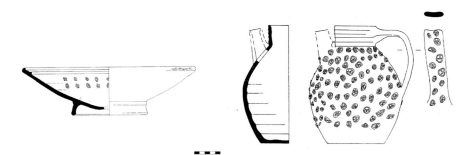

FIGURE 19.7   Comparing "Glazed White Ware" (on the left) and "Forum Ware" (on the right). Re-elaborations of drawings after Hayes 1992, p. 22, Fig. 7.8 and Whitehouse 1965, p. 57, Fig.16.2a
© LABORATORY OF MEDIEVAL ARCHAEOLOGY, UNIVERSITY OF CA' FOSCARI VENICE

3   *Spolia*, the Legacy of Byzantium and the Ancient World

The problem of the relationship between Venice and Byzantium is also a problem regarding the relationship between the lagoon community and its history, a past which is best remembered for its not so noble origins. In fact, Venice was never a Roman city, nor did it have any material proof linking it to Rome. Moreover, Byzantium represented a clear, natural connection with the ancient world and, in a certain way, a reference to Byzantium would have also been an indirect link to that past era. Thus, the problem is to establish whether the emerging Venetian elite actually felt the need to establish a link with the past and, in this case, when this need would have started to be noticed in the material documentation. It is generally considered that this link was of a natural, almost predictable nature. However, this is not exactly the case. An analysis of this situation shall be analysed from two perspectives: the first regards the existence of a city wall; the second refers to the use of *spolia*.

An indisputable element attesting to the establishment of a link that was also ideological to the Byzantine world is the material evidence of an element of which there is no longer any trace, yet which was described in the *Istoria Veneticorum*. This text describes the building of a part of a city wall along the Grand Canal as well as a length of chain to close off the canal itself (Figure 19.8).[47] This large iron chain was positioned across the canal at S. Maria di Zobenigo, attached to one end of the outer face of the city walls and, at the other end, to the side of St Gregory's church.[48] There is an interesting parallel with Constantinople, a replica of what was present in the capital of the empire.[49] Since the episode was associated to the life of Duke Pietro Tribuno, with whom the Venetian citizens' character was ratified, it appears evident that these walls were more likely to attest to the existence of a new city than as a defence against external threats.[50] Thus, perhaps it is not by chance that its presence is cited in only one source (*Istoria Veneticorum*). The *Istoria Veneticorum* is the oldest known text that recounts the events of the duchy

---

47   Reference to this can be found in *Istoria Veneticorum* III, 39 and relates to the period of the duchy of Pietro Tribuno (†911 A.D.). The text explicitly attributes building works ("edificare cepit") to Pietro Tribuno's efforts—and it is only here in the *Istoria* that the author (probably John the Deacon: see footnote 51) refers to the settlement as a *civitas* ("civitas aput rivoaltum"). See also Cessi 1963, 305.

48   The profile of this wall is described as being essentially linear (*Istoria Veneticorum* III, 39): "Predicte vero civitatis murus a capite rivuli de Castello usque ad ecclesiam Sancte Marie, que de Iubiniaco dicitur, extendebantur". The location of the *rivolus de Castello* is not known exactly (yet it can be assumed with a certain approximation), unlike those referring to the church of Santa Maria Zobenigo and St Gregory. Various hypotheses exist regarding the wall's course, summarised in Fig. 8, but we must immediately stress that no material evidence of this exists, despite the various 'archaeological objects' accredited to it over the years (such as the wall discovered in 1822 near Olivolo: Casoni 1856. In general, on this topic, see Gelichi 2016a.

49   Djurić 1995, 195.

50   Ortalli 1981, 85.

up to the beginning of the eleventh century (when it was composed perhaps by a certain John the Deacon).[51] It is possible to define it as a founding text, in the sense that it contains a whole concentration of events, episodes and characters, appropriately chosen with the aim of constructing the identity of a community. On this occasion, it is not essential to test its factual veracity, but what is important is the fact that John acknowledged the element that had to represent the community. In any case, even if it had existed, as one tends to believe, as a functional masonry structure used to control traffic on the Grand Canal, this structure must also have had a symbolic function, certifying the fact that Venice had become a city. But, until that moment, towards the end of the tenth century, there is very little that can help us corroborate the idea of the conscious construction of an identity founded on a past that was initially Roman and then Byzantine.

Another interesting case could be the use of antique *spolia*.[52] The re-use of ancient materials can take place according to two main methods: the first is purely functional, while the other is of a functional/ideological nature. Even a seemingly exclusively functional use for *spolia* can in reality can conceal a wish to link with the past, which is revealed in the simple fact of its recovery and re-use. However, in the absence of 'active' stone quarries as well as new brick factories, the re-use of ancient materials represents a need, almost an obligation in certain periods, since certain buildings require construction using durable materials.

The re-use of ancient materials is a well-known phenomenon in Venice and its Lagoon[53] (Figure 19.9). The case history under discussion, although with a variety of accents,[54] managed to provide a sufficiently clear overview of the use that was made of stone and ancient building materials throughout the history of the city. From a contextualisation, it is possible to achieve a differentiated overview of the behaviours of Venetian labourers as well as the customers who

---

51 With regards to the work and its author, see Berto 1999, 7–12.
52 On the concept of *spolia* and their use in the Middle Ages, see Settis 1986a; Greenhalgh 1989; De Lachenal 1995; Greenhalgh 2008. Finally, see the recently published Brilliant & Kinney 2011; Mathews 2015. With regards to a history of the Latin term, see the recent paper published by Uytterhoeven 2018.
53 Brown 1996. See a recent conference: Centanni & Sperti 2015.
54 Pensabene 2015 devotes attention to these specific topics (despite its title the publication appears to be of a more general nature); Calaon 2015 pays more attention to a better analysis of the problem from a social-anthropological and contextual viewpoint (in an archaeological sense); finally, Calvelli 2015 deals with the re-use of ancient epigraphs.

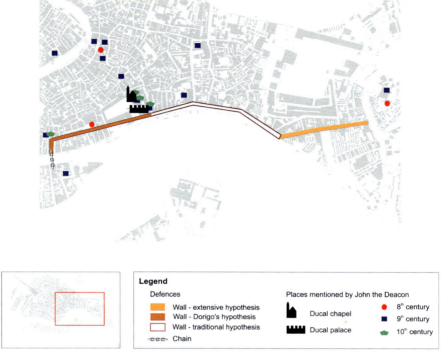

FIGURE 19.8 Map indicating the line of Venice's hypothetical city walls
© LABORATORY OF MEDIEVAL ARCHAEOLOGY, UNIVERSITY OF CA' FOSCARI VENICE

were at the root of the use of *spolia*.[55] The re-use of stones for new purposes over time can be interpreted as part of constructing a different identity.

There is no doubt that building materials taken from antique buildings were re-used in Venetian building construction in the Early Middle Ages; a number of famous written documents attest to this. Among these are Giustiniano Particiaco's last will and testament, which makes explicit mention of the practice.[56] However, this re-use of building materials seems to be almost exclusively of a pragmatic nature. Somehow, this situation positions Venice and the behaviour of its Lagoon elite populations once again within an entirely

55   As mentioned in Calaon 2015.
56   This text is very famous. With regards to one of its editions, see Cessi 1942, n.53, 93–99.

FIGURE 19.9
Roman inscription reused in a Venetian palace
© LABORATORY OF MEDIEVAL ARCHAEOLOGY,
UNIVERSITY OF CA' FOSCARI VENICE

Italian context: in fact, it was precisely from the Late Middle Ages that the use of ancient materials became apparent and persistent.[57]

This is a far cry from the abundance of exposed marble and stonework that characterised Venice, especially after the Fourth Crusade.[58] The direct access to the 'antiquities' of Constantinople, although not only for instrumental purposes associated with navigation,[59] had to favour the arrival of a substantial number of *spolia* into the Lagoon. In this case, these did not include only inscriptions and marble dating back to Roman times, but also stones dating back to either Late Antiquity or the Middle Byzantine period originating from the most remote lands of the empire. It would have actually been these more or less ancient *spolia* that covered the entire new city, now made of bricks and stone, with a touch of antiquity (and Byzantine style). This referred to a sort of late recovery of what was considered ancient and 'Byzantine' rather than a kind of continuity. It was also a phenomenon that, not too surprisingly,

---

57   Also in this case there is a rich bibliography, see Parra 1983; Esch 2001; and the very recent publication by Mathews, 2018.
58   The problem is particularly evident in the monument that is the symbol of the city, and that is St Mark's Church, to which an entire volume was recently devoted, analysing several aspects of its architecture, including the profile relating to the use of the *spolia*. See Maguire & Nelson 2010 volume in its entirety. Mathews 2015, 72–79.
59   See Lazzarini 2015, 136.

became more frequent the moment Venice abandoned its more or less formal dependence on Byzantium.

In short, both of the cases analysed appear to support the idea that a persistent, intentional juxtaposition with the past (whether of a Roman or Byzantine nature) originated from a relatively late period in the history of the Lagoon settlement.

4   Burials and Kinship Memories

A further interesting field that could be used to put this issue to the test is that of funeral rites. There are no direct written sources that tell of these procedures, and excavations carried out in lagoon cemeteries are rather rare or, in any case, underrepresented (Figure 19.10).[60] However, it is possible to analyse this phenomenon from another viewpoint by taking into consideration a particular 'container' that the Venetian aristocracy used with a certain frequency: the sarcophagus.[61] This makes it possible to develop a few considerations on funeral rituals and the cultural and ideological references that are specifically linked with them.

The Venetian aristocracy adopted the sarcophagus as the container for their burials (Figures 19.11–12).[62] Even a quick look at known examples shows

---

60 The excavation of the *Lazzaretto Nuovo* cemetery is an exception, yet it is a rather special context, and, in any case, it dates back to the Late Middle Age and modern period: Fazzini 2004, 157–58. The University of Western Australia and Perth (UWA) Centre of Forensic Science (https://www.lazzarettonuovo.com/nuove-scoperte-sui-veneziani-antichi-con-lo-scavo-di-antropologia-2018/) is currently taking care of the excavations in this cemetery. Data originating from the partial excavations carried out in the Lagoon come from the Island of St Laurence of Ammiana (contexts dating back to the Late Antiquity and Early medieval periods: Ferri 2012, 35–36; by St James in Paludo (context dating back to the Late Middle Ages: Bertoldi & Sisalli 2014, 151–56); and with reference to the Lagoon graves of the monastery of St Hilary and Benedict of Gambarare (context dating back to the Early Middle Ages: Bertoldi and Rasia 2017). On the human skeletons discovered in Torcello in the excavations of the 1960s: Corrain 1961; Corrain & Capitanio 1966–67, 1–15.

61 Unfortunately sarcophagi are often no longer in their original location. See some general yet opportune clarifications made in Wood 1996, 14–18.

62 The phenomenon had been reported for some time and there is a rather significant amount of literature on this topic; however, at this moment, there is a lack of overall studies on this phenomenon. In addition to the data sheets in the archives on Early Middle Age sculptures found in the Lagoon, the phenomenon has been addressed, although not comprehensively in Polacco 1980, 25–27 and Agazzi 2005; and, more recently, also in Tigler 2013. A more recent re-interpretation of the phenomenon from a different perspective can be seen in Gelichi 2015a, 260–66.

FIGURE 19.10 Monastery of St Hilary and Benedict in Gambarare, early medieval grave
© LABORATORY OF MEDIEVAL ARCHAEOLOGY, UNIVERSITY OF CA' FOSCARI VENICE

that this custom seemed to be well-established and diffuse in the lagoon and immediate surrounding areas starting from the ninth century.[63] The use of sarcophagi, therefore, undoubtedly guides us to antiquity. This is not only because, in general, the sarcophagi used or reused were themselves ancient, but also because the sarcophagus was a traditional and ancient mode of burial. However, a number of observations can be made.

The first is that these sarcophagi were, almost always, reworked. This means that it was intended to be understood as a container dating back to Antiquity[64] while also supporting new messages. These new messages were delegated to both the decorations and, in certain cases, to inscriptions. In short, though reused, these are objects that we can define as being new, in the sense that they have been regenerated and re-functionalised.

---

63 Gelichi, Ferri & Moine 2017, with a table that illustrates an initial schematic collection of data (tab. 2).

64 To date, an overall study of these artefacts is lacking, and therefore many questions still need to be answered, starting from, for example, the kind of lithotypes that were used. Another aspect that would be very interesting to study in further detail regards the fact whether these are, as is customary, ancient re-used sarcophagi or if, in certain cases, these are new objects (for example, as occurs in other European countries, such as France, where there is a conspicuous production of sarcophagi in the Early Middle Ages: Cartron, Henrion & Scuiller 2015).

FIGURE 19.11   Venice, Museo Archeologico Nazionale, sarcophagus from monastery of St Hilary and Benedict in Gambarare (after Polacco, *Marmi*, p. 27, n. 12)

FIGURE 19.12   Venice, Museo Archeologico Nazionale, sarcophagus from monastery of St Hilary and Benedict in Gambarare (after Polacco, *Marmi*, p. 25, n. 10)

The second aspect that must be highlighted is the fact that these objects were most likely to have been designed to be seen. Naturally, we are well aware of the fact that many sarcophagi dating back to Late Antiquity were buried (also those with decorations):[65] decorations and texts, however, that alone, are not sufficient to justify their exhibition. However, there are certain elements that encourage the hypothesis that the objects under examination should have been seen; and therefore, were made to be seen. An element that bears witness to this theory consists of the decorations and inscriptions that, whenever present, can always be found only on one side of the sarcophagus, as if it were meant to be put against a wall. A second reason is that it considers a context that is believed to have represented a precedent for this phenomenon, and that is the complex of St Apollinaris in Ravenna, which hosts the sarcophagi of a series of Archbishops from Ravenna, dating back to between the second half of the seventh and the ninth century (Figures 19.13–15).[66] Some of these sarcophagi date to Antiquity, some to the Early Christian Era, and others were re-worked during the eighth century, such as the ones preserving, for example, the remains of Archbishop Felix (709–23), or John and Gratiosus (784–88) (Figure 19.14).[67] Thus, it is not unlikely that this group of sarcophagi preserved even today in the Basilica of St Apollinaris in Classe could have served as an example; replicas of which can also be found in Ravenna dating to the following century in different fields and religious contexts (Figures 19.15–16).[68]

However, if the Byzantine territory is examined, it is important to notice how this phenomenon did not appear to have existed in Constantinople (and, in general, in the Byzantine world) where, instead, there were significant prototypes, such as the sarcophagi of emperors made of porphyry, but no new or re-worked sarcophagi dating back to either the Early Middle Ages or the Middle Byzantine Period.[69]

---

65   By way of example, mention can be made of the case of one of the sarcophagi discovered in the church of St Victor in Marseilles: Boyer et al. 1987.

66   Farioli Campanati 1986.

67   With regards to these sarcophagi, see Zucchini & Bucci 1968, 56–57 (the sarcophagus of *Felix*), 58 (the sarcophagus of John) (Fig. 19.13) and 58–59 (the sarcophagus of *Gratiosus*) (Fig. 19.14). The tomb of bishop *Maurus*, that was situated in the narthex, is accurately described by Andrea Agnello who focuses on the contents of a commemorative inscription engraved on a "slab of highly polished porphyry" which lies at the foot of the sarcophagus; other sarcophagi must have been accompanied by wall-mounted epitaphs: Farioli Campanati 1986, 168.

68   See yet another extensive case study in Zucchini & Bucci 1968, covering various urban contexts.

69   For an analysis of the phenomenon of the use of sarcophagi in the Middle-Late Byzantine periods, see Pazaras 1988.

FIGURE 19.13   Sant'Apollinare in Classe (RA), sarcophagus of Archbishop *Iohannis* (after Valenti Zucchini and Bucci, *"Corpus"*, p. 58, Fig. 60)

FIGURE 19.14   Sant'Apollinare in Classe (RA), sarcophagus of Archbishop *Gratiosus* (after Valenti Zucchini and Bucci, *"Corpus"*, pp. 58–59, Fig. 61)

FIGURE 19.15 Ravenna, Museo Arcivescovile, sarcophagus of *Gregorius* and *Maria* (after Valenti Zucchini and Bucci, *"Corpus"*, p. 59, Fig. 62)

FIGURE 19.16 Ravenna, Museo Nazionale, sarcophagus (after Valenti Zucchini and Bucci, *"Corpus"*, p. 60, Fig. 65)

The use of sarcophagi in Venice reiterated behaviours that were stratified and consolidated in the city's elite, yet which lead, once again, towards more western pattern of behaviour. In fact, the use of sarcophagi in Venice and in the lagoon areas between the ninth and tenth centuries was related to areas in the North Adriatic and more closely linked to Ravenna but, once again, not Byzantium.

5 Byzantine Venice?

At this point, it is important to ask oneself what a Byzantine-Venetian nature means, or what could it have meant to the extent to which it existed, and to what extent it characterised the behaviour of the Venetian elite, compared to, for example, those belonging to the contemporary communities on the mainland. The further away one moves from written texts and formal references that since their origins have compared the Lagoon elite with those originating from Constantinople, the more distance can also be perceived in several aspects of daily life, both public and private in nature, as well as in the ideological sphere, when this can still be recognised in the materiality of archaeological documentation. This is also fully understandable, considering the geographic area and the socio-political context in which the community was formed and developed. Furthermore, right from the very beginning of the Carolingian Age, the Venetian elite fully integrated into an international market that fixed its gaze on both the Mediterranean and Europe, as is clearly shown by the fact that coins were minted bearing the names of Frankish kings.[70] If anything, some of the choices (that have been highlighted in this study) referring both to the funerary and convivial spheres, regard another koine and types of traditions that are essentially those referring to the North-Adriatic maritime context. It is in this kind of great gulf that the connection that links society and populations must be identified: and, in all this, perhaps it will be Ravenna (rather than Byzantium or Rome) which will be considered a point of reference. In this respect, and only in this respect, a relationship with Byzantium re-emerges as something that is yet part of the DNA of these populations.

It seems then that there was more distance between Byzantium and Venice than may have been believed and that this Oriental sheen was only a late acquisition, evidence of a more practical and political strategy of a city which, having once acquired and consolidated its autonomy and power, looked for historical symbols which would legitimate and confirm it. At that point, those symbols were distant and even "harmless".

Bibliography

Primary Sources
Giovanni Diacono. *Istoria Veneticorum.* Ed. L. A. Berto. Bologna 1999.
Rabano Mauro, *De Rerum Naturis Cod. Casin. 132/Archivio dell'Abbazia di Montecassino.* Ed. G. Cavallo. Pavone Canavese 1995.

---

70 Stahl 2000. This fact, variously explained (see, for example, Rösch 1992, 551–52, 570), poses a few problems of a political nature, since Venice was, following the Treaty of Aachen (812), formally recognised as part of the Byzantine Empire: thus, as far as this can be explained also on grounds of practicality (the need of the Venetians to trade with the mainland), remains a fact of particular significance.

S. Petri Damiani, *Opp. Tomus seu Pars III—Opuscula Varia, Opusculum Quinquagesimum, Institutio Monialis. Ad Blancam ex comitissa sanctimonialem*, in J-P. Migne, *Patrologia Latina* (Paris, 1844–1855).

Secondary Sources

Agazzi, M. 2005. "Sarcofagi altomedievali nel territorio del dogado veneziano", in Quintavalle (ed.) 2005, 565–75.

Ardizzon, V. & M. Bortoletto 1996. "Recipienti in ceramica grezza dalla laguna di Venezia", in Brogiolo & Gelichi (eds) 1996, 33–57.

Arena, M. et al. (eds) 2001. *Roma. Dall'Antichità al Medioevo. Archeologia e Storia*. Milan.

Arthur, P. 1997. "Un gruppo di ceramiche alto medievale da Hierapolis (Pamukkale, Denizli), Turchia Occidentale", *Archeologia medievale* 24, 531–40.

Arthur, P. 2007. "Pots and boundaries on cultural and economic areas between Late Antiquity and the Early Middle Ages", in Bonifay & Tréglia (eds) 2007, 15–28.

Berto, A. 2001. *Il vocabolario politico e sociale della* Istoria Veneticorum *di Giovanni Diacono*. Padua.

Berto, L. A. 1999. "Introduzione", in *Istoria Veneticorum* Berto, 7–12.

Bertoldi, F. and P. A. Rasia 2017. "Lo scavo e lo studio dei reperti osteologici umani", in Moine, Elisa & Primon (eds) 2017, 173–87.

Bertoldi, F. & C. Sisalli 2014. "Le sepolture di San Giacomo in Paludo", in Ferri & Moine (eds) 2014, 151–56.

Bon, M. 2011. "La fauna domestica tra dati archeologici e fonti scritte. I dati scientifici", in Bon, Busato & Sfameni (eds) 2011, 127–42.

Bon, M., D. Busato & P. Sfameni 2011. *Forme del vivere in laguna. Archeologia, paesaggio, economia della laguna di Venezia*. Riviera del Brenta.

Bonifay, M. & J.-C. Tréglia (eds) 2007. *LRCW2. Late Roman Coarse Wares, Cooking Wares and Amphorae in the Mediterranean. Archaeology and Archaeometry*. Oxford.

Bourdieu, P. 1990. *The Logic of Practice*. Palo Alto.

Boyer, R. et al. 1987. *Vie et mort à Marseille à la fin de l'Antiquité. Inhumations habillées des VE et VIE siècles et sarcophage reliquaire trouvés à l'abbaye de Saint-Victor*. Marseille. 45–93.

Brilliant, R. & D. Kinney (eds) 2011. *Reuse Value. Spolia and Appropriation in Art and Architecture from Constantine to Sherrie Levine*. London.

Brogiolo, G. & P. Delogu (eds) 2005. *L'Adriatico dalla Tarda Antichità all'Età Carolingia*. Florence.

Brogiolo, G. P. & S. Gelichi (eds) 1996. *Le ceramiche altomedievali (fine VI–X secolo) in Italia Settentrionale: produzioni e commerci* (6 Seminario sulla ceramica tardo antica e alto medievale nell'Italia centro-settentrionale, Monte Barro & Galbiate 1995). Mantua.

Brown, P. F. 1996. *Venice and the Antiquity. The Venetian Sense of the Past*. New Haven & London.

Brubaker, L. & K. Linardou (eds) 2007. *Eat, drink, and be merry (Luke 12.19)—Food and wine in Byzantium*. Abingdon-on-Thames.

Calaon, D. 2015. "Tecniche edilizie, materiali da costruzione e società in laguna tra VI e XI secolo. Leggere gli *spolia* nel contesto archeologico", in Centanni, M. & L. Sperti (eds) 2015, 85–111.

Calaon, D., E. Zendri & G. Biscontin (eds) 2015. *Torcello scavata. Patrimonio condiviso*. Venice.

Calvelli, L. 2015. "Reimpieghi epigrafici datati da Venezia e dalla laguna veneta", in Centanni, M. & L. Sperti (eds) 2015, 113–34.

Carile, A. & G. Fedalto 1978. *Le origini di Venezia*. Bologna.

Cartron, I., F. Henrion & C. Scuiller (eds). 2015. *Les sarcophages de l'Antiquité tardive et du haut Moyen Âge: fabrication, utilisation, diffusion*. Bordeaux.

Casoni, G. 1856. "Sulla destinazione di un'antichissima opera murale scoperta a Venezia", *Istituto Veneto di Scienze, Lettere e Arti* 6, 209–34.

Centanni, M. & L. Sperti (eds) 2015. *Pietre di Venezia. Spolia in se spolia in re*. Rome.

Cessi, R. 1942. *Documenti relativi alla storia Veneziana anteriori al 1000. 1. I secoli V–IX*. Padua.

Cessi, R. 1963. *Venezia ducale. I Duca e Popolo*. Venice.

Christie, N. & H. 2016. Herold *Fortified Settlements in Early medieval Europe. Defended Communities of the 8th–10th centuries*. Oxford.

Corrain, C. 1961. "Prime notizie sui nuovi reperti scheletrici umani a Torcello", *Bollettino dell'Istituto di Storia della Società e dello Stato Veneziano* 3, 64–80.

Corrain, C. & M. Capitanio 1966–67. "I resti scheletrici della necropoli medievale di Torcello (Venezia)" *Memorie di Biogeografia Adriatica* 7, 1–15.

Costantini, M. 2007. *L'acqua di Venezia. L'approvvigionamento idrico della Serenissima*.

Cozza, F. (ed.) 2014. *Vicende stratificate a Murano. Un susseguirsi di sedimentazioni naturali e antropiche nell'area dell'ex Conterie*. Padua.

Cozza, F. & G. Valle 2014. "Gli apporti dell'uomo: sedimenti e strutture", in Cozza 2014, 18–58.

Cracco, G. & G. Ortalli (eds) 1992. *La storia di Venezia, 1: Origini—Età Ducale*. Rome.

D'Amico, E. 2011. *Byzantine Finewares in Italy (10th to 14th centuries A.D.): Social and Economic Contexts in the Mediterranean World*. Unpublished Ph. D. Dissertation, Durham University.

Dark, K. 2001. *Byzantine Pottery*. Stroud.

De Lachenal, L. 1995. *Spolia. Uso e reimpiego dell'antico dal III al XIV secolo*. Milan.

Díaz-Andreu, M. & S. Lucy 2005. "Introduction", in Díaz-Andreu et al. (eds) 2005, 1–12.

Díaz-Andreu, M. et al. 2005. *The Archaeology of Identity. Approaches to Gender, Age, Status, Ethnicity and Religion*. Abingdom & New York.

Djurić, I. 1995. *Il crepuscolo di Bisanzio. La fine dell'Impero Romano d'Oriente (1392–1448)*. Rome.

D'Onofrio, G. 1995. "Per una filologia delle illustrazioni del 'De rerum Naturis' di Rabano Mauro", in Rabano Mauro, *De Rerum*, 99–176.

Duval, Y. & J.-C. Picard (eds) 1986. *L'inhumation privilégiée du IVe au VIIIe siècle en Occident* (Actes du colloque, Créteil 1982). Paris.

Esch, A. 2001. "L'uso dell'antico nell'ideologia papale, imperiale e comunale", in *Roma antica nel Medioevo. Mito, rappresentazioni, sopravvivenze nella 'Respublica Christiana' dei secoli IX–XIII* (Papers from the 14th International Conference of Studies, Meldola 1998). Milan, 2001, 3–26.

Farioli Campanati, R. "Le tombe dei vescovi di Ravenna dal tardoantico all'alto medioevo", in Duval & Picard (eds) 1986, 165–72.

Fazzini, G. (ed.) 2004. *Venezia. Isola del Lazzaretto Nuovo*. Venice.

Ferri, M. 2012. "Il cimitero tardoantico e altomedievale", in Gelichi & Moine 2012.

Ferri, M. 2017. "I materiali dallo scavo 2010 (UTS 1000 e UTS 4000)", in Moine, Corrò & Primon (eds) 2017, 158–68.

Ferri, M. & C. Moine (eds) 2014. *L'isola di domani. Cultura materiale e contesti archeologici a San Giacomo in Paludo (Venice)*. Florence.

Frugoni, C. 2001. *Medioevo sul naso. Occhiali, bottoni e altre invenzioni medievali*. Rome-Bari.

Garavello, S. 2012. "8.2.3. Le ossa animali", in Gelichi and Moine (eds) 2012, 33–4.

Garavello, S. 2018. "Zooarchaeology", in Gelichi, S. Cadamuro & A. Cianciosi (eds) 2018, 38–40.

Gasparri, S. 1997. "Venezia fra l'Italia bizantina e il regno italico: la *civitas* e l'assemblea", in Gasparri, S. et al. (eds) 1997, 61–82.

Gasparri, S. 2011. "Anno 713. La leggenda di Paulicio e le origini di Venezia", in Israel 2011, 27–45.

Gasparri, S. et al. (eds) 1997. *Venezia. Itinerari per la storia della città*. Bologna.

Gasparri, S. & S. Gelichi (eds) 2017. *The Age of Affirmation: Venice, the Adriatic and the Hinterland Between the 9th and 10th centuries*. Turnhout.

Gelichi, S. 2014. "Early medieval Italian Glazed Pottery: A Byzantine Legacy? An Overview", in *Glazed Ware in the Black Sea and Mediterranean as a source for the Studies of Byzantine Civilization*. Sevastopol.

Gelichi, S. 2015a. "Venice in the early middle ages. The material structures and society of the 'civitas aput rivoaltum' between the 9th and 10th centuries", in La Rocca and Majocchi (eds) 2015, 251–71.

Gelichi, S. 2015b. "La storia di una nuova città attraverso l'archeologia: Venezia nell'alto medioevo", in West-Harling (ed.) 2015, 51–98.

Gelichi, S. 2016a. "Castles on the Waters? Defences in Venice and Comacchio during the Early Middle Ages", in Christie & Herold (eds) 2016, 263–76.

Gelichi, S. 2016b. "Nuove invetriate alto-medievali dalla laguna di Venezia e di Comacchio", in Lusuardi Siena et al. (eds) 2016, 297–317.

Gelichi, S. 2018. "Islamic pottery in the neighbourhood of the Venetian lagoon. A contribution on the relationship between Venice and the Eastern Mediterranean during the 11th–12th centuries", in Nowakiewicza, Trzecieckiego & Błaszczyka (eds) 2018, 115–28.

Gelichi, S., A. Cadamuro & A. Cianciosi (eds) 2018. *In Limine. Storie di una comunità ai margini della laguna*. Florence.

Gelichi, S., M. Ferri & C. Moine 2017. "Venezia e la laguna tra IX e X secolo: strutture materiali, insediamenti, economie", in Gasparri & Gelichi (eds) 2017, 79–128.

Gelichi, S. & C. Moine (eds) 2012. *Isole fortunate? La storia della laguna nord di Venezia attraverso lo scavo di San Lorenzo di Ammiana*, Archeologia Medievale 39, 9–56.

Gelichi, S. & C. Negrelli (eds) 2017 *Adriatico altomedievale (VI–XI secolo). Scambi, porti, produzioni*. Venice.

Gelichi, S. & L. Sabbionesi 2018. "A tavola con i vescovi", in Gelichi, Cadamuro & Cianciosi (eds), 2018, 86–90.

Gelichi, S. et al. 2017. "Importare, produrre e consumare nella laguna di Venezia dal IV al XII secolo", in Gelichi & Negrelli 2017, 23–114.

Gilchrist, R. 2012. *Medieval Life. Archaeology and the Life Course*. Woodbridge & Rochester.

Gonçalves, M. J. & S. Gómez Martínez (eds) 2015. *Actas do X Congresso International A cerâmica medieval no Mediterrâneo* (Silves 22nd–27th October 2012). Silves.

Greenhalgh, M. 1989. *The Survival of Roman Antiquities in the Middle Ages*. London.

Greenhalgh, M. 2008. *Marble Past, Monumental Present: Building with the Antiquities in the Mediaeval Mediterranean*. Leiden.

Hahnloser, H. R. & R. Polacco (eds) 1994. *La Pala d'Oro*. Venice.

Hall, S. 1996. "Introduction: who needs "Identity"?", in Hall & Du Gay (eds) 1996, 1–17.

Hall, S. & Du Gay, P. 1996. *Questions of Cultural Identity*. London.

Hayes, J. 1992. *Excavations at Saraçhane in Istanbul II. The Pottery*. Princeton.

Israel, U. (ed.) 2011. *Venezia. I giorni della storia*. Rome.

Jevtić, I. & S. Yalman (eds) 2018. *Spolia reincarnated. Afterlives of Objects, Materials, and Spaces in Anatolian from Antiquity to the Ottoman Era*. Istanbul.

La Rocca, C. 2015. "Foreign dangers. Activities, responsibilities and the problem of women abroad", *Early medieval Europe* 23, 410–35.

La Rocca, C & P. Majocchi (eds) 2015. *Urban Identities in Northern Italy (5th International Seminar of the Inter-university Centre for History and Archaeology in the Early Middle Ages)*. Turnhout.

Lavan, L., E. Swift & T. Putzeys (eds) 2007. *Objects in Context, Objects in Use. Material Spatiality in Late Antiquity*. Leiden.

Lazzarini, L. 2015. "Il reimpiego del marmo proconnesio a Venezia", in Centanni, M. & L. Sperti (eds) 2015, 135–57.

Lorenzoni, G. 1965. *La Pala d'Oro di San Marco*. Florence.

Lusuardi Siena, S. et al. (eds) 2016. *Archeologia classica e post-classica tra Italia e Mediterraneo. Scritti in ricordo di Maria Pia Rossignani*. Milan.

Maguire, H. & R. S. Nelson 2010. *San Marco, Byzantium and the Myths of Venice*. Cambridge, MA.

Mathews, K. R. 2015. "Decorating with Things: *Spolia* ad Material Culture in the Italian Maritime Republics, 1100–1300", *bfo-Journal* 1, 4–13.

Mathews, K. R. 2018. *Conflict, Commerce, and an Aesthetic of Appropriation in Italian Maritime Cities, 1000–1150*. Leiden.

Mazzucato, O. 1972. *La ceramica a vetrina pesante*. Rome.

Moine, C., E. Corrò & S. Primon (eds) 2017. *Paesaggi artificiali a Venezia. Archeologia e geologia nelle terre del monastero di Sant'Ilario tra alto Medioevo ed Età Moderna*. Florence.

Nowakiewicza, T., M. Trzecieckiego & D. Błaszczyka (eds) 2018. *Animos labour nutrit. Studia ofiarowane Profesorowi Andrzejowi Buko w siedmdziesiata rocznice urodzin*. Warszawa.

Oikonomides, N. 1990. "The Contents of the Byzantine House from the Eleventh to the Fifteenth Century", *DOP* 44, 205–14.

Ongania, F. 1911. *Raccolta delle vere da pozzo in Venezia*. Venice.

Ortalli, G. 1981. "Il problema storico delle origini di Venezia", in *Le origini di Venezia. Problemi esperienze proposte*. Venice.

Ortalli, G. 1992. "Il ducato e la '*civitas Rivoalti*': tra carolingi, bizantini e sassoni", in Cracco et al. (eds) 1992, 725–90.

Ortalli, G. 2005. "Realtà veneziana e bizantinità Latina", in Brogiolo & Delogu (eds) 2005, 309–11.

Parani, M. 2010. "Byzantine Cutlery: An Overview" *DChAE*, 139–64.

Pazaras, Th. 1988. Ανάγλυφες σαρκοφάγοι και επιτύμβιες πλάκες της Μέσης και Ύστερης Βυζαντινής περιόδου στην Ελλάδα (*Relief Sarcophagi and Tomb Slabs of the Middle and Late Byzantine Period in Greece*). Athens.

Paroli, L. 1992a. "La ceramica invetriata tardo-antica e medievale nell'Italia centro-meridionale", in Paroli (ed.) 1992b, 33–61.

Paroli, L. (ed.) 1992b. *La ceramica invetriata tardoantica e altomedievale in Italia* (Seminar Papers, Certosa di Pontignano 1990). Florence.

Parra, M. C. 1983. "Rimeditando sul reimpiego: Modena e Pisa viste in parallelo", *Annali della Scuola Normale Superiore di Pisa* 13, 453–83.

Pensabene, P. 2015. "Reimpieghi e percezione dell'"antico", recuperi e trasformazioni", in Centanni, M. & L. Sperti (eds) 2015, 15–59.

Pertusi, A. 1965. "Venezia e Bisanzio nel secolo XI", in *La Venezia del Mille* (Florence, 1965), 143–46.

Penzo, A. 1995. "I pozzi", *Archeo Venezia*, 5.4.

Pluskowski, A., K. Seetah & S. Garavello 2014. "Ossa animali di mammiferi e di uccelli dal monastero e dal priorato", in Ferri & Moine 2014, 145–50.

Polacco, R. 1980. *Marmi e mosaici paleocristiani e altomedievali del Museo Archeologico di Venezia*. Roma.

Quintavalle, A. C. 2005. *Medioevo: immagini e ideologie* (Papers from the International Conference of Studies, Parma 23rd –27th September 2002). Milan.

Ravegnani, G. 1992. "Insegne del potere e titoli ducali", in Cracco & Ortalli (eds) 1992, 838–46.

Ravegnani, G. 2006. *Bisanzio e Venezia*. Bologna.

Riedl, A. 1979. "La fauna degli scavi di Torcello (1961–1962)", *Atti del Museo Civico di Storia Naturale di Trieste*, 31, 75–154.

Rizzi, A. 1981. *Vere da pozzo di Venezia*. Venice.

Rizzi, A. 1992. *Vere da pozzo di Venezia volumi I e II*. Venice.

Rizzi, A. 2007. *Vere da pozzo di Venezia: i puteali pubblici di Venezia e della laguna*. Venice.

Romei, D. 2001. "Ceramiche di VIII–X", in Arena et al. (eds) 2001.

Rösch, G. 1992. "Mercatura e moneta", in Cracco, G. & G. Ortalli (eds) 1992.

Seetah, K. & A. Pluskowski 2014. "Resti archeozoologici", in Calaon, Zendri & Biscontin (eds) 2014, 103–48.

Settis, S. 1986a. "Continuità, distanza, conoscenza: tre usi dell'Antico", in Settis (ed.) 1986b), 373–486.

Settis, S. (ed.) 1986b. *Memoria dell'Antico nell'arte italiana. II. Dalla tradizione all'Archeologia*. Turin.

Stahl, A. M. 2000. *Zecca. The mint of Venice in the Middle Ages*. Baltimore & London.

Talbot Rice, D. 1930. *Byzantine Glazed Pottery*. Oxford.

Talbot Rice, D. 1958a. "Byzantine Pottery", in Rice 1958b.

Talbot Rice, D. (ed.) 1958b. *The Great Palace of the Byzantine Emperors. Second Report*. Edinburgh.

Trigler, G. 2103. *Scultura e pittura del medioevo a Treviso, I. Le sculture dell'alto medioevo (dal secolo VI al 1141) a Treviso, nel suo territorio e in aree che con esso ebbero rapporti. Tentativo di contestualizzazione storica*. Trieste.

Uytterhoeven, I. 2018. "*Spolia, -iorum*: From Spoils of War to Reused Building Materials: The History of a Latin Term", in Jevtić & Yalman (eds) 2018, 26–50.

Vassiliou, A. 2016. "Middle Byzantine chafing dishes from Argolis", *DChAE* 37, 251–76.

Volbach, W. F. 1994. "Gli smalti della Pala d'oro", in Hahnloser & Polacco (eds) 1994, 1–72.

Vroom, J. 2003. *After the Antiquity. Ceramics and Society in the Aegean from the 7th to the 20th centuries B.C. A case-study from Boeotia, Central Greece*. Leiden.

Vroom, J. 2005. *Byzantine to Modern Pottery in Aegean. An Introduction and Field Guide*. Utrecht.

Vroom, J. 2007a. "The Archaeology of Late Antique Dining Habits in the Eastern Mediterranean: A Preliminary Study of the Evidence", in Lavan, Swift & Putzeys 2007, 313–61.

Vroom, J. 2007b. "The changing dining habits at Christ's table", in Brubaker & Linardou 2007, 191–222.

Vroom, J. 2008. "Dishing up history: early medieval ceramic finds from the Triconch Palace in Butrint", *Mélanges de l'Ecole française de Rome. Moyen-Age*, 291–305.

Vroom, J. 2015. "The Archaeology of consumption in the Easter Mediterranean: a ceramic perspective", in Gonçalves and Gómez Martínez (eds) 2015, 359–67.

West-Harling, V. 2015. *Three Empires, three cities. Identity, material culture and legitimacy in Venice, Ravenna and Rome, 750–1000.* Turnhout.

Whitehouse, D. 1965. "Forum Ware: a distinctive type of early medieval glazed pottery in the Roman Campagna", *Medieval Archaeology* 9, 55–63.

Whitehouse, D. 1968. "The medieval glazed pottery of Lazio", *Papers of the British School at Rome* 35, 40–86.

Wood, I. 1996. "Sépultures ecclésiastiques et sénatoriales dans la vallée du Rhône (400–600)", *Médiévales* 31, 13–21.

Zucchini, G. V. & M. Bucci. 1968. *"Corpus" della scultura paleocristiana bizantina ed altomedievale di Ravenna, II. I sarcofagi a figure e a carattere simbolico.* Rome.

PART 5

Performed Spaces: Spatialities of Cultural Practices

Editorial Note on Part 5

This section explores the entanglements between space, culture, and performativity. Five case studies exemplify relations between cultural practices of everyday life and the production of social space. The authors discuss spatial aspects of performativity and performativity of cultural spaces with special focus on rituals and sacred space—in brief, performative conceptions of culture from a spatial perspective. Margaret Mullett investigates the meaning of medieval tents, based on a scrutiny of ways in which the spaces inside and around Byzantine tents were experienced. Mullet reflects on tents' mobility, fleetingness, privacy, versatility and mutability, and she explains the connection of these features through Byzantine settlement, politics, and culture. She epitomizes the tent as 'a mobile empire' in which everything had to be rethought in terms of space and reduced to essentials. Béatrice Caseau shows how the space of early Christian churches was differentiated as 'sacred' from other spaces only because it was performed as such. Caseau emphasizes that notions of sacred space were up for negotiation: performances of different spaces inside and outside the church buildings changed over the centuries in pace with changing definitions of different levels of sanctity. Two chapters explore ways in which the space of the Byzantine capital was being performed through religious practices, on the one hand, and urban design and architecture on the other. Helena Bodin's literary study investigates the Theotokos as a city and the idea of a living city in hymnography. Isabel Kimmelfield presents the variety of factors that gave rise to churches and ritual activities outside the city walls. Both chapters highlight the role of movement and participation in the making of sacred spaces. Last but not least, Liz James bridges the space between viewer and viewed through the idea of Byzantine mosaics as unstable and moving images. With parts of them appearing and disappearing with the changing light during the day, they surprise the viewer and manage to capture the attention. Thus, they are 'performing' while, at the same time, they stimulate different performances and experiences of the space in which they are hosted.

Tents in Space, Space in Tents

Margaret Mullett

We think of the Byzantine Empire as rooted in marble and mosaic on the Bosporos, but for much of the Middle Byzantine period the capital and the court moved with the emperor as he campaigned in Asia Minor, Syria, and later Macedonia.[1] Narratives of the period are full of tents, and manuscript illuminations show the Byzantines with their ephemeral structures.[2] Tent poems comment on the way tents appeared to the Byzantines and how they were experienced.[3] The empire continued to function during the campaigning months of the year, and tents represented a space which reflected and influenced uses of settled space by the Byzantines. Bureaucracy, diplomacy, ceremonial, worship all took place in soft architecture for part of the year, and maintained a mobile empire.[4] In this, Byzantium was not unusual among the states of the Mediterranean; tents were popular diplomatic gifts and had ceremonial functions; court culture in many contemporary states was rooted in tents, and Byzantium in some ways more resembled its neighbours on the move than our concept of a fixed capital at Constantinople.[5]

If "space is a representative strategy"[6] what does it matter that crucial events are portrayed as happening in tents rather than built structures, that tents were inscribed with poems,[7] that the ceiling of the audience hall in Palermo was painted with images of tents,[8] or that manuscripts represent

---

1 See Mullett forthcoming a.
2 Heher 2019.
3 For tent poems see Mullett 2018 and for the experience of tents Mullett 2013b.
4 Mullett forthcoming a.
5 Mullett 2013a.
6 Crang & Thrift 2000a, 1.
7 More accurately perhaps embroidered, as in Manganeios Prodromos poem 146, see Anderson & Jeffreys (1994, 12–13) and Theophylact of Ochrid poem 12, Gautier (ed.) 1983, 367. There is an Ottoman parallel: Atasoy, 2000, 44: A 'supreme command tent' made during the reign of Sultan Ahmet I in 1611 had an outer shell of crimson and an inner shell of satin with a small pattern and couplets of verse in needlework.
8 Brenk 2010, Figs. 889 and 935.

metaphors of siege and diplomacy?⁹ What kind of Byzantine space is being represented here?

The most explicit answer is in a riddle which appears in many collections but first among the poems of Christopher of Mytilene:

> Ἄπετρος εἰμὶ καὶ κινούμενος δόμος
> ἐν γῇ βεβηκώς, γῇ δὲ μὴ συνημμένος·
> οὐ πηλός, οὐκ ἄσβεστος ἐξήγειρέ με,
> πρίων δὲ καὶ σκέπαρνος οὐ τέτμηκέ με,
> εἰ μὴ κορυφὴν καὶ τὰ βάθρα μου λέγεις.
> φῶς ἔνδον ἕλκω, καίπερ ὢν πεφραγμένος
> λοξοὺς συνιστῶντάς με κίονας φέρω.
> τῶν κιόνων μοι πάντοθεν κλονουμένων,
> τὸ σχῆμα σῴζον ἀβλαβὴς ἑστὼς μένω.
> τὸ καινόν· εἴ με καὶ καταστέψεις βίᾳ,
> οὐκ ἂν καταρράξῃς με, σῶός εἰμί σοι·
> ἀνίσταμαι γὰρ καὶ μένω πάλιν δόμος.

> I am a house with no stone and I move about.
> I go on the earth, but I'm not attached to it.
> Neither mud nor plaster raised me.
> Neither saw nor axe cut me—
> Unless you're speaking of my head or my base.
> I draw light in though I am fenced all about.
> The columns I bear stand together obliquely.
> Though on every side my columns are disturbed
> I remain, keeping my shape and standing undamaged.
> Here's what's new about me: if you use force to cast me down,
> You wouldn't shatter me; I am safe for you
> For I stand up and again remain a house.¹⁰

The riddle emphasizes mobility, rootlessness, boundedness, resistance to the elements and the flexible, resilient durability of tents. All these have a bearing on space, space within the tent and the space occupied by the tent in

---

9   Metaphors for both siege and diplomacy appear in the Madrid Skylitzes; siege in fols. 151r and 151v, Tsamakda, Figs. 381–382; fol. 14 or, Tsamakda, Fig. 339; fol. 214r, Tsamakda, Fig. 507; fol. 229r, Tsamakda, Fig. 543. Diplomacy appears in fol. 75v, Tsamakda, Fig. 184, beginning and ending in a tent; on diplomacy see Mullett 1992, 203–16.

10 Christopher of Mytilene, poem 71. *On a tent,* Kurtz (ed.) 1903, 45.

landscape. Other texts allow us to see these double facets in terms of transitions, transformations, identity and community. But first they allow us to see the physical characteristics of a tent in space. The riddle touches on the fundamental issue of light, without which neither space nor tent are visible.[11] The tent draws in light, whether through the entrance or through silken walls is not clear, and in its permeability counteracts the bounded space it occupies. Its space is also defined by sound: the account in Michael Psellos of his visit to the tent of Isaac I Komnenos with its rousing acclamations suggests awareness if not manipulation of acoustics:

> Μείζονι οὖν σκηνῇ ἐντυγχάνομεν ὁπόση καὶ στρατοπέδῳ καὶ ξενικαῖς ἀρκέσειεν ἂν δυνάμεσιν· περιεστήκεσαν δὲ ταύτην ἔξω πολύ τι πλῆθος, οὐκ ἀργοὶ καὶ συγκεχυμένως ἑστηκότες, ἀλλ' οἱ μὲν ξίφη περιεζώννυντο, οἱ δὲ ἀπὸ τῶν ὤμων ῥομφαίας βαρυσιδήρους ἐπέσειον, καὶ ἄλλοι δὲ δόρατα ἠγκαλίζοντο, ἐφεξῆς ἑστηκότες καὶ κατὰ κύκλους, καὶ βραχύ τι ἀπ' ἀλλήλων διεστηκότες, φωνὴ δέ τις παρ' οὐδενὶ ἐξηκούετο [...] Οὗτος τῇ εἰσόδῳ καὶ ἡμῖν προσεγγίσασι στῆναι κελεύσας, ἐντός τε τῆς τοῦ βασιλέως σκηνῆς ἐγεγόνει, καὶ μικρὸν ἀναμείνας χρόνον, ἔξεισί τε, καὶ μηδὲν πρὸς ἡμᾶς εἰρηκώς, ἀθρόον τὴν πύλην ἀναπετάννυσιν ἵν' εὐθὺς καταπλήξῃ τῷ ἀπροσδοκήτῳ τῆς θέας. Ἦν γὰρ δὴ πάντα τυραννικὰ τῷ ὄντι καὶ φρίκης μεστά· τὰ μὲν οὖν πρῶτα κατάκροτοι τὰ ὦτα τοῖς τοῦ πλήθους ἀλαλαγμοῖς γεγόνειμεν, αἱ δὲ φωναὶ οὐχ ὁμοῦ ξύμπασαι, ἀλλ' ἡ πρώτη τάξις πληροῦσα τὴν εὐφημίαν τῇ ἐφεξῆς ἐδίδου τὸ σύνθημα, κἀκείνη τῇ μετ' ἐκείνην, καὶ ἦν τοῦτο καινὸν ἀσύμφωνον· εἶτα δὴ ἐπειδὴ ὁ τελευταῖος κύκλος ἠλάλαξεν, αὖθις ὁμοῦ ξύμπαντες συμπεφωνηκότες μικροῦ δεῖν ἡμᾶς κατεβρόντησαν.

We found him in a bigger tent this time, big enough for an army and its mercenary forces as well. Outside and all around stood a great multitude of men, not at ease or mingled together but drawn up in ranks in a series of concentric circles with a short interval between each group. Some were armed with swords, others with the heavy iron romphaia, others with lances. Not a sound was heard from any of them. [...] when we had drawn near, the captain of the emperor's personal bodyguard told us to stand at the entrance while he himself went inside the tent. After a short pause he came out again, and without a single word to us, threw open the tent door, suddenly. The sight that met our eyes within was astonishing.

---

11 As we were reminded in Lioba Theis' paper, "Space and light in Byzantium: twelve principles", at the conference.

TENTS IN SPACE, SPACE IN TENTS 463

> It was so unexpected, and truly it was an imperial spectacle, capable of overawing anyone. First our ears were deafened by the roars of the army, but their voices were not all raised at once: the front rank acclaimed him first, then the second took up the cry, then the next rank and so on. Each rank uttered its own cry with a different intonation from the rest. Then after the last circle had shouted there was one united roar which hit us almost like a clap of thunder.[12]

Yi-Fu Tuan asks, 'Is a sense of distance and space created out of the ability to hear?'[13] Often, as in recent acoustic projects,[14] we think of structures affecting sound; here sound defines the space of the tent. Size, we note, also plays its part; the bigger tent was large enough for an army plus mercenary forces.

There is some evidence that size did matter where tents were concerned, especially with respect to allies or enemies of the empire. The story of Tancred and Alexios I Komnenos' tent, told in both Anna and Ralph of Caen's *Gesta Tancredi*, is about the size of the tent not its contents:

> ἀκιζόμενος οἷον, ἐνατενίσας πρὸς τὴν σκηνήν, ἐν ᾗ ὁ βασιλεὺς προὐκάθητο (ἦν γὰρ κατὰ μέγεθος ὁποίαν οὔπω τότε οὐδεὶς ἐθεάσατο), "ἐὰν ταύτην", ἔφη, "πλήρη χρημάτων μοι δώσεις καὶ ἄλλα ὁπόσα τοῖς ἅπασι δέδωκας κόμισι, τελέσω τὸν ὅρκον κἀγώ".

> With apparent indifference, fixing his gaze on the tent in which the emperor held the seat of honour (a tent more vast than any other in living memory), he said "If you fill it with money and give it to me, as well as the sums you have given to all the other counts, then I too will take the oath".[15]

Ralph's version is different: Alexios had offered any gift Tancred should name, but he named Alexios' imperial tent,

---

12   Michael Psellos, *Chronographia*, 7. 22, 23, Renauld (ed. tr.), 1926, II, 95-96, Sewter (tr.) 1966, 288.
13   Tuan 1977, 14. Note the answer in Hadjiphilippou 2013, 5: "hearing is a very incorporating sense. It is omnidirectional, not focused like vision. The sense of hearing creates a three-dimensional atmosphere".
14   For example Pentcheva (ed.) 2017.
15   Anna Komnene, 11.3.2, Reinsch & Kambylis (ed.) 2001, 329–330, Sewter & Frankopan (tr.) 2009, 304–5.

Erat namque regi tentorium, quod, art e simul et natura mirabile, duplicem spectator iactabat stuporem: ad haec, urbis instar, turrita atria camelos xx gravi sarcina non fraudabant; capacitas conveniendae multitudini oportuna; apex tantum ceteris preminens, "quantum lenta solent inter viburna cupressi".

A tent that was marvellous both by art and by nature so that it cast a double spell on its viewers. It looked like a city with a turreted atrium. It required twenty heavily burdened camels to carry. It could hold a multitude, and its apex soared above the others "just as the cypress is accustomed to soar over the yielding roses".[16]

It was a request too far. "He desires nothing other than my palace, which is unique in the world. What more can he ask except to take the diadem off my head and place it on his own? " After sneering at Tancred's lack of reception space and noting the transport problems it would bring, Alexios compares Tancred to the ass dressed in a lion's skin of the fable. "[...] let him obtain his own tent and leave off any hope of gaining this one".[17]

And another story is told in the *Book of Gifts and Rarities* about Sayf al-Dawlah, that he possessed a brocade tent that accommodated five hundred persons. "Once he made a truce with the Byzantine emperor stipulating that he could enter the latter's country with a tent (khaymah) and this was the tent [he brought]".[18] But it was true for private individuals as well as potentates. Digenes' is very large in Grottaferrata, "an enormous tent all sewn with gold" in the Russian Devgeni.[19]

We should not assume that everyday tents even for emperors reached the size of Alexander the Great's dining tent for one hundred.[20] If we look at the provision in Text C of the *De cerimoniis* we see that four solid gold plates, two gold vases and two solid gold jugs were to be taken for foreign potentates, plus

---

16 Ralph of Caen, *Gesta Tancredi*, ch. 77, ed. d'Angelo, 22. Bachrach & Bachrach (tr.) 2005, 42.
17 Ralph of Caen, Gesta Tancredi, ed. d'Angelo 22–23, Bachrach & Bachrach (tr.) 2005, 42–43.
18 *Kitab al-Hadaya wa al-Tuhaf, Book of Gifts and Rarities,* ch. 95, Al Hijjawi al-Qaddumi (tr.) 1996, 113.
19 *Digenes Akrites, Grottaferrata*, 4.908; Jeffreys (ed.tr.) 1998, 120–121; for the Russian version see Kuz'mina (ed.) 1962, Haney (tr.) 2012, 2, 3, 21, 23.
20 Spawforth, 2007a, 82–120 esp. the appendix, Alexander's state tents, 112–20.

two silver visitors' chamber pots.[21] Perhaps we should think more in terms of intimacy and compactness, and perhaps we should imagine that everything on campaign had to be rethought in terms of the space and reduced to the essentials. The whole bureaucracy of the empire did not accompany the emperor; central officials who did included the *epi ton deeseon*.[22] Ceremony likewise needed to be rethought.[23] Rhetoric was reduced to harangues; liturgy was tailored to the occasion with prayers for the eve of battle, but also needed to encompass funerary, baptismal and regime-change ritual. Receptions, audiences and embassies could be accommodated in the emperor's tent, and we are told about negotiations like those in Anna with Bohemond for the Treaty of Devol.[24] It may be that changes in imperial ceremony have something to do with the increasing practice of bringing the whole court on campaign as much as shifting spatial arrangements in Constantinople; prokypsis for example ensures visibility for the emperor away from the imperial box at the hippodrome, and can be engineered easily with a frame and a curtain.[25] Entertainment must have been reduced to story-telling, joke-sharing, minstrelsy and juggling rather than the more ambitious spectacles and illusions of the palace in Constantinople.[26]

We can certainly say that tents play with scale.[27] On the one hand, for processions, the limited city-scape of the capital is transformed into the large-scale theme geography of the empire, and a limited *prokinsos* from building to building becomes a long march with icons and candles at the head and dignitaries lined up in order, with new ceremonies written for the army as it reaches a new theme and the theme officials turn out to greet the arriving emperor. On the other, ceremonies normally played out in the huge spaces of Great Palace, Great Church and hippodrome have now to fit in or around the emperor's tent.[28] In these ways tents in space expand scale and the space in tents causes

---

21   Constantine Porphyrogennetos, Text C: *Osa dei ginesthai tou megalou kai hypsilou basileos ton Romaion mellontos phossateusai*, 275–79; 216–17, Haldon (ed.) 1990, 112, 108.
22   Text C 496, Haldon (ed.) 1990, 126. On who traveled see Mullett forthcoming a. On the *epi ton deeseon*, Oikonomides 1972, 322.
23   See Mullett, forthcoming b.
24   Anna Komnene, *Alexiad,* 13.9.4–5, Reinsch & Kambylis (eds), 409, Sewter (tr.) 380–1.
25   On prokypsis see Jeffreys 1987, 38–53; Macrides 2011, 234 and n.103; eadem 2012 at notes 117–18.
26   On entertainment see Mullett 2018b; for a concert on the steppe see Rorex & Wen Fong 1974, poem 7 and discussion in Mullett forthcoming c.
27   On space as vastness see Tuan 1977, 16 and on spaciousness, 51–66.
28   See Mullett forthcoming b.

urban activity to contract, even with tents as massive as Alexander the Great's large tents.

1 Transformations

These great tents were also a case of spatial transformation. Only recently was it realised that the hundred-seater dining tent, the hundred-throng reception tent and the hundred-bedded marriage tent could all have been the same tent.[29] We are used to specialization in the Ottoman tent complex, where as well as reception and sleeping tents there were specially shaped tents for prisons, kitchens, lavatories—and executions.[30] And Chinese conceptualization of nomad encampments allowed for specialist tents for birthing, concerts and reception.[31] But it may be that Byzantine tents were more like Alexander's, in purpose if not in size.

We hear of and see tents for various purposes in Byzantium: War tents as seen in the Madrid Skylitzes are shown also in Old Testament manuscripts, some decorated with warriors, and drawn up in military *taktika* with diagrams to show their positioning in the camp.[32] A hunting tent is shown in the Venice *Kynegetika* associated with bird-snaring; it is however the best parallel for Manganeios Prodromos' elaborate description of the tent of the sebastokratorissa Irene with its parrots and peacocks and foxes, which appears to be a tent taken on campaign in Macedonia by the sebastokratorissa.

145
Εἰς τὴν σεβαστοκρατόρισσαν, ἐπὶ τῇ σκηνῇ αὐτῆς ζῶα διάφορα ἐχούσῃ ἐντετυπωμένα

---

29   Spawforth 2007a, 9.
30   Atasoy 2000, 62–63, Fig. 11 shows an illumination in the album of feasts of sultan Achmed III showing the Imperial tent complex in the grounds of Okmeydani in 1720 for the circumcision of princes. TSMA3593, 10b–11a. Taken with some surviving examples and the register kept by Abdullah Aga, the chief officer of the Corps of Tentmakers for the year 1714, BOA KK 6715, H1126, it is possible to identify in Fig. 12 an execution tent, Fig. 52 a terracotta-coloured kitchen tent and Fig. 55 the box-like lavatory tents.
31   Rorex & Wen Fong 1974, poems 7 (concert), 10 (birthing), 5 and 12 (reception), 13 (cooks' yurt).
32   See for example the siege of Nikephoros Phokas at Mopsuestia, Madrid Codex vitr. 26–2, fols. 151r and v, see Tsamakda 2002, Figs. 381–82; for the Old Testament see e.g. the book of Kings, Vat.gr. 333, fol. 18v, Lassus, 1973, Fig. 31; for the camp diagrams *Peri strategias*, Dennis (ed.tr.), 1985, 257–60 from Vat.gr. 1164, fols 236v, 237, 237v, 238.

Δέσποινα, μοῦσα τῶν μουσῶν, ἀκρόπολις τοῦ κάλλους,
τὰ πρόθυρά σου τῆς σκηνῆς πεπλήρωνται χαρίτων.
Ἔρωτες πλήττουσιν χορδάς, σιγῇ κιθαροδοῦσιν,
δοκοῦσι παίζειν σάτυροι, σκυρτῶσιν ἱπποκράται,
5 αἱ μοῦσαι συγχωρεύουσι, πηδῶσι νηρηίδες,
ὄρνιθες ὑπερίπτανται, κυνηγετοῦσιν ἄλλοι
τῆς Ἰνδικῆς τὰ χρυσέα πτηνὰ συναναπτάντα.
Ὁ χρυσοπτέρυξ ψιττακός, τοῦ κάλλους ὁ λυχνίτης,
πρὸς τὴν χρυσέαν σμάραγδον ἐρίζει τῶν ταώνων,
10 καὶ πρὸς τοὺς γαύρους ὄρνιθας καὶ τῶν πτερῶν τὸν κύκλον·
τὴν τοῦ χρυσοῦ χλωρότητα τὴν ἐν τοῖς μεταφρένοις
συναντιπαρατίθησι καὶ συμπαραδεικνύει.
Ἀλώπεκες αἱ πονηραὶ τοὺς δόλους ἐκλιποῦσαι
τῇ λύρᾳ προσανέχουσιν, ὀρχοῦνται πρὸς κιθάραν.
15 Τίς οὖν εἰς τὸ προτείχισμα καὶ τὴν αὐλαίαν ταύτην
οὐκ ἀπιδὼν καταπλαγῇ καὶ μᾶλλον ἀπορήσει;
Ἂν γὰρ εἰς τὸ προσκήνιον αἱ χάριτες τοσαῦται,
πόσον λοιπὸν ἐν τῇ σκηνῇ τῆς χάριτος τὸ θαῦμα,
τῆς ἀπολύτως καὶ μιᾶς καὶ πρώτης τῶν χαρίτων;
20 Ἔρωτες ἔξω παίζουσιν, ἔρωτες ἔνδον ἄλλοι,
αὐχένας ὑποκλίνουσι καὶ γόνυ τῇ δεσποίνῃ,
ἐπὶ τὸ δουλικώτερον ὑποσχηματισθέντες.
Καὶ χάρις σου ταῖς χάρισι καὶ ταῖς ὑπεροχαῖς σου
καὶ δόξα ταῖς χάρισι καὶ τοῖς κοσμήμασί σου·
25 Ἔρως ἐρώτων πέφηνας, χάρις χαρίτων ἔφυς,
σειρὴν σειρήνων γέγονας, μοῦσα μουσῶν ἐφάνης·
οὐκ ἔχεις ἀντεξέτασιν μετὰ θνητῶν γυναίων.
Μετὰ μουσῶν σε προσκυνῶ, τιμῶ μετὰ σειρήνων,
μετὰ χαρίτων σέβομαι, ταῖς ὥραις σε συνάπτω,
30 μεθ' Ἥρας, μετὰ Θέτιδος, μετὰ τῶν οὐρανίων·
ἔρρωσο, χάρις καὶ σειρὴν καὶ μοῦσα Καλλιόπη.

Manganeios Prodromos, *On her tent which had different animals depicted on it*

My lady, Muse of Muses, akropolis of beauty,
The porch of your tent is filled with delights.
Cupids are plucking strings and quietly strumming the kithara,
Satyrs seem to play, centaurs gambol,
The Muses join in the dance, the Nereids are leaping,
Birds fly above, while others hunt

the golden birds of India which fly together.
The gold-feathered parrot, jewel of beauty,
vies with the golden emerald of the peacocks,
And with those proud birds and the circle of their feathers
contrasts and makes comparisons together
with the freshness of the gold upon their backs.
Cunning foxes, abandoning their wiles,
devote themselves to the lyre, dance to the kithara.
Who then could look at this porch and curtain
and not be amazed, in fact dumbfounded?
For if the delights in the entrance are so great,
How great must be the marvel of delight inside the tent,
She who is absolutely unique and first of the Graces?
Cupids play outside while inside there are other cupids
submitting with bent necks on bended knee to their mistress,
taking on a more servile aspect.
And thanks be to your brilliance and the virtues that adorn you.
You were born Cupid of Cupids and Grace of Graces,
you have become Siren of Sirens, you have proved Muse of Muses.
You cannot be compared with mortal women.
I revere you with the Muses, I honour you with the Sirens,
I do reverence to you with the Graces, I link you with the Hours,
with Hera, with Thetis, with the immortals.
Greetings, Grace and Siren and Muse Kalliope![33]

Tents were required for certain ceremonies, especially in the liminal areas between field and City, like the tents set up in the meadow by the Golden Gate in Text C or the elegant tents in the *Eiseterioi* manuscript which received foreign brides in the Philopation before bringing them into the City.[34] And tents are associated firmly with love as well as marriage: in Grottaferrata Digenes the hero and heroine take to the frontier with their wedding-present tent,

Καὶ τένδαν χρυσοκέντητον, ὡραίαν, παμμεγέθη,
ζῴων ἔχουσαν συγκοπάς, πολυμόρφους ἰδέας,

---

33 Manganeios Prodromos, poem 145, ed. tr. M. Jeffreys in Anderson & Jeffreys 1994, 11–13.
34 Text C, 742–47, Haldon (ed.) 1990, 140–42; Vat.gr. 1851, fol. 6r. On the poem see Jeffreys 1981, 101–15; on the manuscript and the illuminations see Hilsdale 2005, 458–83; see her excellent discussion on 472.

τὰ σχοινία μεταξωτά, ἀργυροῖ δὲ οἱ πάλοι,

A beautiful tent, very large, embroidered with gold
Decorated with multiform shapes of animals
And the ropes were of silk and the poles of silver.[35]

in an idealised setting for al fresco love enhanced by the scents and sounds designed to entice and enhance pleasure in the future.

περὶ τῆς κλίνης πέμματα ἐκάπνιζον παντοῖα,
μόσχοι, νίται καὶ ἄμβαρα, καμφοραὶ καὶ κασσίαι,
καὶ ἦν πλείστη <ἡ> ἡδονὴ καὶ ὀσμὴ εὐφροσύνης·
τοσαύτην ὁ παράδεισος τὴν τερπνότητα εἶχεν.
Ἐν ὥρᾳ τῇ μεσημβρινῇ πρὸς ὕπνον ἀνετράπην
ῥοδόσταμμα τῆς εὐγενοῦς ῥαντιζούσης με κόρης,
ἀδονίδων καὶ τῶν λοιπῶν ὀρνίθων μελῳδούντων.

Around the bed were burning spices of all kinds,
Musk, nard and ambergris, camphor and cassia,
and great was the pleasure and the scent of joys.
Such were the delights this garden offered.
At the hour of noon I turned to sleep,
While the high-born girl sprinkled rosewater over me
and the nightingales and other birds sang.[36]

In Niketas Choniates, love in a tent has taken place in the recent past and death at the hands of angry kinsmen threatens Andronikos I Komnenos who with one leap escapes.

> Once when he was lying in the woman's embraces in his tent at Pelagonia, Eudokia's blood relations, on being so informed, surrounded the tent with a large number of armed troops and stood guard over the exit, intending to cut him down on the spot. Eudokia was well aware of the plot, even though her mind was occupied with other matters for she had either been alerted by one of her kinsmen or warned in some other way of the ambush planned against her corrupter. Contrary to the nature

---

35   *Digenes Akrites, Grottaferrata*, 4.908–10, Jeffreys (ed. tr.) 1998, 120–21.
36   *Digenes Akrites, Grottaferrata*, 6.38–43, Jeffreys (ed. tr.) 1998, 154–55.

of women, she was quick-witted and gifted with sagacity. While in the embraces of Andronikos, she informed him of the plot. Shaken by what he heard, he leaped out of bed and girding on his long sword, deliberated on what he should do. Eudokia proposed to her lover that he don female attire and that she should order aloud and by name one of her maidservants to bring a lantern to the tent, and that as soon as the ambushers heard her voice he should exit and make his escape. However he was not convinced by her persuasive argument, afraid that he might lose his way, be taken captive, and be led before the emperor, ignobly dragged by the hair, and worse, made to suffer a womanish and inglorious death. Hence, unsheathing his sword and taking it in his right hand, he cut slantwise through the tent, leaped forth and in one mighty bound, like a Thessalian, hurdled the barrier that chanced to be standing in front of the tent and the space occupied by the stakes and ropes; the ambushers were left agape: by escaping both obstacles the prey transformed defeat into a marvel.[37]

Though one passage looks forward to sex and the other moves on from it, both emphasise the tent, either its sensory accoutrement or its practical supports; both easily assume tents are associated with (physical) love.

These are common functions of tents in many other societies. The early photographs of the American civil war home in on tents as emblematic of councils of war.[38] Mughal rulers and aristocrats show off and compete with their hunting tents as well as their courage and speed.[39] Sofia Coppola's *Marie Antoinette* (2006) shows the princess en route for Versailles from Austria escorted into a border tent by female members of the French royal house.[40] And a cursory

---

[37] Niketas Choniates, *Chronike diegesis*, van Dieten (ed.) 1975, 104–5, Magoulias (tr.) 1984, 60.

[38] E.g. https://www.archives.gov/files/research/military/civil-war/photos/images/civil-war-021.jpg accessed 3 December 2019. The National Archives collection of Mathew B. Brady also shows visits of e.g. President Lincoln as taking place in tents, and also portraits of generals in the field in front of their tent.

[39] See for example images from the *Akbar-nama*, showing preparation for a hunt with a sayaban and a cheetah-awning, V and A IS 2–1896–15 and another showing Akbar punishing Hamid of Bakkar at a deer hunt with a spectacular harem enclosure behind, V and A IS 2–1896–55, both c. 1590; see Andrews 1999, Figs. 190 and VII.

[40] Sofia Coppola, *Marie Antoinette*, 2006, https://www.imdb.com/title/tt0422720/ accessed 2 December 2019. For a reading of the scene see SB, "Otherness in the handover of Marie Antoinette", *From behind the fourth wall: criticism from a collective of La Trobe University cinema students* https://frombehindthefourthwall.wordpress.com/2013/10/21/otherness-in-the-hand-over-of-marie-antoinette/ accessed 2 December 2019.

internet search for books on tents makes it quite clear that tents are strongly associated with sex.[41] So functions are shared, but not always specialist structures. In Byzantium specialist soft architecture was reserved for the chapel and the imperial tent. Michael Psellos notes after the negotiations with Isaac Komnenos "a special imperial tent will have to be set aside for his use".[42] Church tents like those described in Pachymeres (the tent of Maria Palaiologina, the illegitimate daughter of Michael VIII) and Joinville (Louis IX's gift to the Mongols) were elaborately decorated and Text C requires sacred furniture for the imperial chapel.[43] Apart from these two exceptions, in Byzantium tents transformed space for different purposes, a vital feature of their versatility and mutability. And we should not forget that tents are, particularly in their superportability, subject to repurpose over time, as Avinoam Shalem has posited for the chasuble of Thomas Becket at Fermo;[44] silks in western cathedral treasuries or Tsar Samuel's shroud may have started life as tents like the uniforms of the *komes tes kortes* in Pseudo-Kodinos. By repurposing, though, they lose their space,[45] but add to their identity.

2   Identity and Community

Tents are personal and particular as we saw with the Sebastokratorissa's tent, the home of the Muse of Muses. It is the classical additions of muses and graces and hybrids to the more generalized flora and fauna that personalizes a learned tent for a learned owner. Tents are recognizable as we see from Pseudo-Kodinos' listing of what each official's tent looks like;[46] they are prize possessions, givers of prestige, rather like the blue felt tent of the Tang official Po Chü-i.

---

41   These range in seriousness from the academic Conway 2017 to fiction of the *Slut in a tent*, *A night in a tent with a stranger*, *Two women one tent* variety via a self-help literature offering useful tips because 'tent sex can be pretty tricky': bring a bigger tent, open the vents, use glow-in-the-dark condoms, turn off the lantern first.

42   Michael Psellos, *Chronographia*, 7.33, Renauld (ed.) 1926, II, 103, Sewter (tr.), 1966, 295.

43   Pachymeres, *Chronikon*, III.3, Failler (ed.), Laurent (tr) 1984, 235.; Joinville, *Histoire*, 29, 93, Pauphilet (ed.), 1952, 235, 311, Shaw (tr.), 1963, 198, 282–83. Text C, 183–4, Haldon (ed.), 1990, 106.

44   Shalem (ed.), 2016, 98–107; idem, 2014, building on Simon-Cahn 1992, 1–5.

45   Pseudo-Kodinos, Macrides, Munitiz & Angelov (eds) 2015, 100. Samuel's peacock-silk shroud found in his tomb at Agios Achilleios at Prespa is displayed in the Byzantine Museum at Thessalonike.

46   Pseudo-Kodinos, Macrides et al. (eds) 2015, 40, 44, 46.

> Poor clerics faced with it will gasp with envy;
> Indigent scholars would certainly cling to it!
> My guests are received there;
> My descendants will hand it on.
> The families of princes may boast of their antiquities,
> But these do not equal my blue felt![47]

This one was a captured tent, all the more precious like the Ottoman tents captured at the siege of Vienna in 1683.[48] And they can themselves be an offensive weapon like the other tent of Sayf al-Dawlah in al-Mutanabbī's poem:

> al-Mutanabbī describes the tent of Sayf al-Dawlah
> Your faithfulness is like the abode
> [Opening lament of lost love and youth ll. 1–18]
>
> Better than the lost freshness of youth altogether,
> is the water of the lightning cloud in a tent upon which I fix my hopes;
>   [i.e. the patron]
>
> Upon it [i.e. the tent] are gardens which no cloud has woven,
> And branches of tree upon which no doves sing;
>
> And upon the margins of every two-sided fabric,
> there is a string of pearls which have not been bored by their arranger;
>
> You see pictures of animals that upon it have come to a truce,
> an enemy fights his opponent, and makes peace with him;
>
> If the wind strikes it, it undulates,
> as if its old horses travel round and its lions stalk prey;
>
> In the picture of the Byzantine with a crown, there is obeisance [lit.= humiliation],

---

[47] Po Chü-i, *The blue felt tent*; and *Departure from the felt tent and hearth*, Ishida Mikinosuke (ed.) 1948, 153–55; Andrews & Watson (tr.) in Andrews 1999, 1, 152–54. On the poet see Waley 1949.

[48] On tents captured at Vienna, Atasoy 2000, 124 and now Dimmig 2019. I am grateful to Lioba Theis for her determination that we should see them all.

to the one of shining visage who wears no crowns but his turbans;
[the patron, Sayf al-Dawlah]

The mouths of kings kiss [the hem of] his shroud,
for his sleeve and fingers are too exalted.[49]

But most of all they create a personal space which can be controlled and replicated anywhere; the emphasis in Byzantine texts on reception is not haphazard, for tents are particularly suited to creating an audience hall where the owner, like Muammar al-Gaddafi while visiting Rome,[50] can be at home on his or her own terms. That space is place, individual, tranquil and serene, engaging all the senses and the quieter emotions.[51] It endorses the view of Gillian Rose that places are significant because they are the focus of personal feelings.[52]

And tents can also create a corporate identity, inducing a sense of community: Alexios I's camp on the move included babies being born and elders dying in that community,[53] and the *taktika* require rations to be in the middle of the tent, spears in the ground at the feet of the soldiers, and a whole file eats and sleeps and prepares to die together.[54] In doing this, tents create and negotiate transitional space between interior and exterior.

3   Transitional and Unstable Space

Camp life and ceremony took place both inside, like receptions, banquets and negotiations, and outside, like the swearing of oaths before battle;[55] flaps and porches drew participants from one to another. Boundaries and space, it is said, are interdependent: "without boundaries, there is no space".[56] Tents blur

---

49   Al-Mutanabbi, Ekphrastic passage describing the tent of Sayf al-Dawlah, *Dīwān al-Mutanabbi* 1994, 256–60; Pomerantz (tr. unpublished), lines 18–24, between an opening lament of lost love and youth (lines 1–18) and a concluding section of praise of the patron (lines 25–42). For a reading of the poem, see Larkin 2008, 35–41.
50   *La Repubblica* 31 May 2009.
51   Compare Lanval's lady's tent and its freedom from the slander and politics of Arthur's court in Marie de France, Calabrese 2007, 83.
52   Rose 1995, 88.
53   Anna Komnene, *Alexiad*, 15.7.1–2, Reinsch & Kambylis (ed.), 481–82, Sewter & Frankopan (tr.), 451.
54   *Peri strategias*, 27, Dennis (ed. tr.), 85.
55   Madrid Skylitzes, fol. 121r, Tsamakda, Fig. 281.
56   Ashihara 1983, 2.

those boundaries; further, there is constant ambiguity in the tent poems as to what is on a tent and what is in a tent.

The sebastokratorissa's tent has a porch which is full of various creatures: first cupids, satyrs, centaurs, muses and nereids play the kithara and dance. Next, above, birds fly and hunt one another; there are golden birds from India, parrots and peacocks. And then there are foxes, this time playing the lyre, dancing to the kithara. Which of these groups are envisaged as represented on the tent? All perhaps, evoking in turn mythological space, avian exoticism and Aesopian anthropomorphism. Animals at any rate are to be expected on the tent, as in the Capella Palatina (in roundels), the Marciana (a pard hunts a deer, a raptor hunts a rabbit), so perhaps the hybrids and deities and foxes are inside, dancing. In Digenes it is the other way round: the hybrids are on the tent and nightingales and other birds sing in the real space of the borderlands. But there is a further contrast in the sebastokratorissa's tent. You find your way through the throng of musicians and dancers to the tent itself and there you discover the Lady, who is the epitome of elegance and learning represented by the hybrids and personifications. But there are also cupids, outside playing, and inside doing obeisance to the Lady, like the genii on the Hestia textile at Dumbarton Oaks.[57] All combine to honour the sebastokratorissa, and to offer her an alternative to the rigours of Balkan campaigning: a world of learning and sophistication. On the tent of Sayf al-Dawlah, gardens, trees, rain and peaceful animals are brought to life by the wind as it makes the material ripple, an image of another world of cool luxury and perfection in the midst of the desert warfare suggested by a hunting lion and a defeated Byzantine emperor: again a desired alternative space is provided by the tent.

Tents are liminal spaces and they bring their own uncertainties: liminal space is the place where transformation occurs but also transgression. It is no accident that tent stories and even tent poems involve sedition: the tent of the fake sebastos John Komnenos in the Life of Cyril Phileotes,[58] the Aaron family in Theophylact,[59] the suspected Sebastokratorissa herself.[60] They are a natural

---

57 Schrenk 2019.
58 Nicholas Kataskepenos, *Life of Cyril Phileotes*, ch. 53.2, Sargologos (ed.) 1964, 249: The Devil [...] showed him through his senses, in the monastery and near his cell, an erected tent. Inside it was a couch, strewn and covered with red rugs, where the sebastos was sitting, surrounded by a crowd.
59 The Aaron family of whom one, Rodomir, is addressed in Theophylact's poems 11 and 12, Gautier (ed.) 1983, 367 were not only descendants of the Bulgarian royal house but were also involved in an assassination attempt on the emperor, Anna, *Alexiad*, 13.1.5–7, Reinsch & Kambylis (ed.), 385–87; Sewter & Frankopan (tr.), 358–59.
60 The Sebastokratorissa's ambitions for her son led to difficulties with Manuel, see Jeffreys & Jeffreys 1994, 42 and Evangelatou, 2014, 241–324. On these examples of possible sedition and others see Mullett 2018a.

locus for subversion, sedition, re-evaluation, reshaping, providing metaphors for transitions like war and peace as in Walter Kittredge's *Tenting Tonight*, written in 1863, the first American protest song.

> We're tenting tonight on the old camp ground,
> Give us a song to cheer
> Our weary hearts, a song of home
> And friends we love so dear.
>
> *Chorus:*
> Many are the hearts that are weary tonight,
> Wishing for the war to cease;
> Many are the hearts looking for the right
> To see the dawn of peace.
> Tenting tonight, tenting tonight,
> Tenting on the old camp ground.
>
> We've been tenting tonight on the old camp-ground,
> Thinking of days gone by,
> Of the loved ones at home that gave us the hand,
> And the tear that said, "Good-bye!"
> *Chorus*
>
> The lone wife kneels and prays with a sigh
> That God his watch will keep
> O'er the dear one away and the little dears nigh,
> In the trundle bed fast asleep.
> *Chorus*
>
> We are tenting tonight on the old camp ground.
> The fires are flickering low.
> Still are the sleepers that lie around,
> As the sentinels come and go.
> *Chorus*
>
> Alas for those comrades of days gone by
> Whose forms are missed tonight.
> Alas for the young and true who lie
> Where the battle flag braved the fight.
> *Chorus*

No more on march or field of strife
Shall they lie so tired and worn,
Nor rouse again to hope and life
When the sound of drums beat at morn.
Chorus

We are tired of war on the old camp ground,
Many are dead and gone,
Of the brave and true who've left their homes,
Others been wounded long.
Chorus

We've been fighting today on the old camp ground,
Many are lying near;
Some are dead, and some are dying,
Many are in tears.

Final Chorus:
Many are the hearts that are weary tonight,
Wishing for the war to cease;
Many are the hearts looking for the right,
To see the dawn of peace.
Dying tonight, dying tonight,
Dying on the old camp ground.[61]

In Byzantium, that imperial society, protest is expressed in (threatened or real) usurpation, and tents are significant here. When Manuel I was in difficulties with Turks in a ravine on the retreat from Ikonion in 1146, his uncle Isaac, *sebastokrator* and *porphyrogennetos,* instead of rushing to his aid went to the imperial tent and waited in the imperial chapel to seize the throne, though he was of course to be disappointed. The chapel was not the audience chamber itself, but a doubly liminal space from which he could emerge to be acclaimed. Like the treatment of Aaron and the Sebastokratorissa in the poems and John Komnenos in the *Life,* this vignette uses tents to suggest perfidy, in this case explicitly: Isaac, we are told, had a long-standing hunger for the throne and had passed that *pothos* on to his sons.[62] The instability and polymorphy of tents

---

61 Kittredge 1864; collected by Kittredge & Foster in Kittredge et al. 1890.
62 John Kinnamos, *Histories*, (ed.) Meineke, 53, tr. Brand, 49.

were a metaphor for political inconstancy; their space for dynastic theatre. In Byzantium, transitions like political and military failure and triumph, accession to empire, and marriage into the empire are all set in tents.[63]

∴

So what kind of Byzantine space is represented here? When we look at tents in Byzantium, we can see that they mediate space, maximizing and minimizing it, transforming it through their own versatility and mutability, reinventing personal and political images, inducing the sense of a community and, as liminal and ephemeral spaces, negotiating interiors and exteriors. But are they a third space?[64] Smooth rather than striated?[65] A heterotopia?[66] I don't think any of these descriptions or ways of looking are sufficient, though the idea of heterotopia deserves more consideration.[67] As Christopher of Mytilene makes clear, tents move. If all spaces are actively produced by the act of moving,[68] the space of tents is recreated by the movement of the tent itself, realigning itself with different landscapes, always the same but capable of transformation.

Bibliography

Primary Sources

Al-Mutanabbi, "Your faithfulness is like the abode". Ed. 'U. Tabbā, *Diwan al-Mutanabbi*. Beirut 1994. Tr. M. Pomerantz (unpublished).

Anna Komnene, *Alexiad*. Ed. D. R. Reinsch & A. Kambylis. *Annae Comnenae Alexias*. CFHB, 40.1, Berlin & New York 2001. Tr. E. Sewter & P. Frankopan, *The Alexiad by Anna Komnene, translated, with Notes and Introduction*. Harmondsworth 2009.

---

63 For failure, see Romanos IV Diogenes after Manzikert languishing in his tent in *Timarion*, lines 514–28, ed. Romano, 68, tr. Baldwin, 56; triumph, the prescriptions in Constantine Porphyrogennetos treatise C, lines 472–747, ed. Haldon 1990, 140–42; accession, Michael Psellos, above, n.12; and marriage, the *Eiseterioi*, see Jeffreys 1981 and Hilsdale 2005.

64 Soja 1996. While our tents are certainly "real-and-imagined", thirdspace is really a way of looking at space rather than distinguishing it.

65 Deleuze & Guattari 1987, 361–2. Our tents do alter spaces as they traverse them, but they have military, hunting or ceremonial routes, so nomadism, let alone nomadology does not help us.

66 Foucault 1986.

67 I attempt this in Mullett forthcoming a.

68 Cresswell & Merriman 2011, 7.

Christopher of Mytilene, poem 71. *On a Tent.* Ed. E. Kurtz 1903, *Die Gedichte des Christophoros Mitylenaios.* Leipzig, 45.

Constantine Porphyrogennetos, *Constantine Porphyrogenitus, Three treatises on imperial military expeditions.* Tr. J. F. Haldon. Vienna 1990.

Digenes Akrites, (Grottaferrata). Ed. & tr. E. Jeffreys, *Digenis Akritis: The Grottaferrata and Escorial Versions.* Cambridge 1998. (Russian version) V.D. Kuz'mina, Devgeno Deianie Moscow 1962. Tr. J. V. Haney, *The Deeds of Devgenii,* 2, 3, 21, 23, accessed 17 December 2019. http://nauplion.net/DEV-TheDeedsofDevgeniiAkrit.pdf 2012.

George Pachymeres, *Chronikon.* Ed. A. Failler, tr. V. Laurent, *Georges Pachymerès. Relations historiques.* Paris 1984.

Jean de Joinville, *Histoire de Saint Louis.* Ed. A. Pauphilet (Paris. 1952). Tr. M. R. B. Shaw, *Chronicles of the Crusades.* Harmondsworth 1963.

John Kinnamos, *Histories.* Ed. A. Meineke, *Epitome rerum ab Joanne et Alexio Comneno gestarum.* Bonn 1836. Tr. C. M. Brand, Deeds of John & Manuel Comnenus by John Kinnamos. New York 1976.

Kitab al-Hadaya wa al-Tuhaf, *Book of gifts and rarities.* Ed. M. Hamīdullāh Kuwait, 1959; tr. G. Al Hijjawi al-Qaddumi. Cambridge, MA 1996.

Manganeios Prodromos poem 146, see Anderson & Jeffreys 1994, 12–13.

Michael Psellos, *Chronographia.* Ed. & tr. E. Renauld, *Michel Psellos Chronographie,* 2 vols. Paris 1926. Tr. E. R. A. Sewter, *Fourteen Byzantine Rulers: The Chronographia of Michael Psellus.* Harmondsworth 1966.

Nicholas Kataskepenos, *Life of Cyril Phileotes.* Ed. E. Sargologos, *La vie de saint Cyrille le Philéote, moine byzantine (†1110).* Brussels 1964.

Niketas Choniates, *Chronike diegesis.* Ed. J. A. van Dieten. Berlin & New York 1975. Tr. H. J. Magoulias, *O City of Byzantium, Annals of Niketas Choniates.* Detroit 1984.

Peri Strategias. Ed. & tr. G. T. Dennis, *Three Byzantine Military Treatises.* Washington, D.C. 1985.

Po Chü-i, *The blue felt tent;* and *Departure from the felt tent and hearth.* Ed. Ishida Mikinosuke, *Tōshi Sōshō: Studies in T'ang history and other Sinological essays.* Tokyo 1948. Tr. P. A. Andrews & W. Watson in Andrews 1999, I, 152–54.

Pseudo-Kodinos. *Pseudo-Kodinos and the Constantinopolitan court: offices and ceremonies,* Ed. R. Macrides, J. A. Munitiz & D. Angelov. Surrey 2015.

Pseudo Luciano, *Timarion.* Ed. R. Romano, *Timarione, testo critic, introduzione, traduzione, commentario e lessico.* Napoli 1974. Tr. B. Baldwin, *Timarion, translated with introduction and commentary.* Detroit 1984.

Ralph of Caen, *Gesta Tancredi.* Ed. G. D'Angelo, *Ranulphi Cadomensis Tancredus.* Turnhout 2011. Tr. B. S. Bachrach & D. S. Bachrach. Aldershot 2005.

Theophylact of Ochrid, poem 12. Ed. P. Gautier, *Théophylacte d'Achrida: discours, traités, poésies.* Thessalonike 1983.

Secondary Sources

Anderson, J. C. & M. J. Jeffreys. 1994. "The decoration of the Sebastokratorissa's tent", *Byzantion* 64, 8–18.

Andrews, P. A. 1999. *Felt Tents and Pavilions. The Nomadic Tradition and its Interaction with Princely Tentage*, 2 vols. London.

Ashihara, Y. 1983. *The Aesthetic Townscape*. Cambridge, MA.

Atasoy, N. 2000. *Otağ-ı Hümayun: the Ottoman Imperial Tent Complex*. Istanbul.

Beihammer, A., S. Constantinou & M. Parani. (eds) 2013. *Court Ceremonies and Rituals of Power in the Medieval Mediterranean*. Leiden.

Brenk, B. 2010. *La cappella palatina a Palermo*. Modena.

Bühl, G. & Williams, E.D. (eds) 2019. *Catalogue of the Textiles in the Dumbarton Oaks Byzantine Collection*. Washington, DC.

Calabrese, M. 2007. "Controlling space and secrets in the *Lais* of Marie de France", in Howes 2007. Knoxville, TN, 79–106. .

Conway, C.M. 2017. *Sex and Slaughter in the Tent of Jael: A Cultural History of a Biblical Story*. New York.

Coppola, S. 2006. *Marie Antoinette*, https://www.imdb.com/title/tt0422720/.

Crang, M. & N. Thrift. 2000a. "Introduction", in Crang & Thrift (eds) 2000b. Abingdon, 1–30.

Crang, M. & N. Thrift (eds) 2000b. *Thinking Space*. Abingdon.

Cresswell, T. & Merriman, P. (eds) 2011. *Geographies of Mobilities: Practices, Spaces, Subjects*. Abingdon.

Deleuze, G. & Guattari, F. 1987. *A Thousand Plateaus*. London & New York.

Dimmig, A. 2019. "Substitutes and souvenirs: reliving Polish victory in 'Turkish' tents", in Fraser (ed.) 2019, 70–90.

Duindam, J., T. Artan, & M. Kunt (eds) 2011. *Royal Courts in Dynastic States and Empires; a Global Perspective*. Leiden.

Ergin, N. & S. Redford (eds) 2012. *Cities and Citadels*. Leiden.

Evangelatou, M. 2014. "Threads of Power: Clothing Symbolism, Human Salvation, and Female Identity in the Illustrated Homilies by Iakobos of Kokkinobaphos", *DOP* 68, 241–324.

Fraser, E. A. (ed.) 2019. *The Mobility of People and Things in the Early Modern Mediterranean*. New York & London.

Foucault, M. 1986. "Of other spaces", tr. J. Miskowiec, *Diacritics* 16, 22–27.

Hadjiphilippou, P. 2013. "The contribution of the five human senses toward the perception of space', Sustainable Design Unit.

Heher, D. 2019. *Mobiles Kaisertum: Das Zelt als Ort der Herrschaft und Repräsentation in Byzanz (10.–12. Jahrhundert)*. Münster.

Hilsdale, C. J. 2005. "Constructing a Byzantine augusta: A Greek book for a French bride", *Art Bulletin 87*, 458–83.

Howes, L.L. (ed.) 2007. *Place, Space, and Landscape in Medieval Narrative*, Tennessee Studies in Literature, 43. Knoxville, TN.

Jeffreys, M. 1981. "The vernacular Eiseterioi for Agnes of France", *Byzantine Papers: Proceedings of the First Australian Byzantine Studies Conference*, Canberra. ByzAus 1, Canberra, 101–15.

Jeffreys, M. 1987. "The Komnenian prokypsis", *Parergon* n.s. 5, 38–53.

Jeffreys, M. J. & E. M. Jeffreys. 1994. "Who was Eirene the sebastokratorissa?", *Byzantion* 64, 40–68.

Kittredge, W. 1864. *Tenting on the Old Camp Ground* (sheet music). Boston.

Kittredge, W. & S. C. Foster (eds) 1890. *The Old Plantation Melodies, illustrated by Mary Hillock Foote and Charles Copeland*. New York.

Larkin, M. 2008. *Al-Mutanabbi; Voice of the 'Abbasid Poetic Ideal. Makers of the Muslim World*. Oxford.

Lassus, J. 1973. *L'illustration byzantine du livre des rois, Vaticanus Graecus 333*. Paris.

Macrides, R. 2011. "Ceremonies and the City; the court in fourteenth-century Constantinople', in Duindam, Artan & Kunt (eds) 2011, 217–23.

Macrides, R. 2012. "The citadel of Byzantine Constantinople", in Ergin & Redford (eds) 2012, 277–304.

Massey, D & Jess, P. 1995. *A Place in the World*. Oxford.

Mullett, M. 1992. "The language of diplomacy", in Shepard & Franklin (eds) 1992, 203–16.

Mullett, M. 2013a. "Tented ceremony: ephemeral performances under the Komnenoi", in Beihammer, Constantinou & Parani (eds) 2013, 487–513.

Mullett, M. 2013b. "Experiencing the Byzantine text, experiencing the Byzantine tent", in Nesbitt & Jackson (eds) 2013, 269–91.

Mullett, M. 2017. "Performing court literature in Byzantium: tales told in tents", in Pomerantz & Birge Witz (eds) 2017, 121–41.

Mullett, M. 2018. "Object, text and performance in four Komnenian tent poems", in Shawcross & Toth (ed.) 2018, 414–29.

Mullett, M. forthcoming a. "Constantinople on the move: tented courts in Byzantium", in Preiser-Kapeller, J., Sykopetritou & Rapp (eds) forthcoming.

Mullett, M. forthcoming b. "Alt-Constantinople: ceremony without the City", in D. C. Smythe & S. F. Tougher (eds) forthcoming, (a Festschrift).

Mullett, M. forthcoming c. "Tents across the border: Byzantine tent poems and the global middle ages".

Nesbitt, C. & M. Jackson (eds) 2013. *Experiencing Byzantium*. Farnham Surrey.

Oikonomides, N. 1972. *Les listes de préséance byzantines des IXe et Xe siècles*. Paris.

Payne, A. (ed.) 2014. *Dalmatia and the Mediterranean: Portable Archaeology and the Poetics of Influence*. Leiden.

Pentcheva, B. (ed.) 2017. *Aural Architecture in Byzantium: Music, Acoustics and Ritual*. Abingdon Oxford.

Pomerantz, M. & E. Birge Witz (eds) 2017. *In the Presence of Power: Courts and Performance in the Premodern Middle East, 700–1600*. New York.

Preiser-Kapeller, J., P. Sykopetritou & C. Rapp forthcoming. *Courts on the Move. Perspectives from the Global Middle Ages*. Vienna.

Rorex R. A. & W. Fong. 1974. *Eighteen Songs of a Nomad Flute; the Story of Lady Wen-Chi; a Fourteenth-Century Handscroll in the Metropolitan Museum of Art*. New York.

Rose, G. 1995. "Place and Identity: A Sense of Place" in Massey & Jess 1995, 87–132.

SB 2013, "Otherness in the handover of Marie Antoinette", *From behind the Fourth Wall: Criticism from a Collective of La Trobe University Cinema Students* (blog), October 21, 2013. https://frombehindthefourthwall.wordpress.com/2013/10/21/otherness-in-the-hand-over-of-marie-antoinette/.

Schrenk, S., "The background of the enthroned: spatial analysis of the hanging with Hestia Polyolbos in the Dumbarton Oaks Collection", in Bühl, G. and Williams, E.D. 2019. https://www.doaks.org/resources/textiles/essays/schrenk.

Shalem, A. (ed.) 2016. *The Chasuble of Thomas Becket. A Biography*. Chicago.

Shalem, A. 2014. "Architecture for the body: some reflections on the mobility of textiles and the fate of the so-called chasuble of Saint Thomas Becket in the cathedral of Fermo in Italy", in Payne (ed.) 2014, 246–67.

Shawcross, T. & I. Toth (ed.) 2018. *Reading Byzantium*. Cambridge.

Shepard, J. & S. Franklin (eds) 1992. *Byzantine Diplomacy*. Aldershot.

Simon-Cahn, A. 1992. "The Fermo chasuble of St Thomas Becket and Hispano-mauresque cosmological silks: some speculations on the adaptive reuse of textiles", *Muqarnas* 10, 1–5.

Soja, E.W. 1996. *Thirdspace: Journeys to Los Angeles and other Real-and-imagined Places*. Malden, MA & Oxford.

Spatharakis, I. 2004. *The Illustrations of the Cynegetica in Venice: Codex Marcianus Graecus Z 139*. Leiden.

Spawforth, A. J. 2007a. "The court of Alexander the Great between Europe and Asia", in Spawforth (ed.) 2007b, *The Court and Court Society in Ancient Monarchies*. Cambridge.

Tsamakda, V. 2002. *The Illustrated Chronicle of Ioannes Skylitzes in Madrid*. Leiden.

Tuan, Y.-F. 1977. *Space and Place: The Perspective of Experience*. Minneapolis.

Waley, A. 1949. *The Life and Times of Po Chü-i*. London.

Variations on the Definition of Sacred Space from Eusebius of Caesarea to Balsamon

Béatrice Caseau

In the *Journal of Early Christian Studies*, Robert Markus published an article entitled "How on Earth Could Places Become Holy? Origins of the Christian Idea of Holy Places".[1] In this article, he refutes Mircea Eliades' idea that all religions have sacred spaces. He points to the fact that in their wish to distance themselves from the notion shared by pagans and Jews concerning temples housing a deity, early Christian writers clearly stated that God needs no house.[2]

> Templum quod ei extruam, cum totus hic mundus eius opera fabricates eum capere non possit?[3]

> "What temple would I erect to Him, seeing that this entire universe, the work of His hands, cannot contain Him?" writes Minucius Felix.[4]

Early Christian writers clearly refused to identify the new Christian religion with previous cults and challenged the notion of sacred space for Christians. This very philosophical position did not last, however. Even before Peace was granted to Christian churches by Emperor Constantine, a literature mixing liturgical and canonical rulings developed, setting rules of behaviour inside churches, and de facto defining a space set apart for religious use, with regulations to separate it from ordinary domestic space, from public spaces and, in a word, from the profane world. Because churches, like temples before them, were defined as areas where behaviour was under the control of specific rules, they became sacred spaces.[5] All sorts of actions deemed improper and

---

[1] Markus 1994.
[2] Acts of the Apostles, 17.24: "The God who made the world and everything in it, being the Lord of heaven and earth, does not dwell in shrines made by man".
[3] Minucius Felix, *Octavius*, texte établi et traduit par J. Beaujeu, Paris, 2002, 54–5.
[4] *The Octavius of Minucius Felix*, 32.1, trans. Clarke, 111.
[5] Sacred implies a separate area, a place where access is under some form of control and where rules of behaviour are specific.

disrespectful were excluded from taking place in such a space, from having sex to eating or acting in a violent manner. These rules defined the space as different and as sacred.

The second process which created a Christian sacred space is a literary one, which compared the newly erected churches to the Jewish Temple of Jerusalem. This second process is set in motion by Eusebius of Caesarea who writes about the renewed church building in Tyre based on the biblical model of the temple of Jerusalem. Just after the end of the persecution, Paulinus, the bishop of Tyre rebuilds the church on a larger scale. The text makes a clear reference to sacred space: the precinct of the church is called a *hieron peribolon*:

Πρόπυλον δὲ μέγα καὶ εἰς ὕψος ἐπηρμένον πρὸς αὐτὰς ἀνίσχοντος ἡλίου ἀκτῖνας ἀναπετάσας, ἤδη καὶ τοῖς μακρὰν περιβόλων ἔξω ἱερῶν ἑστῶσιν τῆς τῶν ἔνδον παρέσχεν ἀφθονίαν θέας.[6]

Towards the rays of the rising sun he spread out a vast and lofty entrance-gate affording a full view of what lay inside even to those who stood far away from the sacred precinct".[7]

The model Eusebius had in mind was the Jewish Temple of Jerusalem, with its different courtyards and its most sacred areas reserved only to priests. This identification of churches with the Temple of Jerusalem eventually led to the identifying of different areas inside churches precincts, some for clerics only, others for laypersons, men and women separately.

In his description, Eusebius defines a space for each category of Christians: catechumens, baptized Christians and clerics. At Tyre, an atrium adorned with porticoes and fountains, separated the outer entrance from the church:

καὶ πρώτη μὲν εἰσιόντων αὕτη διατριβή, κόσμον ὁμοῦ καὶ ἀγλαΐαν τῷ παντὶ τοῖς τε τῶν πρώτων εἰσαγωγῶν ἔτι δεομένοις κατάλληλον τὴν μονὴν παρεχομένη.[8]

---

[6] Eusèbe de Césarée, *Histoire ecclésiastique*, livres VIII-X, texte grec, traduction et notes par G. Bardy, Paris, 1993, 93-94.
[7] Eusebius of Cesarea, *Ecclesiastical History*, X, 4, 38, trans. Mango 1986, 5.
[8] Eusèbe de Césarée, *Histoire ecclésiastique*, livres VIII-X, texte grec, traduction et notes par G. Bardy, Paris, 1993, 94.

This is the first halting-place for those who enter, affording both beauty and splendour to everyone, and serving as an appropriate station for those who as yet lack the first initiation.[9]

It is unlikely that catechumens in Tyre remained in the atrium while the liturgy took place, but Eusebius imagines an ideal church, where each group has a proper and separate place.

When describing the new church at Tyre, Eusebius insisted on the notion of gradual sacredness, from the less sacred in the atrium to the most sacred in the sanctuary. Like in the Temple of Jerusalem, these different spaces were opened to different categories of Christians. The highest members of the clergy (bishops, priests, and deacons) occupied the altar area, which was the most sacred location. On the altar, bread and wine offered by the faithful were transformed into Body and Blood of Christ. Eusebius emphasized the necessity to fence this area and restrict access to it:

τὸ τῶν ἁγίων ἅγιον θυσιαστήριον ἐν μέσῳ θείς, αὖθις καὶ τάδε, ὡς ἂν εἴη τοῖς πολλοῖς ἄβατα, τοῖς ἀπὸ ξύλου περιέφραττε δικτύοις εἰς ἄκρον ἐντέχνου λεπτουργίας ἐξησκημένοις, ὡς θαυμάσιον τοῖς ὁρῶσιν παρέχειν τὴν θέαν.[10]

He placed the sanctuary, the Holy of Holies, in the centre, and so that this too should be inaccessible to the multitude, he fenced it off with wooden lattices perfectly fashioned with artful workmanship—an admirable sight to the beholder.[11]

Inside many Late Antique churches, chancel barriers were indeed added to mark the separate area of the sanctuary. Unlike later Byzantine or Russian iconostasis, they did not intend to block the view, but to delineate a threshold between two areas of different sacredness. Their sheer presence was enough to mark boundaries, create liminal spaces, and suggest the notion of a separate area of the utmost sacredness, not freely accessible.

The right to access the different areas of a church complex differed based on clerical or lay status and on the sex. Restricted access is an indication of the area's level of sacredness and also reveals status in the Christian community. Unlike entrance to the atrium, entrance to the church interior space was not

---

9   Eusebius of Cesarea, *Ecclesiastical History*, x, 4, 40, Mango 1986, 5.
10 Eusèbe de Césarée, *Histoire ecclésiastique*, livres VIII-X, texte grec, traduction et notes par G. Bardy, Paris, 1993, 96.
11 Eusebius of Cesarea, *Ecclesiastical History*, x, 4, 44, Mango, 1986, 6.

granted indiscriminately to all. Members of the clergy, either the lowly doorkeepers or deacons, controlled who came in, a necessary precaution in times of persecution. Altogether, it was important to let curious and interested non-Christians watch what was going on, but at the same time, in order to avoid protests or violence, it was necessary to allow only well-intentioned persons inside the building. Pagans, Jews, and Christians of other faiths could hear the first part of the liturgy if they wished to. They probably remained at the back of the church, or possibly in the narthex with the excommunicated members of the community. Listeners from other religions, catechumens and excommunicated persons had to leave before the Eucharistic celebration. The fourth-century compilation of church orders known as *Apostolic Constitutions* records a common dismissal for those who are not believers and those who are "listeners" in the community.[12] Sacredness was defined spatially and temporally.

Church orders also insisted on making spatially visible another hierarchy among members of the Christian community: clerics, baptized Christians and non-baptized Christians had, ideally, different sitting or standing areas. The catechumens had not received baptism; thus, they could sing the prayers and hear readings and sermons, but they had to leave before the consecration of bread and wine, the Eucharistic elements. Their place was behind the faithful, and sometimes in the narthex.

The *Apostolic Constitutions* records a clerical wish to allocate a specific area of the church nave also to the different age groups and they insisted on separating the sexes:

> ἐν τῇ Ἐκκλησίᾳ οἱ μὲν νεώτεροι ἰδίᾳ καθεζέσθωσαν, ἐὰν ᾖ τόπος, εἰ δὲ μή, στηκέτωσαν ὀρθοί· οἱ δὲ τῇ ἡλικίᾳ ἤδη προβεβηκότες καθεζέσθωσαν ἐν τάξει, τὰ δὲ παιδία ἑστῶτα προσλαμβανέσθωσαν αὐτῶν οἱ πατέρες καὶ αἱ μητέρες· αἱ δὲ νεώτεραι πάλιν ἰδίᾳ, ἐὰν ᾖ τόπος, εἰ δὲ μήγε, ὄπισθεν τῶν γυναικῶν ἱστάσθωσαν· αἱ δὲ ἤδη γεγαμηκυῖαι καὶ τὰ τέκνα ἔχουσαι ἰδίᾳ ἱστάσθωσαν· αἱ παρθένοι δὲ καὶ αἱ χῆραι καὶ αἱ πρεσβύτιδες πρῶται πασῶν στηκέτωσαν ἢ καθεζέσθωσαν.[13]

> In church, the young will sit separately if there is room, otherwise they shall remain standing; the elder shall sit at their rank, children shall stand and their fathers and mothers shall take care of them; the young girls will sit apart if there is room, otherwise they shall stand behind the women; the married women accompanied by children shall stand apart;

---

12 Apostolic Constitutions 8.6.
13 *Les Constitutions apostoliques*, t. 1, Livres 1 et 2, introduction, texte critique, traduction et notes par M. Metzger, Paris, 1985, 316.

virgins, widows and elderly women shall stand or sit in front of the other women.[14]

In some regions, such as Syria, archaeology has revealed that separate entrances existed, possibly for men and women.[15] Doorkeepers or deacons could be in charge of allocating different sections for the faithful coming to the liturgy, based on rank, sex and age.[16]

This spatial organization for members of the community and visitors is mostly found in normative texts and we cannot be sure it was enforced everywhere. It represents an ideal spatialization of the community in the eyes of clerics. Archaeology confirms however that some spaces such as the sanctuary were delineated. The area of the main altar where the Eucharist was offered and where Christ himself resided in the bread and wine remained the focal point of the sacred. The materiality of the chancel barriers around this focal space was the signal of a separate, restricted area, sometimes raised above the level of the nave and usually richly adorned.[17] In Byzantium between the fifth and the seventh centuries, canon law confirms and enforces the exclusion of laypeople from the sanctuary.[18] Also excluded were members of the lower clergy, usually below the rank of deacon. Another focal point of sanctity was the tomb of a saint or a reliquary, to which more or less controlled access was granted and which could also be delineated by steps or chancels.[19]

Training and teaching were required to make sure the faithful understood the different levels of sanctity of church areas. As a consequence, once the sanctuary was identified as the most sacred area, it devalued somewhat the other areas of the church building or inside the sacred enclosure. In Late Antique healing shrines, the sick and the disabled sometimes lived inside this enclosure, often in the atrium on which rooms sometimes opened. They could be accompanied by spouses, servants, and, for the wealthiest, their own doctor. At night, they would be brought inside the church, as close as possible to the relics of a saint for the ritual incubation.[20] Somehow, these crowds gathering inside churches for festivals: pilgrims coming for a few days, the sick and their companions, and the begging poor created a mixed crowd whose behaviour was not up to the high standards expected from the most demanding clerics.

14 Apostolic Constitutions 2. 57. 10.
15 Sodini 2006, 232; Briquel Chatonnet 2013a, 28; Koury & Riba 2013, 41–84; Lassus, 1947.
16 Caseau, 2005, 15–27.
17 Bogdanovic 2017; Sodini 2006, 235.
18 *The Council in Trullo* canon 69.
19 Yasin 2009; 2011, 5–17.
20 Pitarakis (ed.) 2018; Talbot 2002; Caseau 2008.

We can follow their condemnation of disapproved behaviours in canon and civil law, which by contrast reveal how to behave in a sacred space and define what the extension of sacred space is.

In 691/692, the council in Trullo promoted 102 canons, some of which helped define proper behaviour expected inside churches. Canon 97 condemns those who live with their wives inside churches:

> Τοὺς ἢ γαμετῇ συνοικοῦντας ἢ ἄλλως ἀδιακρίτως τοὺς ἱεροὺς τόπους κοινοποιοῦντας, καὶ καταφρονητικῶς περὶ αὐτοὺς ἔχοντας, καὶ οὕτως ἐν αὐτοῖς καταμένοντας, καὶ ἐκ τῶν ἐν τοῖς σεβασμίοις ναοῖς κατηχουμενείων ἐξωθεῖσθαι προστάσσομεν. Εἰ δὲ τις μὴ τοῦτο παραφυλάξοι, εἰ μὲν κληρικὸς εἴη, καραιρείσθω, εἰ μὲν λαϊκός, ἀφοριζέσθω.

> In the case of those who cohabit with their wives or otherwise heedlessly profane sacred places and conduct themselves contemptuously whilst dwelling in them, we command that they should be expelled even from the quarters of the catechumens in venerable churches. If anyone does not observe this, if he is a cleric, he shall be deposed, if a layman, excommunicated.[21]

This canon is found among other canons concerning lay people. The end of the canon, however, includes the possibility that members of the clergy live with their wife inside the church. Many possibilities come to mind for clerics living on the premises: either they settled with their wife in one of the side rooms or in a building attached to the church. As for laypersons, we already mentioned that during Late Antiquity and into the Middle Ages, healing sanctuaries allowed sick people to sleep inside churches close to a reliquary or a saint's tomb in the hope of a miraculous cure, either receiving the visit of a saint and a therapeutic program in a dream, or simply waking up healed. Both possibilities account for the canon's notion of people sleeping inside a church. The canon, however, does not condemn sleeping inside a church but behaving contemptuously whilst dwelling in them, and most of all sleeping with one's wife. What is at stake here is the possibility of sexual relations. Having sex was not allowed inside a church and the bishops who gathered in 691 wanted to recall the rule. In their eyes, it amounts to a disrespectful reduction of the sacred space (*hieros topos*) to an ordinary profane space (*koinos*). The canon gives us a hint that the so called "quarters of the catechumens" could be used by some married clerics

---

21   Canon 97, *The Council in Trullo*, ed. and trans. Featherstone 1995, 178–9.

FIGURE 21.1 Istanbul, Byzantine Cathedral of Hagia Sophia, photograph of the catechoumena
AUTHOR'S COPYRIGHT

as their home. The bishops gathered at the council in Trullo decide that the sacred space in churches extended to the "quarters of the catechumens". This canon is particularly interesting because it shows a variation on the definition of sacred space. It concerns not only the sanctuary and the nave of a church but other areas as well.

Where were these premises for catechumens? For Eusebius of Caesarea, at Tyre, the area for catechumens was the atrium, and it is very possible that in other church complexes, rooms opening onto the courtyard or atrium, at one point a place for teaching, and perhaps accommodating catechumens during their baptismal preparation, were later also used to accommodate clerics and their families when the baptism of children put an end to the teaching of adult catechumens. Starting in the sixth century, other areas of churches were called catechumena or catechoumeneia: the upper galleries of churches, where some women gathered during the liturgy.[22] As we shall see, it is difficult to assert where exactly these "quarters of the catechumens" were, and perhaps they were not in the exact same place in all the churches or were moved to different areas of the church enclosure over time. To answer this question and help us

---

22   Taft 1998.

identify these quarters, can we rely on the commentaries of twelfth-century canonists on the canons of the council in Trullo?

Between the end of the eleventh century and the middle of the twelfth century, three authors commented on the *nomocanon* as it was edited by Theodore Vestes in 1089/90: Zonaras, Balsamon and Aristenos.[23] They commented on the 102 canons of the council in Trullo. What did they understand was at stake in canon 97? How did this canon help them define sacred space and think about the relation between civil and canon law?

Before becoming a monk, John Zonaras had been the head of the imperial chancery (*protoasekretis*) and he had also presided over an important court of law, the hippodrome court. He knew civil law. Besides writing a book of history and theological and hagiographical writings, he provided an interesting commentary on Byzantine canon law. Zonaras comments on canon 97 of the council in Trullo in this manner:

> Ἱεροὺς τόπους οὐ τοὺς θείους ναοὺς ἐνταῦθα καλεῖ, ἀλλὰ τὰς περὶ αὐτοὺς κατοικίας, οἷά εἰσι τὰ λεγόμενα κατηχούμενα. Οὐδεὶς γὰρ οὕτως ἂν εἴη τολμητίας ὡς ἐντὸς ναοῦ συνοικεῖν γαμετῇ. Ἐν οἰκίαις δὲ πάνυ συνημμέναις ναοῖς καὶ ἐν τοῖς κατηχουμένοις ᾤκουν τινές, μὴ σεμνῶς ἴσως βιοῦντες, καὶ καταφρονητικῶς εἶχον περὶ τοὺς τόπους τοὺς ἱερούς, ἀδιακρίτως οἰκοῦντες ἐν αὐτοῖς, ἀντὶ τοῦ μὴ διαστέλλοντες μηδὲ διαχωρίζοντες μέσον ἁγίου καὶ βεβήλου. Τοὺς οὖν οὕτως ἔχοντας ἐξωθεῖσθαι τῶν κατηχουμένων ὁ κανὼν διατάττεται καὶ τοὺς μὴ φυλάττοντας αὐτόν, κληρικοὺς μέν, καθαιρεῖ· λαϊκοὺς δέ, ἀφορίζει. Ὅτι δὲ καὶ τὰ συγκείμενα τοῖς θείοις ναοῖς προνομίων ἀξιοῦνται φησὶ τὸ δωδέκατον κεφάλαιον τοῦ α΄ τίτ. τοῦ ε΄ βιβλίου, περιέχον οὕτω· «Μέχρι τῶν ἐπὶ τῆς δημοσίας ἀγορᾶς τῆς ἐκκλησίας ὅρων τὸ ἀσφαλὲς ἐχέτωσαν οἱ προσφυγόντες, τοῖς ἐνδοτέροις λουτροῖς ἢ κήποις ἢ οἰκήμασιν ἢ στοαῖς ἢ αὐλαῖς χρώμενοι καὶ κωλυέσθωσαν ἐντὸς τοῦ ναοῦ ὑπνοῦν ἢ ἐσθίειν».

Here are called sacred places not the divine churches, but the buildings that surround them, which are the so-called spaces of the catechumens. No one would be foolhardy enough to live inside a church with his wife. Some would live in houses adjoining the churches and in rooms intended for catechesis in a manner that was perhaps indecent and contemptuous of holy places, living there without discernment, that is to say, without differentiating and separating the sacred from the profane. The canon orders that those who behave in this way should be expelled from the

---

23 Messis 2020, introduction.

premises intended for catechumens. The canon deposes those who do not observe it, if they are clerics, and deprives them of communion, if they are lay people. The fact that the buildings adjoining the church are worthy of privilege is expressed in chapter 12, title 1, book 5, chapter 12 (of the *Basilica*), which contains the following: "That the refugees should be safe as far as the limits of the church towards the public market, and that they should use the baths, gardens, houses, porticoes and courtyards within this space, but that they should not be allowed to sleep and eat inside the church".[24]

Zonaras clearly extends the notion of sacred space to buildings surrounding a church that he calls premises intended for catechumens. In his definition, they cannot be identified with upper galleries in churches. From the rest of his comments, however, and his citation of the *Basilica*, we can deduce that his definition of a space "worthy of privilege" includes spaces outside the church, such as the ones mentioned by Eusebius of Caesarea: courtyards, porticoes and rooms adjoining a church. He summons a civil law on asylum to explain how they apply not only to churches but to a large area around them.[25] On the one hand, he does not believe that people would have sex with their wife inside a church; in his time, on the other hand, he believes that some persons can live in houses close by, and even in areas for catechumens. He does not seem to disapprove of it. Recalling the fact that people can sleep and eat in these areas if they are asylum seekers, he makes a distinction between the church building itself where it is forbidden to eat and sleep with a wife and these other buildings. Asylum seekers seldom came as couples, but those who asked for protection often came as individuals and they did not stay long enough to organize a family life for themselves. So why call on this text? Did Zonaras intentionally misinterpret the canon in order to let persons live with their wife as a family inside church precincts as long as it was not inside the church? All buildings inside a sacred precinct benefit from a special status and require people to maintain decorum and proper behaviour, but the restriction concerning sleeping and eating concerns only the church and, perhaps, buildings physically adjoining it, as if sacredness expanded through wall contact.

Balsamon's commentary is even longer and more informative on what defines a sacred space. We know more about Baslamon than about Zonaras. Balsamon lived in the twelfth century in Constantinople, where he was

---

24   Zonaras, commentary on canon 97 of the Council in Trullo, in Messis 2020, 506. (B V, 1, 11).
25   Macrides 1988, 509–38.

deacon of the Hagia Sophia church, then nomophylax and chartophylax of the patriarch. He was also head of monasteries and eventually became patriarch of Antioch around 1185–90. He had vainly hoped to become patriarch of Constantinople.

He comments on canon 97 of the council in Trullo in these terms:

> Ἱεροὶ τόποι λέγονται οἱ ἀφωρισμένοι τῷ Θεῷ, ἤγουν οἱ θεῖοι ναοί, οἱ πρόναοι, τὰ κατηχουμενεῖα καὶ τὰ περὶ αὐτά. Μηδὲ γὰρ εἴπῃς ἱεροὺς τόπους πάντας τοὺς προσκυρωθέντας ταῖς ἐκκλησίαις, ἤγουν ἐνοικικὰ καὶ λοιπὰ οἰκήματα. Τινὲς γοῦν κατέχοντες ναοὺς κατῴκουν ἀδιαφόρως μετὰ γυναικῶν ἐν τοῖς περὶ αὐτοὺς κατηχουμενείοις καὶ οἰκήμασι μὴ διαστέλλοντες μέσον ἁγίου καὶ βεβήλου, ἀλλ' ἀδιακρίτως τούτοις κεχρημένοι. Ὅθεν καὶ διωρίσαντο οἱ ἅγιοι πατέρες τοὺς οὕτω καταφρονητικῶς κοινοποιοῦντας τοὺς ἱεροὺς τόπους μὴ μόνον ἀπὸ τῶν ἐκκλησιῶν ἐξωθεῖσθαι, κἂν ἔχωσι δίκαια ἐπ' αὐταῖς, ἀλλὰ καὶ ἀπ' αὐτῶν τῶν κατηχουμενείων· διὰ γὰρ τοῦτο οὐδὲ εἰς νομοθεσίαν ἔφερον τὸ ἐκβάλλεσθαι τούτους ἀπὸ τῶν ναῶν, ὡς εἰδότες εἶναι αὐτὸ ἀναμφίβολον. Ὅτι δὲ ἤθελον οἱ ἔχοντες τὰς ἐκκλησίας, κἂν τὰ κατηχουμενεῖα κατέχειν, εἶπον οἱ πατέρες ὡς οὐ μόνον ἀπὸ τῶν ἐκκλησιῶν, ἀλλὰ καὶ ἀπὸ τῶν κατηχουμενείων ἐξωθοῦνται. Καλῶς δὲ οὐκ ἐμνήσθησαν ἐκκλησιῶν, ἀλλὰ ἱερῶν τόπων· τὸ γὰρ καταμένειν μετὰ γυναικὸς ἐν ἐκκλησίᾳ ἀσεβέστατόν ἐστι καὶ οὐδὲ εἰς ἐνθύμησιν ἦλθε τοῖς πατράσι τὸ τολμηθῆναι ὅλως παρά τινος τοιοῦτον ἀσέβημα. Κοινοποιοῦνται δὲ οἱ ἱεροὶ τόποι διὰ τοῦ καταμένειν μετὰ γυναικῶν, δι' ἀλαλαγῆς μελισμάτων ἀσχημόνων καὶ ἀπρεπῶν καὶ διὰ κατασκευῆς παρακελλίων ἢ μαγειρείων ἢ ἄλλων τοιούτων. Τοὺς μέν τοι παραβάτας τοῦ κανόνος, κληρικοὺς μὲν ὄντας, καθαιρεῖσθαι διορίζονται· λαϊκοὺς δέ, ἀφορίζεσθαι. Ἀνάγνωθι καὶ τὸ ιβ' κεφ. τοῦ α' τίτλου τοῦ ε' βιβλίου ὅπερ κατεστρώθη εἰς τὴν ἑρμηνείαν τοῦ οστ' κανόνος· καὶ μὴ ἐναντιωθῇ σοι διδάσκον ὅρια τῆς ἐκκλησίας εἶναι τὰ λουτρὰ καὶ τοὺς κήπους καὶ τὰς στοὰς ταύτης καὶ διὰ τοῦτο μὴ δύνασθαί τινα ἀφέλκειν ἐκ τούτων τοὺς πρόσφυγας· κατὰ τοῦτο γὰρ καὶ μόνον δοκοῦσι καὶ ταῦτα τῆς ἐκκλησίας μέρη, ἐπείτοι γε καὶ αὐτὸ τὸ κεφ. διορίζεται ἐν τούτοις καὶ ὑπνοῦν καὶ ἐσθίειν, ἅπερ εἰς τὸν ναὸν ἐκωλύθησαν γίνεσθαι. Τὸ μέντοι κα' κεφ. τοῦ αὐτοῦ βιβλίου καὶ τίτλου καὶ ἀπὸ τῆς ἐκκλησίας καὶ ἀπὸ τῶν ὅρων αὐτῆς ἐξέλκειν διορίζεται τοὺς ἀνδροφόνους, τοὺς μοιχοὺς καὶ τοὺς ἅρπαγας· τοῖς γὰρ τοιούτοις τόπος ἀσυλίας οὐκ ἔστιν, ὅτι, φησίν, οὐ τοῖς ἀδικοῦσιν, ἀλλὰ τοῖς ἀδικουμένοις οἱ νόμοι βοηθοῦσιν. Ἀνάγνωθι καὶ τὴν ογ' νεαρὰν τοῦ βασιλέως κυροῦ Λέοντος τοῦ φιλοσόφου παρομοίως κολάζουσαν καὶ τοὺς ἐπιτρέποντας τὴν εἰς τὰ κατηχουμενεῖα κατοικίαν.[26]

---

26   Balsamon, commentary on canon 97 of the Council in Trullo, Messis 2020, 507–8.

Places consecrated to God that is divine churches, areas in front of churches (*pronaos*), areas for catechumens and related places are called sacred places. Do not say that every place attributed to a church is a sacred place, such as the buildings it rents and so on. Some people who had churches in their possession lived disrespectfully with women in the premises for catechumens and in other buildings around the churches without differentiating between the sacred and the profane. The Holy Fathers ordered that those who desecrated sacred places with contempt should be expelled not only from the churches (even if they had rights over them), but also from the premises intended for catechumens; it was for this reason that they did not legislate on the expulsion from the churches themselves, because they knew that this would go without saying. Since those who owned the churches wanted to own for themselves at least the premises for the training of catechumens, the Fathers said that they would be expelled not only from the churches but also from the premises for the catechumens. It is good that they did not refer to the churches but to the sacred places; cohabiting with a woman inside a church is a very ungodly thing and the Fathers did not even think that anyone would dare to commit such ungodliness. Sacred places are desecrated, when people live there with women, when they sing shameless and unseemly tunes, and when adjoining rooms, kitchens and other similar buildings are built. They order that the transgressors of the canon, if they are clerics, be deposed and if they are laymen, be deprived of communion. Read also chapter 12, title 1, of book 5, quoted in the commentary to canon 76; do not consider it a contradiction, when it states that the baths, gardens and porticoes are within the inclusive limits of the church and for this reason refugees cannot be removed from there; only in this respect are these parts considered as parts of the church, since the same chapter permits sleeping and eating there, which is forbidden inside the church. Chapter 21 of the same book and the same title decrees that murderers, adulterers and kidnappers are to be removed from the church and its boundaries; there is no place of refuge for these categories of criminals, for, he says, the laws help not those who commit injustice, but those who suffer it. Read also the novel 73 of Emperor Kyr Leo the philosopher, who punishes in the same way those who believe they are allowed to live in the premises for catechumens.

First, it seems clear that Balsamon builds on Zonaras' commentary. He cites the same text from the *Basilica* but also adds his own elements. For example, he cites a law written by Leo VI on the exact same topic: that no one should live with women in the *catèchoumena* (κατηχούμενα) of churches. By adding this other source, Balsamon shows his extensive knowledge of civil law.[27] Leo VI had been very willing to introduce the decisions of canon law into civil law. The Novella 73 represents the introduction in civil law of canon 97 forbidding couples from living in sacred places. Leo VI adds a useful detail: he explains that the *catèchoumena* are in fact the upper galleries in churches. Contrary to Zonaras, he does not identify them as buildings adjoining a church. Leo also tells a story from the recent past: when his father ascended the throne, it was not uncommon for people to live (or at least sleep) there, and Emperor Basil had given a *prostagma* to forbid it. Novella 73 also intends to stop this same practice, whether it concerns a priest living with his wife or laypeople sleeping inside churches. Leo VI also condemns clerics who allow such a practice, which is an indication that these living arrangements had the approval of local clerics and perhaps concerned some of them. Churches provided lodgings for clerics, and since most of them were married, these lodgings were family residences.

Aristenos is the only one of the three canonists who proposes excluding celibates from sleeping inside a church; the two other canonists only exclude couples, and so did Leo VI. They are concerned with sex, which they consider a pollution and a profanation of the church building. This idea that sex and the sacred cannot peacefully coexist is clearly visible in different rules around Eucharistic practices. Communion is forbidden to lay persons who had sex the night before. Consecrating the host is also forbidden to priests who had sex the night before. This notion that sex is polluting and creates an obstacle to a relation with God is so well entrenched that neither Zonaras nor Balsamon imagine that people would deliberately have sex inside a church. They could, however, use other buildings attached to a church, such as the *catèchoumeneia*, which are not considered as sacred.

Leo VI and Balsamon do not use the same word and they do not have the same definition of the area for catechumens. Leo VI, like Zonaras, mentions *catèchoumena* (κατηχούμενα) while Balsamon writes *catechoumeneia* (κατηχουμενεῖα). For Leo, *catèchoumena* are galleries inside a church, and perhaps also for Zonaras, while for Balsamon, they seem to be rooms located outside of the church. Although they refer to catechumens, they were most likely service rooms in the Middle Byzantine Period.

Perhaps inspired by Zonaras, Balsamon's definition of sacred spaces is more inclusive than that of Eusebius of Caesarea. He includes not only the church building (*naos*) but also the narthex (*pronaos*) and the *catechoumeneia*

---

27 Leo VI, Novella 73, eds Noailles & Dain 1944, 260–3.

(κατηχουμενεῖα), which I shall call secondary rooms. Like Zonaras, but in a clearer manner, he relies on civil law to extend rules of purity (no blood, no sex) to a large area outside the church itself. The exclusion of women corresponds to both requirements of ritual purity.

Yet, Balsamon makes a clear distinction between sacred space and ecclesiastical property. Buildings belonging to a church but not attached to it, like houses or shops in the city and farms and lands in the countryside are not considered sacred spaces. The location and a contact with the church itself matter. He considers sacred space any building attached to a church. It seems coherent with the notion of sacred by contact. A space in contact with the church benefits from the sacredness of the church. Sacredness radiates or diffuses in space. If so, where does it stop?

Both Zonaras and Balsamon build on canon 97 to extend sacred space to a larger area than the church itself. Being very learned, and perhaps again inspired by Zonaras, Balsamon knows that another legal tradition concerning asylum can be useful for this purpose to extend sacred spaces outside the church building. The laws on asylum define a perimeter outside the church where it is not legal to arrest refugees.

Asylum in a church is made a law in 419 by Honorius. A perimeter (fifty feet) around the church and the church itself are protected by law: it is now a sacrilege to arrest someone in this area. In this text, the right of asylum is stated as well as the sanctity of churches.[28] While for pagan temples, the sanctuary started with the temenos, for churches also, the protected area starts with the outer doors of the enclosure in the law of 431 signed by Theodosius and sent to Antioch.[29] In Syria and in Asia Minor, *horoi*, boundary stones discovered around sanctuaries were set up to mark the territory under protection.[30] This extension of the area considered out of reach from armed soldiers came in part from the desire to prohibit refugees from sleeping and eating inside churches, while protecting them. The sanctity of churches which were now considered the temple of God—*summi Dei templa* or *sanctissimum Dei templum*—, meant that decent behaviour and a sense of decorum should be maintained at all times inside the *naos*. No banquets, no sex should take place inside a church, no animals could be allowed in a sacred place. Members of the clergy should make sure that the refugees have a place to sleep and to eat outside the church itself. If the refugees refuse to comply, they should be expelled. The constitution also insists on the absence of arms inside the church enclosure. The

---

28 Sirmond 13, "Ex quo loco quisque tenuerit exeuntem, sacrilegi crimen incurrat".
29 CTh. 9, 45, 4 in 431, c.966–8.
30 Feissel 2000, 103; Perrin 1999, 680.

refugees, as well as the soldiers, should not bring weapons inside the sanctuary. The refugees should trust in the power of religion, while armed soldiers should ask the bishop for permission to enter the sacred enclosure. The law of 431 became the reference for matters related to asylum in the Byzantine Empire. It is cited in the Acts of the council of Ephesus[31] and has been included in the *Codex Justinianus* and later in the *Basilica*.[32] The *Basilica* even extended the area under legal protection to include baths, gardens, houses, porticoes and courtyards, and also an area that goes from the church to the limit of the market. In these areas protected by law, one can be a refugee and live there, which means eat and sleep there. It is legally part of the church and sacred in the sense that committing violence in this area would be a crime.

Following this legal tradition, Zonaras and Balsamon make a distinction between buildings attached to the church itself which are sacralised by this contact and other buildings inside a church precinct where the rules are not so strict and where one can eat and sleep. However, they insist that even in these other buildings and in this extended area, it is still important to preserve ritual purity and not allow sexual activity.

Commenting on canon 97 served their goal, but other canons of the council in Trullo also served their wish to control what happens inside church precincts. Two other canons of the council in Trullo, one dealing with merchants selling inside the church enclosure and the second forbidding banquets inside churches, serve their purpose of extending sacred space. Canon 74 forbids eating inside a church, following canon 28 of the council of Laodikeia:

> Ὅτι οὐ δεῖ ἐν τοῖς κυριακοῖς ἢ ἐν ταῖς ἐκκλησίαις τὰς λεγομένας ἀγάπας ποιεῖν καὶ ἔνδον ἐν τῷ οἴκῳ ἐσθίειν καὶ ἀκούβιτα στρωννύειν. Οἱ δὲ τοῦτο ποιεῖν τολμῶντες ἢ παυσάσθωσαν ἢ ἀφοριζέσθωσαν.

> That no one is to hold so-called charity feasts in houses of the Lord or churches (*kyriakois*), or to eat, or to make up banqueting couches inside the <sacred> house. If any persons dare to do this, they shall cease, or they shall be excommunicated.[33]

While commenting on this canon, the three canonists understand the word *kyriakon* differently. For Zonaras and Aristenos, *kyriakon* is another word for the church building, the House of the Lord. For Balsamon, *kyriakon* is a space

---

31 Acts of the Council of Ephesus, ed. Schwartz 1928, 61–5.
32 C.J., 1, 12, 3, ed. Krueger 1906, 65–7.
33 Canon 74, *The Council in Trullo*, ed. trans. Featherstone 1995, 156.

dedicated to God. He explains that every place destined for the Lord is called a *kyriakon*, even if it is not a church, but the area in front of the church or another sacred place. For him, the canon commands that no feasting should take place in churches and related places inside the sacred enclosure. This canon serves his wish to once again extend sacred space from the church itself to an area around the church, even if this interpretation is in contraction with the asylum laws, unless one distinguishes between the solitary eating of asylum seekers and the feasting of a group. At the end of the seventh century, the bishops were also concerned with meals organized after the celebration of liturgical feasts, a practice that often ceased to take place during the Middle Ages, except in few areas, such as Armenia. During Balsamon's lifetime, however, the problem was a different one: feasting, for example, could be organized inside a sacred enclosure by aristocrats to whom a convent had been given in *charistike*.[34] It is very possible that Balsamon has in mind the settlement of aristocrats, along with their lifestyle, inside monastic enclosures. He could also refer to food distributions at church doors, taking place inside church precincts, for saint's festivals.[35] Balsamon does not develop what he means, so we cannot go much further in this direction, but those are possible interpretations.

The second canon which helps him extend the notion of sacred space outside of the church building itself is canon 76 of the council in Trullo:

Ὅτι οὐ δεῖ ἔνδον ἱερῶν περιβόλων καπηλεῖον ἢ βρωμάτων εἴδη προτιθέναι ἢ ἐμπορεύεσθαι.

Ὅτι οὐ χρὴ ἔνδον τῶν ἱερῶν περιβόλων καπηλεῖον ἢ τὰ διὰ βρωμάτων εἴδη προτιθέναι ἢ ἑτέρας πράσεις ποιεῖσθαι τὸ σεβάσμιον τῆς ἐκκλησίας φυλάσσοντας· ὁ γὰρ σωτὴρ ἡμῶν καὶ θεὸς διὰ τῆς ἐν σαρκὶ πολιτείας παιδαγωγῶν ἡμᾶς μὴ ποιεῖν τὸν οἶκον τοῦ Πατρὸς αὐτοῦ ἐμπορίου οἶκον παρεκευλεύσατο· ὃς καὶ τῶν κολλυβιστῶν τὸ κέρμα ἐξέχεε καὶ τοὺς τὸ ἱερὸν κοινοποιοῦντας ἀπήλασεν. Εἴ τις οὖν ἐπὶ τῷ προκειμένῳ ἅλῳ πλημμελήματι, ἀφοριζέσθω.

[That] no one can keep a tavern, nor display victuals, nor transact any commerce within sacred precincts, thus preserving the reverence due to churches. For our God and Saviour, teaching us through his life in the flesh, instructed us to *Make not my Father's house a marketplace* (*Jn 2: 16*); and he poured out the changers money and drove away those who

---

34   Darrouzès 1966, 150–65; Gautier 1975, 77–132; M. Angold 1995; Ahrweiler 1967, 1–27.
35   Caseau 2015, Nourritures terrestres, nourritures célestes. La culture alimentaire à Byzance, Paris, 2015, 224–38.

profaned the temple. If anyone is found to have committed the aforesaid transgression, he shall be excommunicated.[36]

Balsamon comments on this canon in the following manner:

Τὴν ἀνάλογον τιμὴν τῶν ἁγίων ἐκκλησιῶν καὶ τῶν περὶ αὐτὰς συντηροῦντες οἱ θεῖοι πατέρες καὶ μὴ ἀνεχόμενοι ὅλως κοινοῦσθαι παρά τινος τὰ ἱερά, διωρίσαντο μὴ προτίθεθαι βρωματικὰ εἴδη ἔνδον τῶν ἱερῶν περιβόλων μηδὲ καπηλεῖον γίνεσθαι ἐν αὐτοῖς μηδὲ ἁπλῶς πιπράσκεσθαί τι ἔνδον τούτων, ἀλλ᾽ εἶναι ἀνεπικοινώνητα παντελῶς τοῖς ἐμπορευομένοις·[...] Διαφόρων δὲ ἁγιωτάτων πατριαρχῶν προσταξάντων ἀπό τε τοῦ Αὐγουστεῶνος καὶ τῶν προσεχεστέρων μερῶν τῷ προνάῳ τῆς ἁγιωτάτης τοῦ Θεοῦ Μεγάλης Ἐκκλησίας τοὺς τραπεζίτας διωχθῆναι καὶ τοὺς ὀψοπώλας καὶ ὀπωροπώλας καὶ τοὺς λοιποὺς ἐμπόρους, εἶπόν τινες ὡς περιβόλους ἐκκλησιαστικοὺς ὁ κανὼν ὀνομάζει τοὺς προνάους ἑκάστου ναοῦ, οὐ μὴν τὰς φιάλας καὶ τὰ ἕτερα μέρη τῶν θείων ναῶν τὰ συνηνωμένα αὐτοῖς. Τοῖς πλείοσι δὲ τοῦτο οὐκ ἤρεσεν· εἶπον γὰρ ὡς, ἐπεὶ ὁ κανὼν ἐκκλησίας οὐκ ἐμνήσθη (τὸ γὰρ ἐν μεσονάῳ ἢ προνάῳ καπηλεῖον γενέσθαι ἢ ἀγορανόμων συνέδριον οὐδὲ εἰς ἐνθύμησίν τινος χριστιανοῦ ἔλθοι, ὡς ἀσεβέστατον), ἀλλ᾽ ἱερῶν περιβόλων ναοῦ, ὀφείλομεν περὶ τούτων τὴν πᾶσαν εἰσάγειν ἀμφιβολίαν· πάντες δὲ ἐκείνους εἶναι ἱεροὺς περιβόλους εἶπον τοὺς μὴ ἀπολυθέντας εἰς ἀλόγων ζώων καταπάτησιν καὶ ἀλλοτρόπως κοινωθέντας. Ἀπὸ μέντοι τοῦ ιβ´ κεφ. τοῦ α´ τίτ. τοῦ ε´ βιβλίου τοῦ λέγοντος· «Μέχρι τῶν ἐπὶ τῆς δημοσίας ἀγορᾶς τῆς ἐκκλησίας ὅρων τὸ ἀσφαλὲς ἐχέτωσαν οἱ προσφυγόντες τοῖς ἐνδοτέροις λουτροῖς ἢ κήποις ἢ οἰκήμασιν ἢ στοαῖς ἢ αὐλαῖς χρώμενοι καὶ κωλυέσθωσαν ἐντὸς τοῦ ναοῦ ὑπνοῦν ἢ ἐσθίειν»· μὴ εἴπῃς καὶ τὰ λουτρὰ καὶ τοὺς κήπους καὶ τὰς στοὰς τὰς συνηνωμένας ταῖς ἐκκλησίαις ἱεροὺς περιβόλους εἶναι, ὡς ἐντεῦθεν κωλύεσθαι καὶ τὸ προτίθεσθαι ὤνια ἐπ᾽ αὐτοῖς. Ταῦτα γὰρ μέρη μὲν τῆς ἐκκλησίας λογίζονται, ἱεροὶ δὲ περίβολοι οὐ λεχθήσονται· καὶ ὡς κοινὰ μὲν τῆς τιμῆς τῶν ἱερῶν περιβόλων οὐκ ἀξιωθήσονται· διὰ δὲ τὸ τῆς ἐκκλησίας προνόμιον, ὁ ἐξ αὐτῶν ἀφαρπάσας πρόσφυγα κολασθήσεται. Σημείωσαι δὲ ὅτι ἐντὸς μόνου τοῦ ναοῦ ἐσθίειν καὶ πίνειν τοὺς πρόσφυγας κεκώλυται. Σημείωσαι δὲ καὶ τὸν παρόντα κανόνα διὰ τοὺς πραγματευομένους εἰς τὰ μυρεψεῖα καὶ εἰς τὰ κουρισκαρεῖα τῆς ἁγιωτάτης Μεγάλης Ἐκκλησίας, πολλῷ δὲ πλέον εἰς τὰ ἐνδοτέρω ταύτης. Ὡσαύτως σημείωσαι τὸν αὐτὸν κανόνα καὶ διὰ τοὺς ἀπερχομένους εἰς τὰς γινομένας ἑορτὰς καὶ πανηγύρεις ὁπουδήποτε καὶ ποιουμένους ἀφορμὴν πραγματειῶν τὴν προσκύνησιν τοῦ τηνικαῦτα ἑορταζομένου ἁγίου· μεγάλης γὰρ κολάσεώς εἰσιν οἱ τοιοῦτοι ἄξιοι. Καὶ ὁ μέγας

---

36 Canon 76, *The Council in Trullo*, ed. trans. Featherstone 1995, 157–8.

δὲ Βασίλειος ἐν τοῖς ἀσκητικοῖς αὐτοῦ μεγάλως ταῦτα κωλύει. Καὶ ἀνάγνωθι τὸ χωρίον τὸ γράφον οὕτω περὶ τῶν ἐν ταῖς συνόδοις πραγματειῶν λέγον ἐν μέρει ταῦτα· «Οὐ μὴν ἐπειδὴ ἕτεροι προλαβόντες παρέφθειραν τὴν κεκρατηκυῖαν ἐπὶ τῶν ἁγίων συνήθειαν καὶ ἀντὶ τοῦ προσεύχεσθαι τόν τε καιρὸν καὶ τὸν τόπον ποιοῦνται ἀγορὰν καὶ πανήγυριν καὶ ἐμπορίαν· καὶ ἕτερα οὐκ ὀλίγα.

The divine Fathers, in order to preserve the honour due to the holy churches and the spaces around them, and not allowing the sacred places to become common places, ordered that no food should be offered for consumption, no cabaret should be opened, nor should anything be sold inside the sacred precincts; these spaces should be completely forbidden to merchants". [...] Since many of the Most Holy Patriarchs ordered the money-changers, fish and fruit sellers and other traders to be driven out of the Augusteion square and the parts closest to the atrium of the Most Holy Great Church of God, some have said that the canon calls the atria of each church sacred enclosures and not the fountains and other parts that are dependent on the holy churches. This interpretation did not please the majority; they said that, since the canon does not speak of the church (the fact of opening a cabaret inside or in the atrium of a church, or of having a tavern or a gathering of merchants there, does not even cross the mind of a Christian, because it is something very unholy), but of the sacred precincts of a church, we must have serious doubts; they said that sacred enclosures are the places that are not abandoned to the trampling of animals or otherwise desecrated. Reading ch. 12, title 1, book 5, which says: "Those who have taken refuge there and use the indoor baths, gardens, houses, porticoes and courtyards are safe up to the limits of the church which give onto the public market; they are prevented from sleeping and eating in the church", do not say that the baths, gardens and porticoes which are joined to the churches are sacred enclosures, so that the display of goods there is prohibited. These parts are considered as parts of the church, but they will not be called sacred enclosures; and as desacralized parts, they will not be worthy of the honour due to the sacred enclosures, but because of the privileges of the church, whoever removes a refugee from this space will be punished. Note that refugees are only prevented from eating and drinking inside the church. Note also the present canon for those who do business in the shops of the perfumers and barbers at the Most Holy Great Church, much more, for those who work inside. Also note this canon for those who go to the celebrations and festivities anywhere and who turn the worship of the celebrated saint into a business occasion; these are worthy of a heavy punishment. Basil the

Great, in his Ascetics, rigorously prevents this. Read also the passage he wrote on commercial activities during the synods, which says in part: "No, certainly not, since others who have gone before have deviated from the habitual worship of the saints and instead of praying at the proper time and place, they make a market, an assembly and a trade"; and many others still.[37]

In this text (slightly abridged here), Balsamon explains two contemporary attitudes in his time concerning the use of sacred precincts. One favours the use of church precincts as spaces where it is possible to buy and sell, or to find food and organize fairs during saint's festivals. The other attitude preserves the sanctity of the spaces immediately outside churches and lets no such activities take place. It seems clear he is on the side of those who want to clear the complete area around churches of commercial activities and extend the notion of sacred space to these large areas defined for asylum seekers to include gardens and baths. In his time, however, shops were present around Hagia Sophia, and fairs were organized around churches or convents for saint's festivals. He is fully aware that his wishes might not be heard.

∴

To conclude, from the time of Eusebius of Caesarea to the time of Balsamon, the definition of sacred space was refined and degrees of sacredness were defined. Christian authors and authorities all agreed on the utter sanctity of the church altar and the sanctuary area around it. They somewhat disagreed on how other spaces inside and outside of the church buildings were to be used and how sacred they should be considered. During the Early Middle Ages, some churches became the focal points of small cities and trade developed in their shadow. During the middle byzantine period, the expansion of trade and fairs was such that it can explain the reaction of Balsamon. The *Timarion* gives us a glimpse of a fair organized during the feast of saint Demetrius in Thessaloniki.[38] Balsamon probably felt that this evolution desacralized churches and used his comments on past canons to reform the Church and curb practices that he disapproved. He had an austere and monastic viewpoint when it came to rules of behaviour inside church enclosures. He was especially hostile to the presence of women, for fear menstrual blood would defile the places where they

---

37 Balsamon, commentaries on the council in Trullo, in Messis 2020, 410–11.
38 *Timarion*, ed. R. Romano, 1974, 54–5.

stood.[39] He did not wish that husbands and wives lived on the premises inside church precincts, in houses or rooms close to a church or attached to it. In this extension of sacred spaces around churches and this insistence on applying almost the same rules of behaviour inside churches and inside buildings close to churches, he wanted to assert a form of rigorist clerical control.

In his commentary on canon 97, Balsamon is probably mostly concerned by privately owned churches. He wishes to have the same canonical rules apply to public churches and private ones, when private owners of these churches found convenient to manage their property as they saw fit and give rooms attached to the church as their living space to married members of the clergy. We find here a trace of the tensions between members of the higher clergy, mostly bishops who have a spiritual control over all churches and private landowners, who want to control their property and use the facilities as is convenient for them. In this battle, clerics loose, because they cannot control what goes on on private lands. Even in urban areas, when chapels were attached to other buildings, such as aristocratic mansions, it was probably very difficult to assert control over the use of secondary rooms.

Shops were located near churches and fairs were organized in their shadow. The example of trade taking place around the Hagia Sophia also shows an evolution which made churches the focal point of some commercial activities. In order to reform these habits and regain ecclesiastical control over church precincts, he wrote these commentaries, extending the notion of sacred space to large areas outside churches. Balsamon wished that the areas around churches be more strictly under the control of clerics, and to gain power over these areas he declared them sacred space. He wanted ritual purity to be the rule around churches: no sex, no food, no ordinary living and no trade. Had he become patriarch of Constantinople, as was his desire, he may have tried to enforce his understanding of sacred space, but he only became patriarch of a city where he could not have an influence. In Constantinople, perfumers remained in the shadow of Hagia Sophia and continued to spread their fragrances around the most holy church of Byzantium.

Bibliography

Primary Sources
Acts of the Council of Ephesus, *Acta Conciliorum Oecumenicorum*. Ed. E. Schwartz, I, 1, 4. Berlin & Leipzig 1928.

---

39 Viscuso 2005, 317–26.

Apostolic Constitutions, *Les constitutions apostoliques*. Ed. M. Metzger. 3 vol. Paris 1985–1987.

Balsamon, *Commentary on the council in Trullo*, in Ch. Messis (ed.) 2020.

Codex Theodosianus, Corpus Iuris Romani AnteIustiniani, vol. 2. Ed. G. Haenel. Bonn 1842, reimp. Darmstadt 1987.

Codex Justinianus, Corpus Iuris Civilis, t.2. Ed. P. Krueger. Berlin 1906.

Council in Trullo, text and translation in *The Council in Trullo Revisited*. Ed. G. Nedungatt & M. Featherstone. Rome 1995.

Eusebius of Cesarea, *Ecclesiastical History*. Tr. C. Mango, *The Art of the Byzantine Empire, Sources and Documents*. Toronto 1986.

Leo VI, New Laws: Les *Novelles de Léon VI le Sage*. Ed. P. Noailles & A. Dain. Paris 1944.

The Octavius of Minucius Felix. Tr. G. W. Clarke. New York 1974.

Pseudo-Luciano, Timarione. Ed. R. Romano, Naples 1974.

Zonaras, commentary on the Council in Trullo, in Ch. Messis (ed.) 2020.

Secondary Sources

Angold, M. 1995. *Church and Society in Byzantium under the Comneni (1081–1261)*. Cambridge.

Ahrweiler, H. 1967. "Charisticariat et autres formes d'attribution de fondations pieuses aux Xe–XIe siècles", *Zvornik Radova vizantinoloshkog Instituta* 10, 1–27.

Aurell, M. & T. Deswarte (eds) 2005. *Famille, violence et christianisation au Moyen Age, Mélanges offerts à Michel Rouche*. Paris.

Bagnoli, M. et al. (eds) 2011. *Treasures of Heaven: Saints, Relics, and Devotion in Medieval Europe*. New Haven & London.

Bogdanovic, J. 2017. *The Framing of Sacred Space: The Canopy and the Byzantine Church*. Oxford.

Briquel Chatonnet, F. 2013a. "Les églises dans les textes", in Briquel Chatonnet 2013a, 11–40.

Briquel Chatonnet, F. 2013b. *Les églises en monde syriaque*. Paris.

Brown, P., O. Grabar & G. Bowersock (eds) 1999. *Late Antiquity. A Guide to the Postclassical World*. Cambridge, MA.

Caseau, B. 2005. "La place des enfants dans les églises d'Orient (3e–10e siècles)", in Aurell & Deswarte (eds) 2005, 15–27.

Caseau, B. 2008. "Ordinary Objects in Christian Healing Sanctuaries", in Lavan, Swift & Putzeys (eds) 2008, 625–54.

Caseau, B. 2015. *Nourritures terrestres, nourritures célestes: la culture alimentaire à Byzance*. Paris.

Caseau, B. 2021. "Sacred Space and Sensory Experience in Late Antique Churches", in Etlin (ed) *The Cambridge Guide to the Architecture of Christianity*. Cambridge.

Cassingena-Trévedy, F. & I. Jurasz (eds) 2006. *Les liturgies syriaques*. Paris.

Darrouzès, J. 1966. "Dossier sur la charisticariat", in Wirth (ed.) 1966, 150–65.

Feissel, D. 2000. "Les édifices de Justinien au témoignage de Procope et de l'épigraphie" *Antiquité Tardive* 8, 81–104.

Gautier, P. 1975. "Réquisitoire du patriarche Jean d'Antioche contre le charisticariat", *RéB* 33, 77–132.

Khoury, W. & B. Riba 2013. "Les églises de Syrie (IVe–VIIe siècle): essai de synthèse", in Briquel Chatonnet (ed.) 2013b, 41–84.

Krueger, D. 2011. "The Religion of Relics in Late Antiquity and Byzantium", in Bagnoli et al. (eds) 2011, 5–17.

Lassus, J. 1947. *Sanctuaires chrétiens de Syrie*. Paris.

Lavan, L., E. Swift & T. Putzeys (eds) 2008. *Objects in Context, Objects in Use. Material Spatiality in Late Antiquity*. Leiden.

Macrides, R. 1988. "Killing, Asylum and the Law in Byzantium", *Speculum* 63, 509–38.

Messis, Ch. 2020. *Le corpus nomocanonique oriental et ses scholiastes du XIIe siècle (Aristénos, Zonaras, Balsamon)*. Paris.

Markus, R. 1994. "How on Earth Could Places Become Holy? Origins of the Christian Idea of Holy Places", *Journal of Early Christian Studies* 2, 257–71.

Perrin, M. 1999. "Sanctuary", in Brown, Grabar & Bowersock (eds) 1999.

Pitarakis, B. (ed.) 2018. *Life is Short, Art Long. The Art of Healing in Byzantium. New Perspectives*. Istanbul.

Sodini, J.-P. 2006. "Archéologie des églises et organisation spatiale de la liturgie", in Cassingena-Trévedy & Jurasz (eds) 2006, 229–66.

Taft, R. 1998. "Women at Church in Byzantium: Where, When-And Why?", *DOP* 52, 27–87.

Talbot, A.-M. 2002. "Pilgrimage to Healing Shrines: The Evidence of Miracle Accounts", *DOP* 56, 153–73.

Viscuso, P. 2005. "Theodore Balsamon's Canonical Images of Women", Greek, Roman, and Byzantine Studies 45, 317–326.

Yasin, A.-M. 2009. *Saints and Church Spaces in the Late Antique Mediterranean: Architecture, Cult, and Community*. Cambridge.

Wirth, P. (ed.) 1966. *Polychronion*. Heidelberg.

"Dwelling Place and Palace"

The Theotokos as a "Living City" in Byzantine Hymns, Icons and Liturgical Practice

Helena Bodin

The Theotokos is the God-bearing Virgin, the Mother of God and the unwedded Bride of the Orthodox Church, celebrated in contemporary liturgical practice as well as in the historical Byzantium and in its capital Constantinople. She is praised in prayers and hymns of various genres and lengths, probably dating from as early as the third century, and prominent from the fifth or sixth century.[1] Christological issues, closely associated with the theological role played by Mary, resulted in new hymns such as the well-known Akathistos hymn. As a rich source not only of Orthodox Christian piety and theology but also of poetry and verbal imagery, Byzantine hymnography is of vital importance in the study of the symbolic aspects of Byzantine culture and its aesthetics, expressed also in architecture.

The aim of this chapter is to explore the spatial qualities of the verbal imagery of Byzantine hymns that contain descriptions and praise of the Theotokos, by examining in particular verbal images associated with the city. When relevant, the visual imagery of icons will also be included. It follows from Orthodox Christian belief that the Theotokos is represented as a woman, who is paradoxically both a Virgin and the Mother of God, but her characteristics and symbolic functions are also emphasized by means of verbal images of various spatial phenomena, which involve artefacts such as vessels or founts as well as cultured land such as gardens and fields.[2] Furthermore, she is imagined as a city, which is modelled on Jerusalem, the holy city, and simultaneously shares important features with a Byzantine cityscape, possibly Constantinople. She provides a city where citizens can find shelter and protection in hardship. The hymns convey the belief that by bearing and giving birth to God incarnate in Christ, the Theotokos provides the fulfilment of every basic human need. Thereby, verbal images help us understand how the Byzantines

---

1 See Ledit 1976; the entries "Hymns" and "Suub Tuum" in O'Carroll 1990; Mango 2000; Peltomaa 2001; Arentzen 2017.
2 Bodin 2013, 2016.

perceived and conceived the world around them, as the editors of this volume frame the interrelation between images and space.

Against this background, I will present and discuss examples from Byzantine hymnography and Orthodox liturgical practice, where the Theotokos is represented as a city with its various architectural structures, or is praised as a "living city". This particular epithet occurs in praises and greetings addressed to the Theotokos, for example in the many hymns for the Annunciation, the Nativity of Christ, or her Dormition. "Living" in this case is a translation of the Greek word ἔμψυχος, meaning that something possesses life because it has been "enspirited" or "ensouled". The historical context of the origin of these hymns is often the city of Constantinople, while their theological argument addresses the new, heavenly Jerusalem (as described in Revelation). But the hymns also introduce associations with daily urban life in Byzantine cities and towns. While praising the Theotokos, participants in the Orthodox services are offered mental images of a Mediterranean urban milieu, of a complete city with architectural structures, such as walls, ramparts, towers, gates, portals, pillars, springs and fountains serving fresh water, a haven or port, a palace with a throne, or a temple with a sanctuary—a temple which in Christian contexts is interpreted as a church.

When performed during Orthodox services, these verbal images in the hymns become spatialized and acquire liturgical functions. Within the sacred space of the church, this imagined city, personified and patronized by the Theotokos, is modelled on the heavenly city of Jerusalem. Eventually, so this process implies, the spatial verbal images of the city activated within the ritual tradition of the Orthodox Church convey and communicate Byzantine cultural memories, that is culturally based, collective memories of life in the city of the Theotokos, namely the Constantinople of former Byzantine times.

The present chapter has its base in the perspective of intermedial studies, where verbal and visual arts—in this case hymns, homilies, icons, liturgical utensils and church architecture—are understood as necessarily interacting and inseparably intertwined, in a way that creates a totality. Such a perspective is not only productive in postmodern and popular cultural aesthetics, but is also characteristic of historical Byzantine culture and of how it guides Orthodox Christian liturgical practice still today.[3] Furthermore, I have been inspired by recent research, in which sacred space in Byzantium is regarded as participative, and by the implications of the associated verbal imagery as

---

3   See further Bodin 2014, 209–14.

it mediates a collective, cultural memory of the lost city of Constantinople within the liturgical practice.

1 Sacred Space and Sacred Places—*Hierotopy* and *Chora*

One such inspiration is the concept of *hierotopy*, coined by Alexei Lidov.[4] A hierotopy is created whenever hymns, icons, architecture and liturgical performance are combined in a way that activates all the senses. It is helpful in understanding the importance of spatiality in Orthodox Christian tradition, since 'hierotopy' is more precise than the general notion of 'sacred space', which is the common translation of ἱερός τόπος in Greek.[5] It offers therefore a tool for examining the particular kind of spatial creativity which was developed in Byzantine liturgy and which forms a prominent feature of Byzantine aesthetics. In Byzantium, the church was, as Lidov has emphasized, "considered a transparent structure and moving spiritual substance".[6] The spatial imagery in liturgical hymns and art thereby contributes to "destroying the barrier between the stable church (its material body) and the dynamic external milieu outside any physical borders. The inner space of the church could be displayed and re-created in squares and streets [...]".[7]

Nicoletta Isar chooses to discuss sacred space in Byzantium by means of another concept, *chora* (Gr. χώρα). In order to understand the Byzantine use of chora, Isar emphasizes the significance of movement, since the Greek verb related to chora describes effects such as making room for and "generating a particular kind of space".[8] Consequently, the Byzantine chora is defined by Isar as "the sacred space of liturgical participation" or as "a sacred performative space".[9] She maintains that space and movement were conceived *together* in Byzantium. Space and beholder were not detached from each other but paradoxically united in the chora, which was conceived of as "a space of 'sacred containment', from which the modern distinction between contained space and container should be removed".[10] Isar refers to the interpretation of chora

---

4   Lidov 2006a.
5   For examples of Byzantine descriptions of sacred spaces, see Béatrice Caseau's chapter and her illuminating discussion of the varied definitions of sacred space in Byzantium.
6   Lidov 2006a, 44.
7   Ibid. 44.
8   Isar 2009, 41.
9   Ibid. 42, 43.
10 Ibid. 44.

in a discussion of Orthodox icons by Marie-José Mondzain, where it is concluded, that "the content and the container coincide" in the icon.[11] As a result, Isar is able to formulate a general principle of participation guiding the perception of sacred space in Byzantium: "Presence is participative; there is no presence per se, but an experienced presence".[12]

From an historical perspective, the Christian concept of sacred place was first introduced in the early fourth century by Eusebios, bishop of Caesarea, who invited his listeners to praise God in the "new-made city that God has built, which is the church of the living God", as Kathleen McVey has demonstrated in her illuminating article on the emergence of symbolic interpretations of early Christian and Byzantine architecture.[13] McVey gives the example of an Ethiopian prayer used in the daily worship, where Mary, "the God-bearer", is praised as "the spiritual city wherein dwelt God the Most High".[14] Ever since the fourth century, architectural elements have been objects of symbolic and spiritual interpretations. At the time of the early pilgrimages, many Christian places of worship had become regarded as holy, and the sacralisation of church buildings was accompanied by literary descriptions of their splendour in the form of ekphrases as well as hymns.[15]

In a way that corresponds with the conclusions of both Lidov and Isar, McVey underlines that the church buildings not only had symbolic functions but also functioned as "living symbols": "these buildings not only pointed toward another, heavenly reality, they also participated in that reality". They played "a mediating role between matter and spirit" and "from the limited to the limitless".[16] The fact that inner and outer space—the inside of the church and the outside cityscape—interact in Orthodox liturgical practice, as described by the Byzantine concept of chora and realized by the creation of hierotopies, also forms the basis of my own analysis of hymns where the Theotokos is represented as a city, or as buildings, or as elements and structures of a city. Single cases of orations, with the function of sermons, often alluding and referring

---

11   Ibid. 42.
12   Ibid. 44.
13   McVey 2010, 46–47. See also references to Eusebios' writings in the chapters by Béatrice Caseau and Isabel Kimmelfield in this volume.
14   McVey 2010, 61.
15   Ibid. 51.
16   Ibid. 63. This chimes well also with Caseau's chapter, where she finds sacredness in Byzantium to be defined both spatially and temporally, and to radiate or diffuse in space.

to liturgical hymns, are also deployed as examples of how the Theotokos was praised in terms of a city.[17]

2 Constantinople as Theotokoupolis

That church buildings functioned as mediating, living symbols, as McVey puts it, was also the case in Constantinople, where the building of churches dedicated to the Theotokos and the popular veneration of her had increased from the middle of the fifth century, resulting in her role as the defender and protectress of Constantinople during the sixth century, not later than during the reign of Justinian I.[18] Cyril Mango refers to a sermon by Theodore Synkellos from the 620s, where it is said that the city deserved the name Theotokoupolis, since the majority of its many churches were of the Virgin Mary.[19]

An early eighth-century oration by Germanos of Constantinople on the occasion of the consecration of the church where important relics—the holy belt (or girdle) of Mary and the swaddling clothes of Christ—were kept, brings up the mutual interrelation between the Theotokos, the church building, and the city, i.e. Constantinople, surrounding the church where the oration was delivered.[20] After an initial apostrophe of the "city of God" and the "city of the Great King" of which "the divine David" sang, Germanos interprets this city as Mary, the Theotokos.[21] He elaborates on the meaning of such a denomination, which he explains as spiritual: "She indeed is a glorified city; she is a

---

17 See Cunningham 2008a, 17–18, for the close relationship between festal sermons and hymnography.

18 Mango 2000, 22. As Cunningham 2008a, 13–15, notes, this process is related to the church's recognition of Mary's importance in Christological doctrine, after the ecumenical Council of Ephesus 431. On the defensive role played by churches (with holy shrines and springs) dedicated to the Theotokos at peripheral and vulnerable locations, see further Isabel Kimmelfield's chapter.

19 Mango 2000, 19–20.

20 This was the church at Chalkoprateia. See further Arentzen 2020; Cunningham 2008a, 26–27; Shoemaker 2008.

21 Germanos refers to Ps 87.3 (86.3 according to Septuagint). Germanos of Constantinople, "Oration on the Consecration of the Venerable Church of Our Supremely Holy Lady, the Theotokos, and on the Holy Swaddling Clothes of our Lord Jesus Christ", in *Wider Than Heaven*, 2008, 247, section 1. Since the present analysis has been made on the basis of translations, I do not include the original Greek texts here but kindly refer the interested reader to available editions.

Sion that is apprehended by the mind".[22] He is very clear on this point: "She is a city which does not enrol its citizens into the power of an earthly and mortal emperor, but which [dedicates them] to the heavenly One, who delivers them to eternal life and offers his own Kingdom to those who follow him".[23] According to Germanos, both the Theotokos ("designated the living City of Christ the King") and "her house" ("her all-holy church") are appropriately called "a glorified city", since such names "assigned to earthly things [...] preserve the memory of the appellation".[24] Thereby, the verbal imagery of the city functions also as a device for creating and preserving memories. As Germanos continues his oration by praising the swaddling clothes and the belt in a long series of apostrophes, without ever losing sight of the Theotokos, he states further that the city is hers and protected by her belt: "O sacred belt, which surrounds and encompasses your city and keeps it unassailable from barbaric attack!"[25] There is no doubt that the city in Germanos' oration is Constantinople. It is protected and sheltered by the Theotokos and preserving memory by means of the appellations of its churches with important Marian relics, yet it is apprehended as living (i.e. spiritual) and glorified. Constantinople is represented as the city of the Theotokos, and she herself is identified with the city.

Next, we will look into three historical situations or contexts linked to Constantinople. All of them are associated with important Byzantine hymns, where the Theotokos is represented as a city or as structures of a city. All are still important today in Orthodox Christian tradition in its various national contexts. Examples will be taken, firstly, from the Akathistos hymn itself, from the *canon* of the Akathistos hymn, and from several *theotokia*; secondly, from the icon and hymn to the protection of the Theotokos (Gr. σκέπη; ChSl. *pokrov*); and thirdly, from the concept of *chora* and its spatial implications with regard to the Theotokos, as revealed in the former Chora church on the outskirts of Constantinople, by its architecture and icons, and as expressed in the Akathistos hymn.[26]

---

22 Ibid. 247, section 2.
23 Ibid. 248, section 2.
24 Ibid.
25 Ibid. 251, section 7. Arentzen 2020 discusses Germanos' sermon in detail in relation to ideas of clothing and the agency of things.
26 For explanations of the genres of Byzantine hymnography, their history and liturgical performance, see Wellesz 1961 and Parry 1999.

3   The Akathistos Hymn and *Theotokia*

The origin of the Akathistos hymn, written in the genre of a *kontakion*, is disputed with regard to both place and time, but it undoubtedly provides a treasure trove of metaphors for the Theotokos, perhaps as early as from the fifth century.[27] Its focus is on her significance in the economy of salvation.[28]

The Akathistos hymn is characterized by its so-called *chairetisms*, the repeated greeting of the Virgin as the "unwedded bride", but spatial verbal images of the Theotokos are also abundant. Some, such as the temple, the tabernacle and the ark, all signifying places where God was present according to Hebrew scripture, draw on typological interpretations of the Old Testament.[29] In Christian tradition they were understood as prefigurations of Mary's womb, where God was incarnated. The Virgin is also greeted as a prefiguration of the Christian baptismal font—as a laver, bowl or vessel, all being various kinds of *container*.[30] When she is greeted as a ladder or a bridge, it is her *mediating* function between the spaces of earth and heaven that is activated instead.[31] Furthermore, there are several spatial verbal images in the Akathistos hymn particularly associated with a city and the shelter it provides, since the Virgin is represented as a rampart, pillar, gate and tower, even as "the Protection of the world" (Σκέπη τοῦ κόσμου).[32] She is also greeted as a haven, a structure that characterizes cities like Constantinople that are situated by the sea.[33]

In most of these examples, the Virgin is meant to fulfil the spiritual aspect of the actual building or structure, which functions as the vehicle of the metaphor. She is greeted, for example, as "Haven for those who fare on the sea of life", "Pillar of virginity", "Gate of salvation", "the unshakeable Tower of the Church", and "a living temple".[34] Buildings and structures such as walls, pillars, gates, towers, temples and havens are brought to mind while the hymn is

---

27   For the Akathistos hymn, its genre and origin, see Wellesz 1957 and Peltomaa 2001. (The early dating is the conclusion of Peltomaa, ch. 4 and p. 216.) For its metaphors, see Maguire 2010, 189–90, 193; Peltomaa 2001, 116–25.
28   See Peltomaa 2001, 107.
29   McVey 2010, 40. For an English translation in liturgical use, see The Akathist hymn to the Theotokos, oikos ψ, in *The Service of the Akathist Hymn*. For the Greek text, see Wellesz 1957; Peltomaa 2001.
30   The Akathist hymn to the Theotokos, oikoi φ and ρ, in *The Service of the Akathist Hymn*, 1991.
31   Ibid. oikos γ.
32   Ibid. oikoi τ, ψ, and λ.
33   Ibid. oikos ρ.
34   Ibid. oikoi ρ, τ, and ψ.

performed. These architectural structures form an imagined cityscape, created by the liturgical performance within the church or chapel, which is situated in turn in the surrounding real city, where such buildings were part of daily life in Byzantine times.

A new *prooimion* was composed and attached to the Akathistos hymn as a thanksgiving after the upheaval of a difficult siege of Constantinople in the seventh or eighth century.[35] This new introductory strophe greets the Theotokos as the "Champion General" (Τῇ Ὑπερμάχῳ Στρατηγῷ).[36] Evidently, the Theotokos is regarded as the patroness of Constantinople in this hymn, as Vasiliki Limberis and Bissera V. Pentcheva have demonstrated.[37] The added prooimion of victory and triumph is essentially an *epinikion*, composed as a speech act performed by the city itself: "To you, our leader in battle and defender, O Theotokos, I, your city, delivered from sufferings, ascribe hymns of victory and thanksgiving". By saying "I, your city", the city dedicates not only hymns but even itself to the Theotokos—in the Akathistos hymn, it presents itself as *her* city. The city of Constantinople praises the Theotokos, who, for *her* part, is represented as an imagined city within the hymn, by means of verbal images involving buildings and structures.

When all the twenty-five strophes of the Akathistos hymn are taken into consideration, that is the prooimion together with its *oikoi* and *kontakia*, two separate cities, different yet overlapping, seem to be activated. One is the real city of Constantinople, miraculously delivered from siege and sufferings. It was in this city that the original liturgical performance of the whole Akathistos hymn took place, and it is also this city which proclaims its "hymns of victory and thanksgiving" to the Theotokos in gratitude for her defence of it in battle. The other is the spiritual city, which is created anew by the chanting of the Akathistos hymn whenever it is performed, even far away from Constantinople in space and time.[38] The performance of the Akathistos hymn thus creates a hierotopy, where the collective, cultural memory of the historical city of Constantinople mingles and overlaps with the spiritual city offered by the many epithets of the Theotokos.

---

35 See Pentcheva 2006, 47, for an overview of this discussion and further references.
36 The Akathist hymn to the Theotokos, kontakion (prooimion), in *The Service of the Akathist Hymn*, 1991.
37 Limberis 1994; Pentcheva 2006.
38 On these double functions of space—the real vs spiritual city— see also Kimmelfield's chapter (with further references), exemplifying how the public space of Constantinople was transformed into religious space.

Even later, in the ninth century, a new hymn written by Joseph the Hymnographer was dedicated to the Akathistos hymn—a hymn was created in order to celebrate another hymn. It was composed in the genre of a *canon*, consisting of eight *odes* with several *troparia*, and was added to a special service celebrated in Lent, where the Akathistos hymn is traditionally performed, in early springtime before Easter. Spatial verbal images of the Theotokos associated with the city are repeated also in this canon: the unwedded bride, that is the Theotokos, is explicitly greeted as the "city of the King", as his "dwelling place and palace", as a gateway and portal, and as a port and haven.[39] In one single phrase she is represented as "the shelter and defence, the wall and rampart".[40]

Spatial verbal images of the Theotokos, originating from the Akathistos hymn, occur also in hymns such as the kontakia by Romanos the Melodist from the first half of the sixth century, as well as in festal sermons and orations like the ones performed by Germanos of Constantinople (quoted above). Romanos the Melodist's kontakion on the Nativity of Christ concludes with the Theotokos' prayer, in which she characterizes herself as "a mighty fortress" and rampart.[41] Similar phrases reverberate in Germanos' oration: "May we have you as our strength and help, wall and rampart, harbour and safe refuge!"[42] In yet another oration, Germanos asks for the right words of praise and finds, among several others: "This one, the hallowed temple of God!" and "This one, the gate facing east [...]".[43]

Furthermore, these spatial verbal images are easily recognized in numerous later *theotokia*. These are very short hymns, consisting of only a single strophe each, which elaborate on the role played by the Theotokos in relation to the feast in question. Again, the door or gate, the wall, the rampart and shelter, as well as the tranquil haven, are present—all metaphors or metonymies used as qualifiers for the Theotokos. For example, in theotokia from the *Pentecostarion*, the liturgical book which covers the joyful hymns sung between Easter Sunday

---

39   The canon of the Akathist hymn, ode 5, troparion 4; ode 1, troparion 2; ode 3, troparion 4; ode 6, troparion 3, in *The Service of the Akathist Hymn*, 1991.
40   Ibid. ode 8, troparion 5.
41   Romanos the Melodist, "The Nativity I", 23, in *Sacred Song from the Byzantine Pulpit*, 1995, 58. For this phrase, see also Romanos' kontakion "On the Nativity of the Virgin Mary", no. 35, oikos ι, in *Sancti Romani Melodi Cantica: Cantica Genuina*, 1963, 279–80.
42   Germanos of Constantinople, "Oration on the Consecration of the Venerable Church of Our Supremely Holy Lady, the Theotokos, and on the Holy Swaddling Clothes of our Lord Jesus Christ", in *Wider Than Heaven*, 252, section 8.
43   Germanos of Constantinople, "Oration on the Annunciation", in *Wider Than Heaven*, 242 and 243, section 6.

and Pentecost, the Virgin-and-Theotokos is repeatedly praised as a wall, a haven, a rampart, gate and shelter: "Be thou my protection and mine unshaken wall, O only Mother of God";[44] "Thee do we have as a wall and a haven";[45] "O all-holy Mother of God, thou rampart of Christians";[46] "Impassable gate of the Lord, do thou rejoice. Rejoice, O rampart and shelter for them that hasten to thee. Tranquil haven and pure Maiden [...]".[47]

While these verbal images are usually—and correctly—regarded as symbols of the spiritual qualities of the Theotokos, my point is rather to emphasize that they contain in addition historical and material, architectural referents to the real city, which surrounded the church where the services were performed. The Akathistos hymn, with its special connection to Constantinople, the city that was successfully rescued from siege by the Theotokos, according to the hymn, is a particularly important source in this respect for later theotokia, together with the biblical texts referred to by such hymns.

4 Pokrov—The Protection of the Theotokos

The celebration of Pokrov, with its particular connection with the Blachernai church, is a feast in the Russian-Orthodox calendar. It is closely associated with the city of Constantinople and inspired by St Andrew the Fool's vision of how the Theotokos spread her veil (more precisely the μαφόριον) over the congregation in the Holy Casket (Ἁγία Σορός) at Blachernai, as narrated in his Life, composed in the tenth century.[48] *Pokrov* is a Church Slavonic word equivalent to σκεπή in Greek. Both are translated as "protection", in the sense of "being covered".[49] The feast of Pokrov therefore concerns the "Protection of the Theotokos", though it is often translated into English as the "Intercession of

---

44   Wednesday of Mid-Pentecost, matins, theotokion, in *The Pentecostarion*, 1990.
45   The Saturday of Souls, Friday vespers, theotokion, in *The Pentecostarion*, 1990.
46   Tuesday of the Blind Man, matins, theotokion, in *The Pentecostarion*, 1990.
47   Sunday of the Blind Man, Great vespers, theotokion, in *The Pentecostarion*, 1990.
48   See "The vision of the Mother of God at Blachernaie" in the Greek edition and translation of Rydén 1995, lines 3732–3758 (p. 253–4). For the maphorion at Blachernai, see also Kimmelfield's chapter. Wortley 2005 provides a valuable survey of the Marian relics at Constantinople.
49   Shalina 2005, 367 et passim, discusses the interrelation between the St Andrew the Fool's vision of the Theotokos' protection (ChSl. *pokrov*, Gr. σκεπή) and the liturgical singing of the Akathistos hymn, in which the Virgin is praised as "the Protection of the world" (Σκεπή τοῦ κόσμου, as quoted above), since they both took place at Blachernai, in the chapel Hagia Soros.

the Theotokos". The Russian icon of Pokrov depicts how the Theotokos spreads her veil as a cover over the whole city, to offer it protection (Figure 22.1).

In this context, the actual protected space may be not only the original city of Constantinople, but any town in Rus' where Pokrov is celebrated. After the Christianization of Rus' from Byzantium, several of its churches were dedicated to the Theotokos, particularly to her Dormition (ChSl. *Uspenie*) but also to Pokrov, a feast which is documented since the late twelfth and thirteenth centuries and celebrated on 1 October.[50] In the troparion, composed in Church Slavonic, of the feast of Pokrov, the faithful 'we' of the hymn cry out to the Theotokos: "Encompass us beneath the precious veil of your protection".[51]

In this hymn, there is no architectural structure—neither a wall nor a rampart—that functions as a metaphor for the protection of the Theotokos. Instead it is her veil, a piece of textile from her own dress, usually covering her body, which protects the city. The image of this veil, both in the hymn and in the icon, deepens further the relationship between the Theotokos and the city of Constantinople. Their symbolical identity is emphasized because the same piece of textile that usually covers and protects *her* body is chosen to protect the city.

In the context of the iconographic motif of Pokrov, it is also interesting to note that textiles, for example those used in baldachins, conventionally appear in the art of Orthodox icons as devices symbolizing and visualizing certain situations going on *inside* a building.[52] Thus it comes about that when the Theotokos is depicted spreading her veil as a protection over the city, the same conventional sign is used as when a room or indoor space is represented in Orthodox iconography. The open, outdoor space of the city becomes covered and delimited by the veil of the Theotokos and forms a protected inner room, a sheltered space. In the artistic and visual imagery of the icon of Pokrov, this protected space beneath the veil of the Theotokos represents the city. In the original and literary historical context of the Life of St Andrew the Fool, it was

---

50 Cf. Spasskii 2008, 362, who reflects that Rus' accepted the Patroness (*Pokrovitel'nitsa*) of the Byzantine capital as the Intercessor (*Zastupnitsa*) and Protection (*Pokrov*) of all cities and of the whole country. For thorough studies of how the celebration of Pokrov and its special iconography evolved in Rus', see Pliukhanova 2008, Shalina 2005, 349–382, and Spasskii 2008, 357–71.

51 English translation of the troparion to the Protection of our Most Holy Lady the Mother of God and Ever-Virgin Mary from The Orthodox Church in America, https://oca.org/saints/troparia/2016/10/01/102824-the-protection-of-our-most-holy-lady-the-mother-of-god-and-ever.

52 For the conventions of icon painting, its spatial organization, semiotics and semantics, see Uspensky 1976.

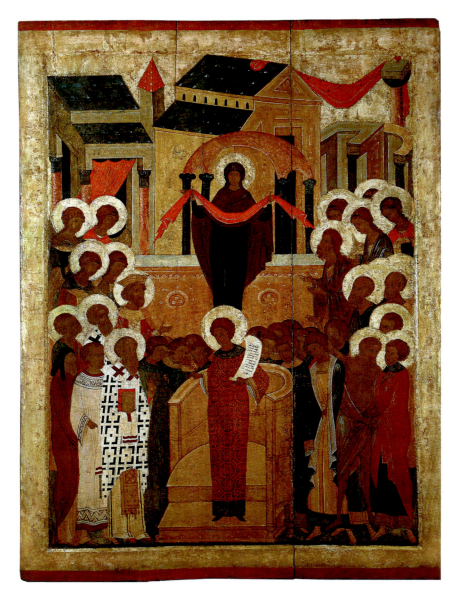

FIGURE 22.1 "Encompass us beneath the precious veil of your protection". *Pokrov* (Protection of the Theotokos). Russian icon, 15th c., Vladimir-Suzdal Museum
PHOTOGRAPH FROM WIKIMEDIA COMMONS. PUBLIC DOMAIN. (HTTPS://COMMONS.WIKIMEDIA.ORG/WIKI/FILE:POKROV_(15TH_C.,_VLADIMIRO-SUZDAL_MUSEUM).JPG)

identified with "The City", that is Constantinople, but in a few centuries, the protection beneath her veil had been distributed particularly to the towns of Rus'. Thereby it became established as what may be regarded as a hierotopy, created as often as the feast of Pokrov is celebrated according to the Russian-Orthodox calendar.

5 Partaking in the *Chora*

In Byzantine hymns, the Theotokos is often presented and represented not only by verbal imagery such as spatial metaphors and metonymies, but also by spatial paradoxes and oxymora. In the well-known hymn, "In Thee, O Full of grace, doth all creation rejoice", corresponding to a likewise well-known iconography (Figure 22.2), the womb of the Theotokos is spatially and paradoxically described as "wider than the heavens",[53] since it circumscribes the only one who is not possible to circumscribe,[54] that is, God depicted here as Christ incarnate.

A similarly complex understanding of the circumscribing and containing function of the womb of the Theotokos is expressed in the Akathistos hymn, where she is represented as the *chora* (Gr. χώρα), the dwelling place and the container of God. Simultaneously, however, God is also mentioned as being impossible to contain, as when the Virgin is greeted as "Container of the Uncontainable God" (Χαῖρε, Θεοῦ ἀχωρήτου χώρα).[55]

This spatial aspect of the Theotokos as *chora* is also relevant to representations of her as a city, since the concept of chora is of symbolic and ritual importance in the Chora church, situated in the former outskirts of Constantinople and restored, renovated and richly adorned by the Byzantine statesman and scholar Theodore Metochites in the early fourteenth century. As Robert Ousterhout has suggested in his explanatory reading of the adornments, icons, architecture and surroundings of the Chora church, the word χώρα may refer to a field, in this case the fields surrounding the church.[56] However, according to Ousterhout, χώρα may also refer to the Theotokos herself, since she is

---

53   English translation of Oktoechos, tone 8, theotokion, from St. Sergius of Radonezh Russian Orthodox Cathedral, http://www.st-sergius.org/services/oktiochos/8-1.pdf. This hymn functions also as a megalynarion in the context of the Liturgy of St Basilios.
54   Cf. "the Uncircumscribed Word". The Akathist hymn to the Theotokos, oikos o, in *The Service of the Akathist Hymn*, 1991.
55   For this English translation, see Ousterhout below. The Akathist hymn to the Theotokos, oikos o, in *The Service of the Akathist Hymn*, 1991, renders it a little differently.
56   Ousterhout 2002, 11. For the importance of Constantinople's peripheries for the development of its religious topography, see Kimmelfield's chapter.

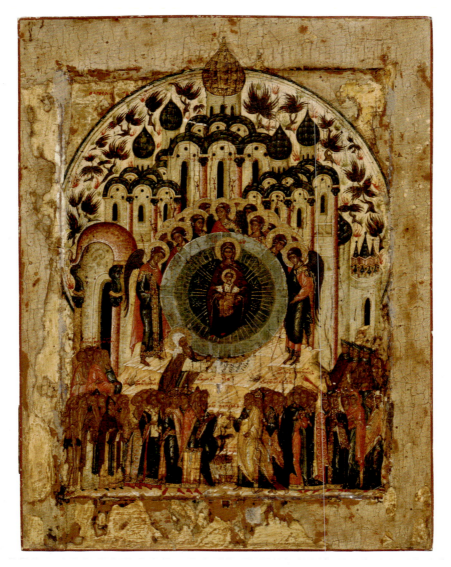

FIGURE 22.2 "In Thee, O Full of grace, doth all creation rejoice". *O Tebe raduetsia*. Russian icon, last quarter of 16th c., Novgorod (?). NMI 297
PHOTOGRAPH @NATIONALMUSEUM, STOCKHOLM

represented in the Blachernitissa icon inside and above the main entrance to the church with Christ in her womb, and with the inscription ἡ Χώρα του Ἀχωρήτου ("Dwelling-place of the Uncontainable" or "Container of the

Uncontainable").⁵⁷ However, as Ousterhout suggests, there is yet a third meaning of χώρα in this church. It may also refer to Christ, as the inscription in the icon of Christ Pantocrator above the door to the inner narthex states. In a quotation taken from the Psalms, Christ is given the epithet of the "land of the living", or "Dwelling-place of the Living", that is, in Greek, the *chora* of the living.⁵⁸

Again, we experience an important spatial verbal image of the Theotokos which functions on several metaphorical and real levels: She is represented as a chora, a container, namely the "Container of the Uncontainable", thereby containing Christ as God incarnate, who thus takes on himself the spatial qualities of a chora, "the land of the living". Moreover, these aspects are revealed in architecture, mosaics and hymns in a church situated in the chora, "in the fields", the fields which welcome the participants of the service when they leave the church. From the chora, a chora has been born, and this event is celebrated in the chora. It comes as no surprise then that Lidov has examined the Chora church as a prominent hierotopy.⁵⁹

This consciously intended, paradoxical relationship between the Theotokos, Christ and the space in which the church is situated is certainly very Byzantine in essence. Similar cases of the use of double or even multiple referents in Byzantine hymnography have been interpreted by Tania Velmans as a hesitation between the container and the contained,⁶⁰ and Thomas Arentzen have discussed examples in the poetic language of Romanos the Melodist in terms of a deliberate ambiguity, concluding that Mary and Christ "share metaphors".⁶¹ As mentioned above, the particular complexity of the Byzantine concept of chora has also been thoroughly discussed by Nicoletta Isar.

The applications of the concept of chora, not only in hymns but also in the Byzantine architectural and iconographical design of the Chora church, would seem to create an exceptionally multifaceted paradox, where level upon level of visual and verbal images collapse into a *mise-en-abyme*, or where the interpreter becomes engaged in a game like with Chinese boxes or Russian nesting dolls. But according to Isar, this device should be recognized rather as an example of how the Byzantines understood space: as movement, and as presence made real by means of experience and participation.⁶² There cannot be any sacred space without its partakers. The oxymoron from the Chora church and

---

57   Ibid. 21, 23 and 27 (Fig. 5).
58   Ibid. 21, 23 and 25 (Fig. 4).
59   Lidov 2006a, 39f.
60   Velmans 1968, 127.
61   Arentzen 2017, 127–28.
62   Isar 2009, 44. See further above.

the Akathistos hymn, "Container of the Uncontainable God", is therefore not primarily an example of theological wit. Instead, it reveals how movement and activity are preferred to containment and stasis in Byzantine aesthetics, and how within Byzantine thought space depends on sense experience and participation, both of which are necessary for the hierotopy and the chora, as these concepts have been introduced and discussed by Lidov and Isar, respectively.

This is also true of the many spatial verbal images for the Theotokos found in Byzantine hymnography. As we have seen, she is represented by means of a variety of places and spaces, such as a garden, a haven, or a city, but that is not enough. She is also the active hostess who invites the believers into her garden,[63] and when she is represented as a haven, it is a haven for "those who fare on the sea of life",[64] a phrase that highlights the fact that this is not a closed or barred haven, but one that offers refuge to humans. Since Byzantine women were surrounded by many restrictions and could be excluded from sacred spaces because of rules of purity, as Béatrice Caseau discusses in her chapter, it is the more thought-provoking that Constantinople's "Champion General" was the Theotokos herself and that the city was protected by a sacred bulwark consisting of her female clothing as relics. When the imagined city of the Theotokos emerges through the spatial verbal imagery in the hymns, performed by the praying congregation, deacon and choir taking part in the Orthodox service, as they praise the Theotokos as a tower, a wall, a palace and rampart, all the participants are invited to seek refuge and shelter within her city. The "living city" of the Theotokos, modelled on the historical Constantinople and the utopian eschatological New Jerusalem, is created anew every time an Orthodox liturgical performance is set in motion, within what Lidov would call a hierotopy and Isar a sacred space or chora.

∴

In Byzantine hymnography the city would seem to function as a spatial paradigm, similar to the concept of chora in Byzantine aesthetics: the Theotokos is represented *as* a city, while she is praised *by* the city itself *within* the city. By means of the metaphorical cityscape created by the hymns praising the Theotokos, an imagined, spiritual, heavenly city is evoked. As has been demonstrated, however, the praising of the Theotokos as a "living city" in hymns and sermons not only carries theological meanings but also activates the Byzantine

---

63 Bodin 2013, 144.
64 The Akathist hymn to the Theotokos, oikos ρ, in *The Service of the Akathist Hymn*, 1991.

city of Constantinople as an enspirited, "living" city in the minds and cultural memory of Orthodox Christians. Since Constantinople is still claimed by Orthodox Greeks as their holy city, as well as by Russian Orthodox pilgrims as a major site, Byzantine verbal imagery, aesthetics and architecture continue to bear not only significant religious impact but also ideological force.

Bibliography

Primary Sources

The Akathistos Hymn. Ed. E. Wellesz, Monumenta musicae Byzantinae. Transcripta. Copenhague 1957.

The Pentecostarion. Tr. the Holy Transfiguration Monastery. Boston, MA 1990.

Romanos the Melodist. *Sacred Song from the Byzantine Pulpit*. Tr. R. J. Schork. Gainesville 1995.

Sancti Romani Melodi Cantica: Cantica Genuina. Ed. P. Maas & C. A. Trypanis. Oxford 1963.

St Sergius of Radonezh Russian Orthodox Cathedral, liturgical resources: http://www.st-sergius.org/services/oktiochos/8-1.pdf Accessed 2021–05–30.

The Orthodox Church of America, "The Protection of our Most Holy Lady the Mother of God and Ever-Virgin Mary—Troparion & Kontakion": https://oca.org/saints/troparia/2016/10/01/102824-the-protection-of-our-most-holy-lady-the-mother-of-god-and-ever Accessed 2021–05–30.

The Service of the Akathist Hymn. Tr. the Holy Transfiguration Monastery. Boston, MA 1991.

Wider Than Heaven: Eighth-Century Homilies on the Mother of God. Tr. M. B. Cunningham. Crestwood, NY 2008.

Secondary Sources

Arentzen, T. 2017. *The Virgin in Song: Mary and the Poetry of Romanos the Melodist*. Philadelphia.

Arentzen, T. 2020. "Conversing with Clothes: Germanos and Mary's Belt", in Frank, Holman & Jacobs (eds) 2020, 57–76.

Bodin, H. 2013. "'Paradise in a Cave': The Garden of the *Theotokos* in Byzantine Hymnography", in Bodin & Hedlund (eds) 2013, 128–47.

Bodin, H. 2014. "'Into golden dusk': Orthodox icons as objects of late modern and post-modern desire", in Nilsson & Stephenson (eds) 2014, 201–16.

Bodin, H. 2016. "'Rejoice, Spring': The Theotokos as a Fountain in the Liturgical Practice of Byzantine Hymnography", in Shilling & Stephenson (eds) 2016, 246–64.

Bodin, H. & R. Hedlund (eds) 2013. *Byzantine Gardens and Beyond*. Uppsala.

Cunningham, M. B. 2008a. "Introduction", in Cunningham 2008b, 13–51.

Cunningham, M. B. (ed.) 2008b. *Wider Than Heaven: Eighth-century Homilies on the Mother of God.* Crestwood, NY.

Ćurčić, S. & E. Hadjitryphonos (eds) 2010. *Architecture as Icon: Perception and Representation of Architecture in Byzantine Art.* New Haven & London.

Di Salvo, M. G., G. Moracci & G. Siedina (eds) 2008. *Nel mondo degli Slavi: Incontri e dialoghi tra culture. Studi in onore di Giovanna Brogi Bercoff.* Vol. 1–2. Firenze.

Frank, G., S. R. Holman & A. S. Jacobs (eds) 2020. *The Garb of Being: Embodiment and the Pursuit of Holiness in Late Ancient Christianity.* New York.

Grabar, A. et al. (eds) 1968. *Synthronon: Art et Archéologie de la fin de l'Antiquité et du Moyen Age.* Paris.

Isar, N. 2009. "Chôra: Tracing the Presence", *Review of European Studies* 1.1, 39–55.

Ledit, J. 1976. *Marie dans la liturgie de Byzance.* Paris.

Lidov, A. 2006a. "Hierotopy: The Creation of Sacred Spaces as a Form of Creativity and Subject of Cultural History", in Lidov (ed.) 2006b, 32–58.

Lidov, A. (ed.) 2006b. *Hierotopy: The Creation of Sacred Spaces in Byzantium and Medieval Russia.* Moscow.

Limberis, V. 1994. *Divine Heiress: The Virgin Mary and the Creation of Christian Constantinople.* London.

Maguire, H. 2010. "Metaphors of the Virgin in Byzantine Literature and Art", in Rhoby & Schiffer (eds) 2010, 189–94.

Mango, C. 2000. "Constantinople as Theotokoupolis", in Vassilaki (ed.) 2000, 16–25.

McVey, K. 2010. "Spirit Embodied: The Emergence of Symbolic Interpretations of Early Christian and Byzantine Architecture", in Ćurčić & Hadjitryphonos (eds) 2010, 39–72.

Nilsson, I. & P. Stephenson (eds) 2014. *Wanted: Byzantium. The Desire for a Lost Empire.* Uppsala.

O'Carroll, M. (ed.) 1990 [1982]. *Theotokos: A Theological Encyclopedia of the Blessed Virgin Mary.* Collegeville, MN.

Ousterhout, R. 2002. *The Art of the Kariye Camii.* London.

Parry, K. et al. (eds) 1999. *The Blackwell Dictionary of Eastern Christianity.* Oxford.

Peltomaa, L. M. 2001. *The Image of the Virgin Mary in the Akathistos Hymn.* Leiden.

Pentcheva, B. V. 2006. *Icons and Power: The Mother of God in Byzantium.* University Park, PA.

Pliukhanova, M. 2008. "V poiskakh istoricheskogo istochnika (Sluzhba Pokrovu)", in Di Salvo, Moracci & Siedina (eds) 2008. Vol. 2, 437–46.

Rhoby, A. & E. Schiffer (eds) 2010. *Imitatio–Aemulatio–Variatio: Akten des internationalen wissenschaftlichen Symposions zur byzantinischen Sprache und Literatur (Wien, 22.–25. oktober 2008).* Wien.

Rydén, L. (ed.) 1995. *The Life of St Andrew the Fool.* Vol. II. Uppsala.

Shalina, I. A. 2005. *Relikvii v vostochnokhristianskoi ikonografii*. Moskva.

Shilling, B. & P. Stephenson (eds) 2016. *Fountains and Water Culture in Byzantium*. Cambridge.

Shoemaker, S. J. 2008. "The Cult of Fashion: The Earliest *Life of the Virgin* and Constantinople's Marian Relics", *DOP* 62, 53–74.

Spasskii, F. G. 2008. *Russkoe liturgicheskoe tvorchestvo*. Moskva.

Uspensky, B. 1976. *The Semiotics of the Russian Icon*. Ed. S. Rudy. Lisse.

Vassilaki. M. (ed.) 2000. *Mother of God: Representations of the Virgin in Byzantine Art*. Milano.

Velmans, T. 1968. "L'iconographie de la 'Fontaine de Vie' dans la tradition Byzantine à la fin du moyen âge", in Grabar et al. (eds) 1968, 119–34.

Wellesz, E. 1961. *A History of Byzantine Music and Hymnography*, 2nd ed. Oxford.

Wortley, J. 2005. "The Marian Relics at Constantinople", *Greek, Roman, and Byzantine Studies* 45, 171–87.

The Development of Religious Topography at Constantinople in the Fourth to Seventh Centuries

Isabel Kimmelfield

Rome's Christian topography developed gradually in the early centuries of the new religion, often within an environment that was less than favourable. The city's religious topography reflected this fact: many of its early important shrines and sites of worship were located outside of the city centre, often beyond the walls, on or near the burial sites of martyrs. As a result, by the time Christianity gained a central and protected place in the empire in the fourth century, an entire way of worship and religious identity had developed at the city's periphery.

But Constantinople, founded as Constantine's eponymous capital on the site of a relatively small Greek city, had no such Christian heritage. The main churches built under Constantine and his immediate successors—Hagia Eirene, Hagia Sophia, and the Holy Apostles (the last two not consecrated until after his death in 360 and 370 respectively)—were possibly the city's first Christian churches, and later legislation under Theodosius I and his successors explicitly banned heretical worship within the city walls.[1] Christianity was thus visible in the centre of urban topography from the city's early years and within a century, heretical (a changing definition) and non-Christian worship had been pushed to the urban periphery, just as Christianity had long found itself excluded at Rome and other cities.

But in the late fourth and early fifth centuries, Constantinople began to develop a tradition of extramural shrines and related patterns of worship, often involving extended processions into the suburbs. This paper will argue that this development—precisely during the period in which the city's Christian identity was being reinforced—suggests that a central urban core of Christian buildings was not considered sufficient to give the capital a truly Christian character. Extramural worship had become a key part of Christian religious identity during the centuries in which worship was perforce

---

1 *Codex Theodosianus*, 16.5.6.

extramural. But Constantinople lacked Rome's Christian heritage, both in the form of long-established worship sites, and in the form of local martyrs around whose *martyria* such extramural shrines could have been based. The importance of peripheral worship to Christians was reflected at Constantinople in a process that at times appeared to emulate the older Christian topography of Rome, while at other times followed a uniquely Constantinopolitan model, which drew from the city itself more than from its Christian heritage.

I divide my study of this phenomenon into two rough chronological periods: the first focussed on the fourth and early fifth centuries, when Roman traditions of civic urban space confronted new Christian interpretations of this space and its use; the second period traces the development of extramural shrines following the initial construction and consolidation of Christian urban topography at Constantinople, from the late fifth century to the early seventh century. In this period, I argue that extramural shrines, no longer needed to shore up a developing Christianisation of the urban space, and instead began to take on more civic roles as spiritual defenders of the city, as well as becoming important features of one of the great centres of Christian pilgrimage. Throughout I will ask, what was the function and meaning of this extramural religious topography? And how did a network of suburban shrines at once both reflect and contribute to Constantinople's particular Christian identity and topography in the early Byzantine period?

1 Worship outside the Walls: Old Rome and New

With the urban core of Rome dominated by important civic monuments—a civicism that was underpinned by religious practices—there was limited space for Christianity to occupy in the city centre in its early centuries. Instead, the religion remained on the urban periphery with early Christian worship at Rome often taking place within private homes. Around the late second or early third centuries, the first exclusively Christian cemeteries appeared in the extramural regions of the city. Here Christian funerary rites could be conducted in anticipation of future resurrection.[2] Martyrs were also naturally buried beyond the walls and although prior to the reign of Constantine these sites were not visited by numerous worshippers nonetheless small monuments were erected.[3]

---

2 Spera 2003, 24.
3 These were sometimes at other sites when actual burial places were inaccessible, as was the case with the earliest cult areas associate with Saints Peter and Paul at what is now the necropolis under the Basilica of Saint Sebastian. Spera 2003, 26–28.

This apparent disinterest in establishing more visible, built-up 'holy sites' was not simply because of prohibitions, but also because of a Christian resistance to such sites, which were associated with pagan and Jewish worship. Early Christians saw Christianity's very spirituality reflected in its turn away from earthly holy sites and towards the heavenly world beyond—an attitude reflected in Eusebius' writings in the fourth century, which saw him wrestling to reconcile this older Christian identity and attitude with Constantine's adorning of cult sites with churches and shrines.[4]

Constantine's imperial patronage and protection prompted a sea change for Christian worship in the fourth century: early *martyria* were embellished and became foci for developing processional urban liturgies that visibly demonstrated Christianity's presence in Rome—despite its continuing absence from the city's monumental centre. Yet this very peripheral nature was an important part of the religion's identity—associated with its greater spirituality, and offering a link between contemporary, free Christians and their persecuted predecessors.[5] Moreover, the very processions required to traverse the city and connect various extramural shrines made Christian worship more public, demonstrating Christianity's triumph through the very topography that had in part been constructed by its early marginalisation.

The situation at Constantinople was very different. Its predecessor, Byzantion, had no established Christian heritage on which to draw under the new emperor's patronage of the religion. Constantine's capital had a church built in its centre, near the imperial palace and hippodrome complex. Constantine had a mausoleum built for himself. Under his son, Constantius II, relics of three of the apostles were transferred here and it was expanded into the Church of the Holy Apostles—a building that stood as an interesting mix of mausoleum, *martyrium* (a traditionally extramural building type) and church. Both of these buildings stood unequivocally within the new city's walls. But we find no records of Christian cemeteries or *martyria* beyond the walls or in the regions along the Golden Horn and the Bosporos that would become its suburbs and likely very little was constructed in the city's early years. These regions appear to have been dotted with a number of pre-Christian cult sites, suggested by Dionysios of Byzantion's extensive second or third-century

---

4 Markus 1994, 258–59.
5 For more on the importance of its history of persecution to Christian identity see Markus 1994, 268–70. Markus argues that martyr cults centred on holy sites developed in the fourth century partly as a way to keep up a sense of connection between the dominant Christians of the period with their martyred, persecuted predecessors. Markus calls this phenomenon 'sanctification of time'.

catalogue.[6] Despite a sixth-century claim that Constantine converted an extramural pagan shrine in the suburb of Sosthenion into a church to St Michael the Archangel, this seems highly unlikely given early Christian resistance to the conversion of temples into churches.[7] Sozomen, writing in the mid-fifth century, reported that Constantine built a church to St Michael, known as the Michaelion, in the suburb of Hestiai or Anaplous, and describes his own personal visit to this site, but apart from this later account, there is little or no evidence of extramural shrines established under Constantine.[8]

Yet, toward the end of the fourth century, we begin to find numerous references to extramural sites of worship. To a degree, this expansion likely reflected the growing population of the city—and of its surrounding suburban regions which served the city both as an agricultural belt to feed the city and as a relaxing retreat for wealthy inhabitants.[9] The increasing extramural population naturally would have required local churches to be built. However, a number of these churches and shrines appear to have been more than sites of local worship; they were integrated into urban worship as well, and received elite and even imperial patronage. Notably, under Theodosius I, the imperial suburb of the Hebdomon, some 10km from the city centre, was adorned with two churches, one dedicated to St John the Evangelist, constructed before 400, and another to St John the Baptist, dedicated in 391 in time to receive the relic of the saint's head.

This transfer of relics was also a new development in the mid-fourth century and underpinned the establishment of churches throughout the Christian world. At Constantinople, this development was particularly important, as it made it possible for a city lacking in local martyrs to develop martyr shrines nonetheless.

---

6 *Dionysios of Byzantion*, ed. Güngerich 1958.
7 John Malalas, *Chronographia*, ed. Dindorf 1831: 4.13. Raymond Janin argued that the Sosthenion church's Constantinian attribution may have been a later invention due to competition with the other church to St Michael in Anaplous/Hestiai (Janin 1969, 436). On the Christian reluctance to make use of pagan holy sites, see Hanson 1978, 257–67.
8 Sozomenos, *Historia Ecclesiastica*, ed, Hansen 2004), 11.3. Raymond Janin argued that the Sosthenion church's Constantinian attribution may have been a later invention due to competition with the other church to St Michael in Anaplous/Hestiai. Janin, 346. Some early churches may have been built outside the original Constantinian walls, however, as there is some indication that the Church of St Mokios may have subsequently become a site of Arian worship after Theodosius' laws pushed their worship from within the old walls. Berger 2013, 180–81.
9 On the agricultural role of the suburban regions see Koder 1995.

2   Processional Liturgy

It is under the patriarch John Chrysostom that the extent and importance of the city's extramural Christian network truly becomes apparent, thanks to the preservation of many of his homilies given in the city and its suburbs. Among other challenges to his leadership of the Constantinopolitan church, Chrysostom faced ongoing resistance from the Arians of the city. Over the decades of the fourth century following Constantine's death, a long-running struggle between different Christian doctrines took place in Constantinople, with alternating Arian and Nicene patriarchs, as well as emperors with varying sympathies. Under Theodosius I in 381, legislation forbade Arian worship within the walls of the city.[10] In defiance, the Arians of the city gathered together within the walls and processed, singing antiphonal Arian hymns, out of the city to their extramural places of worship. Such a public display through the city attracted onlookers who were tempted to join the crowds, and so Chrysostom led competing processions against the Arians, seeking to drown them out with hymns preaching the Nicene Creed. This public religious debate ultimately turned violent, with the emperor Arcadius obliged to step in and ban the Arians from processing through the city.[11] The appeal of this type of worship, however, remained: Chrysostom conducted many processions through the city during his six-year tenure as patriarch and this type of processing and hymn-singing became a key part of the processional liturgy of Constantinople for centuries.

The processions conducted by Chrysostom supported his own stated aims to make the civic body of the city coterminous with the Christian body, to transform public space into religious space, presenting himself as the true successor of Constantine, as the founder of a truly Christian Constantinople.[12] Such efforts did not stop at the city walls—many of Chrysostom's recorded processions travelled well beyond the city limits, as far away as a church to St Thomas at Drypia, approximately 14.5km to the west of the city.[13] Another

---

10   *Codex Theodosianus*, 16.4.10, 16.5.6 and 16.5.8.
11   Socrates, *Ecclesiastical History*, VI.8.
12   Andrade 2010, 161–63. Caseau in this volume elabourates on the creation of sacred space, notably through prescribed permissible actions within certain spaces, or rules regarding what spaces certain categories of worshipers were permitted to access. Processions like Chrysostom's extended this performative nature of sacred space beyond individual buildings or complexes into public spaces, demonstrating how sacred space can be created anywhere through specific activities on a temporary basis as well as being located in a fixed point. Similar questions regarding the 'activation' of sacred space inform studies on the use of icons in Orthodox worship. See Pentcheva, 2006.
13   John Chrysostom, *Homilia dicta postquam reliquiae martyrum*, PG 63, 468–72.

crossed over the Bosporos, to the Church of Sts Peter and Paul at Rufinianai.[14] This last procession indicates the impact distinctive nature of Constantinople's geography, ringed on three sides by water, had on the manner in which extramural worship took place. As a coastal city, the sea was as much (if not more) a route of passage as the roads that fanned out through the city's gates. Given the long history of marine trade through the Bosporos, it is unsurprising that as Constantinopolitan Christian liturgical practices developed these should include movement across the waterways as well as over land.[15] This movement through and beyond the city helped to build a Christian space that was not located within discrete buildings, but rather enacted across an extended urban landscape, helping to weave the sacred into the topography of the city and into daily movements through this space.[16]

Many of these extramural shrines were graced with martyr relics providing them with a holy significance and legitimacy they may otherwise have lacked. It is notable how many important relics were translated to these extramural shrines—despite the presence of multiple important churches in the city centre. The relics of Sts Peter and Paul were deposited in their suburban church by the courtier, Rufinus, the owner of the palace in which the shrine was located.[17] Chrysostom's procession to Drypia marked the occasion of the deposition of relics at the church—and so important was the event that the empress joined the long night-time procession and the emperor arrived for the service the next day.[18] The head of St John the Baptist was first brought to Constantinople at the order of Valens, but Sozomen reports that the mules carrying the relic stopped outside of the city near Chalkedon and refused to travel further. Under Theodosius I an attempt was made to move the head again—but to a suburban church in the Hebdomon, not to the city centre.[19] Together with Chrysostom's extramural processions, these extramural relic depositions suggest a conscious effort on the part of both emperors and patriarchs to consolidate Constantinople's extramural religious landscape. This may suggest

14   John Chrysostom, *Contra ludos et theatre*, PG 56, 261–70.
15   For more consideration of the liturgical use of Constantinople's waterways, see Mayer 1998.
16   Bodin in this volume explores this relationship between city space and sacred space in the praise of the Theotokos as a city, demonstrating how urban space – familiar to worshipers in their daily life – formed a powerful metaphor to express the sacred, while at the same time ensuring that the sacred was embedded in daily life.
17   This transfer likely took place no earlier than 389. *John Chrysostom*. Wendy Mayer & Pauline Allen 2000, 23.
18   Indicated in a second homily for this service the following morning: John Chrysostom, *Homilia dicta praesente imperatore*, PG 63, 473–78.
19   Sozomenos, *HE*, VII.21.

that churches in the city centre were not enough to establish Constantinople as a Christian city. For this to happen, the civic space within and beyond the walls had to be equally co-opted by Christian activity, as at Rome.

The development of extramural religious sites may also reflect an effort to Christianise the old cult-sites indicated by Dionysios, ensuring that Constantinople was not merely a Christian outpost situated within a pagan hinterland, but rather the central point of a well-established sacred network. These extramural churches would also have served a growing suburban population as the immediate environs of Constantinople were affected by the growing city and its needs which required an increase in agricultural production and the development of a number of watercourses to feed a thirsty city lacking a significant natural freshwater source.[20] These sites were also not simply part of a network of movement back and forth from the central point of Constantinople, but also stopping points en route to the city from further afield. As increasing numbers of pilgrims and other travellers journeyed along the roads and waterways to Constantinople, it is unsurprising to find that these peripheral outposts became important sacred destinations in their own right.[21]

Interestingly, the emphasis on the extramural sites of Constantinople took place in the same period during which we find the increasing building of churches within the walls in other major cities in the empire.[22] This development seems to have taken place alongside and as a result of the increasing role of bishops within the urban, civic life of cities. At Constantinople, on the other hand, Chrysostom sought to demonstrate his control over the city in the opposite manner: by processing between churches and outside of the city. It thus seems that for Constantinopolitans it was as important that the religious topography of their city be seen to extend beyond the centrally-located

---

20 Crow and Bardill 2008.
21 Mention of suburban shrines can be found in a number of pilgrim accounts from the middle and later Byzantine periods, but also in earlier periods. The *martyrium* of St Euphemia at Chalkedon, for example, is already mentioned in the late fourth century by the Egeria in her famous *Itinerary*. Egeria, *Itinerarium* 23.7–8.
22 For example, extensions made to the Great Church at Antioch, located close by the imperial palace in the new part of the city. The original Great Church had been built under Constantine and dedicated in 341, while an older 'apostolic' church was located within the walls of the old city. Thus, the early fourth century had already seen intramural church building at Antioch, but the most notable subsequent developments following 341 were extramural churches, notably a church for St Babylas at Daphne (an apparent effort to undermine the influence of the temple of Apollo there), and a later church to the same martyr just across the river from the city. Downey 1961, 434.

churches as it was in other cities for Christian topography to be seen to extend into the urban core.

While it is a step too far to suggest that there was a programmatic effort at Constantinople to reproduce the Christian topographies of other cities, there is at least one instance identified by Cyril Mango that suggests that an awareness of the specific sacred landscape of other cities influenced the topography and liturgical practices of Constantinople. In the fourth and fifth centuries, Ascension Day was celebrated across the Golden Horn at the Church of the Maccabees at Elaia or Elaiôn, whose name, 'olive tree' or 'olive grove', evoked the Mount of Olives at Jerusalem.[23] Socrates, writing around 439, asserted that "from an ancient custom the whole population annually assembled for the celebration of our Saviour's ascension" at Elaia, indicating the importance to Constantinopolitans of emphasising the antiquity of their religious topography and processions. The explicit nature of this link to another city's religious topography is unique, but suggests that it was not absent from the minds of Constantinopolitans as they constructed their own city's religious landscape. Although by the tenth century, the site of this celebration had shifted from this slightly more out-of-the-way location (it required a water crossing) to the Church of the Theotokos of the Pege, even this latter church was located outside of the Theodosian Walls and the Ascension Day service continued to be led by the patriarch and attended by the emperor.

Disputes between various creeds also influenced the development of extramural churches. Prior to the expulsion of Arians from the city centre, other groups had been similarly driven from the city under Arian patriarchs and emperors and many of the earliest references to extramural churches at Constantinople arise in this context.[24] Thus the identity of early suburban churches was fraught with internal Christian conflict, as some of these buildings had passed back and forth between Nicene and non-Nicene ownership multiple times by the end of the fourth century.[25] The story of the transfer of the head of John the Baptist hints at these struggles—and the efforts of Theodosius I and his successors to stamp out remaining non-Nicene worship in the city and its surroundings. Sozomen reports that the head was initially found by "monks of the Macedonian heresy" in Cilicia.[26] When Theodosius

---

23   Mango 2009, 168; Socrates, *Ecclesiastical History*, VII.26.
24   Socrates and Sozomen are particularly keen in their *Ecclesiastical Histories* to emphasise which group owned which church at any given point in time.
25   For the story of a Novatian church that was physically moved outside of the city and then back into it under different emperors, see Socrates, *Ecclesiastical History*, II.38.
26   Sozomenos, *HE*, VII.21.

later sought to move the head from near Chalkedon, it was guarded by a holy virgin, Matrona, who was also of the Macedonian heresy. Resistant to the move at first, she ultimately relented, but she would not be persuaded to renounce her religious sentiments. But a presbyter charged with performing sacerdotal functions over the coffin—another Macedonian heretic—was persuaded to turn to the Nicene Creed, declaring that "if the Baptist would follow the emperor, he also would enter into communion with him".[27]

This account indicates the manner in which the translation of relics and erection of churches in the suburbs of Constantinople provided a field on which competing Christian sects jockeyed for power and influence. While heretical creeds could be expelled from the city centre, it was not wise to let them develop unchallenged in the suburbs either.[28] Chrysostom's long-ranging extramural processions and imperially-commanded translations of relics to extramural churches indicate the degree to which the ruling powers of the city saw that extramural religious topography was as important as intramural in establishing hegemony over the city.[29]

3   Protecting the City

A few decades after Chrysostom's death, a shift is evident in the symbolic meaning and role of suburban shrines: the liturgical processions that developed at the city now took place not only in honour of regular feast days and relic translations, but also to commemorate the salvation of the city.[30] Thus, in a city which lacked a Christian heritage of peripheral worship and *martyria*, the city came to form the basis of its own processional liturgy. In particular, these processions focussed on the divine protection enjoyed by the city, not due to the presence of particular martyrs, but due to the city's own sacred nature. The idea of Constantinople's divine favour developed gradually, and

---

27   Sozomenos, *HE*, VII.21.
28   See, for instance, Theodosius I exiling a heretic, Eunomius, to banishment after Eunomius had taken up residence in the suburbs and held church in private houses. Eunomius' suburban residence was not considered distant enough to prevent his heretical influence at Constantinople. Sozomenos, *HE*, VII.17.
29   On the propagandistic uses of liturgical processions, see Baldovin 1987, 182–86.
30   Such processions include commemorations of the sparing of the city from earthquakes thanks to processions led by the emperor outside the city walls (which were as much exculpatory demonstrations as they were a means of escaping the dangers of the built-up urban space during an earthquake). See below for the flights to the Hebdomon in 437 and 447.

ultimately became attached in particular to the figure of the Theotokos.[31] This development is reflected in two important extramural shrines that were established and adorned by imperial patronage toward the end of the fifth century and beginning of the sixth: the Church of the Theotokos of the Pege and that of the Theotokos of Blachernai. Both of these shrines were located at the sites of holy healing springs and Procopius rhetorically located them at either end of the Theodosian Walls "in order that both of them may serve as invincible defences to the circuit-wall of the city".[32]

This is an early sign of the defensive role that came to be attributed by the seventh century to Constantinople's extramural shrines. Early indications of this role are evident in a regular procession to the Hebdomon, which took place to commemorate a mid-fifth-century earthquake during which the populace had fled to safety on the plain beside the Hebdomon.[33] Regular processions on the 26 January thereafter commemorated this event and gave thanks to God—although the distance travelled by these commemorative processions appears to have been shrunk as they terminated at an otherwise unknown church to the Theotokos just beyond the Constantinian walls.[34] But an earlier earthquake, around 437, in which the populace had also spent a period of some days at prayer on the plain of the Hebdomon, was commemorated with a full procession to this suburb on the 25th of September. This procession commemorated both the salvation of the city and the Trisagion hymn which had been miraculously delivered to the populace during their time in prayer through a levitating child.[35] The celebration of the Trinitarian Trisagion again indicates the role of suburban worship in strengthening Orthodox hegemony in the city by spreading its influence and origins beyond the city centre and into the urban periphery. At the same time, this extended procession carried connotations of expiation and supplication in the face of God's wrath—by

---

31 On this see Cameron 1979; Mango 2000; Peltomaa 2001; Bodin in this volume.
32 Procopius, *De aedeficii*, 1.111, 41.
33 *Chronicon Paschale*, 589, 79. John Malalas also records this event in his sixth-century *Chronographia*, 363.20–365.2. This is likely the earthquake that took place in 447, although the *Chronicon Paschale* dates it to 450.
34 *Typikon*, I, 213. The church of the Theotokos mentioned here is not attested elsewhere, and its precise location remains unknown: Janin 177–78.
35 Theophanes, *Chronographia*, 93; *Typikon* I, 45–49. The *Typikon* makes no explicit reference to an earthquake on this occasion, only to a 'panic' or a 'terror' (φοβῶν), suggesting that the Trisagion was considered the more central object of celebration at the service. A later earthquake in 447 resulted in a similar procession out to the Hebdomon, and the *Chronicon Paschale* reports that this was commemorated annually at the Kampos Tribunalis next to the suburb. *Chronicon Paschale*, 587, 589.

making so arduous a journey to a peripheral church, Constantinopolitans demonstrated their piety to God and ensured continuing divine favour for their city. Worship at suburban shrines thus helped to shore up the divine defences of the city from an early point in Constantinople's history. With the shrines to the Theotokos at Pege and Blachernai, this concept was further consolidated into the idea suggested by Procopius that these extramural shrines themselves defended the city.

The role of suburban shrines as spiritual defences came to a head during the Avar attacks on Constantinople in the early seventh century. Two sermons by Theodore Synkellos indicate this development. The first, dating after the first Avar raid against the city, in 623, describes the removal from the church at Blachernai of the *maphorion*, the robe of the Theotokos, within the walls for safe-keeping.[36] But only three years later, the Avars attacked again, this time aided by Persian allies. Following the city's salvation, Theodore once again wrote a commemorative sermon, but this time the Theotokos comes to the fore as the defender of Constantinople. She is portrayed as actively fighting the attackers on the walls and her two extramural shrines at Pege and Blachernai appear in the sermon as key points on the defences of the city where the Theotokos herself drove back the enemy.[37] Following the siege, the Blachernai church was enclosed within the walls of the city, although Pege remained extramural and, as we have seen, continued to serve as the site of the Ascension Day service led by the patriarch.[38]

This moment indicates the culmination of a shift that had started in the late fifth century. Fourth- and early fifth-century shrines appear to have been part of an effort to spread and strengthen the influence and visibility of Christianity—and in particular Orthodox Christianity—in a city that lacked a historical Christian presence. These early extramural shrines were often raised to prominence through the translation of the relics of martyrs otherwise unconnected to Constantinople. As a result, these shrines and their associated processions can be seen as roots embedding the increasingly Christian city in its surroundings, drawing strength and legitimacy from a wider network reaching out beyond the city walls.

But once this network was firmly established and the core it supported strongly rooted, later extramural shrines began to take on a different role. They were locally-based, like *martyria*, but instead of being located on the sites of

---

36   Synkellos, *In depositionem pretiosae vestis*, 751–88. For a consideration of the attribution of this sermon to Synkellos, see Cameron 1979, 45–46.
37   Synkellos, *De obsidione Constantinopolitana*, sect. 19, 82.
38   *Chronicon Paschale*, 726, 181.

martyr's tombs, they were located near natural features that served the city, sometimes on particular historic occasions: a plain that had served as a refuge for the populace during the earthquake, holy springs that offered healing. The figure of the Theotokos as guardian of the city gradually developed over this time, and the later shrines of the Pege and Blachernai supported this development. Now the extramural shrines took up an additional role: spiritual defenders of the city. This mirrored the military role of the extramural space in which they stood: a buffer zone that could be used to fight off attacking enemies. This shift reflected the increasing pressures in the seventh century on Constantinople from numerous sieges which ravaged its hinterland and even its close suburbs, forcing the city to close upon itself and drawing the concept of 'city' closer to its protective walls.[39] While their extra-mural location made these shrines vulnerable, the location also, paradoxically, made them into defensive sites as well, their very material vulnerability demonstrating the power of Constantinople's spiritual defences at a time when these were so desperately needed.

∙ ∙ ∙

Constantinople had nothing to rival Rome's history as a Christian city when it was founded by Constantine on the site of Byzantion. Yet, within a few short centuries it had become an important centre of worship and pilgrimage, drawing visitors as well as holy men to its many churches, monasteries, and shrines. This was due in part to its role as capital to the empire, home of the emperor and to the patriarch who both led and participated in important religious rituals, processions, and other acts of worship. Constantinople's reputation was further enhanced by a deliberate programme of importing relics which lasted for centuries, providing the city with an unrivalled collection by the time of the Fourth Crusade. Yet all these external elements needed a core and, in the absence of local martyr traditions (although such traditions were soon developed) or a pre-Constantinian Christian heritage in the region, the city itself became this core, and the city in turn became the favoured city of the Theotokos, providing it at once with both divine protection and a claim to distinction among other great cities with apostolic connections.[40]

---

39   Kimmelfield 2016, 109.
40   On the development of local martyr traditions, see Berger 2013. Constantinople, too, was provided with a legendary apostolic origin, but this appears always to have been secondary to the city's special relationship with the Theotokos. Mango 2000, 23. For an extended examination of Constantinople's apostolic tradition see Dvornik 1958.

The shrines that appeared in the suburbs from the late third and fourth centuries onward may to a degree have reflected Roman models of extramural shrines, but only inasmuch as they provided the spatial field on which to conduct similar processional urban liturgy as that found in Rome. But where the Roman shrines were focussed on *martyria*, Constantinople's extramural religious topography was dominated by sites dedicated to the Theotokos and other major saints such as John the Baptist and Michael the Archangel. These sites were chosen not due to local burials, but rather due to the presence of holy springs or other important natural features—a way of tapping into existing cultural memory, but overlaying it with Christian meaning.

This placement of shrines on locally-acknowledged sites helped to weave the city's developing Christian topography firmly within Constantinople's particular local context. It also established a model for future emphasis on the city itself as the Christian focal point of the region: it was the development of Constantinople's urban centre that 'Christianised' its suburban space rather than the other way around, as at Rome and other cities. At the same time, it was important for the central city's Christian identity that it possessed an extramural network of religious sites that could function as did those at other cities, where they were the earliest sites of Christian worship, gradually influencing the city centre. But the effort to assert Constantinople's legitimacy and antiquity as a Christian city ultimately led to a focus on the divine favour of the city itself, as the true originator of Christian worship in the region.[41] This is seen in both the nature of extramural shrines and in the nature of the processions to them: they protected the city and built up its identity as a centre of Christianity. Thus, rather than the city and worship being moulded around extant extramural shrines, Constantinople's extramural shrines were part of the larger construction of the Christian urban topography of the city—their importance and sacred nature was partially supported by translated relics, but ultimately underpinned by the city itself and the divine favour and protection it enjoyed.

---

41 See Sozomen's eulogy to Constantinople as a city whose development under a Christian emperor made it more pure and potent in its Christian identity thanks to its lack of the trappings of pre-Christian worship. Sozomenos, *HE*, 2.3. Baldovin 1987, 233. Baldovin notes that more obviously than at either Rome or Jerusalem, Constantinopolitan liturgy 'reflected historical occasions in the post-Constantinian life of the city".

Bibliography

Primary Sources

Caesarea, *Procopius*, 7 vols. Tr. H. B. Dewing. London 1953–1954.
Chronicon Paschale 284–628 AD. Ed. & tr. M. Whitby & M. Whitby. Liverpool 1989.
Chrysostom, John, *John Chrysostom*. Ed. & tr. W. Mayer & P. Allen. London 2000.
Dionysios of Byzantion. *Dionysii Byzantii Anaplous Bospori*. R. Güngerich, ed. Berlin, 1958.
Egeria, *Itinerarium*. Ed. P. Maraval, SC 296. Paris 1982.
Malalas, John, *Chronographia*. Ed. L. Dindorf. Bonn 1831.
Socrates, *Ecclesiastical History*. Ed. & tr. P. Maraval, *Socrate de Constantinople. Histoire Ecclésiastique*, SC 477, 493, 505, 506. Paris 2004–2007.
Sozomenos, *Ecclesiastical History*. G.C. Hansen, ed. *Historia ecclesiastica: Kirchengeschichte*. Fontes Christiani FC 73–74. Brepols, 2004.
Synkellos, Theodore, *In depositionem pretiosae vestis*. Ed. E. Combefis, *Historia Haeresis Monothelitarum, Bibliothecae Patrum Novum Autuarium*, 751–88. Paris 1648.
Synkellos, Theodore, *De obsidione Constantinopolitana*. Ed. F. Makk, *Traduction et commentaire de l'homélie écrite probablement par Théodore le Syncelle sur le siège de Constantinople en 626*. Szeged 1975.
The Theodosian Code and Novels and the Sirmondian Constitutions. Ed. & tr. C. Pharr. Princeton 1952, repr. 1969.
Theophanes Confessor, *Chronographia*. Ed. Carolus de Boor. Leipzig 1883–1885.
Le Typicon de la Grande Église: Ms. Sainte-Croix no. 40, Xe siècle, vol. 1. Tr. J. Mateos Rome 1962–1963.

Secondary Sources

Andrade, N. 2010. "The Processions of John Chrysostom and the Contested Spaces of Constantinople", *Journal of Early Christian Studies* 18.2, 161–89.
Baldovin, J. F. 1987. *The Urban Character of Christian Worship: The Origins, Development and Meaning of Stational Liturgy*. Rome.
Berger, A. 2013. "Mokios und Konstantin der Große. Zu den Anfängen des Märtyrerkults in Konstantinopel", in Leontaritou, V. A., K. A. Mpourdara, E. S. Papagianni (eds) 2013, *Antecessor. Festschrift für Spyros N. Troianos*. Athens, 165–85.
Cameron, A. 1979. "The Virgin's Robe: An Episode in the History of Early Seventh-Century Constantinople", *Byzantion* 49, 42–56.
Crow, J. & J. Bardill 2008. *The Water Supply of Byzantine Constantinople*. London.
Dvornik, F. 1958. *The Idea of Apostolicity in Byzantium and the Legend of the Apostle Andrew*. Cambridge, MA.

Janin, R. 1969. *La géographie ecclésiastique de l'Empire Byzantin; Première partie: Le siège de Constantinople et le patriarcat œcuménique; T. III: Les églises et les monastères*, 2nd ed. Paris.

Kimmelfield, I. 2016. "Defining Constantinople's Suburbs through Travel and Geography", *Scandinavian Journal of Byzantine and Modern Greek Studies* 2, 97–114.

Koder, J. 1995. "Fresh vegetables for the capital", in C. Mango and G. Dagron (eds), *Constantinopole and its Hinterland: Papers from the Twenty-Seventh Spring Symposium of Bysantine Studies*. Oxford, 49–56.

Mango, C. 2009. "Constantinople's Mount of Olives and Pseudo-Dorotheus of Tyre", *Nea Rhome* 6, 157–70.

Mango, C. 2000. "Constantinople as Theotokoupolis, in Vassilaki (ed.) 2000, 17–25.

Markus, R. A. 1994. "How on Earth Could Places Become Holy? Origins of the Christian Idea of Holy Places", *Journal of Early Christian Studies* 2, 257–71.

Mayer, W. 1998 "The Sea Made Holy: The Liturgical Function of the Waters Surrounding Constantinople", *Ephemerides Liturgicae* 112, 459–468.

Peltomaa, L. M. 2001. *The Image of the Virgin Mary in the Akathistos Hymn*. Leiden.

Pentcheva, B. V. 2006. "The Peformative Icon", *The Art Bulletin* 88.4, 631–655.

Spera, L. 2003. "The Christianization of Space along the via Appia: Changing Landscape in the Suburbs of Rome", *American Journal of Archaeology* 107.1, 23–43.

Vassilaki, M. (ed.) 2000. *Mother of God: The Representation of the Virgin in Byzantine Art*. Milan.

Mind the Gap

Mosaics on the Wall and the Space between Viewer and Viewed

Liz James

Art, especially monumental art, creates a temporal and historicising space that helps to define meaning. Images are located in space and in a space, or indeed a series of spaces: a mosaic on the wall is set in a building, exists in the space that is that building, and is looked at across the space between it and the viewer.[1] This paper will begin to explore some of the exchanges between works of art and the places where their meanings are defined, some of the ways in which the spaces of and around wall mosaics were performed in Byzantium, through considering how mosaics work to be visible in the space of the church.

To do this, I need to start with space and place. Space, the void, the large undifferentiated space, the physical and social landscape that is all around us, can be translated and given cultural meanings through everyday place-bound social practices. It can be turned into 'lived space', in part through being named and identified, by being broken down into something smaller and more manageable: something social geographers have labelled 'place'.[2] Certain places have been given stronger meanings, names or definitions by society than others. These are the places with a close intimate emotional engagement of people and place, a strong 'Sense of Place'.[3] Byzantine churches can be seen as fitting this model, as buildings that translate 'space' into 'place' and, more than that, that may convey this more numinous 'sense of place'. They fit Nigel Thrift's idea of lived spaces, live spaces, places in which people performed meaningful acts.[4] Through those acts, both individual (personal devotion) and official (the Liturgy), the church could gain its sense of place, of being special, of that close

---

1 Additionally, in itself, it offers the image of a particular space (though space will not permit me to go into this). Often mosaics are described as creating a heavenly space, both within the picture plane itself and within the church building, a part of the created image of a bigger 'heavenly space".
2 Lefebvre 1991; Soja 1996.
3 For 'sense of place', Tuan 1977 and 1979.
4 Thrift 1996.

emotional intimacy, the indefinable 'feel' of a church. My contention is that mosaics play a role in this.

In this context however, I want to start with the idea that creating place from space is in part about creating order and asserting control. If, with Michel de Certeau, we accept the idea that place can be understood as an ordered and ordering system, stable with a self-regulating set of rules reached through spatial practices, then a church is (among other things) an official space created by 'authority'.[5] The building serves as an ordering system; it institutes a set of relations for official or proper ends (the Christian worship that takes place within it, whether liturgy or private prayer). This is reinforced (or indeed established) by its decoration. As Lefebvre put it: "monumental buildings mask the will to power and the arbitrariness of power beneath symbols and surfaces which claim to express collective will and collective thought".[6] A church has an 'official' capacity that comes from those with the power to dictate the ordering system: who goes where; who sees what; who makes the rules; and who enforces them, both then and now. Which spaces were available for monks, for women, for emperors: the decoration in the church can serve to emphasise and reinforce these aspects.[7] Modern visitors to churches experience something of this controlling system: as tourists, as women, as non-pilgrims; when certain spaces are barred to them, relics closed away from them, when they are scolded for sitting and crossing their legs, told they are improperly dressed; or even when they are checked by their own anxieties about right and wrong behaviour in a 'sacred' space. Yet de Certeau also offered an escape from this officious mundanity. In contrast to the authoritarian aspects of an idea of place as manageable, controlled and ordered, he proposed that we understand space as endlessly mutable, never fixed or immobile. A city street is created

---

5   de Certeau 1984, especially the chapter "Walking in the City", 91–110. Here de Certeau argues that 'the city' is created by the strategies of governments and institutions whilst 'walkers' at street level take shortcuts through the plan of the city in ways not intended by authority. His wider argument is that everyday life (the 'quotidien') works through people infiltrating the territory of others, using the rules and products that already exist in culture in a way that is influenced, but never wholly determined, by those rules and products and involving a level of creative resistance to these structures. The best introduction to these ideas that I know is Phineas and Ferb's song 'Aerial Area Rug': (https://disney.fandom.com/wiki/Aerial_Area_Rug).
6   Lefebvre 1991, 143.
7   We tend to read this in terms of the iconography of the images: for example, Tronzo 1994 and Barber 2001 on the 'washing of feet' mosaic in Nea Moni; Maguire 1992; Borsook 1990 on the iconography around the Royal Box in the Cappella Palatina. The very materials used can mark off areas of a church: see Majeska 1978; Barry, 2007. L. Webb 2017 considers how mosaics (specifically that of the Transfiguration) and the Liturgy might have interacted.

and defined as a place by official planning but it can be translated into a space by those who walk it, ignoring the official signs and rules, walking on the grass rather than round it. So too a church itself is a mobile space with room to undermine authority; the interior can be more ambiguous and transitive than first experienced. People move around inside it for various reasons (private prayer; veneration of a special icon at a special time, for example), able to find their own way around, making their own routes and footpaths, and transgressing the rules, nipping in to the locked chapel to pray.

De Certeau's is a model that offers a way of thinking about one possible role for the monumental decoration of a church. The mosaics (which are really my interest here) in a church are themselves defined and articulated by their location and their relationship with that ecclesiastical space.[8] They can be conceived of as both ordered and ordering. We understand that mosaics were put onto church walls in some sort of order and to tell some sort of story, that there was a master plan and that the interpretation of that plan allows the audience to bridge the gap between the wall and the viewer. Moreover, it is as a part of this ordering of space that we see that mosaics have meaning.

In this context, we can gain access to two obvious types of meaning. One is the readings that we think the Byzantines gave to their images, interpretations present in the written sources. Texts of whatever sort always order images and create order from them and about them. Ekphraseis are a particularly potent source of such meanings. As descriptions that aimed to make the thing described vivid to the beholder or auditor, ekphraseis offer particular, directive ways of understanding the building or the work of art. Ekphraseis of buildings (and indeed of works of art) order space and translate it into place; space can be sequential or linear; it might be a thematic tour; it can be given specific meanings and cultural connotations.[9] The authors of ekphraseis claim to tell the hidden truths encapsulated by the work of art, and one of our tasks as scholars is to uncover these meanings and hidden stories, be they theological, propaganda or whatever.[10] For example, with Constantine of Rhodes and his account of the Church of the Holy Apostles and its mosaics, one of the stories about the mosaics that it is possible to see Constantine as telling is about how

---

8   If a mosaic is moved to another space, it becomes something else. A mosaic in an art gallery is everything that a mosaic in a church is not: it is flattened out and located in a space designed for looking rather than in a space whose primary purpose is to worship God, not to look at art. Nelson 1989 made this point in relation to icons.
9   Veikou 2018. This is what Macrides & Magdalino 1988 and R. Webb 1999 and 2017 do. Also see Foskolou 2018 on multiple meanings.
10 James & Webb 1991; Webb 2009.

they support the validity of Christian religious art through an emphasis on the image of Christ's humanity, divinity and Incarnation depicted in them.[11] Here, the mosaics help in the creation of an Orthodox space, a place where images prove the Christian message of salvation and redemption. Theological texts in their turn present images as teachers, as books for the illiterate, as miraculous.[12] Images were there to reinforce faith: pictures of the Word Incarnate giving conviction to faith in the Incarnation.[13] They were there to underpin the liturgy; they were instruments of contemplation to focus the mind and attention of worshippers; a way of remembering God and offering him glory, reverence and greeting to God, locating an historical, Incarnate God in time and space/place.[14]

A second type of systematic meaning that we give to the mosaics is that derived from the images themselves. Art historians like creating order and controlling works of art. In the case of the Middle Byzantine church, Otto Demus' development of a system of church decoration serves to order the undifferentiated church space.[15] Using Hosios Loukas, Nea Moni and Daphni as his case studies, Demus made the case that the decoration in a Middle Byzantine church was organised along two interlocking axes, east to west and top to bottom, and in three zones. The holiest of images, images such as the Pantokrator in the dome and the Mother of God and Child in the apse, were in the east end of the church and the dome. In the middle was the 'Feast Cycle', scenes from the life of Christ, arranged as a celebration of the feasts of the church in liturgical order. Lowest down and furthest west was the saint, a sanctoral cycle. Demus' authoritive system brilliantly and convincingly bridged the gap, the actual physical space, as well as the imaginary space, between the image, the mosaic and its audience.

There are also interpretations based on intentions, above all on what we think patrons meant when they paid out for mosaics. We are sure that they expected a return. Their images were intended to be admired, the verses

11   Constantine of Rhodes, *On Constantinople and the Church of the Holy Apostles*, 209–216.
12   "What Scripture is to the educated, images are to the ignorant, who see through them what they must accept; they read in them what they cannot read in books": Gregory the Great, *Letter* to Bishop Serenus of Marseille: book 11, letter 10 in (ed.) Norberg, 873–76. Nilus of Sinai in the fifth century suggested that images in a church helped the illiterate become mindful of the "manly deeds" of those who have served God and be roused to emulation: *Letter to Prefect Olympiodorus*, PG 79, 577–80 and tr. in Mango 1975, 33. For mosaics making expanses of text visible/viewable see Elsner 1994.
13   A phrase I borrow from Mathews' 1998 important article, at 16.
14   Barber 2002.
15   Demus 1948.

associated with them to be read; the mosaics surrounding them to be appreciated (hopes for the afterlife and desires to show one's self off for a variety of reasons) by both God and humanity alike. If these interpretations of donor images are at all correct, then the donor's intention was not necessarily to paper his or her church as lavishly as possible.[16]

But how well mosaics might work as a codification is another story. Mosaics might well have had a didactic function, but in practical terms, standing in the church itself, it can be very hard to see what story is being told through mosaics unless the audience knows in advance (or is told). Sometimes the church space itself might get in the way: at Hosios Loukas, the walls are so tall that mosaics begin about ten metres above the floor; at Nea Moni the dome cuts off lines of sight into the apse and side chapels. Dirt and darkness make it easier to ignore than to decipher the mosaics, coupled with the expectation that the worshipper is directed how to use the space to concentrate. Moreover, an icon is easier to contemplate prayerfully than a mosaic, and easier to teach a Bible story from. Demus' system has been critiqued on many occasions: it is an unemotional view of images, but holy images evoked emotions; it is not a Festival Cycle, and so on.[17] And issues around interpretations of texts and images are a library in their own right. It is consistently clear from Byzantine written sources that almost any plausible story could be attached to any image. Thus, whatever the 'real' reason for its painting, an icon of Mary in Jerusalem was best-known for barring the way into church of the woman who became St Mary of Egypt. Similarly, whatever the 'real' story was, the mosaic in Hosios David in Thessaloniki was understood in the twelfth century as an image of Christ commissioned by the emperor's daughter and hidden in a period of persecution, only to be recovered after Iconoclasm.[18] Once images were in a church, the patron's intentions could fall by the wayside, forgotten or ignored, not used for teaching, not venerated.[19] But still the mosaics remain there, silent, suggesting that there is no such easy sense of ordering and no way of knowing for sure what the images meant to their original audience. In these contexts, the gap between image and viewer seems massive.

---

16   On donors, see Franses 2019.
17   Mathews 1998 on emotions; Kitzinger 1998 on the Feast Cycle; Connor 2016 uses Demus; James 2017 questions him.
18   Mary of Egypt's icon is described in her *vita*, chs 15–17, tr. Ward 1987, 46–48; Hosios David: Ignatius Monachus, *Narratio de imagine Christi* and tr. in Mango 1975, 155–56; discussed in James 2011. On thinking through and with images, especially in the contexts of memory, and how images shape memory see Brubaker 2006.
19   Franses 2019.

Indeed, were mosaics ever anything more than expensive wallpaper, status symbols for rich patrons that no one ever looked at? Are we wasting our time looking to bridge the gap between them and their audiences? Answering this gets me back to the idea of mosaics as non-ordering, as creating place not space. Robin Cormack has made the point that it is rare that accounts of mosaics feature in narratives either of churches or of religious rituals. Icons are an increasing presence; mosaics, after their initial installation, lose their role (if they had one) in worship and prayer.[20] Photius' seventeenth *Homily* talks about the mosaic of the Mother of God in Hagia Sophia. It is taken as a key text for interpreting the importance of images after Iconoclasm through its account of the reality revealed by the image of Mary, confirming the truth of the Incarnation and hence the validity of religious images.[21] However, when Michael the Deacon described the church in the twelfth century, he ignored the mosaic completely, spending his words on the marbles of the church.[22] What had mattered to one author in the ninth century was no longer of the same concern to the latter writer writing for a different purpose. Where did that leave the mosaic? Was Mary merely wallpaper by the twelfth century? Were there no reasons for noticing the mosaic? Where we often talk of the 'power of images' in Byzantium, here are images that just occupy the background. From texts about images, above all the debates around Iconoclasm, what mattered in religious images were issues about the relation between the divine and human, concerns around form and likeness, essence and subject, materiality and spirituality, ideas about the role of images as a vehicle for union with God.[23] But these concepts often fit icons and smaller works of art better than they fit monumental images on church walls. The veneration of icons is a close-up relationship. It is possible to touch, kiss and caress an icon, to light a candle or burn incense in front of it, to bridge the gap in these ways between prototype, image and viewer. It is not as easy to venerate or honour a mosaic in this way, given that usually mosaics are well above people's heads. Indeed, the Iconoclasts put images up high to avoid the risk of worship.[24] Some theological ideas about images—for example, as ways of remembering holy people, or as

---

20 Cormack makes the suggestion of 'wallpaper': Cormack 2017, 115. It is a typically challenging Cormack question that I have taken away from the mosaics of the fourteenth century that he applied it to.
21 Photius, *Homily* 17. On this see REF.
22 Michael the Deacon in Mango & Parker 1960.
23 There is a huge literature on this: Barber 2002 is an excellent starting point. Also Elsner 1998.
24 Elsner 1998, 382.

a means of locating the Incarnate Christ in time and place—work well enough for mosaics. Others do not. Other than the Mother of God in Hagia Sophia, the wall mosaic is not the medium through which honour is offered to the prototype through the image. As far as I know, there were no miracle-working mosaics in Byzantium, as there were miracle-working icons, and no one explicitly said that their vision of a saint was like that in the mosaic. Indeed, Byzantine theology might well imply that the physical visuality of mosaics was just wallpaper to the theology of icons. What then were mosaics for?

By 'wallpaper', Cormack articulates the idea that the monumental images in a church, whatever their regulating function, were invisible to the audience, a background to the space that they used.[25] It is tourists and art historians who take their time to crane their necks upwards, often paying less attention to the icons. Worshippers are supposed to be concentrating on higher things, venerating God through the holy icons, not gawping towards the mosaics. Further, it is very easy to be a spectator without paying attention to the spectacle: the everydayness of images is banal; even the physicality, glamour and beauty of the materials, the marbles, the gold, pales after a time.[26] When this stuff is utterly familiar, seen every week, every day, when it is up there above the head, filling a space, then audiences do not really look at it. Or rather, they look but do not see. It is perhaps not surprising that it was not the congregation of Hagia Sophia but the envoys of Khan Vladimir who believed that the angels descended from the walls to join in the liturgy: they were Rus barbarians, whilst the sophisticated Constantinopolitan congregation had seen it all before.[27]

In this way, Cormack's comparison exposes a different sort of gap, one in which we write of the intentionality of images or of those who commissioned or wrote about the images, and one where we accept their silence about works of art as indicating their indifference to those images. Indifference is where I want to start from. That the mosaics exist is an indication of some worth and there is enough evidence in accounts of buildings to suggest that there were times when people (even if only the author) did look at images. Nevertheless, these ekphraseis only filled the hole between images and audience briefly, a bodily performance creating and occupying space, in some cases even a site-specific performance.[28] When that space between the image on the wall and the audience was filled not with a Constantine of Rhodes telling people what to see and understand, but with the Liturgy, or with silence, could mosaics

---

25 Cormack 2017, 115.
26 James 2017, 122–30.
27 *Russian Primary Chronicle Laurentian Text,* Ch. 108, 111.
28 On performativity and space see Rose 1999. Walker White 2015 does not discuss site.

cross the gap? Despite Cormack's compelling wallpaper metaphor, I want to argue that mosaics possessed the power in themselves as things, as objects, as works of art, to step into that space without human help. This reverses the way in which I have been discussing mosaics so far, where it has been about human agency and human intentions, the ways in which people—the Byzantines, art historians, whoever—cross the gap to give life to the mosaics, to animate them into something more than wallpaper.[29] But what happens when we treat mosaics as things that can act and can make people act, considering them, in Bruno Latour's term, as 'actants'?[30] W.J.T. Mitchell articulated how we often behave as if we believe that pictures are animate, sentient, desiring as if they can act as animated beings: 'What do pictures want?'[31] In (Byzantine) art history, this is an approach often framed to be around small and portable images, but to tackle Cormack's challenge I want to put mosaics in the place of the animate image.[32]

How then might mosaics break through the barrier of mundanity? What about the moments of revelation and clarity that might shatter the everydayness of mosaics? Bill Brown, in discussing how and when objects get noticed, argued that "We begin to confront the thingness of objects when they stop working for us: when the drill breaks, when the car stalls [...]".[33] In other words, things intrude into our consciousness when they fail to do their job. Patricia Cox Miller expanded on this with relics to suggest their physicality as the site of spiritual presence and power, and elsewhere I have suggested that this was one moment when an icon might be noticed: when it did something rather than just stood there, when it bled or averted its face.[34] At that point, these things can no longer be taken for granted as part of the everyday world where functioning objects and pictures on walls are so familiar as not to be noticed.

---

29 Appadurai 1986.
30 Bruno Latour on the agency of things, attributing social agency to 'actants', both human and not human, and on setting things free: see for example, Latour 1996. In Latour 1999, he discusses how scientific and technical work can be made invisible by its own success: when something works, attention is directed to the output and not the way in which it was produced.
31 Gell 1998; Mitchell 2005. But on animated things, see Bogost 2012 which looks to develop an 'object-orientated ontology' with things at the centre of being and human perception as only one way in which objects might relate; Bennett 2010 is (among other things) a political theorising of the non-human in events; and the eloquent expression of the tension between the human and non-human, Pratchett 1996).
32 Thus O'Malley 2005 on altarpieces; Drpić 2018 on enkolpia; Peers 2013, where the things are all portable objects.
33 Brown 1998 and 2001. The quotation is Brown 2001, 4.
34 Cox Miller 2009, esp. 1–3; James 2013.

There are two stages here. Its very existence as a physical object, a relic or a mosaic, a sensuous presence (Brown's 'thingness'), was what gave an object the power to act or, put another way, gave it agency, the ability to influence what people around it did and how they behaved.[35] Yet when do people notice images? When they do something, when they demand we pay them attention. When they cause trouble (Iconoclasm for example), when they are new (Mary in Hagia Sophia), when they feature in dreams and visions (when they cause St Artemios to be recognised because he looks like his icon), when they find a way to cross over from taken for granted.

So, images are to be noticed, are disruptive of space and place, when they look different, when their appearance is not what the viewer expects. This is not far from Michael Fried's view that paintings have first to attract beholders, then stop them to look, and then hold them there.[36] For Mitchell, this was characterised as 'mastery'; I would prefer to label it 'attention-seeking'.[37] It is attention that minds the gap. Not to be wallpaper, mosaics need to look or even to be different to attract a viewer. So how can mosaics disrupt order, short of falling onto the viewer's head? The easiest and most obvious way is visually, by changing their appearance, rendering the familiar unfamiliar. That is something that comes easily to mosaics, but which is rather more difficult to render into words on the page.[38] We are all familiar with the well-worn idea of the icon's eyes following you round a church. But mosaics too can move in different ways. They move best through those slippery visual qualities of light and dark, shadow and colour—elements of the story of art that art historians have not always taken seriously, and elements that are all non-human. In many ways, the interaction between light, colour, dark and shade defines Byzantine mosaics: they simply have to be explored in terms of these qualities. They are works of art whose visual properties revolve around the interplay of light and dark, the effects of lights on colours and not thinking about mosaics in their settings, not thinking about how they 'work' in a building, in interaction with light and dark, is to rule out at least half the picture. I've discussed elsewhere how the Byzantines valued the brightness of colour, the flashing qualities of

---

35   Gell 1998 sees agency as the ability of objects, specifically works of art, to influence the field of social action in ways which would not occur if those objects did not exist. For use of Gell, see eg O'Malley 2005 on altarpieces as agents and R. Webb 2017 on buildings as agents from a written perspective.
36   Fried 1980, 92; also discussed in Mitchell 2005, 36.
37   And if this is a nice pair of gendered perspectives, I can't help that.
38   For art history as ekphrasis only, see Elsner 2010.

light; this is about how those qualities brought art to their attention. This is about how mosaics look, not what we think they say.[39]

It has been well-said that Byzantine mosaics are 'painting with light'. But the type of light affects the appearance of an image, the feel of a building. The debate about the colour of 'That dress' on You-Tube—was it black and blue or white and gold?—highlights both the changeability of colour and the effect that this can have in drawing attention.[40] That dialogue between light and material is common to mosaics. The Mother of God in the apse of Hagia Sophia can move from a sombre dark blue to a brilliant gold depending on what sort of light falls on her. We are used to seeing mosaics lit by steady electric lights, usually at a level so we can see clearly what is depicted in the image. This lighting that kills the visual effects of mosaics. Because every mosaic is made from thousands, millions, of small cubes of glass inserted manually, each tessera is a sort of mirror reflecting and absorbing light. The very randomness of their insertion means each surface reflects and acts differently, and when the light changes, so does the mosaic. Steady electric lighting offers little chance for differential reflections. Further, many mosaics have gold backgrounds. Gold glass tesserae are highly reflective—but only when the gold catches the light. High overhead lights make the image very clear but ensures that the gold looks yellow, dull and solid, charmless.[41]

When low lighting is used, the mosaics become very different. Suddenly the picture is no longer dormant. It stops being clear. Details that were barely visible or noticeable suddenly become striking, focal points for the audience. Others hover on the border of visibility. Colours change. Light flashes and shimmers across the image—it is impossible to convey by photographs—and surfaces and figures spring to life, the image moves, is unstable, even alive. Let me try and describe this with a couple of scenes from Hosios Loukas (Figure 24.1). Lit directly, the Nativity in the south-east pendentif is a bright, colourful, bustling scene, Mary and Child in the centre in a cave in the rocks, Joseph and the Magi led by angels to bottom left, angels and shepherds to the right, the baby's first bath down at the bottom, the star at the top. There are

---

39 As Mitchell 2005, 203, said, the lives and loves of images cannot be answered without some reckoning with the media in which they appear. He wasn't thinking about mosaics but it works pretty well for them.
40 On 'the dress' and its effect, see its own Wikipedia entry: https://en.wikipedia.org/wiki/The_dress (consulted 26/06/19).
41 'Charmless' is Rico Franses' entirely apposite word: Franses 2013, 178; also see Franses 2003. Pentcheva 2010, 128–139 shows how the metal icon of St Michael in the Treasury of San Marco, Venice, moves and is transformed under candle light.

MIND THE GAP: MOSAICS ON THE WALL 547

reds, blues, bright colours and appealing details—the shepherd playing his pipe, top right for example. The gold is part of the background with the green of the earth below it. Dim the lighting, however, and the colours vanish and the gold shines out: the halos of Mary, Joseph and the Child—suddenly revealed as the three central characters. The straw in the manger and the star and the rays from the star above combine to highlight the Christ-child whose story this is. Gold details reveal the attendant angels holding cloths and hint at the arriving Kings. Right in the centre (depending on the lighting) the gold gradually begins to glow intensively rather than shine.

A similar transformation is apparent with the mosaic of the Baptism, where the curve of the pendentive collects light in the centre—the dove descending on Christ's head and the gold cross in the waters of the Jordan, details easy to miss in full light, suddenly become focal points. And in the apse, take the light away and what glows against its blue background is the divine child, Christ Incarnate, his mother a ghostly blur behind, her halo and the five gold stars on her shoulders and the gold hems of her robes are clearest, and then, if you look long enough, a golden glow around her body. Gradually, with a prolonged look, the images glow, as if lit from within. The whole focus and balance of the image alters as the background actually becomes the brightest part of the

FIGURE 24.1   Church of Hosios Loukas, Phokis, Greece, general view of the south-east pendentif
PHOTOGRAPH © REBECCA RAYNOR

images, the part that demands attention, which draws the viewer in. The same happens with the icons on the iconostasis: when a low-powered light source is placed at about head-height, as would have been the case in the dark of morning or evening when candles illuminated the works, the gold catches the light, and comes alive with a warm, even, glow. Mosaics were never lit as they are now. During church rituals, the space was lit with candles and lamps, a low ambient flickering lighting, with the gold in its fully reflective state becoming a shimmering, glowing field. Matter and material, those things that Byzantine theology was so insistent must be inanimate, becomes alive.[42]

How far we might want to see this as the mosaic 'acting for itself' depends on how far we are comfortable with ideas of animate objects. It is true that a whole series of technical devices were employed by artists that created effects such as these.[43] It is rare, for example, that gold backgrounds are solid sheets of gold tesserae: that would create a brassy, stolid feel. Instead, silver tesserae or colourless glass tesserae or amber tesserae are used. Tesserae are angled in different ways in different locations. In Hagia Sophia in Istanbul, the windowsills of the west windows in the inner narthex are tilted in such a way as to catch the direct afternoon sunlight, and the tesserae of the windowsills in the apse in the same church are angled to direct light up into the apse mosaic. At the Church of the Nativity in Bethlehem, tilting the tesserae picks up light from the windows opposite. Some mosaics are in dark and poky buildings and here choices about colours have a specific purpose. In the sixth-century monastery of Mar Gabriel and in some vaults of the Rotunda at Thessaloniki, silver tesserae were used rather than gold to lighten mosaics and make them more visible. Often in haloes (as at Hosios Loukas), the gold tesserae are set running in a circular fashion around the figure's head, rather than in the horizontal lines of the background. It serves to focus and reflect light, as well as to differentiate the halo from the general background. But in the narthex mosaic at Hagia Sophia, the lines of gold continue horizontally through the haloes of Christ and emperor alike, and the haloes themselves are marked out by one or two circular lines in a contrasting colour. In the Deesis panel in Hagia Sophia, the trefoil ripple effect of the gold background continues into the haloes of the three figures of Christ, the Mother of God and St John the Baptist, but the gold of the cross inscribed in Christ's halo is set in straight, slightly spaced lines and that means that the cross, perhaps unexpectedly, stands out clearly and assertively. All of

---

42 On the vitality of matter as a political issue see Bennett 2010. Much of the debate about images and iconoclasm is really about icons (wooden panel paintings). The place of monumental art in these debates isn't quite the same in my view, but that is a different story.

43 James 2017, chapter two.

these are potential visual hooks for the viewers, elements of the mosaic that, in the right light, catch that light differently and seek attention.[44]

How far mosaicists 'knew' that these would be the effects created by their laying of mosaics is unclear. Whether architects and mosaicists worked together in building a medieval church is unknown; nor do we know how far some of the visual effects created by architecture and lighting were fortuitous.[45] While some thought must have been given to the lay-out, design and contents of the mosaic, to be sure that it fitted the space for which it was intended and displayed what was required, how far there was a full plan is another matter. In some churches—Hosios Loukas is one—it appears that the mosaics are a planned programme. In other churches, mosaics are jammed into tight and inappropriate spaces (as seems to be the case with the mosaic of the emperor Alexander in Hagia Sophia), or reflect changes to plans, or even were installed ad hoc. In Hagia Sophia in Constantinople and in San Marco in Venice, mosaics were installed in a piecemeal fashion over centuries without an obvious plan. At Torcello, windows on the west wall were blocked in order to create the space for the massive eleventh-century Last Judgement mosaic. I would guess that there were deliberate choices and accidental results. Plan or no plan, and whether the Byzantine audience recognised the planning and technical skill of the artists or not, because a mosaic is a fluid snakeskin on the walls of a building, it is always subservient to the shape of that building and affected by the different angles of surfaces within the building, as well as by the lighting of the building. These could never be wholly predictable: light changes throughout the year and is never the same two days together.

This gets us back to space and place, order and confusion. Because of their interactions with light and shadow that mosaics are not passive but active and dynamic. Their dynamism changes the space around them. Even if we do not notice the details, in low light the clarity of mosaics is replaced by a numinous effect, things are vaguer and more shadowy, vision is destabilised and confused, the image moves. Is it any wonder that the angels appeared to descend from the mosaics in Hagia Sophia? These extraordinary effects are part of what constitutes the mystical atmosphere of the scenes and their setting. In the disruption, mosaics play with space and place. The familiar ordered place can become strange and mysterious, less controllable. What does a viewer, a

---

44 Mitchell 2005, 235.
45 For mosaics, Andreescu-Treadgold 1992 suggests mosaicists worked in an ad hoc way; James 2017 thinks there was more planning. For architects, see Ousterhout 2000; Buchwald 2004. Nesbitt 2012 argues for deliberate changes to church plans to change the nature of light in the building.

worshipper, do with this sense of visual uncertainty? The mosaic will glint even when it is not looked at; it may eventually catch your eye but does it matter if not? Does art only have a meaning through being looked at?[46] The work of art is intended to provide an adequate rendering of the visible world in visual language that is common to a given space and moment in time. But, as Charles Barber has argued, we need to go beyond the artist and viewer to the possibility that the icon—or indeed the mosaic—manifests an experience that lies beyond its manufacture and the occasions when it was viewed—the conditions that permit the subject to disclose itself in painting.[47] So what happens when you try to bring knowledge of Christ into human experience, a presence beyond representation?

If I were to spin a story around this, it would be of how space is lived experience but mosaics in their movement will create place whether or not there is anyone in the space to give them attention. They are subtle, inconstant things whose very fabrics are light and dark. The materials of the mosaics, the glass, the gold, were transformed into light, a light that carried a spiritual significance in Byzantium. In Christianity, the saints might shine like stars; Christ, the light of the world, was transfigured and revealed in his divinity on Mount Tabor through light; his divine light stood in contrast to the dark of ignorance; the Kingdom of Heaven is a place of light and splendour. Colour, as in the Christian world, was light made material and so the very light effects that were created by mosaics were themselves symbolic of God and the light of God. Mosaic colours speak of light and darkness, the gold backgrounds of so many mosaics was the very substance of divinity itself. And equally Byzantine images, Byzantine mosaics, are full of shadows as well as light, changeable and mutable. But the darkness was not simply negative and the absence of light was not evil. Rather, Byzantine theology is all about obscurity, about the impossibility of knowing God, that God is the divine darkness whose substance is unknown, that we see through a glass darkly, that the light shines in the darkness.

It has to be admitted that sometimes people noticed mosaics and wrote about them and that sometimes they did not. Perhaps more often than not mosaics were a sort of wallpaper, especially if they were old and grubby and had been there for any length of time. Because, really, what people went into churches for was the liturgy—and that idea of the church as a theatre for the liturgy would indeed turn images into backdrop. Nonetheless, that backdrop is nevertheless a part of the story, a part of the overall narrative (of which

---

46 Mitchell 2005, 49.
47 Barber 2002 and 2007.

ekphraseis were a part) going on within the church building. Wallpaper—the type, be it anaglypta, flock, woodchip or even yellow—can define the feel, the ambience of a room. If the icon mediates between man and God, the mosaic creates the space/place for that mediation, the magical space under the dome to encounter the divine, not to work out puzzles in iconography, the space transformed not by the viewer looking at the images but by being surrounded by them.[48] But mosaics themselves do something. They are 'moving images', parts of them appearing and disappearing as the light changes during the day and they change regardless of the desires and actions of their audience. This is what surprises the viewer and manages to draw and capture attention. Byzantine religious art set out to be a true representation of the divine; these images themselves and of themselves wordlessly tell a story and reveal the deeper meanings that art set out to convey. They create the space and cross it to us, simply by being. Next time you are in a Byzantine church turn the lights off and sit there and let the mosaics creep down your back. That 'moment of being' when the person becomes aware of the space and of the experience of the space, the moment when the images get the attention they wish for. Then come and tell me that they're not alive.

Bibliography

Primary Sources

Constantine of Rhodes, *On Constantinople and the Church of the Holy Apostles*, with a new edition of the Greek text by Ioannis Vassis. Ed. L. James. Farnham 2012.

Gregory the Great, *Letter* to Bishop Serenus of Marseille. Ed. D. Norberg, *S. Gregorii Magni Registrum epistularum*. Turnhout 1982.

Ignatius Monachus, *Narratio de imagine Christi in monasterio Latomi*. Ed. A. Papadopoulos-Kerameus, *Varia graeca sacra*. St Petersburg 1909; repr. Leipzig, 1975.

St Sophronius, *The Life of our Venerable Mother Mary of Egypt*. Tr. B. Ward, *Harlots of the Desert*, 46–48. Oxford 1987.

Michael the Deacon, *Ekphrasis*. Tr. C. Mango & J. Parker, "A Twelfth-Century Description of Hagia Sophia", DOP 14, 233–45. 1960.

Michael Psellos, *Chronographia*. Ed. D. R. Reinsch, *Michaelis Pselli Chronographia*. Berlin 2014.

Nilus of Sinai, *Letter to Prefect Olympiodorus*. PG 79, 577–80.

---

48   Mathews, 'The sequel to Nicaea II', 19. My thanks to Michelle O'Malley, as so often, and to Myrto Veikou, for their thoughts and encouragement, and to Reviewer 2, who articulated the key point for me in one sentence!

Photius, *Homilies*. Ed. B. Laourda, *Phōtiou Homiliai*. Thessaloniki, 1959. Tr. C. Mango, *The Homilies of Photios, Patriarch of Constantinople: Translation and Commentary*. Harvard 1958.

The Russian Primary Chronicle Laurentian Text. Ed & tr. S. H. Cross & O. P. Sherbowitz-Wetzor. Cambridge, MA 1953.

Secondary Sources

Andreescu-Treadgold, I. 1992. "The mosaic workshop at San Vitale", in Iannucci and Fiori (eds) 1992, 31–41.

Appadurai, A. (ed.) 1986. *The Social Life of Things: Commodities in Cultural Perspective*. Cambridge.

Barber, C. 2001. "Mimesis and memory in the narthex mosaics at the Nea Moni, Chios", *Art History* 24, 323–37.

Barber, C. 2002. *Figure and Likeness. On the limits of representation in Byzantine Iconoclasm*. Princeton.

Barber, C. 2007. *Contesting the logic of painting. Art and understanding in eleventh-century Byzantium*. Leiden.

Barry, F. 2007. "Walking on water: cosmic floors in antiquity and the middle ages", *The Art Bulletin* 89, 627–56.

Bennett, J. 2010. *Vibrant Matter. A political ecology of things*. Durham & London.

Bogost, I. 2012. *Alien Phenomenology or What it's like to be a thing*. Minneapolis & London.

Borsook, E. 1990. *Messages in Mosaic*. Oxford.

Brown, B. 1998. "How to do things with things (a Toy story)", *Critical Inquiry* 24, 935–64.

Brown, B. 2001. "Thing theory", *Critical Inquiry* 28, 1–22.

Brubaker, L. 2006. "Pictures are good to think with: looking at Byzantium", in Odorico, Agapitos & Hinterberger (eds) 2006, 221–40.

Buchwald, H. 2004. "Job site organization in thirteenth-century Byzantine buildings", in Cavaciocchi (ed.) 2004, 625–67.

Cavaciocchi, S. (ed.) 2004. *L'edilizia prima della rivoluzione industrial secc XIII–XVIII*. Prato.

Connor, C. 2016. *Saints and spectacle: Byzantine mosaics in their cultural setting*. Oxford.

Cormack, R. S. 2017. "After iconoclasm—forwards or backwards?", in Eastmond & Hatzaki (eds) 2017, 103–17.

Cox Miller, P. 2009. *The Corporeal Imagination*. Philadelphia.

de Certeau, M. 1984 [1980]. *L'Invention du Quotidien*. Tr. S. Rendell, *The Practice of Everyday Life*. Berkley.

Demus, O. 1948. *Byzantine Mosaic Decoration*. London.

Drpić, I. 2018. "The enkolpion: object, agency, self", *Gesta* 57, 197–224.

Eastmond, A. & M. Hatzaki (eds) 2017. *The Mosaics of Thessaloniki Revisited*. Athens.

Eastmond, A. & L. James (eds) 2003. *Icon and Word*. Farnham.
Elsner, J. 1998. "Image and Iconoclasm in Byzantium", *Art History* 11, 471–91.
Elsner, J. 1994. "The viewer and the vision: the case of the Sinai apse", *Art History* 17, 81–102.
Elsner, J. 2010. "Art History as Ekphrasis", *Art History* 33, 10–27.
Foskolou, V. 2018. "Decoding Byzantine ekphraseis on works of art. Constantine Manasses' description of earth and its audience", *BZ* 111, 71–102.
Franses, R. 2003. "When all that glitters is not gold: on the strange history of viewing Byzantine art", in Eastmond & James (eds) 2003, 13–24.
Franses, R. 2013. "Partial Transmission" in Peers (ed.) 2013, 175–87.
Franses, R. 2019. *Donor portraits in Byzantine art. The vicissitudes of contact between human and divine*. Cambridge.
Fried, M. 1980. *Absorption and theatricality*. Chicago.
Gell, A. 1998. *Art and Agency: An Anthropological Theory*. Oxford.
Iannucci, A. M. and C. Fiori (eds) 1992. *Mosaici a S Vitale e altri restauri: Atti del Convegno Mosaici a S Vitale e altri restauri*. Ravenna.
Jackson, M. & C. Nesbitt (eds) 2013. *Experiencing Byzantium*. Farnham.
James, L. 2011. "Images of text in Byzantine art: the apse mosaic in Hosios David, Thessaloniki", in Krause & Schellewald (eds) 2011, 255–66.
James, L. 2013. "Things: Art and Experience in Byzantium", in Jackson & Nesbitt (eds) 2013, 17–34.
James, L. 2017. *Mosaics in the medieval world*. Cambridge.
James, L. & R. Webb, 1991. "'To understand ultimate things and enter secret places': ekphrasis and art in Byzantium", *Art History* 14, 3–17.
Kazhdan, A. P. 2006. *A History of Byzantine Literature, vol. 2, 850–1000*. Ed. C. Angelidi. Athens.
Kitzinger, E. 1988. "Reflections on the Feast Cycle in Byzantine art", *CahArch*, 36, 51–74.
Krause, K. & B. Schellewald (eds) 2011. *Bild und Text im Mittelalter*. Vienna.
Latour, B. 1996. "On interobjectivity", *Mind, Culture and Activity* 3, 228–45.
Latour, B. 1999. *Pandora's Hope: Essays on the Reality of Science Studies*. Cambridge.
Lefebvre, H. 1991 [1974]. *La production de l'espace*. Tr. D. Nicholson-Smith, *The Production of Space*. Oxford.
Macrides, R. & P. Magdalino 1988. "The architecture of ekphrasis: construction and context of Paul the Silentiary's ekphrasis of Hagia Sophia", *Byzantine and Modern Greek Studies* 12, 47–82.
Maguire, H. 1992. "The Mosaics of Nea Moni: An Imperial Reading", *DOP* 46, 205–14.
Majeska, G. P. 1978. "Notes on the archaeology of St Sophia at Constantinople: the green marble bands on the floor", *DOP* 32, 299–308.
Mango, C. 1975. *The Art of the Byzantine Empire 312–1453*. Toronto.
Massey, D., J. Allen & P. Sarre (eds) 1999. *Human Geography Today*. Cambridge.

Mathews, T. F. 1998. "The sequel to Nicaea II in Byzantine Church Decoration", *Perkins Journal of Theology* 41, 11–21.

Messis, C., M. Mullett & I. Nilsson (eds) 2018. *Storytelling in Byzantium: Narratological Approaches to Byzantine Texts and Images*. Uppsala.

Mitchell, W. J. T. 2005. *What do pictures want? The lives and loves of images*. Chicago.

Nelson, R. S. 1989. "The Discourse of Icons, Then and Now", *Art History* 12, 144–57.

Nesbitt, C. 2012. "Shaping the sacred: Light and the experience of worship in Middle Byzantine Churches", *Byzantine and Modern Greek Studies* 36, 139–60.

Odorico, P., P. A. Agapitos & M. Hinterberger (eds) 2006. *L'écriture de la mémoire. La littérarite de l'historiographe*. Paris.

O'Malley, M. 2005. "Altarpieces and agency: the altarpiece of the Society of the Purification and its 'invisible skein of relations'", *Art History* 28, 417–41.

Ousterhout, R. 2000. *Master Builders of Byzantium*. Princeton.

Peers, G (ed.). 2013. *Byzantine Things in the World*. Yale.

Pentcheva, B. 2010. *The Sensual Icon. Space, ritual and the senses in Byzantium*. Philadelphia.

Pentcheva, B. (ed.) 2017. *Aural Architecture in Byzantium: music, acoustics and ritual*. London.

Pratchett, T. 1996. *Feet of Clay*. London.

Rose, G. 1999. "Performing space", in Massey, Allen & Sarre (eds) 1999, 247–59.

Soja, E. 1996. *Thirdspace: journeys to Los Angeles and other real-and-imagined places*. Oxford.

Thrift, N. 1996. *Spatial Formations, Theory, Culture and Society*. London.

Tronzo, W. 1994. "Mimesis in Byzantium: notes towards a history of the function of the image", *RES* 25, 61–76.

Tuan, Y.-F. 1977. *Space and Place: the perspective of experience*. Minneapolis.

Tuan, Y.-F. 1979. *Landscapes of Fear*. Oxford.

Veikou, M. 2018. "'Telling spaces' in Byzantium: ekphraseis, place-making and 'thick description'", in Messis, Mullett & Nilsson (eds) 2018, 15–32.

Walker White, A. 2015. *Performing Orthodox Ritual in Byzantium*. Cambridge.

Webb, L. 2017. "Transfigured. Mosaic and liturgy at Nea Moni", in Pentcheva (ed.) 2017, 127–42.

Webb, R. 1999. "The aesthetics of sacred space: narrative, metaphor and motion in *ekphraseis* of church buildings", *DOP* 53, 59–74.

Webb, R. 2009. *Ekphrasis, imagination and persuasion in ancient rhetorical theory and practice*. Farnham.

Webb, R. 2017. "Spatiality, embodiment, and agency in ekphraseis of church buildings" in Pentcheva (ed.) 2017, 163–75.

PART 6

Imaginary Spaces: Byzantine Storyworlds

∴

Editorial Note on Part 6

This section deals with spatial imaginaries encountered in Byzantine images and texts, offering different perspectives on how to deal with spatiality and worldmaking in both literary and material culture. In the first chapter, Rico Franses applies a phenomenological approach to the examination of Byzantine nature scenes in his study of the *Menologion* of Basil II. Franses discusses the pictorial representations of landscape as dynamic elements of varying degrees of flux, working always in conjunction with the human body. In the next two chapters, we return to the recurring issue of mobility and its meanings in Byzantine cultural expressions. David Westberg, in his study of Palladius' *Historica Lausiaca*, takes on a cognitive perspective as he argues for a connection between the monks' mindsets and their physical movement in the narrative. Yulia Mantova turns to a series of Middle Byzantine hagiographical texts, through which she explores changes in the literary techniques used for the textualization of travel. Paolo Cesaretti and Basema Hamarneh are also concerned with hagiography and issues of textual spatiality. In their case study on two Lives of Holy Fools, they argue for a strict connection between the perception of space and eschatological concerns. The section closes with a study by Brad Hostetler on spatialities of Byzantine epigraphy. Hostetler offers an analysis of inscriptions as spaces visually perceived by the reader, focusing, on the one hand, on the performative dimension of an epigram within a space—in this case, an object (a Byzantine reliquary enkolpion)—and, on the other hand, on the epigram's contribution to that space's (the enkolpion's) performativity.

The Phenomenology of Landscape in the *Menologion* of Basil II

Rico Franses

There are no 'pure' landscapes in Byzantine art. Scenes of nature there are aplenty, but all of these contain dominating human figures that serve as the central narrative focus of the picture. This chapter attempts to show, however, that in the case of the *Menologion* of Basil II (at least), landscapes are always much more than simple backdrops. Space, in these scenes, never appears as something that is taken for granted. It is never a static, neutral medium that we move around in and through, as though it did not exist. Frequently, it is a dynamic element, in varying degrees of flux. Crucially, in relation to several of the themes taken up in this volume, that flux is always in conjunction with the body–the space of the body, the body in its natural environment, and, most significantly, the way in which each of the body and space come to mutually transform each other as they interact. What emerges from the analysis of all these elements is one key aspect of (to use the felicitous phrase of the editors) the Byzantine spatial imaginary.

In keeping with one of the goals of this volume of producing a theoretically up-to-date dialogue with other scholarly fields, to help us understand this spatial imaginary we make use of a second spatial imaginary, one articulated at a different time (20th-century modernity), in a different medium (verbal, as opposed to visual form) and in a different discipline (the philosophical school of phenomenology). The authors discussed here are Gilles Deleuze, Henri Maldiney, and Erwin Straus. This approach is adopted not because phenomenology is taken as providing the master-key that will unlock "the truth" of Byzantine practices; rather, in the course of my research into both the images and phenomenology, I began to notice overlaps between the two that allowed me to understand each better when viewed through the screen of the other. If, in their encounter, the result is that Byzantine spatiality is theorized—in effect, the argument being made below is that Byzantine landscapes constitute a form of phenomenological investigation in and of themselves—the reverse is also true. Phenomenology can be said to be "Byzantinized", as we see how several of the concepts that it is grappling with turn out to have been concerns of, and given concrete visual instantiation by, the entirely unrelated (and much earlier) culture. There can be no doubt that all the modern authors discussed here (who themselves often reference Byzantine art) would be the first to agree that Byzantium shows us some of the ways in which space, conceived of as both a natural and a human phenomenon, can be conceptualized and experienced.

The *Menologion* of Basil II is a celebrated manuscript containing 430 illustrations, mostly of saints of the Orthodox Church (Biblioteca Apostolica Vaticana, Vatican, Vat. gr. 1613, late tenth century). At first sight, the apparently endless recurrence of figures can seem monotonous. However, on closer inspection the pictures reveal themselves as anything but rote repetition, each being carefully considered in terms of its composition and spatial dispositions. The saints appear in a variety of positions and activities, most strikingly either standing singly in frontal representation, as the Empress Theodora II (p. 392 of the *Menologion*, Figure 25.1), or undergoing martyrdom, as in the Execution of Autonomous (p. 30, Figure 25.2). However, there are also other scenes where they appear in an outdoor setting, often facing a modest church, as Isidore of Pelusium (p. 371, Figure 25.3).[1]

Of these scenes, let us concentrate on the Execution of Autonomous and St Theodora. From the point of view of the positioning of the figures in relation to the architectural setting, these scenes make for an interesting comparison. Theodora is manifestly placed within the precinct drawn by the architectural framework, clearly on the same floor plane as the columns, which is marked by a uniform band of light green. By contrast, however in the martyrdom scene, despite the presence of an elaborate cityscape, the execution takes place not within the city confines, but unmistakably outside of it. This can be seen in the uneven ground as well as the rocky mound to the right. As a first proposition, then, we may say that in this manuscript a distinction is being drawn between something that looks very much like the twentieth-century structuralist division of Claude Lévi-Strauss between Nature and Culture.[2] Although these terms may not be fully appropriate to a Byzantine context, we may paraphrase this as a distinction between the architectural spaces that signify both sanctity and civilization, and the places where those features are absent, as in the space of nature, where barbarity may occur.

---

[1] The text that has become the standard for the art-historical study of the manuscript is Ševčenko 1962. More recently, see Zakharova 2008. It should be noted that the convention for referencing the pagination of the manuscript is not by folio number, as is the usual case for manuscripts, but by page number.
[2] See for example Lévi-Strauss 1983.

FIGURE 25.1   Empress Theodora II, *Menologion* of Basil II, Biblioteca Apostolica Vaticana, Vatican, Vat. gr. 1613, p. 392. Reproduced by permission of Biblioteca Apostolica Vaticana, with all rights reserved.

This conception of two different kinds of space also corresponds to a difference in the physical character of those spaces. Inside the built environment, the floor surface is absolutely flat and the space is regularized, calm, and static. Outside in nature, however, the space is more unsettled. This is visible in the uneven groundline just mentioned, and especially in the jagged shape of the rock, which contrasts with the straight lines and geometry of the city and its wall behind. At first sight, it might appear that this more agitated effect has been deliberately created to reflect the violence of the iconography. However, our other nature scenes prove the case to be rather more complex. In the picture of Isidore of Pelusium, the winding paths, the rise and fall of the hills, and again, the jagged rocks all give an air of ceaseless, irregular motion (Figure 25.3). In this manuscript, we can say, nature is always in a state of unrest, even when the iconography is innocuous.

Despite the fact that the human activities do not always match up exclusively with the spatial settings—it is true that violence, when it occurs, does take place in nature, but not every human activity set there is violent—our structuralist division between Civilization and Nature does, nonetheless, remain valid. We see now, however, that it applies less to people and more

FIGURE 25.2 The Execution of Autonomous, *Menologion* of Basil II, Biblioteca Apostolica Vaticana, Vatican, Vat. gr. 1613, p. 30. Reproduced by permission of Biblioteca Apostolica Vaticana, with all rights reserved.

specifically to the character of the space: calm and ordered vs. irregular and unsettled. Let us consider further these different kinds of spaces.

The conception of the differing character of space echoes the findings of the group of phenomenologist writers mentioned above. The *Stanford Encyclopedia of Philosophy* defines phenomenology as "the study of structures of consciousness as experienced from the first-person point of view".[3] Within this, a key line of inquiry, and the one with which we are primarily concerned, investigates the development of our sense of space through our sensory interactions with the physical world. Our authors all pursue this theme, albeit from slightly different perspectives. Henri Maldiney (1912–2013) can be most firmly located within the field of phenomenology, having spent his career as a Professor of Philosophy in Belgium and France. Gilles Deleuze (1925–1995), considered one of the pre-eminent French philosophers of the twentieth century, although sometimes disavowing adherence to the school of phenomenology, certainly drew heavily on its tradition. He is widely acknowledged as having expanded its thinking in radical new directions. Erwin Straus

---

3 Smith 2013.

FIGURE 25.3   Isidore of Pelusium, *Menologion* of Basil II, Biblioteca Apostolica Vaticana, Vatican, Vat. gr. 1613, p. 371. Reproduced by permission of Biblioteca Apostolica Vaticana, with all rights reserved.

(1891–1975) was a German-American neurologist, who, although not a professional philosopher, had a keen interest in phenomenological psychology. His work was fundamental to both Maldiney and Deleuze. Examining the thought of these figures allows us to approach our images with fresh eyes, and reveals them to be concerned with spatial issues in ways that have not previously been explored.

Significantly for this essay, which attempts to draw together both philosophical analysis and visual art, two giants of the late nineteenth-century art world exert a powerful influence over both Maldiney and Deleuze. The first is the art historian Alois Riegl and the second is the artist Paul Cezanne. To begin with Riegl, in his book *The Late Roman Art Industry*, originally published in 1901, he draws a distinction between two different kinds vision, one of which he labels 'haptic', the other 'optic'. Although the distinction itself will not play a major role in our own analysis of Byzantine spatiality, almost all of the concepts that do prove useful to us emerge most fully in the theoretical discussions around the terms. It is therefore worth examining them in greater detail.

Haptic, deriving from Greek verb ἅπτω (*hapto*), relates to touch, and Riegl sees haptic vision as bearing similarities to the way in which we perceive objects through the sense of touch. Optic vision, by contrast, he considers to operate more in consonance with the way in which he understands the eye to perceive things in its own intrinsically natural mode. He associates each of these forms of vision with the distance of the eye from the object that it looks at. The further away we are from that object, he notes, the more prone we are to seeing not only the thing itself, but a host of other optical effects as well, primarily the play of light and shadow which obscures the clarity of the item. The closer we are to it, however, the less opportunity there is for these interferences to show through, and the closer we come to perceiving the object in its 'true', unmediated state. For Riegl, this unmediated sense of the item itself is also the one that we obtain through touch, where we feel the thing directly, getting to know its material solidity, its contours, and, most importantly, its three-dimensional form, without anything intervening between it and ourselves. Haptic vision thus delivers a world that is clear, well-defined, and stable. Optic vision, on the other hand, renders a world that is vague, indefinite and inherently unstable, as objects lose their material individuality and blur into the environment.[4]

For Riegl, the prime example of haptic vision is Egyptian art, which offers an uncluttered sense of the object itself by emphasizing simple, clear outlines. Especially in the low relief typical of the genre, no optical effects such as shadows and silhouettes are allowed to disrupt one's perception, and hence one's sense of apprehending the object as one might do through touch. His prime example of optic vision is Late Antique Roman art, which renders complex figures in high relief with deep undercutting and foreshortening. This produces an unclear, constantly shifting visual field of protruding, wavering silhouettes and dark, undercut shadows, all difficult to grasp and comprehend.[5]

As mentioned, the optic/haptic distinction is taken up in some detail by two of the major figures we are concerned with, Maldiney and Deleuze. Maldiney follows Riegl faithfully in his understanding of the characteristics of each of the modes, but Deleuze, while agreeing with them about optic vision, rings considerable changes on the notion of the haptic.[6] Rather than seeing it as providing stability, he regards it as being even more unsettling and un-fixed than the optic. Deleuze bases himself in this connection on the ideas of another art historian, Wilhelm Worringer, who, in a celebrated book entitled *Form and Gothic*, studies the specific qualities of the linear forms that appear in Northern Medieval art, especially in the Gothic style. The essential feature of the Gothic line, he finds, is its extreme irregularity, twisting and turning back on itself,

---

[4] Riegl 1985, 22–7. In the English translation, Riegl's "haptic" is rendered as "tactile".
[5] Ibid. See further 51–132.
[6] See Maldiney 1973, 255–70.

never finding or following its own natural course, and always defying a clear, simple geometry.[7] In the intense, restless energy of this line, Deleuze sees the mark of an agitated hand with a nervy compulsion that, when liberated of control and left to its own devices, produces patterns more complex and intricate than the eye can naturally follow. This volatile, continuously shifting domain constitutes for Deleuze the essence of the haptic—or, as he often terms it, the tactile.[8]

If neither optic nor haptic vision independently provides a stable world for Deleuze, such a thing is still available, except that it is only produced through the joint operations of tactile and optic vision together. In this respect, tactile and optic are complementary, each correcting the fluctuations and uncertainties of the other.[9] Deleuze's philosophical interest, however, lies not with that constant world, but rather, with its unstable component fields, especially the haptic. And he finds there a greater degree of uncertainty than anything envisaged by either Maldiney, or, indeed, Riegl himself.

Before proceeding with our investigation, however, let us note one essential point. As much as Deleuze overturns some of the fundamental conceptions under discussion, there is one key issue on which he, Riegl, Maldiney, and indeed Straus (as we will shortly see) remain firmly in agreement. Irrespective of which attributes are assigned to which individual mode of vision, all believe that, in our lived experience, *space comes to us divided*. Each considers that we distinguish between two different kinds of space, one that is calm and stable, and one that is unstable and in flux. It will be noted that this distinction corresponds very closely to the one that we discovered in the *Menologion*, where the architectural scenes show a well-organized, quiescent space and the nature scenes show one that is variable, in motion, and inconstant. Byzantine art and the phenomenologists seem to be on the same page here, exploring closely related issues and arriving at similar conclusions. Let us examine each in further detail.

For all of the authors we are considering, underlying the distinction between the two kinds of space is another, even more fundamental issue. All hold to what might be called a theory of primary sensory chaos. This concerns the idea that in the first instance, we perceive not defined, quantifiable space or objects, but a confusing melee of fragmentary sensory stimuli. It is only in the wake of this initial disorder that the familiar components of our conventional world begin to take shape for us, and emerge into a recognizable whole. This

---

7 Worringer 1920, 46–54.
8 Deleuze 2003, 85–91.
9 Ibid 88.

understanding of the functioning of the senses also means that they are always linked (at each of their ends, so to speak) to both the world of chaos and that of stability. There is thus always latent in our awareness of the world some of that initial disorder of primary perception.[10]

Maldiney in particular has a specific interest in the process that takes place as we move away from the state of chaos and arrive at our standard apprehension of a more settled world. In his examination of this transition, he accords special status to certain works of art that he maintains take as their subject this very process of coming into perception. To this process itself he gives the name "form", and although he uses the term as a noun, it should best be understood as a verb, as in "being formed", or "something taking form". Maldiney further draws a crucial distinction between 'form' and 'image'; for him, the image is what we might think of today simply as a picture, a representation of the 'real' world as we know it. For Maldiney, however, such an image is what *results from* its form; the picture-image is the end product of the action of form. Some paintings however, rather than showing an image, make manifest the form, tracing the progression itself of a dawning awareness, an unfolding, as the more familiar world of objects and space draws into view. A key term for the discussion of form is thus 'becoming', as the emphasis is placed not on the final result—the image—but on the passage towards that result.[11]

Maldiney's conception can best be traced in the late works of Cezanne; indeed, Cezanne may well be listed as the Master Phenomenologist, the artist in whose wake all our philosophers are trailing as they attempt to account for his achievements. In a painting such as the view of Mont Sainte-Victoire now in the Kunsthaus, Zurich, at first glance, the general but blurry shapes of a mountain can be discerned, yet the canvas as a whole also seems to be covered by a flurry of random marks (1902–1906, Figure 25.4). After a few moments' contemplation however, those marks resolve themselves further into discernible entities. This is visible in the sky and clouds above as well as the mountain itself. However, the effect is most pronounced in the fore- and middle ground, where the marks coalesce into the shapes of trees and even small buildings. At each point in the painting, the same mark serves both as a registration of something like a primordial sensation—it appears as an optical flare not forming part of any recognizable object—and simultaneously, as the building block, a

---

10   Riegl 1985, 21–22; Maldiney 1973, 237–39 and 243–44; Straus 1963, 312–23, 351–53. This is also a recurring idea that is widespread in all Deleuze's works; see for example Deleuze 2003, 78.

11   Maldiney 1967, 209–14, especially 210–11. See also Maldiney 1973, 232–54, especially 242 and 249. See also Straus 1963, 322.

FIGURE 25.4 Paul Cezanne, La Montagne Sainte-Victoire, 1902–1906. Oil on canvas, 63 x 83 cm. Kunsthaus Zurich. Purchased with a contribution of Emil Bührle, 1946.

constituent element, of the landscape itself. As a result, the scene seems to be in the course of distilling out of that welter of primary marks, and it appears as though, in this process, the world is coming into being, taking its form, before our eyes.[12]

Returning now to our Byzantine nature-scapes, close examination shows that they too deal with a related phenomenon, although as will become apparent, there are also significant differences. We mentioned earlier that in a scene such as Isidore of Pelusium, the space itself is in a state of unrest. Looking more closely, we can expand this by noting that not only is the terrain marked by steep and abrupt geographical features, but, at certain points, it appears that something deep within the essential stuff of the land itself is in upheaval and motion. The craggy rocks, noted earlier, are preceded by shooting lines that seem to have carried them rapidly upward in an eruption from their

---

12 For more on this subject, see the two essays by Maurice Merleau-Ponty, "Eye and Mind" and "Cezanne's Doubt", both in Merleau-Ponty 1993.

subterranean home. The agitation continues as well in the lowest level of the ledge in front of Isidore, where the rocks run down and back towards him, whereas on the upper level of the same outcrop, they surge upwards and away from him (Figure 25.3). By comparison, in the Cezanne, although one might feel that there is movement within the picture, that motion comes not from the earth itself, which is largely static. Rather, as encapsulated by Maldiney with his concept of form, it emerges from the visual field as a whole in the process of its transformation into an image. If anything, we might say that there is a sense of the scene rushing towards us as it forms itself within our perception, even as the ground itself remains still.

The specific 'deep' motion that we see in the Byzantine scene can still be elucidated in reference to Maldiney, however some preliminary comments from Straus are also required. As mentioned, Straus, too, writes about primary sensory confusion, and in his discussion of the topic, he gives an example of someone in a landscape at twilight, or in darkness or fog. He describes how, at that moment, before recognizing the features of a known space, "I am still in the landscape. My present location is still determined by the next adjacent location; I can still move. But I no longer know *where* I am, I can no longer determine my position in a panoramic whole".[13] Maldiney, too, expands on this moment of both stillness and confusion: "In the midst of an enveloping plenitude, we are *here*; this is the promordial spatiality that includes no system of reference, no coordinates, no point of origin". He then further asks us to think about what happens when the observer, in this state of indeterminacy, starts to move: "In this progression [...] not only do we walk without a goal [...] but our walking is integrated in space, with no concern for any sense of orientation or previously established points in geographical space".[14]

At this juncture, let us pause and consider further that first instant, in between rest and movement. As we have seen, even before I begin to move, the landscape already looks as if it is unstable and in motion, in process, as it 'slides' into perception. In addition to this, however, as I start forward, each subsequent point that I look at is also subject to the same sense of unfolding, of coming into being. As a result, each new perception arising from my movement begins before the previous one has ended. Thus, as I progress, each instant's unfolding into being links up with the previous one, blending seamlessly with it, so that the whole landscape appears to be in one continuous process of unfolding, the points within it joined together in a continuous line

---

13 Straus 1963, 319.
14 Maldiney 1967, 203–4.

of becoming. It is exactly this phenomenon, this process, I believe, that we see in the Byzantine nature scenes. We find it in the shooting lines running up to each outcrop, as well as in the outcrops themselves, each one consisting of a grouping of smaller, almost identical units, all of them in motion, all of them culminating in the furthermost, uppermost one. In all of these, it is as though a sequence of movements of coming into perception, each one slightly later in time and slightly further along in space, are elided with each other and drawn together into a unity that has become landscape.

This sense of progressive unfolding within the landscape is also indicative of a further, perhaps even more extraordinary phenomenon discussed both by Maldiney and Deleuze. If, in the first instance, the coming into existence of the scene is related to our burgeoning perceptual awareness, there is also a second sense of coming to existence that is, somehow, independent of perception. As the scene distils out into our consciousness, so another, separate awareness begins, one in which it appears as though that process of formation is also taking place only in relation to the landscape itself; it seems as though that landscape is forming itself, emerging into being of itself. Within the shooting lines and the compounded rock formations described above, each adjacent point is linked to the previous one as though it depended on that earlier one for its very existence. And each preceding point carries the subsequent one within it as a potentiality, functioning as the springboard, the energy source, for it, like a series of building waves. It is as if all are linked along a continuous, moving chain of being that carries its source within itself, so that the process of coming into being, into form, takes place through its own agency. This is a landscape undergoing its own self-actualization; in Maldiney's terminology, this is an act of autogenesis, of forms forming themselves.[15]

We thus have two different ways in which the phenomenological world seems to unveil itself, each bringing with it a different sense of what space *is*. In the first of these, we are aware of our own involvement in the process of spatialization; here we see space still in the making in relation to our perception, and we thus see how space emerges into being *for us*. In the second, space feels as though it is coming into existence independently, as though it is generating *itself*. To use the phenomenologist's vocabulary again, this is space in its conception; it is how space would have to conceive of itself in order to build itself. In this second sense, space becomes transformed into a magical, enchanted entity, not as if in an Alice-through-the-looking-glass fantasy world,

---

15   For Maldiney, see Maldiney 1967, 211. For Deleuze, see Deleuze 2003, 41. See also Bogue 2013, 125. The Bogue book constitutes an excellent introduction to many of the themes discussed in this article.

but as a three-dimensional material configuration endowed with its own powers of self-creation and self-sustenance. Both of these modalities of space are omnipresent in our nature scenes, in the rippling lines, the eruptions, the energy, the life that is coursing through the landscape. All these are the living earth both appearing to me as my senses generate it for me, and bringing itself into existence, thinking itself into being. And, as a reflection on the topic of spatiality in general, we might say that it is both of these modalities in play simultaneously with each other (although not necessarily in phase with each other), that constitutes a major part of spatiality itself.

In addition to these conceptions, the phenomenological account provides one further level of analysis that is of relevance to us. It concerns not only the exterior world but also the perceiving subject. For Straus, the act of perception does not entail a pre-formed, pre-extant subject who is waiting to understand what is happening in the landscape in front of him or her. Rather, the subject themself only comes into existence through and with the process of perception; indeed, for Straus, it is one and the same process. Thus, the dawning awareness of which we have been speaking extends not only to the unfamiliar landscape, but to the perceiver themself. "In sensory experience as I become aware of the world around me, I also, simultaneously become aware of myself as a sensing subject", says Straus. And he continues:

> In sensory experience, there unfolds both the becoming of the subject and the happenings of the world. I become only insofar as something happens, and something happens (for me) only insofar as I become [...]. In sensing, both self and world unfold simultaneously for the sensing subject.[16]

Straus further expands on this process by stressing how closely associated the not-quite-yet subject is with the not-quite-yet world. He uses the term '*mitsein*', that is, 'being-with', to describe the way in which that subject and its surroundings are so imbricated with each other that there is no clear differentiation either between the self and the world or, indeed, between objects in the world themselves.[17]

With this idea of the subject-as-process, we round out our theoretical investigation. Combining Straus' conceptions with those of Maldiney seen earlier, we arrive at what might be called the full phenomenological account of spatiality.

---

16   Straus 1963, 351.
17   Straus 1963, 351–52, 354 and 356.

Process, unfolding, is everywhere: in the two layers of which we spoke above, whereby the world seems to emerge both in relation to my perception and in relation only to itself, and in the subject itself coming into being along with the almost-but-not-quite identical worlds of each of those layers. All these processes supervene upon each other simultaneously, linked by an umbilical cord that conjoins them at every step as they call each other into existence. It is all this, we might say, that constitutes spatiality itself.

With Straus' conceptions of the subject and the world being born together, let us return again to our outdoor scenes. In the martyrdom picture of Autonomous, we mentioned the undulating ground on which the figures stand, but let us examine this in greater detail. It will be noted immediately that this undulation is not a 'natural' effect of the earth, but rather coincides with the placement of the feet of the figures; indeed, it is not too much to say that the ground gives way under the press of human contact (Figure 25.2). By contrast, in the architectural scene of Theodora, the ground on which the figure stands is hard and uniform; it does not yield to human contact (Figure 25.1). In the Autonomous representation, space is thus shown as being interactive with, responsive to, humans. It deforms, it seems to be labile and plastic. As with Straus and Maldiney, we have a sense of space as not being fixed, determinate, or indeed, finished, but rather still in process. It does not exist as an independent item 'out there', but as something that 'happens' in consonance with, in interaction with, the body.

Yet, there are also differences between the way in which space is represented in these paintings and the way in which it is conceived within modern phenomenological theory. The Strausian model discussed above considers that the body and the world are each closely intertwined, each mutually affecting the other. However, the Autonomous scene does not go quite that far. Here, it is not a mutual interaction that unfolds, but, rather, humans who cause the ground to be displaced. There is no reverse action upon the body. In these pictures, we thus learn not only about a specific conception of space, but conversely, also a specific conception of the body. Space is malleable, but the human is, so to speak, primary. He is solid and unyielding, producing a pronounced physical effect on his surroundings.

In the Isidore scene, however, we do see spatial configurations that come closer to the modern phenomenological understanding. In this picture, the main figure is placed in a dip formed by a descending hillside behind him, and an ascending one in front of him. He thus stands at the nadir of an inverted triangle (Figure 25.3). It cannot be claimed that the weight of the saint has caused the ground to subside, but equally, his position in relation to his environment is certainly not accidental. One would do well to recall here our earlier analysis of the landscape in motion, in the process of making itself. With Isidore, it is not only the individual currents rippling within the ground, but indeed, the entire landscape as a whole that seems to be moving, sliding towards the right. The hill behind him rises and then descends towards him, just as the hill in front rises also to the right, away from him. At a minimum we may say that the saint here is the fulcrum of the shifting ground, that its movement, including its descent and ascent, is determined by its relation to him.

In connection with this, we should also return to the comments of Straus and Maldiney as they imagine someone coming to perception in a landscape, and simultaneously beginning to move. Maldiney notes that in this circumstance, we do not so much walk *through* that space as *in* it. 'Through' implies for him a fixed, inert space that we transit through, entering at one end and exiting at the other. Moving 'in' space, however, carries a sense whereby it moves with us. "My relation to the landscape is circular", he writes. "It envelopes me below a horizon determined by my 'here', and I am only here because of it".[18] The Isidore scene is surely making a similar point; the 'here' of the saint is marked by the specific place that he occupies within the rise and fall of the land, but that rise and fall is also clearly determined by himself as it pivots around and below him, and as it comes into perception for him. If we were to imagine him moving, we feel that the landscape, too, in its current shape may also move as well, with him always at the nadir. Body and landscape are bound together, each the condition of existence of the other, each locked in an eternal now and here, no matter how much time passes and no matter where they go.

The author who has taken these ideas of our chiasmatic relationship with the living landscape to their furthest extent is Deleuze. If Straus and Maldiney are concerned with the integration of the body and the landscape, Deleuze thinks of that relationship as one of forces between different elements. Indeed, our earlier comments about energy pulsing through the landscape as it seems to be coming into being can also be reframed in a Deleuzian vocabulary of forces and flux.[19] This applies as well to the Autonomous scene, where the feet of the protagonists are figured as exerting force on the surrounding space, which in turn, takes up that force and is pressed, moulded, by it (Figure 25.2).

Yet, once we have begun to speak of forces, our understanding of scenes such as this begins to change. We can also say that figure and space are conjoined by that force, and the part of the body that is exerting it, the foot, is intrinsically linked to the ground that is first displaced beneath it, but then

---

18 Maldiney 1967, 204.
19 References to forces play a major part in almost all of Deleuze's writings. See for example Deleuze 2003, 40–46. For more on the subject, see Bougue 2013, 111–30.

rises up around it, enfolding it. In the Autonomous picture, this effect is not strong enough to alter the primary sense of the foot as the component that is the origin of the force, but other scenes in the manuscript show elements of the body much more firmly interlinked with their surroundings. In order to understand this idea of an especially close connection between part of a figure and part of the environment, it is necessary to detour briefly through one of Deleuze's key concepts, elaborated initially in conjunction with Félix Guattari, the body without organs.

We usually think of our bodies as single, coherent, unified entities, all parts conjoined with the others by skin, bone, muscle, nerves, and organs that operate to keep the whole system functional. This, say Deleuze and Guattari, we might call the body *with* organs, a phrase they borrow from the French avant-garde theatre figure and poet Antonin Artaud. But, Deleuze and Guattari, again borrowing from Artaud, ask you not to think of your body—so familiar to you—as the body-with-organs, but as a body estranged from you, a body *without* organs. To arrive at this conception, they draw upon the phenomenological tradition we have been examining above, especially the work of Straus, where the body itself is not an independent entity, but is constantly intertwined with its environment in a mutual dance of becoming. They write that the body without organs would not have all its parts inherently connected to each other. Rather, it would be "crisscrossed with axes and thresholds, with latitudes and longitudes and geodesic lines, traversed by gradients marking the transitions and the becomings, the destinations of the subject developing along these particular vectors".[20] Such a body without organs, we might say, is a body conceived in the flux of its intensities, exceeding its boundaries, and becoming enmeshed with its surroundings.

With these ideas in mind, let us turn to a further scene in the *Menologion*, The Discovery of the Head of John the Baptist. To the left of the picture stands a crowd of people, in the midst of which is the Emperor Constantine and a priest with a censer. To the right, two workers, one with a pick and one with a spade, uncover a basket in which is contained the head of John the Baptist. We begin to see the effect of the body without organs in the feet of the workman to the right. As with the Autonomous representation, they have caused the ground to subside, however, for the rear foot, so pronounced has this effect become and so securely ensconced is it now in its pocket of earth, that foot and

---

20 Deleuze & Guattari 1977, 19. For the body without organs in general, see the same publication, 9–16. See also Deleuze & Guattari 2005, 149–67, and Deleuze 2003, 32–39. See also Bogue 2013, 124–30.

PHENOMENOLOGY OF LANDSCAPE IN THE *MENOLOGION* OF BASIL II   573

earth form a single unit. Joined by a vector of force, the combined elements separate out from the overall structure of a body with organs, the foot more intensely connected to the earth below than the body above (Figure 25.5).

Additional elements in the scene allow us to expand this analysis even further, into our reading of the landscape itself. In this respect, let us look more closely at the roughly oval area formed by the black hole in which is placed the basket, extending slightly outward on either side, especially to the right. Within this zone, the primary element is the basket itself. Situated, as was Isidore, at the nadir of the 'V' formed by the descending mountainside on the left and the rising terrain to the right, it seems to sink, pressing down ever further into the hole in the ground from which it is purportedly emerging. So unbearably heavy is it that the rocky outcrop to the right, surely not accidentally painted in bright red, seems as though it is being squeezed upwards and outwards by its relentless downward pull. Yet, these are not the only forces in play. The foremost leg of the worker to the right pushes back down and to the left, countering the movement of the outcrop and blocking its trajectory. The diagonal thrust of the spade, too, works against the outcrop, just as it seems to compound the downward draw of the basket.

FIGURE 25.5   Discovery of the Head of John the Baptist, *Menologion* of Basil II, Biblioteca Apostolica Vaticana, Vatican, Vat. gr. 1613, p. 420. Reproduced by permission of Biblioteca Apostolica Vaticana, with all rights reserved.

When seen in this way, we may say that the area circumscribed by an imaginary line running from the front foot of the worker, up to his hand on the spade, across the top of the black hole with its fluctuating upper lip, and then back down the mountainside to the left, constitutes a discrete visual zone of its own. All the elements within it are locked in a micro-storm of forces that binds them together pictorially as an inseparable unit (indeed, so intense is that zone that even the censer is drawn mysteriously, magnetically towards it). Here, again, the lower leg of the worker, his hand, and the foremost section of the spade belong more to the hole and the basket than they do to anything else to which they are 'naturally' attached. In this zone, we see both body and landscape traversed by the gradients, axes and thresholds to which Deleuze and Guattari refer. And this, too, we will say, is spatiality, body and earth bound together in flux, the flux of their mutual intensities.

∴

In conclusion, we have so far seen a number of ways in which Byzantine nature scenes make manifest a form of spatial thinking that bears close similarity to that of modern phenomenology. In the first instance, we discussed how our world is born for us, both in relation to our burgeoning perception, and also only unto itself, as an entity brought into existence through autogenesis. In the second, we considered the manner in which our larger sense of location in space comes into being through an imbrication of body and space together that frequently reconfigures the very nature of that body, that space, and the material world. These analyses should be set against the conventional view of Byzantine art, where space is often thought of as the missing dimension, the feature that drops out of the visual vocabulary as attention is focused on the immaterial aspects of spirituality. But on the evidence of what we have seen, there can be no doubt about how important space itself is within Byzantine visual thinking. It is not necessarily a space that we post-Renaissance moderns easily recognize, indeed, it may well not even have been a space that the Byzantines themselves recognized from their daily experience, but it is certainly consistent spatial thinking, of that there can be no doubt.[21]

In the early sections of this paper, we touched on several subjects that we have not had time to develop. Prime amongst them are the differences between civilization and nature, and the optic and the haptic. All warrant

---

21   For more on the notion of visual thinking as a mode of conceptualization, and its relation to other modes such as verbal thinking, see Franses 2021.

further exploration, and we should add as well a further topic of major importance, the overarching theological implications of each. Underpinning all of these issues, however, is the key point in our analysis, the notion of space coming to us divided, either in calm, stable form, or in its more agitated form. In this paper we have concentrated primarily on the latter, and in doing so have followed phenomenological theory, which generally seems to consider that 'other' space to be far less interesting. Yet, there is clearly much more to be said about it, not least because of the sheer number of scenes in which it appears in the *Menologion*; the Byzantines are certainly exploring each of these modes in equal measure. No doubt an in-depth analysis of these representations will demonstrate as complex an engagement with the core questions of the body in space that we have been examining. A consideration of both modes together will surely reveal unforeseen riches in the Byzantine lifeworld of spatiality.

Bibliography

Secondary Sources

Bougue, R. 2013. *Deleuze on Music, Painting, and the Arts*. London.

Deleuze, G. & F. Guattari 1977. *Anti-Oedipus: Capitalism and Schizophrenia*. Trs. R. Hurley, M. Seem & H. R. Lane. Minneapolis.

Deleuze, G. & F. Guattari 2005. *A Thousand Plateaus: Capitalism and Schizophrenia*. Tr. B. Massumi. Minneapolis.

Deleuze, G. 2003. *Francis Bacon: The Logic of Sensation*. Tr. D. Smith. London.

Franses, R. 2021. "To Not Know God. Geometrical Abstraction and Visual Theology in Islamic Art", in E. Baboula and L. Jessop (eds), *Art and Material Culture in the Byzantine and Islamic Worlds. Essays in Honour of Erica Cruikshank Dodd*. Leiden, 265–85.

Lévi-Strauss, C. 1983. *The Raw and the Cooked*. Tr. J. Weightman & D. Weightman. Chicago.

Maldiney, H. 1967. "The Aesthetic of Rhythms", in Maldiney 2013, 201–30.

Maldiney, H. 1973. "Art and the Power of the Ground", in Maldiney 2013, 231–70.

Maldiney, H. (ed.) 2013. *Regard Parole Espace*. Paris.

Merleau-Ponty, M. 1993. *The Merleau-Ponty Aesthetics Reader: Philosophy and Painting*. Ed. G. Johnson. Evanston, IL.

Riegl, A. 1985. *Late Roman Art Industry*. Tr. R. Winkes. Rome.

Ševčenko, I. 1962. "The Illuminators of the Menologium of Basil II", *DOP* 16, 244–70.

Smith, D. 2013. "Phenomenology", in *The Stanford Encyclopedia of Philosophy*, accessed 10 September, 2019. https://plato.stanford.edu/entries/phenomenology/.

Straus, E. 1963. *The Primary World of Senses: A Vindication of Sensory Experience*. Tr. J. Needleman. London.

Worringer, W. 1920. *Form Problems of the Gothic*. New York.

Zakharova, N. 2008. "Los ocho artistas del Menologio de Basilio II", in I. Pérez Martín (ed.), *El Menologio de Basilio II, Città del Vaticano, Biblioteca Apostolica Vaticana, Vat. gr. 1613. Libro de estudios con ocasión de la edición facsímil*, dirigido por F. d'Aiuto. Vatican, 131–95.

Pachon's Progressive Return
Figurativity, Framing and Movement in Historica Lausiaca 23

David Westberg

In chapter 23 of the *Historica Lausiaca*, Palladios recounts his meeting with the monk Pachon, who tells him the story of how he attempted suicide in the desert rather than lose the battle against his sinful thoughts. On the basis of the structure of Pachon's wandering in the desert, I shall investigate his story, its possible figurativity, its intertextual connections and how the structure of Pachon's movement relates to movements of some other monks in the *HL*. First the textual passage:

> 3. […] Ἐπὶ δώδεκα ἔτη μετὰ τὸ πεντηκοστὸν ἔτος οὐ νύκτα μοι συνεχώρησεν, οὐχ ἡμέραν, ἐπιτιθέμενος. Ὑπονοήσας οὖν ὅτι ἀπέστη μου ὁ θεός, διὸ καὶ καταδυναστεύομαι, ᾑρετισάμην ἀποθανεῖν ἀλόγως ἢ πάθει σώματος ἀσχημονῆσαι. Καὶ ἐξελθὼν καὶ περιελθὼν τὴν ἔρημον εὗρον σπήλαιον ὑαίνης· εἰς ὃ σπήλαιον ἔθηκα ἐμαυτὸν ἐν ἡμέρᾳ γυμνόν, ἵνα ἐξελθόντα φάγῃ με τὰ θηρία. 4. […] καὶ ὡς προσεδόκων βρωθῆναι ἀνεχώρησαν ἀπ' ἐμοῦ. Πεσὼν οὖν διὰ πάσης νυκτὸς οὐκ ἐβρώθην· λογισάμενος δὲ ὅτι ἐφείσατό μου ὁ θεός, αὖθις ὑποστρέφω εἰς τὴν κέλλαν. […]

> For twelve years after my fiftieth year it [the demon] did not leave me neither by night nor by day, assaulting me. So as I supposed that God had departed from me, and because of that I was oppressed, I decided to rather die irrationally than to disgrace myself though a passion of the body. And as I walked away and walked around the desert I found a hyena's cave. I placed myself naked at the cave in the day, so that the beasts would eat me as they came out. […] and as I was expecting to be devoured, they withdrew from me. Thus, lying during the whole night I was not devoured. I reckoned that God had spared me, and turned back again to my cell. […]

In despair Pachon goes to a desolate place, walks around aimlessly, encounters an animal, interprets its lack of aggression as a sign that God still cares for him, and returns. However, after his return just quoted, Pachon's problems continue, so he decides to make the same attempt again and the story is immediately repeated with slight variations.

> 5. [...] Μικροψυχήσας οὖν καὶ ἀπευδοκήσας ἐξῆλθον εἰς τὴν πανέρημον ἀλώμενος· καὶ εὑρὼν ἀσπίδα μικρὰν καὶ λαβὼν αὐτὴν προσφέρω τοῖς γεννητικοῖς μορίοις, ἵνα κἂν οὕτω δηχθεὶς ἀποθάνω. Καὶ προστρίψας τοῦ θηρίου τὴν κεφαλὴν τοῖς μορίοις, ὡς αἰτίοις μοι τοῦ πειρασμοῦ, οὐκ ἐδήχθην. 6. Ἤκουσα οὖν φωνῆς ἐλθούσης ἐν τῇ διανοίᾳ μου, ὅτι "Ἄπελθε, Πάχων, ἀγωνίζου· διὰ γὰρ τοῦτο ἀφῆκά σε καταδυναστευθῆναι, ἵνα μὴ μέγα φρονήσῃς ὡς δυνάμενος, ἀλλ' ἐπιγνούς σου τὴν ἀσθένειαν μὴ θαρρήσῃς τῇ σῇ πολιτείᾳ, ἀλλὰ προσδράμῃς τῇ τοῦ θεοῦ βοηθείᾳ". Οὕτω πληροφορηθεὶς ἀνέκαμψα, καὶ μετὰ θάρρους καθίσας καὶ μηκέτι φροντίσας τοῦ πολέμου εἰρήνευσα τὰς ἐπιλοίπους ἡμέρας. Ὁ δὲ γνούς μου τὴν καταφρόνησιν οὐκέτι μοι ἤγγισεν.

> So, depressed and despairing I walked away to the outer desert, roaming. And finding a small cobra and taking it, I bring it towards my private parts, so that I would in this way be bitten and die. And I pressed the beast's head against these parts, as [they were] the cause of my temptation, but I was not bitten. 6. So, I heard a voice entering into my thought: "Go away, Pachon, keep fighting! For because of this I allowed you to be oppressed, so that you would not be high-minded because of your ability, but, as you understand your weakness, not confide in your way of life but come running for God's help". In this way I was assured and returned, and in confidence I settled and no longer worrying about the enemy I have lived in peace for my remaining days. And he [the demon], knowing my contempt, no longer approached me.

The structure is common to both episodes: departing—walking around—encountering—returning. The second time the language is more emphatic: Pachon leaves for the "outer desert" (εἰς τὴν πανέρημον rather than τὴν ἔρημον) and he does not just "walk around" (περιελθών) but "roams" (ἀλώμενος). Such small variations create slightly higher tension in the second walk and transmit a sense of Pachon's increased despair. What I have labelled 'encounter' is more emphatic as well. A similar event as in the first journey takes place (a wild animal refrains from hurting him), but the second time Pachon does not only *e silentio* interpret what is in fact a non-event as a divine intervention merely because it runs contrary to his expectations, as he did the first time. The second time he also hears a supernatural voice explaining the meaning of his suffering. The second walk also turns out to be effective, Pachon is cured, and he returns to a life of tranquillity.

In the following chapter I analyse Pachon's desert wandering with an aim to illuminate the interpretative consequences of this movement for the story as a whole. I begin by suggesting that Pachon's walk in the desert and back can be interpreted symbolically and figuratively. To do so, I take my cue from cognitive theories about metaphor and figurativity, but I also argue that Pachon's story presents problems to these (semantic) theories and that they need to be complemented with (pragmatic) historicising and intertextual analyses. This is followed up with respect to the story about Pachon in the second and third part of the chapter. In the second part, I suggest that the figurative interpretation of Pachon's movement is triggered by the structure of the movement, which evokes an intertextual metaphor which is strongly embedded in Christian culture, viz. that of the Christian as a sheep. This metaphor can in itself be framed in different ways. Depending on which parts are actualised, it can be projected back not only on Pachon's movement but also onto other movements in the HL. These mechanisms are explored in the third part of the chapter, where I investigate how the mindsets of different wandering monks determine the schema and the framing of their movements. This procedure allows for a typology of movements (and interpretations of these movements) in the HL. Beyond my attempt to illuminate the Pachon story as such, my point is to use this story as a test-case for showing how the triggering of a figurative interpretation is in itself an important clue to how the interpretation is carried out and that metaphor (or figurativity generally) is never only a matter of semantically mapping two conceptual domains, but that an historically embedded pre-understanding will determine how this mapping is framed.

1   The Problem of 'Intuitive' Figurality

A hypothesis for my discussion in this chapter is that the physical movement of Pachon corresponds to a spiritual movement. Just as his body roams in the desert, his soul is confused; and like his body his soul is in danger but ultimately saved. Through his walk in the desert Pachon has developed and reached a higher degree of spiritual maturity in his reliance on God. This seems to be the point of the story, and Pachon is willing to share his experience for the edification of others. The movement through the physical world and the experiences structured by this movement bring about Pachon's spiritual progression. His outward movement is paralleled by an inner one.

But how can we know that this is the case? Such an analogy between physical and spiritual is a typical example of what in cognitive linguistics is referred to as "domain mapping". An abstract domain is "mapped" onto a concrete domain on the basis of some perceived similarities between the two. The abstract domain and its functions are thereby conceptualised through the concrete domain. Such domain mapping is often understood as "metaphorical", and it lies at the heart of Cognitive (or Conceptual) Metaphor Theory (CMT).[1] The analogy between the physical and spiritual domains can within this framework be analysed as a cognitive metaphor of the kind SPIRITUAL DEVELOPMENT IS PHYSICAL MOVEMENT, which involves a mapping from the tangible and embodied physical domain to the abstract psychic domain. The metaphor in turn relies on more basic ones such as MENTAL STATES ARE LOCATIONS and MIND IS BODY.[2]

The problem with such an analysis in Pachon's case is that the target domain (Pachon's spiritual state) is not explicit. There is no comparison involved in the text itself, such as "Pachon made spiritual *progress*" or "*advanced* in his faith". Such examples would provide more obvious cognitive metaphors in the Lakoff-Johnson tradition. To some degree, this could be a result of the fact that CMT typically looks at isolated metaphorical expressions and not on narratives. Does this lack of an explicit target domain imply that we cannot interpret Pachon's roaming as a reflection of his inner state?

To justify the suggestion that Pachon's movement mirrors his soul, we could point to instances in the *HL* where the metaphor SPIRITUAL DEVELOPMENT IS PHYSICAL MOVEMENT is explicitly thematised within the narrative. We find such a discussion about the metaphorical use of outward movement to describe mental change in the story about the holy man Sarapion. He visits a female ascetic and the following conversation takes place (*HL* 37.13.4–7):

"Τί καθέζῃ;" Λέγει αὐτῷ· "Οὐ καθέζομαι ἀλλὰ ὁδεύω". Λέγει αὐτῇ· "Ποῦ ὁδεύεις;" Λέγει αὐτῷ· "Πρὸς τὸν θεόν".

"Why are you sitting here?" She says to him: "I am not sitting, but travelling". He says to her: "Where are you travelling?" She says to him: "To God".

In this case, the very topic of the discussion is that there is no physical movement involved, but that the woman's spiritual development can nevertheless be

---

1   The classical work is Lakoff & Johnson 1980 together with Lakoff 1987. For a more recent and systematic synthesis within the framework of cognitive linguistics as a whole, see Croft & Cruse 2004, Ch. 8 "Metaphor"; cf. also Kövecses 2010, Langacker 2016.
2   These are examples of what Grady 1997 refers to as 'primary metaphors'. For states as locations, see e.g. Radden 1996.

described as a journey to God in metaphorical terms.[3] Such explicit instances of the mapping of a physical journey onto spiritual progress shows that the metaphor of 'inward travel' was at least not alien to Palladios.[4] This is not surprising, since it is a very common metaphor across cultures.[5] Nevertheless, the availability of the metaphor to Palladios does not satisfactorily explain why it should be employed also in Pachon's case.

In Pachon's case the theme is not the incongruity of travelling without moving; there is no evident figurality in the story. The walk does literally take place and there is no explicit comparison between inward and outward movement. By looking at the Sarapion episode we may claim that Palladios had access to the metaphor SPIRITUAL DEVELOPMENT IS PHYSICAL MOVEMENT and thereby more confidently suggest that there is a metaphoric or figurative *potential* also in the Pachon narrative, but not if and how it is actualised in spite of the target domain not being specified. It seems *intuitively* reasonable to interpret Pachon's walk as an analogy, a kind of parable as it were. But more precision is needed if we are to make a valid analysis.

Intuition is often taken for granted in the analysis of metaphor, when it comes to the recognition of a metaphor as such.[6] This is pointed out especially in the case of mappings where the target domain is not explicit, but it applies to figurative language in general.[7] Dancygier and Sweetser remarks on the fact that "it is not always the case that both source and target domain are expressed linguistically".[8] Their example is the phrase "John kicked the can down the road", i.e. procrastinated. "An automatic metaphor-extraction mechanism could have real trouble dealing with such an example, where no

---

3   One may note that the verb for 'travelling' used here, ὀδεύω (lit. 'going by road'), occurs only once and in is literal sense in NT (in the parable about the good Samaritan). LSJ s.v. has no examples of metaphorical usage, which is a bit surprising since ὁδός ('road') has a long metaphorical history to which ὀδεύω would easily assimilate (cf. LSJ s.v. ὁδός III). The connection between metaphorical ὁδός and ὀδεύω is however found in *Barn.* 19.1 (on travelling the road of light), and metaphorical ὀδεύω is fairly common in the Church fathers (Lampe s.v.).
4   It may even be argued that it sustains the entire project of *HL*; the journey through Egypt that Palladios describes is also the one that Lausos, for whom the work was written, will carry out through his reading, cf. Dietz 2005, 134–5.
5   See, e.g. Bernstorff 2012.
6   E.g. Camp 2008, 14 ('an intuitively felt gap between literal and intended meaning').
7   I have used (and will use) the term 'figurative' and 'figurativity' in this article for the sake of convenience. It is, however, a problematic term as it suggests a contrast to 'literal', which in turn suggests a truth-value, i.e. carries problematic ontological connotations. For alternatives that analyse figurativity in terms of lingustic deviance and interpretative relevance, see esp. Sperber & Wilson 1995 (orig. 1986) and also Black 1993 (orig. 1979).
8   Dancygier & Sweetser 2014, 134.

clear linguistic "domain clash" marks the involvement of separate source- and target-domain frames. But actual language users in everyday contexts generally have no problem choosing the right meaning". Again, the suppletion of a target domain happens intuitively or automatically in context.

A classical example within cognitive linguistics of a literary work where such an intuitive understanding is required are the closing lines of Robert Frost's poem "The Road Not Taken" (1915). Just as is the case with the story about Pachon the reader must supply a target domain onto which the source domain can be mapped:

> Two roads diverged in a wood, and I—
> I took the one less travelled by,
> And that has made all the difference.

A discussion of these lines is found at the very outset of Lakoff and Turner's *Moore Than Cool Reason: A Field Guide to Poetic Metaphor* (1989): "we *typically* read him as discussing options for how to live life" and that this reading "comes from our *implicit knowledge* of the structure of the LIFE IS A JOURNEY metaphor" whereupon the authors turn to an analysis of the mappings involved.[9] Steen, likewise, suggests that "the Robert Frost poem presents an extended metaphorical comparison (or even a mini-allegory) that only uses language from the source domain of the journey, leaving the target domain of life entirely implicit".[10] Once it has been established—by intuition or implication—that a metaphor is indeed at work, the mappings can be investigated in detail; for this reason, texts of this type are seen as 'extended metaphor.'

I would say, however, that it is infelicitous from the perspective of literary analysis to merge instances of explicit and implicit target domains, even if one would argue that the mappings are the same once the metaphor is 'detected'. This can, I think, be clarified by a comparison with another forking-roads episode: Xenophon's account of Prodicus' story about Heracles at the crossroads, from the *Memorabilia*. Xenophon's text is, in contrast to Frost's, explicitly allegorical. At the very outset of the story (*Mem.* 2.1.21) we are told that the it concerns a choice εἴτε τὴν δι' ἀρετῆς ὁδὸν τρέψονται [οἱ νέοι] ἐπὶ τὸν βίον εἴτε τὴν διὰ κακίας ("whether in their life they [youths, like Heracles] will take the road through virtue or that through vice"), and the two starkly contrasting female figures who appear are not only described in emblematic fashion (i.e.

---

9   Lakoff & Turner 1989, 3 (both emphases mine). For a recent criticism of Lakoff & Turner's reading, see Qu 2018, esp. 70–73.
10   Steen 2009, 197.

deviating from standard language use and hence suggesting figurative interpretation), but also identify themselves explicitly as personifications of vice and virtue.[11] Though the metaphor LIFE IS A JOURNEY is fundamental both in the case of Xenophon and Frost, to simply note that the target domain is left "entirely implicit" and yet analyse it as if it were explicit, ignores the qualitative difference between Frost's poem and Xenophon's story, the historical conventionalisation of the metaphor, and the possible intertextual play between Frost's text and other texts (such as Xenophon's), that may actually explain the 'intuition' behind a figurative interpretation.

'Forking roads in a forest' should thus be seen as a motif whose figurative or metaphorical interpretation has been conventionalised within a specific cultural tradition, over a period of time—from explicitly allegorical presentations that link the two domains, such as Xenophon's, over Dante ('When I had journeyed half of our life's way, / I found myself within a shadowed forest, / for I had lost the path that does not stray') to Frost. Theories of metaphor and figurative language cannot therefore disregard the history, reception and elaboration of the metaphors, if we are to understand why an implicit domain can nevertheless be supplied, in which cases this is likely (especially in the case of ancient texts), and the cultural background against which even a highly conventionalised metaphor can be exploited for novel purposes.[12]

2 Pachon as a Lost Sheep

Returning to Pachon and his roaming walk in the desert, if we want to specify the analogy between physical and spiritual as a mapping, we need two domains. We postulate that the target domain is Pachon's spirituality, which in turn may serve as a paradigm for our own, which is what makes the story beneficial, even if we do not walk in the desert ourselves. Nevertheless, just as

---

11   Xen. *Mem.* 2.1.21–33.
12   For example, Lakoff & Turner 1989, 3, remarks on the poet's claim in "The Road Not Taken" "to do things differently than most other people do", a point further elaborated in Culler 2015, 338: "The belief that the less-traveled road is not just the more adventurous choice but also the better one is deeply embedded in a conformist culture in which everyone believes in the uniqueness of the individual and the value of that uniqueness". On the other hand, is there any poet in any time who has suggested that taking the broader, more travelled road is the more interesting alternative? The point, as I see it, is rather the (historically informed) interpretative adaptability of what walking the narrow path entails—ranging all the way from a virtuous decision on the basis of long-term vs. short-term benefit to a romantic refusal to be like everybody else.

in "The Road Not Taken", the analogy cannot be inferred from the propositional level of the text's utterances. The spiritual domain must somehow be activated. But what activates it and on which textual level?

As with the Frost poem, I would suggest that the activation is primarily intertextual, based on the reader's competence and exposure to similar texts that are so culturally entrenched that their activation as interpretative paradigms can be regarded as 'intuitive' (which is not to say that they cannot be analysed). In the case of Pachon the domain of spirituality is activated—made available for mapping—because the reader is familiar with other stories that are based, not necessarily on a motif in the form of a scene as in "The Road Not Taken", but on a similar spatial structure of departure and return which in the earlier (inter)texts has been metaphorically linked to spiritual development more explicitly.

Figurative interpretation, or the understanding of a story like Pachon's as an analogy with *both* a literal and a symbolic meaning, is then determined by the reader's competence, which in turn is based on the exposure to similar patterns in previous texts, in this case within the framework of late antique Christian culture. This shifts the focus from semantic to pragmatic considerations, where the 'common ground' between author and reader guides the interpretation. From a cognitive perspective, this may be seen as an extension of the axiom that language is always under-determined and dependent on context.[13]

Which, then, are the likely candidates for 'intuition' about symbolic movements in this case? First, it may be noted that the structure of departure and return as part of a spiritual journey toward a higher plane of understanding is central to both the educational journey (including pilgrimage) and initiation rites.

Pachon, however, is not a pilgrim on a grand tour. Although his movement follows a pattern of departure and return, it is differently *framed*. And although the starting-point for Pachon's physical wandering, like the pilgrim's, eventually is also his goal, he is not aware of this fact when he sets out. Pachon's movement cannot therefore be subsumed within a "Journey Frame" with Pachon as Traveller. A component of this frame is the metaphor KNOWLEDGE IS A LOCATION, which includes the assumption that the process of learning is the purposeful movement towards that destination. Unlike the pilgrim, Pachon is *lost* (though eventually found). He has no purpose of improving himself— the fact that this comes about is the result of God's intervention, in spite of Pachon's plan to simply die in the desert. This is also a component that distinguishes Pachon's circular movement from the initiate's, even if the movement

---

[13] On common ground in cognitive linguistics, see e.g. Croft & Cruse 2004, 60.

of initiation involves the crossing into a liminal space similar to Pachon's sojourn into the 'outer desert' and his supernatural encounters with the wild animals. But the reasons for leaving are still very different. Again, Pachon is not on a deliberate quest for enlightenment (pilgrimage), nor does he want to put himself to any kind of test (initiation).

On the basis of the circular movement and the fact that Pachon is lost, roaming on his way toward destruction but ultimately saved, I find it more reasonable to read Pachon's story against the likening of sheep gone astray, a comparison that is central to Christian discourse and ubiquitous in Christian texts. This, then, would be a possible culturally embedded intertext for Pachon's story based not on its setting but on the very structure of the movement from safety to danger and back, in connection with issues of faith and trust in God.

But we should also note that this is only one particular among several possible instantiations or framings of CHRISTIANS ARE SHEEP. There are at least two main versions of the metaphor CHRISTIANS ARE SHEEP. Either the fact is underlined that (a) the sheep is part of a flock and cared for by a shepherd, or that (b) the sheep is intended for sacrificial slaughter. The most obvious example of the latter, sacrificial metaphor within a Christian understanding is of course Christ himself, the archetypal Christian as it were.[14] The two versions (CHRISTIANS ARE SHEEP and CHRIST IS A SHEEP) are sometimes found in conjunction, creating a rhetorical effect as in 1 Clem. 16.6–7: "We have all wandered astray like sheep; each has wandered on his own path. The Lord handed him over for our sins, but he did not open his mouth because of his mistreatment. He was led like a sheep going to slaughter".[15] By extension, all Christians can also be seen as sacrificial sheep when subject to persecution which they, like the silent sheep and like Christ, face with meekness.

Various aspects of the sheep's nature and circumstances are thus highlighted in the different mappings. "A sheep", Isidore of Seville remarked, "is a mild livestock animal, with wool, a defenceless body, and a peaceful temperament, and it is so called from sacrifice [i.e. *oblatio* as the etymology for *ovis*], because at first the ancients offered not bulls, but sheep, in sacrifice".[16] The sheep's mildness is important primarily for the sacrificial metaphor, while the fact that the sheep is a livestock animal forms the basis for the metaphor of flock and shepherd. The most salient feature of the sheep is its defencelessness, which is important for both metaphors. This is the symbolism of the lamb or sheep also

---

14 The sacrificial metaphor is the one most prevalent in the Old Testament, e.g. Isa 53:5, 7, and of course important for the typological interpretation of Jesus' death.
15 [Clement], *First Letter to the Corinthians* 16.7. Tr. B. Ehrman, *The Apostolic Fathers*, Vol. 1, Cambridge, MA, 2003, 63. Also in Augustine, *City of God* 18.29.
16 *Etym.* 12.1.9. Tr. Barney et al., *The Etymologies of Isidore of Seville*. Cambridge 2006, 247.

in the tradition of Aesop's fables (where the sheep's innocence and feebleness of mind and body are played out against the capacities of the wolf, lion and fox). In the case of the flock-and-shepherd metaphor, it is the sheep which has left its flock and shepherd and is lost and in great danger.[17]

CHRISTIANS ARE SHEEP can thus be employed in various ways, and the degree to which these instalments are interconnected varies as well. The imagery can become more complex through the adding of hierarchical layers. If, for example, the Bishops rather than God Himself are the shepherds, or if they are posited on an intermediate level, we not only move from one shepherd and flock to many, but also to a less potent version of the shepherd, who can now himself go astray or be killed, etc.: "But woe to the shepherds if any of the sheep are found scattered. And if the shepherds themselves are found scattered, what will they say to the Lord of the flock?"[18] The metaphor can also combine with other metaphors and frames entrenched in Christian discourse. Gregory of Nazianzus, for example, accomplished this by quoting Jeremiah's words (12:10) about shepherds destroying the vineyard.[19] In other instances, such combinations form mixed metaphors. Ignatius, in his letter to the Philadelphians, warns that many seemingly trustworthy wolves attempt to catch the sheep that are running God's race. Here, the metaphor CHRISTIANS ARE SHEEP is conventionalised to such a degree that it (in these specific textual contexts) almost reverts into SHEEP ARE CHRISTIANS, and the tension between source domain and target domain is dissolved.[20] In 2 Clem. 5.3–4, for example, the metaphor is short-circuited (CHRISTIANS ARE SHEEP ARE CHRISTIANS): "Peter replied to him, 'And what if the wolves rip apart the sheep?' Jesus said to Peter. After they are dead, the sheep should fear the wolves no longer".[21]

---

17 Another contrast is that between sheep and goats, where the goat symbolises the sinful humans, as in the eschatological discourse of Mt 25:46. Isidore, when enumerating the various animals to which Christ is likened, notes that, apart from "the Lamb for his innocence, and the Sheep for his submissiveness", he is also the "Goat for his likeness to sinful flesh" (*Etym.* 7.2.42–44). Later in the emblematic tradition the goat can symbolise the faithful Christian as well.

18 *Shepherd of Hermas*, parable 108.6. Tr. B. Ehrman, *The Apostolic Fathers*, Vol. II, Cambridge, MA, 2003, 461.

19 Greg.Naz. *Or.* 21.

20 On mixed metaphors of this kind and their cognitive function, see Gibbs (ed,) 2016. Cf. e.g. Maguire 1987, 8: 'It was natural for the patristic writers to employ several images to describe one concept, for they realized that the concepts they wished to express were too complex to be rendered satisfactory by one image alone".

21 [Clement], *Second Letter to the Corinthians* 5.4. Tr. B. Ehrman, *The Apostolic Fathers*, Vol. I, Cambridge, MA, 2003, 171–172.

With regard to the parable of the lost sheep, we may regard the metaphor CHRISTIANS ARE SHEEP as a metaphoric instalment, or fleshing out, of the movement schema:

getting lost → roaming in danger of being destroyed → being brought back to safety,

which is also Pachon's schema. The common structure, the 'lost-and-found' frame, would thus 'back-project' metaphoricity also on Pachon's story. As implied late antique readers in possession of this specific cultural competence, we understand that Pachon is like a sheep who has gone astray but is brought back by the shepherd—Ἰησοῦς ὁ Χριστός, ὁ τῆς ἀνθρωπίνης πλάνης διορθωτής ("Jesus Christ, who sets straight the human wandering" as Palladius states in his *Dialogue on the life of John Chrysostom*)[22]—and that this is what makes his physical wandering correspond to his spiritual development.

An important aspect of the metaphor CHRISTIANS ARE SHEEP is that the sheep which has gone astray and is in danger is not simply rescued by the good shepherd, but also belong to a flock to which it is returned (the shepherd never herds a single sheep). The flock, i.e. the Christian community, to which the sheep belongs is not highlighted in the story about Pachon, but its importance for him becomes clear when we compare his movements with those of other monks in the *HL*.

3   Mindsets as Determinants for Movement Frames

Pachon is saved thanks to God's intervention; other monks in *HL* are presented as less fortunate. The stories of these failed ascetics—Valens, Heron and Ptolemaios—are told in *HL* 25–27 and their fate is also discussed in *HL* 47.[23] While Pachon is restored to a life within the Christian orbit and has matured spiritually, the movement of Heron and Ptolemaios is endless; they drift further and further away, constantly moving but without making progress (Valens is stopped before he is able to leave). In contrast to Pachon, these monks have

---

22   Ed. P.R. Coleman-Norton, *Palladii dialogus de vita S. Joanni Chrysostomi*, Cambridge 1928, p. 78.23–4.

23   Guillamont, Guillamont & Géhin suggest in their edition of *On Thoughts* (1998, 32 and 234 n.3) that Evagrios alludes specifically to Valens and Heron in *On Thoughts* 23 (more on this passage below). Whether this is the case or if Palladios' description of Valens, Heron and Ptolemaios should be seen as examples of the predicament Evagrios describes in general terms is difficult to say.

set off not because of their despair, but because of their pride.[24] Deluded by their ascetic accomplishments they have fallen prey to their own pride and turned their backs on the community in general and, as is explicitly pointed out, communion in particular.[25]

There is a constant and delicate balance in *HL* and other monastic literature between the anchoretic search for God undistracted by the company of others and the dangers of relying on one's own inner strength in this search, beyond the structure and regulations that communal life provides. This balance between solitude and community seems to reflect the real-life situation. In Nitria, for example, the monks lived far enough from each other as to be out of sight, but close enough to be able to convene every week.[26] Also within the anachoretic setting, community thus had a regulating function, and the ultimate symbol of this function was communion.[27]

---

24   In Heron's case pride is eventually combined with *acedia* which is ultimately what sets him roaming. The narrative about Heron falls into two parts, one (26.1–2) in which Heron is disrespectful towards monastic teachers, Evagrius in particular, and also has to be chained because he refuses communion, and another (26.2–5) in which he is an accomplished ascetic explicitly partaking in communion but eventually succumbing to *acedia*. I find the transition between these two parts a bit harsh, but I have not found any comments on a lack of inner logic in the story, and Driscoll in his summary (1997, 265) does not seem to find it disturbing (he simply joins the two parts with 'Yet as the story unfolds [after Heron was put in chains], Palladius still feels constrained to give him further his due [i.e. as an accomplished ascetic]".). In addition to the three monks mentioned, the fallen virgin of *HL* 28 should be mentioned. She too fails because of her pride or arrogance (28.1 ὑπερβολῇ ὑπερηφανίας), but not much is said about her except that she engages in sexual intercourse. In contrast to his evaluation of Valens, Heron and Ptolemaios, who are presented as great but failed ascetics, Palladius also makes the apparently misogynic remark that the virgin—though she remained enclosed for six years—was actually only pretending to be pious, out of vanity.

25   Hunt's remark (1982, 67) that Heron "was clearly overdoing it" is therefore not quite to the point. Heron is not crushed because he tries too hard and fails, but because he has the wrong attitude to begin with.

26   *HM* 20.7, discussed in Rapp 2016, 93 who also points to Palladius' comments (*HL* 16.1) on the problems involved in maintaining this balance as Nitria grew. On the importance of topography for the layout of monastic settlements, see Binns 1994, 191 (comparing Egypt and Palestine). For the construction of the "cultural" (rather than "symbolic" or literary) monastic landscape, see Brooks Hedstrom, this volume.

27   The balance between *anachoresis* and communal life addresses a tension at the very core of Christian monasticism between the salvation of the individual and salvation for the group (which ultimately included all Christians). The responsibility of the monastic leader or teacher as mediator between these poles was a matter for discussion and immediately connected to issues of spiritual authority. Pachomius, for example, was willing to impart to the monastic leader a larger responsibility for the salvation of the monks within the Pachomian community, but a lesser one with regard to the anachoretes; see Rousseau 1999, 98–99.

The anti-social behaviour of Valens, Heron and Ptolemaios, whose pride drive them to the extent that they refuse communion bring the Messalians to mind.[28] This sect considered the Eucharist and other sacraments to be of no benefit, seeing "the possibility of restoration only through assiduous prayer".[29] In addition, the Messalians "gathered together the various deviant monastic practices that clerics despised" and which canon 4 at the council of Chalcedon (451) was an attempt to regulate: "wandering in cities, begging, refusing to acknowledge clerics".[30] Both the contempt for authorities and the refusal to partake in communion can be found in the story about Heron:

> ὃς καὶ αὐτὸς μετὰ πόνους πολλοὺς τύφῳ βληθεὶς ἐξετραχηλιάσθη καὶ κατὰ τῶν πατέρων ἐφρόνησε μέγα, ὑβρίσας καὶ τὸν μακάριον Εὐάγριον, λέγων ὅτι "Οἱ πειθόμενοι τῇ διδασκαλίᾳ σου ἀπατῶνται· οὐ χρὴ γὰρ διδασκάλοις ἑτέροις προσέχειν παρεκτὸς τοῦ Χριστοῦ". Ἀπεχρήσατο δὲ καὶ τῇ μαρτυρίᾳ πρὸς τὸν σκοπὸν τῆς ἑαυτοῦ μωρίας, καὶ ἔλεγεν ὅτι 'Αὐτὸς ὁ σωτὴρ εἶπε· "Μὴ καλέσητε διδάσκαλον ἐπὶ τῆς γῆς". Ὃς ἐπὶ τοσοῦτον καὶ αὐτὸς ἐσκοτώθη ὡς καὶ αὐτὸν ὕστερον σιδηρωθῆναι, μὴ θέλοντα μηδὲ τοῖς μυστηρίοις προσέρχεσθαι.

> After many toils he was struck with delusion and went out of control. He greatly scorned the fathers, and raged against the blessed Evagrius, saying "Those who obey your teachings are deceived; for it is not necessary to pay attention to other teacher except Christ". He misused the (Biblical) testimony too with an aim to his own foolishness and said "The Saviour has said himself: "Do not call (anyone) a teacher upon earth". He was in such a state of darkness that he was later put in chains, as he did not even want to proceed to communion.

For the psychological aspects of estrangement, Evagrios of Pontus provides the theory. In his work *On Thoughts*, Evagrios remarks on the danger in seeking solitude for the wrong reasons (*On Thoughts* 23):

> Μηδεὶς τῶν ἀναχωρούντων μετ' ὀργῆς ἢ ὑπερηφανίας ἢ λύπης ἀναχωρείτω μηδὲ φευγέτω τοὺς ἀδελφοὺς ὑπὸ τοιούτων λογισμῶν ἐνοχλούμενος· γίνονται γὰρ καὶ ἐκστάσεις ἀπὸ τῶν τοιούτων παθῶν, τῆς καρδίας ἀπὸ νοήματος εἰς νόημα καὶ ἀπὸ τούτου ἐφ' ἕτερον καὶ ἀπ' ἐκείνου ἐπ' ἄλλο κατὰ μικρὸν

---

28 Caner 2002, 83–125 discusses the radical asceticism of the Messalians as it conflicted with the authority of the institutionalised church.
29 Booth 2014, 10.
30 Booth 2014, 10. See further Caner 2002, 206–208 (and Ch. 6 generally).

ἐμπιπτούσης εἰς βάραθρον λήθης. Πολλοὺς γὰρ ἔγνωμεν τῶν ἀδελφῶν περιπεσόντας τούτῳ τῷ ναυαγίῳ, οὓς οἱ λοιποὶ μετὰ δακρύων καὶ προσευχῆς αὖθις εἰς τὸν ἀνθρώπινον ἐπανήγαγον βίον· τινὲς δὲ καὶ ἀνεπάνακτον λήθην λαβόντες οὐκέτι ἴσχυσαν καταλαβεῖν τὴν πρώτην κατάστασιν καὶ μέχρι τῆς σήμερον ἡμεῖς οἱ ταπεινοὶ βλέπομεν τὰ τῶν ἀδελφῶν ἡμῶν ναυάγια·

Let no anchorite take up the anchoritic life out of wrath or pride or grief, nor let him flee the brethren while tormented by such thoughts. From such passions arise distractions of the mind, when the heart moves from this concept to another and from that one to yet another, and from that one to still another, falling by degrees into a pit of forgetfulness. We have known many of the brethren caught up in this shipwreck, whom the others retrieved with tears and prayer to a life that befits humans. But some, who had embraced forgetfulness irretrievably, were no longer able to return to their former state and to this day we behold with downcast spirits the shipwreck of our brethren.[31]

This predicament, of course, is also Pachon's, who flees the other monks while tormented by grief (λύπη), although he does so in order to kill himself rather than to become an anachorete. Evagrius has long been recognised as a major influence on Palladios and also appears in the *HL*.[32] Evagrian psychology and its relation to Palladios is also a much-researched field of study, and I shall not go further into it here than is required to study how the monks' movements are structured.

An important point in Evagrius with regard to the various movements is that the vices (*logismoi* in Evagrius' terminology) of pride and grief differ from each other. The monk who is overcome by grief still has the ability to learn, to develop, and return. Pride, by contrast, leads to incessant roaming, with the monk becoming more and more estranged from the Christian community. This drift can be stopped, sometimes by force, as in the case of Valens, who is put in chains for a year while the other monks pray for him and so never actually goes so far as to leave the community. In Heron's case, chaining proves ultimately ineffective. He is eventually saved by a disease which causes his genitals to rot

---

31 Tr. Casiday 2006, 104–105.
32 Binns 1994, 59 on Palladius: "a self-confessed admirer of the Origenist theologian Evagrius Ponticus" with furher references in n.4. In *HL* 23 Palladios presents himself as a personal disciple of Evagrios and in *HL* 47 Palladius recounts a visit by himself, Evagrius and Albanus to Paphnutius on precisely the issue of why seemingly advanced ascetics could fail.

and fall off, upon which he "turned his mind back to God". Ptolemaios is never saved (as far as the *HL* tells).

In contrast to Pachon, the 'failed ascetics' start out from a different presumption; their original mindset, the particular *logismos* that makes them leave, determines their fate. Valens, Heron and Ptoelemios are driven by pride and self-sufficiency rather than grief, as Pachon is. Both Heron and Ptolemaios end up travelling to big cities. In her discussion of the travelling monk Sarapion (*HL* 37), Georgia Frank compares him to these failed ascetics and remarks that "Palladius never mocks Sarapion's intensely physical journey" and that he does not "add Sarapion to his catalogue of fallen heroes". But this is not surprising: there is a marked difference between Heron and Ptolemeaios on the one hand, and Sarapion on the other. 'Movement' and 'travelling' as such cannot be seen in isolation from the framing as a whole. Although Heron and Ptolemaios too are engaged in 'intensely physical journey', they cannot on this account be compared to Sarapion. In a comparison with Heron and Ptolemaios, the aimless journeying is not really the problem—self-sufficiency is.[33]

Though constantly *en route* (37.5 ταῖς συνεχέσιν ἀποδημίαις), Sarapion never leaves the Christian community, but remains in the fold (and rather brings more people into it). He is not 'lost' nor has he 'gone astray'. It may also be noted that Sarapion's travels do not provoke figurative interpretation as Pachon's does—his apparently aimless physical wandering does not correspond to spiritual disorientation. Sarapion is not affected with pride and does not display its primary symptom, refrainment from communion. On the contrary he is a missionary and in possession of the strength that mission requires. As an itinerant teacher, Sarapion does have subversive traits, however. Caner points to Sarapion as an early example of an apostolic monk (and remarks that "such wanderers were accommodated in orthodox tradition primarily by being relegated to the ranks of the *saloi* (Fools for Christ)").[34]

The journey, or the activity of journeying, is therefore not important in itself, but only as a component of a larger schema which determines the interpretation. The spatial schema underlying Sarapion's story is very different from those of Valens, Heron and Ptolemaios. Pachon, on the other hand, is—like Valens, Heron and Ptolemaios—lost, but his original mindset of grief rather than pride eventually brings him back to the flock.

The differences are reflected also in the choice of individual words. Sarapion is rather neutrally said to be περιερχόμενος τὴν οἰκουμένην, "walking around in

---

[33] See Frank 2000, 67 (but I do not quite follow the argument about the "true pilgrim" on pp. 66–67).

[34] Caner 2002, 245.

the (inhabited) world". The same word is used for Pachon's first walk, although he is 'walking around in the desert', a liminal space. The second time Pachon departs the stakes are higher, he is now described as ἀλώμενος, 'roaming', a verb (ἀλάομαι) which carries stronger connotations of being lost and confused.[35] The verb is only used four other times in the HL. The first is in 21 Eulogios, in which a certain Kronios recounts how he, because of *acedia*, ran away from his monastery and roamed until he ended up on the mountain of St Antony. The second instance is in 27 Ptolemaios, already discussed as one of the failed ascetics. The third instance is 29 Elias, which is in many ways a parallel story to Pachon's: plagued by carnal desire Elias leaves the female monastery he has founded and begs for death in the desert, but after a symbolic castration by three angels in a vision, he is able to return. The final instance is HL 34 about a female holy fool, a nun pretending to be possessed by a demon and therefore 'roaming' in the monastery's kitchen. In all of these instances the word ἀλάομαι is strongly negatively connotated, directly reflecting a confused mindset (even if it is feigned in the last instance), suffering from vices such as *acedia*, pride and grief. Ἀλάομαι carries much the same connotations as πλανάω. Πλανάω is used twice by Palladius, in the same contexts as ἀλάομαι; we find in the story about 29 Elias, again to describe a roaming in the desert (HL 29.2 ἐπλανᾶτο ἀνὰ τὴν ἔρημον ἐπὶ ἡμέρας δύο), and in HL 34 about the female holy fool where it is used by an angel to rebuke the holy Piterum for the way he sits and "roams the cities in his mind" (ἀνὰ τὰς πόλεις πλανᾶσαι τῇ διανοίᾳ) instead of being as pious as the nun he is thereby encouraged to visit. Both ἀλάομαι and πλανάω are also used metaphorically from early on but they are unevenly distributed. Ἀλάομαι is not found in either the Septuagint or the New Testament, while πλανάω occurs rather frequently, not least in connection with the sheep gone astray.[36]

∴

In this chapter I have attempted to show that the understanding of Pachon's story as symbolic is problematic. It should not simply be taken as 'intuitive' or as an 'implicit extended metaphor', but the analogy can be intertextually activated on the basis of its structure. In particular, the parable about the lost sheep provides the implied reader of HL 23 with a spiritual target domain. I have also compared the structures of Pachon's movement with those of other

---

35 I have not looked further into the use of the two verbs in other Christian literature of Palladius' time, but the use of ἀλάομαι should probably be taken as another signal that we should read Pachon's movement as both literal and symbolic.

36 In connection with sheep, see Ps. 118:176, Isah. 53:6; 1 Pet. 2.25.

monks in the *HL* on the basis of their mindset as they start out in order to show that different mindsets, or rather *logismoi* in the Evagrian sense, determine how the structure of the monks' movements are framed.

Bibliography

Primary Sources

Evagrios. *On Thoughts*. Ed. A. Guillaumont, C. Guillaumont & P. Géhin, *Évagre le Pontique. Sur les pensées*. Paris 1998, 148–301. Tr. A. M. Casiday, *Evagrius Ponticus*. Abingdon & New York 2006, 89–116.

Palladios. *The Lausiac History*. Ed. G. J. M. Bartelink, *Palladio. La storia Lausiaca*. Verona 1974. Tr. R. T. Meyer, *Palladius: The Lausiac History*. New York 1964.

Secondary Sources

Baicchi, A., R. Digonnet & J. L. Sandford (eds) 2018. *Sensory Perceptions in Language, Embodiment and Epistemology*. Cham.

Binns, J. 1994. *Ascetics and Ambassadors of Christ: The Monasteries of Palestine 314–631*. Oxford.

Black, M. 1993. "More about Metaphor", in Ortony (ed) 1993, 19–41.

Booth, P. 2014. *Crisis of Empire: Doctrine and Dissent at the End of Late Antiquity*. Berkeley, Los Angeles & London.

Brône, G. & J. Vandaele (eds) 2009. *Cognitive Poetics: Goals, Gains and Gaps*. Berlin & New York.

Camp, E. 2008. "Showing, Telling and Seeing: Metaphor and 'Poetic' Language", *Baltic International Yearbook of Cognition, Logic and Communication* 3, 1–24.

Caner, D. 2002. *Wandering, Begging Monks: Spiritual Authority and the Promotion of Monasticism in Late Antiquity*. Berkeley, Los Angeles & London.

Casad, E. H. (ed.) 1996. *Cognitive Linguistics in the Redwoods: The Expansion of a New Paradigm in Linguistics*. Berlin & New York.

Croft, W. & D. A. Cruse. 2004. *Cognitive Linguistics*. Cambridge.

Culler, J., 2015. *Theory of the Lyric*. Cambridge, MA & London.

Dancygier & E. Sweetser, 2014. *Figurative Language*. Cambridge.

Dietz, M. 2005. *Wandering Monks, Virgins, and Pilgrims: Ascetic Travel in the Mediterranean World, A.D. 300–800*. University Park, PA.

Driscoll, J. 1997. "Evagrius and Paphnutius on the Causes for Abandonment by God", *Studia Monastica* 39, 259–86.

Frank, G. 2000. *The Memory of the Eyes: Pilgrims to Living Saints in Christian Late Antiquity*. Berkeley & Los Angeles.

Gibbs, R. (ed.) 2016. *Mixing Metaphor*. Amsterdam & Philadelphia.

Grady, J. E. 1997. "THEORIES ARE BUILDINGS revisited", *Cognitive Linguistics* 8, 267–90.

Hunt, E. D. 1982. *Holy Land Pilgrimage in the Later Roman Empire AD 312–460*. Oxford.

Kövecses, Z. 2010. *Metaphor: A Practical Introduction*, 2nd ed. Oxford.

Lakoff, G. 1987. *Women, Fire, and Dangerous Things: What Categories Reveal about the Mind*. Chicago & London.

Lakoff G. & M. Johnson 1980. *Metaphors We Live By*. Chicago & London.

Lakoff, G. & M. Turner. 1989. *More than Cool Reason: A Field Guide to Poetic Metaphor*. Chicago & London.

Langacker, R. W. 2016. "Metaphor in Linguistic Thought and Theory", *Cognitive Semantics* 2, 3–29.

Maguire, H. 1987. *Earth and Ocean: the terrestrial world in early Byzantine art*. University Park, PA.

Ortony, A. (ed.) 1993. *Metaphor and Thought*. 2nd ed. Cambridge.

Qu, W. 2018. "Do Metaphors Mean or Point? Davidson's Hypothesis Revisited", in Baicchi, Digonnet & Sandford (eds) 2018, 59–74.

Radden, G. 1996. "Motion metaphorized: The case of *coming* and *going*", in Casad (ed.) 1996, 423–58.

Rapp, C. 2016. *Brother-Making in Late Antiquity and Byzantium: Monks, Laymen, and Christian Ritual*. Oxford.

Rousseau, Ph. 1999. *Pachomius: The Making of a Community in Fourth-Century Egypt*. 2nd ed. Berkeley.

Sperber, D. & D. Wilson 1995. *Relevance: Communication and Cognition*. 2nd ed. Oxford & Cambridge, Mass.

Steen, G. 2009. "From linguistic form to conceptual structure in five steps: analyzing metaphor in poetry", in Brône & Vandaele (eds) 2009, 197–226.

von Bernstorff, W. 2012. "Weg / Straße", in G. Butzer & J. Jacob (eds) 2012, *Metzler Lexikon literarischer Symbole*, 2nd ed., 476–78. Stuttgart & Weimar.

Spaces Within, Spaces Beyond

Reassessing the Lives of the Holy Fools Symeon and Andrew (BHG 1677, 115z)

Paolo Cesaretti and Basema Hamarneh

This paper* addresses some of the contexts, strategies and processes of transformation and representation of the concepts of space within the two narratives of the Holy Fools Symeon and Andrew (BHG 1677, 115z),[1] which can be considered a hagiographic corpus of its own.[2] In historical terms, the two *Lives* are strictly interrelated since that of Andrew, dated according to Lennart Rydén's studies to the tenth century, though allegedly set in the fifth century,[3] it is modelled appositely by its author in order to match that of Symeon, written in the seventh century.[4] The two texts deserve specific attention as they present rich documentation on the subject of *spatiality*; they explore the apparently fixed oppositions between materiality, addressed in our discussion as "spaces within", and the spiritual/paradisiac dimension that will be considered here

---

* This contribution stemmed from a common research project and a monograph on visuality in the Lives of the Holy Fools Symeon and Andrew. The authors wish to thank Ingela Nilssen and Myrto Veikou for their kind invitation to take part at the conference in Uppsala, and are grateful for the comments and suggestions of the reviewers.

[1] We have followed the critical editions by Rydén, *Leben des Symeon* and Rydén, *Andrew* (with English translation) respectively. English translation of passages from *Life of Symeon* according with Krueger, *Symeon*.

[2] See Cesaretti, *Metodi*, 38–9.

[3] The *Life of Andrew* presents several anachronisms that point to a later date as argued by Rydén, *Date Andreas*; Rydén, *Andrew*, i, 46; Efthymiadis, *New Developments*, 159–60; Cesaretti, *Metodi*, 32–4; Cesaretti, *Vingt ans après*.

[4] The hagiographer presents Andrew as τρέχων δὲ ἔκτοτε ἐν τῇ πλατείᾳ τῆς πόλεως ἦν παίζων κατὰ τὸν πάλαι Συμεῶνα ἐκεῖνον τὸν θαυμαστόν ("he ran his race in the streets and squares of the city, playing in the manner of the admirable Symeon of old", Rydén, *Andrew*, II, 28–9, ll. 223–4). Grosdidier de Matons, *Thèmes*, 302–11; Rydén, *Byzantine Saints*, 256–7. Moreover, the life of Andrew contains some possible echoes to other early hagiographies such as the *Life of John the Almsgiver* and that of *Isaac the Recluse* (Rydén, *Basil*, 579–80; Magdalino, *Literary Text*, 91); closer affinities with the 10th century *Life of Basil the Younger* have been well pointed out by Rydén, *Basil*. See also discussion in Magdalino, *Literary Text*, 100–1, 108. Moreover Cesaretti, *Vite dei saloi*, 326–7 (n. 837), 338–9 (n. 886).

as "spaces beyond", though the two concepts are developed according to peculiar chrono-spatial coordinates.[5]

1   Spaces 'Within'

According to Leontios of Neapolis, spatiality is projected on various levels that are conveyed to follow the spiritual evolution of Symeon, whom the text calls "a true imitator of Christ", in order to make it more credible.[6] The physical environment reproduced by Leontios is dominated initially by the Holy City of Jerusalem and the monasticism of the Judean Desert, elements that may seem to be drawn from the real experience of the hagiographer,[7] though details of the material context of his setting are not provided.[8] These aspects can be evidenced for example in the realistic description of the route descending to Jericho and the monastery of St Gerasimus,[9] whereas no evidence of eyewitness knowledge is provided of the desert beyond the River Jordan,[10] of the journey from Jerusalem to Emesa, or later of Emesa itself. Symeon's pilgrimage, far from representing a late antique or early medieval interpretation of the

---

[5] This is mostly intended by the authors (Leontios bishop of Neapolis in the seventh century in the case of the *Life of Symeon*; the fictional author who defines himself as "Nicephorus, priest of Hagia Sophia" – see below, n. 39 and context – in the case of the *Life of Andrew*) through specific settings of spaces (Emesa, Constantinople) and time (through emperors such as Justinian in the case of Symeon and Leo I in the case of Andrew). These coordinates allowed the readers not only to follow a progressive evolution of the personality of the saint and of his sainthood, but also provided tools to visualize and relate him to a specific context. However, in the case of the life of Symeon one has the impression that the set of stories in Emesa does not develop according to logical chronological connections. See Cesaretti, *Metodi*, 47; Hamarneh, *Città*, 61–2.

[6] Rydén, *Introduzione*, 40, 41 (Greek text in Rydén, *Leben des Symeon*, 123, 23–4); see as well Cesaretti, *Metodi*, 42–3. The same concept is again expressed by Leontios in his *Bios of John the Almsgiver*: Cavallero, *Juan*, 214; Hamarneh, *Città*, 64. A comparison between Jesus in Jerusalem and Symeon in Emesa is found in Krueger, *Symeon*, 108–25. It is worth pointing out here how Christological typology is brought to a comic effect to exalt the action of the Holy Fool. See Hamarneh, *Città*, 61; Krueger, *Comedy*, 30; on biblical quotations and intertextuality Krueger, *Hagiographers' Bible*, 177–89.

[7] Hamarneh, *Città*, 62.

[8] It is likely that they were deemed unnecessary, since his readers were probably familiar with similar narratives. See Magdalino, *Literary Text*, 85. On Jerusalem in the *Life of Symeon* see Cesaretti, *Vite dei saloi*, 66 (n. 45), 101–2 (nn. 244–45), 152.

[9] Literary echoes are in any case not negligible. See Cesaretti, *Vite dei saloi*, 68 (n. 57), 69 (n. 3), 72–3 (n. 81).

[10] Leontios only mentions that Symeon spent 29 years in the desert (Greek text in Rydén, *Leben des Symeon*, 142, 8). See Cesaretti, *Vite dei saloi*, 97–8 (n. 228).

chōra, is solely a prelude to the monastic experience, and that in turn is a prelude to holy foolery, a correlation that is bound to be immediately perceived as a divinely guided action.[11]

The second part of the narrative setting[12] depicts a paradoxical quality of holiness within a frame of cultural traditions partially reshaped by Christianity within the polis.[13] Leontios identifies Emesa as the physical location of the story or the 'space within' his narrative. The deeds and the actions of the 'historically real' figure of Symeon are confined to the Syrian city and its environs. Nevertheless, defined physical boundaries are clearly and deliberately omitted;[14] Emesa is merely 'a frame' with no specific landmarks and seems more likely the reflection of an image of a medium-sized city in the Eastern Mediterranean.[15]

---

11   The *Bios* introduces divine agency when Symeon and John meet and make friends while on pilgrimage to the Holy City, when they draw lots and choose the way descending to the River Jordan, and finally when they reach the monastery of Gerasimus and find its gates open allowing them to enter. Greek text Rydén, *Leben des Symeon*, 124–6. See Hamarneh *Città*, 62.

12   On the narrative structure of the text see the recent remarks by Cesaretti, *Vite dei saloi*, 59 (n. 1), 101 (nn. 243–4), 104 (n. 266).

13   On the urban setting: Magdalino, *Literary Text*, 86; Patlagean, *Ancienne hagiographie*, 121; Hamarneh, *Città*, 64. As shown by several scholars (Rydén, *Introduzione*, 40–1; Krueger, *Symeon*, 108–25; Cavallero, *Simeón*, 25–7, *al.*; Rapp, *Cypriot Hagiography*, 408), Leontios of Neapolis with his hagiographic texts introduces the possibility that a holy life could be led in the city instead of the desert. This may be connected with the fact that threats to the monasteries of the Judaean desert, after the Persian invasion in 614 CE and the Arab conquest in 635 CE, obliged hagiographers to seek alternative settings. Piccirillo, *Arabia*, 224; Hamarneh, *Hagiography and Archaeology*, 52. The dramatic aftermath of the Persian invasion, the destruction of the Holy City, and the monasteries is mentioned by Leontios in the *Life of John the Almsgiver*. See Dawes – Baynes, *Three Byzantine Saints*, 202–4.

14   The text does not allow any of the classical monuments of Emesa to be placed within a city map. Rydén, *Cities*, 116.

15   The hagiographer relates probably to a text (*paterikon*) composed in Emesa, as indicated by the vague reference to a river (Orontes?) not far from the walls (where ten hippodrome attendants washed their clothes) and the use of Syriac language by some of the protagonists. See Mango, *Hagiographer*, 30–1; Efthymiadis – Déroche, *Greek Hagiography*, 75; Cesaretti, *Vite dei saloi*, 65 (n. 42); Cesaretti, *Metodi*, 43; Hamarneh, *Città*, 64. One may speculate that since Emesa had apparently no historical saint of its own, and its being free of any prior religious implications, may have constituted one of the reasons for selecting it as the physical space of the hagiographic setting. The impact of physical circumstances on spatiality is discussed also in Veikou – Nilsson – James, *Space Matters*, in this volume. Surprisingly the *Life of Symeon* does not refer to the most important relic of the head of St John the Baptist discovered at Emesa in AD 453 (*Chronicle* of Marcellinus Comes [Croke 1995]; *Chronicon Paschale* [Whitby – Whitby 1989, 82], Chronicle of Pseudo-Zachariah [Brooks 1919–1924, v. 2, 192; Greatrex *et al.* 2011, 415], and Piacenza Pilgrim [Wilkinson 2002, 150]).

In the hagiographic perspective, Leontios develops rather a social setting of a humble and marginalized humankind bound in a frame that lacks perfection,[16] he equally expresses disdain and opposition towards the physical context of the classical world, its monuments and institutions (agora, theatre, baths, circus etc.), capable of inducing one to sin and to temptation.[17] It is no coincidence that various episodes narrated in the *Life* involve heretics (monophysites/acephalous Severians), Jews and those who are possessed by demons.[18] There is also reproach for those who led lifestyles deemed incompatible with Christian values and the canons of his time, such as circus attendants (if the interpretation of *dēmotai* is correct),[19] actresses and dancers, amulet makers and prostitutes.[20] Symeon, therefore, through his simulated foolery,[21] prevented virtually the entire city from sinning; Leontios in fact in his epilogue indicates that Symeon was a "new Lot" sent to a corrupt city where he had to fulfil a prophetic mission emphasized by his foresight of destinies.[22]

The narrative as a whole, and through the non-definitions of chrono-physical space,[23] conveys an image of the fading world of Late Antiquity, of the gradual decay of its institutions, moving towards a new spatiality dominated

---

16   Hamarneh, *Città*, 70.
17   The *Life* of Symeon does not explicitly mention a circus in Emesa; it prefers to linger instead on that professional background. The circus attendants are described as being of doubtful morality, modest origin and therefore, on several occasions, are subject to the moralisations of the Holy Fool. Hamarneh, *Città*, 139–40.
18   The socio-religious structure of the society as described in the *Life of Symeon* does not include pagans but rather Jews and monophysites (Rydén, *Cities*, 140; Kennedy, *Last Century*, 147). The Arab authors Baladhurri and Ibn al-Athir report that a large Jewish community resided in the city (Hitti, *Origins*, 206). Déroche argued that a focus on themes connected to anti-Judaism was made appositely for the purpose of persuasion and conversion. Déroche, *Apologie*, 381–452; Krueger, *Comedy*, 44.
19   Rydén, *Cities*, 139; on the interpretation of the term citizens/δημόται as urban middle class and most ardent supporters of the circus colors see Zuckerman, *Le cirque*, 84–6; Kaplan – Kountoura-Galaki, *Economy and Society*, 397.
20   The hints in Leontios' text attest to the continuity of the Late Antique way of life in Emesa, where people are reported as going to taverns, dancing and watching spectacles. Rydén, *Cities*, 140.
21   The Greek language, despite its ability to produce abstract terms, has not developed a widely used noun corresponding to the adjective *salos*, which is a technical term for the "holy fool". In our paper we refer to "foolery" after Ivanov, *Holy Fools*. See Cesaretti, *Vite dei saloi*, 392.
22   In an intratextual reference (Cesaretti, *Vite dei saloi*, 126, n. 386), the hagiographer asserts that Symeon was fully resolved in the salvation of souls, as well as in making prophetic statements by acting as a fool without proclaiming his virtues. See Hamarneh, *Città*, 65.
23   The urban space in the life of Symeon is open and public, yet perceived as one physical, social, economic and ethical. Saradi, *City*, 424.

by the ideology of the Church.[24] Yet, within a much wider frame, the life of Symeon emphatically challenges the tendency established by earlier hagiographies, namely those staged in the fifth to sixth centuries. These narratives, while vividly describing prominent urban topography, social activity and professions, strongly emphasize the unwillingness of the holy men to reside in cities. Such concepts are reflected in the *Historia Lausiaca* of Palladius, in the *Life of St Isaac* (BHG 955), in that of *St Alexander Akoimetos* (BHG 47), and in the *Spiritual Meadow* of John Moschus; while in the case of the *Life of St Matrona of Perge* (BHG 1221) the rejection of urban life is negotiated through holy vision.[25] Symeon instead chooses the city, although the hagiographer provides no hint as to the reasons for his specific preference.[26]

2 Spaces 'Beyond'

In an asymmetrical parallel, the *Life of Andrew* introduces a discernible change of trend in spatial definitions. Although set in a largely undefined late antique context,[27] it presents insights into the cultural, social and religious experience of the tenth century.[28] The text in fact creates a new vision of spatial concepts that are mainly reflected in spiritual, imaginary and mentally-pictured landscapes that seem to prevail over a more material focus.

In the case of the *Life of Andrew*, the literary characterization of the fictional saint is structured within a 'real urban landscape' dominated and defined by the boundaries of the imposing Byzantine cityscape of Constantinople.[29] The realistic description of the urban life of the capital, its religious institutions

---

24   Admittedly, cities in hagiographies are either mentioned as plain topographic references or places rejected by the saints. Seiber, *Urban Saint*, 15–22; Saradi, *City*, 421.
25   Dagron, *Les moines*, 232–3; Saradi, *City*, 423–24; Saradi, *Constantinople*, 42–55.
26   Here again one may notice the prefiguring of a specific construction of sainthood, in which nothing is left to chance. See Mango, *Hagiographer*, 26–7; Krueger, *Symeon*, 31; Cesaretti, *Vite dei saloi*, 104.
27   The hagiographer pretends to be a contemporary of Andrew, who lived during the reign of Leo I (457–74). In a similar way the *Life of St Niphon* BHG 1371z was written in the tenth century, but set in the fourth. Rydén, *Date Niphon*, 39; Ivanov, *K datirovki*, 72–5; Kazhdan, *Byzantine Literature 850–1000*, 200–3; Efthymiadis, *Hagiography*, 126–7; Angelidi, *Dreams*, 26.
28   Rydén, *Date Andreas*, 130–6; Cesaretti, *Vingt ans après*, 34; Saradi, *City*, 434.
29   Andrew exclaims when he sees himself in a paradisiac vision: "ἡ κατοίκησίς μου ἐν Κωνσταντινουπόλει ὑπῆρχε" ("I used to live in Constantinople", see Rydén, *Andrew*, II, 46–47, l. 507). Constant references to landmarks of the imperial capital suggest that the life of Andrew was actually composed for a local audience. Magdalino, *Literary Text*, 100.

and venerated saints aims at providing historical reliability to the fictional figure of the holy fool.[30] Yet that urban landscape is anachronistic in turn: the hagiographer draws inspiration from the *thaumata* of the imperial capital,[31] builds links with the remote epoch of emperor Leo I showing indirectly how the idea and the ideals of holy foolery withstand time, and at the same time takes advantage of his fiction in order to "use" Andrew as a sort of "spokesman" of his own instructive intent.[32]

One can observe how the hagiographer privileges the description of microspatial realities as settings for his moralistic stories. In this regard taverns, porticoes, streets, markets and brothels (in one case) are spaces of continuous interaction between the *salos* and the humble society of the capital dominated by sin and lust and yet even more incompatible with the Christian rule of life.[33]

It must be pointed out that, unlike the former *Bios* (that of Symeon), there is a profound change in the attitudes towards the Christian community as a whole (whom Andrew reproaches and blames, instead of edifying) as well as towards public spaces. Landmarks like the Hippodrome are rejected as vehicles of superstition and their socio-cultural value is slipping away;[34] the statues are infested by demons; colonnades and porticoes are dwellings of the marginalized and the poor; there are no public spectacles, social gatherings or public bathing.[35] Space is instead firmly dominated by the Church, which governs social behaviour, and imposes its daily rhythms onto social life in a way that finds no parallel in the *Bios* of Symeon.[36]

Andrew is an expression of this mutation: he attends church for worship, venerates icons and relics, takes part in liturgical processions,[37] and severely targets the landmarks that bear witness to the pagan past, addressed as "forms

---

30 Saradi, *Byzantine City*, 110; Hamarneh, *Città*, 71.
31 Rydén, *Date Andreas*, 137–41; Magdalino, *Beauty of Antiquity*, 104–5; Magdalino, *Apocryphal Narrative*, 89–90; Hamarneh, *Città*, 78–9.
32 Rydén, *Introduzione*, 49; Cesaretti, *Metodi*, 52.
33 Saradi, *City*, 435.
34 Saradi-Mendelovici, *Christian Attitudes*, 56–7; Dagron, *Hippodrome*, 310–22; Angelidi, *Dreams*, 33; Cesaretti, *Metodi*, 33–4; Hamarneh, *Città*, 78. A similar attitude towards the monumental features of Constantinople is expressed in the *Life of St Stephen the Younger* (BHG 1666) and in the *Life of Patriarch Euthymios* (BHG 651). Saradi, *City*, 432–3.
35 Rydén, *Andrew*, i, 39–40; Saradi, *City*, 434.
36 The *Life of Symeon* mentions only one church, while the imperial capital as represented in the *Life of Andrew* is far richer in ecclesiastical foundations and certainly conveys a different historical context. See Cesaretti – Hamarneh, *Testo agiografico*, 117–18 ("Chiese").
37 Grosdidier de Matons, *Thèmes*, 307–9.

of the idols" (τῶν εἰδώλων τοῖς αἰσθητοῖς ἐντρανίζων ἔστηκα).[38] The hagiographer, who calls himself "Nicephorus, priest of Hagia Sophia",[39] avoids mentioning and representing in his narrative members of the clergy in charge of the functions and maintenance of the shrines;[40] he privileges instead *prefiguration* and vivid interactions with the holy figures physically appearing in the churches of the capital. Such reciprocity is expressed and reinforced through direct dialogues and detailed visual descriptions. The skillful construction allows "Nicephorus" to introduce vertical spatiality, a manifestation of Andrew's sainthood, within a mystical though constant interplay between earth and heaven, which is one of the typical marks of a certain Constantinopolitan hagiographical production of the mid-tenth century, especially when merged with a fictitious late antique setting.[41]

The account describes heaven as an enhanced vision of earthly reality. This 'space beyond' is rich in suggestive visual detail, elements that may present variations according to divine condescension to the protagonist and his pupil Epiphanius respectively.[42] Andrew in fact passes from dream to ecstasy

---

[38] The episode unfolds at the forum in front of the great door of the Senate: "...'You fool in your spirit! I am looking at the visible idols, but you are a spiritual 'thong-leg', and a serpent, and of the viper's brood, for your soul's axles and your heart's spiritual legs are crooked and going to Hades' ...". Rydén, *Andrew*, II, 141 (Greek text II, 140, ll. 1924–30). Nicephorus relates to the theme of the idols in the section of erotapokriseis: "Zeus, Apollo, Hermes, Kronos, Hera, Artemis, and the whole catalogue of idols are called dead and blind. The prophet calls them dead because they are stones and gold and silver; they have never lived nor will they ever live at all" (Rydén, *Andrew*, II, 233, ll. 3409–13 of the Greek text) and again in the account of martyr Theodore (Rydén, *Andrew*, II, 288–92, ll. 4196–264). The fear of idolatry turns out to be a particularly sensitive topic in the post iconoclast era. Magdalino, *Myth*, 210; Hamarneh, *Città*, 78.

[39] Magdalino has discussed the issue of the fabricated model or a literary construction that existed only in the mind of the hagiographer. See Magdalino, *Literary Text*, 85–6; Cesaretti, *Vingt ans après*, 31.

[40] According to Magdalino, the lives of Symeon and Andrew intend to highlight the contrast between *hidden holiness*, which is invisible to the eyes of the world, and the corruption underlying the *visible sanctity* of the official clergy. Magdalino, *Literary Text*, 93; Grosdidier de Matons, *Thèmes*, 322–3; Hamarneh, *Città*, 72.

[41] See the remarks by Kazhdan, *Byzantine Literature 850–1000*, 185–209. Needless to say, each and every one of the six texts grouped by Kazhdan in the eight chapters of his work ("Three Constantinopolitan *Vitae* of the mid-tenth century") presents distinguishing and specific features. In this respect the simulacrum of the late antique city as shown in the *Life of Andrew* deserves to be appreciated as a sort of a mark of authority. Cesaretti, *Metodi*, 59 ("un calco esibito").

[42] Paradise, located in the world beyond according to the life of Philaretos the Merciful (dated to the beginning of the ninth century) is described as marvelous garden. Fourmy – Leroy, *vie de S. Philarète*, 161.29–165.10; Maguire, *Paradise Withdrawn*, 28.

providing emotional sensations with the concrete sensorial experience of immateriality (including *synaesthesia*); the latter is dominated by boundless space and light,[43] and a wonderful garden described as follows:

> Κατενόουν δὲ ἐμαυτὸν ὥσπερ ἄσαρκον· οὐ γὰρ ἐνόμιζον σάρκα φορεῖν. Χιτὼν δέ μοι προσῆν ἀστράπτων, χιονοειδὴς καὶ διάλιθος· σφόδρα δὲ ἐτερπόμην ἐπὶ τῷ κάλλει αὐτοῦ. Τὰ δὲ ἐπὶ τῆς κορυφῆς μου κατενόουν, καὶ ἦν ἐκ παντοίων ἀνθέων πεπλεγμένος μοι στέφανος διάχρυσος ἐκφεγγίζων, καὶ ὑποδήματα ἐπὶ τῶν ποδῶν μου. Ζώνην δὲ ἤμην διεζωσμένος ὡς κόκκινον φοβερόβαφον. Ἔστιλβε δὲ ὁ ἀὴρ τοῦ παραδείσου ἐκείνου ἀρρήτου φωτὸς τῇ ἰδέᾳ, ὑπορροδίζων ἀνθήμασιν. Εὐωδία δὲ παραλλασσομένη ξενοπρεπῶς τοῖς αἰσθητηρίοις καὶ τῇ ὀσφρήσει μου ὑπήντα κατευφραίνουσα. Ὥσπερ δὲ βασιλεὺς οὕτως ἤμην διακινῶν ἐν τῷ κήπῳ τοῦ θεοῦ, καὶ ἐτερπόμην μεγάλως ὑπὲρ ἄνθρωπον ἐμαυτὸν στοχαζόμενος.

I noticed that I was disembodied, as it were, for it did not seem to me that I was wearing flesh. Yet I was dressed in a dazzling garment, white as snow and set with precious stones, and I was greatly delighted by its beauty. I looked at my headgear: it was a wreath plaited of all sorts of flowers, interwoven with gold and radiant. There were sandals on my feet and I had a girdle around my waist, marvellously red, as it were. The air in the garden glowed with an indescribable light, shimmering with the colour of roses. A strangely changing aroma reached my senses and filled my nostrils with delight. I moved in the garden of God like a king, enjoying immensely the feeling of being above the human condition.[44]

The narrative continues evoking trees that sway like waves in perennial flowering; a river; gentle olfactory experiences spread by prodigal, fragrant and coloured winds; a glittering sky at sunset; and delightful melodies that lead the enchanted observer in front of the Redeemer's Cross or Throne, the focal point of the paradisiac setting.[45] This description was probably inspired by the

---

43 Baun, *Tales*, 403; Cesaretti – Hamarneh, *Testo agiografico*, 150 ("Lampade"). The multisensory experience can be perceived as a deliberate change of the parameters of performed spatiality in which both body and mind of the protagonist are engaged in unison. Additional aspects of performed spaces are addressed in: Veikou – Nilsson –James, *Space Matters*, in this volume.

44 Rydén, *Andrew*, II, 47–49, ll. 512–22 of the Greek text. Maguire, *Paradise Withdrawn*, 23–4 and Maguire, *Heavenly City*, 41–2. As well as: Cupane, *Heavenly City*, 53–68.

45 Cesaretti – Hamarneh, *Testo agiografico*, 92 ("Paradiso"). Contextually, the highest possible spatial and social hierarchy.

model of authority of the Imperial Palace of Constantinople, with its luminous majesty and its lovely gardens, though somehow distant and unreachable.[46] Nevertheless, the palatine metaphor allows the author to shape heaven in a tangible form of earthly spatiality, within the speculum of a hagiographic narrative context.

3 Inner 'Space'

The last aspect of our discussion will briefly consider the function of space in its inner psychological aspect that derives from the action of the holy fools within the urban societies of Emesa and Constantinople. While rejecting extant moral patterns that oblige city dwellers to conformity, these two *saloi* risked social sanctions.[47] Leontios states that Symeon "was most pure, just as a pearl which has travelled through slime unsullied"[48] yet he kept the company of women, especially prostitutes:

> Ἦν δέ τις πλησίον Ἐμέσης μένων πρωτοκωμήτης, καὶ ὡς ἤκουσεν τὸν βίον αὐτοῦ, λέγει· "πίστευσον, ἐὰν ἴδω, νοῶ ἐὰν προσποιητός ἐστιν καὶ ἐάν τε ἐν ἀληθείᾳ ἐστὶν ἔξηχος". Παραγενόμενος οὖν εἰς τὴν πόλιν κατὰ συγκυρίαν ηὗρεν αὐτόν, ὅτι ἐβάσταζεν αὐτὸν μία προϊσταμένη καὶ ἄλλη ἐλούριζεν αὐτόν. Εὐθέως δὲ ἐσκανδαλίσθη ὁ πρωτοκωμήτης καὶ εἰς ἑαυτὸν διελογίζετο καὶ ἔλεγεν Συριστί· "ἆρα αὐτὸς ὁ Σατανᾶς οὐ πιστεύει, ὅτι πορνεύει μετ' αὐτῶν ὁ ψευδοαββᾶς οὗτος;" Καταλιπὼν οὖν αὐτὰς εὐθὺς ὁ Σαλὸς ἔρχεται πρὸς τὸν πρωτοκωμήτην ἀπέχοντα ἀπ' αὐτοῦ εἴτι ῥίπτει λίθον τις καὶ δέδωκεν αὐτῷ κόσσον. Ἐγύμνωσεν δὲ τὰ ἱμάτια αὐτοῦ καὶ εἶπεν πρὸς αὐτὸν βαλλίζων καὶ συρίζων· "δεῦ παῖξον, ταπεινέ, ὧδε δόλος οὐκ ἔστιν". Ἔγνω οὖν ἐκεῖνος, ὅτι τὰ ἐν τῇ καρδίᾳ αὐτοῦ ἐνόησεν, καὶ θαυμάσας, καθότι ἤρχετο εἰπεῖν τινι τὸ πρᾶγμα, ἐδεσμεῖτο ἡ γλῶσσα αὐτοῦ καὶ οὐκ ἠδύνατο φθέγξασθαι.

---

46   Carile, *Imperial Palaces*, 90–1; Cesaretti – Hamarneh, *Testo agiografico*, 92–3 ("Paradiso"). Hamarneh, *Città*, 72; Heaven perceived in terms of palaces adorned with mosaics and marbles also appears in the *Life of Basil the Younger* (BHG 263–264) see Magdalino, *Literary Text*, pp. 107–12; also Veikou – Nilsson – James, *Space Matters*, in this volume.

47   The borderline behaviour of Symeon and Andrew within the cities deliberately contrasts with the patterns established by the social canons of their time and seem to manifest as theatrical mannerism. Constantinou, *Holy Actors*, 252–5; Hamarneh, *Città*, 61.

48   Greek text Rydén, *Leben des Symeon*, 122,19–20; transl. Krueger, *Symeon*, 133. Context and discussion in Cesaretti, *Vite dei saloi*, 61, n. 19.

There was a certain village headman living near Emesa, and when he heard about Symeon's way of life, he said, "Believe me, if I saw him, I would know if he's pretending or if he really is an idiot". Therefore, he came to the city and found Symeon by chance while one prostitute was carrying him and another was whipping him. Immediately the village headman was scandalized, and he reasoned with himself and said in Syriac, "Does Satan himself not believe that this false abba is fornicating with them?" At once, the Fool left the women and came toward the village headman, who was about a stone's throw away from him, and hit him. And stripping off his tunic, he danced naked and whistled. And he said to him, "Come here and play, wretch, there's no fraud here!" By this the man knew that Symeon had seen what was in his heart, and he was amazed. Every time he started to tell someone about this, his tongue was bound, and he was unable to utter a sound.[49]

He walked naked into the women's bath:

Ἀποδύεται τὸ ἱμάτιον αὐτοῦ καὶ ἐπιτίθει αὐτὸ εἰς τὴν κεφαλὴν αὐτοῦ δήσας αὐτὸ εἰς αὐτὴν ὡς φακιόλιν. Καὶ λέγει αὐτῷ ὁ κύρις Ἰωάννης· "φόρεσον, ἀδελφέ, ἐπεὶ ὄντως ἐὰν γυμνὸς περιπατεῖς, ἐγὼ μετὰ σοῦ οὐκ ἔρχομαι". Λέγει αὐτῷ ὁ ἀββᾶς Συμεών· "ὕπαγε, ἔξηχε, ἐγὼ ἔργον πρὸ ἔργου ἐποίησα. εἰ δὲ οὐκ ἔρχῃ, ἴδε ἐγὼ προλαμβάνω σε μικρόν". Καὶ ἀφήσας αὐτὸν προεποίησεν ὀλίγον. Δύο οὖν λουτρὰ ἦσαν ἐγγίζοντα ἀλλήλοις, ἓν ἀνδρῶον καὶ ἓν γυναικεῖον. Εἴασεν οὖν τὸ τῶν ἀνδρῶν ὁ Σαλὸς καὶ ὥρμησεν εἰς τὸ γυναικεῖον ἑκουσίως. Ἔκραζεν οὖν αὐτὸν ὁ κύρις Ἰωάννης· "ποῦ ὑπάγεις, Σαλέ; μεῖνον, τῶν γυναικῶν ἐστιν ἐκεῖνο". Στραφεὶς οὖν ὁ θαυμάσιος λέγει αὐτῷ· "ὕπαγε, σὺ ἔξηχε, ἐκεῖ θερμὸν καὶ νερὸν καὶ ὧδε θερμὸν καὶ νερὸν καὶ τίποτε περισσὸν οὔτε ἐκεῖ οὔτε ὧδε ἔνι" καὶ δραμὼν εἰσῆλθεν ἀναμέσον τῶν γυναικῶν ὡς ἐπὶ κυρίου τῆς δόξης. Ὥρμησαν δὲ πᾶσαι κατ' αὐτοῦ καὶ τύπτουσαι αὐτὸν ἐξήνεγκαν.

He stripped off his garment and placed it on his head, wrapping it around like a turban. And Deacon John said to him, "Put it back on, brother, for truly if you are going to walk around naked, I won't go with you". Abba Symeon said to him, "Go away, idiot, I'm all ready. If you won't come, see, I'll go a little ahead of you". And leaving him, he kept a little ahead. However, there were two baths next to each other, one for men and one for women. The Fool ignored the men's and rushed willingly into the

---

49   Greek text Rydén, *Leben des Symeon*, 156,11–22; transl. Krueger, *Symeon*, 160.

women's. Deacon John cried out to him, "Where are you going, Fool? Wait, that's the women's!" The wonderful one turned and said to him, "Go away, you idiot, there's hot and cold water here, and there's hot and cold water there, and it doesn't matter at all whether (I use) this one or that". And he ran and entered into the midst of the women, as in the presence of the Lord of glory. The women rushed against him, beat him, and threw him out.[50]

He threw nuts in church, overthrowing merchant's benches;[51] he even deliberately neglected fasts[52] and relieved himself in public:

Ὅλος δὲ ἦν ὥσπερ ἀσώματος καὶ μηδὲ ὑφορώμενος τὴν ἀσχημοσύνην μήτε τὴν τῶν ἀνθρώπων μήτε τὴν τῆς φύσεως. Πολλάκις γοῦν τῆς γαστρὸς αὐτοῦ τὴν οἰκείαν χρείαν ἐπιζητούσης ποιῆσαι εὐθέως μηδένα ἐρυθριῶν ἐπὶ τῆς ἀγορᾶς πρὸς τόπον ἐκαθέζετο ἐπὶ πάντων, κἀντεῦθεν πεῖσαι βουλόμενος, ὡς ὅτι τῶν κατὰ φύσιν φρενῶν ἐξεστηκὼς τοῦτο ἐργάζεται.

It was entirely as if Symeon had no body, and he paid no attention to what might be judged disgraceful conduct either by human convention or by nature. Often, indeed, when his belly sought to do its private function, immediately, and without blushing, he squatted in the market place, wherever he found himself, in front of everyone, wishing to persuade (others) by this that he did this because he had lost his natural sense.[53]

---

50   Greek text Rydén, *Leben des Symeon*, 148,27–149,10; transl. Krueger, *Symeon*, 153–4.
51   "On the next day, which was Sunday, he took nuts, and entering the church at the beginning of the liturgy, he threw the nuts and put out the candles. When they hurried to run after him, he went up to the pulpit, and from there he pelted the women with nuts. With great trouble, they chased after him, and while he was going out, he overturned the tables of the pastry chefs, who (nearly) beat him to death. Seeing himself crushed by the blows, he said to himself, 'Poor Symeon, if things like this keep happening, you won't live for a week in these people's hands'". Transl. Krueger, *Symeon*, 151.
52   One of the stories narrated by Leontios (Greek text Rydén, *Leben des Symeon*, 156,23–157,4) mentions that Symeon consumed food on Holy Thursday and when questioned by a deacon he showed him forty *noumia*. The *follis*, which equals forty *noumia*, symbolizes the forty days of fasting that Symeon had endured.
53   Greek text Rydén, *Leben des Symeon*, 148,13–17; transl. Krueger, *Symeon*, 153. The episode stresses on the concept of the neglect of the space of proper body as instrument of achieving hidden sanctity. See the introduction by Myrto Veikou, Ingela Nilsson and Liz James in this volume.

All together, these provocative and irrational behaviours caused violent reactions expressed in mocking, beating and mistreatment.[54] Andrew for his part, though far less offensive, is exposed to the same harshness: people strike him on his neck, push him, spit on him and beat him, sometimes for diabolic instigation; boys made fun of him by smearing charcoal ink on his face and dragging him with a rope around his neck.[55]

The hagiographers clearly juxtapose two concepts in which the denial of the "value" of the respective societies of Emesa and Constantinople was paralleled in turn by the denial of the "value of the sanctity" of Symeon and Andrew.[56] This paradox rose to a crescendo in (for Symeon) converting and (for Andrew) biasing the transgressors, heretics and sinners, or in other words, reflecting the expectations of the readership and the mission/function of the hagiographic narrative. A clear example of this is the story narrated by Leontios in his *Life of Symeon*:

Ἦν δὲ πάλιν ἅπαξ καθήμενος μετὰ ἀδελφῶν καὶ θερμαινόμενος πλησίον τοῦ καμινίου τοῦ ὑελοψοῦ. Ἦν δὲ ὁ ὑελοψὸς Ἑβραῖος. Καὶ λέγει τοῖς πτωχοῖς παίζων· "θέλετε ποιῶ ὑμᾶς γελάσαι; ἰδοὺ κατὰ ποτήριον ὃ ποιεῖ ὁ τεχνίτης ποιῶ σταυρὸν καὶ κλάνεται". Ὡς οὖν ἔκλασεν ἐνορδίνως κἂν ἑπτά, ἤρξαντο γελᾶν οἱ πτωχοί, καὶ εἶπαν αὐτῷ τὸ πρᾶγμα καὶ ἐδίωξεν καυτηριάσας αὐτόν. Ὡς οὖν ἀπήρχετο, ἔκραζεν αὐτὸν λέγων· "ὄντως, μάνζηρε, ἕως οὗ ποιήσῃς εἰς τὸ μέτωπόν σου σταυρόν, ὅλα συντρίβονται". Καὶ κλάσας πάλιν ἄλλα δεκατρία ἐνορδίνως κατερράγη καὶ ποιεῖ σταυρὸν εἰς τὸ μέτωπον αὐτοῦ, καὶ οὐκέτι ἔκλασεν τίποτε. Ἐκ τούτου οὖν τοῦ τρόπου ἀπῆλθεν καὶ ἐγένετο Χριστιανός.

Another time he was sitting with his brothers (in poverty) and warming himself near a glassblower's furnace. The glassblower was Jewish. And

---

54 Krueger has recently argued that Leontios' presentation of his hero works as a comic inversion of the biblical narrative. Krueger, *Comedy*, 36–8. The attitude towards the body as spatial category (respected, valued, mistreated, and neglected) is discussed by Messis in this volume.

55 "Blessed Andrew, however, after leaving Epiphanios' house, struggled in the hidden places and streets of the city, where no one knew him, chilled by unbearable frost and numb with cold, hated by all, so that the boys of the city, beating, dragging and slapping him without mercy, put a rope around his neck and dragged him along in full view of everybody, making ink from charcoal which they smeared on his face". (Rydén, *Andrew*, II, 93, ll. 1217–23 of the Greek text). Rydén, *Date Niphon*, 46; Cesaretti – Hamarneh, *Testo agiografico*, 127 ("Volto"). In a similar way the mistreatments, in the case of Andrew, were not intended to amuse the audience but instead to elicit sympathy and pity. Krueger, *Comedy*, 41.

56 The two Fools, although occupying a higher hierarchy in the eyes of God, are deliberately denied that recognition through distancing and social constraints.

Symeon said to the beggars, joking, "Do you want me to make you laugh? Behold, I will make the sign of the cross over the drinking glass which the craftsman is making, and it will break". When he had broken about seven, one after the other, the beggars began to laugh, and they told the glassblower about the matter, and he chased Symeon away, branding him. As he left, Symeon screamed at the glassblower, saying, "Truly, *mànzere*, until you make the sign of the cross on your forehead, all your glasses will be shattered". And again after the (glassblower) broke thirteen others, one after the other, he was shattered and made the sign of the cross on his forehead. And nothing ever broke again. And because of this, he went out and became a Christian.[57]

• • •

To conclude, the two lives considered here are a uniquely interwoven hagiographic corpus, as it provides several elements that underscore the prominence of two surprisingly and symmetrically opposed aspects of spatiality. Although some elements may appear in other hagiographic texts, these two *Bioi* are unequalled in their shared intent, in the form of sanctity they manifestly support, and in the way they communicate acts and criticism. On the one hand, the character of Symeon, while provided with a historical setting, stands out against the evanescent background of Emesa and moves according to defined geo-spatial 'horizontal' coordinates. On the other hand, the story of Andrew, a "holy man who is merely a literary text",[58] is set in a Constantinople-centred ideology and culture, privileging a 'vertical' dialogue between earth and heaven, evincing an interplay of factual and metaphorical spatiality. Likewise, the change in perspective indicates the persistence and the shift of the theme of holy foolery from the periphery (Emesa) to the centre (Constantinople) and a medieval effort to regenerate ancient ideals. Indeed, in the *Life of Andrew* the late antique elements must be perceived as iconic markers of the authority of the distant past in which Symeon, the exemplary *typos* of Andrew, had actually lived.[59] In this way, these archetypal markers contribute to the real purpose of the text, i.e. they enable the reader to perceive dogmatically correct representations of non-earthly realities. Furthermore, tracing pre-arranged boundaries and circumscribing them to a single urban centre allows historians

---

57   Greek text Rydén, *Leben des Symeon*, 163,7–15; transl. Krueger, *Symeon*, 165–6.
58   After Magdalino, *Literary Text*.
59   See above, n. 41 and context.

not only to identify the circulation of the narrative (the readership),[60] but also to point out how the perception of space (private, personal, public, collective, material and imaginary) is strictly connected with salvation paradigms and eschatological concerns wisely entrusted by the two hagiographers to the figures of their heroes.

Bibliography

Primary Sources

Rydén, Lennart, *Das Leben des heiligen Narren Symeon von Leontios von Neapolis*. Uppsala 1963.

Rydén, Lennart, *The Life of St Andrew the Fool*, 2 vols. Uppsala 1995.

Secondary Sources

Angelidi, C. 2015. "The Dreams of a Woman: An Episode from the Life of Andrew the Fool", in Antonopoulou, Kotzabassi & Loukaki (eds) 2015, 25–38.

Angelidi, C. & G. T. Calofonos (eds) 2014. *Dreaming in Byzantium and Beyond*. Farnham.

Antonopoulou, T., S. Kotzabassi & M. Loukaki (eds) 2015. *Myriobiblos. Essays on Byzantine Literature and Culture*. Boston, Berlin & München.

Baun, J. 2007. *Tales from Another Byzantium: Celestial Journey and Local Community in the Medieval Greek Apocrypha*. Cambridge.

Berger, A. & S. A. Ivanov (eds) 2018. *Holy Fools and Devine Madmen. Sacred Insanity Through Ages and Cultures*. München.

Brooks, E.W. 1919–1924. *Historia ecclesiastica Zachariae Rhetori vulgo adscripta*. Louvain.

Carile, M. C. 2009. "Imperial Palaces and Heavenly Jerusalem: Real and Ideal Palaces in Late Antiquity", in Lidov (ed.) 2009, 78–102.

Cavallero, Pablo A. 2011. *Leoncio de Neápolis, Vida de Juan el limosnero*, rev. ed. Buenos Aires.

Cavallero, P. A., T. Fernández & J. César Lastra Sheridan (eds) 2009. *Leoncio de Neápolis, Vida de Simeón el loco*, rev. ed. Buenos Aires.

Cesaretti, P. 2014. *Leonzio di Neapoli: Niceforo prete di Santa Sofia, Vite dei saloi Simeone e Andrea, a cura di Paolo Cesaretti*, Testi e Studi Bizantino-Neoellenici 19. Roma.

---

60 According to Rapp, the audience assumes the role of a substitute text as a medium in the transmission of the teaching of the holy men. Thus, the author's primary aim was not just the making of a saint by celebrating the subject of his narrative but rather to make saints out of those who encounter his work. Rapp, *Author*, 123.

Cesaretti, P. 2016. "I metodi dell'evidenza. Le vite dei saloi Simeone e Andrea tra allusioni e calchi", in Cesaretti & Hamarneh 2016, 33–59.

Cesaretti, P. 2016. "The Life of St Andrew the Fool by Lennart Rydén: vingt ans après", *Scandinavian Journal of Byzantine and Modern Greek Studies* 2, 31–51.

Cesaretti, P. & B. Hamarneh 2016. *Testo Agiografico e Orizzonte visivo. Ricontestualizzare le vite dei saloi Simeone e Andrea (BHG 1677, 115z)*. Roma.

Constantinou, S. 2011 & 2014. "Holy Actors and Actresses: Fools and Cross-Dressers as the Protagonists of Saints' Lives", in Efthymiadis (ed.) 2011a & 2014a, 343–62.

Croke, B. 1995. *The Chronicle of Marcellinus: Text and Commentary. Byzantina Australiensia 7*, Sydney.

Cupane, C. 2014. "The Heavenly City. Religious and Secular Visions of the Other World in Byzantine Literature", in Angelidi & Calofonos (eds) 2014, 53–68.

Dagron, G. 2011. *L'Hippodrome de Constantinople. Jeux, peuple et politique*. Paris.

Dagron, G. 1970. "Les moines et la ville. Le monachisme à Constantinople jusqu'au concile de Chalcédoine (451)", *TM* 4, 229–76.

Dawes, E. & Baynes, N.H. 1977. *Three Byzantine Saints. Contemporary Biographies translated from Greek*. Crestwood – New York.

Déroche, V. 1995. *Études sur Léontios de Neapolis*. Uppsala.

Déroche, V. 2010. "L'Apologie contre les Juifs de Léontius de Néapolis", in Déroche & Dagron (eds) 2010, 381–452.

Déroche, V. & G. Dagron (eds) 2010. *Juifs et chrétiens en Orient byzantin*. Paris.

Efthymiadis, S. (ed.) 2011a & 2014a. *The Ashgate Research Companion to Byzantine Hagiography; Periods and Places*, vol. 1. *Genres and Contexts*. Farnham.

Efthymiadis, S. 2011b & 2014b. "Hagiography from the 'Dark Age' to the Age of Symeon Metaphrastes (Eighth-Tenth Centuries)", in Efthymiadis (ed.) 2011a & 2014a, 95–142.

Efthymiadis, S. & V. Déroche 2011 & 2014. "Greek Hagiography in Late Antiquity (Fourth-Seventh Centuries)", in Efthymiadis (ed.) 2011a & 2014a, 35–94.

Efthymiadis, S. & A. K. Petridis (eds) 2015. Μυθοπλασίες. Χρήση και πρόσληψη των αρχαίων μύθων από την αρχαιότητα μέχρι σήμερα (*Proceedings of Use and Reception of Greek Myths in ancient, Byzantine and modern Greek history, literature and art, European Cultural Centre of Delphi, 28–30 January 2010*). Peristeri.

Fourmy, M.H. & M. Leroy, "La vie de S. Philarète", *Byzantion* 9 (1934): 85–170.

Giankou, T. X. & C. Nassis (eds) 2015. Κυπριακή Αγιολογία: Πρακτικά Α' διεθνούς συνεδρίου. Paralimni.

Greatrex, G., Phenix, R.R., Horn, C.B., Brock, S.P. & W. Witakowski 2011. *The Chronicle of Pseudo-Zachariah Rhetor: Church and War in Late Antiquity*. Liverpool.

Grosdidier de Matons, J. 1970. "Les thèmes d' edification dans la Vie d' André Salos", *Travaux et mémoires* 4, 277–329.

Hamarneh, B. 2016. "Una città per il salos. La costruzione agiografica dell'orizzonte urbano", in Cesaretti & Hamarneh 2016, 60–82.

Hamarneh, B. 2020. "Between Hagiography and Archaeology: Pilgrimage and Monastic Communities on the Banks of the River Jordan, in Pilgrimage to Jerusalem. Christians, Jews and Muslims", in Rapp et al. (eds) 2020, 41–56.

Howard-Johnston, J. & P. A. Hayward (eds) 1999. *The Cult of Saints in Late Antiquity and the Early Middle Ages: Essays on the Contribution of Peter Brown*. Oxford.

Hutter, I. & H. Hunger (eds) 1984. *Byzanz und der Westen. Studien zu Kunst des europäischen Mittelalters*. Wien.

Ivanov, S. A. 1999. "K datirovki žitija sv. Nifonta", *Visantijskii Vremennik* 58, 72–75.

Ivanov, S. A. 2006. *Holy Fools in Byzantium and Beyond*. Tr. S. Franklin. Oxford & New York.

Kaplan, M. & E. Kountoura-Galaki 2014. *Economy and Society in Byzantine Hagiography: Realia and Methodological Questions*, in Efthymiadis (ed.) 2011a & 2014a, 389–418.

Kazhdan, A. P. 2006. *A History of Byzantine Literature (850–1000)*. Ed. C. Angelidi. Athens.

Kennedy, H. 1983. "The Last Century of Byzantine Syria: A Reinterpretation", *Byzantinische Forschungen* 10, 141–83.

Krueger, D. 1996. *Symeon the Holy Fool. Leontius' Life and the Late Antique City*. Berkeley, Los Angeles & London.

Krueger, D. 2017. "The Hagiographers' Bible: Intertextuality and Scriptural Culture in the Late Sixth and the First Half of the Seventh Century", in Krueger & Nelson (eds) 2017,177–89.

Krueger, D. 2018. "From Comedy to Martyrdom: The Shifting Theology of the Holy Fools from Symeon of Emesa to Andrew", in Berger & Ivanov (eds) 2018, 29–48.

Krueger, D. & R. S. Nelson (eds) 2017. *The New Testament in Byzantium*. Washington D.C.

Lidov, A. M. (ed.) 2009. *New Jerusalems. Hierotopy and Iconography*. Moskva.

Littlewood, A., H. Maguire & J. Wolschke-Bulmahn (eds) 2002. *Byzantine Garden Culture*. Washington, D.C.

Magdalino, P. 1999. "'What we heard in the Lives of the saints we have seen with our own eyes': the holy man as literary text in tenth-century Constantinople", in Howard-Johnston & Hayward (eds) 1999, 83–112.

Magdalino, P. 2012. "The Beauty of Antiquity in Late Byzantine Praise of Constantinople", in Odorico & Messis (eds) 2012, 101–21.

Magdalino, P. 2014. "Apocryphal Narrative: Patterns of Fiction in Byzantine Prophetic and Patriographic Literature", in Roilos (ed.) 2014, 87–101.

Magdalino, P. 2015. "The Myth in the Street: the Realities and Perceptions of Pagan Sculptures in Christian Constantinople", in Efthymiadis & Petridis (eds) 2015, 205–22.

Maguire, H. 2002. "Paradise Withdrawn", in Littlewood, Maguire & Wolschke-Bulmahn (eds) 2002, 23–35.

Maguire, H. 2012. "The Heavenly City in Ekphrasis and Art", in Odorico & Messis (eds) 2012, 37–48.

Mango, C. 1984. "A Byzantine Hagiographer at Work: Leontios of Neapolis", in Hutter & Hunger (eds) 1984, 25–41.

Odorico, P. & Messis, Ch. (eds) 2012. *Villes de toute beauté. L'Ekphrasis des cités dans les littératures byzantine et byzantino-slaves*. Paris.

Patlagean, E. 1968. "Ancienne hagiographie et histoire sociale", *Annales. Économies, Sociétés, Civilisations* 23.1, 106–26.

Pettersson, A. et al. (ed.) 2006. *Literary History: Toward a Global Perspective*, vol. 2: *Literary Genres: An Intercultural Approach*. Berlin.

Piccirillo, M. 2002. *L'Arabia Cristiana. Dalla provincia imperiale al primo periodo islamico*. Milano.

Rapp, C. 2015. "Author, Audience, Text and Saint: Two Models of Early Byzantine Hagiography", *Scandinavian Journal of Byzantine and Modern Greek Studies* 1, 110–29.

Rapp, C. 2015. "Cypriot Hagiography in the Seventh Century: Patrons and Purpose", in Giankou & Nassis (eds) 2015, 397–411.

Rapp, C. et al. (eds) 2020. *Pilgrimage to Jerusalem: Journeys, Destinations, Experiences across Times and Cultures*. Mainz & Frankfurt.

Roilos, P. (ed.) 2014. *Medieval Greek Storytelling. Fictionality and Narrative in Byzantium*. Wiesbaden.

Rydén, L. 1983. "The Date of the Life of Andreas Salos", *DOP* 32, 127–55.

Rydén, L. "The *Life of St Basil the Younger* and the Date of the *Life of St Andreas Salos*", *Harvard Ukrainian Studies* 7, 568–856.

Rydén, L. 2014. "Introduzione", in Cesaretti 2014, 33–54.

Rydén, L. 1993. "Gaza, Emesa and Constantinople. Late Ancient Cities in the Light of Hagiography", in Rydén & Rosenquist (eds) 1993, 133–44.

Rydén, L. 2006. "Byzantine Saints' Lives as a Literary Genre", in Pettersson et al (ed.) 2006, 248–78.

Rydén, L. & J. O. Rosenquist (eds) 1993. *Aspects of Late Antiquity and Early Byzantium*, Papers Read at a Colloquium Held at the Swedish Institute in Istanbul (31 May–5 June 1992). Uppsala.

Saradi, H. G. 2006. *The Byzantine City in the Sixth Century. Literary Images and Historical Reality*. Athens.

Saradi, H. G. 2014. "The City in Byzantine Hagiography", in Efthymiadis (ed.) 2011a & 2014a, 419–52.

Saradi, H. G. 1995. "Constantinople and its Saints (IVth–VIth c.). The Image of the City and Social Considerations", *Studi medievali* 36, 87–110.

Saradi-Mendelovici, H. 1990. "Christian Attitudes toward Pagan Monuments in Late Antiquity and their Legacy in Later Byzantine Centuries", *DOP* 44, 47–61.

Seiber, J. 1977. *The Urban Saint in Early Byzantine Social History*. Oxford.

Whitby, M. & Whitby, M. 1989. *Chronicon Paschale 284–628 AD*. Liverpool.
Wilkinson, J. 2002. *Jerusalem Pilgrims Before the Crusades*. Warminster.
Zuckerman, C. 2000. "Le cirque, l'argent et le peuple. À propos d'une inscription du Bas Empire", *RÉB* 58, 69–96.

Textualization of Space and Travel in Middle Byzantine Hagiography

Yulia Mantova

The Spatial Turn in the humanities has provided us with numerous theoretical approaches for dealing with spatiality and its various cultural representations. The most recent findings in this field have been thoroughly explored by Myrto Veikou in her in-depth paper on the *Life of St Lazaros*,[1] in which she demonstrates how Henri Lefebvre's analytical concept of *lived space* can be applied to the study of Byzantine literature. The present paper aims to uncover the *lived spaces* which are present in hagiography.

The term textualization has been borrowed from Marie-Laure Ryan's article in *The Living Handbook of Narratology*.[2] The textualization of space can be understood as a set of techniques used by authors in order to construct a narrative space through which to immerse the reader within their narrative world. I will develop and focus on one particular technique which deals with the movements of characters, exercising it further in order to reveal the ways in which hagiographers have represented the process of travelling.

Movement is one of the most notable means through which space is projected. In this paper, I seek to explore whether hagiographers represent their heroes' travel as a continuous process of movement or as a detached set of locations at which they arrive and depart.

In one of his early works, Alexander Kazhdan compares the different techniques employed by the Byzantines in order to represent space in the fine arts and in literature.[3] According to Kazhdan, both formats have a number of common features, the most crucial being the prevalence of symbolic space over and above realistic description of the environment. In a similar manner to the static and stable compositions of Byzantine frescos and icons, writers tended to depict relocations as a set of static conditions, i.e. movement from one place to another were presented as separate scenes of departure and arrival rather than as a continuous process.

---

1 Veikou 2017.
2 Ryan 2014.
3 Kazhdan 1968, 183–84.

The extensive recent research conducted by Veronica della Dora in her *Landscape, Nature, and the Sacred in Byzantium* reaches a somewhat similar conclusion. Despite the fact that the spatial perceptions of the Church Fathers and their medieval successors were rooted in Greco-Roman topographies, their understanding of nature and the cosmos was distinctively symbolic. Thus, the repetition of pre-existing biblical topoi prevailed over the faithful description of the physical environment.[4]

But does that mean that Byzantine writers had a single universal artistic pattern for embedding travel into their narratives? I will trace how the hagiographers of the Middle Byzantine period adhered to the above-mentioned principle. Besides, as I explore a number of texts containing lengthy journeys,[5] I will also focus on diachronic changes, a task which has become increasingly viable since scholars have moved beyond previous received wisdom regarding the permanency and inalterability of hagiographical literature.

1   From the Seventh to the Tenth Century

One possible starting point for this investigation is the seventh century *Life of Theodore of Sykeon*.[6] The matter of fact is that Theodore made three pilgrimages to Jerusalem and some other journeys. This lengthy vita is a unique source, and its historical value has long been widely acknowledged, since it provides many details regarding the social and economic life of the empire. In addition to this, the author, Gregory of Sykeon, demonstrates a good awareness of the geographical and topographical peculiarities of particular territories, e.g. the towns of Pessinous and Germia.[7] Therefore, it enables the reader to consider the narrative space created by him to correlate quite well with the reality. Nevertheless, as soon as we turn to Theodore's pilgrimages, it becomes obvious that the idea of journey as a process did not appeal to the writer at all. Instead, we are offered what Kazhdan describes as separate scenes either leaving one place or arriving at another.[8] Gregory does not describe the pilgrimages as a

---

4   Della Dora 2016, 35.
5   A specific group of texts containing much of required material has been already defined, see Euthymiades 1999; Malamut 1993; Kültzer 2000; Kültzer 2002; Kaplan 2002; Pratsch 2005; Talbot 2001.
6   *Vita Theodori Sykeotae* Festugière.
7   Waelkens 1971.
8   *Vita Theodori Sykeotae*, § 24, §50–52, §62.

subject around which to develop a gripping story, and this clearly reveals one of his artistic approaches.

Moving further, I would like to examine the *Life of St Gregory of Akragant* (8–9 cc.)[9] who constantly relocates between the most important locations of the Christian Oikoumene. Among his destinations are Rome, Jerusalem, Constantinople, Palestine, Antioch and others. One very specific feature of this *Life* is the crucial role of travel for constructing the plot and the composition. The routes of the protagonist and other characters shape the storylines, move the plot forwards and interweave with one another so as to create a thrilling nonlinear composition.

At the age of eighteen, Gregory hears the voice of an angel urging him to leave on a pilgrimage. The angel instructs him to proceed to the harbour immediately and to find the ship which had been prepared for his travels. We are then presented with details of the circumstances surrounding his departure including some topographic peculiarities of the town of Akragant (modern Agrigento). The youth escapes from home and comes across a ship which had sailed from the sea port into the town centre along the river in order to supply sweet water. After a long conversation with the captain (who immediately tries to verify his juridical status in order to sell him as a slave), Gregory sets sail. Upon arrival in Carthage, he lodges at the house of the captain, who is amazed by the youth's piety and repents of his criminal intention. In Carthage, Gregory comes across some monks from Rome, who offer to accompany him to the Holy Land. At this point the hagiographer takes us back in time and explains that all the previous events had been organized by divine will. It turns out that these monks had been staying in their monastery in Rome and were not planning to go anywhere, but an angel appeared and announced to them that they had to go to Carthage, to find a youth named Gregory from Akragant and guide him to Jerusalem. The author offers a basic description of the different places along their route and the amount of time which it takes them to get to their destination, but the story does not end here. The hagiographer leaves Gregory in Palestine and continues with an account of the return journey of the monks back home. At first, it is not quite clear to the reader why he does this because the protagonist of the story is completely forgotten. Eventually, we are given an explanation later in the narrative. The monks arrive at Gregory's home monastery in Akragant and encounter his parents there right at the moment when they are offering a prayer devoted to their lost son. One of the monks realizes that these people were crying about Gregory and, over a period of time, while

---

9   *Vita Gregorii Agrigenti,* Berger (ed.) 1995.

he explains about their pilgrimage, everybody who is present, including the parents of the saint have a chance to learn what happened to Gregory. That is how the author solves a typical hagiographical collision arising from a hero's escape from the parents, who do not understand what had happened to their beloved son and suffer greatly. In our case, the lines of travel lead to a happy ending, since the parents find out that their child is alive and safe. Being very thorough, the author reports on the final part of the monks' journey and their arrival in Rome.

An unusual trait of the travel narrative in this vita is how much attention the author devotes to reporting the time frame of the trips. In every case the author notices how many days the travel lasted or adds the dates of arrival for all the places which he mentions along the route. What is remarkable is that this is done for every relocation, even those which are completed by marginal characters, e.g. the papal inspectors who are sent from Rome to Sicily to investigate a slander against the saint.[10] Albrecht Berger has evaluated the plausibility of the specified time frames,[11] but for my purpose here this aspect is not of particular importance. It is obvious that the author does not aim to imply the supernaturally fast traversal of space since he describes substantial periods of time. For my purposes, it is worth noting that the hagiographer deliberately wanted to insert this kind of detail into his story. Thus, despite the fact that the process of travel itself is still basically neglected, Leontios nevertheless develops his own individual way of bringing some sense of continuous movement into the travel narrative.

Next, I will consider the texts which have a more certain date of origin within either the ninth or the tenth century. It should be emphasized at the start that this period was highly significant for hagiography. A general revival of cultural and literary life, in conjunction with turbulent events in church history, gave rise to a number of hagiographical works. A situation which has naturally led to an increase in the number of sources able to provide interesting material for my research. Within this period, we find descriptions of exile and persecution caused by iconoclasts, of escapes from Arab raids, from pirates and from political rebellions, of pilgrimages, of business trips, and finally of saints who chose to embark upon constant wandering (ξενιτεία) as part of their ascetic practice.

Such a large number of texts makes it impossible to scrutinize each individual account separately. At the same time, it enables an evaluation of which of

---

10 *Vita Gregorii Agrigentini*, 252.
11 Berger 1995, 51–52.

the travel narrative features can be considered typical or, on the contrary, rare and unusual.

It can clearly be seen that all the texts, including those previously described, have a common feature in terms of their representation of the route network. Despite some examples in which the journey has no intermediary geographical points in between the departure and the destination, the authors generally display a tendency to add these points in some form. What is more significant is that the number of such points varies greatly between texts. While some of them contain only a few waypoints along the journey, others demonstrate a much more intensive route network, with some listing consecutively almost all inhabited localities or outstanding landmarks which the hero passed by. As examples, we can recall St Gregentios' tour around Northern Italy and Rome,[12] Elias the Younger's constant movement around the South of Italy,[13] and two sailings of Symeon of Mytilene from Lesbos to Constantinople.[14] In my opinion, this tendency to list a sequence of place names in order to represent the journey reflects the Byzantines' general geographic perceptions they had inherited from antiquity. Traditionally, this model of description is called *chorographic* or *hodologic* in nature and is characterized by a prevalence of verbal descriptions over and above cartographic maps and an accompanying habit of thinking about travel in terms of itineraries.[15] One notable example of such a description is the supernaturally fast sea voyage undertaken by the magician Iliodoros in the *Life of St Leo of Catania*.[16] This one-day magical relocation from Sicily to the capital mentions several intermediate points along the route, and it is quite obvious that these points reflect some kind of mental map shared by the people of the epoch.[17] Moreover, there is a suggestion that itineraries or guide-books could be used directly as sources for hagiographical travel. The most notable example is the *Life of St Gregentios* which contains a detailed and credible description of Rome and its suburbs.[18]

Depending on the text, therefore, there can either be numerous or, on the contrary, few points described along the route. However, can we observe

---

12 *Vita Gregentii*, §2–6 Berger.
13 *Vita Eliae*, §26–30, §39–40 Rossi Taibbi.
14 *Vita Davidis, Symeonis et Georgii*, §19, 26 van den Gheyn.
15 Dora traces this tradition back to Strabo and adduces a rich bibliography on the question, della Dora 2016, 16–18. See also Podossinow 1993.
16 *Vita Leonis*, §12 Longo.
17 An observation made by M. McCormick (2002).
18 *Vita Gregentii*, 296–342. Berger suggests the author had a guide on Rome at his disposal and used it while working on this part of the text. Ibid. 33. For a more detailed analysis of this text see Mantova 2018.

anything taking place in between these points? Do we see any signs of the traversal of space? A further common feature of travel textualization within this period is that the reader is offered the chance to get a closer look at the heroes' movement, a kind of a zoom-in effect, which arises when the hagiographers discuss situations of emergency during the journey which are usually solved by means of the supernatural abilities of the saints, or sometimes by the intervention of the angels who help them to cope with various perils. These episodes might involve pacifying storms, coping with underwater damage to a ship, overcoming heat and thirst, or taming wild animals.[19]

The second factor which heightens authors' attention to the travel narrative is the necessity of organizing the plot. One of the most frequently exploited models is the attachment of a saint's remarkable actions to his movement from one place to another. The basic scheme can be presented as follows: the saint intends to go somewhere — he starts moving — he meets visionaries or someone in need (people possessed by demons, or afflicted by sickness or some kind of disaster, etc.) — he then helps the miserable people out of their trouble (healing, exorcism, presenting required items or food, etc.) or obtains spiritual growth after communicating with visionaries. This model is very frequently used in the *Lives of Gregentios, Eustratios*,[20] and *Theodore of Sykeon*. In addition to such sequences, descriptions of travel can also be triggered by individual twists in the plot. In the *Life of St Germanos of Kosinitsa* the protagonist has to construct a church. While completing the mission, he runs out of money and is unable to pay the workers, who become enraged, grab Germanos and drag him down from the mountain to the nearest village. This journey takes them a lot of time and effort and, feeling thirsty and tired, they eventually reach the foot of the mountain, where they discover a pleasant landscape awaiting them. The travellers decide to stop there and get some rest, but when they get closer, they realize that the place has been already occupied by other people who have chosen it for the same reasons. These people, who turn out to be imperial officials on their state mission, discover the circumstances of the earlier incident, pay out the required sum of money and free the saint from his captivity by the workers.[21]

Thus far, I have reviewed different features of hagiographical travels outside of their original context, i.e. the texts to which they belong. This might give the somewhat misleading impression that episodes which represent movement are spread evenly through the different lives. However, this is not the

---

19 A wide range of examples are collected in Pratsch 2005, 256–86.
20 *Vita Eustratii,* Papadopoulo–Kerameus (ed.) 1897.
21 *Vita Germani,* 9*–10*.

case, since there are many texts which do not describe travel in detail at all. For example, the vitae of *Nicholas Stoudites*,[22] *Joseph the Hymnographer*,[23] and *Theodore Stoudites*[24] contain only a few such episodes, which are hidden in the general body of the narrative. In contrast, other lives include far more travel elements and grant them much greater space, i.e. the stories of Gregentios, Elias the Younger, and Gregory of Decapolice[25] whose lives were devoted to constant ascetic wanderings.

Ascetic discourse influences the development of another motif which is very important within hagiographical journeys. The travellers usually have to deal with several specific difficulties, such as obtaining food and finding shelter where they can spend the night. In the earliest texts this motif is somewhat rare, but in the later ones it stands out quite notably. Gregory of Decapolis has to constantly think about his daily bread, and the author describes how he is able to cope with his situation. In this regard, the *Life of St Gregentios* is rather intriguing. He faces the same problems as other travellers, but all of them are perfectly handled by his mighty yet invisible guide. Gregentios' wandering leads to his spiritual growth taking place through communication with numerous visionaries and holy fools and through gaining the required life experience necessary to obtain the bishopric. Surprisingly, the combination of wandering and asceticism receives quite the opposite interpretation in the *Life of Nicholas Stoudites*. In this account, the saint's travels are understood simply as a cruel necessity caused by his exile and are deprived of any halo of sanctity; relocation is simply a negative circumstance, which the saint would otherwise happily avoid. In this sense, the hagiographers of Nicholas' patron, Theodore Stoudites, have a similar attitude to travel. The author of the initial version, Michael the Monk, focuses special attention on the saint's exile in Smyrna. The journey was barely tolerable for the saint, due both to his grave physical condition and to the cruelty of the guards, who forced the captives to keep moving for whole days at a time and who put fetters onto their feet during the night.[26]

To conclude my overview of the textualization of travel in hagiographies of the ninth and tenth centuries, I would like to turn to the *Life of St Theoktiste of Lesbos*.[27] As one of the most famous hagiographical texts of the period, this life

---

22 *Vita Nicolai Studitae*, PG 1862.
23 *Vita Iosephi* (BHG 944), Papadopoulo-Kerameus; *vita Iosephi* (BHG 945), PG 1862.
24 *Vita Theod. Stud.* (BHG 1755), PG 1860; *vita Theod. Stud. a Michaele* (BHG 1754), PG 1860.
25 *Vita Gregorii Decapolitae*. Dvornik.
26 *Vita Theod. Stud.a Michaele*, 297, 300; The edition of this text, so called Vita A, saves these data without any changes, *vita Theod. Stud.*, 201.
27 *Vita Theoktistae*, AASS Nov., t.4, 1925.

has already attracted intensive scholarly attention, including particular consideration of the travel motif.[28] However, in the context of my research, the most remarkable feature of this text is the outstanding attention to the physical environment that is demonstrated by the author, Nicetas Magister. Even from a formal point of view the text looks much more like a personal travel account than a classical vita. Immediately after the proemion, instead of the story of the heroine's childhood and family, the reader is offered an exciting tale about the circumstances of the sea voyage which brought the author to the island of Paros. What is even more important is that Nicetas fully realizes that his narrative differs greatly from a regular vita. He explicitly states through Symeo speech that it lacks quite a lot of the typical information for a vita, and that even the date of death for Theoktiste is unknown. Presumably, this could be understood as a manifestation of the author's intentions. Nicetas could have invented all those missing details and there would be nothing extraordinary about doing so, but he chooses to leave the life as it is. He puts traditional hagiographical canons aside and acknowledges that this method can be applied for the composition of a vita too.

The text does not contain any long-distance journeys, and the story is localized within the limits of the island, but the author nevertheless creates the feeling of being on the road with masterful skill. He describes his surroundings in almost minute detail: some natural peculiarities,[29] the harbour,[30] the church,[31] the scenery where he talked to Symeon, which is presented in the platonic locus amoenus style.[32] All these features create an illusion of presence for the reader. This effect is achieved by the author's active usage of ekphrasis and his deployment of a deeply sincere authorial voice to convey his personal sensations and thoughts. This manner of description is one which is subject to much broader development in later periods, and, in this regard, the vita could be seen as a link to both the hagiographical travels and the famous lay travel accounts of the twelfth century.[33]

---

28 Euthymiades 1999; Mullett 2002; Nilsson 2010; Högel 2018.
29 *Vita Theoctistae*, 228.
30 Ibid. 226.
31 Ibid. 226.
32 Ibid. 227.
33 K. Jazdzewska comes to a similar conclusion, but on a more general level. Jazdewska 2009, 279.

2   The Eleventh and Twelfth Centuries

From the middle of the eleventh century onwards, hagiography starts to lose its position of prominence among other genres. Nevertheless, travel descriptions can still be found within hagiographic narratives. Some of the most interesting material comes from the eleventh-century lives of *St Nicon the Metanoite*,[34] *St Lazaros of Galesion*,[35] and two famous twelfth-century lives of *St Leontios of Jerusalem*[36] and *Cyril Phileotes*.[37]

On the one hand, the texts continue to share similar features to those which I considered earlier, i.e. the writers inform the reader of the basic locations along the route and describe travel miracles. However, these narratives demonstrate a strikingly different balance between descriptions of movement which arises as a result of miraculous interventions or plot constructing, on the one hand, and travel episodes which are added without serving any particular such purpose on the other. The author of the life of St Nikon includes several miraculous travel scenes. We read about the saint crossing a turbulent river[38] and covering a vast distance between two towns supernaturally fast.[39] At the same time, the text abounds with travel episodes which have nothing to do with miracles. The hagiographer enriches the story with several ekphraseis devoted to different locations which depict their natural and geographic peculiarities.[40]

Turning to the next text, the *Life of St Lazaros from Mount Galesion*,[41] it is necessary to mention that despite the fact the saint was mainly a stylite, the major part of the Life is devoted to his pilgrimage across Asia Minor to the Holy Land. In this narrative, the method of travel description is transformed quite distinctly. The whole story evolves into a continuous depiction of movement through space. It would be unfair to say that no wonders appear over the course of the relocation, but the fact is that these miracles are completely lost among numerous other travel episodes. These are chases, attempts to hide from the pursuers, and nights spent under the sky. The difficulties of the journey are not merely mentioned in passing, they shape the storyline, ultimately

---

34   *Vita Niconis*, Sullivan (ed.) 1987. The dating is disputable, yet the middle of the eleventh century seems more plausible, see Sullivan 1987, 18.
35   *Vita Lazari*, AASS Nov., t. 3, 1910.
36   *Vita Leontii*, Tsougarakis.
37   *Vita Cyrilli*, Sargologos.
38   *Vita Niconis*, 66.
39   Ibid. 102, 142.
40   In details the text is researched in Mantova 2018.
41   See Veikou 2017 for an extensive analysis of the spatial peculiarities of the text.

becoming the story itself. Moreover, overcoming these difficulties does not always involve the working of miracles. The author immerses the reader into the atmosphere of the journey by describing it in a cinematographic manner, i.e. he manages to arouse a vivid and almost physical feeling of being on the move by adding plenty of tiny details, such as the time of day, weather conditions, sounds, tactile sensations, etc. Some of the most thrilling episodes in St Lazaros' life involve encountering a bear on a foggy mountain,[42] interacting with a dog which followed the saint for several days,[43] an argument with an impious monk,[44] the young Lazaros' escape from home which is followed by a night spent in a chapel surrounded by wolves,[45] and another escape from a malicious monk in which the youth has to climb a mountain at night moving purely on the basis of touch.[46]

Along with some customary problems concerning food or shelter, we are told about quite specific incidents such as an encounter with camel drivers near Tiberias. After noticing Lazaros and his companion Paul come into the city in the morning, the camel drivers wait for them for a whole day, since they have figured out that the monks would leave the city with some bread. After the monks go out of the gates, the gangsters attack them in order to steal the bread. The outcome of the conflict differs significantly from that which we might imagine on the basis of the earlier literature. The travellers give a part of their bread to the robbers, which they hope might be enough. Unfortunately, the robbers are not satisfied, so Lazaros simply offers to give them all the bread in order to avoid the danger. Luckily, Paul manages to shout at the attackers so harshly that they prefer to retreat.[47]

Finally, turning to the later sources, it is noticeable that the *Lives of St Cyril Phileotes* (12 c.) and *Leontios of Jerusalem* (early 13th c.) differ from one another considerably. Nevertheless, they share a common feature in terms of their textualization of travel and space. The most striking dissimilarity from the earlier epoch is the interjection of the travellers' subjective emotions into the narrative. As a result, the authors enrich their stories with some elements which had not previously been considered worth mentioning. St Cyril joins the crew of a ship and sets sail in order to test the strength of his spirit, but, instead of commonplace miracles such as pacifying storms, the reader is confronted with

---

42   *Vita Lazari*, 517.
43   Ibid. 518.
44   Ibid. 511.
45   Ibid. 510–11.
46   Ibid. 511–12.
47   Ibid. 516.

the sufferings of a normal man exhausted from fasting, self-flagellation and his demanding obligations on board.[48] According to Margaret Mullett, this change in tone is not due to the fact that the readers of the period has lost their interest in confrontations with a storm, but rather that such descriptions were just one of the possible ways to present the motif of a sea voyage.[49] On the other hand, this kind of variation clearly indicates that there was some transformation in the literary devices used for the textualization of travel.

As for Leontios, his numerous journeys represent the process of travel without a strong connection either to miracles or to the development of the plot. Travels constitute an ordinary part of the saint's life, especially after he becomes an abbot in the Monastery of St John the Theologian on the island of Patmos. Here, the sea becomes mainly a force of nature which influences Leontios' plans. If the winds are adverse, he has no alternative but to wait until the weather gets better,[50] and when a storm blows great gusts and sends his vessel back to the shore, the hero just stays on the island.[51]

Another aspect to which the hagiographer devotes considerable attention is that of Leontios' financial problems during his journey to Jerusalem, which are vividly depicted in much detail. Following the normal route towards the Holy Land, the saint turns up on Cyprus intending to sail to Acre. Having resided in the Monastery, which belonged to the Patriarchate, he finds it to be in poor spiritual and material condition. Moreover, the imperial tax gatherer Triandafillos demands that the whole income of the monastery be given away and threatens Leontios with imprisonment. After the saint rejects his demands, the taxman takes away the Patriarch's mule, the only means of transport in his possession. These different peripeteia occupy a considerable portion of the narrative and immerse us deeply into the atmosphere of the hero's journey.

One further episode is of particular importance due to its stark contrast to the previous tradition. While the saint was staying on Cyprus, the hagiographer mentions, *en passant*, the pleasant nature of the journey, a type of description which is, conceptually, highly unusual: "Once, the great [man] headed to one of his possessions in order to visit it and its inhabitants and to enjoy a free change of place for, as someone said, change is sweet in all things (ἐλευθερίας δὲ ἀπολαῦσαι ἐκ τῆς τοῦ τόπου μεταβολῆς ἡδύ τι γὰρ ἡ πάντων μεταβολή, ἔφησέ τις).[52] Judging from TLG data, such an expression did indeed exist, and Aristotle,

---

48   *Vita Cyrilli*, 57–65.
49   Mullett 2002, 280. For a complete and in-depth investigation of this text see Mullett 2004.
50   *Vita Leontii*, §17.
51   Ibid. §58.
52   Ibid. §74, lines 1–4.

in his *Rhetoric*, gives a clear explanation of the phrase stating that change is pleasant.[53]

This kind of perception of travel is totally different from that represented in the arduous and spiritually important wanderings described in the texts of the ninth and the tenth centuries. In addition, it is remarkable that the *Life of St Leontios* transmits a highly subjective impression of the Holy Land. After a long journey, the hero finally reaches his destination, but the narrative does not lapse into a sense of pathos due to being at the sacral centre of the world. Instead, the author concentrates on opposition with the part of the hostile Latins who tried to kill Leontios.[54]

In this regard, the manner of textualization greatly resembles some of the pure 'travelogue' texts which appeared in Byzantium in the twelfth century. These include John Phokas' pilgrimage,[55] Constantine Manasses' poem on his diplomatic mission to Palestine,[56] Nicholaos Mesarites'[57] letter about his trip to Nicaea, George of Antioch's letters from Bulgaria,[58] and several others. Each of these narratives pays a great deal of attention to everything that is seen, heard, smelt, touched or sensed by the travellers along the road. The environment and the space around the heroes is adorned with myriads of tiny details, and this is accompanied by a wide range of descriptions relating to different people's emotions and sensations. Even a modern reader can be fascinated by the vividness and literary strength of such descriptions, which are remarkable examples of what can be described as a reconstruction of *lived space*. To a great extent, the particular effect of these descriptions is produced by their subjectivity. Catia Galatariotou has even offered to rate these sources according to the extent of their subjectivity.[59]

A later interpretation of Manasses' poem by Ingela Nilsson is very different.[60] Nilsson does not see the poem as a personal travel account but rather as a highly rhetorical literary product composed in order to praise the capital and, by implication, the court, in a very creative manner. This point of view is convincingly supported by the fact that Manasses uses themes and motifs which were in high demand among many literati of the epoch. Nevertheless,

---

53 Aristotle, *Rhetoric* 1.11.20.
54 *Vita Leontii*, §85–86.
55 Ioannes Phokas, Ἔκφρασις, Troitskiy.
56 Constantinus Manasses, Ὁδοιπορικόν, Horna.
57 Nicholaos Mesarites, *Descriptio itineris Nicaeam*, Heisenberg.
58 Gregorii Antioch, *ep.*, Darrouzès.
59 Galatariotou 1993.
60 Nilsson 2014a; Nilsson 2014b.

if we look at the literary implementation of these motifs, we still face the same set of peculiarities: emotional intensity and highly descriptive writing, which are achieved through extensive usage of ekphrasis, either in order to depict the external environment or internal psychological state. As a result, the most important feature to note is that in all of these different travelogues we can clearly discern either the authorial personality or a rhetorical elaboration of the author's self. Within this framework, hagiographers of the twelfth century belonged to their literary epoch and shared the tastes of their lay contemporaries.

∴

To sum up, I would like to return once again to Kazhdan's statement regarding the sparse representation of space in Byzantine literature in order to suggest that the wider situation is more complex than his research suggests. It is evident that the literary approach to the textualization of travel and space underwent a degree of development. This can broadly be described as a smooth transition from highly schematic representations towards descriptions which begin to contain a much greater range of detail as they are enriched with accounts of the subjective emotions of travellers over the course of the twelfth century. *Narratio* was the most frequent and typical form for the textualization of space in Byzantine travel narratives. However in later periods *descriptio* in the form of ekphrasis and descriptions of the subjective impressions of the travellers find their way into the texts. These narratives therefore allow us to shed greater light on *lived space* in a Byzantine context.

These findings are in full accordance with Kazhdan's ideas regarding the evolution of Byzantine culture in the eleventh and twelfth centuries, which have been so fruitfully developed over recent decades. In order to see this, it is worth turning, first of all, to Stratis Papaioannou's monograph devoted to Michael Psellos,[61] which transforms Kazhdan's statement on the increasing attention paid to the inner psychological world of the heroes.[62] Papaioannou convinces us that Psellos artistically constructed his own authorial self just like any other of his characters. However, what is especially important for our research is that emotional sensitivity and sensibility were crucial features of this created personality. Psellos developed rhetorical techniques in order to describe the realm of the corporeal senses, and such an achievement was both

---

61 Papaioannou 2013.
62 Kazhdan 1985, 219–20.

successfully adopted and widely used in various texts in the twelfth century. In the case of travel narratives, both hagiographic and non-hagiographic, the reader is constantly pushed into following along with the hero in their thirst or hunger, in the cold or in the heat, as they feel pain after walking or after riding a mule whose chine galls against the rider's bottom, or as they smell the disgusting alcohol-laden breath and listen to the drunken songs of neighbours in the xenodochium. Consequently, the image of space that we reconstitute through our perception of these literary journeys loses its discrete character and instead gains a higher degree of continuity.

It appears that this mode of description aligns with broader creative developments in rhetorical and, especially, ekphrastic skill in the twelfth century, as has been conclusively demonstrated by Nilsson[63] and Panagiotis Agapitos.[64] Peculiarities in the educational process, the artistic capabilities of different authors and the specific interests of readers contributed to the formation of thematic, stylistic and narrative features which we now identify as essential characteristics within the literature of the twelfth century. To the widespread depictions of battles, erotic passion, disease and death, we might now add one more theme — that of the journey.

Finally, observations regarding diachronic changes around the travel motif are of importance for our general understanding of hagiography and enable us to specify particular issues in the evolution of the hagiographical topos. Perhaps, evolution within the topoi and creative playing with their boundaries are some of the ways in which hagiography managed to develop and stay afloat in the eleventh and the twelfth centuries. In his survey of the hagiography of the period, Symeon Paschalidis[65] notes that a decrease in the volume of new vitae does not also imply a concomitant decrease in the literary quality of the genre. Hagiographers moved further, and both the thematic content and expressive means deployed within their rhetoric correspond to the most up-to-date developments in other genres. Moreover, in some cases, the saints' lives might even have been a trigger for this development, since descriptions of travel evolved within this genre long before they begin to emerge in the famous twelfth century travelogues. Hagiography may have lost its preeminent position as a result of complex social and cultural changes, but hagiographers of the period certainly did not want to surrender, and instead continued their struggle in the highly competitive literary atmosphere of the eleventh and twelfth centuries.

---

63 Nilsson 2014b.
64 Agapitos (forthcoming).
65 Paschalidis 2011.

Bibliography

Primary Sources

Constantine Manasses, Ὁδοιπορικόν. Ed. K. Horna, *Das Hodoiporikon des Konstantin Manasses*, BZ 13, 325–47. 1904.

Gregory of Antioch, *Epistulae*. Ed. J. Darrouzès, "Deux lettres de Grégoire Antiochos Écrites de Bulgarie vers 1173", *Byzantinoslavica* 23, 276–84. 1962.

Gregory of Antioch, Ed. J. Darrouzès, "Deux lettres de Grégoire Antiochos Écrites de Bulgarie vers 1173", *Byzantinoslavica* 24, 65–73. 1963.

Gregory the Cellarer, *Vita Lazari*. Vita S. Lazari in monte Galesio, AASS Novembris, t. 3. Bruxelles 1910, 508–88. Tr. R. P. H. Greenfield, *The Life of Lazaros of Mt. Galesion: An Eleventh-century Pillar Saint*. Washington D.C. 2000.

John Phocas, Ἔκφρασις. Ed. I. E. Troitskiy, *Ioanna Phoki skazaniye vkratse, Pravoslavny Palestinskiy sbornik*, VII, issue 2, 1–28. Saint-Petersburg 1889.

John the Deacon, *Vita Iosephi* (BHG 945). Vita S. Iosephi auctore Ioanne, PG, t. 105, 940–75. Paris 1862.

Leontios of St Sabas, *Vita Gregorii Agrigenti*. Ed. A. Berger, *Leontios presbyteros von Rom, Das Leben des heiligen Gregorios von Agrigent*. Berlin 1995.

Michael the Monk, *Vita Theod. Stud.* (BHG 1754). Vita et Conversatio S. P. N. et confessoris Theodori abbatis monasterii Studii a Michaele Monacho conscripta, PG, t. 99, 233–328. Paris 1860.

Nicetas Magistros, *Vita Theoctistae*. Ed. H. Delehaye, AASS Novembris, t. 4, 224–33. Bruxelles 1925.

Nicolas Mesarites, *Descriptio itineris Niceam*. Ed. A. Heisenberg, "Reisebericht des Nikolaos Mesarites an die Mönche des Euergetisklosters in Konstantinopel", in *Neue Quellen zur Geschichte des lateinischen Kaisertums und der Kirchenunion*. München, 1923, 35–46.

Theophanes, *Vita Iosephi* (BHG 944). Ed. A. Papadopoulo-Kerameus, *Zhitiye Iosipha Pesnopevtsa monakha Pheophana, Sbornik grecheskikh I latinskikh pamyatnikov, kasayuschikhsya Photiya Patriarkha*, t. 2, 1–14. Saint-Petersburg 1901.

Vita Cyrilli Phileotae. Ed. E. Sargologos, "La Vie de Saint Cyrille le Philéote moine byzantin (†1110)" *Subsidia Hagiographica* 39, 43–264. 1964.

Vitae Davidis, Symeonis et Georgii. Ed. J. van den Gheyn, "Acta graeca Ss. Davidis, Symeonis et Georgii", AB 18, 209–59. 1899.

Vita Eliae Iunioris. Ed. G. Rossi Taibbi, *Vita di Sant' Elia il Giovane*. Palermo 1962.

Vita Eustratii. Ed. Papadopoulo-Kerameus, Ἀνάλεκτα Ἱεροσολυμιτικῆς σταχυολογίας, t. 4, 367–400. Saint-Petersburg 1897.

Vita Germani. Vita S. Germani Cosinitzae, AASS Mai, t. 3, 6*–10*. Paris & Roma 1866.

Vita Gregentii. Ed. A. Berger, *Life and Works of Saint Gregentios, Archbishop of Taphar*. Berlin 2006.

Vita Gregorii Decapolitae. Ed. F. Dvornik, *La Vie de St Grégoire de Décapolite et les Slaves macédoniens au IX siècle.* Paris 1926.

Vita Leonis Catanensis. Ed. Longo, *La vita di S. Leone vescovo di Catania e gli incantesimi del mago Eliodoro.* Rome 1990.

Vita Leontii. Ed. D. Tsougarakis, "The Life of Leontios Patriarch of Jerusalem: Text, Translation, Commentary", in *The Medieval Mediterranean. People, Economies and Cultures, 400–1453*, vol. 2. Leiden, New York & Köln 1993.

Vita Nicolai Studitae. PG, t. 105, 863–925. Paris 1862.

Vita Niconis. Ed. D. F. Sullivan, *The life of Saint Nikon.* Brookline, MA 1987.

Vita Theod. Stud. (*BHG 1755*). Vita et Conversatio S. P. N. et confessoris Theodori praepositi Studiarum, PG, t. 99, 113–232. Paris 1860.

Vita Theodori Syceotae. Ed. A.-J. Festugière, "Vie de Théodore de Sykeôn", *Subsidia Hagiographica* 48.1, 1–161.

Secondary Sources

Agapitos A. P. forthcoming. "'The Force of Discourses:' Literary Production in the Komnenian Era", in van den Berg & Zagklas (eds) forthcoming.

Della Dora, V. 2016. *Landscape, Nature, and the Sacred in Byzantium.* Cambridge.

Euthymiades, S. 1999. "Νοεροί και πραγματικοί ταξιδιώτες στο Βυζάντιο του 8ου, 9ου και 10ου αιώνα", *Byzantina* 20, 155–65.

Efthymiadis, S. (ed.) 2011. *The Ashgate Research Companion to Byzantine Hagiography. Volume I: Periods and Places.* Farnham.

Galatariotou, C. 1993. "Travel and Perception in Byzantium", *DOP* 4, 221–41.

Greenfield, R. P. H. 2000. *The Life of Lazaros of Mt. Galesion: An Eleventh-century Pillar Saint, Introduction, translation, and notes.* Washington D.C.

Högel, C. 2018. "Beauty, Knowledge and Gain in the Life of Theoktiste", *Byzantion* 88, 219–36.

Jazdzewska, K. 2009. "Hagiographic Invention and Imitation: Niketas' Life of Theoktiste and Its Literary Models", *Greek, Roman, and Byzantine Studies* 49, 257–79.

Kaplan, M. 2002. "Les saints en pèlerinage à l'époque mésobyzantine (7e–12e siècles)", *DOP* 56, 109–27.

Kazhdan, A. P. 1968. *Vizantiyskaya kultura.* Moscow.

Kazhdan, A. P. & A. Wharton 1985. *Change in Byzantine Culture in the Eleventh and Twelfth Centuries.* Berkeley, Los Angeles & London.

Kültzer, A. 2002. "Byzantine and Early Post-Byzantine Pilgrimage to the Holy Land and to Mount Sinai" in Macrides (ed.) 2002, 149–65.

Kültzer, A. 2000. "Reisende und Reiseliteratur im Byzantinischen Reich", *Symmeikta* 14, 77–93.

Macrides, R. (ed.) 2002. *Travel in the Byzantine World. Papers from the Thirty-fourth Spring Symposium of Byzantine Studies, Birmingham, April, 2000.* Newcastle-upon-Tyne.

McCormick, M. 2002. "Byzantium on the Move: Imagining a Communications History", in Macrides (ed.) 2002, 3–32.

Malamut, E. 1993. *Sur la route des saints Byzantines*. Paris.

Mantova, Y. 2018. "Space Representation in the Life of St Gregentios and the Life of St Nikon the Metanoite" in Rigo, Trizio & Despotakis (eds) 2018, 157–65.

Mullett, M. 2002. "In Peril on the Sea: Travel Genres and the Unexpected" in R. Macrides (ed.) 2002, 259–84.

Mullett, M 2004. "Literary biography and historical genre in the Life of Cyril Phileotes by Nicholas Kataskepenos", in Odorico & Agapitos (eds) 2004, 387–409.

Nilsson, I. 2010. "The Same Story, but Another. A Reappraisal of Literary Imitation in Byzantium" in Rhoby & Schiffler (eds) 2010, 195–208.

Nilsson, I. 2014a. "Komnenian Literature" in Sakel 2014 (ed.), 121–32.

Nilsson, I. 2014b. *Raconter Byzance: la littérature au XIIe siècle*. Paris.

Odorico, P. & P. A. Agapitos (eds) 2004. *Les Vies des Saints à Byzance: Genre littéraire ou biographie historique? Actes du IIe colloque international philologique EPMHNEIA. Paris, 6–8 juin 2002*. Paris.

Papaioannou, S. 2013. *Michael Psellos: Rhetoric and Authorship in Byzantium*. Cambridge.

Paschalidis, S. A. 2011. "The Hagiography of the Eleventh and Twelfth Centuries", in Efthymiadis (ed.) 2011, 143–71.

Patrich, J. (ed.) 2001. *The Sabaite Heritage in the Orthodox Church from the Fifth Century to the Present*. Leuven.

Pratsch, T. 2005. *Der hagiographische Topos: Griechische Heiligenviten in mittelbyzantinischer Zeit*. New York & Berlin.

Podossinow, A. V. 1993. "Kartographia v Vizantii", *Vizantiyskiy vremennik* 54, 43–48.

Rhoby, A. & E. Schiffler (eds) 2010. *IMITATIO– AEMULATIO — VARIATIO. Akten des internationalen wissenschaftlichen Symposions zur byzantinischen Sprache und Literatur*. Wien.

Rigo, A., M. Trizio & E. Despotakis (eds) 2018. *Byzantine Hagiography: Texts, Themes & Projects*. Turnhout.

Ryan, M.-L. 2014. "Space" in *The Living Handbook of Narratology, Interdisciplinary Centre for Narratology*, Hamburg. Accessed 20 November 2018. http://www.lhn.uni-hamburg.de/article/space, 22.04.2014.

Sakel, D. (ed.) 2014. *Byzantine culture: papers from the conference "Byzantine days of Istanbul" held on the occasion of Istanbul being European Cultural Capital 2010, Istanbul, May 21–23 2010*. Ankara.

Sullivan, D. F. 1987. *The life of Saint Nikon*. Brookline, MA.

Talbot, A.-M. 2001. "Byzantine Pilgrimage to the Holy Land from the Eighth to the Fifteenth Century" in Patrich (ed.) 2001, 97–110.

Tsougarakis, D. 1993. *The Life of Leontios, Patriarch of Jerusalem, Text, translation and commentary*. Leiden, New York & Köln.

Van den Berg, B. & N. Zagklas (eds) forthcoming. *Byzantine Poetry in the Long Twelfth Century*. Cambridge.

Veikou, M. 2017. "Space in Texts and Space as Text: A new approach to Byzantine spatial notions", *Scandinavian Journal of Byzantine and Modern Greek Studies* 2, 143–77.

Waelkens, M. 1971. "Pessinont et le gallos", *Byzantion* 41, 349–52.

The Visual Structure of Epigrams and the Experience of Byzantine Space

A Case Study on Reliquary Enkolpia of St Demetrios

Brad Hostetler

In the Middle and Late Byzantine periods, it became fashionable—even expected—for wealthy patrons to have their works of art and architecture adorned with epigrams.[1] These poetic embellishments served as dedicatory prayers, as expressions of identity, and as comments on the monuments that they adorned. As inscriptions, they are also visual, designed to be perceived and read *in situ*, and thereby facilitating a reader's engagement with the inscribed space.[2] Byzantine readers followed texts carved into marble cornices, traced words hammered onto icon frames, and charted verses across multiple sides of objects.

In her seminal 2001 article, Amy Papalexandrou drew our attention to the spatial and performative dimension of Byzantine epigrams.[3] She demonstrates that these texts were designed to be read aloud, and that their arrangement on the exteriors and interiors of churches embody and reflect the processions and liturgies that inhabited these spaces. An underlying assumption of her thesis is that epigrams were read; however, reading epigrams *in situ* is easier said than done. The medium, the ornamental nature of the script, the distance of the words from the viewer, the placement of text on multiple surfaces, as well as the style and linguistic register of the poetic composition, are obstacles to recognizing words and comprehending their meaning.[4]

---

1 The foundational work on Byzantine epigrams is Rhoby 2009–2018. See also Drpić 2016a, an important art-historical study on the relationship between epigrams, patronage, and devotion.
2 For an excellent overview on questions related to reading and viewing epigrams in their inscribed contexts, see Drpić & Rhoby 2019.
3 Papalexandrou 2001. For other studies that consider the relationship between Byzantine epigrams and their spatial setting, see Nelson 2007; Rhoby 2011b; Drpić 2016a, 202–19; Pallis 2017; and Leatherbury 2019. See also the recent studies that explore, more broadly, the visual aspects of inscriptions: James (ed.) 2007; Aavitsland & Seim (eds) 2011; Eastmond (ed.) 2015; Bedos-Rezak & Hamburger (eds) 2016; and Stavrakos (ed.) 2016.
4 For studies on the visual, and non-textual, perception of inscriptions in Byzantium, see Lauxtermann 2003, 272–73; James 2007; Drpić 2016b; Rhoby 2017.

One way in which inscribed verses were made more accessible for the reader was the development of placement conventions. These conventions allowed the reader to find the starting point of an epigram on a monument or object and to anticipate how the end of one verse and the beginning of the next would be mapped onto a multi-faceted construction. The development of placement conventions must have had a reciprocal cause-and-effect. They may have been a natural outgrowth from the ways in which readers expected to navigate spaces, while also training readers to experience specific spaces in particular ways.

This chapter takes a closer look at these conventions: what they are, and how they facilitated a reader's experience with Byzantine space. My focus is on reliquaries, a category of inscribed objects that Papalexandrou and others have recognized as being spatial in nature, but whose epigrams have not been fully analyzed for their spatial properties.[5] Byzantine reliquaries were frequently adorned with images and texts, inside and out.[6] The faithful encountered a reliquary's visual and verbal program of adornment while wearing, handling, turning, and opening the container and accessing the relics. I examine the ways in which the conventions of epigram placement directed a specific experience and comprehension of a reliquary's space, and demonstrate that placement conventions could be exploited and broken in order to bring greater focus to particular spatial features.

As we shall see, reading an epigram on a reliquary is not an isolated action, but one that also involves touching the object, opening the lid, looking at iconography, smelling fragrant oil housed in many of these containers, and listening to the words of the epigram read aloud.[7] Depending on the type of reliquary—an object of personal devotion or one for communal use—these actions may be performed and experienced by one person or shared with others. We do not know the precise viewing contexts of each and every reliquary. For this reason, I will be using the term "reader" when referring to any person who would read an epigram and the term "viewer" when referring to one who would look at, and handle, a reliquary. My intention in using these two terms is to simply distinguish between these two actions for the purpose of clarity.

There were many variables that factored into the display of an epigram, including the choice and size of the artwork, the medium and type of script used, and the text's location within the inscribed space. But the ways in which

---

5 Papalexandrou 2001, 271n47, 275n60; Pentcheva 2008; Pentcheva 2010, 160–71; Bogdanović 2011, 289–94; Elsner 2015; Veneskey 2019.
6 For an overview, see Klein 2015. For epigrams on reliquaries, see Hostetler 2016.
7 A foundational study on the multisensory experience of art and space is James 2004.

verses were organized, distributed, and arranged generally followed three conventions. One object that clearly illustrates all three is a silver-gilt and niello casket in the Treasury of San Marco in Venice (Figure 29.1).[8] This rectangular box features a lid attached to the base by two hinges on the back and a locking arm on the front. It may have functioned as a reliquary for the four martyrs of Trebizond— Akylas, Eugenios, Kanidios, and Valerianos—depicted in repoussé on the lid with Christ.

The San Marco casket is inscribed with an epigram written in dodecasyllable, the dominant verse form used for Byzantine epigrams.[9] This meter is composed of twelve syllables per verse with a natural pause, or caesura, after the fifth or seventh syllable, and a stress accent on the penult. The epigram on the casket features a total of twelve verses that wrap the perimeter of the base in two parallel lines. The reader would first trace the upper line of text around all four sides, then follow the lower line in like manner. The majuscule letters, executed in niello, are given diacritics and ligatures, features that became more common in Byzantine epigraphy beginning in the eleventh century.[10] The content of this epigram is not important for my purposes as I will focus only on the ways in which the verses are arranged on the object.[11]

The first convention of epigram placement is the symmetrical arrangement of verses. On the San Marco casket, the 12-verse epigram is split into two parallel lines of six verses each (Figure 29.2). The long sides each feature a total of four verses, two for the upper line and two for the lower line. The short sides each contain a total of two verses, one for each line. Taken together, the ratio of verse distribution between the long and short sides is 2:1, which neatly corresponds to the ratio for the casket's dimensions: 28 cm in length and 14 cm in width.[12]

The second convention concerns verse breaks. If an epigram is displayed on more than one part of an object, then a break in the inscribed text corresponds to the end of a verse; for smaller objects with limited surface area, this break may also occur at a verse's caesura. On the San Marco casket, the epigram

---

8   Tesoro di San Marco, inv. no. 33. Rhoby 2009–2018, 2:Me85 with additional bibliography. This casket has been variously dated to the eleventh and twelfth centuries and to the fourteenth and fifteenth centuries. The virtual object is available at Meraviglie di Venezia, http://www.meravigliedivenezia.it/en/virtual-objects/TSM_025.html (accessed 23 December 2019).
9   The characteristics of dodecasyllable are summarized in Rhoby 2009–2018, 1:60.
10 Mango 2008, 149.
11 For the epigram, see Rhoby 2009–2018, 2:Me85; Drpić 2016b, 59–61.
12 The casket has a height of 9 cm.

FIGURE 29.1 Reliquary Casket of the Four Martyrs of Trebizond, 11th/12th or 14th/15th centuries. Tesoro di San Marco, Venice (inv. no. 33)
PHOTO: ARCHIVIO FOTOGRAFICO DELLA PROCURATORIA DI SAN MARCO PROCURATORIA DI SAN MARCO. COURTESY OF THE PROCURATORIA DI SAN MARCO

begins with the upper line on the front to the right of the locking arm. The first verse reads from left to right, ending at the front-right corner. Verse 2 continues around the corner on the short right side, forming the upper line of text and ending at the back-right corner. On the long back side, verses 3 and 4, each bisected by a hinge, form the upper line of text. Verse 5 forms the upper line on the short left side. Verse 6 is displayed on the front, beginning at the front-left corner and ending to the left of the locking arm. Verses 7–12 form the lower line of text, following the same pattern of verse divisions as the upper line.

The third convention of epigram placement is the inclusion of markers that guide the reader, such as a cross to mark the starting point of an epigram and a dot pattern to identify verse divisions. Both of these features are found on the San Marco casket. The beginning of verse 1 is indicated by a cross, placed to

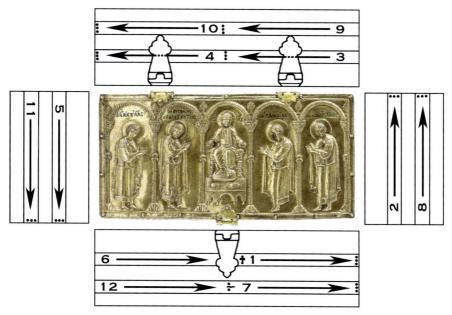

FIGURE 29.2   Reliquary Casket of the Four Martyrs of Trebizond, diagram indicating the placement of verses. Tesoro di San Marco, Venice (inv. no. 33)
PHOTO: ARCHIVIO FOTOGRAFICO DELLA PROCURATORIA DI SAN MARCO
PROCURATORIA DI SAN MARCO, WITH DRAWING BY BRAD HOSTETLER.
COURTESY OF THE PROCURATORIA DI SAN MARCO

the right of the locking arm, and the verse breaks, at the corners of the box, are marked by a pattern of three vertically aligned dots. In this way, the physical features of the casket also provide visual cues for the reader to find the starting point of the epigram at a logical position on the front, next to the locking arm, and to trace the verses along all four sides. On the back, the three-dot markers are clearly visible at the centre, dividing verses 3 and 4 in the upper line and, again, verses 9 and 10 in the lower line. On the front, the separation between the end of verse 6 and the beginning of verse 1 is indicated not by dots, but by the locking arm, where we started. When the reader reaches this point, they jump down to the lower line where they find a marker represented by a horizontal wavy line between two dots. From this point, the reader continues with verse 7, tracing the perimeter of the box and returning to the front.

What purpose did these conventions serve? One was aesthetic. Symmetry is a feature prevalent in Byzantine art, including in the iconographic composition on the lid of the San Marco casket. It was part of an object's beautification, and that beauty mirrored the order of God's created universe.[13] The other purpose that these placement conventions served was to aid in the reading process.[14] For the San Marco casket, they allowed the reader to find the beginning of the epigram on the front next to the locking arm, to trace the path of text, verse-by-verse, around the corners of the object, and on all of its sides. Through this process of reading the inscription, viewing the images, and turning the object, the reader is able to comprehend the casket's program of text, iconography, and space.

In order to understand the ways in which conventions of epigram placement play into the process of experiencing Byzantine space, I focus on a group of reliquaries that possess a specific spatial logic and signification. Reliquary enkolpia of St Demetrios are designed as schematic representations of the martyr's tomb and shrine in Thessaloniki.[15] The individual objects vary in details, but most include a lid featuring an image of St Demetrios. When opened, this lid gives way to the interior and a second set of doors. Behind these doors is a compartment that houses a second image of the martyr, shown dead within his tomb, just as he was imagined to appear in his tomb in Thessaloniki. The double image and the multi-layered nature of these spatial objects allowed the owner to experience Demetrios' shrine in miniaturized, portable form.[16] These objects were also equipped with internal reservoirs that housed the myron and blood of the martyr, making the conceptual pilgrimage experience a material reality. While the formal mimetic qualities of reliquary enkolpia of St Demetrios have attracted much scholarly attention, the epigrams have not been given the same amount of scrutiny.[17] Six reliquary enkolpia of St Demetrios are inscribed with epigrams; my focus in this essay will be on two.[18] I examine the ways in which placement conventions shape the spatial experience of these objects and how they enhance their mimetic interpretation. In this way, the reliquary enkolpia of St Demetrios—through their forms, images, and inscriptions—produce spatial imaginaries that appropriate, interpret,

---

13 Kazhdan (ed.) 1991, 3:1988–89 (s.v. "Symmetry" by A. Kazhdan & A. Cutler). A patron's act of artistic adornment and God's act of creation were seen as "complementary gestures"; see Drpić 2016a, 120–24.
14 For a discussion of late antique verse inscriptions, their epigraphic features, and their legibility and use, see Agosti 2015.
15 Grabar 1950, 7–8; Grabar 1954, 312–13; Bauer 2013, 351–52.
16 Carr 2002, 82; Bogdanović 2011, 289–94; Elsner 2015, 25–31; Veneskey 2019.
17 The exception is Veneskey 2019, who focuses primarily on the eleventh-century ciborium reliquary at the Moscow Kremlin Museums, inv. no. M3–1148.
18 Hostetler 2016, 52–58 documents nine Middle Byzantine reliquaries of St Demetrios inscribed with epigrams, six of which are confirmed to be enkolpia.

FIGURE 29.3
Reliquary Enkolpion of St Demetrios, view of the front showing the image of St. Demetrios and verses 1 & 2, 12th–13th cent
PHOTO: © DUMBARTON OAKS, BYZANTINE COLLECTION, WASHINGTON, DC (BZ.1953.20)

and shape a pilgrim's experience of the tomb at Thessaloniki, but at portable, human-friendly scale.

We begin with the reliquary enkolpion now at Dumbarton Oaks.[19] This twelfth- or thirteenth-century gold and enamel medallion features a bust image of St Demetrios on the front (Figure 29.3). He wears a cuirass covered by a chlamys, and bears a lance in his right hand and a sheathed sword in his left. The military saints Sergios and Bakchos are depicted on the back, dressed in long tunics covered by chlamydes (Figure 29.4). Each holds a small martyr's cross in their right hand; their left hands are raised to their chests. The suspension ring at the top of the medallion unscrews and the front opens by a hinge at the lower end (Figure 29.5). The interior of the object, made of gold, contains a pair of doors that enclose a second relief image of St Demetrios (Figure 29.6). Here he is shown recumbent and within a niche, as he is imagined to appear in his tomb at Thessaloniki.

The exterior of the reliquary enkolpion is inscribed with a four-verse, twelve-syllable epigram executed in cloisonné enamel.

Σεπτὸν δοχεῖον αἵματος Δημητρίου
σὺν μύρῳ φέρει πίστις ἡ τοῦ Σεργίου·
αἰτεῖ σε καὶ ζῶν καὶ θανὼν ῥύστην ἔχ[ειν]
σὺν τοῖς δυσὶν μάρτυσι καὶ ἀθλοφόροις.

---

19   Dumbarton Oaks Museum, BZ.1953.20. The dimensions, including the suspension ring, are 4.4 x 2.8 x 0.6 cm. Hostetler 2020, 276–80; Rhoby 2009–2018, 2:Me112 with additional bibliography.

FIGURE 29.4
Reliquary Enkolpion of St Demetrios, view of the back showing the image of Ss. Sergios & Bakchos, 12th–13th cent
PHOTO: © DUMBARTON OAKS, BYZANTINE COLLECTION, WASHINGTON, DC (BZ.1953.20)

FIGURE 29.5
Reliquary Enkolpion of St Demetrios, interior view showing inner doors closed, 12th–13th cent. Dumbarton Oaks, Byzantine Collection, Washington, DC (BZ.1953.20)
PHOTO: BRAD HOSTETLER. COURTESY OF DUMBARTON OAKS, BYZANTINE COLLECTION, WASHINGTON, DC

2   The faith of Sergios carries, together with the myron,
1   the venerable container of the blood of Demetrios.
    He asks to have you as a deliverer in both life and in death,
    together with the two victorious martyrs.[20]

The first two verses tell us that a man named Sergios owned and wore this reliquary enkolpion. The myron and blood of St Demetrios were contained within a reservoir, accessible through the screw hole stopped by the removable

---

20   Rhoby 2009–2018, 2:Me112.

THE VISUAL STRUCTURE OF EPIGRAMS 639

FIGURE 29.6
Reliquary Enkolpion of St Demetrios, interior view showing inner doors open, 12th–13th cent. Dumbarton Oaks, Byzantine Collection, Washington, DC (BZ.1953.20)
PHOTO: BRAD HOSTETLER. COURTESY OF DUMBARTON OAKS, BYZANTINE COLLECTION, WASHINGTON, DC

suspension loop.[21] In the second two verses, the wearer Sergios seeks the protection of St Demetrios and the "two victorious martyrs". The latter phrase can be understood as a reference to Ss Sergios and Bakchos, whose images are shown on the back.

The placement of the epigram adheres to the three conventions outlined above. The first two verses are symmetrically displayed as a circular frame around the image of St Demetrios on the front of the medallion. The start of the epigram is marked by a cross, placed at a logical starting point above the martyr's head at the 12:00 position. Verse 1 forms the right half of the circular frame, ending at the opposite end from where it began at the 6:00 position. Verse 2 forms the left half of this circular frame, covering from the 6:00 to 12:00 positions. The epigram continues on the narrow width of the medallion (Figure 29.7). The beginning of verse 3, while not indicated by a cross or dots, is clearly and logically positioned, to the right of the suspension loop. Verse 3 covers one-half of the medallion's narrow width from the 12:00 to the 6:00 positions. Verse 4 is displayed in like manner, covering the other half from the 6:00 to the 12:00 positions, and ending to the left of the suspension loop. The small size of the letters and the multi-faceted placement of the verses make this epigram a challenge for any reader. However, the reading process is aided

---

21   Bauer 2013, 340, Fig. 8 illustrates the way in which these reliquary enkolpia were equipped with a reservoir for the myron and blood.

FIGURE 29.7 Reliquary Enkolpion of St Demetrios, multiple views of the side showing verses 3 & 4, 12th–13th cent. Dumbarton Oaks, Byzantine Collection, Washington, DC (BZ.1953.20)
PHOTO: AFTER GRABAR 1954, FIGS. 31–34. COURTESY OF DUMBARTON OAKS, BYZANTINE COLLECTION, WASHINGTON, DC

by the use of placement conventions. The symmetrical arrangement and division of verses mapped onto the form of the reliquary enkolpion guide the reader around the object, from verse to verse, so that the epigram's meaning can be comprehended.

The structured placement of the epigram also helps direct the reader, presumably the wearer Sergios, and his navigation of the enkolpion's miniaturized space. The first two verses, displayed on the front, direct Sergios' attention to that which is contained inside the enkolpion by identifying the object as a container (δοχεῖον) that houses the myron and blood of St Demetrios. In so doing, these verses draw his attention to that which is unseen: to the interior space of the reliquary enkolpion and to the liquid relics of the martyr. Sergios engages with the interior space via three senses. The first is touch: he unscrews the suspension loop and opens the front panel only to find a second set of doors inside the reliquary enkolpion. The second sense is smell: as soon as the suspension loop is unscrewed, the aroma of the myron emerges from the reservoir. The third sense is sight: the successive openings of the reliquary enkolpion are marked by images and materials, from the enamel image of St Demetrios on the front panel to the golden doors inside the enkolpion to the relief image of the martyr lying in his tomb. This sensory engagement with the miniaturized space of the reliquary enkolpion is activated by the first two verses that direct Sergios' attention to the interior space.

Verses 3 and 4 placed on the narrow width of the medallion direct Sergios' attention to the exterior space of the reliquary enkolpion through the change of address and through placement. In verses 1 and 2, Sergios and St Demetrios are referenced in the impersonal third-person voice. This changes in verses 3 and 4 where St Demetrios is addressed directly in the second person, and where he is called upon to protect the owner with the help of Ss Sergios and Bakchos. Verses 3 and 4, beseeching Ss Demetrios, Sergios, and Bakchos, are therefore neatly placed between the cloisonné enamel images of these martyrs depicted on the front and back of the medallion. Reading these verses required Sergios to trace the circumference, rotating the medallion in his hands, then turn it to the front and back to fully comprehend the text's relationship to the images.

The epigram on the Dumbarton Oaks reliquary enkolpion features a two-part arrangement that engages with the interior and exterior space of the object. The first part includes the two verses placed on the front, directing Sergios to that which is housed within the container. The second part includes the two verses placed on the narrow width, addressing the martyrs depicted in enamel on the front and back of the reliquary enkolpion. This two-part arrangement suggests another potential viewing context that includes Sergios wearing the enkolpion and another reader standing in front of him. When worn, the front of the medallion with the image of St Demetrios and verses 1 and 2 would face outward, and the words on the narrow width—verses 3 and 4—would be oriented toward Sergios as the wearer. Viewed in this way, we can see a hierarchy of text directed to two potential readers. The verses on the front may be directed to any reader standing in front of Sergios as they are prominently positioned and maintain the impersonal voice that describes the reliquary's contents. The verses on the narrow width, oriented toward Sergios, are more personal in nature. They are removed from the immediate perspective of the other reader and ask for St Demetrios' protection. When the enkolpion is worn in this manner, the images of the "two victorious martyrs", one of whom is Sergios' namesake, would have been placed against his heart. In this way, the two-part arrangement of the epigram and the orientation of the letters define two distinct spaces of the object's exterior directed to two different readers: one that was more prominent and directed toward any potential reader standing in front of Sergios and the other that was more personal and directed to, and in contact with, Sergios.

The Dumbarton Oaks reliquary enkolpion is an object that adheres to conventional epigram placement in order to direct the viewer's navigation of, and experience with, the interior, exterior, and bodily spaces of the object. However, placement conventions may also be intentionally broken in order to effect a specific reading of an epigram and experience with an object's space. A reliquary enkolpion of St Demetrios, now in the treasury of the Halberstadt

Cathedral, is a testament to this practice.[22] This eleventh-century rectangular silver box takes a different form than the Dumbarton Oaks medallion, but it shares many of the same fundamental features, including two images of St Demetrios, a multi-layered construction, an internal reservoir that housed myron and blood, and an epigram displayed on the exterior.

The sliding lid on the front features a repoussé image of an orant St Demetrios dressed in a tunic covered by a chlamys (Figure 29.8).[23] The reservoir that housed the liquid relics was accessed by the screw hole at the upper short end, but the suspension ring that originally stopped this hole no longer survives.[24] The interior of the box features two compartments covered by doors (Figure 29.9). The upper pair of doors features images of Ss Nestor and Loupos, disciples of the martyr. The image of the anargyros St Damianos on the extant lower door suggests that he was likely paired with St Kosmas. The upper compartment contains a relief bust image of St Demetrios shown dead with his hands crossed at the chest (Figure 29.10). The lower is now empty, but may have housed an additional relic, perhaps cloth or earth stained with the martyr's blood.[25]

The form and iconography of this reliquary enkolpion, like others of St Demetrios, recall the martyr's shrine in Thessaloniki. The shoebox-like shape resembles that of the *krabbation*—the silver coffin, couch, or table that various Early, Middle, and Late Byzantine sources identify as the martyr's tomb and shrine in or near the famous polygonal ciborium in his basilica in Thessaloniki.[26] The repoussé image of the orant St Demetrios on the lid of the reliquary recalls the silver embossed image of the martyr that was featured on the *krabbation*, as well as the imagery that can still be found in the seventh-century mosaics of the basilica.[27] The multi-layered and sensorial nature of the object—from the sliding lid and hinged doors to the reservoir housing the fragrant myron—leads the wearer on a journey that simulates the movement

---

22 Domschatz Halberstadt, inv. no. 24. The dimensions are 10 x 6 x 3 cm. Rhoby 2009–2018, 2:Me5 with additional bibliography.

23 The back of the box is partially damaged. It features the Tree of Life iconography inscribed with the following a tetragram (ΑΠΜΣ) that may be deciphered as Ἀρχὴ Πίστεως Μυστηρίου Σταυρός (the beginning of faith is the Cross of mystery); Rhoby 2009–2018, 2:156n56.

24 Bauer 2013, 340, Fig. 8. Evidence of the suspension ring was noted by Grabar 1950, 6.

25 Bauer 2013, 351.

26 Bauer 2013, 369–73; Veneskey 2019, 23.

27 Bakirtzis (ed.) 2012, 145, 148, 149.

FIGURE 29.8 Reliquary Enkolpion of St Demetrios, oblique view showing the lid with the image of St. Demetrios, 11th cent. Kulturstiftung Sachsen-Anhalt, Domschatz Halberstadt, Inv.-Nr. DS024
PHOTO: AFTER JANKE 2006, 162. COURTESY OF KULTURSTIFTUNG SACHSEN-ANHALT

a pilgrim would make to, within, and around the martyr's basilica.[28] The Halberstadt reliquary enkolpion functioned as a miniaturized space that could virtually transport the wearer to its monumental prototype.

One feature that cannot be overlooked within the reliquary enkolpion's production of space is the three-verse epigram, inscribed in two parallel lines on three sides of the object.

> Οὐχ αἷμα μόνον, ἀλλὰ καὶ μύρον φέρω
> τάφος ὁ παρὼν μάρτυρος Δημητρίου
> ῥῶσιν παρέχων τοῖς πόθῳ εἰληφόσιν.

---

28   Elsner 2015, 28; Veneskey 2019, 33.

FIGURE 29.9
Reliquary Enkolpion of St Demetrios, oblique view showing the lid removed, inner doors closed, and the epigram on the side, 11th cent. Kulturstiftung Sachsen-Anhalt, Domschatz Halberstadt, Inv.-Nr. DS024
PHOTO: BERTRAM KOBER/
PUNCTUM. COURTESY
OF KULTURSTIFTUNG
SACHSEN-ANHALT

Not only blood, but also myron I carry,
(I) the present tomb of the martyr Demetrios,
granting strength to those who have received with devotion.[29]

There are a number of textual strategies at play in this epigram that enhance the mimetic nature of the object. The most direct of these is the identification of the reliquary enkolpion as the "tomb of the martyr Demetrios". Whereas other epigrams describe reliquaries of St Demetrios as an *image* of the tomb, this epigram purports that the reliquary *is* the tomb.[30] The use of first person to make this claim is also significant. Byzantine epigrams written in the voice of the object appear most often in funerary contexts, a tradition handed down from Ancient Greek epitaphs.[31] It is no coincidence that for reliquaries,

29 Rhoby 2009–2018, 2:Me5.
30 See Rhoby 2009–2018, 2:Me99 (v. 1, τοῦ κιβωρίου τύπος); Hostetler 2016, B10 (v. 10, τάφου τύπον σοῦ).
31 Drpić & Rhoby 2019, 438–40.

FIGURE 29.10
Reliquary Enkolpion of St Demetrios, interior view showing the inner doors open, 11th cent. Kulturstiftung Sachsen-Anhalt, Domschatz Halberstadt, Inv.-Nr. DS024
PHOTO: BERTRAM KOBER/PUNCTUM. COURTESY OF KULTURSTIFTUNG SACHSEN-ANHALT

epigrams that speak in the voice of the object are only found on reliquaries of St Demetrios, further suggesting its funerary and tomb-like meaning.[32] Jesper Svenbro suggests that the use of first person in Ancient Greek epitaphs was not meant to imbue the monuments with a sort of animism, but rather to equip them with a deictic function for the reader, representing "hereness".[33] In other words, an epigram's deicity draws the reader's attention to the shared "hereness" with the object, making them aware of their situation within the spatial setting. This spatial relationship between reader and object is evident in Middle Byzantine epitaphs written in the first-person, such as the verse inscription on the tenth-century sarcophagus for a *synkellos* named Michael.[34]

32   See Rhoby 2009–2018, 2:Me99 and 4:532. For epigrams in the voice of the relic, see Rhoby 2009–2018, 2:Me6 and 2:Me91.
33   Svenbro 1993, 41–43.
34   Ayasofya Müzesi, inv. no. 288. Other examples are discussed by Rhoby 2011a.

Τύμβος ἐγὼ προλέγω βιοτήν, τρόπον, οὔνομα τοῦδε·
σύγκελλος Μιχαὴλ μοναχὸ(ς) σοφὸς ὄλβιος ὧδε
ἄχθος ἀπορρίψας βεβαρηότα δεσμὸν ἀλύξας
ποσσὶν ἐλαφροτάτοισι διέστιχεν, ᾗχι χορεύει,
5 πιστότατος θεράπων μεγαλήτορος ἀρχιερῆος
Νικολέω γεγαὼς πινυτόφρονος ὅστις ἔτευξε
τόνδε νεὼν ὑψίστῳ ἐπουρανίῳ βασιλῆι.

I, a grave, proclaim the way of life, character, and name of this (man):
Michael *synkellos*, a wise and blessed monk here,
who cast off the burden, and escaped the shackles that weighed him down,
(and) with most-nimble feet he went, where he (now) dances,
5 having been a most-faithful servant of the great-hearted Archpriest,
wise Nikolaos, who built
this temple to the most-high heavenly ruler.[35]

Michael's epitaph includes a number of deictic words and phrases, including "this man" (v. 1, τοῦδε), "this temple" (v. 7, τόνδε νεών), and "here" (v. 2, ὧδε). The deicity draws the reader's attention to their proximal relationship and spatial "hereness" of the tomb, Michael's corpse, and the monumental setting. The epigram on the Halberstadt reliquary enkolpion is written in a similar linguistic and funerary tradition. It calls the reader's attention to "the present (παρὼν) tomb", making them acutely aware of the object's identity and the space they share with it.[36]

The spatial dimension of the reliquary enkolpion is also suggested by the word φέρω (I carry). The most direct understanding of this word is as an ekphrastic comment on the containing-function of the object by informing the reader that the reliquary *carries* the blood and myron of the saint. As with the Dumbarton Oaks reliquary enkolpion, the reader's attention is then drawn to that which is not immediately visible: the interior space of the container and to the relics. Inscribed on the exterior of the box, it invites the reader to journey within the reliquary, by opening the lid, unscrewing the suspension loop, and finding St Demetrios and his sacred myron and blood.

The word φέρω also serves as an ekphrastic comment on the object's function as an enkolpion. In Middle and Late Byzantine epigrams inscribed on enkolpia,

---

35 Rhoby 2009–2018, 3:TR64, with translation adapted from Ševčenko 1987, 462.
36 Deictic words are found in epigrams for other reliquaries of St Demetrios; see Rhoby 2009–2018, 2:Me33 (discussed below) and 4:532. See also Hostetler 2016, A18 and A54.

this word is consistently used to describe the portable nature of the object and its position near the heart of the wearer.[37] One example is an epigram written by the poet Manuel Philes for a reliquary enkolpion of St Demetrios owned by Demetrios Angelos Doukas Palaiologos (ca. 1295–ca. 1343), the youngest son of Andronikos II Palaiologos and *despotēs* of Thessaloniki.[38]

Τῷ δεσπότῃ τὰ στέρνα, Θετταλῶν πόλις·
Δημήτριον γὰρ εἰς χρυσοῦν φέρει τάφον
Ζωηφόρον βλύζοντα μυρίπνουν χύσιν.
Ὁμώνυμος δ' οὖν ἐστι Παλαιολόγος.

The chest on the *despotēs* (is) the city of the Thessalians;
for it carries (φέρει) Demetrios in a golden tomb,
who gushes forth a life-bringing and sweet-scenting flood.
So then, (this) Palaiologos bears the same name (as the saint).[39]

The reliquary no longer survives, but the first two verses make clear that this object was an enkolpion carried against the wearer's chest. Philes makes use of spatial metaphors to describe the object and its position on the body of the wearer. If the enkolpion is the tomb of the martyr, then the *despotēs'* chest is the city of Thessaloniki.

For the Halberstadt reliquary enkolpion, these two readings of φέρω direct the reader to two aspects of the object's space. As an ekphrastic comment on the reliquary's containing function, the word draws the reader's attention to the interior space where the myron, blood, and the image of St Demetrios are housed. As a description of the enkolpion's portability, φέρω—rendered in the first person and presumably spoken by the wearer—gestures toward the object's exterior space, where it was pressed against the heart of the wearer.

Up to this point, we have looked only at the content of the epigram on the Halberstadt reliquary enkolpion, but the placement of the text also facilitates the reader's experience with the object's space. Looking at the lid of the reliquary with the image of Demetrios oriented upright, we find that the epigram's three verses are displayed in two parallel lines on the left, lower, and right sides

---

37 Hostetler 2016, 142. On the relationship between an enkolpion and the heart of the wearer, see Drpić 2018.
38 Trapp et al. (eds) 1976–1995, 9:21456.
39 Manuel Philes, *Carmina*, ed. Miller 1855–1857, 1:134. This epigram is in a series of twelve (Manuel Philes, *Carmina*, ed. Miller 1855–1857, 1:133–36) that may all refer to a single reliquary; see Frolow 1953; Hostetler 2022, 778–781.

of the box (Figure 29.11). This placement adheres to two of the three conventions. The beginning is identified by a cross, placed to the left of the first word on the upper line on the left side. In terms of symmetry, the three verses are broken into six segments and are placed on the box in the following order: 1) left side, upper line, 2) lower side, upper line, 3) right side, upper line, 4) left side, lower line, 5) lower side, lower line, 6) right side, lower line.

Convention would suggest that breaks in the inscribed text would correspond to verse or caesurae breaks; however, this convention is not consistently followed. The first segment—the upper line on the left side—includes the first half-verse, or hemistich, of the epigram, οὐχ αἷμα μόνον (not only blood), as well as the first two letters of the second hemistich ἀλ/λὰ (but). In order to complete this word, the reader must turn the reliquary 90 degrees to read the upper line of text on the lower short side. This side is also unconventionally broken, bearing an incomplete hemistich: ἀλ/λὰ καὶ μύρον (but also myron). The last word of this hemistich, the verb, is missing and can only be found by turning the reliquary another 90 degrees. Here, on the right side of the reliquary, the word φέρω (I carry) is included with the complete first hemistich of verse 2: τάφος ὁ παρὼν (the present tomb). After completing one cycle around the reliquary, the reader returns back to the left side to trace the lower line sequence. From here to the end, the placement follows convention: each segment is inscribed with one hemistich. The second hemistich of verse 2 forms the lower line on the left side: μάρτυρος Δημητρίου (of the martyr Demetrios). The first hemistich of verse 3 forms the lower line on the lower side: ῥῶσιν παρέχων (granting strength). The second hemistich of verse 3 forms the lower line on the right side: τοῖς πόθῳ εἰληφόσιν (to those who have received with devotion).[40]

What explains the break of ἀλλὰ and the separation of the verb φέρω from its hemistich? I suggest that these uncharacteristic breaks were intentionally included in order to instruct the reader on the proper reading sequence of the epigram. They forced the reader to continue turning the reliquary enkolpion in order to complete the words and phrases and to fully comprehend the meaning of the upper line. Once the first cycle was complete, and the reader was instructed on the proper reading sequence around the box, the reader could then trace the lower line of text in the same manner, but this time with the text divided according to convention: at the caesurae and verse breaks.

The epigram needed to instruct the reader because there was no standard reading sequence for epigrams inscribed on reliquary enkolpia of St

---

40 εἰληφόσιν is masculine, but we cannot be certain whether this is an indication of a specific gendered audience or an address to any potential reader.

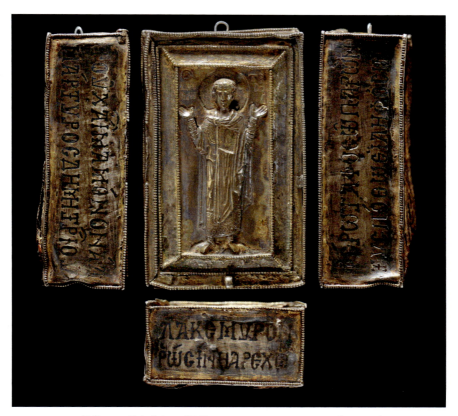

FIGURE 29.11 Reliquary Enkolpion of St Demetrios, composite image showing the arrangement of the epigram on three sides, splayed out, 11th cent. Kulturstiftung Sachsen-Anhalt, Domschatz Halberstadt, Inv.-Nr. DS024
PHOTO: BERTRAM KOBER/PUNCTUM, COMPOSITING BY BRAD HOSTETLER. COURTESY OF KULTURSTIFTUNG SACHSEN-ANHALT

Demetrios. The Vatopedi Monastery owns a twelfth-century reliquary enkolpion of St Demetrios that is similar in form to that of the Halberstadt reliquary enkolpion (Figure 29.12).[41] Rather than having its epigram displayed as two parallel lines on the sides, the Vatopedi reliquary enkolpion features a sequence of six framed narrative scenes from the life of St Demetrios, each accompanied by a short descriptive epigram inscribed within the interstitial spaces around the figures. These scenes and accompanying verses can be

---

41   The dimensions are 11.7 x 6.5 x 6.5 cm. See Bauer 2013, 351–55; Rhoby 2009–2018, 2:Me37–42 with additional bibliography.

followed in one continuous circuit around all four sides of the box: left side, lower side, right side, and upper side. The epigram on the eleventh-century reliquary enkolpion of St Demetrios at the Lavra Monastery exhibits yet another reading sequence.[42] The form of this reliquary is also similar to that of the Halberstadt and Vatopedi reliquaries. The left, lower, and right sides of the box are inscribed with a three-verse epigram in two parallel lines (Figure 29.13).[43]

Τὸ σεπτὸν αἷμα μάρτυρος Δημητρίου
ἐνταῦθα θείῳ συντετήρηται μύ[ρῳ]
πίστιν βεβαιοῦν Ἰωάννου καὶ πόθο[ν].

The venerable blood of the martyr Demetrius
has been preserved here with the divine myron
confirming the faith and love of John.[44]

While the placement of this epigram is similar to that seen on the Halberstadt reliquary, the reading sequence is quite different. Each verse is confined to one side of the box. The first verse is inscribed on the left side with the first hemistich forming the upper line and the second hemistich forming the lower line. The second and third verses follow this pattern on the lower and right sides, respectively.

The epigrams on the Halberstadt, Vatopedi, and Lavra reliquary enkolpia demonstrate that there was not one standard reading sequence used for objects of this type. It was therefore necessary for the epigram on the Halberstadt reliquary enkolpion to teach the reader the proper reading sequence by including unconventional breaks that forced them to turn the object in order to make sense of the text. Through this process of turning the reliquary enkolpion in one's hands, the epigram also allowed the reader to experience and contemplate the full dimensions and space of the object. As we have seen, the multiple layers and doors made reliquary enkolpia of St Demetrios interactive and

---

42   The dimensions are 4.3 x 2.5 x 1.3 cm. See Loverdou-Tsigarida 2004; Bauer 2013, 359–66; Veneskey 2019, 24–25; Rhoby 2009–2018, 2:Me33 with additional bibliography.
43   I have not examined the Lavra reliquary enkolpion, and therefore do not know the proper orientation of the upper side vis-à-vis the other sides of the reliquary. For the purposes of Figure 29.13, I have chosen to orient the upper side so that the labeling inscriptions may be read in the published illustration without rotating the page.
44   This edition revises Rhoby 2009–2018, 2:Me33, using the images published in Bauer 2013, 365 and the partial transcription in Loverdou-Tsigarida 2004, 395. The upper side also features inscriptions that label the reservoir(s) for the liquid relics: ἅγιον αἷμα, ἅγιον μύρον (holy blood, holy myron).

FIGURE 29.12   Reliquary Enkolpion of St Demetrios, 12th cent
PHOTO: COURTESY OF THE HOLY AND GREAT MONASTERY OF VATOPEDI, MOUNT ATHOS

performative spaces that evoked the movements that a pilgrim would make around, in, and through the Basilica of St Demetrios in Thessaloniki. Running their fingers over the surface of the repoussé image of St Demetrios on the lids of the Halberstadt, Vatopedi, and the Lavra reliquary enkolpia offered a material and tactile connection between the miniaturized model tomb in their hands and the repoussé icon of the martyr that adorned the *krabbation* at the basilica. The epigram on the Halberstadt reliquary enkolpion enhances this engagement with the object, directing a reading sequence around the perimeter and forcing the reader to navigate and experience the miniaturized and intimate space.

An epigram's well-ordered visual structure certainly enhanced the beauty of a work of art, but, as we have seen, it also made the text more accessible. It helped the reader find the beginning of an epigram and to trace the words along multiple sides of an object, directing the reader's movement of, and through, inscribed space. As conventions of epigram placement developed in Byzantine epigraphic culture, they were exploited for specific effects. Either by committing to, or breaking from, placement conventions, epigrams could be "programmed" to effect a reader's experience with Byzantine space. For reliquary enkolpia of St Demetrios, epigrams—through their rhetoric,

FIGURE 29.13 Reliquary Enkolpion of St Demetrios, composite image showing all four sides, splayed out, 11th cent
PHOTO: ATHANASIOS LAVRIOTIS, COMPOSITING BY BRAD HOSTETLER. COURTESY OF FRANZ ALTO BAUER AND THE HOLY MONASTERY OF THE GREAT LAVRA, MOUNT ATHOS

arrangement, and display—helped define and reinforce the mimetic and symbolic nature of these spatial objects. While the focus in this chapter has been on specific inscribed contexts, the conventions of epigram placement and the ways in which they could be utilized are found in all types of spaces, monumental and minor. By recognizing these conventions—what they are, and how they were manipulated—we can see the ways which epigrams were integral to the production, meaning, and experience of Byzantine space.[45]

Bibliography

Primary Sources

Manuel Philes, *Carmina*. Ed. E. Miller, *Manuelis Philae Carmina*, 2 vols. Paris, 1855–1857.

Secondary Sources

Aavitsland, K. B. & T. K. Seim (eds) 2011. *Inscriptions in Liturgical Spaces*. Rome.

Agosti, G. 2015. "La *mise en page* come elemento significante nell'epigrafia greca tardoantica" in Maniaci & Orsini (eds) 2015, 45–86.

Bakirtzis, Ch. (ed.) 2012. *Mosaics of Thessaloniki, 4th–14th Century*. Tr. A. Doumas. Athens.

Bauer, F. A. 2013. *Eine Stadt und ihr Patron: Thessaloniki und der Heilige Demetrios*. Regensburg.

Bedos-Rezak, B. M. & J. F. Hamburger (eds) 2016. *Sign and design: Script as Image in Cross-Cultural Perspective (300–1600 CE)*. Washington.

Berti, I. et al. (eds) 2017. *Writing Matters: Presenting and Perceiving Monumental Inscriptions in Antiquity and the Middle Ages*. Berlin.

Bogdanović, J. 2011. "The Performativity of Shrines in a Byzantine Church: The Shrines of St Demetrios", in Lidov (ed.) 2011, 275–316.

Carr, A. W. 2002. "Icons and the Object of Pilgrimage in Middle Byzantine Constantinople", *DOP* 56, 75–92.

Drpić, I. 2016a. *Epigram, Art, and Devotion in Later Byzantium*. Cambridge.

Drpić, I. 2016b. "*Chrysepes Stichourgia*: The Byzantine Epigram as Aesthetic Object", in Bedos-Rezak & Hamburger (eds) 2016, 51–69.

Drpić, I. 2018. "The Enkolpion: Object, Agency, Self", *Gesta* 57, 197–224.

Drpić, I. & A. Rhoby 2019. "Byzantine Verses as Inscriptions: the Interaction of Text, Object, and Beholder", in Hörander et al (eds) 2019, 430–55.

Eastmond, A. (ed.) 2015. *Viewing Inscriptions in the Late Antique and Medieval World*. Cambridge.

---

45 An early version of this paper was presented at the Summer Workshop in Byzantine Epigraphy at the British School at Athens in 2014, and it benefitted from many discussions that followed over the course of that week. My appreciation is due to the editors of this volume, Ingela Nilsson and Myrto Veikou, to Lynn Jones for reading numerous drafts, to Andreas Rhoby for providing feedback on my edition of the epigram on the reliquary of St Demetrios at the Lavra, and to Jenny Tie for our many fruitful discussions.

Elsner, J. 2015. "Relic, Icon, and Architecture: The Material Articulation of the Holy in East Christian Art", in Hahn & Klein (eds) 2015, 13–40.

Frolow, A. 1953. "Un nouveau reliquaire byzantin (*Manuelis Philae Carmina*, I, pp. 133–37)", *REG* 66, 100–10.

Grabar, A. 1950. "Quelques Reliquaires de saint Démétrios et de martyrium du saint à Salonique", *DOP* 5, 3–28.

Grabar, A. 1954. "Un Nouveau Reliquaire de saint Démétrios", *DOP* 8, 305–13.

Hahn, C. & H. Klein (eds) 2015. *Saints and Sacred Matter: The Cult of Relics in Byzantium and Beyond*. Washington D.C.

Hörandner, W. & A. Rhoby (eds) 2008. *Die kulturhistorische Bedeutung byzantinischer Epigramme: Akten des internationalen Workshop (Wien, 1.–2. Dezember 2006)*. Vienna.

Hörander, W. et al (eds) 2019. *A Companion to Byzantine Poetry*. Leiden.

Hostetler, B. 2016. "The Function of Text: Byzantine Reliquaries with Epigrams, 843–1204" PhD diss., Florida State University.

Hostetler, B. 2020. "Towards a Typology for the Placement of Names on Works of Art", in Lauxtermann & Toth (eds) 2020, 267–90.

Hostetler, B. 2022. "Epigrams on Relics and Reliquaries", in Spingou (ed) 2022, 751–788.

James, L. 2007. "'And shall these mute stones speak?': Text as Art", in James (ed.) 2007, 188–206.

James, L. (ed.) 2007. *Art and Text in Byzantine Culture*. Cambridge.

James, L. 2004. "Senses and Sensibility in Byzantium", *Art History* 27 (2004), 522–537.

Janke, P. 2006. *Ein heilbringender Schatz: die Reliquienverehrung am Halberstädter Dom im Mittelalter: Geschichte, Kult und Kunst*. Munich.

Jeffreys, E. et al (eds) 2008. *The Oxford Handbook of Byzantine Studies*. Oxford.

Kazhdan, A. (ed.) 1991. *The Oxford Dictionary of Byzantium*. Oxford.

Klein, H. 2015. "Materiality and the Sacred: Byzantine Reliquaries and the Rhetoric of Enshrinement", in Hahn & Klein (eds) 2015, 231–52.

Kypraiou, L. (ed.) 2004. Θωράκιον: Αφιέρωμα στη μνήμη του Παύλου Λαζαρίδη. Athens.

Lauxtermann, M. 2003. *Byzantine Poetry from Pisides to Geometres. Texts and Contexts*. Vienna.

Lauxtermann, M. & I. Toth (eds) 2020. *Inscribing Texts in Byzantium: Continuities and Transformations*. London.

Leatherbury, S. 2019. *Inscribing Faith in Late Antiquity: Between Reading and Seeing*. London.

Lidov, A. (ed.) 2011. *Spatial Icons: Performativity in Byzantium and Medieval Russia*. Moscow.

Loverdou-Tsigarida, K. 2004. "Λειψανοθήκες του Αγίου Δημητρίου στη Μονή της Λαύρας", in Kypraiou (ed.) 2004, 391–98.

Mango, C. 2008. "Epigraphy", in Jeffreys et al (eds) 2008, 144–49.

Maniaci, M. & P. Orsini (eds) 2015. *Scrittura epigrafica e scrittura libraria: fra Oriente e Occidente*. Cassino.

Nelson, R. 2007. "Image and Inscription: Pleas for Salvation in Spaces of Devotion", in James (ed.) 2007, 100–19.

Pallis, G. 2017. "Messages from a Sacred Space: The Function of the Byzantine Sanctuary Barrier Inscriptions (9th–14th centuries)", in Berti et al. (eds) 2017, 145–58.

Papalexandrou, A. 2001. "Text in Context: Eloquent Monuments and the Byzantine Beholder", *Word and Image* 17, 259–83.

Pentcheva, B. 2008. "Räumliche und akustische Präsenz in byzantinischen Epigrammen: Der Fall der Limburger Staurothek", in Hörandner & Rhoby (eds) 2008, 75–83.

Pentcheva, B. 2010. *The Sensual Icon: Space, Ritual, and the Senses in Byzantium*. University Park, PA.

Rhoby, A. 2009–2018. *Byzantinische Epigramme in inschriftlicher Überlieferung*, vols. 1–4. Vienna.

Rhoby, A. 2011a. "Inscriptional Poetry: Ekphrasis in Byzantine tomb epigrams", *Byzantinoslavica—Revue internationale des Etudes Byzantines* 69/3, 193–204.

Rhoby, A. 2011b. "Interactive Inscriptions: Byzantine Works of Art and their Beholders", in Lidov (ed.) 2011, 317–33.

Rhoby, A. 2017. "Text as Art? Byzantine Inscriptions and Their Display", in Berti et al (eds) 2017, 265–83.

Ševčenko, I. 1987. "An Early Tenth-Century Inscription from Galakrenai with Echoes from Nonnos and the Palatine Anthology", *DOP* 41, 461–68.

Spingou, F. (ed) 2022. *Sources for Byzantine Art History*, vol. 3, *The Visual Culture of Later Byzantium (c.1081-c.1350)*. Cambridge.

Stavrakos, Ch. (ed.) 2016. *Inscriptions in the Byzantine and Post-Byzantine History and History of Art*. Wiesbaden.

Svenbro, J. 1993. *Phrasikleia: An Anthropology of Reading in Ancient Greece*. Tr. J. Lloyd. Cornell.

Trapp, E. et al (eds) 1976–1995. *Prosopographisches Lexikon der Palaiologenzeit*, 12 vols. Vienna.

Veneskey, L. 2019. "Truth and Mimesis in Byzantium: A Speaking Reliquary of St Demetrios of Thessaloniki", *Art History* 42, 16–39.

Afterword

Byzantine Spacetime: A Rough Guide For Future Tourists to the Past

Adam J. Goldwyn and Derek Krueger

To look through space is to look through time. As David Lowenthal writes, "If the past is a foreign country, nostalgia has made it 'the foreign country with the healthiest tourist trade of all'".[1] And although Byzantinists may not be entirely nostalgic about living in the time and space they study, we are happy to visit, to become those whom Lowenthal calls tourists "to the past".[2] Like all tourists, however, tourists to the past "imperil the object of their quest".[3] Although Lowenthal is warning against the ways in which nostalgia can romanticize the past, the principle that scientists call the "observer effect"—that observation of a phenomenon alters the phenomenon being observed—is equally applicable to a photon in the double-slit experiment that complicates quantum physics and the destroy-to-preserve rescue archaeology in downtown Istanbul.

What does an attempt to map Byzantine spatialities tell us about our own cartography of the past, of our work as Byzantinists? What we know about Byzantium must be understood from our position as viewers through Byzantine spacetime, and we must understand how our role as observers of the past alters it. While artefacts from the past survive into the present, knowledge about them—what they mean—can only come to the present filtered through the refracting agent of the human mind. And the human mind is not a static thing, but a changing one: epistemologies change, experiences change, ideologies and technologies change, not only culturally over time (and across space), but also through the idiosyncratic gaze of each unique observer. Indeed, the seemingly fixed concept of space is especially potent for considering this mutability. We could, of course, speak here of geology—the way that the shifting of tectonic plates, erosion, changing waterways, and other forces have moved the physical spaces of Byzantine monuments such as the Byzantine basilica, perhaps of Saint Neophytos, once part of Nicaea, now submerged beneath Lake Iznik.[4] We could also speak of the changing meaning of objects in situ as the cultural spaces in which they were embedded shifted from Byzantine control

---

1 Lowenthal 1985, 4.
2 Lowenthal 1985, 4.
3 Lowenthal 1985, 4.
4 Şahin & Fairchild 2018.

to various successor states—Umayyad, Seljuk, Crusader, Ottoman—and again to the various modern nation-states in whose borders they now reside and that often attribute different historical significance to the remnants of the past they see, and different historical narratives. These visions are not only individual, but cultural and collective, ways of seeing the past that a group sees together. We could speak, also, of the physical transfer of objects such as the Antiochan floor mosaics now installed at Dumbarton Oaks in Washington, DC, across an ocean of which the Byzantines could never have conceived, or, at the other end of the spectrum, the faces of the seraphim in the pendentives of Hagia Sophia, which had been covered by a thin layer of paint by order of the Ottoman sultan in 1609 and remained that way until 2009—well-known to a Late Byzantine and even an early Ottoman audience but invisible to subsequent generations.[5]

It is perhaps more interesting to speak of the shift of the experience of space between the Byzantines themselves and modern scholars of Byzantium. Consider, for instance, this book itself. As we write under lockdown during the coronavirus pandemic of 2020, a draft of this book nevertheless travelled electronically from Sweden to two locations in the United States. Having received the book—or a simulacrum thereof which takes up no actual physical space— we then had a video conference across the 1300 miles between Greensboro, NC and Fargo, ND, with drafts shuttling instantaneously back and forth. Can we, under shelter-in-place conditions in which it is easier to communicate across the globe than with neighbours across the street, understand the conception of space in a Byzantine context in which the letters of John Chrysostom, Theodore Stoudites, or Photius were written in exile in physical form and carried on foot or horseback or sailing ship to their recipients? Can we, who can stroll the virtual streets of downtown Istanbul and Thessaloniki with Google Street View from our homes, understand the conception of space for those for whom such travel required the embodied experience of movement?

Byzantium as spacetime can be seen in the transhistorical and transgeographic nature of the discipline. Indeed, the first Byzantinists could be said to be the last Byzantines, figures like Andronikos Kallistos, a refugee from the 1453 fall of Constantinople who died in London in 1476, surrounded by the vast collection of manuscripts he had brought with him to England. Andronikos' views of Byzantium, however, his epistemological and phenomenological positionality, differ from our own, as ours—we hope!—will differ from those of the future. But the Byzantines themselves engaged in space travel. Their romances transported them to the wonders of a pagan world both known and

---

5 Teteriatnikov 2015.

unknown.[6] Their philological and allegorical studies of Homer carried them from an oddly alien text to a more familiar storyworld.[7] Their liturgical calendar and its rites escorted Byzantine Christians on pilgrimage, week after week and year after year, to Bethlehem at Christmas, to Eden to begin the journey of Lent, and to Jerusalem for Great and Holy Week to witness the death and resurrection of Jesus. Ritual offered them entry into distant and salvific holy lands.[8] Meanwhile, saints' lives and fictional journeys to the underworld booked them on tours of hell and heaven, and offered them a travel guide to the arduous journey from this world to the next.[9]

In the spirit of collapsing Byzantine spacetime, we offer some principles, drawn from the various meditations on space within this volume, to guide the tourists to the past who visit from as yet unknown futures:

1   Byzantine Spacetime Travel Requires Physical Spacetime Travelling Devices

Even we digital spacetime travellers of the early twenty-first century, who move across the world through clouds of electrons, radio frequencies, and satellites, must rely on the spacetime travel technology of the Byzantines—a text or textile, a sherd, a pigmented fragment of masonry—to visit the remains of a medieval village, and thus build a new section of a virtual Byzantium already in progress. In Darlene Brooks Hedstrom's and Joanita Vroom's essays, the archaeological imagination transports us to Byzantine kitchens—monastic and domestic spaces. Through their digging and surveying we can imagine experiencing the parameters of the space, the heat of the ovens, the purposeful shaping of the cooking vessels, the smell of the food, the feel of the utensils in the hands. We move toward Byzantine bodies sensing in time, sensing in space. Our own scholarly care and curation lends details to a historical novel set in a collectively researched past, a place of both precision and fancy. Tomek Labuk and Charis Messis remind us here that these bodies are also spaces with

---

6   As, for instance, when Velthandros travels from the historical city of Tarsus to the fictional Lover's Castle by following a star submerged in a river (*V&C* 231–51).
7   As, for instance, when John Tzetzes allegorizes the "oxen of the sun" as "plow oxen" (*All. Od.*1.10–16) or when Eustathios of Thessaloniki describes the way the handshakes of the Achaians and Trojans are reflected in the modern customs of the Byzantines and Latins (α121; in Cullhed 2016, 139–41).
8   Krueger 2014, 66–105; Krueger 2014.
9   Marinis 2016.

innards and surfaces, boundaries to cross, spots for pleasure and pain. These space bodies are not alien from the realms they inhabit. We can touch, in the literal sense of the word, their physical remains and the remains of the things they left behind. But to touch has another, metaphorical meaning as well in which the power dynamic is reversed. We can touch their physical remains, but they cannot touch ours; they touch our emotions, but we cannot theirs. We think we can handle them, but we know they cannot handle us. The devices of space travel work differently in transtemporal ways.

2   The Space We Explore Changed and Changes in Time

Adam Izbedski's essay challenges us to think about the mutability of the environment and the changing ways in which humans exist within broader biomes, habitats, and environmental spaces. Places become unstable indicators of the past. The historian of climate and its impact on human natural history teaches that places exist only in time. Richard Hodges' consideration of Butrint takes into account that a river runs through it, debouching from its sandy bed into the Adriatic, but we have known since Heraklitos that you cannot step into the same river twice. Topography may determine life in a place, but over time that topography changes and its effects change. This sort of change accelerates with human intervention, with the construction and maintenance of cities, the diversion of water courses, the building of bridges and roads. The website "Byzantium 1200" (http://byzantium1200.com) aggregates collective understandings of the cityscape of Constantinople in a moment that never quite existed, when all the buildings looked like they did when they were built, rather than how they had altered or deteriorated by the eve of the Fourth Crusade. A powerful imaginative tool, it finds its power to illustrate through its tolerance of inaccuracy. A. Tayfun Öner's videos "Water Supply of Constantinople" and "Wondrous Waters of Constantinople", both curated for exhibitions in Istanbul, carry the viewer from the city's water sources in the mountains of Thrace through aqueducts and tunnels, through pipes and cisterns, and into taps and fountains of the metropolis.[10] To follow the water is to

---

10   "Wondrous Waters of Constantinople," video created by A. Tayfun Öner for Life Is Short, Art Long: The Art of Healing in Constantinople, an exhibition curated by B. Pitarakis at the Pera Museum, Istanbul, 10 February–26 April 2015. Scientific consultant: B. Pitarakis, CNRS, Paris (UMR 8167 Orient et Méditerranée). Financial sponsor: "Labex Resmed Investissements d'Avenir" (https://www.youtube.com/watch?v=uX4UJv-eIjQ); and "Water Supply of Constantinople," video created by A. Tayfun Öner for Waters for a Capital: The

admire the massive human reorganization of place that made urban life possible. To reimagine this intervention, the harnessing of an entire watershed, in computer-assisted illustration shows the power of research to reimagine basic realities. The artist renders Byzantium in a style that adapts techniques honed for virtual realities and video games, creating Byzantium as a storyworld in which the water flows and the people—the architects and engineers, the stonecutters and bricklayers, the inhabitants—are eerily absent. The real and the imagined, the unreal and the illustrated meet in a thirdspace where we acquire or attempt historical understanding.[11] The watercourses of Byzantium, like Byzantium itself, are neither here nor there. Byzantium 1200 never existed. The Byzantine spatialities of the postmodern imagination, what Homi Bhabha might term "the location of culture", are scholarly renderings.[12]

3   Our Disciplines of Historical Understanding Depend on Spatial Metaphors

Byzantium becomes a place or a series of places arrayed in time. We enter them in a tradition of scholarship. The spacetime metaphor and the methods of archaeology are helpful here, allowing us to consider the ways in which an intellectual stratigraphy develops, in which we layer our new insights over the pasts of our own scholarly disciplines, compressing, grinding, refining, and erasing them. Often the boundaries of our scholarly practices are clearer to us than the territory that we explore. Hans-Georg Gadamer looked toward the horizons of the human sciences, the humanities. "A horizon is not a rigid frontier, but something that moves with one and invites one to advance further".[13] A horizon's apparent edges deceive. Disciplines both facilitate our attempts to fuse our horizons with theirs, to chart contiguous territories, and impede our ability to be entirely confident that we have come close enough to their spaces to apprehend them or the people who populated them. Are we looking from our vantage point toward theirs? Peering past our horizon to see them beyond their horizon, our horizons blurring, a miasma between us? Between past and

---

Water Supply Systems of Byzantine Istanbul/Constantinople: New Approaches and Methodologies, exhibition curated by J. Crow & D. Maktav at Anamed, Koç University Research Centre for Anatolian Civilizations, Istanbul, 9 November 2012–18 February 2013 (https://www.youtube.com/watch?v=7pGl RuoyQpM).

11   Soja 1996.
12   Bhabha 1994.
13   Gadamer 1975, 217.

present; between here and there? Or are we both looking at the same objects, looking at things, and not at other viewers at all? Does this distance of the object from the horizon, let alone from the viewer, not replicate itself?

Liz James observes that in observing Byzantine mosaics, the mind is directed toward the gap between the mosaic and the viewer, while somehow missing the gaps between the tesserae themselves, an insight not only into Byzantine visual practice, but also a suitable metaphor for scholarly perception. Our observation of Byzantine mosaics, of Byzantium itself, is inevitably spaced in two gaps, as we perceive Byzantium through the space of time, assembling a fragmented vision of the past. For and through this double displacement we generate our diagrams, assemble our paradigms, snap our photos, craft our prose. We then present our perceptions of Byzantium across another space, from the podium to the assembled scholarly conferees, to readers of pages printed and webbed, crossing other gaps. We know that the map is not the territory, even as we know an image can render its subject present. Like the dislocated heroes of Theodore Prodromos' twelfth-century novel *Rhodanthe and Dosikles*, we must ask over an over if we have indeed read Hermes accurately, as the foot-winged god of interpretation brings messages across the gap, from one space to another, about the past and the future.[14]

4 Travel from Topography to Landscape Overlays Place with Meaning and Narrative

We label a space with trade routes, migration patterns, metes and bounds— making places out of evidence and inference for the difference of place in different times. Nick Kardulias shows how humans imbue the natural world with cultural significance, and how through the physical processes of landscaping, mining, deforestation, fortification, and other forms of topographical alteration humans give changing meanings over time to the same spaces. Just as important, he shows how the theoretical and material practices of landscape archaeology shape what is knowable about place. World systems theory emphasizes regional and global links and reifies concepts of centre and periphery, while the constraints of money, personnel, and technology limit the mechanisms by which the twenty square kilometres around Malloura can offer insight into a deep history of Cyprus and the Mediterranean as a whole. Over a long history, Byzantine organization of the land changed. The grand urbanism

---

14   Theodore Prodromos, *Rhodanthe and Dosikles* 3:69–75, 323; 6:395, 471.

of Late Antiquity, its public spaces and large edifices, gave way to new emphases on the countryside, the rural, the village, the estate, the monastery. By the Middle Byzantine centuries, the people of the Eastern Mediterranean basin had redefined the urban, with fewer open squares, with smaller buildings, with towers and walls.[15] Spaces change, far from being static; our mapping captures transition.

5   Beware the Byzantine Butterfly Effect

In 1952, Ray Bradbury published "A Sound of Thunder", a short story about a man named Eckels who in 2055 goes on a "time safari" to hunt Tyrannosaurus Rex.[16] When Eckels and the hunters first set out, the time tourists reflect on how a fascist candidate has only recently been defeated in the Presidential election. Upon returning from the past, however, Eckels finds himself in a new present, one in which the fascist had won. The reason, Bradbury reveals in the conclusion, is that Eckels had brought something from the past with him into the present: a dead butterfly, crushed beneath his boot. The so-called "butterfly effect" has become a near-universal lesson for time-travellers, one Byzantinists should heed as well: beware of digging around in the past, and beware what of the past is brought back to the present. Take, for instance, the case again of Butrint, whose Byzantine history, and whose place on the periphery of Byzantium, Hodges so carefully details in this volume. Each stage of its excavation revealed much not only about the history of the site, but also about the historical moment of its excavation. The first major archaeological survey at the site was sponsored by the Italian government between 1928 and 1936 under the leadership of Benito Mussolini and his Partito Nazionale Fascista (National Fascist Party), which sought to connect southern Albania to the ancient Trojans under Aeneas, who would go on to found Rome.[17] As the meaning of place became subservient to ideological and political claims, archaeology became the tool of fascist propaganda and the justification for military and imperial expansion.

Under Albania's post-War Communist dictatorship, Butrint came to mean something different; Hodges has argued, "Given Albania's obsession with fortification, as an isolated country at odds with most European countries, it is

---

15   For a good overview, see Brubaker 2001; Ousterhout 2019, 333–51.
16   Bradbury 1952.
17   For the context of this in the broader history of Trojan War reception in modern Albania, see Goldwyn 2016.

hardly surprising that it was Butrint's well-preserved defences that caught the imagination" of the country's archaeologists in the 1970s.[18] Now, Butrint is a Unesco World Heritage Site; it became Albania's first such monument in 1992, the same year as the country's first multi-party elections, which ended the Communist military dictatorship that had governed the country since the end of World War II. The dictatorship had turned Albania into one of the most isolated countries in the world; 1992 was also the first time in thirty years its athletes competed in the Olympics. The transition of the archaeological site gained a significance greater than the sum of its stones: it became a symbol of Albanian (re)integration into the global community. Although with varying degrees of malevolence, each of these instances suggest the needs of the present in making decisions about which parts of the past to visit. Ugolini's decision to excavate Butrint over other sites was made with the needs of the Italian fascists in mind; the subsequent decision to focus on Butrint's walls served Albania's Communist identity as a nation under siege; the 1992 decision to include it as a UNESCO World Heritage Site coincided with parallel moves in the spheres of athletics and politics.[19]

Indeed, in somewhat different terms, the Byzantine writer most concerned with the relationship of past to present made a similar point. The twelfth century politician-turned-refugee, Niketas Choniates, wrote that "history can be called the book of the living and the written word a clarion trumpet, like a signal from heaven, raising up those long dead and setting them before the eyes of those who desire to see them".[20] But whose Byzantium is this? In *Romanland: Ethnicity and Empire in Byzantium,* Anthony Kaldellis reframes the conceptual, geographic, and political boundaries of the discipline under a new name: Romanland, Romanía.[21] Seeking a Byzantium neither orientalised nor exoticized and yet quite different from the medieval west, he examines the strategies of coercion and persuasion, of inclusion and exclusion, by which the Roman state in the medieval eastern Mediterranean exerted control over territory and identity.

Even as we scholars construct a postmodern model of Byzantium in digital space, others claim the territory of Byzantium for an illiberal agenda.[22] In

---

18 Hodges 2013, 5.
19 See, for instance, Gilkes 2006.
20 Chon. *Hist.* 2.
21 Kaldellis, 2019.
22 As, for instance, the "New Byzantium Project," which advertises itself as "a premier organization for pro-white advocacy in the 21st century". (https://jasonkessler.us/2017/09/24/announcing-the-formation-new-byzantium/). The organization is listed as a hate group

recent years, right-wing bloggers have filled a corner of the internet, claiming Byzantium for white supremacy and Christian nationalism.[23] Once again, we are forced to confront our own positionality—spatially and temporally—but also in terms of the socio-economic spaces we inhabit. We write in a fraught moment, as protesters fill the streets of cities across the United States (including our own cities of Fargo of Greensboro) and across the globe to protest racial injustice and police violence. As the observer effect proves, study alters the object of study, and Byzantium is no different. One of the central debates in Byzantine Studies today is also at the heart of the Black Lives Matter movement: who qualifies as a member of the state, deserving of its privileges and protections, and who does not. Byzantium for whom? Whose Byzantium? Who should occupy this Byzantium? And what space should this Byzantine spatiality occupy?

Bibliography

Primary Sources

Bradbury, Ray, "A Sound of Thunder" *Collier's*. June 28, 1952.

Eustathios of Thessalonike, *Parekbolai on the Odyssey 1–2*. Ed. & tr. E. Cullhed. Uppsala 2014.

Niketas Choniates, *Nicetae Choniatae historia*. Ed J. van Dieten. Berlin 1975. Tr. H. Magoulias, *O City of Byzantium, Annals of Niketas Choniates*. Detroit 1986.

Theodore Prodromos, *Rhodanthe and Dosikles*. Ed. M. Marcovich, *Theodori Prodromi de Rhodanthes et Discilis amoribus libri IX*. Leipzig 1992. Tr. E. Jeffreys, *Four Byzantine Novels*, 19–156. Liverpool 2012.

Tzetzes, John, *Allegories of the Odyssey*. Tr. A. Goldwyn & D. Kokkini. Cambridge, MA 2019.

Velthandros and Chrysandza. Ed E. Kriaras, Βυζαντινὰ ἱπποτικὰ μυθιστορήματα, 101–30. Athens 1955. Tr. G. Betts, *Three Medieval Greek Romances*, 5–32. New York 1995.

Secondary Sources

Bhabha, H. K. 1994. *The Location of Culture*. London.

Brubaker, L. 2001. "Topography and the Creation of Public Space in Early Medieval Constantinople", in De Jong (ed.) 2001, 31–43.

De Jong, M. (ed.) 2001. *Topographies of Power in the Early Middle Ages*. Leiden.

---

by the Southern Poverty Law Centre (https://web.archive.org/web/20180404004211/ https://www.splcentre.org/fighting-hate/extremist-files/ideology/white-nationalist).

23 See, for instance, Goldwyn 2018 or the Goldwyn 2022 update to that piece.

Hahn, C., & H. A. Klein (eds) 2015. *Saints and Sacred Matter: The Cult of Relics in Byzantium and Beyond*. Washington D.C.

Hansen, I. L., R. Hodges & S. Leppard (eds) 2013. *Butrint 4: The Archaeology and Histories of an Ionian Town*. Ed. I. L. Hansen, R. Hodges & S. Leppard. Oxford & Oakville.

Hodges, R. 2013. "Excavating away the 'poison': the topographic history of Butrint, ancient *Buthrotum*", in Hansen, Hodges & Leppard (eds) 2013, 1–22.

Gadamer, H.-G. 1975. *Truth and Method*. Tr. & ed. G. Barden & J. Cumming. New York.

Galary, M. & C. Watkinson (eds) 2006. *Archaeology Under Dictatorship*. New York.

Gilkes, O. 2006. "The Trojans in Epirus: Archaeology, Myth and Identity in Inter-War Albania", in Galary & Watkinson (eds) 2006, 33–54.

Goldwyn, A. 2016. "'Go Back to Homer's Verse': Iliads of Revolution and Odysseys of Exile in Albanian Poetry", *Classical Receptions Journal* 8.4, 506–28.

Goldwyn, A. 2018. "The Byzantine Workings of the Manosphere" *Eidolon*, June 11, 2018. https://eidolon.pub/the-byzantine-workings-of-the-manosphere-37db3be9e661.

Goldwyn, A. 2022. "Byzantium in the American Alt-Right Imagination: Paradigms of the Medieval Greek Past among Men's Rights Activists and White Supremacists", in Parnell, Stewart & Whately (eds) 2022, 424-39.

Kaldellis, A. 2019. *Romanland: Ethnicity and Empire in Byzantium*. Cambridge, MA.

Krueger, D. 2014. *Liturgical Subjects: Christian Ritual, Biblical Narrative, and the Formation of the self in Byzantium*. Philadelphia.

Krueger, D. 2015. "Liturgical Time and Holy Land Reliquaries in Early Byzantium", in Hahn & Klein (eds) 2015, 111–31.

Lowenthal, D. 1985. *The Past is a Foreign Country*. Cambridge, UK.

Marinis, V. 2016. *Death and the Afterlife in Byzantium: The Fate of the Soul in Theology, Liturgy, and Art*. New York.

Ousterhout, R. G. 2019. *Eastern Medieval Architecture: The Building Traditions of Byzantium and Neighbouring Lands*. New York.

Parnell, D., M. E. Stewart & D. Whately (eds) 2022. *Handbook of Identity in Byzantium*. London.

Şahin, M. & M. R. Fairchild 2018. "Nicea's Underwater Basilica", *Biblical Archaeology Review* 44.6, 30–38.

Soja, E. W. 1996. *Thirdspace: Journeys to Los Angeles and Other Real-and-Imagined Places*. Oxford.

Teteriatnikov, N. 2015. "The Last Palaiologan Mosaic Program of Hagia: The Dome and Pendentives", *DOP* 69, 273–96.

Index

Abydos 224
Achaia 372–4, 384, 394
Acharnai 344
Achris 222
Acıgöl 416, 419
Açıksaray 159
Acre 623
Adramyttion 415, 420
Adriatic Sea 76, 139, 142, 145, 148, 369–70, 373, 377–78, 382, 434, 448–49, 659
Aegean Sea 76, 120, 132, 194, 201, 271–73, 278, 372, 415, 420, 433
Aer 410–11
Aethiopia 371–2
Aetna 76
Aexoni (Glyfada) 342, 344, 349
Africa 75, 77, 119, 197, 224, 229, 275, 370, 372, 376, 434
Afyonkarahisar 409, 413
Agathangelos 220–21
Agia Paraskevi 346
Agrigento 171, 615
Aigaion Pelagos, theme 231, 421
Aigion 386
Akhisar 165, 167
Akragant 615
Akroinon 409, 413, 419
Akşehir 413
al-Andarin. *See* Androna
Alaşehir 409
Albania 113, 128–49, 173, 181, 224, 662–63
Albanon hapan 222
Aleppo 269, 409
Alexander the Great 78, 464, 466
Alexandria 63, 90, 195, 226, 313, 323
Alexios III Angelos 36, 394
Alexios I Komnenos 52, 60, 362, 400, 407, 411–21, 463, 473
Alexios II Komnenos 63
Alimos. *See* Halimous
Ali Pasha 142, 145
al-Mutanabbi 472
Alonissos 195
Alps 76
Amarna 323

Amaroussion/Maroussi. *See* Athmonon
Amathous 276
America 266–68, 402–3, 470
Amnias River 251
Amorion 178, 413
Anastasios I 57, 294
Anastasios of Sinai 44, 46
Anatolia 76, 113, 120–22, 152, 256, 269, 271, 273, 275, 291, 293, 400–21
Anchialus 376
Androna (al-Andarin) 245, 250
Andronikos Asan 365
Andronikos Kallistos 657
Andronikos I Komnenos 31, 412, 469
Andronikos II Palaiologos 359–66, 401, 647
Andronikos III Palaiologos 364
Ankara 412
Anna Komnene 52, 223, 230, 407, 411, 413–14
Annisa (Uluköy) 251–53
Antikythera 178
Antioch, ducate of 409
Antioch of Pisidia (Yalvaç) 416–7
Antioch on the Maeander (Yenişer) 417, 419
Antioch on the Orontes (Antakya) 250, 408–9, 417, 491, 494, 615
Apameia (Dinar) 250, 416, 419, 421
Apollonia 135
Apollonius of Rhodes 75
Appian 393
Arakli (Herakleion) 344
Arethas of Kaisareia 389
Argolid 263
Argos 177
Aristenos 489, 493, 495
Aristotle 23–4, 210, 623
Arsenios Autoreianos 364
Asia 117–18, 223–24, 231, 271, 376
Asia Minor 80, 101, 231, 273, 275, 278, 357, 372, 376, 379, 400–21, 433, 460, 494, 621
Askanian Lake 410
Asparuh 381
Aswan 329
Athanasios I 364
Athens 23, 90, 173, 203, 242, 339–51
    Agora 173–79, 195, 199, 203

Athienou 260–83
Athmonon (Amaroussion/Maroussi) 342–44, 349
Athos Mount 254–57, 393
   Lavra Monastery 650
   Vatopedi Monastery 649
Atlas 76, 227–8
Attaleia 415, 417, 420
Attica 339–51
Avkat 178
Aydın 419

Balkans 113, 130, 250, 288, 306, 357, 369–82, 410, 474
Balsamon 222, 482–500
Banaz. *See* Panasion
Basil I 60
Basil II 62, 557–75
Basil of Caesarea 74, 80–3, 251–53
Basil the Great 79, 92, 498–99
Bergama. *See* Pergamon
Bessarion 216
Bethlehem 548, 658
   Church of the Nativity 548
Beyşehir Lake. *See* Pousgouse
Bithynia 271, 401, 405, 410–13, 420
   Olympus 410
Black Sea. *See* Pontus
Boeotia 177, 190, 263, 345
Boğazköy 185
Bohemond 407, 465
Bolvadin 413
Bosporos 460, 524, 527
Bulgaria 379–80, 624
Buondelmonti 148
Butrint 113, 128–49, 181, 184–5, 659–63
   Lake 143, 147
Byzantion 219, 524, 533

Cairo 195, 269
Cappadocia 79–80, 113, 152–68, 185–6, 219, 245, 256, 401
Caria 271, 401, 417
Caričin Grad 288, 302, 306
Carthage 77, 615
Casius Mount 76
Cephissus (Kifisos) 341, 348
Chalandri. *See* Flya
Chalkedon 527, 530

Chalkis 177
Charax 419
Chassia 343
Cherson 222
   theme 222, 231
Chersonesos 178, 373
China 277
Chios 117
   Nea Moni 540–41
Chlemoutsi Castle 190
Chliara (Kırkağaç) 409, 415–16
Chonai 254, 417–20
Christopher of Mytilene 461, 477
Cicero 77–9
Cilicia 400, 407–8, 529
Cithaeron 76
Clement of Alexandria 25, 85
Constans II 378–80
Constantia 276
Constantine I 372, 482, 525
Constantine V 51, 59
Constantine VI 60
Constantine Manasses 624
Constantine IX Monomachos 56, 225
Constantine of Rhodes 539, 543
Constantine VII Porphyrogennetos 179, 390, 393
Constantinople (Istanbul) 11, 51, 54–5, 57, 60, 63–4, 107, 121, 179, 195, 215–16, 218–19, 224, 247, 291–92, 294, 305, 307, 357–66, 373, 377, 380–81, 388, 390, 405, 407–9, 411–12, 415, 426, 430, 432–33, 439, 442, 446, 449, 460, 465, 479, 490–91, 500, 503–19, 522–34, 548–49, 599, 603, 606–7, 615, 617, 656, 657, 659
   Anaplous/Hestiai 525
      Michaelion Church 525
   Bebaia Elpis Monastery 361
   Blachernes, palace 359–65
   Blachernes, Theotokos Church 531
   Chora Monastery (Kariye Camii) 179, 361–2, 508, 515, 517
   Christos Philanthropos Monastery 361
   Elaia/Elaion, Church of the Maccabees 529
   Forum of Constantine 30
   Golden Gate 359, 364
   Golden Horn 363, 524, 529
   Great Palace 362–64, 366, 465, 603

INDEX   669

Hagia Irene Church   195, 522
Hagia Sophia / Great Church   10, 11, 215–16, 360, 363, 365–66, 465, 491, 499–500, 522, 542–49, 601, 657
Hagios Andreas ἐν τῇ Κρίσει Monastery   364
Hagios Philippos Church   57
Hagios Polyeuktos Church   195
Hebdomon   525, 527, 531
   St John the Baptist Church   525, 527, 548
   St John the Evangelist Church   525
Hippodrome   44, 51–2, 54, 58, 65, 363, 465, 489, 524, 600
Hodegon Monastery   364
Holy Apostles Church   360, 363, 522, 524, 539
Kontoskalion   360
Kynegoi   365
Lips Monastery (Fenari Isa Camii)   361
Mese   359
Milion   52
Pammakaristos Monastery   361
Panagia Mouchliotissa (of the Mongols) Church   361, 365
Petra   365
   Saint John Prodromos Church   363, 365
Rufinianai, Church of Saints Peter and Paul   527
Theodosian Walls   529, 531
Theotokos of the Pege Church   529, 531
Constantius II   524
Corfu   131, 141–43, 145–46, 148
Corinth   177, 190, 195, 381, 387, 389–92, 394
Crete   271, 302, 342, 372, 374
Cyclades   374
Cyprus   178, 241, 262–83, 409, 415, 623, 661
Cyriacus of Ancona   148
Çandir Yayla. *See* Galatia
Çankırı. *See* Gangra
Çanlı Kilise   159, 164–65, 167
Çuka e Ajtoit   141

Dacia Fluvialis   372
Dacia Ripensis   372
Dalmatia   372, 374
Damaskios   212
Danube   76, 369–72

Daphni   346–47, 351, 540
Dara   220, 241, 288–310
Dardania   372
David Komnenos, strategos   62
David of Thessaloniki   213
Dayr al-Bala'yzah   327
Dazkırı. *See* Lakerion
Deabolis   222
Dekeleia   343–44, 348
Demetrios Angelos Doukas Palaiologos   647
Democritus   78
Denizli   417
Derinkuyu   167
Diaporit   147
Dinar. *See* Apameia
Dindymon Mount   76
Dionysios of Byzantion   524
Dodona   146
Dorylaion (Eskişehir)   410, 412–13, 421
Drava River   369
Drossia   348
Drypia   526–27
   St Thomas   526
Dubrovnik   148

Eber   413
Egaleo   339
Egeria   76
Egypt   26, 201, 226, 241, 272–73, 276, 313–32, 372, 375–76, 541
   White Monastery in Upper Egypt   322
Eleusis   345–46
Elis   384
Emesa   64, 596–97, 603–4, 606–7
Emirdağ   413
Ephesos   101, 103, 178, 254, 414–15, 417, 420
Epiphanios   226
Epirus   131–2, 142–44, 372, 374
   Nova   372
   Vetus   372
Episkopi   277
Erdemli   162
Erzincan-Kemah Castle   188
Eski Gümüş   167
Eskişehir. *See* Dorylaion
Esna   326
Euboea   190
Eumathios Philokales   415, 417
Euphrates   178, 188, 370, 400, 407

Europe   119–20, 190, 202, 222–24, 231, 265, 268, 270, 277, 369, 371, 403, 449, 662
Eusebios of Caesarea   483, 488, 490, 493, 499, 506
Eustathios Kamytzes   416
Eustathios of Thessaloniki   216, 228, 408
Euthymios Malakes   408
Euthymios the Younger   64
Euthymios Tornikes   35–7, 39
Evagrius of Pontus   376, 382, 589–90
Evciler   419

Faliron. *See* Phalerum
Fayyum   325
Felix   446
Flya (Chalandri)   349

Galatia (Çandir Yayla)   255
Galesion Mount   99, 101, 103, 108
Gangra (Çankırı)   410
George of Antioch   624
George the Monk   58, 222
Germanos   507–8, 511, 618
Germia   614
Geyve   410
Gihon   226, 370–71
Giovanni Orseolo   426
Gitani   146
Glyfada. *See* Aexoni
Gortyn   302
Gotsarnoe   178
Gökırmak   251
Graecia   372–76, 378, 382
Greece   79, 130–32, 135, 145, 173, 177–78, 181, 190, 194, 203, 209, 224, 250, 263, 267, 370, 372–77, 433
Gregory Kamateros   347
Gregory of Nazianzus   80, 82, 84, 88–90, 92, 251, 586
Gregory of Sykeon   614
Gregory the Cellarer   98–108
Guy of Ibelin   178
Guy of Lusignan   276

Hadrian   76
Haemus   76, 370
Halberstadt, Cathedral   642
Halebiyye. *See* Zenobia
Halimous (Alimos)   342, 344, 349
Hallaç Manastırı   154–59, 164–66

Halys River   408
Hamam Çayı   418
Hattuša. *See* Boğazköy
Helenoupolis   410–11
Hellas   347, 372–76
Heraclitus   78
Herakleion. *See* Arakli
Herakleios   218, 373, 375
Hermos (Gediz) River   409, 414, 416
Herodotus   224, 385
Hesychius   29
Hierapolis   178, 255, 417–18
    Martyrion of Philip   255
Hieron   369
Himara   148
Hippodromes   79, 597
Hipponax   22
Holy Land   101, 276, 377, 615, 621, 623–24
Hosios David Church   541
Hosios Loukas Monastery   540–41, 546, 548–49
Huneberc of Heidenheim   377
Hymettus   339, 341, 349

Ikonion   62, 476
Ilgın   413
Illyricum, prefecture of   372–78, 382
India   226, 371, 468, 474
Indus River   370–71
Ioannina   143, 145–46
Ionian Islands   143, 231
Ionian Sea   143
Irene Doukaina   52, 361
Irene sebastokratorissa   466
Isaac I Komnenos   276, 462
Isaac Komnenos sebastos 61
Isauria   222
Isidore of Seville   373, 375–77, 382, 585
Iskios   343
Ister   369
Italy   5, 7, 117, 130–31, 135, 142–43, 145, 185, 202, 279, 294–95, 298, 305, 372, 376–78, 382, 437, 617

Jericho   596
Jerusalem   72, 92–3, 100, 407, 411, 483–84, 503–4, 518, 529, 541, 596, 614–15, 623, 658
    Mount of Olives   529
John Chrysostom   72–4, 85–7, 90, 92, 216, 526, 587, 657

INDEX

John Eleemon 63
John Geometres 54
John VII Grammatikos 59
John Italos 213
John Kantakouzenos 63, 364–65
John Klimax 25, 27, 40
John II Komnenos 408, 410, 412, 414
John Komnenos 'the Fat' 31, 35
John Malalas 227
John of Biclar 375–76, 382
John of Damascus 216
John of Ephesus 374–76, 382
John Phokas 624
John XVI Philagathos 53
John the Deacon 440
John Tzetzes 61
John Zonaras 489–90, 492–95
Joppa 87–90, 92
Jordan 11, 547, 596
Joseph the Hymnographer 511, 619
Josephus Flavius 29
Judean Desert 255, 596
Julius Caesar 144, 225
Justinian I 49, 215, 248, 253, 294, 360, 372, 507
Justinian II 58, 378–81

Kaikos River 414, 416
Kaisariani 349
Kalavryta 394
Kastamon 250–51
Kastellorizo 196
Kavouri 339
Kaystros (Küçük Menderes) River 409, 414, 416
Kekaumenos 221
Kelainai. See Apameia (Dinar)
Kelbianon 416
Kellia 326, 328
Kephalenia, theme 231
Kephissia (Kifisia) 343–44
Kırkağaç. See Chliara
Kibotos 410–11
Kifisos. See Cephissus
Klaudioupolis 412
Kleisthenes 341
Kogamos River 415–16, 418, 420
Kolossai 417
Kolossi 277
Kom el-Nana 323

Komnenoi 358, 362, 365
Konya 403, 405–6, 413–14, 416, 421
Kordes River 292, 307
Korinthia 263
Kosmas Indikopleustes 228, 370, 378
Kotor 148
Kotyaion (Kütahya) 416
Kouklia 277
Kourion 275
Koutsopetria 263, 275
Kuru Çay 418
Kuyucak 417
Küçük Menderes. See Kaystros
Kütahya. See Kotyaion
Kypros, theme 231
Kyrenia Range 280
Kythera 178

Laconia 178
Laconian Helos 386
Lagopesole 196
Lakedaimon 387, 389–90, 392, 394
Lakerion (Dazkırı) 419
Lakkoi 343
Lampe 416
Lampoudios 31
Laodikeia 417–20, 495
Laodikeia on the Lykos (Denizli) 417
Lapithos 276
Larnaka 275, 280
Lazio 79, 437
Leo III 49, 377
Leo VI 49, 492–93
Leo of Synada 53
Leo the Deacon 152, 168, 371
Leontios of Neapolis 596–98, 603, 606
Lesbos 617
Levant 273, 281, 400
Libye 224
Limassol 178
Littoria 241, 288–310
Longibardia 231
Lopadion 410–12
  Lake 410
Louis VII 417
Louis IX 471
Louma 419
Lucian of Samosata 79
Lycia 271, 401, 415
Lydia 76

Macedonia   372, 374, 460, 466
   Prima   372
   Secunda   372
Maeander (Menderes) River   409, 414–21
   Valley   405, 410, 418
   theme   417
Magnesia on the Meander   101
Malagina   410–12
Malatya   404
Maleas Peninsula   390–91
   Cape   386
Malloura   260–83
Manganeios Prodromos   466–67
Mani   390
Manuel Boutoumites   411
Manuel I Komnenos   62, 408, 412–13, 415, 418, 476
Manuel Philes   647
Manyas. See Poimanenon
Manzikert   407
Marcus Aurelius   78–9, 82
Maria Palaiologina   471
Maroussi/Amaroussion. See Athmonon
Mas'ūd   406, 412
Matthew Blastares   222
Matthew, evangelist   72
Mauretania   76
Maurice   60
Mavrucan   162
Maximianoupolis   196
Maximian   56
Maximos the Confessor   84, 87–8
Mediterranean   2, 75, 100, 113, 119–20, 130, 138, 141, 143, 146, 148–49, 171, 180, 190, 194–95, 202, 204, 241, 244, 263, 267, 269–70, 272, 276, 281, 302, 378, 449, 460, 504, 597, 661, 663
Mekece   410
Melanoudion   421
   theme. See Mylasa and Melanoudion theme
Menander the Guardsman   376, 382
Menidi   343
Mesaoria   269, 280
Mesogeia   346
Mesopotamia   266, 288, 291, 299, 304
Messogis Range   417
Metabole   410
Meteora   254

Michael III   59
Michael Anemas   52
Michael Choniates   344
Michael Kekaumenos   415
Michael VIII Paleologos   359, 363, 471
Michael Psellos   31–4, 39, 212, 223–25, 227–29, 322, 462, 471, 625
Michael the Deacon   542
Middle East   121, 400
Miletus   417
Monemvasia   377, 389, 391
Montecassino   428
Morea   384, 394
Mycenae   136–37
Mylasa   421
   Mylasa and Melanoudion theme   417
Myra   254
Myriokephalon   418–20
Mysia   415

Naqlun   325
Nauplion   222
Near East   187, 272
Nebo Mount   88
Neokastra, theme   415, 421
Nicaea   213, 410–12, 624, 656
Nicholas Mesarites   31, 35–7, 624
Nicomedia   410–12
   Gulf of   410–11
Nicosia   178, 280
Nikephoros   58, 224
Nikephoros Blemmydes   213
Nikephoros III Botaneiates   411
Nikephoros Chrysoberges   35, 37
Nikephoros Gregoras   360–64
Nikephoros Kallistos Xanthopoulos   361, 363
Nikephoros I Komnenos Doukas   379
Nikephoros II Phokas   58
Niketas Choniates   31, 35, 37, 63, 213, 219, 406–7, 418, 469, 663
Niketas Magistros   620
Niketas Stethatos   220
Nikon "Ho Metanoeite"   62
Nile   26, 33, 119, 226, 319, 370–1

Odo of Deuil   362, 417
Onchesmus (Saranda)   131–32, 134, 146
Opsikion, theme   415, 421

INDEX 673

Ortahisar 154
Otto III 53

Pachymeres 359, 361, 363–4, 471
Pagrati 344
Pala d'Oro 429–30
Palaiologoi 357–58
Palermo 460
Palestine 615, 624
Palladios 103, 577–93
Pamukkale 178
Panakton 177
Panasion (Banaz) 419
Pannonia 375
Paphlagonia 218, 250, 412
Paphos 275–76
Parnitha 339, 345, 348–49
Paros 620
Patmos, St John Theologian Monastery 623
Patras 381, 386–87, 389, 391–92, 394
Pausanias 385, 391, 393
Pavlass river 138, 143, 145
Peloponnese 60, 62, 143, 190, 247, 345, 347, 357, 373, 378, 381, 384–95, 410
Pelopos 222
Pelusium 226, 559–60, 566
Pentacheir 419
Pentapolis 418
Penteli 339, 349
    Spelia complex 349
Perama 339
Pergamon (Bergama) 176, 178, 409, 415
Pessinous 176, 178, 614
Peter the Hermit 411
Phalerum (Faliron) 341
Philadelpheia 409, 415–16, 418, 420
Philip of Macedon 76
Philo Judaeus 24
Philomelion (Akşehir) 413
Phison River 370–71
Phoinike 131, 134–35, 143, 146
Photios 220, 228, 542, 657
Phrygia 271, 401, 410, 413, 416, 421
Phyle 345
Pier Damiani 426–28, 432
Pietro Tribuno 439
Piraeus 341, 343–44, 348
Pisa 200, 202, 384

Plato 23–4, 77
Poikilon Mount 339
Poimanenon (Manyas) 409, 411
Poliana 178
Politika 190
Polybius 134–35, 370
Polybotos 413
Pontus (Black Sea) 76, 90, 120, 178, 251, 370, 420
Pousgouse (Beyşehir) Lake 414
Praevalitana 372
Prespa 222
Prima Iustiniana 288, 302, 306
Procopius 220, 224, 300, 304, 307, 372–73, 377, 382, 531–32
Propontis 224, 372, 410–11
Pseudo-Callisthenes 78
Pseudo-George Sphrantzes 223
Pseudo-Kaisarios 371
Pseudo-Kodinos 363–64, 471
Pseudo-Methodius 371
Pyla 263, 275
Pythagoras 24, 78

Qilij Arslan II 413, 418

Rabano Mauro 428
Ralph of Caen 463
Ravenna 446, 448–49
    St Apollinaris 446
    St Apollinaris in Classe 446
Resafa 302, 306–7
Rhine 370
Rhyndakos River 410, 412, 420
Richard I 276
Rogoi 148
Romania 226–28
Romanos III Argyros 31, 407
Romanos IV Diogenes 400
Romanos the Melodist 511, 517
Rome 53, 69, 76–77, 135, 146, 195, 225, 291, 434, 437, 439, 449, 473, 522–24, 528, 533–34, 615–17, 662
    Crypta Balbi 195

Sagiada 131
Sagoudaous (Söğüt) 412, 413
Salamis 276
Samos, theme 231

Sandıklı Ovası 418
Sangarios River 410, 412, 420
Saranda. *See* Onchesmus
Sardinia 393
Sardis 415–16
Saronic Gulf 339
Sava River 369
Selime 159, 167, 186
Seneca 78
Serbia 288
Sergios I 218
Sevastopol 178
Shāhinshāh (Saisan) 407, 413, 417
Sicily 60, 76, 120, 378, 382, 616–17
Sidon 378
Siggidon 376
Sikelia, theme 231
Simonides 76
Sinai Mount 11, 94, 201, 255
    St Catherine's Monastery 201, 255
Sinope 120
Sirmium (Srmska Mitrovica) 226–27
Slawinia 377–78, 382
Smolenon 222
Smyrna 414–16, 619
Socrates 529
Socrates of Constantinople 30
Soğanlı Dere 164
Söğüt. *See* Sagoudaous
Soloi 276
Sozomen 525, 527, 529
Sozopolis (Uluborlu) 405, 417, 419
Sparta 387
Stari Bar 148
Stephen Hagiochristophorites 61
Strabo 76, 369–70, 385–86, 391
Styllo, Cape 140
Sultan Mountains 410, 420–21
Sumela 255
Symeon of Bulgaria 55
Synesios 227
Syracuse 377
Syria 76, 187, 245, 250, 288, 291, 306–7, 375–76, 434, 460, 486, 494, 597

Tabor Mount 550
Tainaron Cape 386
Tangripermes 414
Taygetos Mount 386, 394
Tessarakonta Martyron Lake 413, 421

Thebes 345
Theobald 428
Theodora II 219, 559, 570
Theodore Dexios 213
Theodore Metochites 361, 515
Theodore Prodromos 408, 661
Theodore Stoudites 217, 619, 657
Theodore Synkellos 507, 532
Theodore Vestes 489
Theodoret of Antioch 63
Theodosios I 59, 494, 522, 525–27, 529
Theodosioupolis 220
Theophanes 51, 227, 231, 378–82
Theophanes Continuatus 219, 230–31
Theophanes of Nicaea 213
Theophilos 59, 219
Theophilos Erotikos 56
Theophylact 60, 474
Theopompus 370
Theotokos Koteine Monastery 178
Thessalia, province 372, 374
Thessaloniki 10, 62, 374–75, 381, 499, 541, 548, 636–37, 642, 647, 651, 657
    Rotunda 548
Thessaly 178
Thomas the Slav 58, 230
Thoule 223
Thrace 372–76, 382, 411, 416, 659
    Long Wall 376
Thrakesion, theme 414, 416, 421
Thrakoon, theme 231
Thronoi 343
Tiberias 622
Tigris River 370
Titus Pomponius 146
Tmolus Mount 76
ton Ausonon 222
ton Illyrion 222
Tralleis 419
Trebizond 255, 633
Turkey 173, 176, 178, 181, 185, 187–88, 288, 291, 294
Tyragion 413–14
Tyre 378, 483–84, 488
Tzachas 414–15
Tzybritze 420

Ulu Burun 269
Uluborlu. *See* Sozopolis
Umm al-Rasas 11

INDEX

Vagnetia 148
Valencia 200
Valens 527, 587, 589–91
Vari 349
Vassiliko 190
Veneto 200
Venice 276, 357, 425–49, 466, 549, 633
   San Marco 429, 549, 633–35
Virgil 128, 134–36, 144, 148
Vivari channel 138, 141–45
Vladimir 215, 543
Vlora 131
Vrina Plain 141–2, 145, 148

Wadi al-Natrun 323, 326
Wadi Sarga 328
West 53, 359, 374

Xenophon 582–83

Yalvaç. *See* Antioch of Pisidia
Yaprakhisar 156
Yassi Ada shipwreck 195
Yenişer. *See* Antioch on the Maeander

Zenobia (Halebiyye) 301–2
Zion 88, 216

Printed in the United States
by Baker & Taylor Publisher Services